HUMAN RESOURCE MANAGEMENT

Theory and Practice | 4th edition

JOHN BRATTON
JEFF GOLD

First edition 1994
Second edition 1999
Third edition 2003
Reprinted three times
Fourth edition 2007
Published by
PALGRAVE MACMILLAN
Houndmills, Basingstoke, Hampshire RG21 6XS and
175 Fifth Avenue, New York, N.Y. 10010
Companies and representatives throughout the world

PALGRAVE MACMILLAN is the global academic imprint of the Palgrave Macmillan division of St. Martin's Press, LLC and of Palgrave Macmillan Ltd. Macmillan® is a registered trademark in the United States, United Kingdom and other countries. Palgrave is a registered trademark in the European Union and other countries.

ISBN-13: 978–0–230–00174–9
ISBN-10: 0–230–00174–2

This book is printed on paper suitable for recycling and made from fully managed and sustained forest sources.

A catalogue record for this book is available from the British Library.

A catalog record for this book is available from the Library of Congress.

10 9 8 7 6 5 4 3 2 1
16 15 14 13 12 11 10 09 08 07

Printed in China

People are the only element with the inherent power to generate value. All the other variables offer nothing but inert potential. By their nature, they add nothing, and they cannot add anything until some human being leverages that potential by putting it into play.

Jac Fitz-enz,
The ROI of Human Capital, 2000, p. xii

After a few years away from their MBA programs, most managers report that they wish they had focused more on people management skills while in school.

Margaret Wheatley,
Leadership and the New Science, 1994, p. 144

This fourth edition is dedicated to Dr Henry Hubert, Thompson Rivers University: educator, mentor and friend. As Dean of the Faculty of Arts, 1995–2004, Henry demonstrated academic leadership, helped to establish an environment conducive to teaching and research, and performed his decanal duties in a collegial, supportive and inspirational manner. His human resource management skills and the warmth of his spirit will be missed – John Bratton

To Susan – Jeff Gold

Contents in brief

Full contents

Part Four

THE EVALUATION CONTEXT   521

List of figures

List of tables

Useful HRM web links

Throughout this text, relevant web links are included where appropriate and the companion website includes a thorough and updated index of useful links on all aspects of the subject. This summary is designed as a useful starting point for researching human resource management via the Internet. All the links below, as well as those from the individual chapters in this book, can be found on the companion website at www.palgrave.com/business/brattonandgold4.

HR journals

Asia-Pacific Journal of Human Resources **www.sagepub.co.uk/journals/details/j0468.html**
HR Magazine (USA) **www.shrm.org/hrmagazine/**
HR Monthly (Australia) **www.ahri.com.au**
HR Professional (Canada) **www.hrprofessional.org**
Human Resource Management International **www.tandf.co.uk/journals/online/**
    1367-8868.html
Human Resource Management International Digest **www.mustafa.emeraldinsight.com**
International Journal of Human Resource Management **www.tandf.co.uk/journals/online/**
    0958-5192.html
Journal of Human Resources **www.ssc.wise.edu/jhr/home.html**
People Management (UK) **www.peoplemanagement.co.uk**

Professional HR associations around the world

Australian Human Resources Institute **www.ahri.com.au**
Canadian Council of Human Resources Associations **www.cchra-ccarh.ca**
Centrum for Personal & Utveckling (Sweden) **www.hrmorg.se**
Chartered Institute of Personnel & Development (UK) **www.cipd.co.uk**
Finnish Association for Human Resource Management **www.henryorg.fi**
Hong Kong Institute of Human Resource Management **www.hkihrm.org**
Human Resources Institute of New Zealand **www.hrinz.org.nz**
Human Resources Norway **www.hrnorge.no**
Institute of People Management (South Africa) **www.ipm.co.za**
Japan Society for Human Resource Management **www.jshrm.org**
National Institute of Personnel Management (India) **www20.brinkster.com/nipm**
Nederlandse Vereniging voor Personeelbeleid (Netherlands) **www.nvp.plaza.nl**
Society for Human Resource Management (USA) **www.shrm.org**
World Federation of Personnel Management Associations **www.wfpma.com**

Human resource planning

Enterprise Resource Planning (USA) **www.erpassist.com**

Flexibility (UK) **www.flexibility.co.uk**
HR Focus (South Africa) **www.hr-focus.com**
Personnel Economics Institute (Sweden) **www.fek.su.se/pei/indexe/html**
Software Source (established by CIPD) **www.softwaresource.co.uk**

Recruitment and selection

Association of Online Recruiters (UK) **www.aolr.org/**
Recruitment and Employment Federation (UK) **www.rec.uk.com/**

Appraisal and performance management

ACAS 'Appraisal Related Pay' **www.acas.org.uk/publications/pub_ab_appraisalpay.html**
Performance Management Association **www.som.cranfield.ac.uk/som/cbp/pma/**
PerformanceReview.com (USA) **performancereview.com**

Learning and human resource development

Academy of Human Resource Development (USA) **www.ahrd.org**
Australian National Training Authority **www.anta.gov.au**
CIPD (UK) **www.cipd.co.uk/HRD/**
European Mentoring Centre **www.mentoringcentre.org/**
HRD Gateway (Asia) **www.hrdgateway.org/hub1/**
Human Resources Development Canada **www.hrdc-drhc.gc.ca/common/homex/shtml**
Human Resource Development in Europe **www.b.shuttle.de/wifo/ehrd/=portal.htm**
Investors in People **www.iipuk.co.uk**
Learning and Skills Council (UK) **www.lsc.gov.uk**
National Training Directory (South Africa) **www.peopledevelopment.co.za**

Reward management

International Foundation of Employee Benefits Plan **www.ifebp.org**
New Earnings Survey (UK) **www.statistics.gov.uk**
Reward Strategies (USA) **rewardstrategies.com**

Trade unions

Australian Council of Trade Unions **www.actu.asn.au**
Canadian Labour Congress **www.clc-ctc.ca**
Commonwealth Trade Union Council **www.commonwealthtuc.org/members.shtml**
Congress of SA Trade Unions (South Africa) **cosatu.org.za**
European Trade Union Institute **www.etuc.org/ETUI/**
Indian National Trade Union Congress **members.rediff.com/intuc/**
International Confederation of Free Trade Unions **www.icftu.org/**
International Centre for Trade Union Rights **www.ictur.labournet.org/**
Trades Union Congress (UK) **www.tuc.org.uk/**

Employee involvement and relations

1998 Workplace Employment Relations Survey **www.dti.gov.uk/er/emar/1998WERS.htm**
Advisory, Conciliation and Arbitration Service **www.acas.org.uk/**
Australian Industrial Relations Commission **www.airc.gov.au**

Commission for Conciliation, Mediation and Arbitration (South Africa) **www.ccma.org.za**
Commonwealth Department of Employment, Workplace Relations and Small Business
    (Australia) **www.dewrsb.gov.au**
Employee Involvement Association **www.eia.com**
European Industrial Relations Observatory On-line **www.eiro.eurofound.ie/**
Institute for Employment Studies **www.employment-studies.co.uk/**
Industrial Relations Services **www.irsonline.co.uk/index_pub.htm**
International Labour Organization **www.ilo.org/**
National Labor Management Association (USA) **www.nlma.org**

Equal opportunities

American Institute for Managing Diversity **www.aimd.org/**
Australian Human Rights and Equal Opportunities Commission **www.hreoc.gov.au/**
Canadian Human Rights Commission **www.chrc_ccdp.ca**
Commission for Racial Equality (UK) **www.cre.gov.uk/**
Department of Labour (South Africa) **www.labour.gov.za**
Equal Opportunities Commission (UK) **www.eoc.org.uk/**
European Institute for Managing Diversity **www.iegd.org/**
European Union **www.europa.eu.int/**
United Nations **www.un.org/**

Health, safety and wellness

Asian-Pacific Regional Network on Occupational Safety and Health Information
    www.ilo.org/public/english/region/asro/bangkok/asiaosh
Association of Societies for Occupational Safety and Health (South and Southern Africa)
    www.asosh.org/
Canadian Centre for Occupational Health and Safety **ccohs.ca**
European Agency for Health and Safety at Work **uk.osha.eu.int/**
Health and Safety Executive (UK) **www.hse.gov.uk/**
Hong Kong Occupational Safety and Health Association **hkosha.org.hk**
International Occupational Safety and Health Information Centre **www.ilo.org/public/**
    english/protection/safework/cis
Occupational Safety and Health Administration (USA) **www.osha.gov/**
National Occupational Health and Safety Commission (Australia) **www.nohsc.gov.au/**

Employment law

Australian Employment Law **www.dewr.gov.au/**
British Employment Law www.emplaw.co.uk **www.hmso.gov.uk/acts.htm**
European Union Law **www.euroli.net/search.html**
International Labour Organisation **www.ilo.org**
South African Employment Law **www.labour.gov.za**
US Employment Law **www.rmlibrary.com/db/lawilabor.htm**

About the authors

Dr John Bratton is Professor of Sociology at Thompson Rivers University, Kamloops, Canada. He was Associate Dean (Research) in the Faculty of Adult and Continuing Education and the first Director of the Workplace Learning Research Unit at the University of Calgary. He has served on the faculties of Leeds Business School at Leeds Metropolitan University, University of Bradford, and the Open University, UK.

His research interests focus on the politics of technology, leadership and workplace learning. John has published articles in journals in Canada, the UK and the USA. He is a member of the editorial board of *Journal of Workplace Learning* and *Leadership*.

In addition to co-authoring the present text on human resource management, now in its fourth edition, he is author of *Japanization of Work: Managerial Studies in the 1990s* (1992) and co-author of the following texts: *Workplace Learning: A Critical Introduction* (2003, with J. Helm-Mills, J. Pyrch and P. Sawchuk), *Organizational Leadership* (2004, with K. Grint and D. Nelson) and *Work and Organizational Behaviour* (forthcoming, with M. Callinan, C. Forshaw and P. Sawchuk).

Jeff Gold is Principal Lecturer in Human Resource Management at Leeds Business School, Leeds Metropolitan University, UK and a Visiting Lecturer at the École Supérieure de Commerce, Amiens, France.

He has published widely on human resource development and issues relating to learning at work and has a strong interest in action learning and the creation of collaborative learning partnerships with organizations to bridge the divide between academic ideas and organization practice. He has acted as a consultant for multinational clients in the USA and Europe. He is co-author, with Alan Mumford, of *Management Development, Strategies for Action* (2004). He is currently working to establish a Northern Leadership Academy, an initiative involving Leeds, Lancaster and Liverpool Universities, which aims to stimulate the demand for leadership and enterprise development in the north of England.

Dear student

Thank you for buying *Human Resource Management: Theory and Practice*. This fourth edition of our bestselling textbook has been written in response to feedback from students and lecturers around the world, so you can be confident that it has been designed with your needs in mind. Whatever level you are studying at, it provides an accessible but critical introduction to HRM that will equip you with a comprehensive knowledge and understanding of the latest relevant theories, practices and functional activities of the subject.

The text is structured in four parts, which are described in detail in the Preface. Each chapter follows a similar structure in order to help you navigate easily through the text. At the beginning of each chapter, we offer **quotes** from academics or practitioners to show the direct relevance of the chapter topic. The **chapter outline** and **chapter objectives** that follow summarize the key concepts that will be covered and the knowledge you will gain.

The main text introduces you to the major concepts and issues before offering critical comment and discussing alternative perspectives. **Reflective questions** encourage you to think critically about key issues and consider broader consequences than we can cover in the space available. **HRM in Practice** examples illustrate current developments or practices in HRM so you can see the application of theory in the real world. We have included **study tips** to help you formulate questions about the subject, and **HRM web links** to help you research topics further and appreciate the application of HR practices in the contemporary workplace.

At the end of each chapter, you will find a **summary** of the chapter content and a list of **key concepts**. These can be used alongside the chapter outlines and chapter objectives to ensure that you have understood the key issues. If you need to recap on any topics, page references are provided to enable you to find the relevant section. There is also a comprehensive **glossary** at the back of the book. We provide details of **further reading** sources to enable you to explore the subject further and **case studies** to highlight the challenges of applying HRM theory in practice. Finally, the **practising HRM** assignments offer you the opportunity to develop the key skills needed for professional success.

The companion **website** to this text can be accessed at **www.palgrave.com/business/brattonandgold4**; this provides extensive **web links** to further resources to help you research the topic, summary lecture notes to accompany each chapter, **skill development exercises** to improve your professional competencies and a searchable **online glossary** to check on definitions of key terms. You can also gain access to a guide to enhancing your study skills.

We hope our hands-on approach to learning helps you to make maximum use of the textbook and be successful in your HRM course and future career. We would welcome any feedback on the text and any suggestions on how we can improve the next edition; please contact us via our email addresses on the companion website.

Good luck with your studies

John Bratton   Jeff Gold

Dear lecturer

Thank you for adopting *Human Resource Management: Theory and Practice*. This fourth edition incorporates changes we have made teaching our own courses – particularly the use of Internet resources – and comments from the many anonymous users and non-users of the third edition, as well as six more lecturers who looked in detail at the manuscript for this new edition. If you are not familiar with previous editions of the book, the Preface provides a complete explanation of our approach to teaching HRM and the structure and content of the text.

This fourth edition has been thoroughly updated, including new material on: the contemporary context of HRM; new employment-related topics, such as flexibility, emotional labour and knowledge work; diversity in work organizations; a new discussion on workplace wellness; partnership strategies; ethics in HRM; and new legislation. Reflecting the growing emphasis on global management, this edition features a new chapter (Chapter 3), International Human Resource Management. For a more detailed description of changes in this edition, see 'New to the fourth edition' in the Preface.

More than ever, *Human Resource Management: Theory and Practice*, fourth edition now not only teaches students, but also elicits their responses. **Reflective questions**, **study tips** and **discussion questions** prompt students to consider **key concepts** and implications. In addition, the student website for the text offers **skill development exercises** and other web resources that encourage students to discover more about HRM on their own.

This new edition includes a variety of supporting materials to help you prepare and present the material in the textbook. The website at **www.palgrave.com/business/ brattonandgold4** offers downloadable teaching supplements including:

- Lecturer notes, teaching tips and lecture enhancement ideas
- PowerPoint lecture slides for each chapter
- Skill development exercises.

To add additional value for your students using *Human Resource Management: Theory and Practice*, fourth edition, we suggest that you make reference to the book during your lecture, for instance identifying relevant sections of the chapter, referring to the **HRM in Practice** and **further reading** features. In addition, ask students to attempt the end-of-chapter **Case study** in preparation for your seminar or in-class discussion.

We would welcome any feedback on these new features or any suggestions on how we can improve the next edition. Please contact us via our email addresses on the companion website.

Best wishes

John Bratton   *Jeff Gold*

Preface

Human Resource Management: Theory and Practice reflects over 50 years of experience of teaching undergraduate and graduate courses on HRM. This book has been written specifically to fulfil the need of introductory undergraduate and graduate courses for an accessible but rigorous, comprehensive analysis of contemporary HRM.

Overview

Many undergraduate textbooks on the market tend to be more prescriptive than analytical. Academically rigorous and practically relevant, this fourth edition gives a comprehensive coverage of contemporary theories and concepts in key HR activities such as strategic human resource management and international HRM, recruitment and selection, appraisal, workplace learning and HR development, rewards management, union–management relations, employee relations, and employee safety and wellness, with a recurrent theme of gender and diversity running throughout the book.

Our aim is to give students aspiring to be managers and leaders in for-profit or non-profit organizations a solid working knowledge of HRM. The intent is to educate and not simply train students. As such, this book encourages students to think critically and evaluate the nature of HRM in order to develop a deeper understanding of employment relations. We do, however, acknowledge that, in an introductory text, there needs to be an opportunity for students to engage in HR-related skill development; therefore, it has a practical element – the 'how to' activities of HRM. For example, it discusses how to recruit and select and how to design training programmes.

Human Resource Management: Theory and Practice has been written for students looking to be managers in the local or increasingly global arena, and therefore draws examples of and literature on HRM from Europe, Canada, the USA, China, India, Japan, South Korea and other countries. This should help students to compare international developments in HRM and to develop a broader understanding of HRM issues and practices.

Approach

It is more than a decade since the first edition of *Human Resource Management: Theory and Practice* was published, yet the management of people in the workplace continues to present challenges to managers and attract considerable research interest and funding from research and professional bodies. The world has, however, altered, and the context, the HR practices and the HRM discourse have changed since 1994.

In the first edition of *Human Resource Management: Theory and Practice*, we made reference to the turbulent business climate caused by increased global price competitiveness, and explored developments in the European Community. A decade on, the processes of globalization have accelerated and continue to integrate markets at both regional and worldwide level. Since 1994, what was known as the European Community has been enlarged by the inclusion of northern states, such as Finland, and eastern states, such as Poland, Hungary and the Czech Republic; the European Union currently comprises 25 states.

In addition, in 1994 in Britain, the Conservative government was in power, pursuing its neoliberalism ideology and policies. Since 1997, with the election of 'New Labour' and its 'Third Way', the management of people at work has been affected by New Labour initiatives in the areas of pay, the Social Charter and union recognition. During the 1980s and 90s, Japanese 'best' management practices were the very essence of avant-garde management theory. In the early 21st century, the Japanese model has been eclipsed by developments in the People's Republic of China and India, two of the world's fastest growing economies. The first edition made no reference to 'knowledge work', but with the mobility of capital and the shift towards more knowledge-based work, the case for 'better' HR policies and practices has been strengthened, both theoretically and empirically.

Two decades ago, scholars debated the meaning of the term 'human resource management' and produced analytical and polar models to contrast the fundamental traits of traditional personnel management and HRM. The debate focused around such questions as 'What is the difference between personnel management and human resource management?' and 'Is human resource management simply personnel management in a new fancy wrapping?', or, as Armstrong (1987) mused, is HRM 'old wine in new bottles?' And relatedly, the question arose of 'What distinguishes "soft" and "hard" versions of HRM?' The concept of 'best' HR practice or 'bundles' of best HR practices became an important part of the discourse on HRM's contribution to organizational performance. The context and the debate, which were largely initiated by John Storey's (1989) seminal book, *New Perspectives on Human Resource Management*, shaped previous editions of *Human Resource Management: Theory and Practice*. In the light of unabated 'downsizing' and 'rightsizing' – euphemisms for layoffs – even in high-tech 'blue chip' companies, and the phenomenon of the 'jobless recovery' (cf Aronowitz, 2005), the theorical debate is somewhat passé. Today, many of the people management practices seem to resemble 'old age' capitalism's priorities and values.

So, as we prepare this fourth edition of *Human Resource Management: Theory and Practice*, what is the established consensus on the key HRM issues facing managers and academics in the first decade of the 21st century? As we discussed in the third edition, an important theoretical issue continues to be the integration of strategic management, organizational restructuring and adult learning in order to create a resource-based theory of competitive advantage.

A second major issue debated is the conceptualization and measurement of the impact of HRM on organizational performance, sometimes referred to as the 'holy grail' (Purcell, 2003). The third edition acknowledged this development and included a new chapter on Evaluating HRM. Measuring the HRM–performance link still remains problematic, especially methodological challenges related to the difficulty of proving causality and 'why' a relationship should exist between HR practices and performance outcomes, known as the 'black box' of workplace behaviour (Legge, 2005; Purcell, 2003).

The third major issue for academics and practitioners is the effect of globalization on the management of people across national boundaries. As the globalization of world markets continues apace, there has been growing interest in international and comparative HRM. The HRM strategies, policies and practices that global companies pursue in response to the globalization process have been keenly scrutinized by an increasing number of researchers. Furthermore, with the increased probability of managers having to manage people in a different national culture and within different business systems, there has been an increased awareness of the importance of comparative HRM research (Budhwar and Boyne, 2004).

A common theme in the literature is the 'convergence' and 'divergence' in HR policies and practices in different regions of the world that has resulted from globalization. The debate has a long antecedence in neoclassical economic theory, but, on balance, the established consensus on this issue is that there are no universal prescriptions for effective HRM: one size does not fit all. The 'societal effects' approach theorizes that global companies are socially constructed in the same way as national companies and organizations, and are thus not 'free agents' able to design their own HR practices unfettered by social institutions. Hence, the emerging favoured explanation for divergence in HR practices is that HR systems are embedded in wider 'sets' of interdependent social and political relations beyond the organization that influence the structure, strategy and HR policies and practices in global companies (Lane, 2000; Paauwe and Boselie, 2003)

In addition, there is growing interest among academics and practitioners in debates about the psychological contract, work–life balance, workplace wellness and the ethics of HRM, in the context of globalization, precarious employment and corporate governance. Running in tandem with the 'new' issues are enduring 'old' issues concerning work intensification, employment insecurity, skill change, emotional labour, job control and job-related stress (Gallie, 2005). 'McWork' is the symbolic term often used to capture these new realities of globalization that engulf young people in the 21st-century workplace.

We believe that this new edition of *Human Resource Management: Theory and Practice* and its companion website, with a new chapter on International Human Resource Management, an increased emphasis on 'wellness', an increased focus on gender and diversity and of course reference to the most recent research and thinking throughout will help the student of HRM to make sense of these developments.

Content

This book is divided into four major parts, which are summarized in the plan of the book opposite. These parts are, of course, interconnected, as shown by a feedback loop linking HRM practices with the external and internal contexts, but, at the same time, they reflect different focuses of study.

Part One introduces the whole arena of HRM. *Chapter 1* discusses the nature and role of HRM and addresses some of the controversial theoretical issues surrounding the contemporary debate on HRM. *Chapter 2* examines the notion of strategic HRM and explores various strategic issues such as leadership, workplace learning and union–management relations. *Chapter 3* examines the impact of globalization on HRM and reviews debates and issues about international and comparative HRM.

Part Two reviews the external contexts that affect HRM policies and actions inside

Plan of the book

Ths book is divided into four major parts. These parts are of course interconnected, as shown by a feedback loop that links HRM practices with the external and internal contexts, but at the same time they reflect different focuses of study (see below).

PART 1 THE HUMAN RESOURCE MANAGEMENT ARENA

Chapter 1   The nature of human resource management

Chapter 2   Strategic human resource management

Chapter 3   International human resource management

PART 2 THE HUMAN RESOURCE MANAGEMENT CONTEXT

Chapter 4   The context of human resource management

Chapter 5   Restructuring work and organizations

PART 3 HUMAN RESOURCE MANAGEMENT PRACTICES

Chapter 6   Human resource planning

Chapter 7   Recruitment and selection

Chapter 8   Performance management and appraisal

Chapter 9   Human resource development

Chapter 10 Reward management

Chapter 11 Union–management relations

Chapter 12 Employee involvement and relations

Chapter 13 Health and wellness management

PART 4 THE EVALUATION CONTEXT

Chapter 14 Evaluating human resource management

Chapter 15 Conclusion: Rebuilding trust and voice

the organization. The economic, social, political and technology contexts are outlined in *Chapter 4*, with further discussion of globalization and new material on the effects of non-standard employment practices, while *Chapter 5* discusses changes in job design and organizational structures.

The discussion in Parts One and Two provides the context of HRM and prepares the groundwork for Part Three.

Part Three examines the key HR practices, including HR planning, recruitment and selection, appraisal, learning and HR development, rewards, union–management relations, employee involvement and relations, and employee safety and wellness. The content of each chapter reflects the latest developments in HR practice. In particular, *Chapter 6*, which covers the principles of HR planning, now includes a much extended section on flexible working, with a discussion of teleworking, outsourcing and offshoring, and a completely new section on diversity management.

Chapter 7 highlights the increased use of assessment centres and psychological tests to measure personality and looks at diversity issues including discrimination on the grounds of age, disability and religion, highlighting the most recent legislation in the UK to counter such discrimination. *Chapter 8* discusses the international growth of organizational performance appraisal systems for both non-manual and manual workers, and *Chapter 9* examines the favoured theories of adult learning and HR development practices.

In the area of reward or compensation management, *Chapter 10* shows that employers have been moving towards a more individualist approach to the wage–effort bargain, with merit pay increasingly replacing traditional wage rates, and that these new pay practices go hand in hand with a more uncertain business environment and new organizational and work configurations, which demand more flexibility.

Within union and employee relations, *Chapter 11* highlights the major changes that are taking place at worksite and national levels, including collective bargaining and partnership strategies. *Chapter 12* provides evidence that organizations are devoting more resources to employee communication programmes and employee involvement, and looks at why managing diversity is important. It also considers ethical concerns in employee involvement. *Chapter 13* examines employee safety and health issues, for example workplace stress, violence and workplace wellness, including smoking in the workplace, one of several wellness issues that has jumped in importance in recent years. It considers the moral responsibilities of employers in this regard.

Part Four discusses whether HR practices can be evaluated in terms of organizational effectiveness and the effectiveness of HR. *Chapter 14* discusses statistical and financial approaches to evaluating HR policies and practices, and highlights the methodological challenges in measuring HRM–organizational and individual effectiveness. The final chapter *(Chapter 15)* considers the standing of HR professionals and their profession and the general moral responsibility of HR practioners and managers.

See below for details of the new material for this fourth edition.

The plan of the book does not assign values to the relationships between HRM contexts, practices and outcomes, and therefore does not claim to be predictive. The model is, however, a useful learning tool that allows the different dimensions of HRM to be studied within a consistent, general framework, upon which this text builds.

Teaching aids

The textual material is complemented by a number of features to help student learning. These include:

Chapter outlines and **chapter objectives** guide the student through the material that follows and allow them to check their progress.

 HRM in Practice examples illustrate current developments or practices in HRM. These are taken from a range of companies and regions to reflect the breadth of application of HR theory.

 Reflective questions challenge the student to think analytically and critically, and to consider the broader relationships and interactions of the topics under discussion.

 Study tips encourage students to challenge mainstream thinking on HRM by formulating critical thinking questions, and identifying and evaluating alternative information and perspectives.

 HRM web links enable students to download statistical information, follow current international developments in HRM practice and even monitor the job market in HRM.

Chapter summaries provide an abbreviated version of the main concepts and theories, which students may find useful for revision and also for checking their understanding of the key points.

Key concepts at the end of each chapter are referenced back to their introduction in the text. Students can use these to check that they understand all the key terms and recap if necessary.

Discussion questions test students' understanding of core concepts and can be used to promote classroom or group discussion of different perspectives.

Further reading references provide elaboration of key topics discussed in the text.

Chapter case studies demonstrate the application of theoretical material from the text and help the student to appreciate the challenges of managing people at work.

Practising human resource management assignments provide individual and group learning activities that focus on skill development so that students can use the HRM theories and concepts they learn to improve their personal and professional lives.

Glossary. A comprehensive glossary (containing more than 200 terms) is provided at the end of the book and on the accompanying website to help the student review and define key terms used in the text.

Bibliography. A bibliography provides the student with a comprehensive list of sources/works cited in the text.

Indexes. At the end of the book, we provide an author index and a general index to help readers search easily for relevant information or references.

New to the fourth edition

Users of previous editions of *Human Resource Management: Theory and Practice* will find that we have retained the overall aims of the previous versions. However, all the material retained from the third edition has been updated and has also been carefully edited to enhance readability. In Part One, we include a new chapter (Chapter 3), which reflects the growing interest in how globalization impacts on the management of people across national boundaries, and the increased probability of business graduates having to manage in an international context and in other cultures. The new chapter examines typologies of global business strategies, international HRM and comparative HRM in Europe and Asia.

In Part Two, Chapter 4 has been renamed and rewritten to provide a more thorough discussion of global trends, the labour market and employment flexibility. Chapter 5 has been renamed and provides a new section on emotional labour.

In Part Three, employment flexibility is covered again in Chapter 7, along with a new discussion on e-HR. Equality and diversity and equal opportunities in European workplaces are also new in Chapter 7. Chapter 9 has an expanded discussion on adult learning, including knowledge management and e-learning, and also includes new material on skills. Chapter 12 now includes material on managing diversity and workplace sexual harassment. We have also updated relevant legislation, particularly in Chapters 7 and 11. Chapter 13 has been renamed and rewritten to introduce new developments about workplace wellness.

In addition, we have increased the interactive nature of the book, with more opportunities for students to check or reinforce their learning and to expand their knowledge outside the printed text. The reflective questions, study tips, HRM web links and practising HRM features described above have all been extended to enhance the learning experience.

Companion website

Lecturers who adopt this textbook for student purchase have access to Palgrave's password-protected website. Log on to find out more at **www.palgrave.com/business/brattonandgold4**. The website offers downloadable teaching support and other resources, including:

- suggested course outlines to demonstrate how to incorporate the text in your teaching
- lecture notes for each chapter that expand the content in the book and provide advice for teaching each topic. This includes lecture enhancement notes, providing new ideas for adding further dimensions to lectures
- PowerPoint lecture slides for each chapter, including key points and definitions, learning objectives and relevant figures and tables, which you can edit for your own use
- lecture notes to accompany skill development exercises
- quick reference grids to locate readily both HRM in Practice articles and case studies in terms of context and topic coverage.

Students also have free access to:

- extensive web links to further resources around the world to help them research topics in more depth
- summary lecture notes to accompany each chapter topic
- skill development exercises to improve their professional competencies
- a searchable online glossary to check on definitions of key terms.

Overall, we are confident that the incorporation of new material and student-focused features will continue to make *Human Resource Management: Theory and Practice* a valuable learning resource. We are also confident that this book will encourage the reader to question, to doubt, to investigate, to be sceptical and to seek multiple causes when analysing the problems and challenges of managing people in the workplace. We would welcome any feedback on the text or any suggestions on how we can improve the next edition. Please contact us via our email addresses listed on the companion website.

JOHN BRATTON
JEFF GOLD

Authors' acknowledgements

No book is ever simply the product of its authors. This book was originally inspired by the teaching and research in which we were involved at Leeds Business School and Thompson Rivers University (formerly University College of the Cariboo), Canada. We continue to be inspired by our students, but we are also indebted to our past and current colleagues at Leeds Business School, University of Calgary and Thompson Rivers University for their ideas and encouragement in the writing of four editions of the book.

The fourth edition of *Human Resource Management: Theory and Practice* has been improved by the comments and suggestions of colleagues, anonymous reviewers and students. We have endeavoured to incorporate their insights and criticisms to improve this edition. We are particularly indebted to the following reviewers for their detailed comments:

Dr Julian Gould-Williams, Cardiff Business School, Cardiff University, UK

Cliff Lockyer, University of Strathclyde Business School, UK

Dr Damian Hodgson, Manchester Business School, University of Manchester, UK

Nina Kivinen, Åbo Akademi University, Finland

Alex Alexandrou, freelance academic and researcher working at Cranfield University, the University of the West of England, University of Bolton, UK, and Toulouse Business School, France

Tan Yoke Eng, The Business School, Canterbury Christchurch University, UK.

John Bratton would like to acknowledge Sabrina Weeks, a sociology undergraduate student at Thompson Rivers University, for her excellent research assistance. She is a bright and diligent young woman who is destined to write a book herself some day. He would also like to thank Keith Forrester, Nick Frost, Keith Grint, Les Hamilton and Sue Hughes, in the UK; Esa Poikela and Annikki Järvinen in Finland; and Linda Deutschmann, Rowna Massey-Hicks, Albert Mills, Anne Phelan, Iwan Saunders, Bruce Spencer and Peter Sawchuk in Canada for their friendship and support. Special thanks also to my children, Amy, Andrew and Jennie, and Carolyn Forshaw, at Thompson Rivers University, wife and partner, who has provided so much valuable insight and unstinting support with all four manuscripts, and others, over the years.

Jeff Gold would like to thank Rick Holden, Stuart Watson, John Hamblett, Vicky Harte and Les Hamilton at Leeds Business School for their undying support. He would also like to express his gratitude to Mike Rix at NTP Meridian, Lloyd and Sallie Davies, Howard Pickard and Hugh Clark at LBBC, David Firth at Treefrog, Andrew Choi at WY Business Link, Peter Mullinger at Croda Chemicals and Steve Francis at Simply Fresh Foods.

Finally, we are grateful for the professional advice and support shown by our publisher, Helen Bugler, throughout the project.

People Management, from which some of the HRM in Practice articles in this book are taken, is the magazine of the Chartered Institute of Personnel and Development, with a circulation of 124,964 every fortnight. It is sent to all CIPD members and is available on subscription. For details and a sample copy, contact the magazine by phone on +44 (0) 20 7880 7650, or fax on +44 (0) 20 7324 2791. Alternatively, visit it online at www.peoplemanagement.co.uk.

Publisher's acknowledgements

The authors and publishers are grateful to the following for permission to reproduce copyright material:

The Bank of England and the Office of National Statistics for Figure 4.3 from *Bank of England Quarterly Bulletin*, Autumn 2001 and *State of the Labour Market Report*, August 2004, respectively.

Blackwell Publishing for Figure 1.3 from *Squires Journal of Management Studies* (2001) **38**(4).

The Canadian Association of University Teachers (CAUT) for HRM in Practice 10.6.

Canadian HR Reporter for HRM in Practice 1.3, 4.4, 10.2, 11.2, 13.5. Reprinted with permission.

Colin Cottell for HRM in Practice 13.3 in the *Guardian*, 28 July 2001. Reprinted with permission.

The Department of Trade and Industry for the bulleted list on page 219.

Emerald Group Publishing Ltd for Figure 6.5 from B. Ball (1997) Career management competences – the individual perspective, in *Career Development International*, **2**(2): 74–9.

For Figure 2.4, Porter's competitive strategies, adapted with the permission of The Free Press, a Division of Simon & Schuster Adult Publishing Group, from Michael E. Porter (1985) *Competitive Advantage: Creating and Sustaining Superior Performance*. © 1985, 1998 Michael E. Porter. All rights reserved.

Elsevier for Table 8.2 reprinted from F. J. Yammarino and L. E. Atwater (1997) Implications of self–other rating agreement for human resources management, in *Organizational Dynamics*, **25**: 40. Reprinted with permission.

Globe and Mail for HRM in Practice 3.2, 4.3, 4.6, 4.7, 4.8, 11.1, 15.1. Reprinted with permission.

Government Actuary's Department for Figure 4.5 from the *The Economist*, 23 March 2002.

The *Guardian* for HRM in Practice 4.2, 13.1. Reprinted with permission.

HRM Guide for HRM in Practice 1.2, 4.1, 11.3. Reprinted with permission.

Neil Merrick for HRM in Practice 1.1.

NTP Ltd for HRM in Practice 9.2.

Organization for Economic Co-operation and Development (OECD) for Tables 4.1 and 4.5, adapted from *OECD Employment Outlook* (2004).

People Management for HRM in Practice 1.1, 2.1, 2.2, 5.1, 5.3, 6.1, 6.2, 6.3, 7.1, 7.2, 7.3, 8.1, 8.3, 8.4, 10.1, 10.4, 12.2, 14.3. All these articles originally appeared in *People Management* and are reprinted with permission.

Richard Pickard and Jim Alexander from LBBC for HRM in Practice 9.3.

Qualifications and Curriculum Authority for Tables 9.1 and 9.2.

Routledge for Figure 1.1 based on a figure from T. Watson *Management, Organization and Employment Strategy* (1986); and for Tables 4.3, 11.2 and 11.6 adapted from Millward et al. (2000) *All Change at Work: British Employee Relations 1980–1998*.

Thomson Learning Ltd for Table 3.2 from C. Brewster (2001) HRM: The comparative dimension, in J. Storey *HRM: A Critical Text*.

Tribune Media Services, Inc. for Figure 4.4, a cartoon by Jeff MacNelly. © Tribune Media Services, Inc. All rights reserved. Reprinted with permission.

John Wiley & Sons Ltd for Figure 1.4, adapted from Fombrun et al. (1984) *Human Resources Management*. Reprinted with permission.

June Williamson for HRM in Practice 9.1.

Every effort has been made to trace all the copyright-holders, but if any have been inadvertently overlooked the publishers will be pleased to make the necessary arrangements at the first opportunity.

List of abbreviations

ACAS	Advisory, Conciliation and Arbitration Service	**IPM**	Institute of Personnel Management
AEEU	Amalgamated Engineering and Electrical Union	**IPRP**	individual performance-related pay
AIDS	acquired immune deficiency syndrome	**JCC**	joint consultation committee
B2E	business to employee	**JIT**	just-in-time
BARS	behaviour-anchored rating scale	**LEC**	Local Enterprise Company
BOS	behavioural observation scale	**LMC**	labour–management committee
BPR	business process re-engineering	**LSC**	Learning and Skills Council
CIPD	Chartered Institute of Personnel and Development	**MNC**	multinational corporation
CoP	community of practice	**NVQ**	national vocational qualifications
CPD	continuous professional development	**OECD**	Organization for Economic Co-operation and Development
EI	employee involvement	**PDP**	performance and development plan
ERP	enterprise resource planning	**RJP**	realistic job preview
EU	European Union	**ROI**	return on investment
EWC	European works council	**SBS**	sick building syndrome
FOE	foreign-owned enterprises	**SOE**	state-owned enterprises
HASAWA	Health and Safety at Work etc. Act 1974	**SHRM**	strategic human resource management
HIV	human immunodeficiency virus	**SIHRM**	strategic international human resource management
HR	human resources	**SMT**	self-managed teams
HRA	human resources accounting	**SRSC**	safety representatives and safety committee
HRD	human resource development	**SVQ**	Scottish Vocational Qualifications
HRIS	human resources information systems	**SWOT**	stengths, weaknesses, opportunities and threats
HRM	human resource management		
HRP	human resource planning	**TEC**	Training and Enterprise Council
HSC	Health and Safety Commission	**TQM**	total quality management
HSE	Health and Safety Executive	**TUC**	Trades Union Congress
ICT	information and communication technology/information and computer technology	**ULR**	union learning representative
		WERS	Workplace Employment Relations Survey
IHRM	international human resource management	**WHO**	World Health Organization
IiP	Investors in People		

The human resource management arena

Chapter one

The nature of human resource management

John Bratton

Human resource management (HRM) is a strategic approach to managing employment relations which emphasizes that leveraging people's capabilities is critical to achieving competitive advantage, this being achieved through a distinctive set of integrated employment policies, programmes and practices.

'The real sources of competitive leverage [are] the culture and capabilities of your organization that derive from how you manage your people.'[1]

'The role of HR is becoming as important if not more than any other executive leadership function.'[2]

'The role of the HR professional is one of creating the space and circumstances for serendipity to occur.'[3]

Chapter outline

Chapter objectives

After studying this chapter, you should be able to:

1. Explain the development of human resource management (HRM)
2. Define HRM and its relation to organizational management
3. Explain the central features of the contract in the employment relationship
4. Summarize the key HRM functions
5. Explain the theoretical issues surrounding the HRM debate
6. Appreciate the different approaches to studying HRM

Introduction

This book is concerned with managing people, individually and collectively, at work. The quotations that opened the chapter provide insights into how the human resource function is viewed by academics and practitioners in the first decade of the 21st century. In recent times, **human resource management** (HRM) has assumed new prominence as concerns persist about global competition, the internationalization of technology and the productivity of labour. It is argued that these market imperatives require managers to change the way in which they manage the employment relationship to allow for the most effective utilization of human resources (HR). Leveraging workers' full potential and gaining the commitment of all employees, including managers, which is considered necessary for competitive advantage, requires change in three aspects of managerial control: organizational design, culture, and HR policies and practices. Current managerial orthodoxy, therefore, argues the need for restructuring towards 'flat' hierarchical structures, an enlargement of job tasks with greater employee autonomy and managerial leadership to shape the more intangible aspects of the workplace, such as beliefs, norms and values. For some, HRM is associated with a set of distinctive 'best' practices that aim to recruit, develop, reward and manage people in ways that create a sustainable commitment to high-commitment management, or what North American academics call 'high-performing work systems'.

The last two decades witnessed considerable practitioner and academic interest in the precise meaning of HRM, its characteristics, its antecedents and its ideological assumptions. The focus of much research explored the 'added value' of the HRM function, the link between 'best' or better HRM practices and business performance, and the role of the HR specialist within that process. The HRM debate has exposed enduring tensions and paradoxes associated with the management of employment relations in the workplace. As business organizations strive for competitive cost structures, most follow the conventional wisdom of business strategy – restructuring, delayering and redundancies – rather than look to the HRM elixir for competitive advantage. In the first decade of the 21st century, when most Western economies are experiencing relative growth and 'jobless recoveries', periodic newspaper reports of large-scale redundancies of professionals, managers and workers have an 'exposé' quality to them. It's as if the theatre curtain is pulled back too early so that we see the stage crew still moving props into position. Business news exposes the reality of executive behaviour and the management of employment relationships: restructuring, outsourcing of work to ever cheaper labour markets, workforce reductions and greater 'flexibility' in the use of people. Whether it is called downsizing, rightsizing or re-engineering, the result is the same; many managerial and non-managerial employees experience career derailment and job loss. For those still in employment, change, insecurity, longer hours and work intensification become the norm. Research and critical debate have pointed to the need to address the tension between the dual imperatives of competitiveness and control, and the consent and commitment of employees. In the HRM literature, the tension is often framed in terms of 'the rhetoric versus the reality' of HRM.

This chapter examines the complex debate about the nature and significance of contemporary HRM. We aim to explore some influential theoretical models developed by HRM scholars that attempt to define HRM analytically by discovering its fundamental traits, contrasting concepts, key domains and goals. To make sense of the HRM discourse, however, it is important for us to briefly examine the history of HRM.

REFLECTIVE QUESTION

Based upon your reading or own work experience, how important is HRM to organizational success?

The history of human resource management

In the management literature, there is an awareness that developments in HRM are mediated by product and labour markets, social movements and public policies that are shaped by past patterns of historical development and current societal changes and beliefs. Fashions come and go, and the same might be said about approaches to people management.

Keynesianism: collectivism and personnel management

The roots of people management can be traced back to the Industrial Revolution in England in the late 18th century. However, we begin our discussion on the history of people management with the economic and political conditions prevailing after the 1939–45 world war. The years 1950–74 were the 'golden age' of Keynesian economic doctrine, as evidenced by the post-war Labour government's commitment 'to combine a free democracy with a planned economy' (Coates, 1975, p. 46). It was a period when both Conservative and Labour governments, anxious to foster industrial peace through conciliation, mediation and arbitration (Crouch, 1982), passed employment laws to improve employment conditions and extend workers' rights, which also encouraged growth of personnel specialists. The Donovan Commission (1968) investigated UK industrial relations and recommended, among other things, that management should develop joint (union–management) procedures for the speedy settlement of grievances.

In the 1970s, new legislation, promoting sexual equality and standards in employment, and the prescriptions contained in the Donovan Commission's report amplified the status of the personnel function. Running parallel with these public policy developments was the rise of productivity bargaining. This had the effect of extending the personnel manager's function into the 'fabric of the business – the improvement of profitability' (Clegg, 1979, p. 100). The Donovan Commission (1968, p. 25) observed the growth in **personnel management**: 'From a tiny band of women factory welfare officers in 1914, personnel managers have multiplied to well over ten thousand today, most of them men.' A decade later, a study found that 46 per cent of the manufacturing establishments sampled had personnel officers with some responsibility for 'dealing with trade unions.' The Second World War increased the demand for labour and personnel specialists, and in 1946 those professionals involved in people management established the Institute of Personnel Management (IPM). Between 1956 and 1989, membership of the IPM rose from 3979 to 35,548 (Farnham, 1990, p. 24).

It is outside the scope of this chapter to analyse why men dominated the HR profession, but Townley (1994) offers one explanation. She argues that gender was a dimension in the relative employment opportunities in the workplace, as 'soft' training positions went to women and senior industrial relations negotiating positions devolved to men. The current debate on HRM is heavily gendered: 'Put bluntly, the focus of HRM – an agenda, in the main, prescribed by men – has been "important" men in one field (academia) talking to, reflecting and reporting on "important" men in another (business)' (Townley, 1994, p. 16). If we accept a feminist critique, the gender dimension has also shaped the way in which personnel management and HRM has been constituted as a subject for study (see, for example, Mills and Tancred, 1992).

HRM WEB LINKS

Go to the website of the HR professional associations (e.g. Australia www.hrhq.com; Britain www.cipd.co.uk; Canada www.hrpao.org; USA www.shrm.org). Then click on the 'Mission Statement' or 'History'. Evaluate the information at the site in terms of the material covering the history of personnel management. What are the origins of the association?

Neoliberalism: individualism and human resource management

The 1980s and 1990s witnessed a period of radical change in both the context and content of the way in which people were managed. Western economies saw the renaissance of 'market disciplines' and a strong belief that, in terms of economic well-being, too much government was the problem. The new economic orthodoxy insisted that the role of government was mainly to facilitate this laissez-faire agenda (Kuttner, 2000). The rise of radical Conservative governments in Britain and the USA provided the political and economic backcloth to the shift in managerial thought and discourse. Whereas it was alleged that traditional personnel management based its legitimacy and influence on its ability to deal with the uncertainties stemming from full employment and trade union growth, HRM, it was contended, emphasized internal sources of competitive advantage.

The seminal book *New Perspectives on Human Resource Management* (1989), edited by John Storey, generated the 'first wave' of debate on the nature and ideological significance of the normative HRM model. Debate focused on 'hard' and 'soft' versions of the HRM model. The 'hard' version emphasizes the term 'resource' and adopts a 'rational' approach to managing employees, that is, viewing employees as any other economic factor, as a cost that must be controlled. The 'soft' HRM model emphasizes the term 'human' and thus advocates investment in training and development, and the adoption of 'commitment' strategies to ensure that highly skilled and loyal employees give the organization a competitive advantage. For some academics, the normative HRM model represented a distinctive approach to managing the employment relationship that fitted the new economic order (Bamberger and Meshoulam, 2000; Beer et al., 1984), and heralded the beginnings of a new theoretical sophistication in the area of personnel management (Boxall, 1992). For detractors, however, the HRM model was characterized as a manipulative form of management control causing work intensification (Wells, 1993), as a cultural construct concerned with moulding employees to corporate values (Townley, 1994). The HRM model, among both its advocates and its detractors, came to represent 'one of the most controversial signifiers in managerial debate' (Storey, 1989, p. 4).

By the late 1990s, a 'second wave' of debate emerged that emphasized the centrality of HRM to organizational success. The literature focused on four distinct themes: the measurement of the effects of HR practices on organizational performance, sometimes referred to as the 'Holy Grail' (Purcell, 2003); the significance of the economic and social context in shaping the HR strategies and practices of organizations; the new organizational forms and relationships; and the importance of 'knowledge' management and learning in the workplace (Mabey et al., 1998b, pp. 2–3). In the academy, the significance of the HRM phenomenon was recognized in the launch and growth of new academic journals, such as the *Human Resource Management Journal* and the *International Journal of Human Resource Management*. Within the HRM profession, the Institute of Personnel and Development (IPD) was formed in 1994 by the merger of the IPM and the Institute of Training and Development. In 2000, the IPD's quest for centrality and credibility was given a boost when it was awarded chartered status and became the Chartered Institute of Personnel and Development (CIPD).

Since its earliest inception, the HRM model has remained highly controversial (Legge, 2005; Storey, 2001). As a set of ideas associated with the totality of the organization's management of work and employees, the HRM model represented the dominant managerialist thinking on the quest for flexibility and labour productivity, ideally without interference from trade unions or government institutions. As such, the emergence of the HRM phenomenon can be seen as a historical outcome of rising neoliberalism ideology and globalization (see Chapters 3 and 4), much as the 'Social Contract' of the 1970s was an outcome of Keynesian economic planning and the 'Old' Labour government–union partnership. Whatever the fashions in management theory, HRM remains highly relevant for students and practitioners of management, given that the raison d'être of HRM is, using a variety of styles and techniques, to leverage people's knowledge and capabilities and manage employment relationships.

Management and human resource management

The term 'human resource management' has been subject to considerable debate, and its underlying philosophy and character is highly controversial. Much of this controversy stems from the absence of a precise formulation and agreement on its significance (see, for example, Storey, 2001). A widely acknowledged definition of HRM does not exist, but we obviously need a definition of the subject matter if we are to understand HRM theory and practice, although we accept that it will be one of several possible definitions. This is our attempt at a definition:

> Human resource management (HRM) is a strategic approach to managing employment relations which emphasizes that leveraging people's capabilities is critical to achieving competitive advantage, this being achieved through a distinctive set of integrated employment policies, programmes and practices.

HRM, as we have portrayed it, underlines a belief that people really make the difference; only *people* or *employees*, among other resources, have the capacity to generate value. It follows from this premise that human knowledge and skills are a *strategic* resource that needs to be adroitly managed. Another distinguishing feature of HRM relates to the notion of *integration*. A set of employment policies, programmes and practices needs to be coherent and integrated with organizational strategy. It follows, therefore, that if the workforce is so critical for organizational success, the responsibility for HRM activities rests with all *line managers* and should not be left to HR specialists (Schonberger, 1982; Storey, 2001). Since most readers of this textbook aspire to be managers rather than HR specialists, this book is oriented towards helping people manage people, individually and collectively, more effectively and equitably, whether they become line managers or chief executive officers. To grasp the nature and significance of HRM, it is necessary to understand the management process and the role of HRM within it. Before we do this, we should explain why managing people or the 'human resource' is different from managing other resources.

The meaning of 'human resource'

First and foremost, people in work organizations set overall strategies and goals, design work systems, produce goods and services, monitor quality, allocate financial resources and market the products and services. Human beings, therefore, become human capital by virtue of the roles they assume in the work organization. Employment roles are defined and described in a manner designed to maximize particular employees' contributions to achieving organizational objectives. Schultz (1981), an economist who won the Nobel Prize in 1979, argued that economic development depended on the application of knowledge; he called this aspect of economics '*human capital*'. He offered this definition:

> Consider all human abilities to be either innate or acquired. Every person is born with a particular set of genes, which determines his [sic] innate ability. Attributes of acquired population quality, which are valuable and can be augmented by appropriate investment, will be treated as human capital. (Schultz, 1981, p. 21; quoted in Fitz-enz, 2000, p. xii)

In management terms, 'human capital' or 'human resources' refers to the traits that people bring to the workplace – intelligence, aptitude, commitment, tacit knowledge and skills, and ability to learn. But the contribution of this human resource to the organization is typically variable and unpredictable. This indeterminacy of an employee's contribution to her or his work organization makes the human resource the 'most vexatious of assets to manage' (Fitz-enz, 2000, p. xii) and goes a long way to understanding Hyman's (1987) assertion that the need to gain both the control and consent of workers will be the leitmotiv of HRM.

The open-ended nature of the human component drives much of the research into organizational behaviour. One set of perspectives, drawing on psychology, suggests that the behaviour of people in the workplace is a function of at least four variables: ability, motivation, role perception and situational contingencies (McShane, 2006). Another set of perspectives, drawing on sociology, emphasizes the problematic nature of employment relations: the interrelated problems of control and commitment (Baldamus, 1961; Watson, 1995). Human capital differs from other resources, partly because individuals are endowed with varying levels of ability (including aptitudes, skills and knowledge), along with personality traits, gender, role perception and differences in experience, and partly as a result of differences in motivation and commitment. In other words, employees differ from other resources because of their ability to evaluate and to question management's actions, and their commitment and cooperation always has to be won. In addition, employees have the capacity to form groups and trade unions to defend or further their economic interest.

HRM IN PRACTICE 1.1

RAIL FIRMS SHUNT 'OLD BR WAY' INTO SIDINGS

NEIL MERRICK *PEOPLE MANAGEMENT*

Great North Eastern Railway (GNER), which operates trains between London and the north-east, celebrated its first birthday earlier this month by announcing that it would spend an extra £1 million on training over the next four years.

The investment, taking the company's annual training budget to £1.25 million, will allow it to place extra emphasis on customer service and to introduce core competencies for managers.

Twenty 'on-board coaches', will work alongside inspectors, caterers and other staff to assist them in meeting new delivery standards. 'Traditionally, managers have told employees what to do,' said Victoria McKechnie, the firm's HR development manager, who worked with many members of the coaching staff when the line was owned by British Rail. 'The idea of appointing coaches is to create a peer group on board the trains that will help to enhance customer service.'

Some of the new money will be spent on a management-training programme, which is being introduced in July to coincide with the new performance management system. The course will revolve around 12 core competencies, including teamworking, creativity and building relationships, that were proposed by managers.

According to McKechnie, the 'old BR way' of sending people on training courses has been abandoned in favour of coaching, mentoring and secondments. Managers and other employees are, with the assistance of the training department, responsible for identifying and meeting their own training needs.

> **'They want to make safety secondary to revenue-raising,' Harries said. 'It is absolutely critical that, if a train breaks down, the people left in control know what they are doing.'**

Midland Main Line (MML) is organising a 'Winning the Future' programme, under which all 600 employees who have direct contact with customers or fill support roles will attend a two-day programme focusing on culture change. About 300 maintenance staff will take part in similar events at their depots.

MML, privatised in April 1996, spends about £800,000 per year on training. Barry Brown, customer services director, hopes that events focusing on culture and attitude change will be held annually, with all staff spending up to five days away from the workplace.

'It's the hearts and minds of front-line managers that have got to change,' he said. 'They are a pivotal influence on the staff below them.'

Richard Greenhill, an IPD vice-president, believes that training is encouraging employees to review traditional roles. 'People can organise themselves more effectively if they are prepared to be flexible and cross boundaries that they didn't cross previously,' he said.

Anglia Railways, privatised in January, has expanded its customer service programme to cover all its 650 staff. The company has also introduced a training scheme for telesales and ticket-office staff. Among the areas covered are proactive selling, such as asking a customer if they want to upgrade to first-class travel. 'In the past, railways have not been very good at selling themselves,' said Peter Meades, Anglia's communications manager.

Laurie Harries, spokesman for the RMT [National Union of Rail, Maritime, and Transport Workers], said that the rail workers' union had always argued for better customer service training, but it was concerned that the rail operators might go too far in ending demarcation. The RMT is opposing proposals under consideration by a Railtrack working party that would see guards spending more time collecting money from passengers, rather than performing other duties.

'They want to make safety secondary to revenue-raising,' Harries said. 'It is absolutely critical that, if a train breaks down, the people left in control know what they are doing.'

The meaning of 'management'

The term **management** may be applied to either a social group or a process. When applied to a process, management conjures up in the mind a variety of images of managerial work. But it would be misleading to define a manager in terms of the tasks that she or he performs. For example, a homemaker plans and organizes tasks in the home, but does this make him or her a manager (Grint, 1995; Hales, 1986; Stewart, 1998)? To answer the question, 'Who is a manager?' depends not upon the tasks people undertake but on their social position in the organization's hierarchy. A manager is an organizational member who is 'institutionally empowered to determine and/or regulate certain aspects of the actions of others' (Willmott, 1984, p. 350). Collectively, managers are traditionally differentiated horizontally by their function activities and vertically by the level in which they are located in their organizational hierarchy. Management has been variously conceptualized as 'the central process whereby work organizations achieve the semblance of congruence and direction' (Mintzberg, 1973), as 'art, science, magic and politics' (Watson, 1986) and a process designed to coordinate and control productive activities (e.g. Reed, 1989; Thompson and McHugh, 2002). To study the complex and contradictory nature of managerial work, we need to examine various theoretical perspectives. The purpose is to develop a more in-depth understanding of the factors that shape the HRM process.

Drawing upon the work of Watson (1986) and Reed (1989), we can identify four major analytical perspectives that have shaped the study of management: the science perspective, the political perspective, the control perspective and the practice perspective (Figure 1.1). Fayol (1949) articulated the notion that management is a science. In his seminal work, Fayol identified a distinct body of knowledge and managerial activities, from planning to controlling, including organizing and directing – the 'PODC' tradition. This offers an idealized image of management as a rationally designed and operationalized tool for the realization of organizational goals.

The *political perspective* provides a view of management that characterizes the workplace as a purposive miniature society with politics pervading all managerial work. By politics we mean the power relationships between managers and relevant others and, in turn, the capacity of an individual manager to influence others who are in a state of dependence. This perspective to studying management offers an approach that examines individual managers as 'knowledgeable human agents' func-

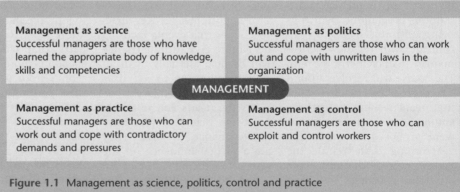

Figure 1.1 Management as science, politics, control and practice
Source: Based on Watson (1986) and Reed (1989)

tioning within a dynamic arena where both organizational resources and outcomes can be substantially shaped by their actions. It reinforces the theoretical and practical importance attached to building alliances and networks of cooperative relationships among organizational members. The political perspective has been criticized for failing to give sufficient attention to 'power struggles' in the workplace (e.g. Salaman, 1979; Willmott, 1984), which is the essence of the 'radical' control perspective on management.

The *control perspective* conceptualizes management as a controlling agent that serves the economic imperatives imposed by capitalist market relations. Managerial control is thus the central focus of management activity. According to this perspective, management structures and labour strategies are instruments and techniques to control the labour process in order to secure high levels of labour productivity and corresponding levels of profitability. This approach to management has come to be associated with the seminal work of Harry Braverman (1974) and the labour process school to which his work has given rise. It recognizes the existence of inconsistent organizational designs and management practices, and these paradoxical tendencies provide the source of further management strategies that attempt to eradicate the tensions that these paradoxes have created. The most important of these paradoxes is considered to be the simultaneous desire for control over and cooperation and commitment from workers.

The *practice perspective* conceptualizes management as an activity aimed at the continual amelioration of diverse, fragmented and usually contested complex practices. According to Reed (1989), it addresses the limitations of the first three perspectives by recognizing that although management is indeed a science, it at the same time involves both a political process and control mechanisms. Furthermore, Reed (1989, p. 21) contends that, within the practice perspective, organizations 'generate both structural and processual contradictions that will be reflected within management practice'. Therefore, managers will be called upon to secure subordinates' discipline and consent simultaneously, and, given the heterogeneous nature of management, they will be divided over how these mutually incompatible objectives are to be achieved. Typically, a nexus of HRM practices and supporting rationales will be constructed to provide the mechanisms by which managers strive to secure control over and commitment from organizational members, in other words to ensure that employees are manageable.

REFLECTIVE QUESTION

What do you think of these four perspectives of management? Do they help to explain managerial behaviour? Do they help us to understand the uncertainties and conflicts found in managing people?

The nature of the employment relationship

The nature of the relationship between individuals and their work organization is clearly an issue of central importance to HRM. Although the term **employment relationship** appears to be self-explanatory, it is complex in nature, containing distinct elements that make it different from other contractual relationships. The employment relationship describes dynamic interlocking reciprocal relations that exist between employees and their employers. Today, employment relationships vary widely from a short-term, primarily but not exclusively economic exchange for a relatively well-defined set of duties and low commitment, to complex long-term relationships defined by a broad range of economic inducements, and also relative security of employment, in return for a broad set of duties and a high commitment from the employee (Coyle-Shapiro et al., 2005; Tsui and Wu, 2005). The employment relationship may be regulated three ways: *unilaterally* by the employer; *bilaterally*, by the employer and trade unions, through a process of collective bargaining; and *trilaterally*, by employers, trade unions and statutes, through the intervention of the government or state (Kelly, 2005). What, then, is the essence of the employment relationship? Research into the employment relationship has drawn attention to relations in the workplace oriented towards the:

- economic
- legal
- social
- psychological.

At its most basic, the employment relationship embraces an economic relationship: the 'exchange of pay for work' (Brown, 1988). When people enter the workplace, they enter into a *pay–effort bargain*, which places an obligation on both the employer and the employee; in exchange for a wage or salary, paid by the employer, the employee is obligated to perform an amount of physical or intellectual labour. The pay–effort bargain is relevant for understanding how far the employment relationship is inherently conflictual or consensual. In the capitalist labour market, people sell their labour and seek to maximize their pay. To the employer, pay is a cost that, all things being equal, reduces profit and therefore needs to be minimized. Thus, as Brown (1988, p. 57) states, 'Conflict is structured into employment relations' as the logic makes the pay to one group the cost to the other. The 'effort' or 'work' side of the contract also generates tensions and conflict because it is inherently imprecise and indeterminate. The contract permits the employer to buy a *potential* level of physical or intellectual labour. The function of management is therefore to transform this potential into actual value-added labour. HR practices are designed to narrow the gap between employees' potential and actual performance, or, as Townley (1994, p. 14) explains:

> Personnel practices measure both the physical and subjective dimensions of labour, and offer a technology which aims to render individuals and their behaviour predictable and calculable ... to bridge the gap between promise and performance, between labour power and labour, and organizes labour into a productive force or power.

The second component of the employment relationship is that it involves a legal relationship: a network contractual and statutory rights and obligations affecting both parties to the contract. Contractual rights are based upon case law (judicial precedent), and the basic rules of contract, in so far as they relate to the contract of employment, are fundamental to the legal relationship between the employer and employee. It is outside the scope of this chapter to give a full exposition of the rules of contract, but there are a number of requirements of a valid contract:

- *Intention*. The parties must have expressly or implicitly intended that their agreement should be binding in law. In the case of a contract of employment, it can be entered into informally or formally. It can emerge as a result of a conversation at the office door, interviews, exchange of letters or negotiation.

● *Agreement.* The parties to the contract must actually have reached an agreement on the basis of an offer and acceptance.

● *Consideration.* This may be defined as an economic value or a promise thereof, and, in the case of a contract of employment, the consideration of the parties is a promise by the employer to pay the agreed salary or wage in return for the employee's promise to work for the employer in accordance with the contract.

● *Consent.* Both parties to the agreement must consent to the terms of the contract. There must be no duress or undue influence applied in respect of either party by the other, and no misrepresentation.

● *Legality.* The proposed contract must be legal both in its object and in the manner in which it is performed. For example, a contract of employment is illegal and therefore invalid if the manner of payment deliberately seeks to defraud the taxation authorities.

In summary, a contract freely negotiated between an individual and her or his employer is central to understanding the employment relationship in English law (Wedderburn, 1986), and the contract of employment is subject to the general contractual rules of common law (see, for example, Selwyn, 2004).

Statutory rights refer to an array of legislation that affects the employer–employee relationship and employer–union relationship: the 'right not to be unfairly dismissed' or the 'right to bargain'. Statutory employment rights provide a basic minimum or 'floor' of rights for all employees. A complex network of UK and European Union statutory rights regulates the obligations of employer and employee even though they are not (for the most part) inserted in formal terms into the employment contract itself. In the event of violation, legal rights can be enforced by some compulsory mechanism provided by the state, for example a tribunal or the courts. For a further discussion on the legal regulation of the employment relations, see 'The state and the employment relationship' in Chapter 4.

REFLECTIVE QUESTION

Based on your own work experience or that of a friend or relative, can you identify three statutory employment rights?

The third distinguishing component of the employment relationship is that it involves a *social* relationship. Managerial and non-managerial employees are not isolated individuals but members of social groups, who respond to 'social norms' that influence their actions in the workplace. This observation of human behaviour in the workplace – documented since the 1930s – is highly relevant given the increased use of teamworking (Kersley et al., 2005). Furthermore, unless the employee happens to be an international soccer or hockey celebrity, the employment relationship typically involves an uneven balance of social power between the employer and the employee. The notion in English law of a 'freely' negotiated individual agreement is misleading. In reality, without collective (trade union) or statutory intervention, the most powerful party, the employer, imposes the agreement by 'the brute facts of power' (Wedderburn, 1986, p. 106). Thus, the social dimension of the employment relationship relates to the issue of power in the workplace.

The fourth component of the employment relationship is a dynamic two-way exchange of perceived promises and obligations between employees and their organization: the **psychological contract** (Guest and Conway, 2002; Herriot, 1998; Kramer and Tyler, 1996; Rousseau, 1995). The concept of the psychological contract was written about in the early 1960s, but in recent years it has become a 'fashionable' framework within which to study aspects of the employment relationship (Guest and Conway, 2002; Sisson and Storey, 2000). One reason for the increased focus on the more cognitive-driven aspects of the employment relationship is corporate restructuring. Organizations seek both flexibility and employee commitment. The restructuring of many corporations has increased 'non-standard' forms of employment (temporary, part time, contract work), which has led to a 'no guarantees' attitude among many organizations (Rousseau, 1995). Yet, when competitive advantage appears to come from leveraging managerial or 'knowledge' workers' intellectual assets, and when those 'human assets' can 'walk out of the door' to work for a competitor, the notion of employee commitment emphasizes the importance of managing the psychological contract (Rousseau, 1995) and why we need to examine this contemporary concept more fully.

The 'psychological contract' is a metaphor that captures a wide variety of largely unwritten expectations and understandings of the two parties about their mutual obligations. Rousseau (1995, p. 9) defines it as 'individual beliefs, shaped by the organization, regarding terms of an exchange agreement between individuals and their organization'. Most discussants view the concept as a two-way exchange of perceived promises and obligations. Guest and Conway (2002) have conducted empirical studies on the psychological contract and define it as 'the perceptions of both parties to the employment relationship – organization and individual – of the reciprocal promises and obligations implied in that relationship' (p. 22). At the heart of the concept of the psychological contract are levers for individual commitment, motivation and task performance *beyond* 'expected outcomes' (Figure 1.2).

The concept of the psychological contract has a number of important features that challenge managers. The organization does not always communicate with one voice,

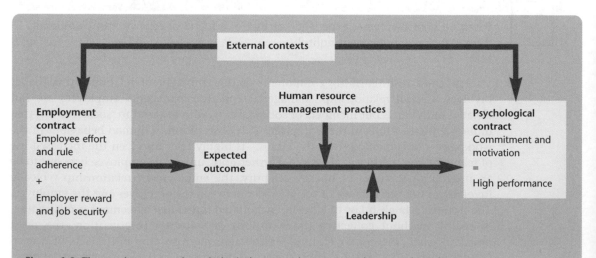

Figure 1.2 The employment and psychological contract between employees and employers

and ineffective communication practices are more likely to create different beliefs about the reciprocal promises and obligations (Guest and Conway, 2002). Thus, individual employees will have different perceptions of their psychological contract, even when the legal contract is identical. Managers, therefore, will be faced with a multitude of potential psychological contracts within the same organization (Bendal et al., 1998). A second feature of the psychological contract that challenges managers is that it reaffirms the notion that the employment relationship is perceived to be one of exchange – the *promissory* exchange of offers and the mutual obligation to fulfil these offers by the organization and employee. As Rousseau (1995, p. xi) observes, 'Promises about the future are the essence of contracts'. Yet, research confirms that senior managers often fail to keep their promises (Guest and Conway, 2002). A third feature of psychological contracts that has been emphasized is that they are shaped by the social and economic context, leadership, communication and HR practices. Rousseau (1995; Rousseau and Ho, 2000), for example, has persuasively shown that HR practices shape the day-to-day behaviours of employees and are 'the major means through which workers and their organization contract with each other. HR practices send strong messages to individuals regarding what the organization expects of them and what they can expect in return' (Rousseau, 1995, pp. 182–3).

Let us try to illustrate how HR practices create contracts. Eleanor has just graduated from university and is considering applying to Zap Airlines for an entry-level management position. She goes to the company's website and reads in its mission statement 'We are a learning organization'; the job advertisement she reads in the newspaper states 'Excellent career prospects'; at the selection interview, Eleanor is told, 'We encourage you to complete an MBA'; two weeks later Eleanor receives a letter offering her the position and detailing her salary and other terms; in the first 12 months, she works hard and frequently completes company work at the weekends; she hears stories from co-workers of other employees on the career 'fast-track' being promoted; at the year-end appraisal interview, she is reassured 'Keep up the good work and you'll be promoted'. In effect, the psychological contract to Eleanor is conveyed through several communication channels: written documents (e.g. mission statement, job advertisement) and oral discussions (e.g. selection interview, 'stories', appraisal interview). Thus, HR practices and organizational communications create both formal (e.g. letter of appointment) and psychological contracts to support organizational strategy. Recent UK research emphasizes the importance of organizational communication practices: 'Effective communication reduces perceived breach of the psychological contract', assert Guest and Conway (2002, p. 35).

? REFLECTIVE QUESTION

What do you think of the concept of the psychological contract? Why does there appear to be more interest in managing the psychological contract? How important is it to manage the psychological contract for (1) non-managerial employees and (2) managerial employees?

Human resource management functions

HRM is a body of knowledge and a set of policies and practices that shape the nature of work and regulate the employment relationship. Drawing on the recent work of

Squires (2001), these practices suggest three basic questions: What do HRM professionals do? What affects what they do? How do they do what they do? To help us answer the first question, we draw on the work of Harzing (2000), Millward et al. (2000) and Ulrich (1997) to identify key HRM functions. These are HR policies, programmes and practices designed in response to organizational goals and contingencies, and managed to achieve those goals. Each function contains alternatives from which managers can choose. The key functions are:

- *Planning:* preparing forecasts of future HR needs in the light of an organization's environment, mission and objectives, strategies, and internal strengths and weaknesses, including its structure, culture, technology and leadership.
- *Integrating:* appropriately integrating or linking HRM with the strategic management processes of the organization and coordinating clusters or bundles of HR practices to achieve the organization's desired goals.
- *Staffing:* obtaining people with the appropriate skills, abilities, knowledge and experience to fill jobs in the work organization. Key practices are HR planning, job analysis, recruitment and selection.
- *Developing:* analysing learning requirements to ensure that employees possess the knowledge and skills to perform satisfactorily in their jobs or to advance in the organization. Performance appraisal can identify employee key skills and 'competencies'.
- *Motivating:* the design and administration of reward systems. HR practices include job evaluation, performance appraisal, pay and benefits.
- *Designing:* the design and maintenance of work systems that are safe and promote employee health and workplace wellness in order to attract and retain a competent workforce and comply with statutory standards and regulations.
- *Managing relationships:* under this heading may be a range of practices, processes and structures that build cooperative relationships among employees. It also includes employee involvement/participation schemes in the workplace. In a union environment, it extends to nurturing cooperative relationships between the employer and the trade union, negotiating collective agreements and administrating the collective agreement.
- *Managing change:* which involves helping others to envision the future, communicating this vision, diagnosing and changing mindsets and mental models, setting clear expectations for performance, and developing the capability to reorganize people and reallocate other resources.
- *Evaluating:* designing the procedures and processes that measure, evaluate and communicate the value-added of HR practices and the entire HR system to the organization.

HRM WEB LINKS

Go to the website of the 2004 Workplace Employment Relations Survey: www.dti.gov.uk/employment/research-evaluation/grants/wers/index.html for data on the job responsibilities of HR specialists. Has there been any change in the functions performed by HR specialists over the last decade? Are HR specialists involved in all key areas of activity above?

HRM IN PRACTICE 1.2

THE 21ST CENTURY CHIEF HUMAN RESOURCES OFFICER (CHRO)

HRM GUIDE, APRIL 2006

Senior HR leaders have a changing role to play with the rise in prominence of issues such as:

- workforce demographics and global talent trends
- corporate scandals and intensifying regulatory challenges
- technology innovations enabling new ways of working
- endless pressures to boost workforce profitability and performance
- increasing globalization

Meet a developing 21st century professional: the Chief Human Resources Officer (CHRO).

A new report from Deloitte Consulting, *Strategist & Steward: The Evolving Role of the Chief Human Resources Officer*, outlines the challenges, processes and performance measures facing today's CHRO. According to the report, the modern CHRO is required increasingly to act as both strategist and steward. To quote Deloitte's media release, they are 'leaders who not only manage the HR function and operations team, but also collaborate directly with the CEO and board of directors on a range of critical business issues.'

Jeff Schwartz, principal and national co-leader of Deloitte Consulting's CHRO Services, said:

'The requirements and perception of HR are changing dramatically as this function's leadership is now expected to play a central role in building and shaping – not just staffing – the enterprise strategy.'

'The role of the CHRO as an enterprise business leader is still evolving – but this transformation has never been more timely or relevant.'

'This is an environment that HR leaders have longed for – where their executive peers would view HR as a business partner, rather than as a back-office administrator. Now CHROs must make sure that they are up to the task. The central challenge for CHROs is to view themselves as business leaders first – i.e. senior business executives responsible for the HR portfolio.' Deloitte Consulting's framework categorizes the CHRO's roles and responsibilities in four major ways:

- *Workforce Strategist*: Integrating business strategy and overall performance are increasingly important tasks.
- *HR Service Delivery Owner*: Despite the increasing focus on wider business issues, CHROs must still provide cost-effective, day-to-day HR administration and operations.
- *Organizational and Performance Conductor*: How do

businesses get the best performance from their employees? Organizations are increasingly complex and performance improvements can be required from departments.
- *Compliance and Governance Regulator*: CHROs must work directly with their boards on employee issues directly related to the critical areas of

- Regulatory compliance
- Ethics

'The role of the CHRO as an enterprise business leader is still evolving – but this transformation has never been more timely or relevant' said William Chafetz, principal and national co-leader of Deloitte Consulting's CHRO Services. 'As human capital-related issues, such as Baby Boomer retirement, generational differences, skills gaps and workforce globalization, continue to challenge a company's overall strategy and bottom line, the CHRO must become an increasingly familiar face and, in may companies, a potent force in the boardroom and executive suite, paving the way toward change, performance and new ways of working.'

Deloitte Consulting's *Strategist and Steward* report is available at http://www.deloitte.com/us/strategistandsteward.

Organizing the human resource function

How the HR function is organized and how much power it has relative to that of other management functions is affected both by external factors (e.g. a shortage of skilled knowledge workers, government employment regulations, social norms) and by internal factors unique to the organization (e.g. business strategy, organizational culture, corporate governance; see Figure 1.3 below). A *regulated-oriented* national business system, with strong trade unions, employment laws on equity and affirmative action and occupational health and safety regulations, elevates the status of the HR manager and strengthens the corporate HR function. In contrast, a *market-oriented* corporate culture, with employee pay based on going market rates, minimum investment in employee training and shorter employment contracts, is associated with outsourcing and decentralization of the HR function, which weakens the corporate HR function (Jacoby, 2005). The size of the organization also appears to negatively affect the extent to which HR services are provided internally by HR specialists from the central HR unit.

Klass et al.'s (2005) study, for example, found that an increasing number of small and medium organizations – defined as enterprises with 500 or fewer employees – have established a commercial relationship with a professional employer organization, which assumes responsibility for the delivery of HR services and interventions, a process usually referred to as 'outsourcing' (see also Chapter 4). They argue that the choice is not between an internal HR department or outsourcing HR services. Instead, small organizations have limited resources so the choice is between obtaining HR expertise and services from an external professional employer organization or foregoing such services. Besides the outsourcing of the HRM function, it would appear that an increasing number of European organizations have transferred responsibility for the HRM function from central internal HR departments to line management, a process referred to as 'decentralization' or 'devolution' (Andolšek and Štebe, 2005; Chartered Institute of Personnel and Development, 2006a; Jacoby, 2005). The espoused HRM canon posits that HR are so critical for organizational success that the responsibility for HRM activities must rest with all managers at all organizational levels and should not be left to HR specialists. As the HRM function has assumed a more strategic role, shifting from the margins of an organization system to its very centre, line management simultaneously appears to be taking on responsibility for HRM activities. As the HR function has assumed a more strategic role, decentralization has meant a transfer of operating authority from the central HR department to line managers (Jacoby, 2005).

The development of strategic HRM (Chapter 2) has fostered this devolution process (Andolšek and Štebe, 2005). The notion of 'strategic' HRM underscores the need for HR strategy to be integrated with other management functions and highlights the responsibility of line management to foster the high commitment and motivation associated with 'high-performing work systems'. The decentralization of HR practices can be explained by line management's new responsibility for implementing a change in organizational culture. Typically defined as the basic set of shared beliefs, values and norms that represents the unique character of an organization, organizational culture provides the context for managerial behaviour. A focus on organizational culture underscores the fact that line managers have a myriad of simultaneous challenges including leveraging workers' full potential and developing shared values, norms and commitment. As part of the integrative process, they are expected to better comprehend the strategic nature of 'best' or better HR practices, to execute them more adroitly (Andolšek and Štebe, 2005), and at the same time to intervene to affect the 'mental models' needed to build a high-performing culture (Pfeffer, 2005). Research reveals that the size of the organization affects the decentralization process. Based on the results of their European study, Andolšek and Štebe (2005) conclude that decentralization is greater in smaller organizations without a developed HRM team of specialists, and where there is less written HR strategy. Furthermore, national systems of employment regulation set the limits or encourage the decentralization of the HRM function: 'the stronger the institutional framework ... the less [sic] options a company may have to impose its own approach to regulating its HRM' (Andolšek and Štebe, 2005, p. 327).

Human resource management practices, contingencies and skills

The peculiarities of national employment systems, national culture and organizational culture are factors that foster the divergent tendencies in HRM practice and inform the second question referred to above, 'What affects what they do?' The HR activities that managers undertake vary from one workplace to another depending upon the *contingencies* affecting management. These contingencies can be divided into three broad categories: external context, strategy and organization. The external category encompasses the economic, political, legal regulations and social aspect (for a full discussion on this, see Chapter 4). The external variables frame the context for formulating competitive strategies (see Chapters 2 and 3). The organization, which is embedded within a national socioeconomic system, is subdivided into size, work and structure, and technology (see Chapter 5). As we have discussed, an organization employing a large workforce is more likely to employ at least one HRM specialist to assist line managers with people-related issues.

It is important to recognize that domestic HR policies and practices are contingent upon external and internal contexts and are highly interrelated. For example, a company responding to competitive pressures may change its manufacturing strategy by introducing 'self-managed' teams. This in turn will cause changes in recruitment and selection, training and reward priorities, for example hiring people perceived to be 'team players', designing cross-functional training and designing a reward system that encourages the sharing of information and learning. HRM practices, therefore, aim to achieve two sets of objective: to improve employee performance and to enhance organizational effectiveness.

The third of our three basic questions, 'How do HR professionals do what they do?' requires us to discuss the means or *skills* by which HR practitioners may accomplish their managerial work. Line managers and HR specialists use technical, cognitive and interpersonal processes and skills to accomplish their work (Squires, 2001; Yukl, 2002). They accomplish their role by mentoring and teaching (Agashae and Bratton, 2001; Senge, 1990). Power is important because it is part of the influence process, as are legal procedures. Communication practices and skills convey the formal and psychological contract to employees (Guest and Conway, 2002). Managing the employment relationship will involve a mix of processes and skills, and individual managers will vary in terms of their capacity or inclination to use them. These processes and skills, therefore, are about human relationships and go some way to explaining different management styles and the distinction between a manager and a leader (Bratton et al., 2004; Kotter, 1990). The three related dimensions of HRM – functions, contingencies and skills – can be brought together and diagrammatically shown in a three-dimensional model (Figure 1.3).

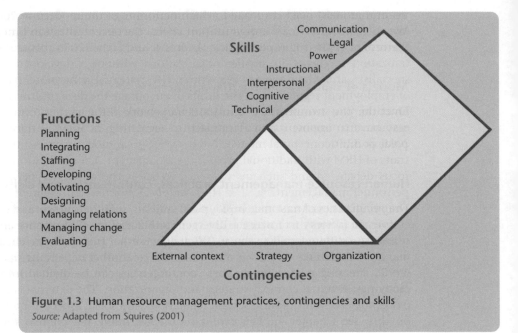

Figure 1.3 Human resource management practices, contingencies and skills
Source: Adapted from Squires (2001)

The model implies not only that HRM is a multidimensional activity, but also that the analysis of it has to be multidirectional (Squires, 2001). We might, therefore, examine the effect of new technology (a contingency) on HR functions, such as training and development, and how HR functions are translated into action, such as learning and communication processes. The model is useful in several ways: it serves as a pedagogical device that allows the reader to discover and connect a specific aspect of HRM within a consistent, general framework; it offers HR specialists a sense of professional 'identity' by identifying professional functions, processes and skills; and it helps the HR specialist to look beyond his or her immediate tasks and be aware of the 'totality of management' (Squires, 2001, p. 482).

HRM WEB LINKS

Go to the website of the HR professional associations (e.g. Australia, www.hrhq.com; Britain www.cipd.co.uk; Canada www.hrpao.org; or the USA www.shrm.org). Click on the 'Accreditation and/or certification' button. Using the information you find, compare the practices that HR professionals are formally accredited to practise with the practices listed in Figure 1.3. Does the information on the website give a comprehensive picture of 'What HRM specialists do'?

Theoretical perspectives on human resource management

Practice without theory is blind. (Hyman, 1989, p. xiv)

So far, we have focused on the meaning of management and the practical contribution that HRM practices make to the functioning of the modern work organization. We will now turn to an important part of the discourse – the search for the defining features of HRM – by exploring the **theoretical perspectives** in this area.

Models of human resource management

Over the past two decades, scholars have debated the meaning of the term 'human resource management' and attempted to define its fundamental traits by producing polar or multiconceptual models. A number of polar models contrast the fundamental traits of HRM with traditional personnel management. The models formulated help to focus debate around such questions as 'What is the difference between HRM and personnel management?' and 'Is HRM simply personnel management in a new fancy wrapping?' or, as Armstrong (1987, p. 32) mused, is HRM 'old wine in new bottles'?

We can identify five major HRM models that seek to demonstrate analytically the qualitative differences between traditional personnel management and HRM (Beer et al., 1984; Fombrun et al., 1984; Guest, 1987; Hendry and Pettigrew, 1990; Storey, 1992). These models fulfil at least four important intellectual functions for those studying HRM:

1. They provide an analytical framework for studying HRM (e.g. situational factors, stakeholders, strategic choice levels, notions of commitment and competence).
2. They legitimate certain HRM practices. A key issue here is the distinctiveness of HRM practices: 'it is not the presence of selection or training but a distinctive approach to selection or training that matters. It is the use of high performance or high commitment HRM practices' (Guest, 1997, p. 273).
3. They provide a characterization of HRM that establishes variables and relationships to be researched.
4. They serve as a heuristic device – something to help us discover and understand the world – for explaining the nature and significance of key HR practices and outcomes.

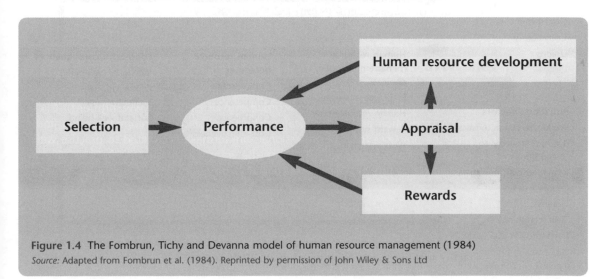

Figure 1.4 The Fombrun, Tichy and Devanna model of human resource management (1984)
Source: Adapted from Fombrun et al. (1984). Reprinted by permission of John Wiley & Sons Ltd

The Fombrun, Tichy and Devanna model of human resource management

The early HRM model developed by Fombrun et al. (1984) emphasizes the interrelatedness and coherence of HRM activities. The HRM 'cycle' in their model consists of four key constituent components: selection, appraisal, development and rewards (Figure 1.4). These four HR activities aim to increase organizational performance. The weakness of Fombrun et al.'s model is its apparent prescriptive nature, with its focus on four HR practices. It also ignores different stakeholder interests, situational factors and the notion of management's strategic choice. The strength of the model, however, is that it expresses the coherence of internal HR policies and the importance of 'matching' internal HR policies and practices to the organization's external business strategy (see Chapters 2 and 3). The notion of the 'HRM cycle' is also a simple model that serves as a heuristic framework for explaining the nature and significance of key HR practices and the interactions among the factors making up the complex fields of HRM.

The Harvard model of human resource management

The analytical framework of the 'Harvard model' offered by Beer et al. consists of six basic components:

1. situational factors
2. stakeholder interests
3. HRM policy choices
4. HR outcomes

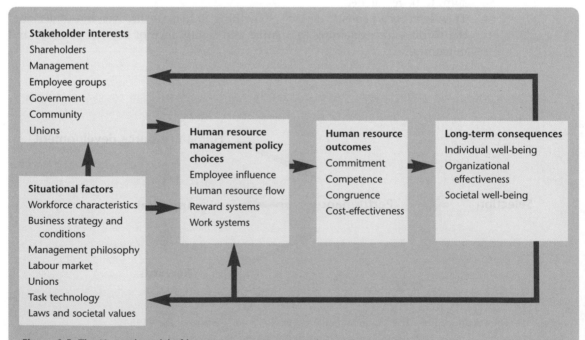

Figure 1.5 The Harvard model of human resource management
Source: Beer et al. (1984)

5. long-term consequences
6. a feedback loop through which the outputs flow directly into the organization and to the stakeholders.

The Harvard model for HRM is shown in Figure 1.5.

The *situational factors* influence management's choice of HR strategy. This normative model incorporates workforce characteristics, management philosophy, labour market regulations, societal values and patterns of unionization, and suggests a meshing of both 'product market' and 'sociocultural logics' (Evans and Lorange, 1989). Analytically, both HRM scholars and practitioners will be more comfortable with contextual variables included in the model because it conforms to the reality of what they know: 'the employment relationship entails a blending of business and societal expectations' (Boxall, 1992, p. 72).

The *stakeholder interests* recognize the importance of 'trade-offs', either explicitly or implicitly, between the interests of owners and those of employees and their organizations, the unions. Although the model is still vulnerable to the charge of 'unitarism', it is a much more pluralist frame of reference than that found in later models.

HRM policy choices emphasize that management's decisions and actions in HR management can be fully appreciated only if it is recognized that they result from an interaction between constraints and choices. The model depicts management as a real actor, capable of making at least some degree of unique contribution within environmental and organizational parameters and of influencing those parameters itself over time (Beer et al., 1984).

HR outcomes are high employee commitment to organizational goals and high individual performance leading to cost-effective products or services. The underlying assumptions here are that employees have talents that are rarely fully utilized at work, and that they show a desire to experience growth through work. Thus, the HRM model takes the view that employment relations should be managed on the basis of the assumptions inherent in McGregor's (1960) approach to people-related issues, which he labelled 'Theory Y'.[4]

The *long-term consequences* distinguish between three levels: individual, organizational and societal. At the level of the individual employee, the long-term outputs comprise the psychological rewards that workers receive in exchange for effort. At the organizational level, increased effectiveness ensures the survival of the organization. In turn, at the societal level, as a result of fully utilizing people at work, some of society's goals (e.g. employment and growth) are attained. A strength of the Harvard model is the classification of inputs and outcomes at both the organizational and the societal level, creating the basis for a critique of comparative HRM (Boxall, 1992). A weakness is the absence of a coherent theoretical basis for measuring the relationship between HR inputs, outcomes and performance (Guest, 1997).

A *feedback loop* is the sixth component of the Harvard model. As we have discussed, the situational factors influence HRM policy and choices. Conversely, however, long-term outputs can influence the situational factors, stakeholder interests and HR policies. The feedback loop in Figure 1.5 reflects this two-way relationship.

The Harvard model clearly provides a useful analytical basis for the study of HRM. It also contains elements that are analytical (i.e. situational factors, stakeholders, strategic choice levels) and prescriptive (i.e. notions of commitment, competence, etc.) (Boxall, 1992).

The Guest model of human resource management

David Guest (1989, 1997) has developed a more prescriptive theoretical framework, reflecting the view that a core set of integrated HRM practices can achieve superior individual and organizational performance. According to Guest, HRM differs from personnel management, and he attempts to identify the major assumptions or stereotypes underpinning each approach to employment management (Table 1.1).

Table 1.1 Points of difference between personnel management (PM) and human resource management (HRM)

	PM compliance	HRM commitment
Psychological contract	Fair day's work for a fair day's pay	Reciprocal commitment
Locus of control	External	Internal
Employee relations	Pluralist Collective Low trust	Unitarist Individual High trust
Organizing principles	Mechanistic Formal/defined roles Top-down Centralized	Organic Flexible roles Bottom-up Decentralized
Policy goals	Administrative efficiency Standard performance Cost minimization	Adaptive workforce Improving performance Maximum utilization

Source: Guest (1987)

HRM, according to the stereotypes shown in Table 1.1, is distinctively different from personnel management because:

- it integrates HR into strategic management, it seeks behavioural commitment to organizational goals
- the perspective is unitary with a focus on the individual
- it works better in organizations that have an 'organic' structure
- the emphasis is on a full and positive utilization of HR.

Implicit in the contrasting stereotypes is an assumption that HRM is 'better'. However, as Guest correctly states, 'this fails to take account of variations in context which might limit its effectiveness ... human resource management can most sensibly be viewed as an approach to managing the workforce' (1987, p. 508).

The central hypothesis of Guest's (1997) model is that if an integrated set of HR practices is applied in a coherent fashion, superior individual performance will result. It also assumes that this will result in superior organizational performance. The 'Guest model' has six components (Table 1.2):

1. an HR strategy
2. a set of HR policies
3. a set of HR outcomes

4. behavioural outcomes
5. a number of performance outcomes
6. financial outcomes.

The model acknowledges the close links between HR strategy and general business strategies: differentiation, focus, and cost (see Chapter 2). The 'core' hypothesis, however, is that HR practices should be designed to lead to a set of HR outcomes of 'high employee commitment', 'high quality' and 'flexibility'. Like Beer et al., Guest sees high employee commitment as a critical HR outcome, concerned with the goals of binding employees to the organization and obtaining behaviour outcomes of increased effort, cooperation and organizational citizenship. Quality refers to all aspects of employee behaviour that bear directly on the quality of goods and services. Flexibility is concerned with employees' receptiveness to innovation and change. The right-hand side of the model focuses on the link between HR practices and performance. Only when all three HR outcomes – commitment, quality and flexibility – are achieved can we expect superior performance outcomes. As Guest (1989, 1997) emphasizes, these HRM goals are a 'package; 'Only when a coherent strategy, directed towards these four policy goals, fully integrated into business strategy and fully sponsored by line management at all levels is applied will the high productivity and related outcomes sought by industry be achieved' (1990, p. 378).

Table 1.2 The Guest model of human resource management (HRM)

HRM strategy	HRM practices	HRM outcomes	Behaviour outcomes	Performance outcomes	Financial outcomes
Differentiation (innovation)	Selection		Effort/ motivation	High: Productivity	Profits
	Training	Commitment		Quality Innovation	
Focus (quality)	Appraisal		Cooperation		
Cost (cost-reduction)	Rewards	Quality	Involvement	Low: Absence	Return on investment
	Job design			Labour turnover Conflict	
	Involvement	Flexibility	Organizational citizenship	Customer complaints	
	Status and security				

Source: Guest (1997)

Guest (1987, 1989, 1997) recognizes a number of conceptual issues associated with the HRM model. The first issue is that the values underpinning the model are predominantly individualist-oriented; 'There is no recognition of any broader concept of pluralism within society giving rise to solidaristic collective orientation' (Guest, 1987, p. 519). The second conceptual issue concerns the status of some of the concepts. For example, the important concept of commitment is suggested to be 'a rather messy, ill-defined concept' (Guest, 1987, pp. 513–14). A third issue is the explicit link between HRM and performance. This raises the problem of deciding which types of performance indicator to use in order to establish these links (see Chapter 14). It has been argued elsewhere that Guest's model may simply be a polar **ideal type**, first developed by the German sociologist Max Weber, towards which organizations can move, thus positing unrealistic conditions for the practice of HRM (Keenoy, 1990, p. 367). It may also make the error of criticizing managers for not conforming to an image that academics have constructed (Boxall, 1992). Furthermore, it presents the HRM model as inconsistent with collective approaches to managing the employment relationship (Legge, 1989).

In contrast, the strength of the Guest model is that it clearly maps out the field of HRM and classifies the inputs and outcomes. The model is useful for examining the key goals usually associated with the normative models of HRM: strategic integration, commitment, flexibility and quality. Guest's constructed set of theoretical proposit-ions can also provide a framework for a critical dialogue on the precise nature of HRM and the tensions between 'hard' and 'soft' versions (Legge, 2005). The constituents of Guest's model linking HRM and performance can be empirically tested by research.

The Warwick model of human resource management

The Warwick model emanates from the Centre for Corporate Strategy and Change at the University of Warwick, UK, and with two particular researchers: Hendry and Petti-grew (1990). The Warwick model extends the Harvard framework by drawing on its analytical aspects. The model takes cognisance of business strategy and HR practices, the external and internal context in which these activities take place, and the processes by which such changes take place, including interactions between changes in both context and content. The strength of the model is that it identifies and classi-fies important environmental influences on HRM. It maps the connections between the outer (wider environment) and inner (organizational) contexts, and explores how HRM adapts to changes in the context. The implication is that those organizations achieving an alignment between the external and internal contexts will experience superior performance. A weakness of the model is that the process whereby internal HR practices are linked to business output or performance is not developed. The five elements of the model, shown in Figure 1.6, are:

1. outer context
2. inner context
3. business strategy content
4. HRM context
5. HRM content.

The Storey model of human resource management

The Storey model attempts to demonstrate the differences between what John Storey terms the 'personnel and industrials' and the HRM paradigm by creating an 'ideal type'. Storey devised the model by reconstructing the 'implicit models' conveyed by some managers during research interviews. We should note that the usage of 'ideal type' is a popular heuristic tool in the social sciences. It is a 'mental construct' and, in its conceptual purity, cannot be found in any workplace. Its purpose is 'to simplify by highlighting the essential features in an exaggerated way' (1992, p. 34). Storey's model characterizes HRM as 'an amalgam of description, prescription, and logical deduction' (Storey, 2001, p. 6). The four main elements in his HRM model (Table 1.3) are:

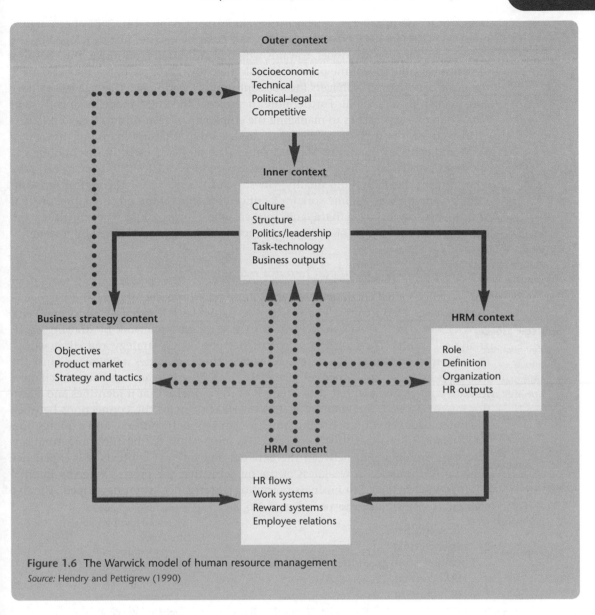

Figure 1.6 The Warwick model of human resource management
Source: Hendry and Pettigrew (1990)

1. beliefs and assumptions
2. strategic aspects
3. the role of line managers
4. key levers.

According to the stereotypes depicted in Table 1.3, HRM attempts to increase trust and employee commitment and aims to go 'beyond the contract'. The strategic aspects of Storey's model show HRM as central to corporate planning. The third component, line management, gives HRM specialists a 'transformational leadership' role in the organization. Research evidence from 15 UK 'core' organizations, studied by Storey (1992), suggests that line managers have emerged in almost all cases as the key players in HR issues. The key levers are shown in the lower portion of Storey's

Table 1.3 The Storey model of human resource management

Personnel and industrial relations (IR) and human resource management (HRM): the differences

Dimension	Personnel and IR	HRM
Beliefs and assumptions		
Contract	Careful delineation of written contracts	Aim to go 'beyond contract'
Rules	Importance of devising clear rules/mutuality	'Can do' outlook; impatience with 'rules'
Guide to management action	Procedures/consistency/control	'Business need'/flexibility/commitment
Behaviour referent	Norms/custom and practice	Values/mission
Managerial task vis-à-vis labour	Monitoring	Nurturing
Nature of relations	Pluralist	Unitarist
Conflict	Institutionalised	De-emphasised
Standardisation	High (for example 'parity' an issue)	Low (for example 'parity' not seen as relevant)
Strategic aspects		
Key relations	Labour–management	Business–customer
Initiatives	Piecemeal	Integrated
Corporate plan	Marginal to	Central to
Speed of decision	Slow	Fast
Line management		
Management role	Transactional	Transformational leadership
Key managers	Personnel/IR specialists	General/business/line managers
Prized management skills	Negotiation	Facilitation
Key levers		
Foci of attention for interventions	Personnel procedures	Wide-ranging cultural, structural and personnel strategies
Selection	Separate, marginal task	Integrated, key task
Pay	Job evaluation; multiple fixed grades	Performance-related; few if any grades
Conditions	Separately negotiated	Harmonisation
Labour–management	Collective bargaining contracts	Towards individual contracts
Thrust of relations with stewards	Regularised through facilities and training	Marginalised (with exception of some bargaining for change models)
Communication	Restricted flow/indirect	Increased flow/direct
Job design	Division of labour	Teamwork
Conflict handling	Reach temporary truces	Manage climate and culture
Training and development	Controlled access to courses	Learning companies

Source: Storey (1992)

model and are issues and techniques strongly featured, explicitly or implicitly, in researcher–manager interviews on HRM. Storey found considerable unevenness in the adoption of these key levers (performance-related pay, harmonization of conditions, the learning company). The 'implicit models' of the managers were used to devise a checklist of 25 key HRM variables to measure the degree of movement from one approach to the other in the 'core' organizations (Storey, 1992).

REFLECTIVE QUESTION

Reviewing the five models, what beliefs and assumptions are implied in them? For example, look at the direction of the arrows in Fombrun et al.'s model: what is the message for managers? What similarities and/or differences do you see? How well does each model define the characteristics of HRM?

Personnel management versus human resource management

It should be clear by now that an important part of the debate on HRM centres on the critical question: 'How does HRM differ from the deeply rooted personnel management model?' In the UK, in particular, it has proved difficult to arrive at an agreed meaning and significance of HRM. For some, HRM represents a new approach to managing people. For others, it is simply a relabelling and repackaging of 'progressive' personnel management (e.g. Blyton and Turnbull, 1992; Noon, 1992).

The review of the HRM models suggests that there is a difference between HRM and traditional personnel management, and these differences are not just a matter of semantics. This assertion is based upon a number of previously stated arguments. First, HRM is, in theory at least, integrated into *strategic planning*; as Hendry and Pettigrew (1990, p. 36) state, 'the strategic character of HRM is indeed distinctive'. Second, the HRM model emphasizes the importance of the *'psychological contract'*. Whereas personnel management is built on a legally constructed exchange – 'you do this work for that level of pay' – HRM attempts to build a cognitive construct concerned with developing a 'reciprocal commitment' and obligation between each of the parties. In this sense, the concept of employee commitment 'lies at the heart of any analysis of HRM' (Guest, 1998, p. 42). Third, the HRM paradigm explicitly emphasizes the importance of *learning* in the workplace. Fourth, HRM has overall focused heavily on the *individual* and the way in which individuals might be motivated and managed to achieve individual and organizational goals. The role of workplace trade union representatives and the *collective* aspects of relations between the workforce and management are marginalized. The rise in prominence of HRM has coincided with a period of decline in trade union membership (Blyton and Turnbull, 1998), which has led critics of HRM to argue convincingly that this approach to employment management represents a renaissance of unitarism or non-union employment strategy (see Chapter 11). Fifth, the theoretical models conceptualize HRM as a *proactive* central strategic management activity that is different from personnel management, with its implied passive connotations. Sixth, three of the HRM models make explicit reference to performance outcomes, and one compelling claim for HRM is that if organizations adopt this distinctive approach to employment management, the organization's financial 'bottom line' will improve.

The positive claim that a coherent 'bundle' of HR practices will, when aligned with organizational strategy, result in higher performance is an area of continuing research (see Chapter 14). The HRM phenomenon is 'highly controversial', certainly among the academic community, and its antecedents, its defining characteristics and its outcomes are much disputed (Storey, 2001). However, as others have suggested (Legge, 2005), what may be of more significance is not the message, but the messenger; HRM represents the 'discovery' of human capital as an asset by chief executives, and the message itself is being taken more seriously. The core argument of this chapter is that it is legitimate to define HRM as a particular approach to the management of the employment relationship with a distinctive set of HR policies and practices designed to produce specific outcomes: securing greater employee commitment and organizational performance.

Over the last decade, there has been incontrovertible evidence of a fall in the importance attached to 'collectivism' and a renaissance of 'individualism' in the management of the employment relationship in UK-based organizations (Kersley et al., 2005; Millward et al., 2000). A symbolic desire by employers to move towards 'individually oriented' cultures is the growth of contingency pay (Bacon and Storey, 1993). Many HRM techniques could exist within either an HRM or a traditional personnel management model, depending upon both circumstances and strategic choice (Keenoy, 1990). But also, the fairly extensive uptake of individual, rather than 'bundles' of, HR practices supports the view that a large proportion of UK organizations are still preoccupied with cost-focus strategies – the so-called 'hard' HRM model (Legge, 2005; Storey, 2001). In appraising the empirical evidence, there appears to be a disjuncture between knowledge of the normative HRM model and management practice. Despite many organizations looking for some magic formula that will provide a competitive advantage, relatively few organizations have integrated HRM planning into strategic business planning, a central element in the HRM model.

HRM IN PRACTICE 1.3

HR HAS MUCH TO CONTRIBUTE TO VOLUNTEER MANAGEMENT

SHANN KLIE, *CANADIAN HR REPORTER*, 22 MAY 2006, PP. 3–4

When Catherine Connelly's mother worked as a school librarian, she was completely dependent on volunteers to run the library programmes successfully. But there were limits as to what she could ask her volunteers to do because the dynamic between volunteers and their managers was very delicate. 'It's almost like they're a guest in your organization,' said Connelly, an assistant professor of HRM and management at the DeGroote School of Business at McMaster University in Canada. 'You can't be as bossy as you would ordinarily be. Volunteers are there doing you a favour.'

But volunteers are immensely valuable to the economy. Unfortunately many organizations have difficulty retaining volunteers and frequently accept low levels of performance, said Connelly. Employ-ers assume the experiences, attitudes and behaviours of volunteers are identical to those of paid employees, but they can't be motivated with promises of financial rewards and they have tenuous links to their organizations, she said.

But even though there are many differences between managing volunteers and paid staff, there are also a lot of similarities and HR professionals can play a big part in effectively managing this increasingly important workforce, said Marlene Deboisbriand, president of Volunteer Canada, an Ottawa-based group that promotes the role and value of volunteering. 'People mostly think of HR as paid human resources, but at least in the voluntary and non-profit sector, it includes voluntary human resources as well', she said.

The same challenges HR faces with paid staff – recruitment, retention, diversity, health and safety, screening and risk management – also apply to the management of volunteers, she said.

In some organizations, the responsibility of managing volunteers falls to the same HR professional who manages paid staff, said Connelly. 'HR has a lot to offer these organizations, but we need to be careful about transplanting HR theories from the business school directly into a voluntary or non-profit organization', she said. She compared volunteers to contract and temporary workers. Volunteers tend to have a more marginal position within the organization and might volunteer at an organization to get a foot in the door or gain work experience, she said.

> The same challenges HR faces with paid staff – recruitment, retention, diversity, health and safety, screening and risk management – also apply to the management of volunteers.

One of the best ways to motivate volunteers is to give them tasks that match the reasons they have for volunteering – be it learning a new skill or being more involved with people, said Connelly. 'You need to be careful that you're giving tasks to volunteers that keep them interested', she said. 'But you still have to very careful about the impact on paid staff. You don't want to be giving all the fun, interesting, nice tasks to volunteers, because then the paid staff will resent the volunteers coming in and taking all the good stuff. No one wants to be stuck just stuffing envelopes.'

In organizations where the management of volunteers falls under the purview of a volunteer manager, usually someone outside of HR, the HR department still has an important role to play, said Deboisbriand. HR needs to build links with volunteer managers, because these managers are doing a lot of the same functions as HR and can benefit from HR expertise, she said. 'It's really important that volunteers receive the proper training, especially if they're working in high-risk jobs in hospitals or as counsellors for disadvantaged populations such as the homeless and drug addicts', said Deboisbriand.

Just as no employer would consider hiring an employee without a thorough interview and screening process, the same applies to taking on new volunteers. But HR and volunteer managers have to walk a fine line because volunteers might find the typical screening process invasive, said Deboisbriand. To date, the management of volunteers hasn't been studied from an HR perspective, said Connelly.

Paradoxes in human resource management

The more critical evaluations of HRM models expose internal paradoxes. Paradox involves ambiguity and inconsistency, two or more positions that each sound reasonable yet conflict or even contradict each other. The use of paradox is one of a number of well-established techniques used by social scientists to engage their audiences and to encourage them to view social reality differently (Crow, 2005). Paradox is inherent in HRM, similar to what Charles Dickens (1859 [1952], p. 21) wrote in *A Tale of Two Cities*:

> It was the best of times, it was the worst of times, it was the age of wisdom, it was the age of foolishness, it was the epoch of belief, it was the epoch of incredulity, it was the season of Light, it was the season of Darkness, it was the spring of hope, it was the winter of despair, we had everything before us, we had nothing before us, we were all going direct to heaven, we were all going direct the other way …

For our purposes here, paradox results when managers, in pursuit of a specific organizational goal or goals, call for or carry out actions that are in opposition to the very goals the organization is attempting to accomplish. Critics of the HRM model have drawn upon the Weberian notion (Weber, 1968) of a **paradox of consequence**. arising from HR policies and practices. For example, new organizational designs have been introduced to improve productivity and employee autonomy. On the other hand, the productivity benefits arising from the new organizational forms are accompanied by a number of deleterious consequences on the psychological contract, which have the effect of undermining other espoused goals such as loyalty and commitment. More broadly, there is ambiguity with regard to whether the main role of the HRM function is a 'caring' or a 'controlling' one (Watson, 1986), and whether these ambiguities are exacerbated by the contradictions of capitalist employment relations and patriarchy (Legge, 2005). Townley (1994), for example, applying the work of Michel Foucault, offers a convincing argument that HR practices produce knowledge about work activities and employees' behaviour that enables the workforce to be more easily controlled. A whole battery of HR practices are designed to make employees more 'governable' and to bring order and stability to organizational life.

Legge's (1995, 2001, 2005) incisive critique of the HRM phenomenon identifies further ambiguities in the 'soft' and 'hard' schools of HRM. As such, she contrasts the 'rhetoric' and 'reality' of HRM where, for example, the rhetoric that asserts 'we are all managers now' owing to 'empowerment' conceals the legitimate question of whether a social group holding privileges and material returns can hold on to power: 'Paradoxically, then, a rhetoric adopted to enhance managerial legitimacy might prove the thin end of the wedge for at least some of its advocates' (Legge, 1995, p. 56). Similarly, the inclusion of the HR director in the strategic management team, the process of 'decentralization' or the act of 'giving away HR management' to line managers, and the outsourcing of HR activities might ultimately lead to the demise of the HR professional (Andolšek and Štebe, 2005; Caldwell, 2001; Klass et al., 2005): the 'Big Hat, No Cattle' syndrome (Fernie et al., 1994). As Legge (2005) points out, all this might undermine the perennial quest of HRM specialists for centrality and credibility. Armstrong (1989) has argued that short-term accounting controls practised in UK companies might well undermine long-term HR goals oriented towards employee development. In addition, the HRM rhetoric on investment in work-based learning is, according to Lyon and Glover (1998), at odds with the reality of 'HRM's organizationally sponsored ageism'.

One notable feature of much of the HRM literature is the tendency for the research and debate on the HRM model to be gender-blind. More recently, however, there has been more interest in the gender implications of HRM models (Dickens, 1994, 1998). Within that interest, Dickens has suggested that the HRM model might undermine the promotion of equal opportunities and that the gender equality assumption in the HRM model, which emphasizes the value of diversity and individual learning and development, is part of the rhetoric rather than the reality. Theoretically, one of the most important consequences of gender analysis in the HRM approach is its power to question research findings and analysis that segregates studies of HRM from those of gender divisions in the labour market (Dex, 1988), patriarchal power (Witz, 1986), issues of workplace inequality (Phillips and Phillips, 1993) and 'dual-role' work–family issues (Knights and Willmott, 1986; Platt, 1997). More importantly, however, including the development of gender in the study of the HRM model has a potential to move the HRM debate forward by examining the people who are deemed to be the 'recipients' of HRM theory and practice (Mabey et al., 1998b). Throughout this book, we emphasize that paradox is an inherent ongoing part of the employment relationship. By illustrating and explaining the inevitable paradoxes, we hope to encourage a deeper understanding and sensitivity with respect to HR-related issues.

Studying human resource management

This book presents a detailed examination of definitions, theories, historical developments and practices in the field of HRM, and in so doing exposes differing *standpoints* found in the management literature. Differing standpoints give rise to different perspectives, which in turn provide meaning, legitimacy and justification for people's actions. When people ask, 'What's your perspective on this?', they might just as well be asking, 'What is your own bias on this?', as each perspective is a particular bias, based on how *you* 'see' the issue and what vested interests are the most important to you (Pratt, 1998). Thus, perspectives are a 'lens' through which we view the world of work and organizations. When we refer to a perspective on HRM, we are speaking of an interrelated set of beliefs, values and intentions, which legitimize actions.

In our treatment of HRM, we present two standpoints: mainstream and critical. Although there are variations and tensions, *mainstream* management analysis makes a number of assumptions. They are that the managerial process takes place in rationally designed organizations to accomplish strategic goals; work organizations are harmonious bodies tending towards a state of equilibrium and order; and the basic task of managers is to manage resources for formal organizational ends. Thus, the mainstream perspective becomes inseparable from the notion of efficiency. The focus of much of the research and literature on management using this 'lens' is about finding the 'winning formula' so that more managers can become 'effective' (Thompson and McHugh, 2002). Common to all variations of mainstream perspectives is a failure to connect management processes to the 'master discourse' on market economics and globalization.

In contrast, *critical* perspectives on management set out to discover the ways in which power, control, conflict and legitimacy impact on employment relations. As is the case with mainstream perspectives, critical perspectives are based on numerous theoretical ideas. Obviously, the starting point is critique per se: the identification of the limitations, paradoxes, contradictions and ideological functions of orthodoxy (see, Clegg and Dunkerley, 1980; Mills and Simmons, 1995; Thompson and McHugh, 2002). In critical social analysis, *historical* and *contextual* considerations are underlined. Consequently, HRM theory and practice can only be understood as part of a management process located within a set of structural contingencies. This approach to studying HRM downplays the 'rhetoric-versus-reality' type of analysis and the clichéd distinctions between 'hard' and 'soft' HRM models by attending to the interplay of economic forces, power and conflict (Watson, 2004). In writing this text, we have found concepts from both mainstream and critical perspectives to be helpful for analysing HRM, albeit through the prism of our own bias. We hope that our approach to HRM will encourage the reader to question, to be sceptical and to seek multicausality when analysing employment relations in the contemporary workplace.

> ### ⚠ STUDY TIP
>
> Evaluating the debate on HRM more effectively means having an appreciation that most scholarly writing is 'embedded' within a dominant perspective (Reinharz, 1988, p. 168). Thus, Reinharz argues, 'we need to treat scientific writing not only as a source of information as defined by the author, but also as a text revealing something about the author'.
>
> Obtain a copy of T. Keenoy's (1990) article, 'Human resource management: rhetoric, reality and contradiction' (*International Journal of Human Resource Management*, **1**(3), 363–84) and a copy of G. Prahalad and C. Hamel's (1990) article 'The core competencies of the corporation' (*Harvard Business Review*, May–June, 79–91). Compare how the authors define HRM and describe its role in the organization. What asides, examples and taken-for-granted assumptions do the authors make? Are the authors 'silent' on some HRM issues (e.g. gender, discrimination, race/ethnicity, ageism)? After comparing the two articles, to what extent do the texts reveal something about the authors' 'lens' or perspective?

● Chapter summary

- In this introductory chapter, we have emphasized the primacy of managing people, individually and collectively, over other resources in the workplace. We have examined the development of the HRM model and emphasized that, since its earliest inception, it has remained highly controversial. In terms of its being a set of ideas associated with the management of employees, we have portrayed the HRM phenomenon as a historical outcome of rising neoliberalism ideology, much as the 'Social Contract' of the 1970s was an outcome of Keynesian economic planning. In the UK and USA, the HRM phenomenon emerged during the political era of Thatcherism and Reaganism (Guest, 1990). As such, HRM reflected an ascendancy of a new political and economic ideology and the changed conditions of national and global capitalism.

- To show the polysemy of the term 'human resource management', we have examined five theoretical models. We have discussed whether HRM now represents a new orthodoxy. Certainly, the language is different. The US models include those of Fombrun et al. and Beer et al. For Fombrun et al., HRM portrays an approach to managing employment relations that emphasizes the interrelatedness and coherence of HR practices; it is also one of the first models to explicitly suggest that specific bundles of HR practices lead to performance outcomes. The Harvard HRM model provides a useful analytical framework for studying HRM. It contains analytical elements, such as situational factors, stakeholder interests and strategic choice, and prescriptive elements stressing notions of employee commitment and competence.

- We have also examined HRM models developed by UK academics including Guest, Hendry and Pettigrew, and Storey. Guest has identified key features of personnel management and HRM that allow for comparative measurement. His model acknowledges the close links between HR strategy and general business strategies. Like Beer et al., Guest sees high employee commitment as a crucial outcome of HRM. The model developed by

Hendry and Pettigrew extended the Harvard framework, drawing on its analytical aspects by connecting the outer (wider environment) and inner (organizational) contexts, and exploring how HRM adapts to changes in the context. Storey sees HRM as a combination of description, prescription and logical deduction. His model of HRM focuses on four key elements: beliefs and assumptions, strategy, the role of line managers and key levers. Storey has also identified the 'Jekyll and Hyde' quality of HRM, or what are called 'soft' and 'hard' versions of HRM (Storey, 1989; Sisson and Storey, 2000).

- Whereas personnel management is built on a legally constructed exchange – 'You do this work for that level of pay' – HRM builds a cognitive construct concerned with developing a 'reciprocal commitment' and obligation between each of the parties. Managing the psychological contract is an important task for managers in the contemporary workplace. On balance, we consider that the 'soft' HRM metaphor is different from personnel management because it represents a different 'mindset' and approach to managing people in the workplace. In essence, 'soft', or what others have called 'high-commitment', HRM sees employees – managerial and non-managerial – as part of the solution rather than the problem. This distinctive approach may be summed up in this way: people empowered and continuously learning are central to organizational success.

- Paradox is an ongoing part of the employment relationship. The more critical evaluations of HRM expose internal paradoxes. Throughout this book, we illustrate and explain some of these inevitable paradoxes to encourage a deeper understanding of HR-related issues.

- Finally, the HRM discourse should be considered within the wider debates on globalization, competitive advantage and changing public policy. Every management function involves the execution of HR activities, so HRM has an enduring role in the task of designing work, resourcing the organization, motivating and controlling all employee groups, and managing the contradictions inherent in capitalist employment relations.

Key concepts

- Employment relationship
- Human resource management
- Ideal type
- Management
- Paradox of consequence
- Personnel management
- Psychological contract
- Theoretical perspective

Chapter review questions

1. What is human resource management and what role does it play in work organizations?

2. To what extent does the emergence of HRM reflect the rise and ideology of neoliberalism?

3. To what extent is HRM different from conventional personnel management – or is it simply 'old wine in new bottles'?

Further reading

Brewster, C., Wood, G., Brookes, M. and Van Ommeren, J. (2006) What determines the size of the HR function? A cross-nation analysis. *Human Resource Management*, **45**(1): 3–21.

Caldwell, R. (2001) Champions, adapters, consultants and synergists: the new change agents in HRM. *Human Resource Management Journal*, **11**(3): 39–52.

Chartered Institute of Personnel and Development (2006a) *Offshoring and the Role of HR*. London: CIPD.

Dickens, L. (1998) What HRM means for gender equality. *Human Resource Management Journal*, **8**(1): 23–38.

Jacoby, S. (2005) *The Embedded Corporation*. Princeton, NJ: Princeton University Press.

Legge, K. (2005) *Human Resource Management: Rhetorics and Realities*. London: Palgrave Macmillan.

Pfeffer, J. (2005) Changing mental models: HR's most important task. *Human Resource Management*, **44**(2): 123–8.

Storey, J. (ed.) (2001) Human resource management today: an assessment. In J. Storey (ed.) *Human Resource Management: A Critical Text* (pp. 3–20). London: Thompson Learning.

Tsui, A.A. and Wu, J.B. (2005) The new employment relationship versus the mutual investment approach: implications for human resource management. *Human Resource Management*, **44**(2): 115–121.

Watson, T. (2004) HRM and critical social sciences. *Journal of Management Studies*, **41**(3): 447–67.

Practising human resource management

Searching the web

Enter the website of an HR-related organization (e.g. www.hrhq.com) and an HR-related magazine (e.g. www.peoplemanagement.co.uk). Write a report outlining the key issues facing managers and HR specialists. To what extent, if at all, do the current issues reflect underlying tensions and contradictions within the HR function?

HRM group project

Form a study group of three to five people, and go to the website of any of the following organizations or one that interests members of the group (Compaq Computer (www.compaq.com); Airbus Industries (www.airbus.com); Wal-Mart (www.walmart.com); Virgin Airlines (www.virgin.com). Then go to the 'Company overview' of the site and look at the HRM department. Evaluate the goals of the HRM department in the light of the material contained in this chapter. Write a report that draws out the common features and identifies any key omissions (e.g. union–management relations) As a guide to your search, ask the following questions. How is the HRM department organized? Do the department's activities correspond to the key functional areas outlined in this chapter? Do the values listed here provide a good guideline for managerial behaviour at the company? Do the HR department's objectives emphasize the strategic role of HRM?

SERVO ENGINEERING

Servo Engineering was founded in 1897 to man-ufacture mining equipment. Over the last 50 years, the company has developed as a leading manufacturer of commercial vehicle compon-ents. In 1965, Servo Engineering became a sub-sidiary of Zipton Holding Ltd, which merged in 1977 with American Ensign. This multinational company has manufacturing plants in the UK, the USA and Germany. In 2006, the UK group had four sites in the UK.

In recent years, the company replaced over half its conventional and numerical control machines with computer numerical control. In addition, the firm organized production into six 'self-managed teams' (SMT). The SMTs were product-centred: for example, one SMT would manufacture a whole component such as vacuum pumps or air compressors. Each SMT operated as a miniature factory within the larger factory, and each SMT had sufficient machinery to complete the majority of the manufacturing stages. Processes outside the scope of the SMT were subcontracted out, either to another SMT or to an external contractor. The number of workers in each SMT varied between 12 and 50. The SMT operated a three-shift system: 6 am to 2 pm, 2 pm to 10 pm, and 10 pm to 6 am. The division of labour within the SMT is as follows. The 'SMT supervisor' had overall responsibility for the SMT. The product-coordinator's job was to ensure the supply of raw materials and parts to meet SMT production targets. The 'charge-hand' acted as progress-chaser. Below the supervisory grades was a hierarchy of manual grades reflect-ing different levels of training, experience and pay. For example, the 'setter' was apprentice-trained and was paid a skilled rate to set up the machines for the semi-skilled operators. Semi-skilled workers received little training. In total, the firm employed 442 people. Just over half the workforce belong to the trade union, AMICUS-AEEU, for collective-bargaining purposes.

The personnel manager at the factory was George Wyke, who had worked for the company for 25 years. Prior to becoming the personnel manager, he had been a union shop steward. He had no formal personnel management qualifica-tions. The company gave SMT leaders consider-able discretion for employee relations. To quote George Wyke: 'What the STM system has done as far as man-management [sic] is concerned, is that it has pushed that responsibility further down the chain, into the SMTs. So where some-body wants disciplining, they don't say to the personnel manager: "I want to sack this bastard. What can I do to get rid of him?" They know what they have got to do. The only time they will come to me is to seek advice on whether they are doing it right or wrong.' Although levels of unemployment were high in the area, the company had difficulty recruiting 'good' people at its factory in Yorkshire. Also, absenteeism and turnover were high, as shown here.

Absenteeism	2005	Turnover rates
5.3	January	34.4
5.7	February	20.4
8.0	March	27.5

The apparent low level of commitment among manual employees can be explained in two ways. First, shop stewards and workers expressed considerable discontent over the bonus scheme: the standard time allowed to complete a particular task was not considered adequate to earn a 'decent' bonus. Second, the way in which the SMTs were designed resulted in operatives performing narrow, repetitive tasks under close supervision. The personnel manager, George Wyke, is due to retire this

Christmas. The plant manager, Elizabeth Bell, has been concerned for some time over employee relations in the factory and the management style of George Wyke and some of the SMT leaders. Elizabeth Bell has decided to seek an external candidate to replace the incumbent personnel manager. Gleaning through the ads in newspapers and journals, she also decided to drop the term `personnel' and advertise for a 'human resource' manager.

Source: Adapted from The motor components company: Japanization in large-batch production. In J. Bratton (1992) *Japanization at Work* (pp. 103–30). Basingstoke: Macmillan – now Palgrave Macmillan.

Discussion questions

1. Describe the main features of George Wyke's approach to managing employment relations. How does Wyke's approach differ from the stereotyped HRM approach?

2. Discuss the contribution that an HRM professional could make to this company.

 ## HR-related skill development

No skill is as important to managers as report-writing. Managers and HR specialists have to write progress reports, proposals, accident reports and evaluation reports to name but a few. You should use a formal report format if your subject matter is important to your organization, if your findings are extensive or if your readership is large or important. Many of the assignments in the sections 'Practising human resource management', ask you to write a formal report. Remember that a formal report, especially if it is to be sent outside the organization, is meant to reflect and maintain the organization's professional image. You will develop your skill at report-writing by going to our website (www.palgrave.com/business/brattonandgold4) and clicking on 'Report writing'.

Notes

1. Jeffrey Pfeffer (1998) *The Human Equation,* p. 5.
2. Maureen Shaw, COE (2002) Quoted in the *Globe and Mail,* January 16, p. M2.
3. Lynda Gratton (2005) Managing integration through cooperation. *Human Resource Management,* p. 153.
4. According to McGregor (1960; *The Human Side of Enterprise.* New York: McGraw-Hill), 'people work because they want to work', not because they have to work. Thus, the Theory Y view of people assumes that when workers are given challenging assignments and autonomy over their work assignments, they will respond with high motivation, high commitment and high performance.

Chapter two

Strategic human resource management

John Bratton

Strategic human resource management is the process of linking the human resource function with the strategic objectives of the organization in order to improve performance.

'If a global company is to function successfully, strategies at different levels need to inter-relate.'[1]

'An organization's [human resource management] policies and practices must fit with its strategy in its competitive environment and with the immediate business conditions that it faces.'[2]

'The [human resources–business strategy] alignment cannot necessarily be characterized in the logical and sequential way suggested by some writers; rather, the design of an HR system is a complex and iterative process.'[3]

Chapter outline

Chapter objectives

After studying this chapter, you should be able to:

1. Explain the meaning of strategic management and give an overview of its conceptual framework

2. Describe the three levels of strategy formulation and comment on the links between business strategy and human resource management (HRM)

3. Explain three models of human resources (HR) strategy: control, resource and integrative

4. Comment on the various strategic HRM themes of the HR–performance link: re-engineering, leadership, workplace learning and trade unions

Introduction

In the first chapter, we examined the theoretical debate on the nature and significance of the human resource management (HRM) model; in this chapter, we explore an approach to HRM labelled **strategic human resource management**, or SHRM. By a strategic approach to HRM, we are referring to a managerial process requiring human resource (HR) policies and practices to be linked with the strategic objectives of the organization. Just as the term 'human resource management' has been contested, so too has the notion of SHRM. One aspect for debate is the lack of conceptual clarity (Bamberger and Meshoulam, 2000). Do, for example, the related concepts of SHRM and **human resource strategy** relate to a process or an outcome?

The strategic HRM debate focuses on several important questions. First, what determines whether an organization adopts a strategic approach to HRM, and how is HR strategy formulated? Of interest is which organizations are most likely to adopt a strategic approach to HRM. Is there, for example, a positive association between a given set of external and internal characteristics or contingencies and the adoption of SHRM? Much of the debate on this question has centred around normative models of 'best fit', that is, aligning HR strategy to the organization's context. One influential 'best-fit' model advocates that HR policies and practices should fit the organization's competitive strategy (otherwise called 'external fit'). Another area of interest concerns the policies and practices making up different HR strategies. Is it possible to identify a cluster or 'bundle' of 'best HR practice' with different strategic competitive models? Finally, much research on productivity in recent years has been devoted to examining the relationship between different clusters of 'best HR practice' and organizational performance (see, for example, Boselie et al., 2001; Guest, 1997; Michie and Sheehan, 2005). Does HR strategy really matter? For organizational practitioners who are looking for ways in which to gain a competitive advantage, the implication of HR strategic choices for company performance is certainly the key factor.

Before, however, we look at some of the issues associated with the SHRM debate, we need first to examine the strategic management process. This chapter also examines whether it is possible to speak of different 'models' of HR strategy and the degree to which these types of HR strategy systematically vary between organizations. We then consider some issues associated with SHRM, including international and comparative SHRM. As for the question of whether there is a positive association between different HR strategies and organizational performance, we are of the opinion that, given the importance and volume of the research surrounding this issue, the topic warrants an extended discussion (Chapter 14). In the current chapter, we address a number of questions, some essential to our understanding of how work organizations operate in the early 21st century work and the role of HRM therein. How do 'big' corporate decisions impact on HRM? Does the evidence suggest that firms adopting different competitive strategies adopt different HR strategies? How does HRM impact on the 'bottom line'? There is a common theme running through this chapter, much of the HR research pointing out that there are fundamental structural constraints that attest to the complexity of implementing different HRM models.

Strategic management

The word 'strategy', deriving from the Greek noun *strategus*, meaning 'commander in chief', was first used in the English language in 1656. The development and usage of the word suggests that it is composed of *stratos* (army) and *agein* (to lead). In a management context, the word 'strategy' has now replaced the more traditional term 'long-term planning' to denote a specific pattern of behaviour undertaken by the upper echelon of the organization in order to accomplish performance goals. Wheelen and Hunger (1995, p. 3) define **strategic management** as 'that set of managerial decisions and actions that determines the long-run performance of a corporation'. Similarly, Hill and Jones (2004, p. 4) define strategy as 'an action a company takes to attain superior performance'. As Boxall and Purcell (2003, p.28) emphasize, we should avoid the mistake of equating strategy with formal plans: 'strategy is best discerned in behaviour'. Strategic management is best defined as a continuous process that requires a constant adjustment of three major interdependent poles: the values of senior management, the environment, and the resources available (Figure 2.1).

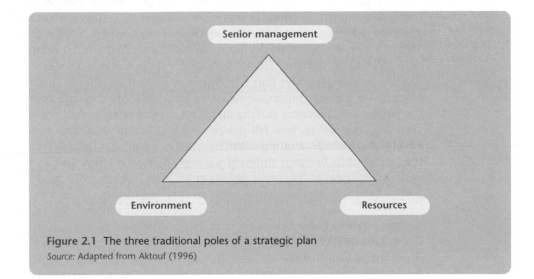

Figure 2.1 The three traditional poles of a strategic plan
Source: Adapted from Aktouf (1996)

HRM IN PRACTICE 2.1

RAISING THE PROFILE OF THE HR AGENDA

MARTIN CLARKE, *PEOPLE MANAGEMENT*, 1 SEPTEMBER 2005

HR professionals need to be more questioning of the function's fundamental values if they are to raise the profile of the HR agenda with top management.

Before engaging in any kind of family debate, my father used to say: 'State your terms'. So here they are: I'm an ex-HR director from the SME sector who cares deeply about people

strategy, and I want to get critical about the HR function.

> **The business context is now too messy and individualised for corporate neatness.**

In my role I routinely ask managers: 'Who believes that their HR function adds strategic

value?' On average, only 15 per cent stand up for their hardworking HR colleagues, and that figure hasn't changed in eight years. So the good news is that there are effective strategic HR leaders among us – but what about the other 85 per cent?

The HR function needs to address three crucial issues urgently. The first is the profession's relentless drive for consistency and alignment. The business context is now too messy and individualised for corporate neatness. One senior manager recently told me that HR had introduced so many policies that intervened between his managers and their staff, that his managers no longer felt a sense of obligation to them.

Second, allied to the drive for consistency is the mantra of best practice. Research at Cranfield reveals a wide disjuncture between HR best-practice priorities and the real needs of the business. Best practice provides safety and reassurance for HR, but can't really enable an organisation to gain strategic advantage.

Third, much research about HR raises concerns about the business acumen of HR professionals. This is not about professional qualifications but about the willingness of HR staff to develop themselves beyond an HR mindset. Interestingly, HR is the least represented of all the 'traditional' functions on the general management programme at Cranfield. Is this because HR people feel budgets should be spent on others, or because they are unwilling to have their own business management expertise challenged?

To redress this, HR specialists need to consider whether the starting point for HR is their own values and practices or those of the business. Managing is full of ambiguity, so HR needs to embrace rather than reduce the complexity of the role. This means devolving power to line managers. Construct your people strategy from a mindset that seeks to create the least number of uniform policies, rather than pursue a level of consistency usually unwanted by your internal customers. Be critical about your department: where does it really add value? Finally, acknowledge that businesses will always be a sea of competing interests.

Model of strategic management

In the descriptive and prescriptive management texts, strategic management appears as a cycle in which several activities follow and feed upon one another. The strategic management process is typically broken down into five steps:

1. mission and goals
2. environmental analysis
3. strategic formulation
4. strategy implementation
5. strategy evaluation.

Figure 2.2 illustrates how the five steps interact. At the corporate level, the strategic management process includes activities that range from appraising the organization's current mission and goals to strategic evaluation.

The first step in the strategic management model begins with senior managers evaluating their position in relation to the organization's current *mission and goals*. The mission describes the organization's values and aspirations; it is the organization's raison d'être and indicates the direction in which senior management is going. Goals are the desired ends sought through the actual operating procedures of the organization and typically describe short-term measurable outcomes (Daft, 2004).

Environmental analysis looks at the internal organizational strengths and weaknesses and the external environment for opportunities and threats. The factors that are most important to the organization's future are referred to as 'strategic factors' and can be summarised by the acronym SWOT – Strengths, Weaknesses, Opportunities and Threats.

Strategic formulation involves senior managers evaluating the interaction between strategic factors and making strategic choices that enable the organization to meet its

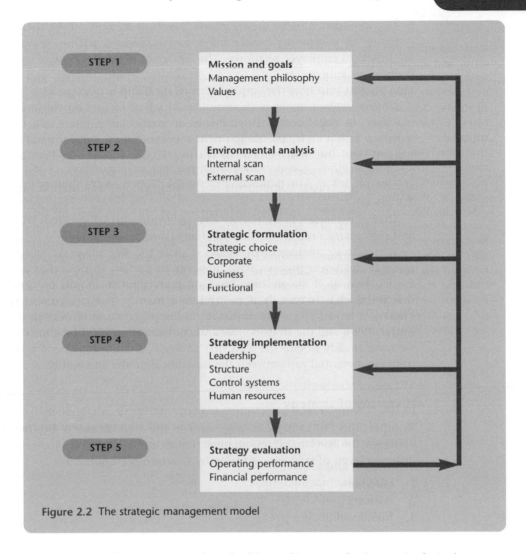

Figure 2.2 The strategic management model

business goals. The process, as described here, draws on the 'strategic choice' perspective (Child, 1972). Some strategies are formulated at the corporate, business and specific functional levels. The concept of 'strategic choice' underscores the importance of asking such questions as who makes decisions and why they are made. It also draws attention to strategic management as a 'political process' whereby decisions and actions on issues are taken by a 'power-dominant' group of managers within the organization. Child (1972, quoted in McLoughlin and Clark, 1988, p. 41) affirms this interpretation of the decision-making process when he writes:

> [When] incorporating strategic choice in a theory of organizations, one is recognizing the operation of an essentially political process, in which constraints and opportunities are functions of the power exercised by decision-makers in the light of ideological values.

In a political model of strategic management, it is necessary to consider the distribution of power within the organization. According to Purcell and Ahlstrand (1994,

p. 45), we must consider 'where power lies, how it comes to be there, and how the outcome of competing power plays and coalitions within senior management are linked to employee relations'. The strategic choice perspective on organizational decision-making makes the discourse on strategy 'more concrete' and provides important insights into how the employment relationship is managed.

Strategy implementation is an area of activity that focuses on the techniques used by managers to implement their strategies. In particular, it refers to activities that deal with leadership style, the design of the organization, the information and control systems, and the management of HR (see Figure 1.2 above). Prominent academics emphasize that leadership (e.g. Kotter, 1996) and HR policies and practices (Schuler et al., 2001) are crucial components of the strategic implementation process (see Table 2.1 below).

Strategy evaluation is an activity that determines to what extent the actual change and performance match the desired change and performance.

The strategic management model depicts the five major activities as forming a rational and linear process. It is, however, important to note that it is a normative model, that is, it shows how strategic management should be done rather than describing what is actually done by senior managers (Wheelen and Hunger, 1995). There is a tendency to underestimate the importance of leadership (Champy, 1996; Kotter, 1996) and the strategic role and contribution of HRM (Schuler et al., 2001). As we have already noted, the idea that strategic decision-making is a political process implies a potential gap between the theoretical model and reality.

Hierarchy of strategy

Another aspect of strategic management in the multidivisional business organization concerns the level to which strategic issues apply. Conventional wisdom identifies different levels of strategy – a **hierarchy of strategy** (Figure 2.3):

1. corporate
2. business
3. functional.

Corporate-level strategy

Corporate-level strategy describes a corporation's overall direction in terms of its general philosophy towards the growth and the management of its various business units. Such strategies determine the types of business a corporation wants to be involved in and what business units should be acquired, modified or sold. This strategy addresses the question, 'What business are we in?' Devising a strategy for a multidivisional company involves at least four types of initiative:

- establishing investment priorities and steering corporate resources into the most attractive business units
- initiating actions to improve the combined performance of those business units with which the corporation first became involved
- finding ways to improve the synergy between related business units in order to increase performance
- making decisions dealing with diversification.

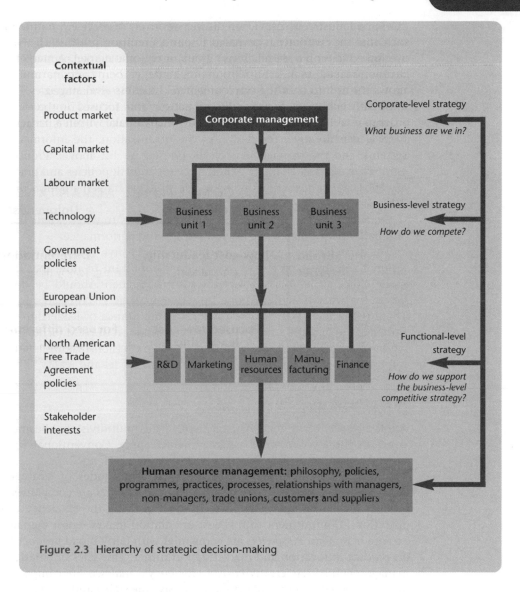

Figure 2.3 Hierarchy of strategic decision-making

Business-level strategy

Business-level strategy deals with decisions and actions pertaining to each business unit, the main objective of a business-level strategy being to make the unit more competitive in its marketplace. This level of strategy addresses the question, 'How do we compete?' Although business-level strategy is guided by 'upstream', corporate-level strategy, business unit management must craft a strategy that is appropriate for its own operating situation. In the 1980s, Porter (1980, 1985) made a significant contribution to our understanding of business strategy by formulating a framework that described three competitive strategies: cost leadership, differentiation and focus.

The **low-cost leadership** strategy attempts to increase the organization's market share by having the lowest unit cost and price compared with those of competitors. The simple alternative to cost leadership is **differentiation strategy**. This assumes that managers distinguish their services and products from those of their competitors in the same industry by providing distinctive levels of service, product or high quality such that the customer is prepared to pay a premium price. With the focus strategy, managers focus on a specific buyer group or regional market. A market strategy can be narrow or broad, as in the notion of niche markets being very narrow or focused. This allows the firm to choose from four generic business-level strategies – low-cost leadership, differentiation, focused differentiation and focused low-cost leadership – in order to establish and exploit a competitive advantage within a particular competitive scope (Figure 2.4).

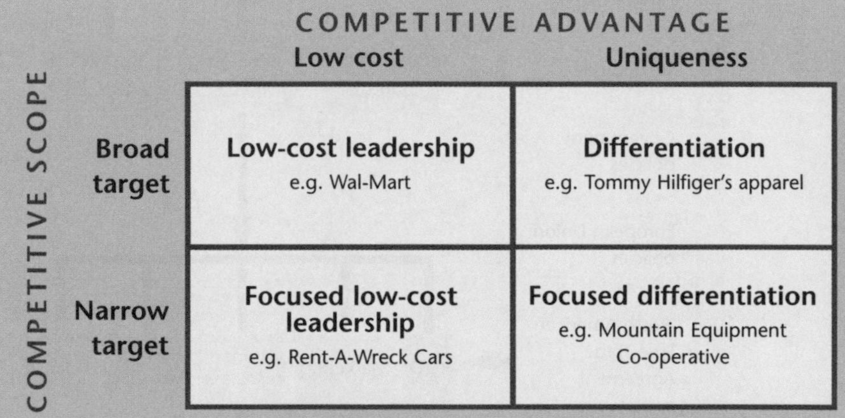

		COMPETITIVE ADVANTAGE	
		Low cost	Uniqueness
COMPETITIVE SCOPE	**Broad target**	**Low-cost leadership** e.g. Wal-Mart	**Differentiation** e.g. Tommy Hilfiger's apparel
	Narrow target	**Focused low-cost leadership** e.g. Rent-A-Wreck Cars	**Focused differentiation** e.g. Mountain Equipment Co-operative

Figure 2.4 Porter's competitive strategies
Source: Adapted from Porter (1985)

Miles and Snow (1984) have identified four modes of strategic orientation: defenders, prospectors, analysers and reactors. *Defenders* are companies with a limited product line and a management focus on improving the efficiency of their existing operations. Commitment to this cost orientation makes senior managers unlikely to explore new areas. *Prospectors* are companies with fairly broad product lines that focus on product innovation and market opportunities. This sales orientation makes senior managers emphasize 'creativity over efficiency'. *Analysers* are companies that operate in at least two different product market areas, one stable and one variable. In this situation, senior managers emphasize efficiency in the stable areas and innovation in the variable areas. *Reactors* are companies that lack a consistent strategy–structure–culture relationship. In this reactive orientation, senior management's responses to environmental changes and pressures thus tend to be piecemeal strategic adjustments. Competing companies within a single industry can choose any one of these four types of strategy and adopt a corresponding combination of structure, culture and processes consistent with that strategy in response to the environment. The different competitive strategies influence the 'downstream' functional strategies.

Functional-level strategy

Functional-level strategy pertains to the major functional operations within the business unit, including research and development, marketing, manufacturing, finance and HR. This strategy level is typically primarily concerned with maximizing resource productivity and addresses the question, 'How do we support the business-level competitive strategy?' Consistent with this, at the functional level, HRM policies and practices support the business strategy goals.

These three levels of strategy – corporate, business and functional – form a hierarchy of strategy within large multidivisional corporations. In different corporations, the specific operation of the hierarchy of strategy might vary between 'top-down' and 'bottom-up' strategic planning. The top-down approach resembles a 'cascade' in which the 'downstream' strategic decisions are dependent on higher 'upstream' strategic decisions (Wheelen and Hunger, 1995). The bottom-up approach to strategy-making recognizes that individuals 'deep' within the organization might contribute to strategic planning. Mintzberg (1978) has incorporated this idea into a model of 'emergent strategies', which are unplanned responses to unforeseen circumstances by non-executive employees within the organization. Strategic management literature emphasizes that the strategies at different levels must be fully integrated. Thus:

> strategies at different levels need to inter-relate. The strategy at corporate level must build upon the strategies at the lower levels in the hierarchy. However, at the same time, all parts of the business have to work to accommodate the overriding corporate goals. (F. A. Maljers, chairman of the board of Unilever, quoted by Wheelen and Hunger, 1995, p. 20)

The need to integrate business strategy and HRM strategy has received much attention from the HR academic community, and it is to this discourse that we now turn.

HRM IN PRACTICE 2.2

CULTURE SHIFT INVIGORATES DELL

ANNA SCOTT, *PEOPLE MANAGEMENT*, 23 MARCH 2006

A culture change at Dell has allowed it to strengthen its position in the marketplace, according to an HR vice-president at the computer company. It has moved from a focus on growth and US-centricity to one on leadership, talent management and a global outlook.

Pat Casey, vice-president for HR in Europe, the Middle East and Africa, said the creation of the new culture was driven by the market downturn following the events of 11 September 2001, lower growth and a flat share price.

'We needed a culture that would have some "glue" that was more than a share price. Ultimately, this became the "Soul of Dell",' he said.

'We now have a programme of creating leaders.'

The 'Old Dell' culture was characterised by growth, and the company was US-centric. 'It was a business model, not a culture,' Casey said. 'For HR it was about hiring and paying people, and filling in forms.'

The 'New Dell' is characterised by leadership and talent management, and 50 per cent of Dell's business is outside the US.

'Eighty per cent of our senior executives have come from within the company. In the Old Dell, 75 per cent came from outside. We now have a programme of creating leaders,' Casey said.

The company also runs a twice-yearly culture survey, 'Tell Dell', which measures every manager on trust, providing feedback, creating alignment, developing capability, work-life balance and managerial effectiveness. No executive is promoted without their Tell Dell scores being taken into account, and their bonus is also affected.

Strategic human resource management

The SHRM literature is rooted in 'manpower' (sic) planning, but it was the work of influential management gurus (e.g. Ouchi, 1981; Peters and Waterman, 1982), affirming the importance of the effective management of people as a source of competitive advantage, that encouraged academics to develop frameworks emphasizing the strategic role of the HR function (e.g. Beer et al., 1984; Fombrun et al., 1984) and attaching the prefix 'strategic' to the term 'human resource management'. Interest among academics and practitioners in linking the strategy concept to HRM can be explained from both the 'rational choice' and the 'constituency-based' perspective. There is a managerial logic in focusing attention on people's skills and intellectual assets to provide a major competitive advantage when technological superiority, even once achieved, will quickly erode (Barney, 1991; Pfeffer, 1994, 1998). From a 'constituency-based' perspective, it is argued that HR academics and HR practitioners have embraced SHRM as a means of securing greater respect for HRM as a field of study and, in the case of HR managers, of appearing more 'strategic', thereby enhancing their status within organizations (Bamberger and Meshoulam, 2000; Pfeffer and Salancik, 1977; Powell and DiMaggio, 1991; Purcell and Ahlstrand, 1994; Whipp, 1999).

REFLECTIVE QUESTION

Why have academics and HR professionals embraced SHRM? Is there a strong business case for the strategic approach to HRM, or is it more the case that academics and HR professionals have embraced SHRM out of self-interest? What do you think of these arguments?

Concepts and models

In spite of the increasing volume of research and scholarship, the precise meaning of strategic HRM and HR strategy remains problematic. It is unclear, for example, which one of these two terms relates to an *outcome* or a *process* (Bamberger and Meshoulam, 2000). For Snell et al. (1996, p. 62), 'strategic HRM' is an outcome: 'as organizational systems designed to achieve sustainable competitive advantage through people'. For others, however, SHRM is viewed as a process, 'the process of linking HR practices to business strategy' (Ulrich, 1997, p. 89). Similarly, Bamberger and Meshoulam (2000, p. 6) describe SHRM as 'the process by which organizations seek to link the human, social, and intellectual capital of their members to the strategic needs of the firm'. According to Ulrich (1997, p. 190) 'HR strategy' is the outcome: 'the mission, vision and priorities of the HR function'.

Consistent with this view, Bamberger and Meshoulam (2000, p. 5) conceptualize HR strategy as an outcome: 'the pattern of decisions regarding the policies and practices associated with the HR system'. The authors go on to make a useful distinction between senior management's 'espoused' HR strategy and their 'emergent' strategy. The espoused HR strategy refers to the pattern of HR-related decisions made but not necessarily implemented, whereas the emergent HR strategy refers to the pattern of HR-related decisions that have been applied in the workplace. Thus, 'espoused HR strategy is the road map … and emergent HR strategy is the road actually traveled' (Bamberger and Meshoulam, 2000, p. 6). Purcell (2001) has also portrayed HR strategy as 'emerging patterns of action' that are likely to be much more 'intuitive' and only 'visible' after the event.

We begin the discussion of SHRM and HR strategy with a focus on the link between organizational strategy formulation and strategic HR formulation. A range of business–HRM links has been classified in terms of a proactive–reactive continuum (Kydd and Oppenheim, 1990) and in terms of environment–HR-strategy–business-strategy linkages (Bamberger and Phillips, 1991). In the 'proactive' orientation, the HR professional has a seat at the strategic table and is actively engaged in strategy formulation. In Figure 2.3 above, the two-way arrows on the right-hand side showing both downward and upward influence on strategy depict this type of proactive model.

At the other end of the continuum is the 'reactive' orientation, which sees the HR function as being fully subservient to corporate and business-level strategy, and organizational-level strategies as ultimately determining HR policies and practices. Once the business strategy has been determined, an HR strategy is implemented to support the chosen competitive strategy. This type of reactive orientation would be depicted in Figure 2.3 above by a *one-way downward arrow* from business-level to functional-level strategy. In this sense, an HR strategy is concerned with the challenge of matching the Philosophy, Policies, Programmes, Practices and Processes – the 'five Ps' – in a way that will stimulate and reinforce the different employee role behaviours appropriate for each competitive strategy (Schuler, 1989, 1992).

Here we draw on Randall et al.'s (2001) recent work to emphasize the strategic 'reactive' role and contribution of HRM. Strategic management plans at corporate and business level provide the context within which HR plans are developed and implemented. HR plans provide a map for managers to follow in order to fulfil the core responsibilities of the HR function, which are to ensure that:

- the organization has the right number of qualified employees
- employees have the right skills and knowledge to perform efficiently and effectively
- employees exhibit the appropriate behaviours consistent with the organization's culture and values
- employees meet the organization's motivational needs.

These four core activities are the leitmotiv of HRM and, according to Randall et al. (2001), constitute the **four-task model of HRM**. The four core HR tasks provide the rationale that guides the strategic choice of HR policies and practices (Table 2.1).

The importance of the environment as a determinant of HR strategy has been incorporated into some 'best-fit' or contingency models. Extending strategic management concepts, Bamberger and Phillips' (1991) model depicts links between three poles: the environment, HR strategy and the business strategy (Figure 2.5). In the hierarchy of the strategic decision-making model (see Figure 2.3 above), the HR strategy is influenced by contextual variables such as markets, technology, national government policies, European Union policies and trade unions. Purcell and Ahlstrand (1994, p. 36) argue, however, that those models which incorporate contextual influences as a mediating variable of HR policies and practices tend to lack 'precision and detail' in terms of the precise nature of the environment linkages, and that 'much of the work on the linkages has been developed at an abstract and highly generalized level'.

Table 2.1 Strategy implementation and the four-task model of human resource (HR) management

HR tasks	Major strategic decisions
Employee assignments and opportunities	• How many employees are needed? • What qualifications will the employees need? • What pay and conditions will attract people to the firm?
Employee competencies	• What competencies do employees have now? • What new competencies will be needed in the future? • How can new competencies be purchased or developed?
Employee behaviours	• What behaviours does the firm value? • What behaviours are detrimental to the strategy? • What behaviours need to be modified or eliminated?
Employee motivation	• How much more effort are employees able and willing to give? • What is the optimal length of time for employees to stay with the firm? • Can productivity be improved by reducing absence and tardiness?

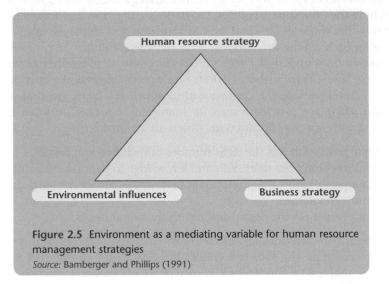

Figure 2.5 Environment as a mediating variable for human resource management strategies
Source: Bamberger and Phillips (1991)

John Purcell (1989) made a significant contribution to research on business–HRM strategy. Drawing on the literature on 'strategic choice' in industrial relations (see, for example, Kochan et al., 1986; Thurley and Wood, 1983) and using the notion of a hierarchy of strategy, he identified what he called 'upstream' and 'downstream' types of strategic decision. Upstream or 'first-order' strategic decisions are concerned with the long-term direction of the corporation. If a first-order decision is made to take over another enterprise, for example a French company acquiring a water company in southern England, a second set of considerations applies concerning the extent to which the new operation is to be integrated with or separate from existing operations. These are classified as downstream, or 'second-order', strategic decisions. Different HR strategies are called 'third-order' strategic decisions because they establish the basic parameters for managing people in the workplace. Purcell (1989, p. 71) wrote, '[in theory] strategy in human resources management is determined in the context of first-order, long-run decisions on the direction and scope of the firm's activities and purpose ... and second-order decisions on the structure of the firm'.

In a major study of HRM in multidivisional companies, Purcell and Ahlstrand (1994) argue that what actually determines HR strategy will be determined by decisions at all three levels and by the ability and leadership style of local managers to follow through goals in the context of specific environmental conditions. In summary, the strategic choice perspective defines an organization's strategy as 'sets of strategic choices', which includes critical choices about 'means and ends' (Boxall and Purcell, 2003, p. 34). Case study analysis has, however, highlighted the problematic nature of strategic choice model-building. The perspective might exaggerate the 'choice' in 'strategic choice', the ability of managers to make strategic decisions independent of the market and the national settings in which they do business (Colling, 1995; Hyman, 1999; Paauwe and Boselie, 2003; Whitley, 1999). The extent to which managers have 'choice' is 'variable' in different settings (Boxall and Purcell, 2003; Paauwe and Boselie, 2003).

Another part of the strategic HRM debate has focused on the integration or 'external fit' of business strategy with HR strategy. This shift in managerial thought, calling for the HR function to be 'strategically integrated', is depicted in Beer et al.'s (1984) model of HRM. The authors espoused the need to establish a close two-way relationship or 'fit' between the external business strategy and the elements of the internal HR strategy: 'An organization's HRM policies and practices must fit with its strategy in its competitive environment and with the immediate business conditions that it faces' (Beer et al., 1984, p. 25). The concept of integration has three aspects:

1. linking of HR policies and practices with the strategic management process of the organization
2. internalization of the importance of HR on the part of line managers
3. integration of the workforce into the organization to foster commitment or an 'identity of interest' with the strategic goals.

Not surprisingly, this approach to SHRM has been referred to as the 'matching' model.

The matching model

Early interest in the 'matching' model was evident in Devanna et al.'s (1984, p. 37) work: 'HR systems and organizational structure should be managed in a way that is congruent with organizational strategy.' This is close to Chandler's (1962) distinction between strategy and structure and his often-quoted maxim that 'structure follows strategy'. In the Devanna et al. model, HRM–strategy–structure follow and feed upon one another and are influenced by environmental forces (Figure 2.6).

The notion of 'external fit' between an external competitive strategy and the internal HR strategy is a central tenet of the HRM model advanced by Beer et al. (1984; see Figure 1.5). The authors emphasize the analysis of the linkages between the two strategies and how each strategy provides goals and constraints for the other. There must be a 'fit between competitive strategy and internal HRM strategy and a fit among the elements of the HRM strategy' (Beer et al., 1984, p. 13). The relationship between business strategy and HR strategy is said to be 'reactive' in the sense that HR strategy is subservient to 'product market logic' and the corporate strategy. The latter is assumed to be the independent variable (Boxall, 1992; Purcell and Ahlstrand, 1994).

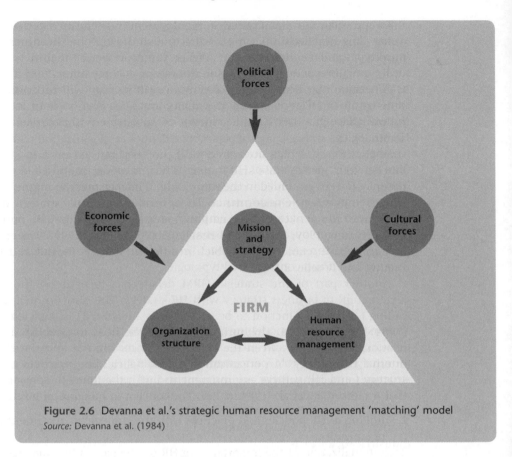

Figure 2.6 Devanna et al.'s strategic human resource management 'matching' model
Source: Devanna et al. (1984)

As Miller (1987, cited in Boxall, 1992, p. 66) emphasizes, 'HRM cannot be conceptualized as a stand-alone corporate issue. Strategically speaking it must flow from and be dependent upon the organization's (market oriented) corporate strategy'. There is some theorization of the link between product markets and organizational design, and approaches to people management. Thus, for example, each of the Porterian 'generic strategies' involves a unique set of responses from workers, or 'needed role behaviours', and a particular HR strategy designed to develop and reinforce a unique pattern of behaviour (Cappelli and Singh, 1992; Schuler and Jackson, 1987). HRM is therefore seen to be 'strategic' by virtue of its 'fit' with business strategy and its internal consistency (Boxall, 1996; Boxall and Purcell, 2003).

Human resource strategy models

This section examines the link between organization/business strategy and HR strategy. 'HR strategies' are here taken to mean the patterns of decisions regarding HR policies and practices that are used by management to design work and select, train, develop, appraise, motivate and control workers. Studying HR strategies in terms of typologies is appealing to academics because conceptual frameworks or models give HR researchers the ability to compare and contrast the different configurations or clusters of HR practices and further develop and test theory (Bamberger and Meshoulam, 2000).

To appreciate the significance of 'typologies', it is useful to recall the work of Max Weber. This sociologist built his theory through the use of abstractions that he called 'ideal types', such as 'bureaucracy'. Weber warned, however, that these abstractions or ideal types never actually exist in the real world: they are simply useful fictions to help us understand the more complex and messy realities found in work organizations. The same is true of HR typologies – they are abstractions that do not necessarily exist in the workplace, but they help the student of management to understand the nature of HR strategies.

Since the early 1990s, academics have proposed at least three models to differentiate between 'ideal types' of HR strategy. The first model examined here – the **control-based model** – is grounded in the way in which management attempts to monitor and control employee role performance. The second model – the **resource-based model** – is grounded in the nature of the employer–employee exchange and, more specifically, in the set of employee attitudes, behaviours and the quality of the manager–subordinate relationship. A third approach creates an integrative model that combines resource-based and control-based typologies.

The control-based model

The first approach to modelling different types of HR strategy is based on the nature of workplace control and more specifically on managerial behaviour to direct and monitor employee role performance. According to this perspective, management structures and HR strategy are instruments and techniques to control all aspects of work to secure a high level of labour productivity and a corresponding level of profitability. This focus on monitoring and controlling employee behaviour as a basis for distinguishing different HR strategies has its roots in the study of 'labour process' by industrial sociologists.

The starting point for this framework is Marx's analysis of the capitalist labour process and what he referred to as the 'transformation of labour power into labour'. Put simply, when organizations hire people, they have only a *potential* or capacity to work. To ensure that each worker exercises his or her full capacity, managers must organize the tasks, space, movement and time within which workers operate. But workers have divergent interests in terms of pace of work, rewards and job security, and engage in formal (trade unions) and informal (restrictions of output or sabotage) behaviours to counteract management job controls. Workers' own countermanagement behaviour then causes managers to control and discipline the interior of the organization. In an insightful review, Thompson and McHugh (2002, p. 104) comment that 'control is not an end in itself, but a means to transform the capacity to work established by the wage relation into profitable production'.

What alternative HR strategies have managers used to render employees and their behaviour predictable and measurable? Edwards (1979) identified successive dominant modes of control that reflect changing competitive conditions and worker resistance. An early system of *individual control* by employers exercising direct authority was replaced by more complex structural forms of control: *bureaucratic control* and *technical control*. Bureaucratic control includes written rules and procedures covering work. Technical control includes machinery or systems – assembly line, surveillance cameras – that set the pace of work or monitor employees' behaviour in the workplace. Edwards also argued that managers use a 'divide and rule' strategy, using gender and race, to foster managerial control.

Friedman (1977) structured his typology of HR strategies – *direct control* and *responsible autonomy* – around the notion of differing logics of control depending upon the nature of the product and the labour markets. Burawoy (1979), another organizational theorist, categorized the development of HR strategies in terms of the transition from *despotic* to *hegemonic* regimes. The former were dominated by coercive manager–subordinate relations; the latter provided an 'industrial citizenship' that regulated employment relations through grievance and bargaining processes. The growth of employment in new call centres has recently given rise to a renewed focus of interest on the use of technical control systems: the electronic surveillance of the operator's role performance (Callaghan and Thompson, 2001; Sewell, 1998).

The choice of HR strategy is governed by variations in organizational form (e.g. size, structure, age), competitive pressures on management and the stability of labour markets, mediated by the interplay of manager–subordinate relations and worker resistance (Thompson and McHugh, 2002). Moreover, the variations in HR strategy are not random but reflect two management logics (Bamberger and Meshoulam, 2000). The first is the logic of direct, *process-based control*, in which the focus is on efficiency and cost containment (managers needing within this domain to monitor and control workers' performance carefully), whereas the second is the logic of indirect *outcomes-based control*, in which the focus is on actual results (within this domain, managers needing to engage workers' intellectual capital, commitment and cooperation). Thus, when managing people at work, control and cooperation coexist, and the extent to which there is any ebb and flow in intensity and direction between *types* of control will depend upon the 'multiple constituents' of the management process.

Implicit in this approach to managerial control is that the logic underlying an HR strategy will tend to be consistent with an organization's competitive strategy (e.g. Schuler and Jackson, 1987). We are thus unlikely to find organizations adopting a Porterian cost-leadership strategy with an HR strategy grounded in an outcome-based logic. Managers will tend to adopt process-based controls when means–ends relations are certain (as is typically the case among firms adopting a cost-leadership strategy), and outcomes-based controls when means–ends are uncertain (e.g. differentiation strategy). These management logics result in different organizational designs and variations in HR strategy, which provide the source of inevitable structural tensions between management and employees. It is posited, therefore, that HR strategies contain inherent contradictions (Hyman, 1987; Storey, 1995b; Thompson and McHugh, 2002).

REFLECTIVE QUESTION

What do you think of the argument that each type of competitive strategy requires a different HR strategy? Thinking about your own work experience, reflect upon the way in which managers attempted to control your behaviour at work. Was each task closely monitored, or was the focus on actual outcome? To what extent, if at all, were different types of managerial control related to the firm's product or service?

The resource-based model

This second approach to developing typologies of HR strategy is grounded in the nature of the reward-effort exchange and, more specifically, in the degree to which managers view their HR as an asset as opposed to a variable cost. Superior performance through workers is underscored when advanced technology and other inanimate resources are readily available to competing firms. The sum of people's knowledge and expertise, and social relationships, has the *potential* to provide non-substitutable capabilities that serve as a source of competitive advantage (Cappelli and Singh, 1992). The various perspectives on resource-based HRM models raise questions about the inextricable connection between work-related learning, the 'mobilization of employee consent' through learning strategies and competitive advantage. Given the upsurge of interest in resource-based models, and in particular the new **workplace learning** discourse, we need to examine this model in some detail.

The genesis of the resource-based model can be traced back to Selznick (1957), who suggested that work organizations each possess 'distinctive competence' that enables them to outperform their competitors, and to Penrose (1959), who conceptualized the firm as a 'collection of productive resources'. She distinguished between 'physical' and 'human' resources, and drew attention to issues of learning, including the knowledge and experience of the management team. Moreover, Penrose emphasized what many organizational theorists take for granted – that organizations are 'heterogeneous' (Penrose, 1959, cited in Boxall, 1996, pp. 64–5). More recently, Barney (1991) has argued that '*sustained* competitive advantage' (emphasis added) is achieved not through an analysis of a firm's external market position but through a careful analysis of its skills and capabilities, characteristics that competitors find themselves unable to imitate. Putting it in terms of a simple SWOT analysis, the resource-based perspective emphasizes the strategic importance of exploiting internal 'strengths' and neutralizing internal 'weaknesses' (Barney, 1991). Over the last decade, the resource-based perspective has become the dominant theory in the strategic HRM discourse (Paauwe and Boselie, 2003).

The resource-based approach focuses on the distinctive competencies – resources and capabilities – in order to account for differences in the organization's performance. An organization's *resources* can be divided into tangible (financial, technological, physical, human) and intangible (brand name, reputation, know-how) resources. To give rise to a distinctive competency, an organization's resources must be both unique and valuable. By *capabilities*, we mean the collective skills possessed by the organization to coordinate the resources effectively. According to strategic management theorists, the distinction between resources and capabilities is critical to understanding what generates a distinctive competency (see, for example, Hill and Jones, 2004). It is important to recognize that a firm may not need a uniquely endowed workforce to establish a distinctive competency as long as it has managerial capabilities that no competitor possesses. This observation may explain why an organization adopts one of the control-based HR strategies.

HRM WEB LINKS

An increasing number of US companies are establishing 'corporate' universities to help to build 'core' competencies. Examples of US corporate universities are Intel

University (www.intel.com/jobs/workplace/worklife/education.htm), and Motorola University (www.motorola.com/motorolauniversity.jsp).

Barney argues that four characteristics of resources and capabilities – value, rarity, inimitability and non-substitutability – are important in sustaining competitive advantage. From this perspective, collective learning in the workplace on the part of managers and non-managers, especially on how to coordinate workers' diverse knowledge and skills, and integrate diverse information technology, is a strategic asset that rivals find difficult to replicate. In other words, leadership capabilities are critical to harnessing the firm's human assets. Amit and Shoemaker (1993, p. 37) make a similar point when they emphasize the strategic importance of managers identifying, ex ante, and marshalling 'a set of complementary and specialized resources and capabilities which are scarce, durable, not easily traded, and difficult to imitate' in order to enable the company to earn 'economic rent' (profits). Jacoby's (2005) engagement in the resource-based debate is new in that he asserts that investment in this approach varies across employers depending on whether or not senior management are insulated from shareholder pressure for short-term growth in shareholder value. The more that executive managers are insulated from shareholder pressure, the higher the likelihood that firms will invest in the resource-based approach to HRM. Figure 2.7 summarizes the relationship between resources and capabilities, strategies and sustained competitive advantage.

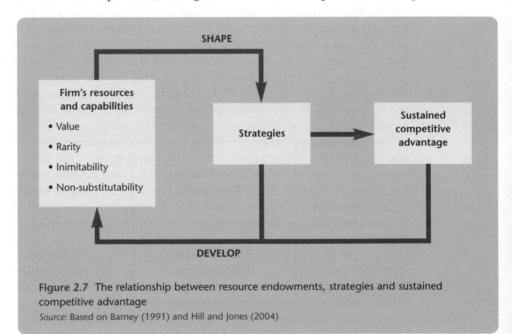

Figure 2.7 The relationship between resource endowments, strategies and sustained competitive advantage
Source: Based on Barney (1991) and Hill and Jones (2004)

REFLECTIVE QUESTION

Based upon your own work experience, or upon your studies of organizations, is continuous learning in the workplace more or less important for some organizations than others? If so, why?

An integrative model of HR strategy

Bamberger and Meshoulam (2000) integrate the two main models of HR strategy, one approach focusing on the strategy's underlying logic of managerial control, the other focusing on the reward–effort exchange. Arguing that neither of the two dichotomous approaches (control- and resource-based models) provides a framework able to encompass the ebb and flow of the intensity and direction of HR strategy, they build a model that characterizes the two main dimensions of HR strategy as involving 'acquisition and development' and the 'locus of control'.

Acquisition and development is concerned with the extent to which the HR strategy develops internal human capital as opposed to the external recruitment of human capital. In other words, organizations can lean more towards 'making' their workers (high investment in training) or more towards 'buying' their workers from the external labour market (Rousseau, 1995). Bamberger and Meshoulam (2000) call this the 'make-or-buy' aspect of HR strategy.

Locus of control is concerned with the degree to which HR strategy focuses on monitoring employees' compliance with process-based standards as opposed to developing a *psychological* contract that nurtures social relationships, encourages mutual trust and respect, and controls the focus on the outcomes (ends) themselves. This strand of thinking in HR strategy can be traced back to the ideas of Walton (1985), who made a distinction between commitment and control strategies (Hutchinson et al., 2000). As Figure 2.8 shows, these two main dimensions of HR strategy yield four different 'ideal types' of dominant HR strategy:

1. commitment
2. collaborative
3. paternalistic
4. traditional.

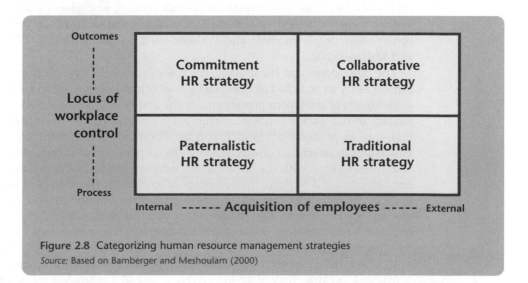

Figure 2.8 Categorizing human resource management strategies
Source: Based on Bamberger and Meshoulam (2000)

The *commitment HR strategy* is characterized as focusing on the internal development of employees' competencies and outcome control. In contrast, the *traditional HR strategy*, which parallels Bamberger and Meshoulam's 'secondary' HR strategy, is viewed as focusing on the external recruitment of competencies and behavioural or process-based controls. The *collaborative HR strategy*, which parallels Bamberger and Meshoulam's 'free agent' HR strategy, involves the organization subcontracting work to external independent experts (e.g. consultants or contractors), giving extensive autonomy and evaluating their performance primarily in terms of the end results. The *paternalistic HR strategy* offers learning opportunities and internal promotion to employees for their compliance with process-based control mechanisms. Each HR strategy represents a distinctive HR paradigm, or set of beliefs, values and assumptions, that guide managers. Similar four-cell grids have been developed by Lepak and Snell (1999). Based upon empirical evidence, Bamberger and Meshoulam suggest that the HR strategies in the diagonal quadrants 'commitment' and 'traditional' are likely to be the most prevalent in (North American) work organizations.

It is argued that an organization's HR strategy is strongly related to its competitive strategy. So, for example, the traditional HR strategy (bottom right quadrant) is most likely to be adopted by management when there is certainty over how inputs are transformed into outcomes and/or when employee performance can be closely monitored or appraised. This dominant HR strategy is more prevalent in firms with a highly routinized transformation process, low-cost priority and stable competitive environment. Under such conditions, managers use technology to control the uncertainty inherent in the labour process and insist only that workers enact the specified core standards of behaviour required to facilitate undisrupted production. Managerial behaviour in such organizations can be summed up by the managerial edict 'You are here to work, not to think!' Implied by this approach is a focus on process-based control in which 'close monitoring by supervisors and efficiency wages ensure adequate work effort' (MacDuffie, 1995, quoted by Bamberger and Meshoulam, 2000, p. 60). The use of the word 'traditional' to classify this HR strategy and the use of a technological 'fix' to control workers should not be viewed as a strategy only of 'industrial' worksites. Case study research on call centres, workplaces that some organizational theorists label 'post-industrial', reveal systems of technical and bureaucratic control that closely monitor and evaluate their operators (Sewell, 1998; Thompson and McHugh, 2002).

The other dominant HR strategy, the commitment HR strategy (top left quadrant), is most likely to be found in workplaces in which management lacks a full knowledge of all aspects of the labour process and/or the ability to monitor closely or evaluate the efficacy of the worker behaviours required for executing the work (e.g. single-batch, high-quality production, research and development, and health care professionals). This typically refers to 'knowledge work'. In such workplaces, managers must rely on employees to cope with the uncertainties inherent in the labour process and can thus only monitor and evaluate the outcomes of work. This HR strategy is associated with a set of HR practices that aim to develop highly committed and flexible people, internal markets that reward commitment with promotion and a degree of job security, and a 'participative' leadership style that forges a commonality of interest and mobilizes consent to the organization's goals (Hutchinson et al., 2000). In addition, as others have noted, workers under such conditions do not always need to be overtly controlled because they may effectively 'control themselves' (Thompson, 1989; Thompson and McHugh, 2002). To develop cooperation and common interests, an effort–reward exchange based upon investment in learning, internal promotion and internal equity is typically used (Bamberger and Meshoulam, 2000). In addition, such workplaces 'mobilize' employee consent through culture strategies, including the popular notion of the 'learning organization'. As one of us has argued elsewhere (Bratton, 2001, p. 341):

> For organizational controllers, workplace learning provides a compelling ideology in the twenty-first century, with an attractive metaphor for mobilizing worker commitment and sustainable competitiveness ... [And] the learning organization paradigm can be construed as a more subtle way of shaping workers' beliefs and values and behaviour.

HRM IN PRACTICE 2.3

AIRLINE HOPES TO CUT COSTS, REGAIN MARKET SHARE

PATRICK BRETHOUR AND KEITH MCARTHUR, *GLOBE AND MAIL*, 20 APRIL 2002, PP. B1, B6

Air Canada unveiled its long awaited discount carrier yesterday, but warned that customers shouldn't expect fares to immediately be lower than those already offered by Air Canada. Steve Smith, president and chief executive officer of Zip Air Inc., said the new airline is being created to cut Air Canada's costs – not to reduce fares. 'Right now, the price is already low, particularly in this market,' he said, adding that prices could fall over time as the new airline reduced expenses.

Observers see the wholly owned subsidiary as a way for Air Canada to lower labour costs and win back market share it has lost in recent years to Calgary-based WestJet Airlines Ltd. Mr Smith said a new business model is emerging in the airline market – as it has in retailing – where lower-cost, no-frills service becomes the norm. He said the full-service model for short flights is 'going

the way of the dinosaur.' Zip is aimed at meeting that challenge in the low end of the market, he said.

'They are hurting the very people who have worked so hard for them and for so long.'

Zip's costs will be at least 20 per cent lower than those at Air Canada's comparable mainline flights, in part because Zip's employees will be making less money than their counterparts at Air Canada. Mr. Smith said wages will be competitive with Zip's competitors in the low-cost market. 'For the employees, they have to understand that they will be working for zip,' he joked.

Pamela Sachs, president of Air Canada component of the Canadian Union of Public Employees, said the union will mount a legal challenge to Air Canada's attempts to pay so-

called B-scale wages to Zip employees. 'Air Canada gives zip by zapping its employees. They are hurting the very people who have worked so hard for them and for so long,' she said.

Other cost-cutting measures at Zip include offering snacks instead of meals, providing no in-flight entertainment and operating only one kind of plane. There will also be less room between seats – 32 inches or 33 inches – although the seats will still have more leg room than the smallest seats at WestJet. The reduction, along with the elimination of business-class seats, will allow Zip to add 17 seats to the 100 seats in the Boeing 737-200. (WestJet has 120 seats in its Boeing 737-200s).

The company will operate independently of Air Canada, although it will buy maintenance services from its parent, as well as using the larger company's pilots.

REFLECTIVE QUESTION

How would you describe the HR strategy at Zip Air (HRM in Practice 2.3)? How does this HR strategy support the business plan? Do you think that Zip Air will be able to mobilize its employees' competencies and commitment to achieve a competitive advantage?

Evaluating strategic human resource management and models of human resource strategy

A number of limitations to current research on SHRM and HR strategy have been identified: the focus on strategic decision-making, the absence of internal strategies and the conceptualization of managerial control.

Existing conceptualizations of SHRM are based upon the traditional rational perspective of managerial decision-making – definable acts of linear planning, choice and action – but critical organizational theorists have challenged these assumptions, arguing that strategic decisions are not necessarily based on the output of rational calculation. The assumption that a firm's business-level strategy and HR system have a logical, linear relationship is questionable given the evidence that strategy formulation is informal, politically charged and subject to complex contingency factors (Bamberger and Meshoulam, 2000; Monks and McMackin, 2001; Whittington, 1993). As such, the notion of *consciously* aligning business strategy and HR strategy applies only to the 'classical' approach to strategy (Legge, 2005). Those who question the classical approach to strategic management argue that the image of the manager as a reflective planner and strategist is a myth. Management's strategic behaviour is more likely to be uncoordinated, frenetic, ad hoc and fragmented (e.g. Hales, 1986).

The political perspectives on strategic decision-making make the case that managerial rationality is limited by lack of information, time and 'cognitive capacity' as well as that strategic management is a highly competitive process in which managers fiercely compete for resources, status and power. Within such a management milieu, strategies can signal changes in power relationships between managers (Mintzberg et al., 1998). Rather than viewing strategic choices as the outcome of rational decision-making, Johnson (1987, cited in Purcell, 1989, p. 72), among others, argues that 'Strategic decisions are characterized by the political hurly-burly of organizational life with a high incidence of bargaining ... all within a notable lack of clarity in terms of environmental influences and objectives.'

Alternatively, strategic decision-making may be conceptualized as a 'discourse' or body of language-based communication that operates at different levels in the organization. Thus, Hendry (2000) persuasively argues that a strategic decision takes its meaning from the discourse and social practice within which it is located, so a decision must be not only effectively communicated, but also 'recommunicated' until it becomes embodied in action. This perspective reaffirms the importance of conceptualizing management in terms of functions, contingencies and skills and the leadership competence of managers (see Figure 1.3). Whatever insights the different perspectives afford on the strategic management process, critical organizational theorists have suggested that 'strategic' is no longer fashionable in management thought and discourse, having gone from 'buzzword to boo-word' (Thompson and McHugh, 2002, p. 110).

A second limitation of SHRM and HR strategy theory is the focus on the connection between external market strategies and HR function. It is argued that contingency analysis relies exclusively on external marketing strategies (how the firm competes) and disregards the internal operational strategies (how the firm is managed) that influence HR practices and performance (Purcell, 1999). Work motivation and commitment are, as ever, central to managing employment relations, but strategizing 'best fit' disregards 'employee interests'. In coping with internal contradictions, the organization not only has to fit HR practices to competitive strategy, but must also integrate business *and* employee needs (Boxall and Purcell, 2003). In an industry in which a flexible, customized product range and high quality are the key to profitability, a firm can adopt a manufacturing strategy that allows, via 'high-performance work systems', for far fewer employees but within a commitment HR strategy regime. This was the strategy at Flowpak Engineering (Bratton, 1992). In this case, the technology and manufacturing strategy became the key intervening variable between overall business strategy and HR strategy.

Drawing upon the early work of Kelly (1985), the major limitation of a simple SHRM model is that it privileges only one step in the full circuit of industrial capital. To put it another way, the SHRM approach looks only at the *realization* of profitability within product markets rather than at complex contingent variables that constitute the full transformation process. As others have argued, we need to avoid being entrapped in rational choice logic and view competitive posture in global markets as 'multidimensional', with resilient companies being agile at cost leadership *and* differentiation (Boxall and Purcell, 2003; Purcell, 1999). In such companies, managing employment relations is less likely to be based on aligning HR practices to, in Porter's terminology, a 'single strategy' (Boxall and Purcell, 2003, p. 55).

Another limitation of most current studies examining SHRM is the conceptualization of managerial control. The basic premise of the typologies of HR strategy approach is that a dominant HR strategy is strongly related to a specific competitive strategy. Thus, the commitment HR strategy is most likely to be adopted when management seek to compete in the marketplace by using a generic differentiation strategy. This might be true, but the notion that a commitment HR strategy follows from a real or perceived 'added-value' competitive strategy is more problematic in practice. Moreover, it is misleading to assume that managerial behaviour is not influenced by the indeterminacy of the employment contract and by how to close the 'gap' between an employee's potential and actual performance level. Reflecting on this problem, Colling (1995, p. 29) correctly emphasizes that ''added-value' [differentiation] strategies do not preclude or prevent the use of managerial control over employees ... few companies are able to operationalize added-value programmes without cost-constraints and even fewer can do so for very long'. Others have gone beyond the 'organizational democracy' rhetoric and acknowledge that 'It is utopian to think that control can be completely surrendered' in the 'postmodern' work organization (Cloke and Goldsmith, 2002, p. 162).

Consistent with our earlier definition of strategy – as a specific pattern of decisions and actions – management's actions create potential 'strategic tensions' subject to paradox (Boxall and Purcell, 2003; Thompson and McHugh, 2002; Watson, 1999). Thus, one strategic decision and action might undermine another strategic goal. Acceding to the imperatives of a global free market, there is, for example, in a recession a tendency for management to improve profitability by mass redundancies – so-called 'downsizing' or 'rightsizing' – and by applying more demanding performance outcomes to the remaining managers and workers at unit level. This pattern of action constitutes a strategy even though manifesting a disjunction between organizational design and employer–employee relations. As Purcell (1989, 1995) points out, an organization pursuing a strategy of acquisition and downsizing might 'logically' adopt an HR strategy that includes the compulsory lay-off of non-core employees and, for the identifiable core of employees with rare attributes, a compensation system based on performance results. In practice, the resource-based approach predicts a sharp differentiation within organizations 'between those with key competencies, knowledge and valued organizational memory, and those more easily replaced or disposed of' (Purcell, 1999, p. 36). In such a case, the business strategy and HR strategy might 'fit', but, as Legge (2005, p. 128) points out, these HR policies and practices are unlikely to engender employee commitment and will cause a misfit with 'soft' HRM values. Thus, achieving the goal of 'external fit' of business and HR strategy can contradict the goal of employee commitment and cooperation.

In essence, the 'best-fit' metaphor for strategic HRM contends that HR strategy is more effective when it is premeditated to fit specific contingencies in the organization's competitive context. It is important to emphasize that, however committed a group of managers might be to a particular HR strategy (e.g. the commitment HR strategy), there are external conditions and internal 'structural contradictions' at work that will constrain management action (Boxall, 1992, 1996; Boxall and Purcell, 2003; Streeck, 1987). All organizations are embedded in national cultures, and HR strategy will therefore be shaped by economic, technological, political and social factors. The kind of analysis explored here is nicely summed up by Hyman's pessimistic pronouncement that 'there is no 'one best way' of managing these contradictions, only different routes to partial failure' (1987, quoted in Thompson and McHugh, 2002, p. 108).

STUDY TIP

Read Chapter 8, Control: concepts and strategies, in Thompson and McHugh's (2002) book, *Work Organizations: A Critical Introduction*, 3rd edition. Why and how do organizational theorists contest theories of management control? To what extent do variations in HR strategy reflect the fundamental tension between management's need to control workers' behaviour while tapping into workers' ingenuity and cooperation?

Dimensions of strategic human resource management

In addition to focusing on the validity of the matching SHRM model and typologies of HR strategy, researchers have identified a number of important themes associated with the notion of SHRM that are discussed briefly here and, with the exception of leadership, more extensively in later chapters. These are:

- HR practices and performance (see also Chapter 14)
- organizational architecture (see also Chapter 5)

- **leadership**
- workplace learning (see also Chapter 9)
- trade unions (see also Chapter 11).

Human resource management practices and performance

Although most HRM models provide no clear focus for any test of the HRM–performance link, the models tend to assume that an alignment between business strategy and HR strategy will improve organizational performance and competitiveness. During the past decade, demonstrating that there is indeed a positive link between particular sets or 'bundles' of HR practices and business performance has become '*the* dominant research issue' (Guest, 1997, p. 264). The dominant empirical questions on this topic ask 'What types of performance data are available to measure the HRM–performance link?' and 'Do "high-commitment-type" HRM systems produce above-average results compared with "control-type" systems?' A number of studies (e.g. Baker, 1999; Betcherman et al., 1994; Guest, 1997; Hutchinson et al., 2000; Ichniowski et al., 1996; Pfeffer, 1998) have found that, in spite of the methodological challenges, bundles of HRM practices are positively associated with superior organization performance.

Organizational architecture and strategic human resource management

All normative models of HRM emphasize the importance of organizational design. As previously discussed, the 'soft' HRM model is concerned with organizational architecture or design that encourages the vertical and horizontal compression of tasks, greater employee autonomy and cooperative, cross-boundary working. Horizontal or cross-boundary working is essentially about the extent and quality of the relationships between employees (Gratton, 2005). The redesign of work organizations has been variously labelled 'high-performing work systems', 'business process re-engineering' and 'high-commitment management'. The literature emphasizes core features of this approach to organizational architecture and management, including a 'flattened' hierarchy, decentralized decision-making to line managers or work teams, 'enabling' information technology and 're-configurable and modular' descriptors of organizational architecture. The HR function, it is argued, plays a crucial role in designing the structures and practices that create levers for horizontal working and shaping workers' behaviour that are more congruent with the organization's culture and goals (Champy, 1996; Gratton, 2005; Hammer, 1997; Hammer and Champy, 1993).

Leadership and strategic human resource management

The concept of managerial leadership permeates and structures the theory and practice of work organizations and hence how we understand SHRM. Most definitions of managerial leadership reflect the assumption that it involves a process whereby an individual exerts influence upon others in an organizational context. Within the literature, there is a continuing debate over the alleged differences between a manager and a leader. According to Kotter (1996), the difference lies in the fact that managers develop *plans* whereas leaders create a *vision*. For Mintzberg (2005, p. 6) , however, it is better not to separate the processes: 'management without leadership is sterile; leadership without management is disconnected and encourages hubris'. And for Grint

(2005, p. 15), management is the equivalent of déjà vu – already seen – whereas leadership is the equivalent of vu jàdé – never seen before.

Much of the leadership research and literature tends to be androcentric in nature and rarely acknowledges the limited representation of ethnic groups and women in senior leadership positions (Ford, 2006; Townley, 1994). The current interest in alternative leadership paradigms variously labelled 'transformational leadership' (Tichy and Devanna, 1986) and 'charismatic leadership' (Conger and Kanungo, 1988) may be explained by understanding the prerequisites of the resource-based SHRM model. In the discourse of the new economy and the resource-based perspective, the prime task of leadership is to tap, organize and transform individual and collective knowledge into profits (Holmberg and Strannegård, 2005), a style of leadership that will develop the firm's human endowment and, moreover, cultivate commitment, flexibility, innovation and profits (Bratton et al., 2004).

A number of writers (e.g. Agashae and Bratton, 2001; Groves, 2005; Kotter, 1996; Senge, 1990) make explicit links between learning, leadership and organizational change, and it would seem that a key constraint on adopting a resource-based SHRM model is leadership competencies. Apparently, 'most re-engineering failures stem from breakdowns in leadership' (Hammer and Champy, 1993, p. 107), and the 'engine' that creates employee 'openness' to organizational change is 'charismatic leadership behaviours' (Groves, 2005, p.274). In essence, the leadership ideology of the new economy exhorts followers to work beyond the economic contract for the 'common' good. In contemporary management parlance, the 'transformational' leader is empowering workers. To go beyond the rhetoric, however, such popular leadership models shift the focus away from managerial control processes and innate power relationships towards the psychological contract and the individualization of the employment relationship.

Workplace learning and strategic human resource management

Within most formulations of SHRM, formal and informal work-related learning has come to represent a key lever that can help managers to achieve the substantive HRM goals of profitability, productivity, flexibility, quality, commitment and social legitimacy (Beer et al., 1984; Boxall and Purcell, 2003; Keep, 1989). As such, this growing field of research occupies centre stage in the resource-based SHRM model. From a managerial perspective, formal and informal learning can, it is argued, strengthen an organization's 'core competencies' and is thus a prerequisite for success – having the ability to learn more quickly than one's competitors is of the essence here (Dixon, 1992; Kochan and Dyer, 1995). More broadly, an investment in workplace learning can enhance the quality of the organization's reputation as an 'employer of choice', which is one aspect of its 'social legitimacy'. There is a growing body of work that has taken a more critical look at workplace learning (Bratton et al., 2003). Some of these writers, for example, emphasize how workplace learning can strengthen cultural control (Legge, 2005), strengthen the power of top managers (Coopey, 1996) and be a source of conflict when linked to productivity or flexibility bargaining and job control (see Chapter 9).

Trade unions and strategic human resource management

The notion of worker commitment embedded in the HRM model has led writers from both ends of the political spectrum to argue that there is a contradiction between the normative HRM model and the trade unions. In the prescriptive management literature, the argument is that the collectivist culture, with its 'them and us' attitude, sits uncomfortably with the HRM goal of high employee commitment and the individualization of the employment relationship. The critical perspective also presents the HRM model as being inconsistent with traditional industrial relations, albeit for very different reasons. Critics argue that 'high-commitment' HR strategies are designed to provide workers with a false sense of job security and to obscure underlying sources of conflict inherent in capitalist employment relations (Godard, 2005). Other scholars, taking an 'orthodox pluralist' perspective, have argued that trade unions and the 'high-performance–high-commitment' HRM model cannot only coexist but are indeed necessary if a high-performing work system is to succeed (see Betcherman et al., 1994; Guest, 1995). What is apparent is that this part of the SHRM debate has been strongly influenced by economic, political and legal developments in the USA and UK, as well as by globalization, over the past two decades (Chapter 4).

The distinction between domestic HRM, strategic HRM and strategic international HRM, and some of the current issues in international HRM within globalized markets and business strategies, are examined in the next chapter.

Chapter summary

- This chapter has examined different levels of strategic management, defining strategic management as a 'pattern of decisions and actions' undertaken by the upper echelon of the company.

- Strategic decisions are concerned with change and the achievement of superior performance, and they involve strategic choices. In multidivisional companies, strategy formulation takes place at three levels – corporate, business and functional – to form a hierarchy of strategic decision-making. Corporate and business-level strategies, as well as environmental pressures, dictate the choice of HR policies and practices.

- Strategic management plans at corporate level and business level provide the context within which HR plans are developed and implemented. These HR plans provide a map for managers to follow in order to fulfil the core responsibilities of the HR function, which involves managing employee assignments, competencies, behaviours and motivation. These prime responsibilities of the HR function constitute the 'four-task model' of HRM.

- When reading the descriptive and prescriptive strategic management texts, there is a great temptation to be smitten by what appears to be the linear and absolute rationality of the strategic management process. We draw attention to the more critical literature that recognizes that HR strategic options are, at any given time, partially constrained by the outcomes of corporate and business decisions, the current distribution of power within the organization and the ideological values of the key decision-makers.

- A core assumption underlying much of the SHRM research and literature is that each of the main types of generic competitive strategy used by organizations (e.g. cost leadership or differentiation strategy) is associated with a different approach to managing people, that is, with a different HR strategy.

- We critiqued here the matching model of SHRM on both conceptual and empirical grounds. It was noted that, in the globalized economy with market turbulence, the 'fit' metaphor might not be appropriate when flexibility and the need for organizations to learn more quickly than their competitors seem to be the key to sustainable competitiveness. We also emphasized how the goal of aligning a Porterian low-cost business strategy with an HRM strategy can contradict the core goal of employee commitment.

- The resource-based SHRM model, which places an emphasis on a company's HR endowments as a strategy for sustained competitive advantage, was outlined. In spite of the interest in workplace learning, there seems, however, little empirical evidence to suggest that many firms have adopted this 'soft' HR strategic model.

- The final section examined a number of important themes associated with SHRM, notably the alleged link between HR practices and organizational performance, organizational design, leadership, workplace learning and the role of trade unions.

Key concepts

- Control-based model
- Differentiation strategy
- Four-task model of HRM
- Hierarchy of strategy
- Human resource strategy
- Leadership

- Low-cost leadership
- Resource-based model
- Strategic human resource management
- Strategic management
- Workplace learning

Chapter review questions

1. What is meant by 'strategy'? Explain the meaning of 'first-order' and 'second-order' strategies.

2. Explain Purcell's statement that 'trends in corporate strategy have the potential to render the ideals of HRM unobtainable'.

3. 'Business-level strategies may be constrained by human resource issues but rarely seem to be designed to influence them.' Discuss.

4. What does a 'resource-based' SHRM model of competitive advantage mean? What are the implications for HRM of this business strategy?

5. What are the linkages, if any, between SHRM, leadership and learning?

Further reading

Boxall, P. (2003) HR strategy and competitive advantage in the service sector. *Human Resource Management Journal*, **13**(3): 5–20.

Boxall, P. and Purcell, J. (2003) *Strategy and Human Resource Management*. London: Palgrave Macmillan.

Clarke, N. (2006) Why HR policies fail to support workplace learning: the complexities of policy implementation in healthcare. *International Journal of Human Resource Management*, **17**(1): 190–206.

Ford, J. (2006) Discourses of leadership: gender, identity and contradiction in the UK public sector organization. *Leadership*, **2**(1): 77–99.

Gratton, L. (2005) Managing integration through cooperation. *Human Resource Management*, **44**(2): 151–8.

Grint, K. (2005) *Leadership: Limits and Possibilities*. Basingstoke: Palgrave Macmillan.

Kamoche, K. (1996) Strategic human resource management within a resource-capability view of the firm. *Journal of Management Studies*, **33**(2): 213–33.

Monks, K. and McMackin, J. (2001) Designing and aligning an HR system. *Human Resource Management Journal*, **11**(2): 57–72.

Purcell, J. (2001) The meaning of strategy in human resource management. In J. Storey (ed.) *Human Resource Management: A Critical Text* (pp. 59–77). London: Thompson Learning.

Schuler, R., Jackson, S. and Storey, J. (2001) HRM and its link with strategic management. In J. Storey (ed.) *Human Resource Management: A Critical Text* (pp. 114–30). London: Thompson Learning.

Practising human resource management

Searching the web

Enter the website of two luxury-car manufacturers, such as Lexus (www.lexus.com/about/) and Volvo (www.volvo.com), both of which compete in the same strategic group. Scan the websites to determine the key features of each company's business strategy. In what ways are their business-level strategies similar and different? Do the companies include HRM in their business-level strategies? If so, how does each company's HR strategy support its business strategy? Enter the websites of two economy-car manufacturers, for example Ford (www.ford.com) and Hyundai (www.hyundai.com). In what ways are their business-level and HR strategies similar to and different from those of the first group?

HRM group project

Form a study group of between three and five people, and search the web for sports equipment retailers such as Balmoral Boards (www.balmoralboards.com.au), Mountain Equipment Co-operative (www.mec.ca), ProSportUK (www.prosportuk.com) and Sportsmart (www.sportsmart.com). After viewing various company websites, discuss the following scenario:

You are advising a group of partners contemplating opening a new sports retail store in your city. Based on your web search, decide what business strategy can best provide your sports store with a competitive advantage to make it a profitable, ongoing operation.

1. Create a strategic group of sports equipment stores in your city and define their generic strategies (for example, cost leadership or differentiation strategy).
2. Identify which sports stores are most successful and why.

3. On the basis of this analysis, decide what kind of sports retail store you would advise your clients to open.
4. On the basis of your understanding of the material in this chapter, decide what kind of HR strategy would best support your chosen business-level strategy and why.

Chapter case study

AIR NATIONAL[4]

Air National's (AN) 1998 Annual Report glowed with optimism. Bradley Smith, CEO, stated in his letter to shareholders, 'As a newly privatized company, we face the future with enthusiasm, confident that we can compete in a deregulated industry.' By April 2000, however, the tone had changed, with a reported pre-tax loss of $93 million. The newly appointed CEO, Clive Warren, announced a major change in the company's business strategy that would lead to a transformation of business operations and HR practices in Europe's largest airline company.

Background

During the early 1980s, civil aviation was a highly regulated market, and competition was managed via close, if not always harmonious, relationships between airlines, their competitors and governments. National flag-carriers dominated the markets, and market shares were determined not by competition but by the skill of their governments in negotiating bilateral 'air service agreements'. These agreements established the volume and distribution of air traffic and thereby revenue. Within these markets, AN dominated other carriers; despite the emergence of new entrants, AN's share of the domestic market in the early 1980s, for example, increased by 60 per cent.

The competition

In the middle of the 1980s, AN's external environment was subjected to two sets of significant change. First, in 1986, AN was privatized by

Britain's Conservative government. This potentially reduced the political influence of the old corporation and exposed the new company to competitive forces. Preparation for privatization required a painful restructuring and 'downsizing' of assets and the workforce, driven largely by the need to make the company attractive to initially sceptical investors. Privatization also offered significant political leverage, which AN was able to deploy to secure further stability in its key product markets. It was this context, rather than the stimulus of market competition, that gave senior management the degree of stability and security needed to plan and implement new business and HRM strategies. The second set of pressures, potentially more decisive, was generated by prolonged economic recession and the ongoing deregulation of civil aviation in Europe and North America.

With these environmental forces, AN attempted to grow out of the recession by adopting a low-cost competitive strategy and joining the industry-wide price war. Bradley Smith, when he addressed his senior management team, stated, 'this strategy requires us to be aggressive in the marketplace and to be diligent in our pursuit of cost reductions and cost minimization in areas like service, marketing and advertising'. The low-cost competitive strategy failed. Passenger numbers slumped by 7 per cent during the late 1980s, contributing to a pre-tax loss. Following the appointment of the new CEO, AN changed its competitive strategy and began to develop a differentiation business strategy (Porter, 1980) or what is also referred to as an 'added-value' strategy.

In 2002, following the September 11 attacks in New York and Washington in which four commercial planes were hijacked and crashed, killing almost 3000 people, international air travel bookings fell sharply. The catastrophes caused the loss of more than 100,000 airline jobs around the world. In addition, early in 2002, new discount airlines started operating in Europe, and there was a costly battle for market share between AN, HopJet Airlines and Tango Airlines.

Air National's new competitive strategy

Under the guidance of the newly appointed CEO, Clive Warren, AN prioritized high-quality customer service, 're-engineered' the company and launched a discount airline that operated as a separate company. The management structure was reorganized to provide a tighter focus on operational issues beneath corporate level. AN's operations were divided into route groups based on five major markets (Exhibit 2.1). Each group was to be headed by a general manager who was given authority over the development of the business, with a particular emphasis on marketing. The company's advertising began also to emphasize the added-value elements of AN's services. New brand names were developed, and new uniforms were introduced for the cabin crews and point-of-service staff.

AN's restructuring also aimed to cut the company's cost base. Aircraft and buildings were sold and persistently unprofitable routes either suspended or abandoned altogether. AN's overall route portfolio was cut by 4 per cent during 2001 alone. Labour costs offered the most significant potential savings, and with 35,000 employees AN's re-engineering included 'one of the biggest redundancy programmes in British history'. Once the redundancy programme was underway, the company was able to focus on product development, marketing, customer service and HR development. The company's sharpened focus on the new 'customer-first' programme prompted a major review of the management of employees and their interface with customers.

Air National's human resources strategy

The competitive and HR strategies pursued by AN mainline business in the wake of this restructuring process are congruent with an HR strategy that emphasizes employee empowerment and commitment. As Clive Warren stated in a television interview, 'In an industry like ours, where there are no assembly lines or robots, people are our most important asset and our long term survival depends upon how they work as part of a team'. In the closing part of her presentation, Elizabeth Hoffman, AN's director of human resources, outlined the need for a new approach to managing AN's mainline employees: 'We must

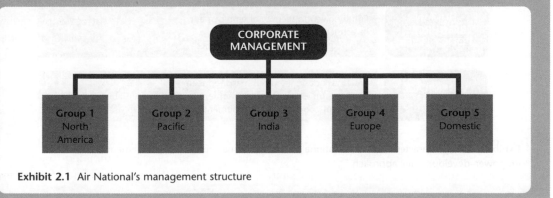

Exhibit 2.1 Air National's management structure

emphasize to our managers that they must give up control if our employees are to improve their performance' (Exhibit 2.2).

As part of the 'new way of doing things', demarcation between craft groups, such as avionics and mechanical engineers, were removed, and staff were organized into teams of multiskilled operatives led by team leaders. Even those middle managers who supported the new work teams found this approach to managing their subordinates uncomfortable, as one maintenance manager acknowledged: 'The hard part is having to share power. I confess, I like to be able to say yes or no without having to confer all the time and seek consensus from the team.'

AN instituted a series of customer service training seminars and invested in training and development. The senior management also developed a 'strategic partnership' with the unions. At the onset of the restructuring process, Clive Warren and Elizabeth Hoffman undertook to 'open the books' to the unions and established team briefings and regular, formal consultation meetings with union representatives. A profit-related pay system was also launched, with the full support of the unions. In addition, senior management held major training programmes,

designed and delivered by leading business school academics, on the importance of trust, motivation and 'visionary' leadership.

Running parallel to these developments was the company's concurrent objective of cost reduction. Between 1996 and 2000, AN shed 37 per cent of its workforce, nearly 25 per cent leaving in 1998. Job cuts were managed entirely through voluntary severance and redeployment. The requirement to sustain and improve performance in the face of such job losses produced, however, a preoccupation with productivity levels, and attempts to alter shift patterns sometimes provoked conflict. Disputes were resolved quickly, usually by the company reminding employees of AN's commitment to job security, training and development, and through senior management 'throwing money at the problem'.

GoJet competitive and human resources strategy

AN also launched its GoJet product in November 2002 to take advantage of the dramatic shift by European and North American passengers towards discount airlines. GoJet planes have more seats because there is less room between the seats and the business-class section has been

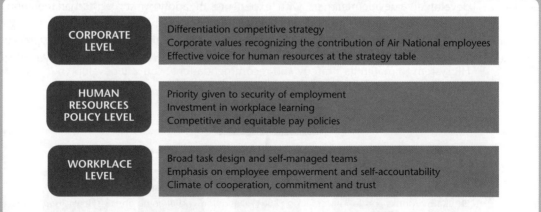

CORPORATE LEVEL	Differentiation competitive strategy Corporate values recognizing the contribution of Air National employees Effective voice for human resources at the strategy table
HUMAN RESOURCES POLICY LEVEL	Priority given to security of employment Investment in workplace learning Competitive and equitable pay policies
WORKPLACE LEVEL	Broad task design and self-managed teams Emphasis on employee empowerment and self-accountability Climate of cooperation, commitment and trust

Exhibit 2.2 Key characteristics of Air National's strategic human resource management and empower–developmental approach

removed, which allows the planes to carry an additional 20 passengers.

GoJet costs will be 20 per cent lower than those of AN's comparable mainline flights partly because GoJet's employees will be paid a lower wage than their counterparts at AN. Clive Warren has, however, said that wages will be competitive with GoJet's competitors in the discount market. Reviewing the developments, Clive Warren considered that AN had been 'transformed by re-engineering'. Deep in debt in the late 1980s, AN went into profit in the first quarter of 1998 and then suffered a loss in the last quarter of 2001 and the first quarter of 2002. The company's aircraft were flying to 164 destinations in 75 countries from 16 UK airports. 'If we are to maintain our market share in domestic and international passenger traffic we have to have a business plan that recognizes the realities of airline travel in the 21st century', said Warren.

Assignment

You are an HR consultant employed by a rival national airline to investigate AN's competitive and HR strategy. Prepare a written report on the following questions:

1. What factors enabled AN's senior management to take a strategic approach to its business and to adopt an empowering-developmental approach to HRM?

2. How useful is the concept of 'strategic choice' in understanding the linkage between AN's competitive and HR strategies?

3. What problems, if any, do you envisage with AN's HR strategy and GoJet's HR strategy? (Rereading HRM in Practice 2.3 might help here.)

HR-related skill development

Case study analysis is an important skill for potential and practising managers to develop: it provides learners with experience of applying strategic management concepts to an organization they have been asked to study or to their own company or organization. Typically, a detailed analysis of a case should include the following: background of the organization, SWOT analysis, nature of the business strategy, an HR system to match its strategy and recommendations. You will develop your skill at analysing a case study by going to www.palgrave.com/business/brattonandgold4 and clicking on 'Analysing a case study'.

Notes

1. F. A. Maljers, chairman of the board of Unilever.
2. Beer et al. (1984) *Managing Human Assets*, p. 25.
3. Kathy Monks and John McMackin (2001) Designing and aligning an HR system. *Human Resource Management*, **11**(2): 57–72.
4. This case is based on 'Experiencing turbulence: competition, strategic choice and the management of human resources in British Airways' by Trevor Colling (1995) *Human Resource Management Journal*, **5**(5), pp. 18–32, and articles in the *Globe and Mail* (2002, April 20).

Chapter three

International human resource management

John Bratton

International human resource management refers to all human resource management practices used to manage people in companies operating in more than one country.

'Definitions of success now transcend national boundaries. In fact, the very concept of domestic business may have become anachronistic.'[1]

'The idiosyncratic national institutional settings are so variable that no common [human resource management] model is likely to emerge in the foreseeable future.'[2]

Chapter outline

Chapter objectives

After studying this chapter, you should be able to:

1. Explain how developments in global capitalism affect corporate and HR strategies within multinational corporations (MNCs)
2. Describe the difference between strategic international human resource management (SIHRM) and international human resource management (IHRM)
3. Explain how SIHRM is linked to different global business strategies
4. Outline some key aspects and contemporary issues in IHRM
5. Explain HRM trends in Europe
6. Explain recent developments in HRM in Asia
7. Comment on whether globalization is driving processes of convergence or divergence in HRM policies and practices

Introduction

In the final quarter of the 20th century, globalization as a set of beliefs or ideologies became infectious. Advocates argued with audacity that neoliberal market economics – an ideology concerned primarily with the maximization of economic efficiency that gives prominence to the role of market forces – along with deregulation and privatization would lead to sustained economic growth. As a result, all societies around the world would reap the benefits in the form of higher living standards and the elimination of poverty. In this global era, old national institutions and processes attempting to regulate national economies, national labour markets and national patterns of employment relations were increasingly displaced by the emergence of new transnational institutions and processes.

The employment relationship has traditionally been shaped by national systems of employment legislation and the cultural contexts in which it operates. However, as the pace of globalization accelerated, the notion of a national system of employment relations began to be openly challenged and to appear out of date (Murray, 2005). This process of globalization has:

- enhanced the integration of markets at both the regional (e.g. the European Union (EU) and North America) and worldwide level
- stimulated new powerful markets in Eastern Europe, the People's Republic of China and India
- increased foreign direct investment by multinational corporations (MNCs) and transnational corporations, as well as, concomitantly, a cross-border integration of their production and services.

As firms increasingly seek to leverage human resources (HR) to compete in global markets, academics and practitioners alike have increasingly begun to explore the international potential of strategic human resource management (HRM). In so doing, they have generally addressed HR policies and practices relating to global and local recruitment and selection, international training and learning, international reward management, performance appraisal and the management of expatriates that define international HRM (IHRM). IHRM can be distinguished from domestic HRM by the fact that these five core HRM activities have to be culturally sensitive and effective in a cross-cultural, multinational environment (Scullion and Linehan, 2005). Comparative HRM, a related but separate field, focuses on providing insights into and an understanding of the nature of and reasons for differences in HR practice across national boundaries (Bamber and Lansbury, 1998; Lansbury and Baird, 2004). The proliferation of interest in both international HRM and comparative HRM springs directly from the globalization of market competition, integrated modes of production, new boundaryless (sometimes virtual) work organizations and the impact of these changes in the global economy on national patterns of employment relations. Interest also stems from developments in management theory and the assumption that strategic HRM is a strategically driven process with immense potential to foster a global mindset or develop global competencies that simultaneously link innovative work practices to the need to deliver competitive cost structures in what may be contracting markets or markets that are being transformed by new entrants (Sparrow et al., 2004).

This chapter begins with some developments in global capitalism and how they play out in terms of employment relations and international HRM in MNCs. We identify three alternative theories relating to the impact of global processes on domestic patterns of employment relations. This is followed by an examination of the international aspects of recruitment and selection, training and development, rewards, performance appraisal, and the management and repatriation of expatriates in companies operating outside their parent country. As we explained in Chapter 1, 'hard' and 'soft' versions of HRM emanated from the USA, so we have not included a further discussion of US HRM in the second half of the chapter, which focuses on recent developments in and an analysis of aspects of HRM in Europe and Asia.

Global capitalism

Over the past 25 years, the number of MNCs has increased eightfold, and foreign direct investment stock has increased twelve-fold. These economic indicators reflect 'a reshuffling of total business investment away from domestic to foreign operations, largely through cross-border acquisitions and mergers' (Cooke, 2005, p. 283). This section explores key concepts in the global business strategy literature as a basis from which to understand the development of IHRM.

Globalization is arguably about the unfettered pursuit of profit (Hertz, 2002). There is nothing in the logic of profit-making corporations and capital accumulation to keep the manufacture of steel in Sheffield, the Ruhr or Pennsylvania, as many managers and non-managers have discovered (Hobsbawm, 1995). Developments in transport and communication have meant that corporations can increase their profits by relocating their operations beyond their parent country. Higher profits can be realized by transferring their distinctive competencies to foreign markets, by economies of scale and by exploiting location economies (Hill and Jones, 2004). The concept of *distinctive competencies* has its roots in resource-based theory (see Chapter 2). MNCs with distinctive competencies can potentially realize higher profits by applying those competencies in foreign markets, where there is no competition or where local competitors lack similar competencies. For example, following the collapse of Soviet Communism, the McDonald's Corporation expanded rapidly in Eastern Europe to exploit its distinctive competencies in managing fast-food operations (Royle, 2005).

REFLECTIVE QUESTION

How does the increasing globalization of markets allow MNCs to increase their profit margins?

Higher profits can be realized through *economies of scale*, which are consistent with the business strategy of low-cost leadership (Porter, 1985). The underlying assumption here is that MNCs that are capable of supplying a global market from a single location are likely to realize economies of scale, and increased profit, more quickly than companies that restrict their marketing to a smaller local economy. Each national (local) economy is embedded within its own social sphere – economic, political, legal and social. Thus, levels of corporate taxation, employment standards and a 'business-friendly' environment can all affect the pursuit of profit. These differences in a country's business environment are known in international management parlance as *economies of location*. In an era of corporate globalization, the portability of capital makes it possible for MNCs to select their production location in an endlessly variable geometry of profit-searching (Castells, 2000; HRM in Practice 3.1) Moreover, the logic of unfettered globalization means that labour-intensive value-added activities migrate from high-wage to low-wage countries, that is, from the rich developed countries such as the USA and Western Europe to poorer developing countries such as China, Bangladesh and India.

HRM IN PRACTICE 3.1

'FOR CHRYSLER, CHINA OFFERS BOTH PROFIT, PERIL'

TOM BROWN, *GLOBE AND MAIL*, 15 AUGUST 2005, P. B5

As he sped through this city in northern Mexico this past week, the incoming head of Chrysler may have been thinking about the advantages of doing business in low-cost labour markets.

Entry-level workers at the high-tech assembly plant operated here by the Chrysler arm of Daimler-Chrysler AG make the equivalent of about $120 (U.S.) a week, a fraction of what its hourly workers in the United States or Canada are paid. That gives Chrysler, the biggest vehicle exporter in Mexico, a definite advantage over some of its competitors. It also goes a long way towards explaining why it builds its popular V8 Hemi engines in Saltillo, and not just multiple versions of the big Dodge Ram pickup truck.

'I still believe the biggest threats are from Asia.'

In remarks to reporters as he flew to Saltillo from Detroit for a visit to the assembly plant, Tom LaSorda, Chrysler's CEO, spoke far more about Asia and China than he did about Mexico, however. Automakers have been pouring billions of dollars into Communist-ruled China to ramp up production there. The lure is the world's fastest growing vehicle market and cut-rate wages that make even Mexico look expensive.

Mr. LaSorda, referring to the day when low-cost cars from China make their debut in North America, said 'I still believe the biggest threats are from Asia, no question, with China being right up there.' 'I saw what Japan did. We've seen what Korea did,' he added. 'China could be next.'

Typologies of global business strategy

The global business strategies of MNCs are all connected to the generic business-level strategies of cost-leadership and differentiation that were examined in Chapter 2. A useful starting point for understanding global business theories is the model developed by Bartlett and Ghoshal (1989). These two international business theorists suggest that global corporations typically face tension from two types of business pressure. On the one hand, MNCs face demands for global *cost reductions* and *integration*, and, on the other hand, demands for *differentiation* and *local responsiveness*. The demand to control costs and integrate has its roots in classical management theory that there is 'one best way' to manage.

Global companies strive for global efficiency by rationalizing their product lines, standardizing parts design and integrating their global manufacturing and control systems. The pressures for integration can be high in technologically intensive enterprises or where the product is universal and requires minimal modification to local needs. This typically occurs with goods such as petroleum, steel and chemicals, and it is also typical in consumer electronics, for instance mobile phones and personal computers. Demands for integration are also high in industries in which there is excess capacity or in which consumers face low switching costs. For example, the demand for integration has been globally intense in the steel industry, in which differentiation is difficult and price is the main competitive variable (Hill and Jones, 2004).

Countering global strategies and organizational efficiency imperatives are local realities and a need for local responsiveness. Companies have to satisfy consumer tastes and preferences in diverse locations, so competitive advantage may be derived from producing a product or service that is more sensitive to national cultures and local tastes in the host countries where the MNC operates. Culture differentiates one locale from another, and the duality of culture – its pervasiveness yet its uniqueness – impacts on global business strategy (Mintzberg et al., 1998). Pressures to be locally responsive arise from *consumer tastes and preferences*, differences in the host country's infrastructure and the regulations of the national business environment imposed by the host government. For example, when the Swedish home furnishing company IKEA entered the US market in the 1990s, it offered cut-price standardized products, which had sold well across Europe, based on huge economies of scale. However, IKEA soon found that it had to be responsive to North American tastes and physiques: IKEA's glasses were too small for North American consumers, who tend to add ice to their drinks, and Swedish beds were too narrow for American body-sizes (Hill and Jones, 2004).

A second set of demands for local responsiveness arises from differences in the host country's *infrastructure*. For example, some EU member states use 240-volt consumer electric systems, whereas in North America 110-volt systems tend to be standard. Thus, differences in the national infrastructure require MNCs to customize domestic electrical appliances. This diversity in infrastructure has been identified as a barrier to European competitiveness and was behind the Single Europe Act of 1986. The Act aimed to stimulate pan-European trade by harmonizing technical standards governing the production and distribution of goods (Hendry, 1994).

A third set of demands for local responsiveness emanates from *nationally based regulatory regimes* constructed and maintained by host governments. The regulation of employment relations, consumer products (e.g. automobile exhaust emissions), ecological controls and local testing (e.g. clinical trials of pharmaceutical products according to domestic standards) may dictate that MNCs be responsive to local conditions. Global corporations can be enticed to relocate by national governments deregulating safety, environmental or employment standards.

In Bhopal, India, for example, there was a major accident that illustrates the dangers implicit in reducing standards to attract MNC investment. A chemical plant owned by the US multinational company Union Carbide engaged in chemical production under conditions that would have been illegal in the USA. On 3 December 1984, the plant experienced a major leak. Within hours, 3000 people were dead, 15,000 more dying in the aftermath. A further 200,000 were seriously injured, and half a million still carry special health cards. Eventually, the MNC paid out just $470 million in compensation (Saul, 2005). More recently, the Indian government gave tax exemptions and deregulated the telecommunications industry in order to increase foreign investment in call centres (Maitra and Sangha, 2005 and see HRM in Practice 3.2).

HRM IN PRACTICE 3.2

BLOW-OUT IN BANGLADESH, TENGRATILA, BANGLADESH

GEOFFREY YORK, *GLOBE AND MAIL*, 1 APRIL 2006, PP. B4–5

The protesters are already gathering at the gate of the gas field as the top executives of Niko Resources Ltd. roar overhead in a float plane, inspecting the remains of the gas blowouts on the scarred earth.

Dozens of villagers are chanting angrily at the gate, waving their fists in the air, as Ed Sampson and Bill Hornaday drive into the compound in their jeep. 'Why is there no drinking water?' the protesters shout. 'Why is there gas coming out in the market? We demand more compensation!'

It's another rough day in Bangladesh for Mr. Sampson, president and chairman of the Calgary-based company, and Mr. Hornaday, its chief operating officer. Already six months behind schedule because of two blowouts last year and a price dispute with the government, the Niko executives are struggling with a political environment that has somehow exploded in their faces.

After investing $100-million to develop two gas fields in Bangladesh over the past three years, Niko was supposed to be reaping another South Asian success story by now. The subcontinent has been crucial to Niko's rise, beginning with its pioneering work over the past 14 years in India. 'We were fantastically successful in rejuvenating fields in India,' Mr. Hornaday said in an interview. 'The plan in Bangladesh was to adopt the same strategy and take it on the road.'

For a company with about $125-million in annual revenue, its $100-million investment in Bangladesh is a significant gamble. In the aftermath of the blowouts, the company has suffered lawsuits, a frozen bank account, verbal attacks by citizen activists, massive government claims for compensation and almost daily denunciations by the media.

Niko's executives admit they failed to prepare themselves for the ferociously partisan climate of hardball politics here. Their ordeal in Bangladesh points to the crucial importance of understanding the political landscape when investing in a foreign country – and never to assume it is similar to Canada.

> **Perhaps the company should never have expected an easy path in Bangladesh.**

The atmosphere in Bangladesh is more 'vindictive' than anything he had anticipated, Mr. Hornaday said. 'I've never experienced anything like it before. It's amazing. Anything happens and someone has to be hanged. It's like a national crisis.'

Perhaps the company should never have expected an easy path in Bangladesh. Although it is the world's eighth-biggest country by population (with 140 million people), this impoverished country is ranked by Transparency International as the most corrupt in the world. And it is a consistent underachiever in foreign investment, attracting less than most other major Asian countries.

After beginning production at its Feni gas field in November 2004, the company assumed it finally had clear sailing. But it all began to go wrong when the two blowouts erupted last year as it developed its Tengratila field in northeastern Bangladesh.

Two blowouts within a few months, however, is a less common event. Niko was pilloried in the Bangladeshi media, even though nobody was killed or seriously injured in either accident. With an election approaching in the country, Niko became a scapegoat for jousting politicians and feuding officials. Critics pointed out that the company had won its contract without a formal competition. 'It was a shock to us,' Mr. Hornaday said. 'We weren't prepared for that kind of aggressiveness – that really nasty stuff. It wasn't something we were accustomed to, even in India.'

Corruption and bribery are commonplace in Bangladesh's media outlets, and Niko's competitors were savvy enough to cultivate the media. Local journalists say it is common to get cash or gifts from gas developers in Bangladesh, including the big multinationals. But Niko refused to distribute any envelopes of cash. 'It's not the Canadian way,' Mr. Sampson said.

Thus, through a wide variety of national or regional policy mechanisms, national governments can effectively shape national business systems and therefore the competitive dynamics within a market (Whitley, 1999). Other economic, political, legal and social factors that may demand local responsiveness are discussed in Chapter 4. Prahalad and Doz (1987, p. 251) suggest that, because governments influence competitive outcomes, 'MNCs can approach strategy as a process of "negotiation" with host governments'. They call this process 'negotiated strategies'. The point we wish to make here is that the cost efficiency–responsiveness strategic mix may well depend on the MNC's calculation to exploit cross-national differences, including the model of capitalism that prevails in the host country and that country's social mechanisms designed to protect the planet and safeguard the health and safety of its people.

The integration–responsiveness grid

Local realities are the classic barrier to universal theories of global efficiency. Two pressures – cost efficiencies and rationalization, and differentiation and local responsiveness – form the two dimensions of the integration–responsiveness grid (Figure 3.1). Bartlett and Ghoshal (1989) and Prahalad and Doz (1987) offer four fashionable typologies – global, multidomestic, international, and transnational – as solutions to the dual pressure for cost efficiency and responsiveness.

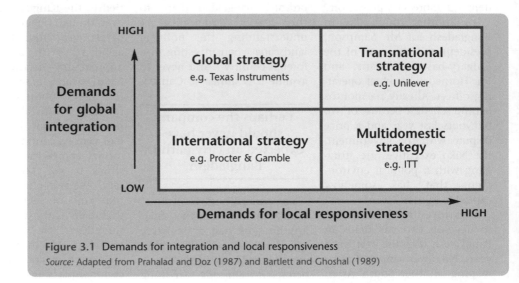

Figure 3.1 Demands for integration and local responsiveness
Source: Adapted from Prahalad and Doz (1987) and Bartlett and Ghoshal (1989)

Global strategy

Global corporations that pursue a **global strategy** focus on increasing profit margins through cost efficiencies arising from economies of scale and economies of location. These MNCs are pursuing a low-cost leadership strategy. The operations of the MNCs will be concentrated in a few favourable host economies and will tend not to customize their goods to local situations. A global strategy is typically associated with high demands for integration and low demands for local responsiveness (the top-left quandrant of Figure 3.1). Texas Instruments, a company that once dominated the market in pocket calculators and digital watches by focusing persistently on cost reductions and price at the expense of understanding consumers' needs, is an example of an MNC that, until 1982, followed a global strategy (Hill and Jones, 2004).

Multidomestic strategy

Companies pursuing a **multidomestic strategy** design their operations to maximize local responsiveness. Thus, these MNCs tend to customize both their product offering and marketing strategy to different local customer tastes and preferences. A multidomestic company such as ITT developed a 'strategic posture and organizational ability that enables it to be very sensitive and responsive to differences in national environments' (Bartlett and Ghoshal, 1989, p. 14). A multidomestic strategy is typically associated with low demands for integration and high demands for local responsiveness.

International strategy

Global corporations pursuing an **international strategy** create competitive advantage through a global diffusion of the company's distinctive competencies where its local competitors lack these resources and the capability to integrate and effectively rationalize their value-added activities abroad. An international strategy is typically associated with low demands for integration and low demands for local responsiveness. MNCs pursuing an international strategy tend to centralize their research and development activities in the parent country but also tend to establish operations in each major national economy in which they do business. The US-based company Procter & Gamble is an example of an MNC that has pursued an international strategy: 'it set up miniature replicas of the domestic organization to adapt P&G products without deviating from the "Procter way"' (Bartlett and Ghoshal, 1989, p. 15).

Transnational strategy

MNCs following a **transnational strategy** strive for competitive advantage worldwide by rationalizing and integrating resources to achieve superior cost efficiencies from economies of scale and economies of location, by being sensitive and capable of responding to local needs, and by sharing knowledge throughout their global operations. In a transnational company, knowledge and distinctive competencies flow *to* and *from* each of the company's operations as part of a larger process of 'global learning' that encompasses 'every member of the company' (Bartlett and Ghoshal, 1989, p. 59). In essence, a transnational company *simultaneously* achieves low-cost leadership and a competitive advantage in terms of differentiation. The effect is 'a complex configuration of assets and capabilities that are distributed, yet specialized [and] the company integrates the dispersed resources through strong interdependencies ... Such interdependencies may be reciprocal rather than sequential' (Bartlett and Ghoshal, 1989, p. 60). Thus, a world-scale production plant in Mexico may depend on world-scale component plants in Australia, France and South Korea; major sales subsidiaries worldwide may in turn depend on Mexico for their finished products. The transnational's resources and capabilities are represented as an *integrated network*, a term emphasizing the significant flows of components, products, resources, information and people. Unilever is an example of an MNC that pursued a transnational strategy with 17 different and largely decentralized detergent plants in Europe alone.

HRM WEB LINKS

Go to the websites of Procter and Gamble UK and Ireland (www.uk.pg.com) and Procter & Gamble USA (www.pg.com/en_US/index.jhtml), ITT (www.itt.com), Unilever (www.unilever.com), Texas Instruments (www.texasinstruments.com) and Hewlett-Packard Co. (www.h-p.com). What is the parent country for these MNCs? How many countries does each MNC operate in?

The integration–responsiveness grid is a simple and impressive heuristic model for explaining the strategic choices shaping the strategies and organizational networks of MNCs. Case study research confirms Barlett and Ghoshal's typology of MNCs that is explained here (see Harzing, 2000), but we should end this introduction to global management strategies with a word of caution. The typologies proposed by Bartlett and Ghoshal depict a theoretical or 'ideal type' of global strategy that MNCs should strive for if they wish to attain superior performance outcomes. But few MNCs truly pursue a transnational strategy. Instead, managing the conflicting pressures for global rationalization and integration (low-cost leadership) and local responsiveness (differentiation) sets the context for IHRM.

International human resource management

In this section, we seek to understand the explicit connection between global competition and HRM in MNCs. We identify three alternative theories relating to the impact of global processes on domestic patterns of employment relations. We explain the concepts of strategic IHRM (SIHRM) and IHRM. We then critically examine the links between global strategic management and SIHRM and IHRM, and examine a model of strategic IHRM first developed by Schuler et al. (1993).

Global capitalism and employment relations

The developments in international capitalism have generated a debate on how globalization impacts on domestic patterns of employment relations. The literature identifies three alternative approaches to this: economic, institutionalist and integrated (Bamber et al., 2004).

The *economic* globalization approach follows the classical premise that global business activity has become so interconnected, and that competitive imperatives are so dominant, that they offer little scope for domestic differences in patterns of employment relations. This simple economic approach predicts that international markets operate in accordance with universal principles and will result in a 'convergence' of national employment relations. Economic imperatives will, for example, drive wages down and erode employment standards.

The *institutionalist* approach to the impact of globalization contends that global forces are more fluid in their dynamics and more contradictory in their outcome. Moreover, nationally based regulatory institutions form an independent dynamic that structures, controls and legitimates business activities and outcomes. Global trends are mediated by national or local institutional regimes and changed into 'divergent' power struggles over particular national employment practices (Hyman, 1999). By highlighting national differences in how societies shape economic and social outcomes, the institutionalist approach emphasizes the heterogeneity of market economies and highlights why 'varieties of capitalism' are likely to persist in the future (Hall and Soskice, 2001; Whitley, 1999). Furthermore, nationally embedded institutions structuring the political economy can confer a comparative competitive advantage, especially in the sphere of learning and innovation (Hall and Soskice, 2001; Hyman, 1999).

STUDY TIP

SIHRM and IHRM often tend to privilege universal management theories at the expense of national culture and realities. Sociologist Diane Crane makes the interesting argument that cultures flow in, around, out and across national borders. She writes that 'The intertwining of local, regional, national, and global cultures are now complex beyond reckoning … Culture may be integrative, but it may also be disintegrative at the same time. It may ally acquiescent citizens under a common regime and common symbols, but it may also prove a focal point for division, contention, and conflict' (Crane, 1994, p. 42).

Then read Javier Quintanilla and Anthony Ferner's (2003) article on global convergence and national identity. In the context of 'globalization' and alleged trends towards 'convergence', to what extent do Crane's observations on national culture impact on the conversion debate? Is conversion a good thing? If so, why? Does the cultural phenomenon negate 'black and white' depictions of convergence or continued diversity? Is diversity in HR practices a good thing?

Bamber et al. (2004) put forward an *integrated* approach to globalization and national patterns of employment relations. This integrated approach suggests that both global economic trends and nationally based institutions are important in structuring national patterns of employment relations. However, because different kinds of market economies are integrated into the global economy in different ways, global economic pressures are likely to be divergent. The integrated approach thus focuses on the effects of global economic developments on the 'interests of different groups of employers, workers and policy-makers within different institutional settings' (Bamber et al., 2004, p. 1483).

International and strategic international human resource management

Before we consider models of SIHRM that have been developed to explain how the HRM function is configured in global companies, it is important to distinguish between IHRM and SIHRM. There are competing definitions of **international human resource management**, although most scholarship in the field has focused on issues associated with the cross-national transfer of expatriates (i.e. how to recruit and manage individual managers in international job assignments; e.g. Shenkar, 1995; Tung, 1988). Kochan et al. (1992) suggested that much of the research tended to be descriptive and lacked analytical rigour, but scholarship has made considerable progress over the past 10 years.

Taylor et al. (1996, p. 960) define IHRM as 'the set of distinct activities, functions and processes that are directed at attracting, developing and maintaining an MNC's human resources. It is thus the aggregate of the various HRM systems used to manage people in the MNC, both at home and overseas'. Scullion (2001, p. 288) defines IHRM as the 'HRM issues and problems arising from the internationalization of business, and the HRM strategies, policies and practices which firms pursue in response to the internationalization process'. More recent definitions have extended the term to cover the need to adapt to local contexts, the global coordination of overseas subsidiaries, global knowledge management and global leadership (Scullion and Linehan, 2005).

IHRM tends to celebrate a Western hegemonic culture, one that emphasizes the subordination of domestic culture and domestic employment practices to corporate culture and corporate HRM practices (Boxall, 1995). As such, many of the contemporary IHRM studies tend to be seen as a managerial tool unashamedly connected to neoliberalism. It is the principal discourse of neoliberalism that gives insights into related debates around labour market rigidities and flexibility, outsourcing, privatization and international HR practices. IHRM is thus the sum of the various HRM policies and practices used to manage people in companies operating in more than one country.

As we showed in Chapter 2, strategic HRM is the process of explicitly linking the HRM function with the strategic management goals of the organization. Thus, **strategic international human resource management** is the process of explicitly linking IHRM with the strategy of the global company. In defining SIHRM, we will follow Scullion and Linehan (2005), who draw on the work of Lado and Wilson (1994), Schuler et al. (1993) and Taylor et al. (1996). Schuler et al. (1993, p. 720) define SIHRM as the 'HRM issues, functions and policies and practices that result from the strategic activities of multinational enterprises and that impact the international concerns and goals of those enterprises'. SIHRM is defined here as:

> The HR policies and processes that result from the global competitive activities of MNCs and that explicitly link international HR practices and processes with the worldwide strategic goals of those companies.

SIHRM builds on strategic HRM that aims to connect HRM explicitly with strategic management processes. In so doing, SIHRM recognizes the need to address the tension between the global and the local. This tension is related to balancing global competitiveness (rationalization and integration) and local responsiveness (flexibility) strategies pursued by MNCs while simultaneously leveraging global learning within and across the MNC. Thus, SIHRM links 'IHRM explicitly with the strategy and with the MNC' (Scullion and Linehan, 2005, p. 23).

A model of strategic international human resource management

We have focused so far on some global business strategies and the meaning of IHRM and SIHRM. We will now identify some conceptual models of SIHRM developed to explain IHRM processes and roles, and how external and internal factors impact on HRM in MNCs. Models of SIHRM have been developed by De Cieri and Dowling (1999), Schuler et al. (1993) and Taylor et al. (1996). In Figure 3.2, we present an integrative model that draws primarily from Schuler et al. (1993) and is informed by the work of Bartlett and Ghoshal (1989) and Taylor et al. (1996).

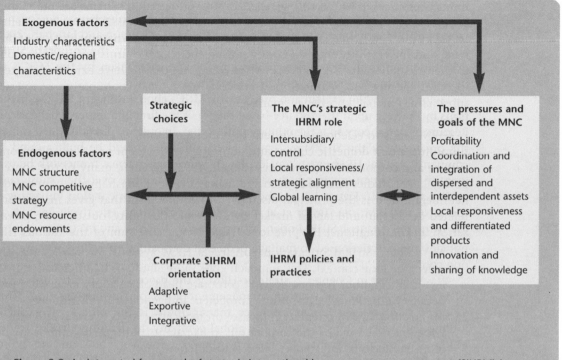

Figure 3.2 An integrated framework of strategic international human resource management (SIHRM) in multinational companies (MNCs)

Source: Adapted from Schuler et al. (1993) p. 722; Scullion and Linehan (2005) p. 31; Taylor et al. (1996) p. 965 and Bartlett and Ghoshal (1989) p. 67

Schuler et al.'s original integrative framework consisted of four core components:

1. exogenous factors
2. endogenous factors
3. SIHRM
4. the pressures and goals of the MNC.

To this, we have added a fifth component – the corporate SIHRM orientation. The lines and arrows in Figure 3.2 denote the reciprocal relationships between exogenous factors, SIHRM and the pressures and goals of the MNC.

Briefly, *exogenous factors* relate to issues external to the MNC. They include, for example, industry characteristics, the technology available, and domestic characteristics such as domestic employment relations. De Cieri and Dowling (1999) argue that exogenous factors exert a direct influence on endogenous factors, SIHRM and the pressures and goals of the MNC. *Endogenous factors* relate to internal organizational issues, such as work design, intraorganizational networks and coordination and control systems.

SIHRM relates to issues of coordination and control, local responsiveness and worldwide learning. It is concerned with 'Developing a fit between exogenous and endogenous factors and balancing the competing demands of global versus local requirements as well as the needs of coordination, control and autonomy' (Schuler et al., 1993, p. 451). *Pressures and goals of the MNC* relate to profitability, the dual demands for cost reductions and local responsiveness, and the global transfer of inno-vation. The model suggests that there are reciprocal relationships between exogenous factors, SIHRM and the pressures and goals of the MNC (Scullion and Linehan, 2005). SIHRM is expected to buttress the MNC's global goals. Finally, the **corporate SIHRM orientation** refers to the general philosophy or approach taken by the MNC's top management in designing its total IHRM system.

Taylor et al. (1996) explain and predict why MNCs choose different SIHRM orienta-tions by drawing upon the resource-based theory of the firm and resource dependence. Resource-based theory adds the primary notion that, in order to provide added value to the organization, the SIHRM system of global affiliates should be built around the company's critical HRM competencies. The resource dependence framework helps to identify those situations in which MNCs will exercise control over their subsidiaries' SIHRM systems. In Figure 3.2, we showed corporate SIHRM orientation impacting on the MNC's SIHRM role. Taylor et al. propose that MNCs can effectively leverage HR following three generic SIHRM orientations: *adaptive*, *exportive* and *integrative*:

1. An *adaptive* SIHRM orientation constructs HRM systems for subsidiaries that reflect the local context. This approach gives more emphasis to differentiation and less to integration. Top managers at corporate head office adopt local HRM prac-tices by hiring knowledgeable and competent indigenous HR practitioners.
2. An *exportive* SIHRM orientation focuses on replicating in its overseas affiliates the HRM practices used by the corporation in its parent country. This approach gives more emphasis to integration and less to differentiation.
3. An *integrative* SIHRM orientation focuses on transferring the 'best' HRM policies and practices from *any* of the company's affiliates worldwide to construct a global HRM system. Taylor et al. contend that the SIHRM orientation of the MNC determines its overall approach to managing the tension between integra-tion and control pressures, and local responsiveness and differentiation pres-sures. The central theoretical argument of the integrative model, therefore, is that IHRM should be explicitly related to the MNC's global business strategy and that its changing forms must be understood in relation to the strategic evolution of the MNC (Scullion and Linehan, 2005; Scullion and Starkey, 2000; Taylor et al., 1996).

REFLECTIVE QUESTION

Go back to Figure 3.1. What type of SIHRM orientation would you expect to find at Texas Instruments, ITT and Unilever? Why?

The integrated model is useful for understanding the link between international business strategy and IHRM in the global corporation, and for identifying a comprehensive range of factors that influence SIHRM in MNCs. However, models are just that: they are a conceptual construct and have been criticized because the alleged direction of the causal relationships within them is uncertain. For example, the argu-ment that exogenous factors exert a direct impact on endogenous factors may privi-lege external factors as *the* actor when MNCs have actually become global giants that wield titanic political power. Arguably, corporations in fact determine the rules of the game, and governments enforce the rules laid down by others (Hertz, 2002). The MNC is *the* actor. Although the framework covers a wide range of relevant issues, the issue of transplanting Western HRM practices and values into culturally diverse domestic environments needs to be researched through a critical lens. Global companies share with their domestic counterparts the intractable problem of managing the employment relationship to reduce the indeterminacy resulting from the unspecified nature of the employment contract. If we adopt Townley's (1994) perspective on IHRM, the role of knowledge to render people in the workplace 'governable' is further problematized by the intertwining of highly complex local, regional, national and global cultures (Crane, 1994).

WEB LINKS

For further information on cultural diversity go to www.ciber.bus.msu.edu, www.shrm.org/diversity and www.shhrm.org/trends.

The Internationalization of the human resource management cycle

The global strategies examined above, in particular the supposed ascendancy of the transnational corporation with global communication networks, has far-reaching implications for the function and practices of IHRM. In leveraging the core HR activities, MNCs must achieve a dynamic balance between the pressures for central control and the pressures for local responsiveness across diverse national locations and intercultural contexts (Adler, 2002a). Here, we extend the HRM cycle in Fombrun, Tichy and Devanna's model (see Figure 1.4) to briefly explore the international aspects of recruitment and selection, rewards, training and development, and performance appraisal, as well as the issue of repatriation. Figure 3.3 shows how four HR practices can be examined as part of an international HRM 'cycle', each contributing to the strategic goals and international performance of both the individual employee and the global organ-

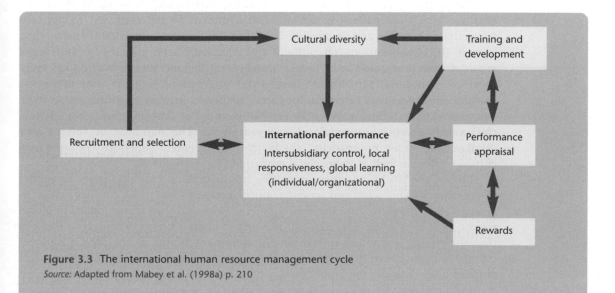

Figure 3.3 The international human resource management cycle
Source: Adapted from Mabey et al. (1998a) p. 210

ization. Unlike Fombrun et al.'s model, however, Figure 3.3 adds a further dimension: cultural diversity. Others have noted that cultural diversity poses a number of new challenges for managing these four HR practices. The MNC typically has a multicultural workforce made up of employees with a variety of ethnic, racial, religious and cultural values and mores. Indeed, it has been suggested that the central modus operandi of the global company is the creation and effective management of multicultural work teams that represent diversity in competencies, levels of experience and cultural and language backgrounds (Rhinesmith, 1993, quoted in Mabey et al., 1998a, p. 210).

REFLECTIVE QUESTION

As we have discussed, the global company is characterized by geographical dispersion, demands for rationalization and differentiation, and cultural diversity. Look at Figure 3.3. When an MNC adopts a global business strategy, what new challenges does it present for managing:

- recruitment and selection
- rewards
- training and development
- performance appraisal?

International recruitment and selection

An MNC does not simply transmit capital: it transmits management 'know-how'. Expatriate managers play a critical role in the transfer of both explicit knowledge and the tacit knowledge of the MNC's practices and management style to the overseas affiliates (Gamble, 2003). The use of expatriates to staff vacant positions in affiliates in host countries is a widespread practice. In the case of European MNCs, 54 per cent of the managers of their overseas subsidiaries are expatriates, and in North American and Japanese MNCs the pattern is similar, with figures of 51 per cent and 75 per cent respectively (Bonache and Fernández, 2005, p. 115). It is not surprising therefore that, in most IHRM publications, recruitment and selection is seen primarily as an issue of *expatriate* selection. *Selection* is, however, important beyond simply staffing key technical or managerial positions. Intercultural phenomena suggest that mastering cultural differences may be crucial for successful organizational performance. As such, it is argued that staffing goes to the central dilemma of centralization (cost efficiencies) versus decentralization (local responsiveness). The handling of this balance invokes issues of 'ethnocentricity', the belief in the inherent superiority of one's own culture or race, as well as 'managerial empathy' (Torbiörn, 2005).

Much of the IHRM literature on staffing has focused on two alternative categories of recruitment and selection: parent country nationals and host country nationals (Tung, 1998). Drawing from these two pools of potential staff seems logical in global recruiting as they mirror the general dilemma of central versus decentral or local, in that the choice is whether to transfer the dominant norms of the MNC's national culture or make use of those of the local culture. In theory, a varied cultural context requires a selective use of parent country nationals and host country nationals across staffing decisions. In practice, however, expatriate selection appears to be more a matter of 'good luck than good management' (Anderson, 2005, p. 580). In addition, because the locus of decision-making is embedded in the local culture and norms where the MNC's corporate office is located, expatriate staff at the company's head office may have little idea what culturally derived expectations are needed to 'fit' the local context (Gamble, 2003). Moreover, informal ad hoc selection practices may be frequent, and decisions of intercultural reach may frequently be affected by illogical elements such as ethnocentrism, ignorance and stereotyping (Torbiörn, 2005).

The low number of women chosen for global assignments provides evidence that staffing decisions in MNCs may often be irrational and sometimes discriminatory. Research shows that, despite equal opportunities legislation and women's increased presence in the organizational hierarchy, the number of female expatriates remains only a fraction of those in senior management positions, and 'only in rare circumstances' are female managers offered global assignments (Linehan, 2005, p. 197). In all capitalist countries, it is argued, men control economic and political power; management is consequently androcentric (HRM in Practice 3.3). Numerous studies (e.g. Adler, 1984, 1994; Caligiuri and Tung, 1999; Linehan, 2000, 2005; Punnett et al., 1992; Taylor and Napier, 1996) point to stereotypical perceptions of women's managerial abilities and business acumen, traditional attitudes towards women's family roles, the need to accommodate dual-career couples, and general discrimination against women as major social barriers to women expanding their career horizons through access to global management positions. Countering one myth, studies by Adler (1987) and Taylor and Napier (1996) found that there were no significant differences between male and female expatriates in their business performance, even in male-dominated cultures such as South Korea and Japan.

HRM IN PRACTICE 3.3

WOMEN FIND OVERSEAS POSTINGS OUT OF REACH

ROSS SHERWOOD, *GLOBE AND MAIL*, 27 AUGUST 2001, P. M6

Female executives who want plum overseas assignments are forced to break through a 'glass border' – a barrier to foreign postings that is not unlike the glass ceiling that stands in the way of promotions, experts say.

'As global assignments increasingly become prerequisites for advancement, glass borders may impede women's progress before they even reach the glass ceiling,' says Ilene Lang, president of Catalyst, an advocacy group to advance women in business. Women hold about 13 per cent of all corporate American expatriate posts, according to a study done by Catalyst. That's a poor showing, says the New York-based group.

Women are victims of 'subtle discrimination'

Authorities cite a variety of obstacles to women becoming global executives. These include misplaced concerns for the safety and effectiveness of female expatriates, as well as the fact that some women have been given little or no opportunity to obtain experience abroad, even with small projects. Women who are selected 'tend to be younger and single and that tells me employers are probably ruling out married women with children,' says Virginia Hollis, vice-president of sales at Cigna International Expatriate Benefits. Women are victims of 'subtle discrimination,' says Linda Stroh, a professor at the Institute of Human Resources and Industrial Relations at Loyola University, in Chicago. 'It doesn't mean that men are screening women out to work abroad. It's an unawareness that women are capable of going.' Also, male executives do not send women abroad 'in the mistakenly paternalistic belief that they are protecting them from environments that may be difficult or dangerous,' says Jean Lipman-Blumen, professor of public policy and organizational behaviour, at the University of Claremont.

Change will not come, though, until 'corporate executives at the top become very proactive in reaching out to women to be considered for [overseas] assignments,' predicts Anna Lloyd, president of the Committee of 200, a group that represents more than 430 female business executives.

REFLECTIVE QUESTION

The term 'glass border' describes the irrational assumptions held by parent-country senior management about the suitability of female managers for overseas appointments. To what extent is gender still relevant as a criterion for selecting female expatriates? If gender is still relevant, what can be done to promote equal opportunity for female managers to undertake international assignments?

International rewards

Reward management (salary, allowances, incentive bonuses) generally needs to support overall business strategy in order to attract, retain and motivate needed employees (see Chapter 10). Managing *international rewards* requires that managers responsible for implementing HR policies and practices are familiar with a range of other issues, including the foreign country's employment law, national labour relations, the availability of particular allowances or benefits, and currency fluctuations in particular host countries. Reward management for expatriates has been a major focus in IHRM research. Much of the literature deals with technical rather than strategic issues of rewards, that is, how to design effective reward/compensation packages for expatriates (Bonache and Fernández, 2005). Part of that technical discussion includes deciding what currency it is beneficial to pay rewards in so that, in terms of tax efficiency, the outcome motivates the expatriate. Bonache and Fernández (2005) present a theory-based approach to expatriate rewards based on the costs and benefits. They argue that when salary and non-salary costs (e.g. training) are taken into account, and in certain circumstances (e.g. the need to exploit company-specific knowledge), expatriates can be a cost-effective solution. Studies suggest that effective performance management requires expatriates to know whether and how their performance in their overseas assignment is linked to pay and the next step in their career (Tahvanainen and Suutari, 2005).

International training and development

The transnational strategy focuses attention on the issue of 'fit' between a MNC's global business strategy and training interventions. Within the global integration versus local responsiveness framework, the notion of strategic alignment suggests that *international training and development* will vary and take one of three forms: centralized, synergistic or local (Caligiuri et al., 2005). MNCs pursuing a global strategy will tend to place greater emphasis on training rather than development. The general objective of the training interventions will be to provide managers and key technical personnel with the competencies needed to transfer the distinctive competencies and organizational culture successfully from the parent headquarters to the subsidiaries. MNCs pursuing a multidomestic strategy tend to transfer almost all HR practices to the host country subsidiaries. Local managers at the affiliate make decisions on the types of training intervention required. MNCs pursuing a transnational strategy clearly require the most complex training and development strategy. The transnational strategy requires that managers be recruited from a worldwide pool of employees, regardless of nationality.

The role of training interventions is to nurture a 'strong' culture, or what Bartlett and Ghoshal (1989, p. 175) call the 'global glue' that counterbalances the centrifugal forces of the decentralized operations and processes. A particular focus in this area has been the predeparture training of expatriates to be 'interculturally competent', which refers to the ability of the effective manager to have both 'communicative competence' – that is, to communicate both verbally and non-verbally with host country nationals – and 'cognitive competence', which avoids the use of crude stereotypes to judge people (see, for example, Mabey et al., 1998). According to Caligiuri et al. (2005, p. 76), training interventions in the transnational MNC aim to help managers 'to work, think and behave synergistically across borders with people from diverse cultural backgrounds'. Irrespective of business strategy, training and development interventions in MNCs typically include cross-cultural training and competencies associated with global leadership. Table 3.1 summarises these interventions and their respective goals. (See Chapter 9 for a further discussion on training and development.)

Table 3.1 Examples of training and development interventions in multinational corporations

Training and development initiatives	Goals
Cross-cultural orientation (predeparture)	Comfortably live and work in host country
Cross-cultural training (in-country)	Increase cross-cultural adjustment
Diversity training	Increase ability to understand and appreciate multiple cultural perspectives
Language training	Fluency in another language
Traditional education in international management	Increase international business acumen and knowledge
Individualized coaching or mentoring on cultural experiences	Build cultural awareness; work on cultural 'blind spots'; develop competencies for becoming an effective global leader
Immersion cultural experiences	Build extensive understanding of the local culture and increase ability to understand and appreciate multiple cultural perspectives
Cross-border global teams with debriefing	Learn skills to be a better leader (or team member) with multiple cultures involved in the team
Global meetings with debriefing or coaching	Learn skills to conduct a better meeting when multiple cultures are involved in the meeting
International assignment rotations with debriefing or coaching	Develop a deep appreciation for the challenges of working in another culture; increase global leadership competence

Source: Caligiuri et al. (2005) p. 77

International performance appraisal

As we discuss in Chapter 8, performance appraisal has become a key feature of the employment relationship. The desire to control and predict an employee's current and potential performance has resulted in both national and global firms developing integrated performance appraisal systems. In keeping with the critical perspective of HRM, some have argued that the diffusion of performance appraisal systems is associated with low trade union density (Brown and Heywood, 2005) and is indicative of increasing employer attempts to individualize the employment relationship and thwart trade union influence (e.g. Gunnigle et al., 1998). Here, we will consider questions of 'why' and 'how' related to *international performance appraisal*. Sparrow et al. (2004) argue that five interrelated organizational 'drivers' – core business cost efficiencies, information exchange, building a global presence, global learning and localized decision-making – are together creating an obvious logic of being as effective as possible across the organization's whole international operations and a need for the cross-national transfer of better HR practices such as performance appraisal. Notably, performance appraisal is the favoured way to ensure that strategic employee competencies, employee behaviour and motivation are performed effectively in the host country.

In Eastern Europe, following the collapse of the Soviet Union in 1991, the 'Washington Consensus' dominated the ideology of most newly elected governments. This was the ideology of wide-scale privatization, deregulation and free markets, all promoted by the International Monetary Fund and the World Bank. The new dominant ideology and the orientation towards the EU urged East European managers into new roles requiring increased autonomy and performance appraisal (Koubek and Brewster, 1995; Prokopenko, 1994). According to Shibata (2002), in Asia, when the Japanese 'bubble economy' collapsed in the 1990s, Japanese companies began to be attracted to the performance appraisal systems long found in North American business organizations. Chou's (2005) study examines the implementation of performance appraisal in the civil service of China in the 1990s. It is suggested that changes occurred to improve personnel practices and government capacity in both central and local government.

How far does performance appraisal in an international context resemble the Anglo-American model and practice? Performance appraisal is a political activity. It is about gathering relevant information on an employee's competencies and behaviour; it is about making judgements on a subordinate's work effort; it is about the level of reward and about career paths; it is about motivation (being inspired by positive appraisal); it is about possible termination of employment. To perform successfully in a host country, a manager requires technical skills, interpersonal skills, adaptability and cultural sensitivity. Expatriate performance in an international context is, however, affected by volatility in the international environment (e.g. fluctuating currency exchange rates), which is outside the expatriate's scope of control, and by cultural and political factors inside the host country (e.g. acts of terrorism).

The complexity of the task is illustrated by Hofstede's (1980) model: who sets what performance criteria for an individualistic, task-oriented Anglo-Saxon expatriate transferred to a collectivist, relationship-oriented Chinese subsidiary? Chou (2005) found that Anglo-Saxon-style performance appraisal was undermined in China because of the collectivist, relationship-oriented or 'Communist neo-traditionalism' sociopolitical culture. The study found that many managers 'manipulated appraisal results' and refrained from rating subordinates' performance as 'unsatisfactory' because of the importance placed on 'reciprocal relationship and organizational harmony' (Chou, 2005, p. 54). The evidence suggests that the internationalization of performance appraisal demands sensitivity to different cultural and sociopolitical experiences. This section also illustrates that the cross-national transfer of Anglo-Saxon HR practices for selection, rewards, training and appraisal will require some degree of cultural sensitivity, as well as consultation with host-country nationals about local suitability (Mabey et al., 1998).

Repatriation

REFLECTIVE QUESTION

If you were an expatriate, how would you feel about returning to your old position in the company after five years working at one of the company's overseas subsidiaries? Can you think of any problems you would encounter on your return to your parent country and company?

Much of the traditional work on IHRM focuses on the additional component in the internationalized HRM cycle, that is, expatriates returning to the parent company – *repatriation*. In the context of strategic IHRM discussed in this chapter, managing expatriates or 'flexpatriates' (Mayerhofer et al., 2004) returning to the parent company may be the least of the challenges facing a global manager. Nonetheless, for many MNCs, the failure to repatriate managers successfully has caused many expatriates to resign from the company owing to what has been termed *re-entry shock*. The complexity of the repatriation problem varies from individual to individual. Linehan and Mayrhofer (2005) point out that a violation of the *psychological contract* may lead to a negative psychological reaction to repatriation. Anecdotal and empirical evidence of re-entry shock indicates that *loss of autonomy*, *loss of status* and *loss of career opportunities*, together with problems of family members readjusting to the parent culture, are often relevant (Adler, 1996; Brewster and Scullion, 1997; Dowling et al., 1999; Linehan and Mayrhofer, 2005; Mayerhofer et al., 2004; Suutari and Brewster, 2003). Even before the attacks on New York in 2001, MNCs had begun to experience difficulty attracting managers to accept overseas assignments. The security issue will be an additional contributing factor in this reluctance to go abroad.

● Comparative human resource management

As with IHRM, the growth of interest in **comparative human resource management** is linked to globalized capitalism. We can define comparative HRM as:

> a systematic investigation of HRM practices in two or more countries to increase knowledge and understanding that has analytic rather than descriptive implications.

Underscoring comparative HRM is the premise that the person who understands only one HRM system understands none or, to borrow a quote, 'a fish only recognizes water when it discovers air'.[3] In terms of critical research, comparative HRM is relatively underdeveloped. If we look at the types of question that mainstream comparative HRM generates – for example, 'Can "best HR practices" that work effectively in one country be transplanted to others?' and 'Does it make sense to refer to a "European" or an "Asian" HRM model?' – there is an explicit assumption that best HR practice can, and indeed should, be transferred to any country irrespective of local realities (Hyman, 1999). Here, we again use the classic five-step HRM cycle (see Chapter 1) to explore mainstream studies of cross-border HR practices in selected European and Asian countries. In addition, we examine three other topics – *trade union organization*, *non-standard employment patterns* and *the role of the HRM function* – that have a high profile in the comparative HRM literature.

HRM in Europe

A comparative survey of HRM in Europe begs the question 'What really constitutes Europe?' (Kirkbride, 1994). The whole of Europe, excluding Russia and Turkey, comprises just 5.5 million km^2 – not much more than half the size of China and the USA. However, in the intensity of its internal differences and contrasts, Europe is said to be unique (Judt, 2005). At the last count, it comprised 46 countries; in 2006, 25 of these were members of the EU, and two new member states – Bulgaria and Romania – will join in 2007. All have their distinct and overlapping histories, politics, cultures, memories and languages. Within the EU, there are 21 official languages. No one, then, can aspire to write a fully comprehensive account of HRM practices in regionalized, polyethnic Europe. Here, we review comparative empirical research drawn mainly from Western Europe (Brewster, 1994, 1995, 2001; Brewster et al., 2000; Scullion, 2001). Space does not permit us to review important developments in HRM in South Africa (see, for example, Donnelly and Dunn, 2006) or in the Central and Eastern European states (see Blanchard et al., 1991; Brewster, 1992; Elenkov, 1998; Martin and Cristescu-Martin, 1999, 2002; Royle, 2005; Weinstein and Obloj, 2002).

The role of the human resource management function

Most observers, especially those academics teaching HRM and HRM professionals, argue that, given the central role of the HRM function in achieving global competitiveness, a senior HR practitioner should have a 'seat at the strategic table' to influence corporate decision-making. As Brewster (2001, p. 265) points out, 'HR membership of the Board is an obvious way to recognize the importance of HRM in corporate strategy decisions'. The data on this show significant variations between selected European countries (Table 3.2). For example, Sweden, Spain, Finland and France report that seven or eight out of ten organizations have a senior HR representative on the board (or equivalent), whereas Germany, Denmark and the UK report fewer than half of all organizations having an HR representative at the strategic table. Brewster (2001) makes an interesting observation with regards to the Netherlands and Germany. In these two EU member states, where workers have rights to elect representatives to the board, top HR representation is relatively low: 'Presumably the employee representatives ensure that the HR implications of corporate strategy decisions are taken into account' (Brewster, 2001, p. 265).

Table 3.2 Percentage of HR representatives at board level, or equivalent, in selected European countries

Norway	66
Sweden	77
Finland	86
Spain	73
France	87
Germany	45
Denmark	48
UK	46
Netherlands	17

Source: Adapted from Brewster (2001) p. 266

WEB LINKS

For further information on comparative HRM, go to www.cipd.co.uk (UK), www.workindex.com/ (USA), www.clc-ctc.ca (Canada) and www.travail.gouv.qc.ca/ (Quebec, Canada).

Selection and equal opportunities

Flexibility in employment relations is now widely accepted as a critical issue in European HRM. The assumption underpinning EU policy statements (such as the 1997 Amsterdam Treaty) and discourse (e.g. the 2000 Lisbon Summit) has been that, with social and employment legislation and the embeddedness of West European trade unions, European labour is highly inflexible, and that this is linked to low levels of productivity (Brewster, 2001). The selection of people must be carried out strategically in order to match organizational needs and within the constraints imposed by national institutional systems. The European HRM agenda emphasizes that selection decisions affect all of the four Cs: competence, commitment, congruence and cost-effectiveness. In enlarged EU contexts, however, the selection process may take on dimensions of importance beyond a matter of providing committed, competent and flexible employees. Strategic selection has to consider the complexities of intercultural phenomena, as well as avoiding 'ethnocentric traps' (Torbiörn, 2005).

It is important to emphasize the centrality of equal opportunities in strategic selection. Equal opportunities in employment is one of the tenets of EU social policy, embodied in the Treaty of Rome (1957) and the Social Charter (1989). Equal opportunities are generally understood to apply to the equal treatment of women and to other dimensions of equality, such as race, ethnicity, sexual orientation and disability. Equality of opportunity in employment encompasses pre-employment, including recruitment and selection practices as well as opportunities to compete for work within a work organization. All EU member states have legislation prohibiting sex discrimination, but HR practice in the area of equal opportunities and support for women is one of the 'most divergent' (Brewster, 1995, p. 320), and the equal opportunity legal framework is 'inevitably limited in its effectiveness' (Rees, W. D. 1998, p. 4). Over 50 per cent of work organizations in the Netherlands and the UK, and over 30 per cent in Germany, Norway and Sweden, monitor the proportion of women in recruitment and promotion. Such monitoring is significantly lower in Denmark, France and Spain (Table 3.3). In most European countries, concern among employers about equal opportunities and discrimination on grounds of race and ethnic origin in paid work remains low (Brewster, 1995).

Table 3.3 Percentage of organizations monitoring the share of women in the workforce in recruitment and promotion, in selected European countries, 1991

	Recruitment	Promotion
Germany	37	14
Denmark	11	11
Spain	24	16
France	25	24
Italy	29	17
Norway	41	31
Netherlands	50	34
Sweden	41	39
UK	53	33

Source: Adapted from Brewster (1994) p. 124

Rewards and trade unions

Across Western Europe, the trends in reward management are clear – the increasing decentralization of pay determination and the growth of flexible reward systems (Brewster, 1994, 1995; Brewster et al., 2000). The diffusion across parts of the EU of performance-related pay systems based on performance appraisal is indicative of employment strategies designed to individualize the employment relationship and exclude trade union representation (Gunnigle et al., 1998). The HR practice of performance-related pay or contingency pay is most widespread in the UK and Denmark, and least prevalent in the Scandinavian countries – Finland, Norway and Sweden – where trade unions play a key role in negotiating the wage–effort bargain. An understanding of the diversity in national trade unions and systems of collective bargaining (see also Chapter 11) is essential for understanding the diversity in European reward systems. It also helps to explain managerial behaviour in MNCs (O'Hagan et al., 2005). As Table 3.4 indicates, the diversity in trade union density – broadly the proportion of the working population organized into trade unions – in selected countries spans the whole continuum from France, which has experienced a steep decline, to South Africa, which has experienced significant growth in the post-apartheid period.

Cross-national differences exist in the way in which trade unions bargain their pay and conditions of employment. Among some EU member states, the so-called 'European model' traditionally involves industry-wide collective bargaining. Survey results disclose that the tradition of determining pay at national or industry level is predominantly a public sector HR/industrial relations practice. In the UK, for example, only 22 per cent of companies negotiate at industry level for manual workers, whereas in Denmark and the Netherlands over 60 per cent of employers still determine pay by negotiating at national or industry level (Brewster, 1995).

Table 3.4 Trade union densities in selected countries, 1985–95

	Union density, 1995 (%)	Change in union density, 1985–95 (%)
South Africa	40.9	130.8
Canada	37.5	1.8
USA	14.2	–21.1
France	9.1	–37.2
Italy	44.1	–7.4
Australia	24.3	–29.6
Hungary	60.0	–25.3
Sweden	91.1	8.7
UK	32.9	–27.7

Source: Adapted from O'Hagan et al. (2005) p. 160

In contrast, in Canada, the USA and the UK, collective bargaining in the private sector is decentralized where negotiations take place at the enterprise level. But these are broad regional trends, and within the EU and North America the collective bargaining processes differ quite significantly (O'Hagan et al., 2005). Empirically based studies support a more subtle approach to globalization. Although there is evidence of an erosion of union power and a tendency for collective bargaining to become more decentralized, changes in employment relations in the developed capitalist economies have not been uniform, and there are still important and enduring differences between capitalist economies (Bamber et al., 2004).

The 'adapt/export' debate on the relations between MNCs and trade unions questions whether MNCs adapt their HR practices according to the situation found in the host country or whether they adhere to the HR practices they use in the parent country. Dowling et al. (1999) argue that ideological reasons and sheer economic dominance explain a tendency found in US MNCs to adhere to a union avoidance strategy and establish 'union-free zones' in the host country regardless of national labour practices. As a counterpoint, Gunnigle et al. (2002) argue that the host country's HR and labour practices , rather than the ideology and culture of the MNC, are the significant factors. In countries such as Canada, Germany, Finland and Sweden, where HR and labour relations practices are more codified, US MNCs face pressure to adopt localized HR practices and, for example, to recognize and negotiate collective agreements with trade unions. In contrast, US-owned MNCs are less likely to localize in host countries with less regulated employment and labour practices, such as the UK and the Republic of Ireland. Studies reveal that national governments that are most dependent on MNCs tend to recognize the significance of their national employment policies for the MNCs' global business strategies (e.g. O'Hagan, 2002; O'Hagan et al., 2005). The point here is that MNCs are likely to take advantage of weak trade union and collective bargaining rights in potential host countries to enhance cost efficiencies.

Training and development

Vocational education and training is increasingly viewed as a strategic HRM activity in the discourse on global management. Moreover, in the EU, following the Amsterdam

Treaty's tenets of employability, adaptability and entrepreneurship, it is an area that has seen considerable government intervention. Manual workers receive the least training, but even for this category of workers, more than 10 per cent of the organizations in 7 out of the 10 countries reported devoting more than five days a year to training. Furthermore, more than 50 per cent of all organizations across Europe reported that they systematically conducted training-needs analysis (Brewster, 1995). The success of vocational education and training initiatives has been mixed (see Chapter 9). Such initiatives reflect a radical change in the role of national governments: a shift from a post-war Keynesian policy of 'full employment' to a less challenging employment policy of 'employability' – equipping people with the requisite skills and knowledge for the workplace.

Flexibility and non-standard employment

Among advocates of neoliberal market economics, *flexibility* has become a cause célèbre. Comparative research has found significant differences, even within major regions and often within certain sectors, in the use of non-standard employment contracts defined as part-time, short-term and temporary agency work, and independent contracting (see Table 4.2). International business scholars refer to this phenomenon as 'labour market flexibility'. Non-regular employment contracts facilitate 'a looser contractual relationship between manager and worker', writes Atkinson (1985, p. 17). To put it more bluntly, flexible contracts permit managers to hire and fire workers as global business circumstances change. In the context of global business strategies, the issue of non-standard employment contracts is of particular relevance for at least two reasons. First, a non-standard employment contract is closely associated with new, more flexible modes of production, such as self-managed work teams, and 'multitasking' typically lowers costs. Second, employers' propensity to use flexible contracts shapes any tendency towards 'convergence' or a 'universal' model of HR practice (Belanger et al., 1999; Clark and Pugh, 2000; Kidd et al., 2001). Faced with the pressure for competitive cost structures, global companies will exploit the diversity in national employment regulation to lower labour costs. MNCs will therefore use flexible employment contracts in different degrees and forms in response to variations in national business systems and culture (see Almond and Rubery, 2000; Rubery et al. 1999).

HRM in Asia

Asia comprises a wide range of countries, national institutional systems and complex diverse cultures. Competitive advantage in most Asian countries is based on cheap manual and intellectual labour, yet others use highly skilled and paid workers. Some Asian countries are marked by cultural homogeneity, whereas others are marked by cultural diversity. Within the Asia-Pacific region, 2200 languages are spoken[4] and people believe in widely different religions and philosophies, ranging from Buddhism, Confucianism and Hinduism to Islam and Christianity (Harris and Moran, 1991). In this section, we review some developments in HRM in the People's Republic of China – referred to hereafter as China – and India, two of the world's fastest-growing economies, which account for a third of the world's population. We shall also consider Japan. Japanese management practices became the very essence of avant-garde management theory in the 1980s and, despite recent economic setbacks, still attract considerable research interest from HRM theorists. In addition, South Korea is briefly examined as an example of an Asian 'tiger'. Unfortunately, space does not permit us to review other important economies in the region, such as those of Australia, New Zealand, Taiwan, Hong Kong, Indonesia, Singapore, Malaysia and Thailand.

REFLECTIVE QUESTION

As you read this section, consider to what degree Western 'best HR practices' can be imitated in an Asian business environment, culture and values.

China

The People's Republic of China is estimated to have a population of 1.4 billion people in 2007. After the USA and Japan, China is considered the biggest economy in the world. Following the death of Mao Zedong in 1976, China has undergone major economic reform to encourage trade, direct foreign investment and technological transfer. Under the leadership of Deng Xiaoping, the Communist centralized planning model has been replaced by a 'socialist market economy' (Ding et al., 2000). China's 'open policy' constitutes one of the most momentous changes in the global economic landscape (Hassard et al., 2004). Between 1985 and 1997, foreign direct investment in China increased at an average annual rate of more than 30 per cent. By 1998, foreign-owned companies, if the statistics are accurate, accounted for 15 per cent of Chinese total investment in fixed assets and employed about 18 million workers (Zhu and Dowling, 2002, pp. 569–70). More recently, China's exposure to globalized capitalism, including its membership of the World Trade Organization and its decision to peg the value of its currency, the yuan, against a basket of currencies, eventually paving the way for a yuan whose value is 'market-driven' (El Akkad, 2005), will cause a dislocation in the labour markets and major changes in employment relations among China's trading partners.

After 1949, when Mao Zedong came to power, Chinese Communism attempted to base the entire economy on state-ownership of the means of production and all-encompassing central planning, without any effective recourse to market or pricing systems (Hobsbawm, 1995). Chinese industrial workers in state-owned enterprises (SOEs) became part of the 'labour aristocracy' as they enjoyed much more generous benefits than other groups of workers (Mok et al., 2002) and were promised 'jobs for life' and 'cradle-to-grave' welfare protection. The symbol of this Soviet-inspired industrial model was widely known as the 'iron rice bowl' – *tie fan wan* (Hughes, 2002; Warner, 1996, 2000). Under this system, pay was linked to seniority rather than individual work performance. The role of the Chinese trade unions was to mobilize workers to reach industrial targets and to protect workers' workplace interests (Warner, 1997). It is argued that this 'iron rice bowl' system encouraged a high degree of 'organizational dependency' (Ding et al., 2000, p. 218). It is reported that although the 'iron rice bowl' regime is gradually being phased out, it continues to impact on HR practices today.

Foreign-owned enterprises (FOEs) and Chinese 'socialist capitalism' have provided a new context in which to manage the Chinese employment relationship. MNCs have transferred to China not only technological 'hardware', but also 'software' such as management 'know-how'. Academics debate whether Chinese HR practices are becoming more 'Westernized' given the logic of market-driven capitalism. In the area of staffing, studies report cases of managers in SOEs being given the authority to recruit, allocate work, reward individual employees more according to their competence, and 'hire and fire' (Benson and Zhu, 1999; Ding et al., 2000). It is noted that, for a large segment of the economy, namely the SOEs, recruitment and selection are 'largely irrelevant'. The 'open door' policy has created 15–20 million 'surplus' workers so most SOEs face surplus rather than shortage labour problems (Hassard et al., 2004). This may partly explain why mobility within the Chinese labour market is reported to be low among manual workers but higher within the managerial classes (Benson et al., 2000; Ding and Warner, 1999; Tsang, 1994).

In the 21st century, FOEs have become the main driving force of the Chinese economy (Mok et al., 2002). In FOEs, there is evidence that staffing practices are becoming less politically driven and more market-driven (Zhu and Dowling, 2002). There is, for example, more focus on whether an applicant possesses personal competencies as opposed to a party card (Communist Party membership). Furthermore, Korean- and Japanese-owned transplants generally avoid workers previously employed at SOEs, and the HR practices employed reflect 'low-commitment' employment relations (Gamble et al., 2004). Shen and Edwards' (2004) study found that foreign MNCs tended to avoid employing home country nationals in key management positions. The speed of economic growth and the legacy of SOEs have meant that investment in formal training remains a low priority within most enterprises (Ng et al., 2004; Tsang, 1994). In FOEs, training focuses on enhancing both working relationships and skill improvements. In contrast, SOEs continue to provide limited skill-deficiency training to their workers (Ng and Siu, 2004).

The reward system is also changing in many Chinese workplaces. There is evidence that the traditional reward system, based on the belief that loyalty (seniority) should be the basis for reward, is increasingly giving way to reward systems that are linked to performance. There is evidence that, within SOE and joint Chinese–foreign ventures, HR practices are moving towards more flexible reward systems that link pay to performance (Benson et al., 2000; Ding and Warner, 1999). Case studies, however, provide evidence that foreign direct investment companies have adopted some 'good' HRM practices from SOEs (e.g. extensive welfare benefits), but have also adopted 'bad' practices (e.g. non-compliance with labour regulations), for which the private sector in China is notorious. This mixed package of HR practices speaks to the need for a more nuanced approach in our study of the impact of China's 'market socialism' on employment relations (Cooke, 2004). Finally, Ding et al. (2000) bring a spatial dimension to the study of Chinese management practices, arguing not only that FOEs are more market-driven in their HR practices than SOEs, but also that enterprises located in coastal and southern cities are much more innovative than their ownership counterparts located in inland and northern China.

Behind the triumph of Chinese 'market socialism', another picture is emerging as ordinary Chinese workers react to the tectonic upheavals of 'marketization'. Strikes and demonstrations have become more frequent as ex-state sector workers – the old 'labour aristocracy' in China – increasingly 'feel betrayed by socialism and marginalized' (Mok et al., 2002, p. 411). Chinese trade unions seem to be playing the role of guardian or 'watchdog' over workers' health and safety. This situation could change in the future with trade unions bargaining for better pay and conditions of employment (Benson et al., 2000). Traditional Communist 'iron rice bowl' employment relations have been eroded in China by powerful national political and global economic forces, and depending on such variables as ownership, location and size, Western-style HRM practices in today's Chinese FOE and joint venture enterprises, although not dominant, appear to be increasingly affecting Chinese workplace life (see Ding et al. 2000; Warner, 2004).

WEB LINKS

For further information on HRM in China, go to www.hr-china.ch.

South Korea

South Korea has an estimated population of 46.5 million people. The country remains largely unknown to many Europeans, but it was the world's 11th largest economy prior to the 1997 Asian financial crisis (Kim and Briscoe, 1997; Rowley and Bae, 2002). South Korean's collective consciousness, philosophical and religious beliefs are informed by Buddhism, Confucianism and Christianity. Chaebol is the Korean term for a large family-owned conglomerate. The chaebol's paternalistic employment relations – almost an 'iron rice bowl' system – are a dominant influence on the South Korean employment landscape (Warner, 2002). Two of the leading chaebols before the recession were the automobile manufacturer Hyundai and the electronics giant Samsung.

Recent studies have identified high systemic rigidities and weak individual-level motivational effects arising from traditional South Korean employment practices. The chaebols have tended to show a lower propensity to utilize high-performance work system techniques than non-indigenous Korean-based enterprises (Bae et al., 2003). Korean management tends to be strongly influenced by Taylorism (see Chapter 5). The chaebols typically recruit and select university graduates for management positions (Kim and Briscoe, 1997). The focus of training and development programmes tends to be more on inculcating trainees into the company's norms and behaviours and less on the development of technical skills. Thus, chaebols spend considerable effort on transforming new employees into 'warrior workers' loyal to the organization. Rewards in chaebols are traditionally based upon seniority. The use of performance appraisal is apparently not widely used, partly because managers are reluctant to give their subordinates critical feedback (Kim and Briscoe, 1997).

With current international management wisdom emphasizing workplace learning, flexibility and innovation, it is not surprising that traditional South Korean management practices have been increasingly highlighted as a possible impediment to South Korea's economic development in the 21st century (Rowley and Bae, 2002; Whitley, 1999). There is, however, growing evidence that the traditional employment practices are changing. Rowley and Bae (2002, p. 539) note the change of direction in Korean HR practices towards more 'Westernized flexible systems', including flexible and external labour markets, performance-based rewards, and shareholding and profit-sharing. Samsung, for example, has changed its promotion, rewards and job design practices (Kim and Briscoe, 1997). Furthermore, Cin et al. (2003) document the growth of employee stock ownership plans. Korean workers have reacted to employers' demands for greater labour flexibility and the phasing out of lifetime employment provision by increased trade union militancy (Morden and Bowles, 1998).

WEB LINKS

For further information on HRM in Asia-Pacific countries, go to www.hkihrm.org (Hong Kong), www.hrinz.org.nz (New Zealand), www.ahri.com.au (Australia) and www.kihrm.ko (South Korea).

India

India was the core of the entire British Empire until the country became independent from Britain in 1947 (Hobsbawm, 1995). The country has an estimated population of over 1 billion. India avoided the worst excess of the Asian financial crisis of 1997–98 and is forecast to become the world's fourth largest economy by 2020 (Budhwar and Boyne, 2004). Between 1947 and 1990, India's economy was state-regulated. The Trade Union Act of 1926, the Royal Commission of 1932 and the Factories Act of 1948 laid the foundation of the HRM function in India (Singh, 2003). In 1991, India experienced a severe reduction in industrial production, low foreign exchange reserves and a double-digit rate of inflation. As a condition for a rescue package, the World Bank and the International Monetary Fund required the Indian government to change from a regulated 'mixed economy' to a 'free-market economy' (HRM in Practice 3.4). The 'liberalization' of the economy and wide-scale privatization of state assets placed considerable pressure on Indian companies to be more competitive and on the HRM function in domestic enterprises to be more 'proactive' and strategic (Budhwar and Boyne, 2004).

HRM IN PRACTICE 3.4

INDIAN ACT THREATENS OUTSOURCING PROWESS

MATT BYRNE, *THE LAWYER*, OCTOBER 2005, P. 7

The revival of a long forgotten law banning women from working through the night is threatening to derail the boom in the Indian outsourcing market.

The labour department of the State of Haryana, neighbouring New Delhi, has cited the Punjab Shops and Commercial Establishment Act 1958 and notified many Curgaon-based call centers to remind them that women employees are not allowed to work night shifts. Section 30 of the Act warns that 'no women shall be required or allowed to work, whether as an employee or otherwise, in any establishment during the night'. IT companies are exempt from the law in Haryana, but the state is claiming that call centers are not IT companies and therefore the law should apply.

...women employees are not allowed to work night shifts...

With women workers accounting for approximately 40 per cent of the call center workforce, the revival of the law could fundamentally threaten the operations of numerous multinational corporations that have outsourced work to the subcontinent. According to David Barrett, whose firm regularly handles outsourcing projects in India, the law could have a significant, but not terminal effect. India is a federal jurisdiction and there is no guarantee that other states will follow the Haryana lead, he said. Although Haryana, and in particular Gurgaon, is a major base for call center outsourcing, there are many others, particularly in the south, where in general the authorities have been far more sympathetic. 'In addition, we're already seeing a move away from outsourcing to India to other jurisdictions – for example, the Philippines, Mexico, Malaysia and, in particular, China, as well as Eastern Europe and the Maghreb countries of North Africa, ' added Barrett.

Underpinning the justification for privatization is arguably the premise that private sector management, because it is exposed to the 'discipline of the market', has superior skills and practices. Budhwar and Boyne (2004) conducted a comparative study of HRM practices in Indian public and private sector organizations. The results of their study show that HR practices in private and public sector organizations are more similar than different (Table 3.5). Despite evidence to show that companies with an emphasis on strategic HRM orientation perform 'significantly better than firms with a lower emphasis' (Singh, 2003, p. 537), the comparative data show a considerable variation between sectors in terms of the role of the HR function at the strategic decision-making level. In private sector enterprises, just over a third – 37.5 per cent – reported that an HR representative had a place on the board of directors, in comparison to only 14.8 per cent of public sector organizations.

Table 3.5 Human resource (HR) practices in Indian private sector and public sector organizations

	Private sector (*n*=81) %	Public sector (*n*=56) %
HR representation at board level	37.5	14.8
External recruitment of white-collar employees	60.7	74.1
Rewards linked to performance	21.0	14.3
Conduct training needs analysis	46.4	66.7
Unionization	53.6	61.5

Source: Adapted from Budhwar and Boyne (2004) pp. 367–9

Budhwar and Boyne's (2004) findings also show that in comparison to private sector companies, public sector organizations in India advertised more externally to recruit their managerial staff. Both public and private sector organizations use the 'word of mouth' method to recruit their blue-collar employees. Indian staffing practices emphasize the importance of cultural variables such as the caste system and religion (Budhwar and Boyne, 2004; Sparrow and Budhwar, 1997). There is evidence that Indian private sector companies are more likely to adopt a skill-based approach to rewards, and that public sector organizations are less likely to link pay to the performance of their employees. In the private sector, there is 'a subtle transition taking place away from seniority-based towards performance-based pay' (Budhwar and Boyne, 2004, p. 358). Lifetime employment and seniority-based pay are still in evidence in the India public sector. In both the private and public sectors, a relatively high proportion of companies and organizations have increased their investment in training their white-collar employees. In the private sector sample, 53.6 per cent of firms were unionized compared with 61.5 per cent in the public sector. Budhwar and Boyne's research appears to suggest that the gap between HR practices in the public and private sectors is frequently insignificant. The data also reveal an increased emphasis on training and development, a preference for recruiting the most qualified candidate for positions, and performance-based rewards.

WEB LINKS

For further information on HRM in India, go to www.20.brinkster.com/nipm.

Japan

Japan's business system is the most advanced of those in the Asia-Pacific countries reviewed here. With an estimated population of 127 million, Japan experienced a rate of economic growth that outpaced the USA's until the 1990s. In the 1980s, the Japanese approach to manufacturing and HR practices attracted considerable attention from academics and managers, mainly because of the success of Japanese global companies in penetrating European and North American automobile and electronic markets. The stereotyped model of Japanese production focused attention around its three core elements: flexibility, quality and minimum waste (see Chapter 5). The 'Japanization' phenomenon generated a cottage industry of books and articles devoted to explaining and understanding Japanese manufacturing and people management, ranging from managerialist texts such as Schonberger (1982) and Wickens (1987) to more critical works such as those of Whittaker (1990), Elger and Smith (1994) and Wilkinson and Ackers (1995).

Investigations into traditional HR practices have usually emphasized six characteristics of Japanese employment relations: recruitment and selection, training, the lifetime employment contract, seniority-based rewards, the consensus decision-making process and enterprise trade unionism. Traditionally, Japanese recruitment and selection practices have always aimed and still endeavour to appoint people who will develop a long-term commitment to the organization. Various screening processes eliminate candidates believed to possess certain 'disqualifiers: including the 'inability to get along with others' or 'radical views' (Bratton, 1992, p. 28). Japanese training and development tends to be company-specific, but it also aims to shape employee commitment to the company. According to Pascale and Athos (1986, p. 52), each new recruit at Mitsushita is indoctrinated with the '"Mitsushita way" from which little deviance is tolerated'. Kono (1984, p. 329) points out that the lifetime employment contract engenders a high level of commitment and loyalty; the sense among employees of 'all being together in the same boat'.

A system of seniority-based rewards is another basic feature of traditional Japanese HR practices. The *nenko joretsu* reward system means that length of service and age – rather than job performance – determine pay. The consensus or *ringisei* approach to decision-making seeks to generate a greater understanding of workplace-based problems/issues and the acceptance of and total commitment to implementing decisions once they have been made (Wickens, 1987).

The sixth pillar of traditional Japanese HR practices is the *kigyobetsu-kumiai*, the enterprise trade union. Japanese trade unions are not organized by industry, occupation, profession or job, but by enterprise. The enterprise union consists solely of the regular full-time employees of a single company, regardless of their occupation. Enterprise unions developed only after the suppression of independent trade unions in post-war Japan (Bratton, 1992).

This view of traditional Japanese HR practices so eulogized by Western managers is, of course, a simplistic and sanitized version of reality, and critics have challenged different aspects of the Japanese HRM model, particularly in the context of globalized capitalism. Whittaker (1990) notes that one of the 'pillars' of Japanese employment – 'lifetime employment' – is highly selective and, where it does exist, excludes part-time, short-term or peripheral workers. Others have noted that, since the 1997 financial crisis, Japanese companies have found it difficult to maintain lifetime employment security and the *nenko* automatic pay increase system (Benson, 1996; Chalmers, 1989; Sano, 1993). There is evidence of change in the way in which Japanese workers are rewarded, with the growing popularity of profit-sharing plans in smaller Japanese companies without trade unions (Kato and Morishima, 2003). Benson (1996) also notes that flexible labour practices are more prevalent in small Japanese firms.

HRM IN PRACTICE 3.5

CEO'S HARMONIOUS-SOCIETY PLAN? FIRE 14,000 STAFF

GORDON PITTS, *GLOBE AND MAIL*, 6 JULY 2005, P. A1

Tomoyo Nonaka blew into Sanyo Electrical Co. as the space-cadet chief executive, a former TV anchorwoman with no management experience but lots of rhetoric about listening to the Earth. Yet the New Age CEO's first act atop the troubled electronics giant smacks of Old Age realism: Sanyo will cut 15 per cent of its workforce of 14,000 jobs.

Ms. Nonaka, 50, one of the most off-the-wall CEO choices in Japanese corporate history, cloaked the layoffs and factory closings in her trademark mystical language. 'Sanyo will become the company that will listen to the Earth's voice and will please the Earth instead of polluting it,' she said.

Sanyo will cut 15 per cent of its workforce of 14,000 jobs

Ms. Nonaka said the restructuring plan, described by Sanyo as 'Think Gaia' – a reference to the Greek goddess of the Earth – would include greater focus on 'ecological co-existence solutions.' The company also unveiled four programs to realize its new vision: Sanyo Blue Planet, Sanyo Genesis III, Sanyo Harmonious Society, and Sanyo Product Circulation.

Observers say Ms. Nonaka's move this year from outside director to Sanyo's CEO is an extreme case of the current appetite for fresh faces to shake up Japan's underperforming companies, instead of the usual line-up of middle-aged Japanese men.

Many Japanese companies have imitated US reward systems, as evidenced by increased use of performance-related pay (Shibata, 2000). Whereas large manufacturing establishments can achieve improved labour productivity by more efficient capital equipment, different contractual relationships dictate that small Japanese firms will tend to adopt forms of HR practice aimed at maximizing flexibility and reducing labour costs (Benson, 1996). The debate over whether the Japanese model will remain intact has to consider firm size as an important variable (see, for example, Berggren and Nomura, 1997; Kuwahara, 1998).

WEB LINKS

For further information on HRM in Japan, go to www.jshrm.org.

The convergence/divergence debate

A common theme in the comparative HRM literature has been 'convergence' and 'divergence' in HR practices, resulting from globalization, in different regions of the world. The debate has a long antecedent in neoclassical economic theory that unfettered flows of international trade would allow rich and poor economies eventually to converge to similar levels of per capita income, as capital investment would migrate from developed economies, where it would be abundant and returns limited, to developing economies, where capital would be scarce and returns higher. This convergence process should also, according to the theory, induce a convergence of national business environments, including HR practices, towards homogeneity. Both the power of capital from the parent country and the weakness and 'receptiveness' of the subordinate host country underpin ideas on how globalization creates uniformity in national business patterns (Rowley and Bae, 2002). The major challenge to a universal vision of order, equilibrium and convergence arises from local rationalities, local realities, local ideologies and local culture (Clegg et al., 1999; Whitley, 1999). Evidence of continued diversity in local or national patterns of economic activity and employment relations has contributed to the notion of 'varieties of capitalism'. For Whitley (1999, p. 3), although the global economy continues to be more interconnected, 'societies with different institutional arrangements will continue to develop and reproduce varied systems of economic organization with different economic and social capabilities in particular industries and sectors'.

We therefore go back to a key question in comparative HRM, that of convergence. Is there evidence of convergence in the different trajectories of HR practices within Europe towards a 'European model' of HRM? Drawing upon the data from a three-year survey of 14 European countries, Chris Brewster, an authoritative observer of European HRM, puts forward the notion of a new 'European HRM model' that recognizes state and trade union involvement in the regulation of the employment relationship. Brewster contends that the European HRM model has a greater potential for 'partnership' between labour and management because, in most EU states, 'the unions are not seen, and do not see themselves, as "adversaries"' (Brewster, 1995, p. 323). Others have persuasively argued that, with the existence of distinct national contexts and cross-cultural differences, the notion of a European HRM model is problematic, and the 'universalist' assumption that Anglo-American HRM techniques are directly transferable is wrong (Elenkov, 1998).

In the same vein, Clark and Pugh (2000) argue that, despite economic pressures toward convergence, strikingly resilient differences in cultural and institutional contexts produce divergent employment relationships. For example, the Netherlands 'feminine' culture encourages the antipathy of Dutch workers toward 'hard' HRM, whereas 'Sweden's strong collectivist culture counters the development of an individualistic orientation to the employment relationship' (Clark and Pugh, 2000, p. 96). Following on from the notion of diversity in national business systems, more reflective observers are increasingly acknowledging that the issues of convergence and divergence in European HRM need 'more careful nuance than has been the case hitherto', and European national institutional patterns are so variable that 'no common model is likely to emerge in the foreseeable future' (Brewster, 2001, p. 268). Thus, cross-national research suggests that national conceptions of better HRM practices remain dominant (Sparrow et al., 2004).

Similarly, studies suggest that there is a considerable divergence of HR practices in Asian economies. Prominent HRM academic Malcolm Warner speaks of a process of 'soft convergence' towards Western-style HR practices in Asian-Pacific economies (Warner, 2002). Paik et al.'s (1996) findings provide strong support for the divergence hypothesis even among the Chinese culture-based countries of Hong Kong, Singapore and Taiwan. Contrary to the convergence hypothesis underpinning globalization, the idea that 'best' HR practices have 'universal' application is untenable when the HRM phenomenon embodies a different national institutional profile and cultural milieu. In the world's third largest economy, China, there have been noteworthy shifts away from the 'iron rice bowl' system to a more 'market-responsive' system of employment relations. Yet, as Hassard et al. (2004) conclude, this is somewhat removed from the HRM ideal type model. At best, it is argued, globalization may be causing an increasing degree of 'relative convergence' across 'regional clusters' such as China, South Korea and Japan, resulting from globally driven market forces (Rowley et al., 2004). However, this relative convergence 'is not necessarily towards some *sui generis* model of Asian HRM (Warner, 2004, p. 620). Inherent in controversies surrounding the notion of a 'European model' of HRM or an 'Asian model' are questions of the limitations and value of cross-national generalizations in HRM (Hyman, 1994). The theory of a universal model of HRM (which often is interpreted as meaning an Anglo-American model of HRM) is challenged by national rationalities, national institutional settings and national, regional and local cultures. HRM varies between countries, by sector, by size and by ownership of the work organization.

Does globalization bring into being a convergence of HR practices? To address this conundrum, we have drawn on Rowley and Bae's (2002) model (Figure 3.4). The two dimensions in Rowley and Bae's framework are the unit of analysis – *country* versus *organizational* level – and the foci – *practices* versus *people*. Changes in HR practices within the organization are mediated by environmental changes and universal 'best

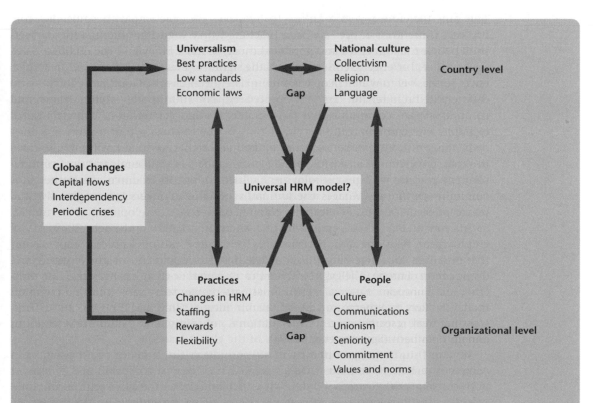

Figure 3.4 Globalization and human resource management (HRM) models
Source: Adapted from Rowley and Bae (2002) p. 543

practices'. However, the framework draws attention to 'gaps' between universalism versus national culture and HR practices newly adopted versus the organizational culture or the 'shared mindset' of people in the workplace. For example, the change from a regulated to a more market-driven form of capitalism in China, India and Singapore with greater flexibility and unemployment would provide a cultural shock for the nationals of these countries.

Different national institutional systems, which comprise laws, frames of reference and core values and norms, can explain 'divergence' between the parent and host local establishments. Sanford Jacoby (2005) argues the case for a persistence of varieties of capitalism and employment management practices. In Japan, for example, institutions are more closely embedded in social relations and shared social values than they are in the USA. Consequently, institutional change to facilitate movements towards US-inspired market-oriented HR practices and employment management has been slow in Japan. Similarly, Rowley and Bae (2002) engage in the convergence/ divergence debate by pointing out the gap between changes in HR practices and what they call the 'shared mindset' of managers and workers. Successful transfer, it is argued, depends upon two processes:

1. the 'implementation' of the HR practices, whereby workers in the recipient organization change their observable behaviours in respect of the transferred practice
2. the 'internalization' of the HR practices, whereby people fully accept and approve the practices.

The gaps therefore reflect a failure to inculcate HR practices with embedded core 'values'. Thus, 'even if there are "best practices", they would not bring positive effects until people fully accepted and approved them,' assert Rowley and Bae (2002, p. 544).

A further challenge to convergence is the significant cultural and subcultural differences in the way in which people communicate. According to Guirdham (2005), these differences include, but are not limited to, communication styles, non-verbal communication, communication rules, politeness and conversation constraints. For example, one communication style or trait is assertiveness – putting forward one's own rights without hampering other individuals' rights – which has been advocated in Western societies as a way for women and members of visible minorities to communicate, especially with people who are inclined to 'put them down'. Assertiveness is culturally specific, and what is assertive and acceptable in one society is aggressive and unacceptable in another (Guirdham, 2005, p. 88).

Sparrow et al. (2004) remind us that there is no reason why some aspects of employment relations and HR practices could not exhibit signs of convergence (decentralized collective bargaining), whereas others would show signs of divergence (trade union density). The gaps between the 'universal' logic of change and HRM practices and embedded national business systems problematize any grand narrative on the conversion to either European or Asian models of HRM and their efficacy. Understanding these gaps between universal theory and idiosyncratic national institutions and cultures becomes a key competency of the global manager.

We can thus be more confident in affirming that the study of international and comparative human resource management is no longer a marginal area of interest (Clark et al., 2000; Sparrow et al., 2004). Increasingly, as the globalization of world markets continues apace, managers will be expected to undertake overseas assignments, and IHRM and comparative HRM research will be an important resource for training expatriate managers (Budhwar and Boyne, 2004). For students of HRM, the highly complex and political nature of the global–local issue affirms the need for an international network of academics to undertake intensive collaborative research in Europe and the Asia-Pacific region. The lessons for managers of recent comparative HRM research are to avoid generalizations of trends towards convergence or continued diversity and to adopt a more nuanced cross-cultural approach to managing people. This approach needs to abandon the 'global' template' (Rowley et al., 2004, p. 930) and recognize that the highly complex processes of managing people across borders frequently contains elements of both convergence and national diversity, as well as being shaped by the contingent requirements of management's 'strategic choice' (Quintanilla and Ferner, 2003).

Chapter summary

- In this chapter, we examined how MNCs profit from the globalization of markets, and explored how global corporations typically face tension from two types of business pressure: on the one hand, pressures for global cost reductions and rationalization and, on the other hand, demands for differentiation and local responsiveness.

- We also discussed four fashionable international business strategies – global, multi-domestic, international and transnational – as solutions to the dual pressure for cost efficiencies and responsiveness. The integration–responsiveness grid (Figure 3.1) suggests that if a business is high on local responsiveness and low on global integration, for example if it is a manufacturer of processed meals, it is likely to be managed with significant local autonomy. On the other hand, a business high on global integration and low on local responsiveness, for example a manufacturer of silicon chips, will be managed, by most companies engaged in that business, on a global scale (Prahalad and Doz, 1987).

- The chapter explained that the driving force behind the growth of interest in SIHRM and IHRM is the resurgence of neoliberalism and the unprecedented growth in global markets.

- Critics argue that unfettered markets have created the new international division of labour, causing the transfer from old industrialized regions of high-wage manufacturing jobs to low-wage developing economies. They also argue that IHRM tends to emphasize the subordination of national culture and national employment practices to corporate culture and HR practices.

- An integrative model, drawn from Schuler et al.'s (1993) work, explored how IHRM should be explicitly linked to the global business strategy of the MNC and that its changing forms must be understood in relation to the strategic evolution of the MNC.

- We discussed how the cross-national transfer of Anglo-Saxon HR practices for recruitment and selection, rewards, training and development, and performance appraisal will require some degree of cultural sensitivity, as well as consultation with host country nationals about local suitability.

- We have also discussed how, despite the economic and political pressures from globalization, a divergence of HR practices continues to be influenced and shaped by national and organizational cultures in the developed and the developing world. Moreover, variations in national regulatory systems, the labour markets, business-related institutions and cultural and polyethnic contexts are likely to constrain or shape any tendency towards 'convergence' or a 'universal' model of 'better' HR practice. The sheer variation of economies, national institutional profiles and cultures makes claims for convergence both simplistic and problematic.

● Within Europe and the Asia-Pacific region, there is significant divergence. One explanation for this diversity is the mediating effect of national, regional and local cultures on 'universal' models of human resource management.

● The evidence examined in this chapter also suggested that the transfer of Anglo-Saxon-style HR practices and values into culturally diverse environments needs to be critically researched. We have indicated that more research is needed to test the links between international business strategy and IHRM. Further research is needed to investigate HR practices in developing countries. The mantra of 'high-commitment' HR practices is hollow and unconvincing when applied to organizational life in the export-processing zones in, for example, India and China.

● In this chapter, it has been easier to formulate questions than answers, and we have taken the easier rather than the more difficult route. Yet there is value in asking questions. Questions can stimulate reflection and increase our understanding of IHRM. Our object here has been to do both.

Key concepts

- Strategic international human resource management
- International human resource management
- Comparative human resource management
- Transnational strategy
- Global strategy
- Multidomestic strategy
- International strategy
- Corporate strategic international human resource management orientation

Chapter review questions

1. What is meant by SIHRM and IHRM?

2. Explain how MNCs address the tension between the dual imperatives of global integration and local responsiveness.

3. Discuss how differences in national institutional systems influence a corporation's decision to locate its profit-making operations.

4. Explain how a need for rationalization and standardization over foreign operations varies with the business strategy and distinctive competencies of an MNC.

5. How helpfully, if at all, do the models covered in this chapter contribute to our understanding of SIHRM?

6. What value is gained from studying comparative HRM?

Further reading

Anakwe, U.P. (2002) Human resource management practices in Nigeria: challenges and insights. *International Journal of Human Resource Management*, **13**(7): 1042–59.

Brown, M. and Heywood, J. (2005) Performance appraisal systems: determinants and change. *British Journal of Industrial Relations*, **43**(4): 659–79.

Geppert, M. and Williams, K. (2006) Global, national and local practices in multinational corporations: towards a sociopolitical framework. *International Journal of Human Resource Management*, **17**(1): 49–69.

Guirdham, M. (2005) *Communicating Across Cultures at Work*. Basingstoke: Palgrave Macmillan.

Hertz, N. (2002) *The Silent Takeover: Global Capitalism and the Death of Democracy*. London: Arrow Books.

Jackson, T. (2002) Reframing human resource management in Africa: a cross-cultural perspective. *International Journal of Human Resource Management*, **13**(7): 998–1018.

Jacoby, S. (2005) *The Embedded Corporation: Corporate Governance and Employment Relations in Japan and the United States*. Princeton, NJ: Princeton University Press.

Rowley, C., Benson, J. and Warner, M. (2004) Towards an Asian model of human resource management? A comparative analysis of China, Japan and South Korea. *International Journal of Human Resource Management*, **14**(4): 917–33.

Pudelko, M. (2006) A comparison of HRM systems in the USA, Japan and Germany in their socio-economic context. *Human Resource Management Journal*, **16**(2): 123–53.

Scullion, H. (2001) International human resource management. In J. Storey (ed.), *Human Resource Management: A Critical Text* (pp. 288–313). London: Thompson Learning.

Scullion, H. and Linehan, M. (2005) *International Human Resource Management*, Basingstoke: Palgrave Macmillan.

Shen, J. (2006) Factors affecting international staffing in Chinese multinationals (MNEs). *International Journal of Human Resource Management*, **17**(2): pp. 295-315.

Sparrow, P., Brewster, C. and Harris, H. (2004) *Globalizing Human Resource Management*. London: Routledge.

Suutari, V. and Brewster, C. (2003) Repatriation: empirical evidence from a longitudinal study of careers and expectations among Finnish expatriates. *International Journal of Human Resource Management*, **14**(7): 1132–51.

Practising human resource management

Searching the web

Enter the website of Proctor & Gamble at www.uk.pg.com/. Go to 'Worldwide operations' and select and visit the websites of the following Procter & Gamble affiliates: Procter & Gamble Australia, Procter & Gamble Brazil, Procter & Gamble Canada, Procter & Gamble Nigeria and Procter & Gamble India. Scan each website to determine the history of the local affiliate. Try to establish how Procter & Gamble first entered each domestic market and how its involvement there subsequently evolved. Read the profiles of key managers.

On the basis of this information, try to establish whether Procter & Gamble use expatriates or hire local managers. In retrospect, what type of corporate SIHRM orientation does Proctor & Gamble adopt for its affiliates?

HRM group project

Form a study group of between three and five people, and search the web for sports equipment retailers such as The North Face Company (www.northface.com). After viewing the company's website, discuss the following scenario.

You are advising a group of ex-students who have developed a new skateboard. They have already established a manufacturing and sales presence in your home market and are now planning expansion into international markets. On the basis of what you have read in this chapter, decide the following:

1. What business strategy should the new company pursue – global, international, multidomestic or transnational?
2. What kind of IHRM strategy should the company follow and why?
3. What information do you need in order to make these kinds of decisions?

Chapter case study

FAEKI[5]

The company

FAEKI, established in 1972 in Finland by Vesa Stroh, has experienced considerable growth since Finland joined the European Union in the 1990s to become one of the largest manufacturers of home furnishings in the EU. The parent company is located in Tampere and employs 1750 employees made up of skilled and semi-skilled workers. Two hundred and thirty employees work in design and development and other highly skilled areas. All employees belong to one trade union. The company has a profit-sharing scheme and an excellent pension scheme.

Since 1972, FAEKI has sold a basic range of typically 'Scandinavian' home furnishings in six stores, only one of which – Helsinki – is inside Finland. The company remains primarily production-oriented, its Finnish management and design group deciding what it is going to manufacture in the most cost-effective way and then how it will sell it to the European homeowner, often with very little market research outside Finland. The company has emphasized its Finnish roots in its European advertising, including the adoption of the colours blue and white, from the Finnish national flag, for its retail outlets and advertising material.

Business strategy

The foundation of FAEKI's success has been to offer consumers good value for money, distinctive branding and a good network of suppliers. A supplier for FAEKI gains long-term contracts and leased equipment from the company. In return, FAEKI demands an exclusive contract and low prices. FAEKI's expatriate managers seconded to the subsidiary standardize products and integrate production to gain maximum savings on the final products at a low cost. FAEKI sells its avant-garde furniture to customers as self-assembly kits. In this way, the company reaps economies of scale from the large production runs. In 2000, only 13 per cent of its sales were generated in Finland, the balance coming from Germany (33 per cent), Sweden (22 per cent), the Netherlands (11 per cent) and the UK (21 per cent). This strategy allows FAEKI to match its competitors on quality but undercut them by up to 30 per cent on price, while maintaining an after-tax return on sales of around 7 per cent.

In 2004, FAEKI decided to establish a factory in Montreal and two retail stores in Canada, followed by six in the USA. The Canadian subsidiary was built on a greenfield site on the east side of Montreal and employed 320 employees by the end of 2005. Informed that trade union density in Canada was well below that of Finland, expatriate managers were told that unionization was a 'non-issue' and that the company's profit-sharing scheme, similar to the Finnish scheme, would ensure employee loyalty and commitment. The production side of the business was meeting output targets. Preliminary reports, however, indicated that the new North American retail stores did not meet sales and profit targets as planned. Finnish home furnishings, which sold well in Western Europe, clashed with Canadian and US tastes and sometimes physiques. In addition, the new Canadian factory was experiencing quality control problems and some challenges in managing the workforce.

Taskforce meeting

Vesa Engeström, the factory manager, called a meeting of the Canadian management team. Yrjö Alvesson, an experienced Finnish marketing manager, gave the first presentation to the assembled FAEKI managers. He explained that sales had not reached expected targets because the standard furniture did not meet North American tastes and preferences. He said, for example, 'Our Finnish kitchen cupboards are too narrow to take large dinner plates needed for pizza. And our beds are too narrow for American preferences.'

Christian Poikela, the HR manager at the Canadian subsidiary, explained that some of the Canadian managers resented the degree of control exerted over how they managed their units. In addition, he had heard through various managers and supervisors that some employees had been overheard talking about 'bringing in a union' to achieve higher wages. Jonathan Pyrch, one of three Canadian-born and Canadian-educated managers present at the meeting, interjected at this point and said, 'The union isn't the problem; it's poor communications. Many staff can't understand the expatriate managers! I've heard that shop-floor supervisors leave their encounters with Finnish managers feeling frustrated by their inability to understand and relate to them.' Poikela also said that shop-floor staff were reluctant to work at weekends. 'The fact that Quebec, like the other provinces in Canada, has its own labour relations statutes makes dealing with Canadian unions more difficult and frustrating, especially if we open a factory in Calgary,' he added. What legal rights do unions have in this province, asked Engeström? 'I'm unsure, but I'll investigate', replied Poikela.

Assignment

Given the pressures facing FAEKI in the marketplace, prepare a report to Christian Poikela:

1. Explaining how FAEKI can be both competitive and locally responsive, detailing why FAEKI's SIHRM orientation should be linked to its international business strategy and what this would mean for the role of the HRM function at FAEKI's Canadian subsidiary.

2. Explaining the types of competency you feel the managers at the Canadian subsidiary need, and whether expatriate or local managers can supply these competencies.

HR-related skill development

Writing a 'justification report' is an important skill for potential and practising managers to develop. It provides learners with experience of applying HRM concepts to an organization they have been asked to study or to their own company or organization. Typically, a justification report includes the following: issue/problem, present system, proposed changes, costs and benefits, and final recommendation. You will develop your skill at analyzing a case study by going to our website (www.palgrave.com/business/brattonandgold4) and clicking on 'Justification report'.

Notes

1. Nancy Adler (1992) Preface. In H. Lane and J. DiStefano (eds) *International Management Behavior*, 2nd edn. Boston, MA: PWS-Kent Publishing, p. vii.
2. C. Brewster (2001) HRM: The comparative dimension. In Storey, J. (ed.) *Human Resource Management*, 2nd edn (pp. 255–71), London: Thomson Learning.
3. The quote is taken from Susan Drummond, 'Beyond cartoons', *Globe and Mail*, 2006, 11 February, p. A23.
4. I am grateful to Professor W. Foley, University of Sydney, Australia, for this information.
5. Adapted from Hill and Jones (2004) *Strategy in a Global Environment*, pp. 243–4.

Part Two

The human resource management context

Chapter four

The context of human resource management

John Bratton

Context refers to all the external forces that exist outside the boundary of the organization and have the potential to affect work organizations and, in turn, shape human resource management strategy, policies and practices.

'An infectious greed seemed to have gripped much of our business community in the late 1990s. It's not that humans have become any more greedy than in generations past. It is that the avenues to express greed have grown so enormously.'[1]

'Every generation believes it is living through great change, and our generation is no different ... [But] What gives contemporary change its power and momentum is in the economic, political and cultural change summed up by the term "globalization". It is the interaction of extraordinary technological innovation combined with worldwide reach driven by a global capitalism that gives today's change its particular complexion. It has a speed, inevitability and force that it has not had before.'[2]

'The belief that we do not have choices is a fantasy, an unfortunate indulgence in abdication.'[3]

'Capitalist globalization is an historical form but not the only possible viable form of globalization.'[4]

Chapter outline

Chapter objectives

After studying this chapter, you should be able to:

1. Explain the importance of studying context for understanding human resource management (HRM)
2. Discuss ways of conceptualizing the nature of context
3. Identify the external contexts that affect HRM policies and actions
4. Understand the implications of these external contexts for the HRM function

Introduction

Managing people at work does not take place in a vacuum. Wider economic, technological, political and social forces influence and shape human resource management (HRM) strategy, policies and practices, global and local economic developments sometimes having an indirect or a 'multiplier' effect. The electrical giant Siemens, for example, overtakes Philips Electronics, so Philips downsizes and lays off workers. Belt-tightening workers then press for cheaper services from local traders and are prepared to work for lower wages, thereby causing an adjustment in the local labour markets and in the HRM decisions and activities of those organizations affected.

Williams (1993) is one of a number of theorists who have argued the importance of understanding the relationship between economic stability or instability and HRM, but it is not just the economic context that matters. New manufacturing and service technologies, new processes (e.g. total quality management and International Organization for Standardization – ISO 9000) and developments in global telecommunications networks have important ramifications for organizational and work design, and for HRM. Just as significant are demographic changes and the restructuring of labour markets that affect the supply of and demand for human resources (HR). Past fluctuations in the birthrate in Anglo-Saxon economies are producing abrupt changes in the composition of the labour force. The proportion of older workers (aged 55 years and above) is beginning to rise as the 'baby-boomers' approach retirement age, and an ageing workforce has significant implications for organizations.

These examples of contextual change strongly suggest that we cannot understand the nature of HRM without understanding the dynamics of the economy and the national institutional system in which it is embedded. Human resource strategies and practices are better understood when they are examined in the broader economic, technological, political and social contexts that help to shape them (Maurice and Sorge, 2000). The financial crash that affected the major Asian economies in 1997, the attack on the World Trade Center on 11 September 2001, the crisis in the equity markets in July 2002, and the dispute between Russia's OAO Gazprom and Ukraine over gas supply in January 2006 are dramatic examples of contextual events that impact on economies and organizations. An analysis of the external environment, the structural changes, the causes of the adjustments and possible outcomes would fill several volumes. In this chapter, however, we clarify what we mean by the term 'context' and assess the causal connections between context and work organizations. In so doing, we provide a modest review of the economic, technological, political and social changes in European and North American economies, and possible ramifications for HRM. The chapter begins with a brief overview of some of the broader changes in global capitalism. This is followed by sections examining developments in labour markets and government interventions, the chapter concluding by considering demographic changes.

REFLECTIVE QUESTION

Go back to Chapter 1 and look at Figure 1.3 (HRM practices, contingencies and skills). Can you think of some recent events that significantly influence the external context of HRM? Why is it important for HR managers to be informed of external developments?

Conceptions of contexts

A fundamental insight of sociology is that people operate in a social context or environment that has a powerful influence on their behaviour. Organizational theorists have applied this idea to formal work organizations by acknowledging the role of external factors or forces in shaping managerial behaviour. But studying the context is not easy. Over the past three decades, analysts have encompassed more and more elements shaping organizational action and have, moreover, recognized that the causal arrows point in both directions: contexts influence organizations, but organizations also affect contexts (Scott, 2003).

The analysis presented here uses an 'open-systems' model to examine the multidimensional and changing nature of context. So what is an open system? A system is a set of interrelated and interdependent parts configured in a manner that produces a unified whole. Cars, plants and societies are said to be systems. That is, they take inputs, transform them and produce an output. Systems may be classified as either 'closed' or 'open' to their environment. Work organizations are said to be open systems in that they acquire inputs (e.g. materials, energy, people and finance) from the environment, transform them into services or products, and discharge outputs in the form of services, products – and sometimes pollutants – to the external environment. Figure 4.1 illustrates a simple open system. A closed system is one that does not depend on its environment, that is, one that is sealed off from the outside world.

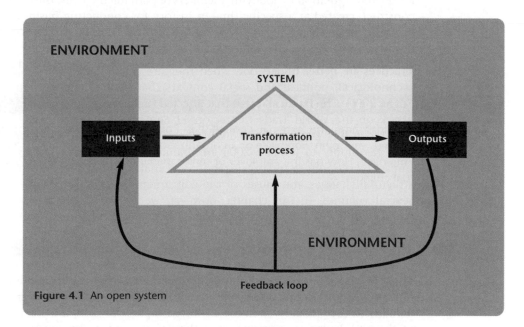

Figure 4.1 An open system

In a broad sense, the context is infinite and includes everything outside the immediate boundaries of the organization. The analysis of external factors is, however, limited to the factors or forces to which the organization is sensitive and to which it must respond to survive (Scott, 2003). Thus, for our purposes, context refers to all the external elements that exist outside the boundary of the organization or 'system' and have the potential to affect and shape formal work organizations and in turn influence HRM strategy, policies and practices. Conceptions of contexts vary by level of analysis as well as by substantive focus (e.g. economic resources or political forces). Levels of analysis include the specific organization, the industry level, the spatial level (e.g. all the organizations in a geographical region) and the global level. The open-system model emphasizes that management action is not separate from the world but is connected to the wider context. As Jaffee (2001, p. 209) states, 'The existing internal structure, strategy, and success of an organization is heavily influenced by environmental forces in which it operates and with which it interacts and competes.' This proposition suggests, first, that those in charge of organizations are externally constrained in their ability to implement any organizational strategy, and second, that any 'one best way' to manage depends on the environment or context in which the organization operates.

The notion that a particular organizational strategy is contingent upon the contextual demands placed upon organizations has been criticized on the grounds of 'environmental determinism' (e.g. Perrow, 1986). The resource dependency theory advances an alternative to contextual determinism. Rather than viewing organizational controllers as largely passive or impotent in relation to contextual forces, it is emphasized that organizations pursue 'proactive strategies' to overcome contextual constraints (Pfeffer and Salancik, 1978). In essence, it is proposed that it is too simple to regard the influence of context as merely a one-way flow. Senior management will attempt to change the external context or environment. A company might, for example, transfer its operations to where there is little competition or few, if any, health and safety regulations. In addition, workers seek to influence government legislation and regulation by lobbying members of parliament. Thus, the context is a social construct, created at a specific time in history for conducting business. Fully understanding the strategic role of HRM requires an understanding of external contexts. A model for examining the complex and dynamic realities of context and its causal connections with HRM is shown in Figure 4.2 (see also Figures 2.3 and 3.2).

REFLECTIVE QUESTION

Consider how the external context has impacted on an organization you have studied, your own workplace or an organization in which a member of your family is employed. How has the employer or senior management responded to such contextual changes?

The economic context

There is a general agreement among commentators that the structure as well as the fundamental dynamics of business have dramatically changed over the past two decades. At the global level, in the advanced capitalist world, the previous dominance of the USA began to give way to a three-way competitive rivalry between North America, the European Union (EU) and the Pacific rim countries, once dominated by Japan and the 'four tigers' of Hong Kong, South Korea, Singapore and Taiwan, but now increasingly dominated by the economic juggernauts of China and India (HRM in Practice 4.1). At the European level, as part of the process of European integration, an expanded EU has introduced a number of measures to remove barriers to free trade and encourage the mobility of capital, services and people. At the national level, in Britain, contextual changes include a further contraction of manufacturing employ-

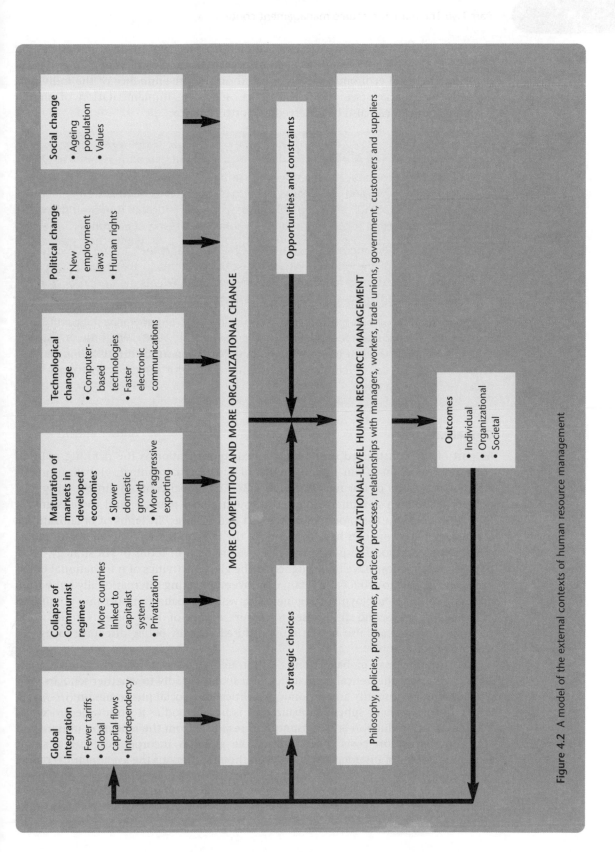

Figure 4.2 A model of the external contexts of human resource management

ment, the wide diffusion and acceptance of microprocessor-based technologies, an increase in the amount of non-standard or **precarious employment** and an entrenchment of a political economic paradigm based on the pre-eminence of the individual and the free market (see HRM in Practice 4.2). The implementation of similar economic policies can also be observed in North America.

STUDY TIP

Underlying the economic–competitive advantage discourse is an emphasis on learning both for work and at work. As the Organisation for Economic Co-operation and Development (OECD, 1997, p. 33) argues, 'a well educated and well trained population is important for the social and economic well-being of countries'.

Go back to the HRM models presented in Chapter 1 and look at the contextual elements in some of the models. What contextual elements in the models help to explain why there is a new focus on workplace learning? Why is the notion of workplace learning changing how businesses see themselves?

Obtain a copy of the Department for Education and Employment's report *The Learning Age* (Department for Education and Employment, 1998). What assumptions underpin the report? What are the implications of the report for the HRM function? What contribution can organizations, and in particular the HRM function, make to wider workplace learning?

Globalization

As part of the constructed economic context, **globalization** is the defining political economic paradigm of our time. In terms of the external context, globalization has affected all aspects of our model (Figure 4.2). The global economy in the early 21st century is more closely interconnected through global markets, and there is greater interdependency in the production of goods and services. In terms of organizational context, global companies have to reconcile the tension between the needs for global coordination and local responsiveness (see Figure 3.2). In terms of HR strategy, HRM policies and practices have to be aligned to the global activities of transnational enterprises and be able to attract and retain employees operating internationally but within different national employment regimes. The word 'globalization' became ubiquitous in the 1990s. It was, and still is, used to capture a range of developments in the world economy, but it must also be the most misused term in public discourse today. So, what is globalization?

First and foremost, globalization is a thoroughly contested concept (Aart Scholte, 2005). Contested theoretical approaches correspond broadly to whether scholars view globalization as primarily an economic, a political or a social phenomenon (Hoogvelt, 2001). In the *economic* sphere, globalization is understood as a worldwide process of integration of production and consumption resulting from the reduction of transport and communication costs. Thus, the whole globe is incorporated into a single economic system of interdependences, even though it retains the asymmetrical nature of the capitalist system, with highly developed and underdeveloped parts. Arguments that build only on these technical conceptions, however, fail to generate new understanding given that, during the period of the gold standard, the world was just as integrated and open as it is today (Hoogvelt, 2001; Saul, 2005).

HRM IN PRACTICE 4.1

CHINA, INDIA AND THE USA WILL DRIVE GROWTH

HRM GUIDE, APRIL 2006

A new research report from the Economist Intelligence Unit predicts that more than half the growth in the world's GDP over the next 15 years will come from China (27%), the US (16%) and India (12%).

The Foresight 2020 research report, sponsored by Cisco Systems, bases its predictions on new long-term economic forecasts, a survey of more than 1,650 executives and in-depth interviews with senior business leaders. Other predictions in the study include:

- The US will average close to 3% growth a year between now and 2020
- In comparison, the 25 European Union countries will average 2.1%
- Japan's growth will average less than 1% a year as its population shrinks
- The EU will compensate for the slower growth rate by territorial expansion, increasing to a union of more than 30 countries

- Average income of the enlarged EU will be just 56% of the US average in 2020
- China will close the gap in economic size with the US by 2020
- In terms of purchasing power parity (PPP) Asia will increase its share of world GDP, from its current 35% to 43% in 2020.

> **'On a per-capita basis, China and India will remain far poorer than Western markets and the region faces a host of downside risks.'**

Laza Kekic, director of forecasting services at the Economist Intelligence Unit, considers talk of the 'Asian century' to be premature:

'On a per-capita basis, China and India will remain far poorer than Western markets and the region faces a host of downside risks,' he says. 'Asia will narrow the gap in wealth, power and influence, but will not close it.'

The report assumes that world economic growth depends on the pace of globalization. If global trade continues to be gradually liberalized, the global economy will be two-thirds larger in 2020 than in 2005. But if globalization reverses or unravels, annual rates of global economic growth would be two percentage points lower. On the other hand, faster liberalization could boost annual global growth by a further percentage point.

Labour-intensive production will continue to shift to lower-cost countries but the report concludes that fears of the death of Western manufacturing are premature. Workers in the low-cost economies will benefit but Chinese average wages, for example, will rise only to about 15% of the developed-country average in 2020 compared with today's 5%.

To download Foresight2020 free of charge, visit
www.eiu.com/foresight2020

Writers who conceptualize globalization in terms of politics and power argue that 'big' business, particularly the growth of transnational networks of investment, production and trade, has relegated national governments to the 'gatekeepers' of free unfettered markets. And without competition from Communist ideology, post-1989 capitalism 'is much harder, more mobile, more ruthless and more certain about what it needs to make it tick' (Giddens and Hutton, 2000, p. 9). Giddens and Hutton call it a 'febrile capitalism' serving the needs of Wall Street and the financial and stock markets; 'Its ideology is that shareholder value must be maximized, that labour markets should be "flexible" and that capital should be free to invest and disinvest in industries and countries at will' (Giddens and Hutton, 2000, p. 10). Critics conceptualize globalization as a hegemonic discourse, an ideology of promised progress that conceals disempowerment and exploitation by the West. Chomsky (1999), for example, argues that national governments have lost power over their own economies as a handful of large corporations are permitted to control natural resources and social life – medical care, education and welfare services – in order to pursue their primary goal, the maximization of profits. In other words, civil society – from politics to social policy to culture – is perceived principally through the 'prism of economics' (Saul, 2005, p. 18).

The 'transformationalist thesis' views globalization primarily as a social phenomenon. The communication revolution – the Internet and e-business – provides the infrastructure for new 'global capitalism', which has brought about the ascendancy of 'real time' over 'physical time', and which deserves to be identified with a new phenomenon – globalization (Castells, 2000). For Castells (1996, p. 96), globalization brings 'the capacity of the world economy to operate as a unit in real time on a planetary basis'. This shrinking of the world to a 'global village' intensifies worldwide social relations (Giddens, 1990). In this usage, globalization enables people to become more able to engage with each other, wherever they may be on the planet. As Aart Scholte (2005) contends, contemporary globalization constructs social connections that transcend territorial boundaries quite distinct from the past, thus, representing 'a shift in the nature of social space' (p. 59). The privileging of one aspect of globalization is to deny the importance of other factors; more especially, it may deflect theoretical and empirical focus away from alternative types of globalization (Sklair, 2002).

HRM IN PRACTICE 4.2

THREAD THAT COULD SPAN GLOBAL GULF

KEVIN WATKINS, *GUARDIAN*, 30 JULY 2001, P. 21

At the age of 18, with three years' education to her name, Shawaz Begum is an authority on globalization. Six mornings a week she leaves her crumbling one-room mud home in the slum area of Ashulia on the outskirts of Dhaka, capital of Bangladesh, and walks to a South Korean-owned factory in the export-processing zone. She spends the next 10 hours sewing garments, including Tesco, Pierre Cardin and Harrods shirts, Nike tracksuits and Levi jeans. Is Shawaz Begum a symbol of globalization or a victim of a world trading system that benefits only the rich? Answer: neither. Debates on world trade are becoming polarized. In one corner stand the 'globaphiles', among them the World Bank, the IMF and northern governments, which hold that increased exports are good

for the poor. In the other are the 'globaphobes', arguing that trade is inherently exploitive and salvation should be sought in less trade and more self-reliance. In Ashulia, both camps appear equally out of touch with reality.

> **What the anti-trade lobby does not understand is that access to northern markets provides real people with opportunities to build a better life.**

Bangladesh is a desperately poor country, with almost half of the population below the poverty line. Yet by comparison with other least developed countries it is a (very) partial success story. In the past 10 years incomes have been rising

at more that 2% a year, poverty is falling – albeit far too slowly – and social welfare indicators are improving.

Garment exports are crucial. From minuscule beginnings at the end of the 1980s, the sector now generates almost 80% of foreign exchange earnings, about 3.7 billion pounds a year. There are 1.7 million people employed in the industry, three-quarters of them women.

In return for clothing western consumers, Shawaz Begum receives $1.70 for her 10-hour day. This is double what she would earn in the informal sector; it keeps a widowed mother in food and a sister in school.

The more serious problem concerns labour conditions. When Bangladeshi women enter an export-processing zone, they leave their human rights at the gate. Membership of a trade union is illegal, government has relinquished the right to carry out health and safety checks, and compliance with minimum wage and social welfare law is voluntary ... What the anti-trade lobby does not understand is that access to northern markets provides real people with opportunities to build a better life. Their alter egos in the World Bank and G8 appear equally incapable of grasping that their complacency, hypocrisy, and failure to act on pledges to make globalization work for the poor undermine the credibility of the international trading system.

Debating globalization

Changes in capitalist globalization have been the subject of different interpretations. One influential school of thought links the changes to the concept of postmodernism: flexible specialization (Piore and Sabel, 1984), disorganized capitalism (Lash and Urry, 1987), post-Fordism (Hall and Jacques, 1989) and neoliberalism, or the 'Washington consensus' (Chomsky, 1999). Lash and Urry (1987) argue that Britain and the USA, among other capitalist societies, are moving into an era of 'disorganized capitalism'. The increasing scale of industrial and financial corporations, combined with the growth of a global market, means that national markets have become less regulated by large nationally based corporations, and individual nation-states have less direct control and regulation over large transnational companies. The themes of post-Fordism, flexibility and disorganization are supportive of the broader themes of the diversity of capital, political management and 'post-bureaucratic' and 'postmodern' work organization (Thompson, 1993; Thompson and McHugh, 2002).

Others have argued that the changes in the global economy are so profound as to constitute 'multiple revolutions'. In the words of Giddens and Hutton (2000, p. 214), 'The open global economy is a precious acquisition offering opportunity, creativity and wealth. But it is a system ... that is precarious and potentially dangerous – it is on the edge.' Still others have emphasized the basic rules of the new global order: 'liberalize trade and finance, let markets set prices ("get prices right"), end inflation ("macroeconomic stability"), privatize' (Chomsky, 1999, p. 20). And, as for the elected government, it should 'get out of the way – hence the population too, insofar as the government is democratic, though the conclusion remains implicit' (Chomsky, 1999, p. 20).

The global and the local

The effects of globalization on income level are readily apparent. Global free trade has enriched a class of senior executives, financial investors and professionals (largely accountants and corporate lawyers). In 1996, the United Nations reported that the assets of the world's 358 billionaires exceeded the combined incomes of 45 per cent of the planet's population (Faux and Mishel, 2000). In 1990, 2.7 billion people were living on less than US$2 a day, whereas in 1998 the number living on less than US$2 daily had increased to an estimated 2.8 billion (Stiglitz, 2002). Moreover, inequality of income and wealth has increased, resulting in an impoverishment of large sectors of the world population. In the advanced industrialized countries, for which comparable data are available, income growth was higher in the 1980s than the 1990s. Over the past two decades, income growth has been substantially below that of the two decades between 1960 and 1980, as shown in Table 4.1.

Table 4.1 Per capita income growth in selected developed countries, 1960–2005

	Annual growth rate per capita income (%)[1]			
	1960–79	1979–89	1989–96	1996–2005[2]
Canada	3.4	1.8	–0.1	2.9
France	3.7	1.6	0.8	1.6
Germany	3.3	1.9	1.3	1.1
UK	2.2	2.2	1.0	2.5
USA	2.3	1.5	1.0	3.4
EU-15[3]	nd	nd	nd	1.7
EU-19[4]	nd	nd	nd	2.6
Total OECD	nd	nd	nd	2.6

Notes:
1. At 1990 price levels and exchange rates
2. Averages for 2001–05 based on OECD projections
3. EU-15, the EU member states prior to expansion in May 2004 (EU = 25 in 2004): Austria, Belgium, Denmark, Finland, France, Germany, Greece, Ireland, Italy, Luxemburg, Netherlands, Portugal, Spain, Sweden and United Kingdom
4. EU-19, as above plus Czech Republic, Estonia, Hungary and Poland
nd, no data
Source: Data from Faux and Mishel (2000) p. 97 and OECD (2004) p. 19

Critics of globalization also point to the inherently exploitive nature of global free trade. In the developing countries, the 'globalization of poverty' has caused local famines to erupt in sub-Saharan Africa, South Asia and parts of Latin America, largely reversing the achievements of post-war decolonization (Chossudovsky, 2003). Naomi Klein (2000, p. xvii), for example, brings together the reality of the so-called 'logo-linked' global economy:

This village where some multinationals, far from leveling the global playing field with jobs and technology for all, are in the process of mining the planet's poorest backcountry for unimaginable profits. This is the village where Bill Gates lives, amassing a fortune of $55 billion while a third of his workforce is classified as temporary workers, and where competitors are either incorporated into the Microsoft monolith or made obsolete by the latest feat in software bundling. This is the village where we are indeed connected to one another through a web of brands, but the underside of that web reveals designer slums like the one I visited outside Jakarta. IBM claims that its technology spans the globe, and so it does, but often its international presence takes the form of cheap Third World labour producing the computer chips and power sources that drive our machines.

In recent years, a significant theme in the globalization discourse has been the increasingly expressed concern for the current and emerging quality of the natural environment (Egri and Pinfield, 1999; Hertz, 2002; Hoogvelt, 2001). Critics of globalization have argued that global free trade has caused worldwide environmental destruction in an asymmetrical pattern. It has been suggested that as the multinational corporations located in the North control the global economy, it is the South and the underdeveloped countries that are, because of the North's greater economic and political power, disproportionately bearing the environmental burden of the new global capitalism (Shiva, 2000).

Despite the environmental costs of atmospheric pollution, North American global corporations continue to influence and shape the external context by lobbying against ratifying the Kyoto Protocol on climate change (HRM in Practice 4.3). Broad social movements, concerned about global inequality and environmental pollution, have also attempted to influence the external context of business through international conferences, commissioned reports, political lobbying and street protests, for example in Seattle, Genoa and Quebec.

HRM IN PRACTICE 4.3

RATIFYING KYOTO ESTIMATED TO COST UP TO 450,000 JOBS

STEVEN CHASE, *GLOBE AND MAIL*, 27 FEBRUARY 2002, P. B6

Ratifying the Kyoto protocol could force plant closing throughout Canada and cost the country's manufacturing sector as many as 450,000 jobs by 2010, the Canadian Manufacturers and Exporters association is warning. 'The cumulative impact of meeting Canada's Kyoto target would be the equivalent of a one-year recession,' the CME says in a report to be released today called 'Pain Without Gain: Canada and the Kyoto Protocol'.

Ottawa is coming under pressure to decide whether Canada will ratify the 1997 Kyoto accord, negotiated in Japan by 150 countries, which requires signatories to cut emissions of global-warming gases by about 6 per cent from 1990 levels by the end of 2012.

The federal government has said it hopes to ratify the deal, but, in the four years since the accord was signed, has yet to develop a detailed plan showing how Canada will meet its Kyoto emissions targets – a delay that's making business groups nervous. 'We've been working on this for over four years of consultation and we still don't

have a reliable economic analysis that can tell us what the costs will be,' said the CME chief economist Jayson Myers. The CME's estimate of 450,000 lost manufacturing jobs – or about 20 per cent of the country's manufacturing base of 2.2 million workers – is based in part on the assumption that

> 'The bottom line is that Canada will not be able to achieve its Kyoto target without damaging economic and employment growth.'

curbing emissions will impose new costs on businesses and reduce their competitiveness compared to the USA. Being less competitive would cost Canadian companies contracts and jobs, the CME reasons. The CME fears that American companies will beat our Canadian companies for jobs and production if Ottawa ratifies Kyoto. 'The jobs will go south and so will the emissions: the production will just be picked up by another country,' Mr. Myers said.

Meanwhile, the group says new technologies that might enable Canada to painlessly meet targets have not yet been invented. 'The bottom line is that Canada will not be able to achieve its Kyoto target without damaging economic and employment growth,' the CME's report says.

The federal government, which insists it can meet Kyoto targets, is currently hammering out new estimates of the Kyoto accord's impact on Canada's economy. 'It is possible, in Canada, to remain competitive and yet make sure that our air is not polluted,' Prime Minister Jean Crétien told the House of Commons yesterday.

The CME suggests in its report that perhaps Ottawa would think twice about ratifying the deal. 'It is not clear that the ... Kyoto protocol is the appropriate mechanism for Canada in responding to the challenges of climate change. Our largest trading partner, the United States, is not covered by the agreement. [And] developing countries are not bound to emissions reductions targets either.'

REFLECTIVE QUESTION

Look at the quotes on the economy and global developments at the beginning of the chapter and HRM in Practice 4.3. What is your own view on global capitalism – unlimited opportunities for wealth creation or an Orwellian nightmare?

These issues of growing inequality and atmospheric pollution, among others, are symptomatic of the deep structure of beliefs regarding the consequences of globalization. As Hutton and Giddens (2000) explore in their book, the trajectory of global capitalism is unpredictable. For example, the string of accounting deceptions in corporate America – Enron, WorldCom Inc. and Adelphia Communications Corp. – destabilized investor confidence and have caused the conventional wisdom of the 1990s, that government should abdicate control and initiative to the private business sector, to be questioned. Commenting on President George W. Bush's speech to the business community in July 2002, one business editorial reflected the shift in thinking like this: 'It has become clear that the scandals represent not just a few bad apples, but an entire system of inadequate corporate and financial reporting. If President Bush is serious about getting tough on big business, he must deal with the conflicts that have undermined investors' faith in the markets.'[5]

Local labour markets, 1970–2005

So far, this chapter has dealt with global and European economic forces that influence trends in employment systems in the early 21st century. External markets simultaneously generate opportunities and constraints for strategic choice in organizations (see Figure 4.2 above). The specific focus of this section is how labour markets affect the scope of strategic choice in HRM. To consider this, we draw on data and critical social scientific analysis emanating primarily, but not exclusively, from the UK and Europe.

The essence of the employment relationship begins with people interacting with organizations through the workings of the **labour markets**. People sell their capacity for work (labour power) for a price, a wage. Employers buy people's capacity to work to produce goods and services. The simplest view of the labour market is that it is an arena of competition involving an *economic exchange* between two equal parties, which constitutes the employer–employee relationship. There is no coercion involved: employers are buying labour power, and employees are willing to sell it. The *demand for labour* – the number of jobs offered by employers – is the total number of employees in employment plus the number of unfilled jobs. The demand for labour is a derived demand in that it is determined by the level of demand for the goods and services produced by the employer in a given market. In capitalism, competing organizations individually decide what goods and services to produce, in what quantity, at what price and so on. When the demand for the firm's goods and services rises – all things being equal – the firm's demand for labour increases, and when demand falls, the firm's demand for labour decreases. The *supply of labour* is the total number of people of legal working age who are in employment and the number of hours that they are able and willing to work. Labour supply is determined by the size of the population, decisions made by individuals and families to engage in paid work, and legal regulations.

Neoclassical economic theory predicts that, providing all things – for example welfare benefits, social norms and values – remain constant, a higher wage will generally attract more people into the labour market, and a lower wage will attract fewer people to sell their labour power. A major ideological achievement of neoclassical economics is the belief that a 'free' labour market will achieve an optimum allocation of human resources. That is, competition between firms for workers and between workers seeking employment results in a 'market wage' that adjusts to the relative changes in labour demand and supply. Although competitive pressures operate to a certain degree in the labour market, employers' employment and reward practices vary considerably within sectors. In practice, **internal labour markets** (which are large organization-based employment systems) rather than competitive forces in the external labour market determine the economic exchange. The conventional notion that markets, including labour markets, operate in accordance with universal principles has been refuted (Whitley, 2000). In reality, the economic contract between the two parties does not reflect the competitive model of the labour market because legal regulations, such as a minimum wage, and the activities of trade unions also put a limit on competition (see Chapter 11).

HRM IN PRACTICE 4.4

PROTESTS AGAINST FRANCE'S NEW JOB LAW ESCALATE

Thousands of students and union members expected to take to the streets again Saturday

CANADIAN HR REPORTER, 17 MARCH 2006

Tens of thousands of French students marched in protest of a new law that makes it easier to hire and fire young workers on Tuesday. More protests, in which the students will be joined by France's main unions, are expected on Saturday.

Last month, the country's right-of-centre government passed a law that it claims will ease the crisis of high unemployment, especially among disadvantaged young people in the suburbs. In France, 23 per cent of those under 26 are jobless and in some suburbs the unemployment rate is nearly 50 per cent.

The 'first job contract' law encourages firms to hire young people with little or no job experience, but it also allows companies to fire workers under the age of 26 within the first two years of employment with little notice or severance.

> **The government's leftist deputies are challenging the constitutionality of the new law**

On Tuesday, teachers, workers, union members and Communist Party members joined university and high school students in marches across Paris.

The government's leftist deputies are challenging the constitutionality of the new law before the Constitutional Council, which can review a law before it receives presidential approval.

Prime Minister Dominique de Villepin's popularity has plummeted to a record low of 36 per cent and members of his own U.M.P. Party have called on him to drop the law. President Jacques Chirac, who under French law is responsible for the country's defence and foreign policy while the prime minister is responsible for domestic issues, has publicly supported de Villepin.

The analysis of the 'social' dimension of the employment relationship, primarily grounded in sociology, highlights the key issues of how employment relationships operate – social relations are not free and equal but coercive and hierarchical, as it is the employer who organizes work and determines the design and pace of work, as well as whether to employ HR at all (substitute employees for machinery) and at what price. In this sense, organizations are not passive agents simply responding to external economic and demographic or social forces. Critical research of labour markets has focused on the role of organizations in altering the nature of the labour market. Three processes – the *restructuring of the economy*, the *polarization of labour markets* and the *globalization of business* – have profoundly changed the demand and recruitment for HR, the traditional patterns of occupational structure, mobility within the labour market and, more generally, the level of job security and well-being afforded by standard employment. We will examine these three processes in turn, exploring the effect they have on millions of people and on HRM.

Restructuring of the economy

An important trend during the second half of the 20th century characterized the labour markets of all industrialized economies: **deindustrialization**. Although some observers question the wisdom of using the term, 'deindustrialization' typically refers to the process by which the number of jobs in manufacturing and the extraction of raw materials declined in both absolute terms and, compared with the volume of service sector activity in the economy, relative terms. A trend observed from the 1950s, this accelerated in the 1980s. In 1950, 35 per cent of the total number of people in civil employment were employed in manufacturing; this had fallen to 26 per cent in mid-1984 and to 23 per cent in 1990 (Millward et al., 1992). The UK's share of world exports of manufactures fell from approximately 17 per cent in 1960 to about 8 per cent in 1986. In the manufacturing sector, UK output increased by 6 per cent in the period 1979–91 compared with the OECD average (excluding the UK) of 35 per cent. In 1983, UK trade in manufacturing went into deficit for the first time since the Industrial Revolution (Hutton, 1996), the UK being placed 20th out of the 21 OECD economies. The UK's share of total OECD manufacturing output declined from 6.5 per cent in 1979 to 5.2 per cent in 1991; over the period 1979–92, the UK was situated at the bottom of the league (Michie, 1992).

During the same period, employment in the service sector increased from 47 per cent to 60 per cent of total employment, and within that, predominantly at the low end, in cleaning, fast food and retail services. The share of employment in private sector services increased from 29 per cent in 1984 to 44 per cent in 1998 (Cully et al., 1999). Much of the growth in service employment has therefore been in what is fashionably referred to as 'knowledge work' (see, for example, Newell et al., 2002) or what Thompson and McHugh (2002, p. 171) rather ingenuously refer to as 'no knowledge' work.

REFLECTIVE QUESTION

According to Bowen (1992, quoted in Needle, 2004, p. 98), 'you cannot pay for Japanese cars with British hairdressing'. What do you think of the argument that a healthy economy requires a healthy manufacturing sector?

Another major trend in the British economy has been the marked shift away from public ownership. *Privatization* was a key component of Conservative government economic policy and has taken different forms. Most prominent has been the sale of public corporations, such as British Telecom (1984), British Gas (1986), British Airways (1987), British Steel (1988), water (1989), electricity distribution (1990), electricity generation (1991), British Coal (1994), British Rail (1996) and Her Majesty's Stationery Office (1996). The successive waves of privatization and contracting out of a wide range of services substantially reduced employment in the public sector. Survey findings show that employment in state-owned corporations fell by 38 per cent, from 1.3 million to 0.8 million, between 1984 and 1990 (Millward et al., 1992; see also Beaumont, 1992), and by 1998 public sector industries accounted for less than one-third (32 per cent) of all employees covered by the Workplace Employment Relations Survey (WERS) of 1998 (Cully et al., 1999). Throughout the 1980s and 90s, then, privatization favoured an organizational strategy that reduced the business to its 'core' operations, and an HR strategy that promoted flexibility and reduced labour costs (Pendleton, 1997a).

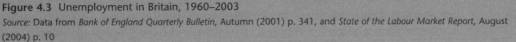

HRM WEB LINKS

Go to the following websites for more information on important economic trends in Britain (www.statistics.gov.uk), Canada (www.statcan.ca/start.html), the EU (www.eiro.eurofound.ie), South Africa (www.statssa.gov.za) and Australia (www.abs.gov.au).

The development of the UK economy, along a trajectory of low investment in manufacturing, low levels of research and development, and privatization, has led to many notable changes in the labour market. On the demand side, the aggregate unemployment rate over the period indicates significant changes in the UK labour market.

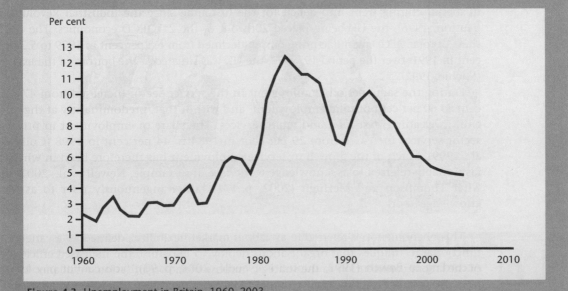

Figure 4.3 Unemployment in Britain, 1960–2003

Source: Data from *Bank of England Quarterly Bulletin*, Autumn (2001) p. 341, and *State of the Labour Market Report*, August (2004) p. 10

Figure 4.3 shows that unemployment started to move gradually upwards in the late 1960s and early 1970s, surging upwards rapidly after 1979, falling rapidly in the late 1980s and increasing rapidly again after 1990. Since 1993, the unemployment rate has been falling, levelling off in 2001 and rising slightly through 2002; at around 5 per cent in 2003, it was, however, at its lowest level since the late 1970s.

Labour market polarization

Another central theme of critical labour market research, which runs parallel to the deindustrialization discourse, is the emergence of a polarized labour market. This theme became evident in the 1970s but was sustained and developed in the 1980s and 1990s by increasing interest in employment policies to make workers more flexible (Rubery, 1988). This theoretical approach claims that labour markets are asymmetrically divided: the better paid, secure jobs and poorly paid, insecure jobs. Early work by Doeringer and Piore (1971) explored how the labour market was polarized or segmented into a 'primary' sector with good jobs offering better pay, security and career progression, and the 'secondary' sector offering something much less. In the 1980s, the debate focused on explaining changes in the labour market resulting from new employment strategies in search of cost minimization. The influential Atkinson (1985) model of the flexible firm proposes that increasing uncertainty and competition has led organizations to restructure their HR into a 'core' workforces and 'peripheral' workforces.

Figure 4.4 One view of the labour market
Source: Vancouver Sun, BC, Canada (1995) June 25

This phenomenon is referred to as 'labour market flexibility', defined as 'a variety of functional techniques that organisations deploy to maximise the increased efficiency of the labour contribution to the strategic purpose of the organisation' (Williams, 1993, p. 1). Atkinson's (1985) flexibility model identifies three types of flexibility: *functional*, *numerical* and *financial*. Those workers on permanent, full-time contracts constitute the core workforce; those on temporary, part-time and fixed-term employment contracts, and self-employed workers, constitute the numerical flexible or 'peripheral' workforce (Figure 4.4). Functional flexibility allows employees to be redeployed between activities and tasks (see Chapter 5), whereas financial flexibility allows employers to pay according to individual and/or organizational performance (Chapter 10). Critics of the flexible labour model have, however, challenged it on both ideological and empirical grounds, and have argued that the notion of 'core' and 'periphery' is confused, circular and value-laden (Hyman, 1988; Pollert, 1988; Williams, 1993).

Despite the criticism, Atkinson's model has been widely cited and used for explaining changes in the labour markets of all the industrialized economies in the EU and OECD. The evidence on labour market polarization and, in particular, numerical flexibility is the growth of *non-standard employment*, including self-employment, part-time work, temporary agency work, temporary or fixed-term contracts and homework (Conley, 2002; Cully et al., 1999; Kersley et al., 2005; Millward et al., 2000; Olsen and Kalleberg, 2004; Standing, 1997; Storey et al., 2002). In 1993, 40 per cent of the UK workforce was employed in three common forms of non-regular employment (Table 4.2). The 2004 WERS survey data show that the use of non-standard forms of employment has become 'commonplace' in British workplaces. Eighty-three per cent of workplaces employed part-time employees (defined as 30 hours or less per week), up from 79 per cent in 1998. Almost one-third (30 per cent) of workplaces had employees on temporary contracts, a similar proportion to that reported in 1998 (32 per cent). Non-regular employment contracts facilitate 'a looser contractual relationship between manager and worker' (Atkinson, 1985, p. 17) or, to put it more bluntly, employers can hire and fire workers as business circumstances change.

Table 4.2 Non-regular forms of employment, selected countries, 1973–93

	Self-employed (per cent of non-agricultural employees)		Part-time (per cent of total employment)		Temporary (per cent of total employment)		Total non-regular (per cent of total employment)	
	1973	1993	1973	1993	1983	1993	1973	1993
USA	6.7	7.7	15.6	17.5	–	–	(22.3)	(25.2)
Canada	6.2	8.6	9.7	17.2	7.5	8.3	23.4	34.1
Australia	9.5	12.9	11.9	23.9	15.6	22.4	(37.0)	(49.2)
Japan	14.0	10.3	13.9	21.1	10.3	10.8	38.2	42.2
Austria	11.7	6.3	6.4	10.1	–	–	–	–
Belgium	11.2	13.3	3.8	12.8	5.4	4.7	20.4	30.8
Denmark	9.3	7.0	(22.7)	23.3	12.5	10.7	(42.5)	44.0
Finland	6.5	9.5	6.7	8.6	(11.3)	13.5	(24.5)	31.6
France	11.4	8.8	5.9	13.7	3.3	10.2	20.6	32.7
Germany	9.1	7.9	10.1	15.1	9.9	10.2	29.1	33.2
Ireland	10.1	13.0	(5.1)	10.8	6.1	9.0	(21.3)	32.8
Italy	23.1	24.2	6.4	5.4	6.6	5.8	36.1	35.4
Netherlands	9.2	8.7	(16.6)	33.4	5.8	10.0	(31.6)	52.1
Norway	7.8	6.2	23.0	27.1	–	–	(30.8)	(33.3)
Portugal	12.7	18.2	(7.8)	7.4	(13.1)	8.6	(33.6)	(34.2)
Spain	16.3	18.7	–	6.6	15.6	32.0	(31.9)	57.3
Sweden	4.8	8.7	(23.6)	24.9	(12.0)	11.9	(40.4)	45.5
UK	7.3	11.9	16.0	23.3	5.5	5.7	28.8	40.9

Source: Standing (1997)

The dominant core–periphery explanatory framework for labour markets lacks a gender analysis. More recently, however, the debate has also turned to exploring how gender, race and ethnicity mediate the way in which the phenomenon of polarization is experienced (Charles and James, 2003; PRI Project, 2004; Vosko, 2000). One of the most significant developments in *labour supply* has been the growing feminization of the labour force. Women's share of total employment increased from 34 per cent in 1959 to 42 per cent in 1980, reaching 48 per cent in 1998 (Millward et al., 2000). The work done by the two sexes remains distinct, with the majority of women workers being engaged in clerical, serving or cleaning work.

Over two decades, survey data suggest that British workplaces became more diversified. The number of workplaces employing a more diversified workforce rose from 36 per cent in 1980 to 48 per cent in 1998 (Millward et al., 2000). Women and people of colour are much more likely to experience precarious non-regular forms of paid work. For example, women made up the whole of the part-time workforce in 44 per cent of British workplaces that employed part-time workers (Kersley et al., 2006). Exploring the concepts of the working poor and precarious or insecure employment caused by the growth of non-standard employment contracts, Vosko's (2000) central argument is that non-standard working is associated conceptually with employment insecurity and is deeply rooted in the history of capitalist employment relations. Indeed, evidence shows that women are overrepresented at the expanding margins of the labour market – the peripheral workforce – and are treated like 'commodities', which has the effect of intensifying the insecurity in the employment relationship (Charles and James, 2003; PRI Project, 2004).

HRM WEB LINKS

Go to the following websites for more information on employment trends in Britain (www.statistics.gov.uk), Canada (www.statcan.ca/start.html and the Canadian Labour Force Development Board www.hrmguide.net/canada/), EU (www.eiro.eurofound.ie), USA (www.stats.gov and www.workindex.com/), South Africa (www.statssa.gov.za) and Australia (www.abs.gov.au).

The globalization of business

The third development and theoretical debate on how organizations are active agents in shaping labour markets centres on the globalization of business. The growth of the global economy has resulted in significant sections of the labour market being influenced by the investment decisions and production and HR strategies of transnational corporations. As we discussed in Chapter 3, transnational corporations, such as Toyota, Ford and Unilever, have established a global network for research and development, production and marketing. Moreover, these corporations integrate global resources and 'outsource' some of their work to 'preferred suppliers' to achieve cost efficiencies while maintaining the capability to respond to local markets. Global companies strive for flexibility, responsiveness and innovation (Needle, 2004; see HRM in Practice 4.5).

HRM IN PRACTICE 4.5

EMPLOYEES URGE BRITISH GAS TO RECONSIDER PLAN TO MOVE 2000 JOBS TO INDIA
Workers campaign for company to keep sites running in Manchester, Oldham and Solihull

PEOPLE MANAGEMENT, 15 AUGUST 2005

Angry British Gas employees are campaigning for the company to reverse its decision to transfer 2,000 back-office jobs to India. British Gas plans to close sites in Manchester, Oldham and Solihull as part of a £430m overhaul of its customer billing system. Unison, the public-services union, is backing workers that are against the move.

Steve Bloomfield, head of utilities at Unison, explained it had been bombarded with letters and emails from people working at affected sites. 'Some are new mothers just returning from maternity leave,' he said. 'In one case both a husband and wife with two young children face losing their jobs. Families in these areas will be left devastated.'

'Families in these areas will be left devastated.'

Workers were particularly upset because they had recently been praised for their loyalty and dedication to the firm. Sir Roy Gardner, chief executive of Centrica, the firm that owns British Gas, commended staff in its 2004 annual report. 'The achievements of our people have been outstanding during 2004, continuing to meet our customers' very diverse needs against the backdrop of a highly competitive marketplace,' he said. 'I would like to join the chairman in thanking all our people for their ongoing and valued commitment.'

Unison has called on the government to act on what it sees as a threat to the UK economy from businesses offshoring jobs to cheaper overseas locations.

These global business strategies strongly affect the nature of local markets and therefore HRM initiatives and practices. The discourse on deindustrialization and privatization, labour market polarization and the globalization of business forms part of a wider debate on the restructuring of labour markets for the traditional skilled manual working class and their trade unions, the formation of occupational classes and the role of national institutional systems. Finally, whatever the academic merits of the debate, the terms 'deindustrialization', 'globalization' and 'employment flexibility' have real meaning for the men and women who live in the industrialized economies. In concrete terms, they often result in more workers experiencing redundancy, long-term unemployment, immense upheaval and dislocation, poverty and despair, employment insecurity and intensification in the pace of paid work.

REFLECTIVE QUESTION

Do you think that 'new technology' inevitably leads to higher productivity and an improvement in the quality of life? How many microprocessor-based pieces of equipment do you use (1) in your home, and (2) in your workplace? How does the diffusion of microprocessor-based technology affect HRM?

The technology context

Over the past two decades, several developments relating to microprocessor-based technology have impacted directly upon the context within which HRM takes place. The terms 'new technology', 'microelectronic technology' and 'information technology' are all interrelated; indeed, these terms are frequently used interchangeably in everyday speech. The importance of 'information technology' arises from the integration between developments in microelectronics and telecommunications. At the end of the 1970s, observers were predicting a 'new industrial revolution' based not on steam but on microelectronics (see, for example, Jenkins and Sherman, 1979). It was judgements of this kind, together with intense media coverage, that prompted governments, industrialists and trade unions to wake up to the significance of microprocessor-based technology.

In the 1990s, developments in information technology have led some social observers to predict that 'thinking machines' will perform 'conceptual', 'managerial' and 'administrative' functions, thereby causing a further shift to 'a near-workerless, information society', the final stage of the 'Third Industrial Revolution' (Rifkin, 1996). When it has been reported that many workers in Britain and North America were actually working more hours each week in 2002 than they were two decades ago, it might be premature to speak of the 'end of work'; what we are more confident about, however, is the reconfiguring of the relationship between technology, globalization and work. Academics have identified at least three different forms of technological change that cause a reconfiguration of the relationship between technology and work (Millward and Stevens 1986). Using the example of microelectronic technology, there are:

1. *Advanced technical change:* new plant, machinery or equipment that includes microelectronic technology (e.g. computer-aided design).
2. *Conventional technical change:* new plant, machinery or equipment not incorporating microelectronic technology (e.g. containerization).
3. *Organizational change:* substantial changes in work organization or job design not involving new plant, machinery or equipment (e.g. self-managed teams).

Using two 'crude' indicators – the computerization of production and the computerization of office work – the WERS98 survey confirmed just how far microprocessor-based technology has become a feature of British workplaces across all sectors of employment (Table 4.3).

Table 4.3 Diffusion of microtechnology in UK workplaces, 1984–98

	1984 %	1990 %	1998 %
Manufacturing microtechnology	44	66	87
Office microtechnology	25	62	90[1]

Note:
1. Panel survey
Source: Based on figures from Millward et al. (2000) pp. 37–8

In 1984, a little over two-fifths (44 per cent) of manufacturing workplaces reported using microprocessor-based technology. The application of advanced technology increased substantially by 1998, when the proportion had risen to 87 per cent. Between 1984 and 1998, microprocessor-based technology was adopted more widely than before in smaller manufacturing workplaces. Among large manufacturing establishments (those employing more than 500 workers), the diffusion of microprocessor-based technology became almost universal, 94 per cent applying the technology. The uptake of microprocessor-based technology in the office (word processors) has been even more spectacular. Just a quarter of the workplaces surveyed in 1984 reported using computerized office equipment, whereas by 1998 the proportion was 90 per cent (Millward et al., 2000). Other research has shown the diffusion of microprocessor-based technology in different sectors of the economy. In financial services, for example, Wilson (1994) reports the adoption of computer-based technology, and in the UK clothing industry Lloyd (1997) describes the widespread diffusion of computer-aided design. The diffusion of microprocessor-based technology became one of the 'most revolutionary developments' within British industry in the last quarter of the 20th century (Millward et al., 2000), a phenomenon that has affected both manual and non-manual workers.

Technological changes have provided the infrastructure for global free trade, as well as radically transforming the nature of work inside the organization for both blue-collar and white-collar employees. Research has been concerned with describing and interpreting the complex interplay between technical innovation, blue-collar and white-collar skills, and the reconfiguration of work structures and social relations, as well as trade union responses to technical change (Batstone et al., 1987; Bratton, 1992; Clark, 1993; Hogarth, 1993; McLoughlin and Clark, 1988). Neither is the analysis of technological change limited to Britain. Studies on the impact of technological change have been conducted in Sweden (Bengtsson, 1992; Lowstedt, 1988), Finland (Penn et al., 1992), Denmark (Clausen and Lorentzen, 1993) and North America (Drache, 1995; Wells, 1993; Womack et al., 1990). Much of this research was initially stimulated by Braverman's publication *Labor and Monopoly Capital* (1974) and the upsurge of interest in the labour process debate that followed in its wake (Thompson, 1989).

Running parallel with the diffusion of microprocessor-based technology, however, is organizational change. The proportion of workplaces experiencing a substantial change in work organization or working practices affecting manual employees increased from 23 per cent in 1984 to 35 per cent in 1998 (Cully et al., 1999; Millward et al., 1992). Of particular relevance here is the influence of Japanese 'lean production' concepts, such as 'just-in-time', total quality management, teamworking and business process re-engineering (see Chapter 5). Business process re-engineering involves the radical redesign of business processes to create simultaneous changes in organizational design, culture, working practices and performance improvements. A number of researchers have documented shifts in work reorganization from traditional job designs based on Taylorist principles and rule-bound procedures towards flexibility and commitment. The Massachusetts Institute of Technology study by Womack et al. (1990), *The Machine that Changed the World*, identifies a work configuration labelled 'lean production' that incorporates Japanese-style manufacturing practices, including flexible work teams. This study has been particularly influential among academics and practitioners, but it has been criticized, not least because of its 'reliance upon an idealised mode of lean production' (Elger and Smith, 1994, p. 3). The logic of this line of argument is that flexible specialization requires a good 'fit' between technology and organization. Although there is a considerable variation in the way in which managers conceptualize 'teamworking', and therefore survey data may exaggerate the use of teams, the 2004 Workplace Employment Relations Survey found teamworking to be a central component of 'high-performance' work practices, over two-thirds (72 per cent) of all workplaces reporting having at least some core workers in formally designated work teams (Kersley et al., 2006, p. 89). In UK manufacturing, the changes in work organization were introduced mostly for business reasons – improvements in productivity, quality, flexibility and cost efficiency – rather than to benefit workers' job satisfaction or skills (Psoinos and Smithson, 2002).

HRM WEB LINKS

Go to the website of the Centre for the Study of Work Teams (www.workteams.unt.edu) for more information on organizational design. The International Sociological Association's Research Committee on Economy and Society conducts research into economic activity at regional, national and international levels, and provides information on the development of work (www.ucm.es/OTROS/isa/rc02.htm).

The political context

Globalization restructures relations between state and capital. (Hoogvelt, 2001, p. 148)

The **political context** in our model is the most complex and the most difficult to analyse, both because of its power to shape the nature of the employment relationship and because of its effects on the other contexts. In what follows, we examine how governments and their agencies – or what is referred to as 'the state' – affect the regulation of employment relations and the working lives of millions of people.

The state and business

The state comprises the executive, parliament, the civil service, the judiciary, the police and the armed forces. It has a monopoly over money supply, taxation and the legitimate use of violence. As an institution, the state, to a large extent, mirrors the concentration of economic power in society at large. As a result of that power, the social elites in whose hands it lies enjoy immense influence in society, in the political system and in the determination of the state's policies and actions (Miliband, 1969). In a social democracy, the state has six major responsibilities:

1. Protecting national sovereignty
2. Establishing a legal system
3. Developing economic policies
4. Building basic services and infrastructure
5. Protecting vulnerable people
6. Protecting the environment.

All these major state activities affect business and managers in some way. The state is not, however, monolithic, and differences can and do occur, as between parliament and the civil service. The impact of state intervention on business is not one way: business managers in turn continually lobby and seek to influence the policies of the state (see Needle, 2004, p. 99).

In this section, we will examine aspects of the state's activity to shape and regulate employment relations, and reconcile the conflict that inevitably arises in employment (HRM in Practice 4.6). In this regard, the state has three roles. First and foremost, it is responsible for economic policy that partly influences labour markets and shapes the economic context within which employees and management interact. Second, the state establishes the legal context of employment relations through legislation and third-party intervention. Employment rights, pay equity, occupational health and safety, union–management relations and pension laws all impinge on HRM activities. Third, it is an employer in its own right (Godard, 2005).

HRM IN PRACTICE 4.6

CHINA FRETS OVER EXPANDING INCOME GAP
Disparity between rich and poor fuels social unrest in worker's paradise

GEOFFREY YORK, *GLOBE AND MAIL*, 9 FEBRUARY 2006, P. A1

China's surging economy is fuelling an 'alarming' and growing gulf between the rich and poor, Beijing has acknowledged as it pledges to take measures to close the income gap in the workers' paradise.

The poorest 29 per cent of China's urban residents are earning less than 3 per cent of total urban income, according to a new study by China's National Development and Reform Commission.

The inequality is even starker when assets are measured. The richest 10 per cent of urban dwellers control 45 per cent of urban assets, while the poorest 10 per cent have only 1.4 per cent. Not only has the gap reached an 'alarming and unreasonable level,' it is 'continually expanding,' the study concludes.

The Chinese government has announced that the narrowing of the income gap will be one of its main priorities this year and will be at the top of the agenda when China's national legislature holds its annual meeting next month. Some sociologists say that the huge wealth gap will cause hatred toward the rich by the poor, one Beijing newspaper warned this week.

The wealth gap has provoked a furious on-line debate among Chinese, with many people outraged at the latest evidence of rising inequalities. Many are convinced that the wealthiest Chinese are corrupt officials and businessmen who ignore the law. 'Kill the rich to help the poor!' one person wrote on the hugely popular Sohu website.

> **The Chinese government has announced that the narrowing of the income gap will be one of its main priorities this year**

'People hate the rich because the rich become rich with dirty money,' another person wrote on the same website. 'If you are rich, you can even become a people's representative in the state council. Haven't you seen how horrible they are?'

With street protests rising to record levels, China's Commu-nist government is worried that the growing gap between rich and poor could provoke more instability this year.

Another new report revealed that there were 87,000 mass protests and other 'public order disturbances' in China last year, compared with 74,000 in the previous year. The number of protests has soared tenfold since 1993 and violent protests increased by 13 per cent last year.

The authorities see a link between the social unrest and the wealth gap. Migrant workers in Shanghai and Beijing live in overcrowded dormitories, while the richest residents drive luxury cars and shop in Louis Vuitton boutiques.

Many of the most violent protests are triggered when peasants or workers lose their land for urban developments that benefit the wealthy.

'In some areas, illegal seizures of farmland without reasonable compensation and resettlement have provoked uprisings,' Chinese Premier Wen Jiabao said this past month. 'This is still a key source of instability in rural areas and even the whole of society.'

While the urban gap is a serious concern, the inequality between China's rural and urban populations is even more severe – 'perhaps the highest in the world,' according to the latest United Nations report on human development in China, released in December.

The focus here is on the first two roles. Most of the HRM literature devotes little attention to the wider politicoeconomic new world order or trilateral regulation; instead, the emphasis is on the employer as the key agent of employment regulation (Kelly, 2005). We believe it important to be aware of the general trend in Britain from *voluntary regulation*, which has normally taken the form of collective bargaining between management and trade unions, to *legal regulation*, through the development of statutory employment protection provisions and individual and collective legal rights (see Table 4.4 below). It is, however, also important to understand the political ideology underpinning state intervention: the 'why' behind state involvement in constructing the context.

The state and neoliberalism

In the final quarter of the 20th century, we witnessed a fundamental shift in political ideology and, subsequently, in the role played by central governments in the Western hemisphere. Indeed, some have argued that the past two decades have comprised the most distinctive political era in recent history (Millward et al., 2000). To appreciate this distinctiveness, we need briefly to describe different types of state intervention in advanced capitalist economies. Drawing on Needle (2004) and Kuttner (2000), we can identify four:

1. facilitative
2. supportive
3. directive
4. neoliberalist (Chomsky, 1999).

During the first three decades of the 20th century, governments 'facilitated' the smooth operation of the markets, largely through taxation and currency protection, shipping and trade production, and law and order. The economic crisis of the 1920s, the Second World War and the threat of Communism ultimately led to the state adopting a more 'supportive' role towards economic activities. State intervention in the economy was strongly influenced by the Keynesian economic doctrine, which believed that the free market is myopic and inclined periodically to 'self-destruct' (Kuttner, 2000). Supportive economic state policies were challenged by the rise of free global trade and inflation.

In the 1960s, Conservative and Labour governments engaged in 'directive' policies, cooperating with employers' associations, for example the Confederation of British Industry, and the trade unions, such as the Trades Union Congress, in order to restructure British business and control inflation. The 1974–79 Labour government's 'social contract' is an example of this collaborative attempt at central planning. A lack of consensus among the trade unions, culminating in public sector strikes – the so-called 'winter of discontent' – ultimately defeated the Labour government and, with it, support for directive economic policies. The intervening 18 years (1979–97) of Conservative governments, led by Margaret Thatcher and her successor John Major, constituted a period of 'neoliberalism' or 'New Right' economic doctrine.

Successive Conservative governments in Britain rejected Keynesian post-war economic orthodoxy and adopted 'supply-side economics'. Advocates of supply-side economics posited the theory that economic growth and employment creation are best achieved by governments withdrawing from economic intervention policies, by dismantling the administrative arrangements for regulating the labour market and by adopting a policy of 'tough love' towards the business sector. The 'love' is for business as a creator of wealth and jobs. The 'toughness' is for business with regard to non-protection and support. According to one management guru, 'Governments, with few exceptions, now realize that protecting business enterprises creates bloated companies unable to compete in global markets' (Champy, 1996, p. 18). Not only was neoliberalism preached and practised in the UK, but the Mulroney government in Canada, the Kohl government in Germany and the Reagan administration in the USA also pursued the economic doctrine.

The New Right regarded the neoliberalist doctrine as the optimal way in which to organize a modern economy. This economic path includes, above all (Kuttner, 2000, pp. 149–50):

> The dismantling of barriers to free commerce and free flows of financial capital. To the extent that there is remnant regulatory role, it is to protect property, both tangible and intellectual; to assure open, non-discriminatory access; to allow any investor to purchase or sell any asset or repatriate any profit anywhere in the world; to remove and prevent subsidies and other distortions of the laissez-faire pricing system; to dismantle what remains of government-industry alliances.

In other words, the role of the state is to assist this laissez-faire agenda. It is much better, argues the New Right, to limit government economic power and allow a 'free' market to enhance both the economic well-being of the individual and his or her individual liberty. Proponents of the neoliberalist economic orthodoxy argue that the market and zero deficits will remove impediments to investment, thereby creating jobs. Furthermore, post-war welfare systems were depicted as a major source of non-wage costs and labour market rigidity (Standing, 1997). Another feature of neoliberalism is the dismantling of the public sector, with criticisms that the public sector 'crowds out' private investment and employment. Moreover, the ideology of supply-side economics provides the theoretical justification for reducing the role and size of government and the privatization of utilities.

The state and the employment relationship

In the UK, over the past 45 years, 30 key UK Acts of Parliament have helped to shape the legal relationship between employers and employees, as well as between employers and employees' collective organizations – the trade unions (Table 4.4). The Conservative government, led by Margaret Thatcher and her successor John Major, systematically eroded, using a 'step-by-step approach', both the rights of employees and the collective rights of trade unions. The principal aim was to promote private enterprise, individualism, greater flexibility in the labour market and managers' 'right to manage'. The individual employment legislation, or 'floor of rights', established in the 1970s was increasingly being viewed by the government as a constraint on enterprise and an obstacle to efficiency and job creation. The Employment Acts of 1980, 1982, 1988, 1989 and 1990, the Trade Union Act of 1984 and the Trade Union Reform and Employment Rights Act 1993 aimed on the one hand to undermine individual employment protection and support for union organization and collective bargaining. On the other hand, however, their purpose was to increase the legal regulation of industrial action and trade union government. This body of legislation, affecting both individual and collective rights, was part of the Conservative government's agenda to reform the context in order to allow national-level neoliberalism to operate.

Table 4.4 Key UK employment legislation, 1961–2005

Year	Act
1961	Factories Act (Safety)
1963/72	Contract of Employment Act
1965	Industrial Training Act
1968	Race Relations Act
1970	Equal Pay Act
1971	Industrial Relations Act
1973	Employment and Training Act
1974	Health and Safety at Work etc. Act
1974/76	Trade Union and Labour Relations Act
1975/86	Sex Discrimination Act
1975	Employment Protection Act
1978	Employment Protection (Consolidation) Act
1980	Employment Act
1982	Employment Act
1984	Trade Union Act
1986	Wages Act
1988	Employment Act
1989	Employment Act
1990	Employment Act
1992	Trade Union and Labour Relations (Consolidation) Act
1993	Trade Union Reform and Employment Rights Act
1996	Employment Rights Act
1996	Employment Tribunals Act
1998	Employment Rights (Disputes Resolution) Act
1998	National Minimum Wage Act
1999	Employment Relations Act
2002	Employment Act
2003	National Minimum Wage (Enforcement) Act
2004	Employment Relations Act
2005	Disability Discrimination Act

In terms of *individual employment rights,* amendments to the Employment Protection (Consolidation) Act 1978 reduced the provision for unfair dismissal. Extending the service qualification needed to make a claim for unfair dismissal from six months to two years reduced the number eligible to apply to the industrial tribunals. In the period 1987–88, there were only 34,233 applications to industrial tribunals compared with 41,244 in 1979 (McIlroy, 1991). A critical study of the law of unfair dismissal indicates that few applications for unfair dismissal were successful at an industrial tribunal, that those applicants who were successful were rarely offered reinstatement or re-engagement, and that the level of compensation was low (Denham, 1990). Denham argues that, in the 1980s, unfair dismissal law offered workers only a very limited degree of protection.

The purpose of the Employment Act 1989 was further to remove many regulatory restrictions, particularly for small businesses employing fewer than 20 employees. Section 15, for example, amended the 1978 Employment Protection (Consolidation) Act to increase from six months to two years the qualifying period of continuous employment after which employees were entitled to be given, on request, a written statement of the reasons for their dismissal. Protection for low-paid employees was further limited by Section 35 of the Trade Union Reform and Employment Rights Act 1993, which in effect abolished wages councils by the repeal of Part II of the Wages Act 1986. For those workers who are in good health, not pregnant and in a secure job, the changes in individual employment rights might seem to be of little consequence, but for those workers in the enlarged peripheral labour market, who are primarily female, curtailment of employment protection is not inconsequential and has adverse implications for employment security.

In terms of *collective employment rights*, the Conservative government's industrial relations legislation sought to regulate the activities of trade unions throughout their 18-year period of office. The process began by repealing provisions for the statutory recognition of unions and by narrowing the definition of a trade dispute in which industrial action is lawful. The phrase 'in contemplation or furtherance of a trade dispute' no longer fulfilled the same function as it did prior to the 1982 Employment Act and, as argued at the time, 'It now denies legitimacy to many disputes which are clearly about industrial relations issues' (Simpson, 1986, p. 192). The policy objective of the statutes was designed to deter strikes and limit their scale, as well as to regulate the unions' membership, discipline and recruitment policies. According to one industrial relations academic, the legislation marked 'a radical shift from the consensus underlying "public policy" on industrial relations during most of the past century' (Hyman, 1987, p. 93). According to the Secretary of State for Employment, the Employment Act 1988 sought to give 'new rights to trade union members', notably protection from 'unjustified' discipline on the part of union members and officials. The government justified the statute in the belief that, in recent years, some British trade unions had meted out harsh treatment to non-striking union members (Gennard et al., 1989). The purpose of the Employment Act 1988 was further to discourage industrial action and reduce the likelihood of 'militant' union leadership (McKendrick, 1988).

The Employment Act 1990 dealt with rights to union membership, the closed shop, unofficial industrial action, the dismissal of strikers and limits of secondary action. The 1990 Act gave those refused employment, on the grounds that they were not, or refused to become, a member of a union, the right to take the union to an industrial tribunal. Furthermore, the Act removed immunity from all forms of secondary industrial action. Thus, the complicated provisions of Section 17 of the Employment Act 1980, which made some form of secondary action lawful, were removed. The Trade Union Reform and Employment Rights Act 1993 had two main purposes: first, to further restrict trade union organization and activity, and second, to enact employment rights arising from EU directives and case law. Sections 1–7 of the 1993 Act related to internal union governance, such as the election of union officials. Sections 13–16 related to union membership, Section 13, for example, permitting employers to provide inducements to employees to opt out of collective bargaining or leave the union. These provisions were included following the decision of the Court of Appeal in two cases: *Wilson* v. *Associated Newspapers Ltd* (1993) and *Palmer* v. *Associated British Ports* (1993).

These changes in industrial relations law were used to tilt the balance of power in an industrial dispute towards the employer (Brown et al., 1997). By the middle of the 1990s, it was unlawful for industrial action to involve secondary action, secondary picketing, action in defence of the closed shop and action in support of union recognition by a third party. It was, however, lawful for an employer to dismiss on a selective basis individuals taking part in industrial action that the union had not authorised. In a scathing critique of the Conservative government's labour policies, Standing (1997, p. 14) argues that:

> nobody should be misled into thinking that the rolling back of protective and pro-collective regulations constitutes 'deregulation'. What supply-siders have promoted is pro-individualistic (anti-collective) regulations, coupled with some repressive regulations and greater use of promotional and fiscal regulations, intended to prevent people from making particular choices or to encourage, facilitate or promote other types of behaviour.

The Conservative government's employment legislation has not, however, gone unchallenged. In the context of a strategically weakened trade union movement, the EU emerged as a countervailing influence on matters affecting the employment relationship. In 1989, the EU **Social Charter** (Appendix A) adopted by all member states except the UK, introduced protection in such areas as improvements in the working environment to protect workers' health and safety, communications and employee involvement, and employment equity. The UK's rejection of the Maastricht Treaty was, insists Towers (1992), the product of opportunism and belief that the Social Charter provisions would impose higher labour costs, leading to bankruptcies and job losses.

During the 18 years of Conservative government, the influence of EU law (see Appendix A) increased steadily (Brown et al., 1997). Although not a comprehensive body of employment legislation, EU employment law does draw on the Western European tradition in which the rights of employees are laid down in constitutional texts and legal codes. Part II of the Trade Union Reform and Employment Rights Act 1993 enacts certain individual employment rights as a result of EU directives and case law. To comply with the European Union Pregnant Workers' Directive, for example, Sections 23–25 amended maternity rights. Sections 26–27 extended the right of employees to receive from their employer a written statement of principal employment details, and Section 28 protects employees against being victimized by their employer for taking specified industrial action related to health and safety.

HRM WEB LINKS

Go to the following websites to compare employment-related legislation in the UK (www.hmso.gov.uk/acts.htm and www.venables.co.uk), Canada (www.lmi-imt.hrdc.drhc.gc.ca and www.law-lib.utoronto.ca/) and South Africa (www.acts.co.za).

Intervention by New Labour

With the election of New Labour in 1997, UK employers have had to accept new labour law initiatives in the areas of rewards, the Social Charter and union representation, which have ramifications for HRM. Shortly after being elected, the Labour government announced that a minimum wage would be imposed in the UK. In 1997, the Labour government restored trade union rights to General Communication Headquarters workers, denied since 1984, and asked the Trades Union Congress and the Confederation of British Industries to explore areas of agreement on union recognition. The 1998 National Minimum Wage Act sets out the procedures for ensuring and enforcing a national minimum wage for all workers. The UK's self-exclusion from the Social Charter in the Maastricht Treaty limited the development of 'social dialogue' between employers and employee representatives at transnational level. In 1999, however, the notion of 'partnership' was developed in the Employment Relations Act (see Chapter 12).

In broad terms, the 1999 and 2004 Employment Relations Acts provide a number of measures to facilitate trade union recognition and organization, collective bargaining and protection to employees if they are dismissed for taking lawfully organized official industrial action. After a long period of 'legal deregulation', the UK government's employment legislation, along with EU directives on European Works Councils and Employee Information and Consultation, has the potential to shape employer approaches to systems of employee representation and employee 'voice' (Dundon et al., 2004). Notwithstanding these developments, and although key elements of human rights – the rights of disabled people, visible minorities and women – have been extended, particularly in Western societies, some writers argue that the rights of workers to bargain collectively in order to have a voice in the workplace have been diminishing during the past 50 years (Adams, 2006).

Finally, we should note in these new 'postindustrial' times a theme emphasized throughout this book – the apparent dissonance between the rhetoric of HRM and evidence of greater exclusion and job insecurity. For, as Kelly (2005, p. 62) argues, contrary to the spirit of 'cooperation' so central to the HRM agenda, 'employer disempowerment and coercion of employees continues to be a widespread feature of contemporary employment relations'. Arguably, if his view is correct, there is a strong case for believing that the trilateral regulation of employment relations is necessary to counter the hierarchical and power characteristic of the 'postindustrial' employment relationship.

HRM WEB LINKS

Go to the following website www.dti.gov.uk/er/employ/index.htm for more information on the 2004 Employment Relations Act.

Critics of New Labour argue that the government has simply continued the agenda of market discipline, deregulation and privatization, and, with more emphasis on performance management, detractors argue that the policies of New Labour have reinforced a process of work intensification observed in the early 1990s (Bach, 2002). Furthermore, it is alleged that New Labour has refused to challenge the hegemony of neoliberalism: 'New labour deals with globalisation as if it is a self-regulating, implacable Force of Nature, like the weather' (Hall, 1998, p. 11).

Others, however, take a more sanguine view. Hutton and Giddens (2000, p. 214) argue that the open global economy offers 'opportunity, creativity and wealth' and that, in the absence of viable alternatives, the role of democratic governments is to improve the current global economy: the so-called 'Third Way'. Partial critics of globalization, like Joseph Stiglitz (2002, p. 223), have argued that 'systems of global governance are essential'. The notion of a Third Way and the need to reinvent a global system of economic governance, one that eschews viewing civilization as a whole only through an economic prism (Saul, 2005), is arguably the most powerful discourse on economic management at this point in our history.

The social context

Changes in the proportion of the population participating in the labour market and changing demographics determine the size and composition of the workforce. In addition, people entering the workplace bring with them different attitudes and values relating to work, parenthood, leisure, notions of 'fairness' and organizational loyalty (HRM in Practice 4.7). It is these human elements which make up the social context of HRM.

HRM IN PRACTICE 4.7

IBM LABELS DIVERSITY A 'STRATEGIC IMPERATIVE'
Hiring women, gays and minorities is about more than doing the right thing
VIRGINIA GALT, *GLOBE AND MAIL*, 24 JUNE 2002, P. B3

Fishing is more fun, says IBM's 'dean of diversity,' but golf is the game of business – which is why, he explains, Big Blue has installed putting greens at some of its on-site day-care centers. Little girls should learn to play golf so they will not grow up to be 'competitively disadvantaged,' Ted Childs, global vice president of work force diversity at International Business Machines Corp., said during a recent visit to the company's Canadian headquarters.

Their mothers are getting golf lessons, too, as IBM drives its diversity initiative in a range of new directions as part of a sweeping corporate strategy aimed at increasing IBM's appeal in the marketplace. Right down to the games children play at the day-care centers, Mr. Childs is presiding over a cultural evolution at IBM – a company that was very white, very male, and very strait-laced when he joined as an affirmative-action hire in the USA 35 years ago.

IBM should be a place where people feel comfortable being openly gay ...

IBM should be a place where people feel comfortable being openly gay and where women and people from minority group backgrounds have equal opportunity for promotion and advancement, said Mr. Childs, who is black. And anyone who has a problem with that need not apply to IBM, he added.

This is driven as much by market realities as it is by a desire to do the right thing, Mr. Childs said in an interview between meetings. IBM's effort to diversify the work force 'has moved from being a moral imperative to being a strategic imperative.'

IBM does business in 164 countries, it has operations in 73 countries and even in its home base of the USA there are now more than 83 million people from visible minority backgrounds. 'This is a larger group than the individual country populations of Canada, Spain, France, Argentina, the United Kingdom, Italy, Egypt, South Africa ... Do we want to do business with those countries? The answer is yes. Do we want to do business with those 83 million? The answer is yes. We're going to see more companies owned by women or by ethnic minorities. If we get to them in their infancy and grow with them, that's how we'll grow. It's about opportunity, the opportunity for IBM to compete.'

Demographic changes provide a starting point for analysing the social context. During the past three decades, the general pattern that has emerged is one of an ageing population as life expectancy for older people has risen at an unprecedented rate. At the same time, those older people have been starting their retirement earlier, some as early as 50 years old (Figure 4.5). Since 1951, the number of Britons of pensionable age has risen by over 40 per cent, from 5.5 million to over 9 million in 2000, or from just under 14 per cent to approximately 18 per cent of the population. The phrase 'ageing population' is, however, often misunderstood. It does not mean that senior citizens are about to become the dominant group in society: demographic data show that the real era of 'grey power' will be in 2018.

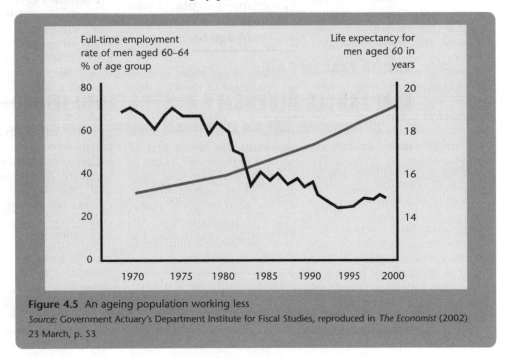

Figure 4.5 An ageing population working less
Source: Government Actuary's Department Institute for Fiscal Studies, reproduced in *The Economist* (2002) 23 March, p. 53

Demographic projections are based on the most basic demographic fact: every year each person gets a year older. Analysing human behaviour according to age offers insights into socioeconomic variables. A 30-year-old, for example, is more likely to be married than a 20-year-old. A 55-year-old probably views work differently from a 25-year-old. The ability to forecast behaviour according to age has the advantage of allowing organizations to know more about the composition of the workforce and their needs. A 55-year-old employee with a teenage family is less likely to be interested in childcare provision than a 25-year-old worker. Demographic data are an important source of information that can help managers in such areas as recruitment and selection, training and rewards management (HRM in Practice 4.8).[6]

HRM IN PRACTICE 4.8

MANDATORY RETIREMENT ATTACKED

RICHARD MACKIE, *GLOBE AND MAIL*, 14 JUNE 2002, P. A11

Governments should ban mandatory retirement at age 65 because it discriminates against people who are capable of working and who often need the money, Ontario Human Rights Commissioner Keith Norton said yesterday.

'Mandatory retirement, where age is used to determine the person's employment status, [is] unacceptable from a human-rights perspective,' Mr. Norton told a Queen's Park news conference. He predicted that governments would come under increasing political pressure to protect those who want to continue working after 65 as the number of older people in the population increases.

Demographic predictions indicate that by 2030, about one in four Canadians will be over age 65. This means 14 million people will be over the mandatory retirement age, from 3.7 million now. Of the 3.7 million, only about 6 per cent continued to work after 65, according to figures for 1996 compiled by Statistics Canada. 'As a political force, those older Ontarians are increasing in their political clout, and a political party that ignores that fact does so at their political peril,' Mr. Norton said.

Governments should ban mandatory retirement at age 65 ...

Lillian Morgenthau, founder and president of the Canadian Association of Retired Persons, which has 400,000 members across Canada, endorsed his arguments. She noted that 35 per cent of those over 65 live in poverty, and stressed that people often need to work to pay for food, housing, health care and transportation. Ms. Morgenthau's organization has 230,000 members in Ontario alone.

The calls for an end to mandatory retirement were made as Ontario's Human Rights Commission announced a policy to counter discrimination against older people. Mr. Norton said that while human rights usually relate to protecting people from discrimination on the basis of race, religion, sex, sexual orientation or physical disability, increasingly there are problems with discrimination on the basis of age.

'Age discrimination does not invoke the same sense of moral outrage as other forms of discriminations, even though it can be as harmful in terms of its social, economic and psychological consequences as other forms of discrimination,' he said. The Supreme Court of Canada has accepted the discrimination implicit in mandatory retirement.

REFLECTIVE QUESTION

Is mandatory retirement an abuse of human rights or just 'common sense'?

Changes in the labour force – the number of people in the civilian working population – derive not only from changes in the size and age distribution of the population, but also from the variations in labour force participation rates. The participation rate represents the labour force expressed as a percentage of the working age population that actually participates in the labour force. In the 'old', 12 member state EU, the participation rate for all adults fell from 67.5 per cent to 65.7 per cent from 1973 to 1993 (Standing, 1997). In contrast, the participation rate among women increased from around 45 per cent to 56 per cent over this period (Cully et al., 1999; Millward et al., 2000; Kersley et al., 2005).

HRM WEB LINKS

Go to the following websites for more information on demographic changes and participation rates in Britain (www.statistics.gov.uk), Canada (www.statcan.ca/start.html and
the Canadian Labour Force Development Board at www.reformmonitor.org), the EU
(www.eurofound.eu.int/ewco), the USA (www.bls.gov and www.workindex.com/),
South Africa (www.statssa.gov.za) and Australia (www.aifs.gov.au/institute/info/trends).
The Institute for Life Course and Aging at the University of Toronto conducts research
on ageing (www.utoronto.ca/lifecourse/research).

The dynamics of culture

Whether people seek employment and how they respond to HR practices, designed
to elicit both the control and the consent of employees, will depend on cultural
values. **Culture** is a concept we explored in international HRM (see Chapter 3).
Parker et al. (2003) remind us that, in everyday language , the word 'culture' is
loaded with evaluative connotations related to social class and status. In this sense,
culture is associated with the arts, refinement and privileged education. Anthropol-
ogists and sociologists emphasize that culture, as a concept to explain social behaviour, has a 'collectivizing effect' and creates differences between populations. A
'culture' is a collective product, consisting of processes and artefacts, produced over
long periods of time by large numbers of individuals, which enable the *past* to be
carried into the *present* and the *future* (Parker et al., 2003). Guirdham (2005) explains
that 'culture' represents an imperfectly shared system of interrelated understandings, shaped by beliefs, customs, values, communications and identities. An understanding of culture shows us that social behaviour in the present is shaped by the
past. Culture also constrains and enables *social action*, and it conditions *social structure* or relatively stable patterns of social behaviour (Figure 4.6). Cultural values
pervade all areas of human life and have a strong influence on the management of
people in different societies.

Europe and North America are culturally diverse. Within their borders lie many
cultures and subcultures formed from divisions such as social class, ethnicity and
gender, these cultures and subcultures in turn all being locally differentiated.

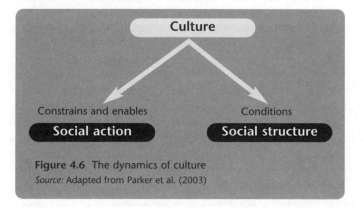

Figure 4.6 The dynamics of culture
Source: Adapted from Parker et al. (2003)

Changing cultural values have an impact on HRM activities. Changes in traditional gender roles and new lifestyles, for example, change participation rates in the labour market and the way in which workers are motivated and managed in the workplace. Whereas affluent working women have difficulty balancing work and home, poorer women on the minimum wage have the most difficult balancing act to perform.

An influential US study draws attention to the issue of balancing paid work and unpaid household work (Hochschild, 1983, 2000, 2003). As the majority of women entered the US workforce, Hochschild documented the effects in dual-career households. In 1975, 47 per cent of all mothers with children under the age of 18 were in paid employment, whereas in 2000 the rate had increased to 73 per cent (Hochschild, 2003). But although American women changed to the new labour market environment, the jobs they went out to and the men they came home to did not change, at least not significantly, argues Hochschild. Furthermore, the issue of 'family-friendly' policies continued to be absent from the national and US corporate agenda. The study reported that women in paid work were still responsible for the majority of housework and childcare even though they also were employed outside the home, hence women worked a 'double shift'. "'Marriage", writes Hochschild (2003, p. xxi), 'has become a shock absorber of tensions borne by this "stalled revolution"'. Platt's (1997) study showed that professional men and women both spend about the same number of hours – about 50 – at work each week, but professional women spend an average of 33 hours a week on housework or childcare, compared with about 19 hours for men. On average, therefore, professional women have about two hours a day less leisure time than men.

In Europe, the data show a similar trend in the employment status of couple families with young children. Over the past two decades, the 'male breadwinner' model has become less the norm, as can be seen from the trends showing the average share of couple families with a child under 6 (or under 15) years containing a sole male full-time earner has fallen from more than 50 per cent in 1985 to only around one-third in 2002. Furthermore, the average share of dual-earner families composed of two full-timers or a full-timer and a part-timer increased steadily from 23 per cent and 14 per cent respectively in 1985 to 32 per cent and 23 per cent in 2002 (Table 4.5). The WERS 2004 survey also found that 11 per cent of employees usually worked more than 48 hours a week, with a greater frequency of this in the private sector and in workplaces without trade union representative (Kersley et al., 2006). This dual-role syndrome can have detrimental consequences for women's health, psychological well-being and family life (Burchell et al., 1999; Felstead et al., 2002; see also Chapter 13).

Table 4.5 Work situation of couple families with a child aged under seven years, 1985–2002

Work status	1985	1990	1995	2002
Two full-timers	23	26	28	32
One full-timer and one part-timer	14	18	19	23
One full-timer with partner not employed	53	48	42	35

Source: Adapted from OECD (2004) p. 45

The notion of a **work–life balance** for employees – the need to balance work and leisure/family activities – is a 'hot' area of HRM research that is receiving increasing attention from policy-makers and managers (Purcell, 2004; Sturges and Guest, 2004). Research on employer work–life balance strategies can have important benefits for organizations (Figure 4.7). Evidence suggests that, in the face of a highly competitive labour market, work–life policies and practices are necessary for attracting, retaining and motivating highly skilled knowledge workers (Scholarios and Marks, 2004). Work–life boundary and work–life balance strategies are closely related to the commitment that knowledge workers 'give' to their employer and are, in addition, necessary for creative and innovative behaviours and organizational cultures (De Cieri et al., 2005).

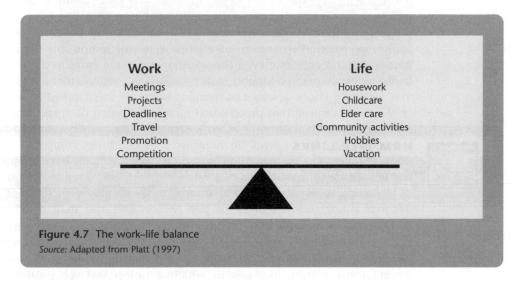

Figure 4.7 The work–life balance
Source: Adapted from Platt (1997)

The EU Social Charter of 1961 obligated member states to ensure 'reasonable daily and weekly working hours' and a progressive reduction in the length of the working week, while the EU directive declares that 'every worker has a right to limitation of maximum working hours'. For the EU-25 as a whole, the statutory maximum working week stood at 48 hours and the average, collectively agreed, normal working week at 38.6 hours in 2005. In the new EU-25, men's average, normal full-time working hours are longer than women's. The average gender differential is 2.1 hours per week (or around 5 per cent). Research indicates that British workers work the longest hours in the EU-15 member states and are unaware of the EU directive setting a 48-hour working week.[7] Not surprisingly, therefore, the UK labour market has been characterized as the 'long hours culture' (Bonney, 2005). Setting a limit on the number of hours an employee must work in a working day and week most directly affects the work–life balance and employee well-being, for example work-related stress (see Chapter 13). One key question related to working time and well-being is whether long working hours or precarious employment make it more difficult to reconcile paid work with family or social commitments. Table 4.6 provides some evidence of employer commitment to work–life balance in 2004.

Table 4.6 Flexible-working and leave arrangements for
non-managerial employees, 1998–2004

	% of workplaces	
	1998	2004
Flexible working arrangements		
Change from full-time to part-time hours	46	64
Job-sharing	31	41
Flexitime	19	26
Homeworking	16	28
Leave arrangements		
Paid paternity leave	48	92
Parental leave	38	73

Source: Data from WERS (2004) and Kersley (2006)

HRM WEB LINKS

Go to the www.eiro.eurofound.eu.int/2005 for more information on the EU Working
Time Developments 2000–4.

The survey data show that the proportion of workplaces providing flexible working
arrangement practices has increased since the 1998 WERS survey. These working time
and leave practices were most likely to be operating in the public sector, in larger
workplaces and in workplaces in which a union was recognized for collective
bargaining purposes (Kersley et al., 2006).

The concept of work–life balance is inherent to Western capitalist economies
because paid work is constituted as a realm separate from that of non-paid domestic
work. Felstead et al. (2002, p. 56) define the work–life balance as 'the relationship
between the institutional and cultural times and spaces of work and non-work in societies where income is predominantly generated and distributed through labour
markets'. Although it is suggested that the work–life balance is particularly relevant to
women in the workforce, men are also increasingly concerned with this. Given,
however, the evidence of growing employment insecurity for many low-paid workers
and the lack of provision for childcare in the UK and North America, the probability
of achieving the goal of a work–life balance seems remote for millions of people.

Change and human resource management

Analysing the context is important because, in various ways, conditions external to
the organization present particular opportunities and constraints related to the
management of work processes and people. Looking back, we can see how the context
and consequently the nature of employment relations in the UK have undergone
major alterations. In the 1960s, changing public policies covering labour markets,

productivity and employment law extended the HRM function (Sisson, 1989). Different HR strategies and practices arose as the result of changes in the political economy. Between 1979 and 1997, the context of British HRM was profoundly influenced by the ideology of neoliberalism: four consecutive Conservative governments dedicated to bolstering employers' 'right to manage', and the emergence of the EU as a political force on the employment front (Millward et al., 1992, 2000).

In recent years, HRM has once again been reshaped by the new political realities caused, it is argued, by a worldwide shift to the left of the global political centre. According to political scientist Daniel Drache, the political centre is moving left with a corresponding change in values and policies. Drache divides political parties into 'market' parties – those which devote their major pledges to cutting taxes and regulations – and 'public' parties – those which mostly promise to increase social spending and rein in business. He argues that, since 1996, in 22 elections in 11 developed countries, the 'market' parties attracted more votes than the 'public' political parties in only three of those elections: Brazil in 1998, Spain in 2000 and the USA in 2004 (Saunders, 2006).

Over the past two decades or so, most work organizations, albeit not precisely at the same time or to the same degree, have faced the effects of free global trade, deregulation of the markets, privatization and, simultaneously, the need to improve productivity, quality and cost efficiencies. The implications of globalization, international and national neoliberalist economic policies, new technology, different political doctrines and social changes are readily apparent. As we discussed in Chapters 2 and 3, depending on which strategic option is chosen – for example cost minimization or 'differentiation' – global economic forces and national institutional regimes will ultimately determine the HR strategy taken by management and the subsequent HRM outcomes (see Figures 2.3, 3.2 and 4.2). High levels of unemployment and structural changes shift the balance of power in individual or collective contract negotiations towards the employer: employees and union representatives become more tractable in order to preserve jobs, and managers find that they are more able to introduce unilateral changes in working practices. In other words, different HR strategies aim to mesh strategic needs with operational requirements (Williams, 1993). More directly, global companies relocating to different parts of Europe and Asia bring to the host country their own management philosophy and practices, the result of which is not only a greater diversity of HR practices, but also pressure on indigenous management to adopt similar best practices (Blyton and Turnbull, 1998).

The changes imposed by globalization have led some writers to take a more pessimistic view. Globalization will potentially cause firms to become 'disembedded' from the society in which they operate and force a *downward* harmonization of employment, health and safety, and environmental standards (Hutton, 1996). Underpinning the analysis of the UK labour market, for example, is the notion that the traditional employment contracts are anachronistic and no longer appropriate for competing in the new economic order. According to Champy (1996), a business process re-engineering guru, the 'new' business model is 'customer-driven' and flexible, and requires a different approach to managing labour. Thus, the neoliberalist economic model extols the flexibility and lack of regulations in the Asian labour markets (see also Wong, 2001). Critics of neoliberalism persuasively argue that the 'contract culture' has induced fear about job insecurity as firms downsize or threaten to relocate to low-wage developing countries (Hutton, 1996, 1997). Moreover, the neoliberalist doctrine is based upon fear and avarice: 'There needs to be fear and greed in the system in order to make it tick' (Hutton, 1996, p. 173), the former to encourage flexibility and the latter to stimulate private enterprise and risk-taking. In the early 1980s, one union leader summed up the effect of high unemployment when he declared 'we've got 3 million on the dole, and another 23 million scared to death' (Bratton, 1992, p. 70). Furthermore, 'unfettered' markets have caused 'inequalities and insecurities' in global labour markets (Faux and Mishel, 2000), and, simultaneously, existing collective trade union rights have been eroded, particularly in the USA, Britain and New Zealand (Standing, 1997).

One of the problems of current shareholder value-driven capitalist globalization is its inherent drive for profit, fostering a 'race to the bottom' in which employment standards tend towards worst rather than best practice. Although in the summer of 2005, popular majorities voted against the ratification of the EU draft constitutional treaty in France and the Netherlands and, increasingly, it would appear, Europeans are demonstrating a reluctance to accept common rules and protect common interests (Jones, 2005), the case for the European regulation of employment standards and corporate governance through EU institutions is powerful.

Increased global competition and a reliance on 'fear' and contingency workers form a paradox. In general, part-time or contingency workers receive less training and pay, and have a low attachment to the organization. Thus, globalization itself may be the best reason for investing in people and giving all workers greater protection (Sukert, 2000). The dialectic of flexibility and cooperation, yet conflict, between employers and workers is key to understanding the renaissance of interest in the 'human' element in production. Interest and support for the new HRM paradigm represent a conviction that HRM has a strategic role to play in gaining competitive advantage, and concomitantly that HRM innovations have an important role to play in creating an organizational culture that builds trust, flexibility, cooperation and a commitment to organizational goals. In the long term, HRM practices and the relative standing of HRM professions in organizations generally are strongly influenced by the prevailing economic and legal contexts that shape employment relationships.

The ramifications of new communication technologies for HRM are also apparent. Microtechnology potentially allows multinational corporations to operate in real time or in chosen time. Increasingly, multinational companies can readily transfer all or parts of their production to wherever the mix of materials, infrastructure, skilled workers, labour costs and regulatory requirements offers the greatest potential to maximize return on investment. Thus, large business organizations are able to supply their operations with components from around the plant, 'in an endlessly variable geometry of value searching. This implies bypassing economically valueless or devalued territories and people' (Castells, 2000, p. 53).

From an HRM perspective, major technological development involves changes in the way in which work is organized and workers are motivated and governed. These changes can take many forms, including flattened hierarchies, decentralized decision-making and flexible work teams. The recipients of these changes will in turn undergo almost constant 'skill disruption' as they switch from one obsolete skill set to enter another, new set (Wallace, 1989). The workplace in the 'new economy' would, therefore, logically give workplace learning a high priority. This transformation presents opportunities for cooperation between managers and workers (and their unions), but such change also has the potential to exacerbate conflict between the parties. Where HRM professionals have played a prominent role in workplace technological change, their inclusion has had a positive impact: 'their involvement was associated with a stronger level of workers' support for the change' (Daniel and Millward, 1993, p. 69). The rationale for different HR strategies can be explained by the labour exigencies of a particular international business strategy.

Taking the globalization of markets and competition together, what are the implications of these economic and technological changes for the recipients of HRM? Using the language of economists, it depends upon whether the recipient is a 'core' or a 'peripheral' employee. As Legge (1998, p. 20) argues: 'if you are a core knowledge worker with skills which are scarce and highly in demand, life may be good – empowerment, high rewards and some element of job security ... For the bulk of the workforce, though, things are not so rosy.' Williams (1993) estimates that, in America, only approximately 20 per cent of the national population is engaged in creation of 'new value-added production'; for the other 80 per cent, employment insecurity will therefore be a permanent feature of work.

Chapter summary

- We have attempted to cover a wide range of complex issues in this chapter. In essence, we have emphasized that the key to understanding managerial behaviour, such as HRM, lies within its context. The external domain influences the structure and functioning of a work organization, and organization decision-makers in turn influence wider society. Guest (1987) argues that interest in HRM in Britain and North America arose as a result of the search for competitive advantage, the decline in trade union power, and changes in the workforce and the nature of work.

- We have emphasized that, in order to understand structural changes in the nature of labour markets, it is important to understand the global forces that have acted upon them and which UK capitalism has itself helped to shape. The global economy has become more integrated. We have also noted three major economic processes that have altered the nature of labour markets: restructuring of the UK economy, the polarization of the labour market and the globalization of business. Although many of our empirical data relate to the UK, the arguments presented here can be applied to all mature postindustrial capitalist societies. For managers, the continuing restructuring of the labour market is having a profound effect on competition and thereby on such HR activities such as HR planning, selection and development.

- Empirical studies show that non-standard employment practices are associated with insecurity, low skills and low employee commitment. In addition, women are overrepresented in the growing peripheral workforce, which has the effect of intensifying insecurity in employment (Charles and James, 2003; Felstead and Gallie, 2004). Studies also suggest that the functional flexibility and non-standard employment contracts discussed in this chapter are 'tactical rather than strategic', primarily designed to minimize labour costs or labour shortfalls, and may actually undermine conditions for long-term competitive goals, a workplace culture of creativity and innovation (Storey et al., 2002).

- New technology and processes such as 'lean' production methods and business process re-engineering impact in complex ways on people and their work, as well as on the HRM function. The Fombrun, Tichy and Devanna HRM model (see Figure 1.4) illustrates the link between external contexts and the search for competitive advantage through employee performance and HRM activities.

● As far as employment law is concerned, the Labour government's support for the EU Social Charter (Appendix A) is beginning to encourage senior management to have more regard for HRM. The UK Employment Act, which received Royal Assent in July 2002, supports the Labour government's commitment to improving organizational performance through 'fairness and partnership' at work. Furthermore, European studies show that HRM is not intrinsically anti-union (Brewster et al., 2000). In addition to legislation on union–management relations, age discrimination is going to be banned from 2006 under a EU directive (*The Economist*, 2002).

● The general indication is that the changing social context of HRM will continue to place more pressure on employers to pay more attention to the issues associated with a diverse workforce – in particular to be more sensitive to the issues and challenges related to an ageing workforce, ethnic minorities, the disabled and work–life balance. Evidence also suggests that, when faced with a highly competitive labour market, work–life policies and practices are needed to attract and retain managerial and knowledge workers and for innovative organizational cultures (De Cieri et al., 2005).

Key concepts

● **Culture**

● **Social Charter**

● **Globalization**

● **Labour markets**

● **Internal labour markets**

● **Deindustrialization**

● **Work–life balance**

● **Precarious employment**

● **Political context**

Chapter review questions

1. How does the notion of an 'open-system' organization help our understanding of the HRM function?

2. Describe the major economic challenges facing HR managers.

3. How have political developments since 1997 affected HRM?

4. How will the 1994 European Works Council Directive affect managers and HRM?

5. What are some of the likely consequences for HRM of an 'ageing' population?

6. How realistic is it to expect employees to achieve the goal of a work–life balance?

Further reading

Aart Scholte, J. (2005) *Globalization: A Critical Introduction*. Basingstoke: Palgrave Macmillan.

Adams, R. (2006) *Labour Left Out*. Ottawa: CCPA.

Chomsky, N. (1999) *Profit over People*. New York: Seven Stories Press.

Hertz, N. (2002) *The Silent Takeover: Global Capitalism and the Death of Democracy*. London: Arrow.

Hoogvelt, A. (2001) *Globalization and the Postcolonial World* (2nd edn). Basingstoke: Palgrave Macmillan.

Hutton, W. and Giddens, A. (2000) *On the Edge: Living with Global Capitalism*. London: Jonathan Cape.

Kersley, B., Alpin, C., Forth, J., Bryson, A., Bewley, H. Dix, G. and Oxenbridge, S. (2006) *Inside the Workplace: Findings from the 2004 Workplace Employment Relations Survey*. London: Routledge.

Saul, J. R. (2005) *The Collapse of Globalism*. Toronto: Viking.

Practising human resource management

Searching the web

On an individual basis, or working in a small group, visit each of the websites listed in the chapter. In addition, there are a number of online business periodicals available that can provide information on the external context of business. Some examples include *Financial Post* (www.nationalpost.com), *Fortune* (www.fortune.com), *Business Week* (www.businessweek.com) and *The Economist* (www.economist.com).

Describe the current external challenges that are forcing work organizations to change the way in which people are managed in the workplace. Bring this information to class, and present your findings and recommendation in an oral report. Discuss any challenges the groups hold in common. Are any of the challenges unique to your country?

HRM group project

Form a group of three or four students. The purpose of this group assignment is to allow you to apply your knowledge of context to a business organization and to consider the implications for HRM. Specifically, students will: (1) carry out research into secondary and primary sources related to the contextual elements discussed in the chapter, (2) apply key principles and theories to a case, and (3) demonstrate academic writing skills. Group members should take responsibility for researching the various aspects of the assignment.

Select an organization of your choice and familiarize yourself with the company's current products, services and global operations. Using one of the popular search engines, such as Yahoo! or Excite, search the web for other timely information about the company. After you have completed your search, make a list of the issues affecting the organization in its external environment. Organize your list into the different contextual elements of one of the HRM models presented in Chapter 1. How would you characterize the nature of the external environment facing the organization (e.g. stable or unstable, certain or uncertain)? A team member(s) should interview at least one manager in an organization in the same sector as your case study.

Based upon your research, the interviewer(s) should probe the nature of the organization's external environment: How do external factors – economic, political or demographic – affect the organization? How do these external factors impact on organizational strategy? How do they affect the HR strategy? Write your findings up in the form of a report.

Chapter case study

OIL TOOL INCORPORATED PLC

Oil Tool Engineering plc was established in West Yorkshire in 1950 and four years later became part of Oil Tool International, an American multinational company engaged in the design, manufacture and marketing of machinery used at the wellhead when drilling for oil and gas, both onshore and offshore. The company, whose corporate headquarters are in Houston, Texas, USA, has other manufacturing establishments in Scotland, Germany, France and Mexico, and employs 4500 people throughout the world.

Oil Tool Incorporated dominated the oil extraction industry for nearly 40 years. After a long period of growth and continual profits, things started to go wrong in 1995. Low productivity, rising production costs, a decline in oilfield exploration and new competitors entering the industry culminated in a £76 million loss for the West Yorkshire plant. At this point, the senior management decided to bring in an outside consultancy firm, Mercury Engineers Inc.

Bill Dorfman, the plant manager, called a meeting with his senior management team and the consultants. Dorfman started the discussion: 'We all know that we have considerable autonomy from the corporate management in Texas. That means we have the task of turning this plant around. If we fail, the plant will close. This is the company's biggest manufacturing operation in the world. But it would only be a question of months before another operation could be bigger. Headquarters have mothballed several of our operations, and the French and German plants could be 'geared up' to our size within 12 months. What has gone wrong, and how do we turn this plant around?'

Yvonne Turner, the marketing manager, began, 'Our sales have fallen in the Middle East because our customers want equipment that is lighter and more mobile. The design and the materials of our block-tree valve haven't changed for 10 years.' She went on, 'The Japanese are engineering equipment that is made with alloy metals and is lighter, stronger and has a microprocessor-based control system.'

Doug Meyer, the manufacturing manager, then jumped in: 'Don't blame us. If the market is changing out there, it's marketing's job to tell us and keep us informed. It's not just our manufacturing practices; we all know our prices are higher because of sterling's high exchange rate. And besides,' he said angrily, 'we lost that last Middle East order because the government refused to give us an export license. Whether there is a war or not, if we don't sell them the machinery, you can be damn sure somebody else will. We ought to get the local MP to have a word with the bureaucrats in the Board of Trade.'

At this point, Wendy Seely, the HR manager, intervened in the discussion, 'Well, I don't know whether we can blame everything on the tension in the Middle East or government in London. I do know, however, that EU directives on pay equity and court decisions on retirement and pensions will push our labour costs up. We must find ways to reduce labour costs and improve quality standards,' she said.

We can't achieve high-quality standards,' retorted Doug Miller, 'because your department stopped training apprentices and we can't find the quality we need using subcontractors.' Feeling defensive, Wendy Seely argued, 'We ended the training programme for apprentices because the local college closed the first-year apprentice course as part of its own cost-saving measures. You can't blame my department for that.'

Bill Dorfman decided to bring the meeting to a close. 'Would each department address the issues discussed this morning? We shall meet in seven days and see whether there is a consensus on the way forward. Remember that we have to be competitive to survive. We have to quit whining and save this plant,' he said.

Source: Adapted from The drilling machine company: Japanization in small-batch production in J. Bratton (1992), Japanization at Work. Basingstoke: Macmillan – now Palgrave Macmillan.

Assignment

Assume that you are a member of the consultancy team. Prepare a report outlining the contextual changes affecting Oil Tool Engineering.

1. What factors from the chapter can help to explain what happened to this company?

2. What information does this case give companies about the importance of scanning the external environment?

3. How can HRM help to solve some of the problems?

HR-related skill development

Most organizations face external contexts that are complex, dynamic and increasingly global. This makes the context increasingly difficult to interpret. To cope with often incomplete and ambiguous contextual data, and to increase their understanding of the general external context, organizations engage in a process called 'external environmental analysis'. All managers, including HR managers, need to be aware of the importance of scanning the external context in a systematic way. You can develop this management skill by going to our website (www.palgrave.com/business/brattonandgold4) and clicking on 'External environmental analysis exercise'.

Notes

1. Alan Greenspan, US Federal Reserve board chairman, reporting to the US Senate Banking Committee, 2002, July 16, and quoted in the *Globe and Mail* (2002, July 17), p. B1.
2. Will Hutton and Antony Giddens (2000) *On the Edge*. London: Jonathan Cape, p. vii.
3. John Ralston Saul (2005) *The Collapse of Globalism*. Toronto: Viking, p. 13.
4. Leslie Sklair (2002) *Globalization: Capitalism and its Alternatives*. Oxford: Oxford University Press, p. 15.
5. *Globe and Mail* (2002) Will Bush bring big business to account? (July 9), p. A12.
6. For a more in-depth examination of how demographics impacts on business and society, see David Foot and Daniel Stoffman (1996) *Boom, Bust and Echo*. Toronto: Macfarlane Walter and Ross.
7. European Trade Union Confederation Factsheet: *Working Time Directive*. www.etuc.org/a/504.

Chapter five

Restructuring work and organizations

John Bratton

Work refers to physical and mental activity that is carried out at a particular place and time, according to instructions, in return for a wage or salary. Differing forms of work organization generate and reflect tension, contradiction and change.

'Mary Newell has worked at the Royal Bank of Canada for 25 years but only recently carved out a niche for herself that meets her own needs, as well as the bank's. Since April 1999, she has worked full time from home, selling credit-card services and debit machines to small and medium-sized businesses.'[1]

'The summer jobs in retail or the service sector – jobs that provide students with little more than pocket change – are no longer a stepping-stone along the career path to the "dream job" in McWorld. They are quickly becoming dead-end careers.'[2]

Chapter outline

Chapter objectives

After studying this chapter, you should be able to:

1. Explain the meaning of the term 'work'

2. Define job design and describe specific job design strategies

3. Understand the theoretical arguments underpinning current organizational and work design practices

4. Explain how the nature of work and different organizational designs affect human resource management activities

Introduction

The study of the design of work and organizations is inseparable from the study of human resource management (HRM). In addition, the way in which managers organize work is a critical internal contingency affecting human resources (HR) activities (see Figure 1.3). A good example of this is the way in which teamworking affects the recruitment and selection criteria for new employees, the workplace learning and training that people need for multitasking, and the design of reward systems. Much organizational theory is closely linked to management behaviour. For example, organizational culture theory informs managers that teamworking has a positive effect on employee attitudes, satisfaction and commitment. Alternatively, team performance theory predicts that favourable teamworking characteristics can enhance an employee's creativity and contribute to workplace innovation (Shalley et al., 2004). Organizational theory is, believes Grey (2005), an agenda that incorporates and validates many assumptions about contemporary organizations and management, as well as about people and how the world of paid employment is organized. Taking HRM to a broader level – by examining the way in which organizations are structured and understanding the links between job design, technology and HR practices – helps to locate HRM in a strategic context (Boxall and Purcell, 2003).

The study of organizational forms has a long history. In the 18th century, the traditional work rhythms and practices of preindustrial society gave way to the division of labour and the discipline of the factory system of work organization. At the turn of the 20th century, the essence of the scientific management movement was the opportunity it afforded for increasing the control over and coordination of workers' effort. In the 1960s, concern about declining productivity, increasing industrial disputes and worker dissatisfaction led to new work structures that emphasized worker autonomy and participation, as well as a variety of functional tasks through 'job enrichment'. Technological change and the processes of globalization produced 'new' systems of work organization in the 1990s. The managerial mantra of the 1990s was flexibility, and studies of organizational innovations such as flexible specialization, cellular production, lean production, team-based horizontal work structures, re-engineering and virtual organizations are now well established in the literature. Much of the rationale for new job designs and work structures was initially developed in the context of the USA and then generalized across North America and European economies. Hammer and Champy (1993), for example, inform us that 're-engineering' is necessary because the world is a different place. To respond more rapidly to global changes, to make organizations compete more aggressively in global markets and to have a workforce that is more flexible and attuned to the needs of customers, senior managers have to fundamentally restructure business processes.

The discourse on 'post-bureaucratic' work organizations – those using a system of work designed to invert bureaucratic principles by adopting decentralized decision-making, fewer managerial levels and flexible work practices – has emphasized competing claims over whether new forms of work organization lead to an 'enrichment of work' or the 'degradation of work'. On the one hand, optimists argue that new work structures 'empower' employees and celebrate the fact that managerial behaviour has shifted from the 'management of control' to the 'management of commitment' (Walton, 1985). On the other hand, detractors argue that some new work arrangements constitute 'electronic sweatshops' (Sewell, 1998) and that employee-empowering work regimes are basically 'a euphemism for work intensification' (Hyman and Mason, 1995). To capture the new realities of the modern workplace, critics often use the term 'McWork', meaning that a vast amount of work experience, especially for young people, women and workers of colour, involves menial tasks, part-time contracts, the close monitoring of performance and entrenched job insecurity.

Some empirically based literature also offers a context-sensitive understanding of the processes of work reconfiguration (Bratton, 1992; Edwards et al., 2001; Geary and Dobbins, 2001). The 'context-sensitive' view makes the point that new work structures do not have a uniform outcome but are likely to be contingent on a number of variables, such as business strategy, union involvement in the change process and the extent to which 'bundles' of HR practices support the new work regime. Geary and Dobbins (2001), for example, argue persuasively that the introduction of work teams brought with it 'a mix of benefits and costs'. In sum, the identification of potential benefits and costs for employees as a result of organizational innovations provides a more complex picture, one that strongly supports the hypothesis that changes in the organization of work can strengthen or threaten the 'psychological contract' (Emmott and Hutchinson, 1998).

In this chapter, we explain job design strategies and emerging organizational forms, as seen by sociologists and industrial psychologists researching the links between motivation, job satisfaction and work design. We examine the meaning of work in contemporary Western society. The broader context of work should be seen as providing essential background knowledge for managers and HR practitioners concerned with current job design techniques and emerging organizational paradigms. We critically evaluate alternative job design strategies, including post-Fordism, self-managed work designs and re-engineering, and examine the implications of different work structures for managing the employment relationship.

REFLECTIVE QUESTION

Look at the quotes on the nature of work at the beginning of this chapter. What is your own experience of work? Have you or your friends had jobs in which you were expected to 'check your brains at the door'? Have you experienced work in a team? How do you feel about working at home? What are the implications of new ways of working for (1) young people, women and workers of colour, and (2) HRM?

The nature of work

Filling in the forms to apply for a student grant is not seen as work, but filling in forms is part of a clerical worker's job. Similarly, when a mature student looks after her or his own child, this is not seen as work, but if she or he employs a child-minder, it is, for the minder, paid work. We can see from these examples that work cannot be defined simply by the content of the activity. So when we refer to the term **work**, what do we mean? We can begin to get a sense of what this question relates to and how society views work by exploring the following definition of work:

> Work refers to physical and mental activity that is carried out at a particular place and time, according to instructions, in return for a wage or salary.

This definition draws attention to some central features of work. First, the notion of 'physical and mental' obviously suggests that the activities of a construction worker or a computer systems analyst are deemed to be work. The 'mental activity' also includes the commercialization of human feeling or emotion (Hochschild, 1983). Second, the tendency for the activity to take place away from our home and at set time periods of the day or night – 'place and time' – locates work within a social context. Third, the social context also includes the social relations within which the activity is performed. When a mother or father cooks the dinner for the family, the actual content of the activity is similar to that performed by a hospital cook employed to prepare meals for patients, but the social relations within which the activity occurs are quite distinct. Hospital cooks have more in common with factory workers or office workers because their activities are governed by rules and regulations – 'instructions' from the employer or employer's agent. Clearly, then, it is not the nature of the activity that determines whether it is considered 'work' but instead the social relations in which the activity is embedded (Pahl, 1988). Fourth, in return for physical effort and/or mental application, fatigue and loss of personal autonomy, the worker receives a mix of rewards, including 'money', status and intrinsic satisfaction. Watson (1986) refers to this mix of inputs (physical and mental activities, and so on) and outputs (rewards) as the 'implicit contract' between the employer and the employee.

Although this definition helps us to identify key features of the employment relationship, it is too narrow and restrictive. First, consider all the activities, physical and mental, that do not bring in a wage or salary. Such activities can be exhilarating or exhausting; they may involve voluntary work for the Citizen's Advice Bureau or encompass the most demanding work outside paid employment – childcare. Again, the same activities – advising people on their legal rights and being paid for it, or being employed in a nursery – would all count as 'work' because of the social relations and the monetary reward. This text concentrates on paid work, and, as a consequence, we largely omit the critically important area of women's unpaid work in the household (Rinehart, 2006).

Second, our definition of work says little about how opportunities for paid work are shaped by gender, ethnicity, age or disability. Women are disproportionately represented in paid work that can be viewed as an extension of their domestic life – catering, nursing, teaching, clerical and retail employment. Ethnic and racially defined minorities experience chronic disadvantage in paid work because of racism in organizations and in recruitment. The likelihood of participating in paid work varies with age and certain types of work. For example, young people are disproportionately represented in more physically demanding paid work. Disabled adults, especially disabled young adults, experience higher levels of unemployment and underemployment (Barnes, 1996).

Third, it is clear that the rewards, satisfaction and hazards of work are highly unequally distributed. Contemporary society rewards employees according to the kind of people they are and the kind of work they do; historically, women receive less money than men in similar work. Work can also be dangerous and unhealthy, but the hazards are not distributed evenly. Despite the publicity surrounding managerial stress, for example, the realities of the distribution of work-related hazards show that they are most prevalent among manual workers. It has been argued that this unequal distribution of work-related accidents represents the systematic outcome of values and economic pressures (Littler and Salaman, 1984).

There is no doubt that the nature and experience of work is changing. As part of the wider process of globalization and the implementation of new managerial strategies, there is an ongoing shift of paid work into the service sector, an increase in information technology and an increasing number of women being drawn into the waged labour force and engaged in emotional labour. Contemporary forms of waged work, particularly in the less developed industrialized economies, are dependent on the integration between work and the family (Moore, 1995). The nature of work in turn affects HRM activities. For example, the pay that an employee receives is related to social attitudes and traditions rather than the actual content of the activity; pay determination requires an understanding of the social division of labour, especially gender divisions of labour (Pahl, 1988). Management decides how the tasks are divided into various jobs and how they relate to other tasks and other jobs, contingent upon different modes of production and technology. Decisions are also made about control systems, the ratio of supervisors to subordinates, the training of workers and the nature of the reward system. HRM is thus both affected by and profoundly affects an individual's experience of work. Clearly, the way in which work is designed impacts on both the effectiveness of the organization and the experience and motivation of the individual and work group. It is this process of job design that we will now consider.

● Classical approaches to job design – scientific management

We begin by studying what others call 'classical' approaches to **job design**, which can be defined as, 'the process of combining tasks and responsibilities to form complete jobs and the relationships between jobs in the organization'. They are considered classical partly because they are the earliest contributions to management theory, but partly because they identify ideas and issues that keep occurring in contemporary literature, albeit using a different vocabulary (Grey, 2005).

Early developments

Innovations in how work is designed have interested academics and managers for centuries. For example, Adam Smith (1723–90), the founder of modern economics, studied the newly emerging industrial division of labour in 18th-century England. For Smith, the separation of manual tasks was central to his theory of economic growth. He argued that this division of labour led to an improvement of economic growth in three ways:

1. Output per worker increases because of enhanced dexterity.
2. Work preparation and changeover time is reduced.
3. Specialization stimulates the invention of new machinery.

In his book, *The Wealth of Nations* (1982 [1776], p. 109), Smith described the manufacture of pins and gave an early example of job design:

> Man draws out the wire; another straightens it; a third cuts it; a fourth points it; a fifth grinds it at the top for receiving the head ... the important business of making a pin is, in this manner, divided into eighteen distinct operations.

In the 19th century, Charles Babbage also pointed out that the division of labour gave the employer a further advantage – by simplifying tasks and allocating fragmented tasks to unskilled workers, the employer could pay a lower wage: 'in a society based upon the purchase and sale of labour power, dividing the craft cheapens its individual parts' (Braverman, 1974, p. 80).

The emergence of the industrial division of labour gave rise to more radical studies of job design. Karl Marx (1818–83) argued that the new work patterns constituted a form of systematic exploitation and that workers were alienated from the product of their labour because of capitalist employment relations and the loss of autonomy at work: 'factory work does away with the many-sided play of the muscles, and confiscates every atom of freedom, both in bodily and intellectual activity' (quoted in Nichols, 1980, p. 69).

Since the beginning of the 20th century, interest in job design has intensified because of the writings of Frederick Taylor on 'scientific management'. Between 1908 and 1929, Henry Ford developed the principles of Taylorism but went further and developed new work structures based on the flow-line principle of assembly work. The human relations movement emerged in the 1920s and drew attention to the effect of work groups on output. Then, in the late 1960s, concern about declining productivity and the disadvantages of scientific management techniques led to the job redesign movement. Current interest and discourse on job design centres around Japanese management, which deals with more than job design as it emphasizes, for example, management style, skill and values, and aims to incorporate job design into an organization's employment strategy. We will now consider each of these approaches in more detail.

Scientific management

The American Frederick W. Taylor (1856–1915) pioneered the **scientific management** movement. This approach to job design, referred to as Taylorism, was also influenced by Henry L. Gantt (1861–1919) and Frank B. Gilbreth (1868–1924). Taylor developed his ideas on employee motivation and job design techniques at the Midvale Steel Company in Pennsylvania, USA, where he rose to the position of shop superintendent. Littler (1982, p. 51) has argued that 'Taylorism was both a system of ideological assertions and a set of management practices'. Taylor was appalled by what he regarded as inefficient working practices and the tendency of workers not to put in a full day's work, what Taylor called 'natural soldering'. He saw workers who did manual work to be motivated by money – the 'greedy robot' – and to be too stupid to develop the 'one best way' of doing a task. The role of management was to analyse scientifically all the tasks to be undertaken and then to design jobs to eliminate time and motion waste.

Taylor's approach to job design was based on five main principles:

1. maximum job fragmentation
2. the divorce of planning and doing
3. the divorce of 'direct' and 'indirect' labour
4. the minimization of skill requirements and job-learning time
5. the reduction of material handling to a minimum.

Thus, the centrepiece of scientific management was the separation of tasks into their simplest constituent elements (first principle). Most manual workers were viewed as sinful and stupid, and therefore all decision-making functions had to be removed from their hands (second principle). All preparation and servicing tasks should be taken away from the skilled worker (direct labour) and performed by unskilled and cheaper labour (indirect labour in the third principle); according to Littler, this is the Taylorist equivalent of Babbage's principle and is an essential element of more work intensification (1982). Minimizing skill requirements to perform a task reduces labour's control over the labour process (fourth principle), and finally, management should ensure that the configuration of machines minimizes the movement of people and materials to shorten the time taken (fifth principle). Taylor's approach to job designs, argues Littler (1982, p. 52), embodies 'a dynamic of deskilling' and offers to organizations 'new structures of control'.

Some writers argue that Taylorism was a relatively short-lived phenomenon, which died in the economic depression of the 1930s. Rose suggests that scientific management did not appeal to most employers – 'Some Taylorians invested a great effort to gain its acceptance among American employers but largely failed' (1988, p. 56) – but this view underestimates the diffusion and influence of Taylor's principles on job designers. In contrast to Rose, Braverman (1974, pp. 86–7) believes that 'the popular notion that Taylorism has been "superseded" by later schools of "human relations", that it "failed" … represents a woeful misreading of the actual dynamics of the development of management'. Similarly, Littler and Salaman (1984, p. 73) have argued that 'In general the direct and indirect influence of Taylorism on factory jobs has been extensive, so that in Britain job design and technology design have become imbued with neo-Taylorism' (HRM in Practice 5.1).

HRM IN PRACTICE 5.1

ONLY 39 PER CENT OF EMPLOYEES HAVE A 'GOOD' JOB

JULIE GRIFFITHS, *PEOPLE MANAGEMENT*, AUGUST 2005

Employers should make roles more appealing to improve worker commitment.

Only 39 per cent of workers think that their job is 'good', according to new research from CIPD.

'Good' roles are defined as 'exciting but not too stressful', according to a new report from the institute, *Reflections on employee well-being and the psychological contract*.

The research explored how employees felt about their job and their relationships with managers and colleagues. It concluded that employers should make jobs more appealing and interesting to improve commitment from employees. 'Most jobs can be made interesting or even exciting if they are well managed,' Mike Emmott, CIPD employee relations adviser, said.

> ## 'Good' roles are defined as 'exciting but not too stressful'

An interesting and exciting job was one with variety and security, and where the role of the employee was clear. Many workers did not believe that their job had these qualities – a fifth of respondents thought that the demands of their job were unrealistic and the same proportion found their jobs either very or extremely stressful.

Nic Marks, head of well-being research at the New Economics Foundation and co-author of the report, said that interest and excitement were key elements in the psychological contract between employers and employees. 'If employees don't feel their role is exciting, this will be reflected in underperformance and their lack of commitment and satisfaction,' he said.

Can you think of jobs in the retail and service sector that would support the charge that work systems in the modern workplace continue to be imbued with neo-Taylorism?

Fordism

Henry Ford applied the major principles of Taylorism but also installed specialized machines and perfected the flow-line principle of assembly work; this kind of job design has, not surprisingly, come to be called **Fordism**. The classical assembly line principle should be examined as a technology of the control of employees and as a job design to increase labour productivity, both job fragmentation and short task-cycle times being accelerated. Fordism is also characterized by two other essential features:

- the introduction of an interlinking system of conveyor lines that feed components to different work stations to be worked on
- the standardization of commodities to gain economies of scale.

Fordism established the long-term principle of the mass production of standardized commodities at a reduced cost (Coriat, 1980).

Speed of work on the assembly line is determined by the technology itself rather than by a series of instructions. Management's control of the work process was also enhanced by a detailed time and motion study inaugurated by Taylor. Work-study engineers attempted to discover the shortest possible task-cycle time. Ford's concept of people management was simple: 'The idea is that man ... must have every second necessary but not a single unnecessary second' (Ford, 1922, quoted in Beynon, 1984, p. 33). Recording job times meant that managers could monitor more closely their subordinates' effort levels and performance. Task measurement therefore acted as the basis of a new structure of control (Littler, 1982).

Ford's production system was, however, not without its problems. Workers found the repetitive work boring and unchallenging, job dissatisfaction being expressed in high rates of absenteeism and turnover. In 1913, for example, Ford required about 13,500 workers to operate his factories at any one time, and in that year alone the turnover was more than 50,000 workers (Beynon, 1984). The management techniques developed by Ford in response to these HR problems serve further to differentiate Fordism from Taylorism (Littler and Salaman, 1984). Ford introduced the 'five dollar day' – double the pay and shorter hours for those who qualified. Benefits depended on a factory worker's lifestyle being deemed satisfactory, which included abstaining from alcohol. Ford's style of paternalism attempted to inculcate new social habits, as well as new labour habits, that would facilitate job performance. Taylorism and Fordism became the predominant approach to job design in vehicle and electrical engineering – the large-batch production industries – in the USA, Canada and Britain.

As a job design and labour management strategy, scientific management and Fordist principles had limitations even when the workforce accepted them. First, work simplification led to *boredom and dissatisfaction*, and tended to encourage an adversarial industrial relations climate. Second, Taylor-style job design techniques carry *control and coordination costs*. With extended specialization, indirect labour costs thus increase as the organization employs an increasing number of production planners, controllers, supervisors and inspectors. The economies of the extended division of labour tend to be offset by the dis-economies of management control structures. Third, there are what might be called *cooperation costs*. Taylorism increases management's control over the quantity and quality of workers' performance, but, as a result, there is increased frustration and dissatisfaction, leading to a withdrawal of commitment on the part of the worker. Quality control can then become a major problem for management. The relationship between controller and controlled can deteriorate so much as to result in a further increase in management control. The principles of Taylorism and Fordism thus reveal a basic paradox, 'that the tighter the control of labour power, the more control is needed' (Littler and Salaman, 1984, pp. 36–7; see also Huczynski and Buchanan, 2001). The adverse reactions to the extreme division of labour led to the development of new approaches to job design that attempted to address these problems, starting with the human relations movement.

● Human relations movement and job redesign

The **human relations movement**, which began to shift managers' attention to the perceived needs of workers, emphasized the fact that job design had to consider the psychological and social aspects of work. This movement grew out of the Hawthorne experiments conducted by Elto Mayo in the 1920s.

Mayo set up an experiment in the relay assembly room at the Hawthorne Works in Chicago, USA, which was designed to test the effects on productivity of variations in working conditions (lighting, temperature and ventilation). The Hawthorne research team found no clear relationship between any of these factors and productivity. The researchers then developed, after the fact, concepts that might explain the factors affecting worker motivation, concluding that more than just economic incentives and the work environment motivated workers: recognition and social cohesion were important too. The message for management was also quite clear: rather than depending on management controls and financial incentives, it needed to influence the work group by cultivating a climate that met the social needs of workers. The human relations movement advocated various techniques such as worker participation and non-authoritarian first-line supervisors, which would, it was thought, promote a climate of good human relations in which the quantity and quality needs of management could be met.

Criticism of the human relations approach to job design were made by numerous writers. Human relations detractors claimed managerial bias and the fact that the human relations movement tended to play down the basic economic conflict of interest between the employer and employee. Critics also pointed out that when the techniques were tested, it became apparent that workers did not inevitably respond as predicted. Finally, the human relations approach has been criticized because it neglects wider socioeconomic factors (Thompson, 1989). Despite these criticisms, however, the human relations approach to job design began to have some impact on management practices in the post-Second World War environment of full employment. Running parallel with the human relations school of thought, though, came newer ideas about work that led to the emergence of a job redesign movement.

During the 1960s and early 1970s, job design was guided by what Rose (1988) refers to as the 'neo-human relations' school and the wider-based 'quality of working life' movement. The neo-human relations approach to job design emphasized the fulfilment of social needs by recomposing fragmented jobs. Advocates of the quality of working life movement put forward five principles of 'good' job design that challenged the core principles of scientific management (Littler and Salaman, 1984):

1. The principle of closure, whereby the scope of the job is such that it includes all the tasks to complete a product or process, thus satisfying the social need of achievement.
2. A good design incorporates control and monitoring tasks, whereby the individual or group assumes responsibility for quality control.
3. Task variety, whereby the worker acquires a range of different skills so that job flexibility is possible.
4. Self-regulation of the speed of work.
5. The design encompasses a job structure that permits some social interaction and a degree of cooperation among workers.

In the late 1970s, competitive pressures compelled an increasing number of Western companies to reassess the way in which work was organized and introduce job enrichment designs. The term **job enrichment** refers to a number of different processes of rotating, enlarging and aggregating tasks. An early example of this process was the use of job rotation, which involves the periodic shifting of a worker from one work-simplified task to another (Figure 5.1). The advantage of job rotation is, it was argued, that it reduces the boredom and monotony of doing one simplified task by diversifying a worker's activities (Robbins, 1989).

An alternative approach to job redesign was the horizontal expansion of tasks, referred to as **job enlargement** (Figure 5.2). Instead of only grilling hamburgers, for

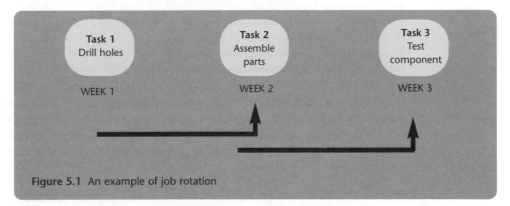

Figure 5.1 An example of job rotation

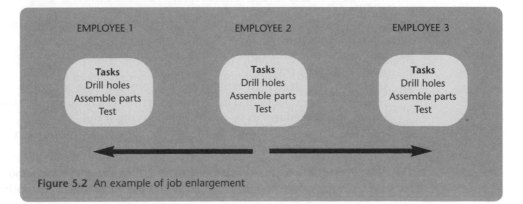

Figure 5.2 An example of job enlargement

example, a griller's job could be enlarged to include mixing the meat for the burger or preparing a side salad to accompany the order. With a larger number of tasks per worker, the time-cycle of work increases, thus reducing repetition and monotony.

A later and more sophisticated effort to address the limits of Taylorism and Fordism was the vertical expansion of jobs, often referred to in organizational behaviour text-books as job enrichment. This approach takes some authority from the supervisors and adds it to the job (Figure 5.3). Increased vertical scope gives the worker additional responsibilities, including planning and quality control. For example, the fast-food worker from our previous example might be expected not only to grill the burgers and prepare the salad, but also to order the produce from the wholesaler and inspect the food on delivery for its quality.

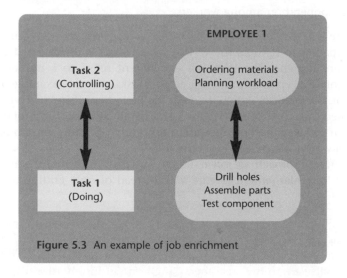

Figure 5.3 An example of job enrichment

Hackman and Oldham's (1980) model of job enrichment – the **job characteristic model** – is an influential approach to job design. This model suggests that five core job characteristics result in the worker experiencing three favourable psychological states, which in turn lead to positive outcomes (Figure 5.4). The five core job characteristics are:

- *Skill variety:* the degree to which the job requires a variety of different activities in carrying out the work, requiring the use of a number of the worker's skills and talents.
- *Task identity:* the degree to which the job requires the completion of a 'whole' and identifiable piece of work.
- *Task significance:* the degree to which the job has a substantial impact on the lives or work of other people.
- *Autonomy:* the degree to which the job provides the worker with substantial freedom, independence and discretion in terms of scheduling the work and determining the procedures to be used when carrying it out.
- *Feedback:* the degree to which the worker possesses information of the actual results of her or his performance.

The chef/manager of a small restaurant would, for example, have a job high on skill variety (requiring all the skills of cooking plus the business skills of keeping

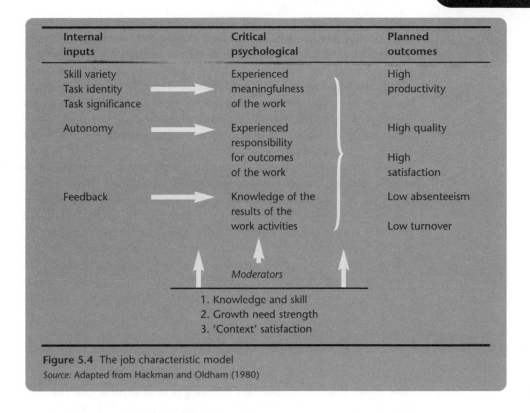

Figure 5.4 The job characteristic model
Source: Adapted from Hackman and Oldham (1980)

accounts, and so on), high on task identity (starting with raw ingredients and ending with appetizing meals), high on task significance (feeling that the meals have brought pleasure to the customers), high on autonomy (deciding the suppliers and the menus) and high on feedback (visiting the customers after they have finished their meals). In contrast, a person working for a fast-food chain grilling hamburgers would probably have a job low on skill variety (doing nothing but grilling hamburgers throughout the shift), low on task identity (simply grilling burgers and seldom preparing other food), low on task significance (not feeling that the cooking makes much of a difference when the burger is to be covered in tomato ketchup anyway), low on autonomy (grilling the burgers according to a routine, highly specified procedure) and low on feedback (receiving few comments from either co-workers or customers).

The model suggests that the more a job possesses the five core job characteristics, the greater its motivating potential. The existence of 'moderators' – knowledge and skill, degree of need for growth and context satisfactions – explains why jobs theoretically high in motivating potential will not automatically generate a high level of motivation and satisfaction for all workers. This means that employees with a low growth need are less likely to experience a positive outcome when their job is enriched. The job characteristic model has been tested by theorists and, according to Robbins (1989, p. 210), 'most of the evidence supports the theory'.

Some theorists have offered a more critical and ideological evaluation of job enrichment. Bosquet, for example, argues that modern management is being forced by labour problems to question the wisdom of the extreme division of labour and factory 'despotism'. Job enrichment (Bosquet, 1980, p. 378) 'spells the end of authority and despotic power for bosses great and small'; this should in turn lead workers liberated from boring jobs to demand total emancipation. An influential study by Friedman (1977) argues that although job enrichment techniques may increase job satisfaction and commitment, the key focus remains managerial control. He maintains that job design strategies such as job enrichment result in individuals or groups of workers being given a wider measure of discretion over their work with a minimum of supervision, and that this 'responsible autonomy' strategy is a means of maintaining and augmenting managerial authority over workers (Friedman, 1977) or is a 'tool of self-discipline' (Coriat, 1980, p. 40) for workers.

Thompson (1989) offers one of the most penetrating critiques of job redesign techniques. Drawing upon the contributions of various theorists and the empirical evidence, he argues that many job enrichment schemes 'offer little or nothing that is new, and are often disguised forms of intensified [managerial] control' (1989, p. 141). With the growth of call centres over the past decade, critical research has drawn attention to 'new' forms of managerial control. It is alleged that sophisticated electronic communication and employee-monitoring systems, electronic eavesdropping on sales–client conversations and peer group scrutiny have created 'electronic sweatshops' or a form of 'electronic Taylorism' (Callaghan and Thompson, 2001; Sewell, 1998).

Contemporary approaches – self-management

According to Grey (2005), contemporary approaches to job restructuring grow out of, draw upon and sometimes react against classical approaches. For many modern theorists, the paradigm shift in work restructuring that has occurred over the past two decades is teamworking. For example, Cloke and Goldsmith (2002, p. 138) argue that 'In the new organizational paradigm, the fundamental unit of structure is not the isolated individual but the collaborative self-managing team.' In Britain, for example, successive Workplace Employee Relations Surveys have reported an increased adoption of teamworking or 'high-involvement' work practices (Cully et al., 1999; Kersley et al., 2006; Millward et al., 2000; see HRM in Practice 5.2). Such new methods of work organization that depart from the 'rational' Fordist model are the focus here and in the next section.

HRM IN PRACTICE 5.2

WORKERS TURN OFF AUTOPILOT AND TAKE CHARGE ON ASSEMBLY LINES OF THE 21ST CENTURY

SHERWOOD ROSS, *GLOBE AND MAIL*, 3 SEPTEMBER 2001, P. B12

Assembly line workers, once told to 'check your brains at the door,' are now prized for their ability to think and act independently, as automation, cross-training and new management styles are leading to greater worker involvement and greater productivity. 'Workers will tell you that things have changed from the early 1990s,' says Aleda Roth, an authority on manufacturing who has visited hundreds of assembly lines all over the world. 'You see a much more productive environment as managers get assembly line workers involved in process improvement and using the new technologies,' says Ms. Roth.

It wasn't always so. Command and control policies, Mr. Donkin says, 'produced results, but it was a wasteful system, wasting most of the human ingenuity residing in the workforce.' A spokesman for DaimlerChrysler Corporation agrees there has been a shift. 'A trend has been to give more responsibility to the [plant] floor and to cascade that responsibility down to empower our people,' says Trevor Hale. 'Nobody knows that job better than the person doing the job.'

At Daimler's Toledo North assembly plant, 'We have a lot of job rotation built in' so that assembly line workers 'understand the big picture of operations in different areas,' Mr. Hales says. There, workers are organized in teams of 10, to learn the jobs of other team members so they can step right in when one of them is absent. Rotating job assignments also help to prevent repetitive motion injuries.

> **'Never tell people how to do things. Tell them what to do and they will surprise you with their ingenuity.'**

The 2,000 hourly workers in the plant are urged to think in terms of making continuous improvements. 'The change never stops,' Mr. Hale says. 'We encourage change in terms of improving quality.'

Manager Vick Crawley says: 'We have moved away from assembly lines where one person would add one piece. Today, people have multiple tasks that they do.' He says the new 'manufacturing cells' system requires more employee training and development than the traditional assembly line arrangement. 'We have kaizen [the Japanese term for continuous improvement] and employees get involved in designing their own cells.' Self-directed work initiatives have been around for some time, of course. As Second World War US General George Patton once wrote: 'Never tell people how to do things. Tell them what to do and they will surprise you with their ingenuity.'

Before we examine some of the alternative work structures designed by managers, it is, however, important to note an analytical caution. Much of the organizational theory literature on newly emerging organizational forms simplifies the analysis to a polar comparison between 'traditional' Fordist and new or 'post-Fordist' work-team characteristics (Jaffee, 2001; Vallas, 1999). An example of binary comparisons between two approaches to work design is shown in Table 5.1. As Jaffee (2001, p. 129) correctly argues, however, the enumeration of lists of binary opposite features 'conform[s] more to conceptual elegance than empirical reality'. Organizational redesign is not a smooth transition from one Weberian ideal-type model to another, and new organizational forms are most likely to resemble a hybrid configuration that welds elements from the old organizational design with parts of the new.

REFLECTIVE QUESTION

You have probably experienced group working as part of your business programme. Have you enjoyed the experience? What are the advantages/disadvantages of group projects? Why have 'team' projects become common practice in many business schools?

Table 5.1 Ideal types of Fordist and post-Fordist work systems

	Fordist	Post-Fordist
1. Technology	• Fixed, dedicated machines • Vertically integrated operation • Mass production	• Micro-electronically controlled multipurpose machines • Subcontracting • Batch production
2. Products	• For a mass consumer market • Relatively cheap	• Diverse production • High quality
3. Labour process	• Fragmented • Few tasks • Little discretion • Hierarchical authority and technical control	• Many tasks for versatile workers • Some autonomy • Group control
4. Contracts	• Collectively negotiated rate for the job • Relatively secure	• Payment by individual performance • Dual market: secure core, highly insecure periphery

If corporate giants, such as the Ford Motor Company, had once been the model of mass production – captured by Henry Ford's famous marketing slogan 'You may have any colour you wish, so long as it's black' – Toyota became the model for reorganizing assembly lines.

The early discourse on the limitations of Fordism is well captured by Michael Piore and Charles Sabel in their book *The Second Industrial Divide* (1984); according to these US authors, the Fordist model is incapable of responding quickly in highly competitive consumer industries. The alternative to Fordism was 'flexible specialization', which presented a revival of the 'craft paradigm'. This neoromantic perspective on organizational change is described (Piore and Sabel, 1984, p. 17) as:

> a strategy of permanent innovation: accommodation to ceaseless change, rather than an effort to control it [based] on flexible – multi-use – equipment; skilled workers; and the creation, through politics, of an industrial community that restricts the forms of competition to those favoring innovation.

The *flexible specialization model* had the following features:

- the small-scale production of a large variety of products for differentiated markets
- the utilization of highly skilled workers exercising considerable control and autonomy over the labour process
- the use of process and information technology
- strong networks of small producers that achieved flexibility and efficiency through collaboration (Appelbaum and Batt, 1994; Piore and Sabel, 1984).

In this scheme, the flexible firm model developed by Atkinson (1984) provoked extensive attention from European policy-makers, management theorists and practitioners. The analysis surrounding the flexible firm model also became de facto British government policy in the late 1980s and 90s (Sisson and Storey, 2000). As we discussed in Chapter 4, the flexible firm model is a variant of the dual labour market approach, but it is important in the flexibility discourse because it gave theoretical legitimacy to flexible employment arrangements and thereby contributed to the growth of non-standard labour. The centrepiece of the *flexible firm model* is formed by three types of flexibility (Chapter 6):

1. functional
2. financial
3. numerical.

In Europe, particularly in the UK, the flexible firm model has been linked with the post-bureaucratic agenda of promoting 'fluidity' by creating 'looser organizational boundaries' that tolerate 'outsiders' coming in to the organization (Felstead and Jewson, 1999).

Japanese management and organizational culture: Japanese-style work design

The 'Japanese threat' so challenged traditional manufacturing strategies in the 1980s that influential management consultants proclaimed the need for Western companies to embrace the 'art of Japanese management' (Grey, 2005). To be competitive, then, organizations had to develop a set of 'shared values', which meant that all managers and other employees were committed to common goals such as high quality. In addition, because employees would be committed to the 'culture of excellence' and 'empowered' to make decisions, fewer supervisors would be needed and operating costs would fall as a result. The adoption of Japanese management practices set off a process of organizational restructuring and concomitant changes in managing the employment relationship (Bratton, 1992; Thompson and McHugh, 2002; Womack et al., 1990).

The mystique of Japanese management is worth considering in some detail because, in the 1980s, it attracted considerable attention from North American and European academics and managers. Two important questions can be raised here: What are the major characteristics of the Japanese model of management? And, do these characteristics constitute the basis of a new phase in job design?

In 1986, the British industrial relations theorist Peter Turnbull described a new 'module' production system at Lucas Electrical (UK). According to Turnbull (1986), the production system employed a new breed of multiskilled 'super-craftsmen'. Turnbull used the term **Japanization** to describe these changes at Lucas Electrical (UK) because they were based on the production methods used by many large Japanese corporations.

In addressing our first question, we see that the Japanese production model has three notable elements:

- flexibility
- quality control
- minimum waste.

Flexibility is attained using module or cellular manufacturing. The system achieves flexibility in two ways: by arranging machinery in a group or 'cell' – cellular technology – and by using a flexible multiskilled workforce. Machines are arranged into a U-shaped configuration to enable the workers to complete a whole component, similar to the group technology principle introduced in the European and US automobile industry in the early 1970s (Coriat, 1980; Littler and Salaman, 1984). The job design underpinning a cellular work structure is the opposite of that of 'Taylorism': a generalized, skilled machinist with flexible job boundaries is a substitute for the specialized machinist operating one machine in one particular workstation.

Quality control is the second component of the Japanese production system. The management philosophy of total quality control attempts to build quality standards into the manufacturing process by making quality every operator's concern and responsibility. Total quality control results in job enlargement as cell members undertake new self-inspection tasks and participate in quality-improvement activities. With this approach, there are savings on labour and raw materials: fewer quality control inspectors, fewer rework hours and less material wasted (Schonberger, 1982).

Minimum waste is the third component of the Japanese production model. Waste is eliminated, or at least minimized, by just-in-time (JIT) production. As the name suggests, this is a hand-to-mouth mode of manufacture that aims to produce the necessary components, in the necessary quantities, of the necessary quality and at the necessary time. It is a system in which stocks of components and raw materials are kept to a minimum, ideally being delivered a matter of days or even hours before their use in the manufacturing process. An important beneficial outcome of JIT production is the reduction in inventory and scrap (Schonberger, 1982).

Turning to our second question, academics differ over whether or not such work practices constitute a significant departure from traditional job design principles (e.g. Elger and Smith, 1994). To help in understanding the debate, we have developed a theoretical framework for examining Japanese production management. As Figure 5.5 shows, the model has six major hypothesized components, which we will examine in turn. These components are:

1. a set of manufacturing techniques
2. a set of dependency relationships
3. a set of HRM policies
4. a set of supplier policies
5. a managerial ideology
6. a series of HRM outcomes.

The *set of manufacturing techniques* comprises cellular technology, JIT manufacturing and total quality control, the principles of which have been discussed above. Japanese manufacturing processes create, it is alleged, a complex web of *dependency relationships* that calls for adroit management (Oliver and Wilkinson, 1988). The cellular system implies a low level of substitutability of the workers and a heightened dependency on a multiskilled workforce. In addition, total quality control heightens dependency when the safety net of the safety inspectors is removed. Furthermore, JIT is vulnerable to delays and stoppages. If the company is operating on a zero or minimum inventory, late delivery or stoppages resulting from strikes will quickly affect the manufacturing process. As Oliver and Wilkinson point out (1988, p. 135), 'A mere work-to-rule or overtime ban could be as disastrous for a company operating a JIT system as could a strike for a company not doing so.'

Implicit in our model is the need for a set of *moderators* to counterbalance the company's dependency on its workforce and suppliers. The organization needs to

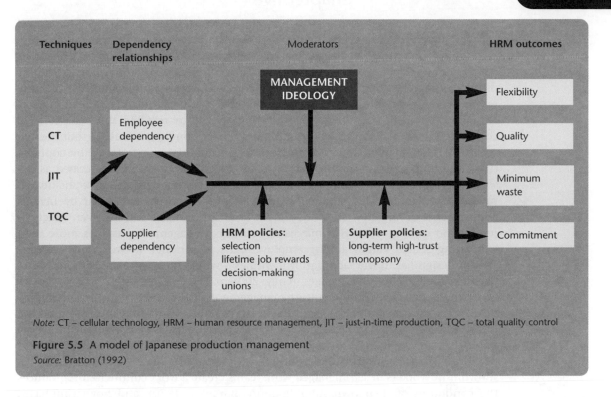

Note: CT – cellular technology, HRM – human resource management, JIT – just-in-time production, TQC – total quality control

Figure 5.5 A model of Japanese production management
Source: Bratton (1992)

develop social mechanisms aimed at exerting sufficient influence over employees' psychological contract to redress the imbalance in the employment relationship (see Chapter 1 for the importance of the psychological contract in HRM). A set of *HR policies* and practices is designed to shape employee perceptions of expectations and obligations beyond the traditional form of the employment relationship based on the cash nexus (Dore, 1973; Guest, 1987). Similarly, a unique set of *supplier policies* relating to the buyer aims to generate a reciprocal obligation between the buyer and the supplier (Oliver and Wilkinson, 1988). *Managerial ideology* and leadership behaviour also act as moderators. Finally, the *HRM outcomes* or performance goals of the system are:

● commitment – the leitmotiv of progressive or 'soft' models of HRM (Legge, 2005): employee commitment rather than compliance to the organization's goals
● flexibility in terms of the employment contract, employee skills and tasks
● minimum waste of materials and time
● the minimum number of quality defects arising from production.

This model illustrates three dimensions – *technical* (task flexibility), *governance* (delegated empowerment) and *culture* (Findlay et al., 2000; Grey, 2005) – believed to underpin the superior, more 'holistic' approach of Japanese management. The cultural or 'normative' dimension of Japanese work practices draws attention to the social and psychological aspects of the employment relationship that aim to generate social cohesion and a 'moral commitment' to common organizational goals (Etzioni, 1988). From the perspective of culture management, self-managed work teams are a 'socialization device' aimed at solving the classical management problem of empowering employees to release creativity, synergy and commitment without reducing management control of the labour process (Geary and Dobbins, 2001; Grey, 2005; Procter and Mueller, 2000; Thompson and Wallace, 1996). Analyses of large Japanese companies have often conceptualized the Japanese corporation as a 'community', and theorists have focused on how workers are socialized into complying with the rules and norms of the 'corporate community' or culture. Japanese managers, for example, constantly remind their workers of the 'competition' inherent in the market. The notion of corporate 'competitiveness' is an ideology that acts to regulate the behaviour of corporate members independently of actual market conditions existing outside the company. The Japanese approach to work organization is characterized by cooperativeness, group problem-solving and attitude control (what may be described as the social organization of work), the system being characterized by a sophisticated production planning. JIT production itself modifies workers' behaviour by heightening a sense of 'urgency' and inducement to avoid mistakes and discover defects in production quickly. Trite as it may seem, culture management proposes more than cultivating shared values among employees; its importance to work and organizational design lies in the fact that 'it identifies a whole range of organizational practices designed to elicit these values' (Grey, 2005, p. 68).

Japanese management and culture management, critics argue, constitute a sophisticated control system designed to influence expectations and obligations beyond the formal effort–reward contract. As Grey (2005, p. 70) persuasively argues, 'the whole purpose of culture management is to re-constitute beliefs – nothing less will do if its promise of the removal of supervision is to be achieved'. Studies have, for example, shown how workers in self-managed work teams create a work culture that reproduces the conditions of their own subordination (Burawoy, 1979), and how team-based work regimes can produce a 'coercive culture system', wherein exists a moral obligation to work hard, to 'put in a full day', without direct supervision, because of peer-group pressure or 'clan' control (Bratton, 1991). In another study of work teams, the workers' discipline was more punitive than that of the managers: 'peer pressure in the groups was very important. [Team members] are tougher on [co-workers] than management' (Wells, 1993, p. 75).

REFLECTIVE QUESTION

Is our model of Japanese management outlined in Figure 5.5. a theory or simply a helpful way of organizing a complex social phenomenon such as culture management?

HRM WEB LINKS

Go to the following websites: the Centre for the Study of Work Teams (www.work-teams.unt.edu), DaimlerChrysler AG (www.daimlerchrysler.com), Amicus (www.amicustheunion.org) and the Canadian Autoworkers Union (www.caw.ca). How do these different companies and unions view the introduction of work teams? Do teams improve performance? Are there any negative outcomes of teamworking for managers or workers?

The classical Japanese management model is no longer avant-garde, and there have been 'multiple' challenges to Japanese employment practices (Jacoby, 2005; Whittaker,

1990;). However, notwithstanding the varied vocabulary that is used to capture work restructuring – much of the most recent literature refers to 'high-performance work systems' – numerous US and European studies show that teamworking has become the dominant reality and is more than a 'passing fad' in management thinking (Fröbel and Marchington, 2005; Jones, 1997; Jurgens, 1989; Kersley et al., 2006; Malloch, 1997; Murakami, 1995). Data, for example, from the 2004 Workplace Employee Relations Survey revealed that 72 per cent of workplaces had some core employees in formally designated workteams (Table 5.2). The use of problem-solving groups was much less common than that of teamworking (21 per cent) and the incidence of teamworking and problem-solving groups had changed little since the previous national survey in 1998. In all, 66 per cent of workplaces reported training some core employees to be functionally flexible, and 48 per cent had trained some core employees in team-working, communication or problem-solving in the previous year.

Table 5.2 Teamwork practices in workplaces (%) 1998 and 2004

Work design practices	1998	2004
Work teams	74	72
Problem-solving groups	16	21
Functionally flexible	69	66
Trained in teamworking	41	48

Source: Kersley et al. (2006) p. 90

In our view, the model shown in Figure 5.5 is a useful heuristic framework for mapping out the 'systematic interlocking' (Thompson and McHugh, 2002) nature of self-managed work teams – technical, governance and cultural aspects – and the prerequisite 'bundle' of HR practices used to manage organizational culture and to socialize the 'empowered' work regime.

Knowledge work and post-bureaucratic designs

Knowledge work

The final quarter of the 20th century witnessed the emergence of so-called 'knowledge work', in which work was no longer about the mass production of tangible commodities but was concerned with the organization's intangible assets – knowledge (Sveiby, 1997). Indeed, it is argued that knowledge is the principal asset of the corporation and of countries (Drucker, 1993). The nature of knowledge work is fundamentally different from what we have traditionally associated with the 'machine age' and mass production and marketing, the alleged differences between the nature of traditional work and knowledge work being illustrated in Table 5.3.

Conventional wisdom says that this alleged shift from traditional to knowledge work has important implications for HRM. Within this context, the argument goes that if an organization's wealth and ability to compete exists 'principally in the heads of its employees, and, moreover, that it effectively "walks out the gates" every day'

(Boud and Garrick, 1999, p. 48), greater attention needs to be given to those HR practices that recruit, motivate and retain core knowledge workers. Similarly, Quah argues that sustainable competitiveness depends not on 'having built the largest factory … [but] on knowing how to locate and juxtapose critical pieces of information, how to organize understanding into forms that others will understand' (1997, p. 4, quoted in Thompson and Warhurst, 1998, p. 1). This realization that knowledge work is fundamentally different has led managers to change strategies, patterns of interaction, HR practices and organizational structures.

Table 5.3 The nature of traditional work and knowledge work

	Traditional work	Knowledge work
Locus of work	Around individuals	In groups and projects
Focus of work	Tasks, objectives, performance	Customers, problems, issues
Skill obsolescence	Gradual	Rapid
Skill/knowledge sets	Narrow and often functional	Specialized and deep, but often with diffuse peripheral focuses
Activity/feedback cycles	Primary and of an immediate nature	Lengthy from a business perspective
Performance measures	Task deliverables	Process effectiveness
	Little (as planned), but regular and dependable	Potentially great, but often erratic
Employee's loyalty	To organization and his or her career systems	To professions, networks and peers
Impact on company success	Many small contributions that support the master plan	A few major contributions of strategic and long-term importance

Source: Adapted from Despres and Hiltrop (1995) and Boud and Garrick (1999)

Post-bureaucratic designs

Underpinning the debates on post-bureaucratic organizations, described below, are the implicit assumptions, first that the nature of work in the 'information age' has radically changed, and second, that organizations will experience superior performance if the typical bureaucratic pyramid model is reconfigured so that management structures are 'delayered' and decision-making is pushed down to the 'front line' (HRM in Practice 5.3). Some writers have described these anti-hierarchical characteristics in organizational design as a shift from 'modernist' to 'postmodernist' organizational practices (Clegg, 1990; Clegg and Hardy, 1999; Grugulis et al., 2003; Hassard and Parker, 1993; Heckscher and Donnelon, 1994).

HRM IN PRACTICE 5.3

COUNCIL MANAGEMENT FORCED TO SHED TIERS

STEPHEN OVERELL, *PEOPLE MANAGEMENT*, 1997

Hackney Council is ridding itself of its 'historical baggage' as part of a radical management overhaul. London's Hackney Council will next week approve a radical organisational shake-up that will see tiers of management axed and top staff forced to reapply for their jobs.

Tony Elliston, Hackney's chief executive, has ambitious plans to see a total management overhaul completed by the beginning of 1998. This is intended to further his aim of pushing the troubled council to the top of Audit Commission league tables.

... units purchasing support services will be free to buy help from the private sector if in-house teams are not up to scratch.

Under the new structure, units purchasing support services will be free to buy help from the private sector if in-house teams are not up to scratch. Personnel services and training, for example, will each operate as a trading unit, effectively as internal consultancies.

There will also be a core central personnel function concerned with top-level recruitment and management and organisational development.

Elliston intends to scrap six director posts and replace them with four new executive directors. These will have no budgets or staff, but will deal with corporate strategy.

The current tier of 15 assistant directors will be replaced with nine service directors responsible for targets and commissioning services. Delivery will be provided by units that will, in turn, buy support services such as legal, training or personnel from trading units operating in an internal market.

Asked about how top staff felt about reapplying for their jobs, Elliston replied: 'Huge changes are going to happen, not just a little here and a little there. If officers can't mirror that in their behaviours, they have got some life choices to make. New staff will be those most able to do the job.'

Elliston said he was keen to avoid traditional titles such as director of education and director of housing. Instead, service directors will be responsible for areas such as learning and leisure, children and families and estate management and development.

'... the only thing that matters is the community getting their services promptly, efficiently and professionally.'

'I do not want to see the creation of fiefdoms,' he said. 'It is only human to want to protect your patch, but they have got to be able to see that the only thing that matters is the community getting their services promptly, efficiently and professionally.'

The shake-up is expected to make initial savings of £5 million, which will be used to extend services or cut council tax bills. Hackney has already trimmed £58 off its bills this year, the largest cut in London. A parallel move towards devolution, with 'one-stop shops' for queries on, for example, housing and social services, is also under way.

Post-bureaucracy is part of an evolving series of 'conversions' associated with post-modern critiques coalesced around an antipathy to 'modernist' tendencies emphasizing functionalism, by which we mean an approach based on assumptions concerning the unitary and orderly nature of work organizations, the notion of totality and grand narratives history. The bureaucratic features of 'modern' organizations are those of 'losing shape' and giving way to a flat, flexible and empowered 'postmodern' organizational form (Clegg and Hardy, 1999). Clegg (1990, quoted in Willmott, 1995, p. 90) outlines the main contrasting features of postmodernism thus:

Where the modern organization was rigid, post-modern organization is flexible ... Where modern organization was premised on technological determinism, postmodernism is premised on technological choices made possible through dedicated microelectronic equipment. Where modernism organization and jobs were highly differentiated, demarcated and de-skilled, postmodernist organization and jobs are highly differentiated, demarcated and multi-skilled.

On the outside, the boundaries of the post-bureaucratic organization are blurred or 'fluid' as managers form temporary 'strategic alliances' with other independent firms that are linked by information technology – an 'integrated collaborative network' enabling flows of information, resources and people (Bartlett and Ghoshal, 1989; Grugulis et al., 2003) or 'virtual' organization (Davidow and Malone, 1992). (See also Chapter 3 on transitional business strategies and international HRM.)

On the inside, these new organizational configurations offer, argue advocates, opportunities for 'flexible' work-related learning, more radical innovation and collaborative patterns of social interaction, allowing organizations to 'reinvent the future' (Hamel and Prahalad, 1994). The concepts of 'workplace learning' and 'organizational learning' are part of the conversation that fuels the postmodern debate on organizations based on the processing of knowledge and information (Huseman and Goodman, 1999; Jaffee, 2001). The notion that an organization 'learns' by processing information fits with the 'brain' metaphor of work organization (Morgan, 1997). The pursuit of flexibility and superior performance through designing a 'learning organization' is discussed in Chapters 2 and 9.

Five key features of Heckscher's (1994) ideal-type conceptualization of the post-bureaucratic organization provide an interesting insight into the internal practices and patterns of social interaction that we can expect to find in these emerging organizational forms. These features are:

1. organizational dialogue, persuasion and trust
2. information-sharing
3. behaviour based on principles
4. communication based on problem-solving
5. peer evaluation.

According to observers, management 'command and control' is replaced by *dialogue, persuasion* and *trust*, which allows a wide range of inputs to arise from the bottom and from across the organization, rather than from the top of the hierarchy. The effectiveness of dialogue, persuasion and trust depends on access to and the *sharing of information* relating to the organization's operations. The behaviour and actions of managers and subordinates are dictated by general *principles* that allow greater flexibility, discretion and adaptation, rather than by formal contractual rules and written procedures. Organizational communications and decision-making are driven by *problems* and *projects* rather than a hierarchical chain of command. In the post-bureaucratic organization, people's performance relies more on *peer evaluation* and negotiated standards of performance than on their immediate supervisor, seniority and formal credentials. Taken together, Heckscher's ideal-type features produce the 'master concept', 'an organization in which everyone takes responsibility for the success of the whole' (1994, p. 24). There appear to be few existing post-bureaucratic organizations, but Heckscher does cite the Shell-Sarnia chemical plant in Ontario, Canada as being the 'most advanced exemplar' of this work regime.

A number of academics are critical of post-bureaucratic, postmodern formulations (see, for example, Reed, 1993; Thompson, 1993; Thompson and McHugh, 2002). Thompson, for instance, accuses postmodern organizational theorists of having fallen victim to technological determinism and mistaking the surface of work organizations for their substance. Thompson argues that the 'leaner' organization actually gives more power to a few: 'Removing some of the middle layers of organizations is not the same as altering the basic power structure ... By cutting out intermediary levels [of management] ... the power resources of those at the top can be increased' (1993, p. 192). One way of doing this is described in the next section.

HRM WEB LINKS

Go to the website for Shell-Sarnia, Ontario, Canada (www.shell.ca) for more information.

STUDY TIP

You may wish to extend your understanding of 'postmodernism' and its implications for HRM by asking to what extent postmodernism represents a 'yearning for alternatives' or a 'distraction' from the critical analysis of current trends in organizations. Read John Hassard's chapter 'Postmodernism and organizational analysis: an overview' in Hassard and Parker (1993).

What do you think of the modern and postmodern discourse? Have the basic principles that originally defined capitalist work organizations (competition, technological change, a tendency to minimize costs, antagonistic employment relations over pay and effort levels) changed? How does your experience of work and organizations align with the popular management rhetoric?

Business process re-engineering

One major development in organizational design, which emphasizes process in a *horizontal* structure – the organization of work by self-managed teams (Figure 5.6) – is **business process re-engineering** (BPR), which falls within the post-bureaucratic genre (Albizu and Olazaran, 2006; Champy, 1996; Hammer, 1997). The BPR movement declares that organizational structures and the way in which work is structured have to be 'radically' changed so that the re-engineered company can become adaptable and oriented towards continuous change and renewal. According to the re-engineering guru James Champy (1996, p. 3), BPR is 'about changing our managerial work, the way we think about, organize, inspire, deploy, enable, measure, and reward the value-adding operational work. It is about changing management itself.'

Re-engineered organizations allegedly have a number of common characteristics (Table 5.4). Central to these organizational forms, argues Willmott (1995), is the 'reconceptualization of core employees' from being considered a variable cost to being represented as a valuable asset capable of serving the customer without the need for a command and control leadership style. With the ascendancy of 'customer

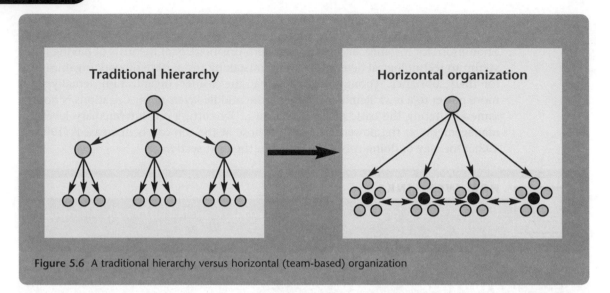

Figure 5.6 A traditional hierarchy versus horizontal (team-based) organization

democracy', employees are encouraged to exercise initiative in creating value for customers and thereby profits for the company. According to Hammer (1997, pp. 158–9):

> Obedience and diligence are now irrelevant. Following orders is no guarantee of success. Working hard at the wrong thing is no virtue. When customers are kings, mere hard work – work without understanding, flexibility, and enthusiasm – leads nowhere. Work must be smart, appropriately targeted, and adapted to the particular circumstances of the process and the customer ... Loyalty and hard work are by themselves quaint relics ... organizations must now urge employees to put loyalty to the customer over loyalty to the company – because that is the only way the company will survive.

Table 5.4 The re-engineered organization

Characteristic	Traditional model	Re-engineered model
Market	Domestic	Global
Competitive advantage	Cost	Speed and quality
Resources	Capital	Information
Quality	What is affordable	No compromise
Focal point	Profit	Customer
Structural design	Hierarchical	Flattened
Control	Centralized	De-centralized
Leadership	Autocratic	Shared
Labour	Homogeneous	Culturally diverse
Organization of work	Specialized and individual	Flexible and in teams
Communications	Vertical	Horizontal

This passage is most revealing. First, it presents the debate on employee commitment, shared commitment and reciprocity in a different light. (We discuss the issue of employee commitment in Chapters 11 and 12.) Second, in the re-engineered organization, responsibility for the fate of employees shifts from managers to customers. In Hammer's (1997, p. 157) opinion, 'The company does not close plants or lay off workers – customers do, by their actions or inactions.'

Unlike earlier movements in work design, such as the quality of working life movement (see above), re-engineering is *market-driven*. In essence, it views the management of employment relations through an economic prism focusing on the relationship between the buyer and seller of services or goods rather than between the employer and employee. Hammer and Champy (1993) emphasize that the 'three Cs' – customers, competition and change – and a shift in the national government policy of 'tough love' towards business have created the need for re-engineering business processes. For Champy (1996, p. 19), using a mixture of language discarded by the political 'old Left' and terminology of the 'new Right', 'a dictatorship of the customariat or ... a market democracy ... is the cause of a total revolution within the traditional, machine-like corporation'.

Practitioners and academics have, however, been critical of re-engineering. One management consultant has criticized the imprecise meaning of BPR and pointed out that senior managers have been using the term 'to legitimize other objectives' (quoted in *Management Today*, February, 1995). Grint and Willcocks (1995) offer a scathing review of BPR, arguing that it is not new and pointing out that it is essentially political in its rhetorical and practical manifestations. Willmott is similarly scornful of BPR, emphasizing that re-engineering is 'heavily top-down' and pointing out that the re-engineered organization, using information technology, while creating less hierarchical structures, also produces 'a fist-full of dynamic processes ... notably, the primacy of hierarchical control and the continuing treatment of employees as cogs in the machine' (Willmott, 1995, p. 91). In his case study analysis of BPR in a hospital, Buchanan (1997) observes that the lack of clarity of BPR terminology and methodology offers 'considerable scope for political maneuvering' by politically motivated actors. A case study of BPR in the public sector found that conflict arose from 'very human needs to justify one's role in the new organization, or individual managers' needs to maintain their power bases within the organization' (Harrington et al., 1998, p. 50). Moreover, within the context of the employment relationship, BPR does not obviate the inherent conflict of interest between the two parties: the employers and the employees. When examined in the context of employment relations, BPR can be interpreted 'as the latest wave in a series of initiatives ... to increase the cooperation/productivity/adaptability of staff' (Willmott, 1995, p. 96).

HRM WEB LINKS

Go to www.bprc.warwick.ac.uk/bp-site.html, the website of the ESRC-funded Business Processes Resource Centre at Warwick University. It was created as a focal point in the UK for the dissemination of current knowledge and research, and to provide access to best practice thinking and application.

HRM IN PRACTICE 5.4

WORKING PART-TIME NO BED OF ROSES: STUDY

VIRGINIA GALT, *GLOBE AND MAIL*, 9 JULY 2001, P. B4

Part-time work is not as idyllic as it may appear to envious full-timers, according to new Canadian research published in the *Harvard Business Review*. 'Professionals who work part-time must go to extreme lengths to make the arrangements acceptable to their employers and colleagues,' wrote academics Vivian Corwin, Thomas Lawrence and Peter Frost.

A common pitfall is the tendency to compress a full-time workload into part-time hours – for part-time pay, they found. Even with the compressed schedule, however, work still encroaches on what is supposed to be family time.

'It is not necessarily a panacea for a striking a balance between work and life,' the researchers wrote. The researchers interviewed a mother who confessed to sending an ill child to school in order to attend business meetings and prove her 'commitment'. They also interviewed a co-worker irked by a part-time colleague who would swan out of the office at noon on Wednesdays, wishing everyone else a good weekend. 'She didn't win many friends,' observed Ms. Corwin, a consultant in leadership development and human resource management and an associate faculty member at Royal Roads University in Victoria.

> **'Professionals who work part-time must go to extreme lengths to make the arrangements acceptable to their employers and colleagues.'**

'Many part-timers are forced to work longer hours than they contracted for, and many suffer under the second-class status of part-time work,' the researchers found as part of a wide-ranging study on how employees in Canada and the USA balance the competing demands of work and home life. 'At the same time, part-time work makes organizations uncomfortable. It raises obvious questions about who will pick up the slack,' they wrote in their *Harvard Business Review* article.

Most part-timer arrangements are ad hoc, many professionals working part-time report that they are overlooked when bonuses are handed out, and may feel 'out of the loop' professionally. 'Most part-timers told us they accepted the consequences of their status as part of the deal. But they also said that sometimes their confidence was eroded, and they questioned whether the arrangement was worth the effort.'

Organizational design and human resource management

The design of organizational structures and the way in which work is performed are critical features of new formulations of HRM. As Guest (1990) points out, underpinning the HRM model is the need to reconfigure organizational structures as the rhetoric is essentially 'anti-bureaucratic'. Guest further emphasizes the concomitant change in job design, believing that HRM takes as its starting point the view that organizations should be designed on the basis of the assumptions inherent in McGregor's (1960) Theory Y. According to McGregor, people work because they want to work rather than because they have to. Thus, the Theory Y view of people assumes that when workers are given challenging assignments and autonomy over work assignments, they will respond with high motivation, high commitment and high performance. In the more critical language of labour process theory, a limited reintegration of conception and execution becomes a source of employee empowerment *and* improved productivity (Sewell, 2005).

Job and organizational design is related closely to all key HRM activities, including recruitment and selection, learning and development, rewards and employee relations; job design is basic to the recruitment and selection function. A company that produces small-batch, high value-added products using skilled labour within a team-based organizational arrangement will clearly have more rigorous recruitment and selection priorities than a company that specializes in large-batch production using dedicated machines operated by unskilled operators supervised in the usual pyramid-shaped organizational hierarchy. Job design affects workplace learning. As one of us has noted elsewhere, high-quality workplace learning is contingent upon the quality of job design (Bratton, 2005). The organizational design or 'architecture' affects employees' capacity to build 'cooperative relationships' and work cooperatively across functional borders (Gratton, 2005).

Several empirical studies have found a strong and consistent association between new forms of work organization, as well as higher levels of technical skills' upgrading and training for their employees, than are seen in those firms operating under 'traditional' work regimes (Adams and McQuillan, 2000; Felstead and Ashton, 2000; Osterman, 1995). Specifically, new forms of work organization require enhanced formal and informal learning in technical, decision-making and team-building skills. Compaq Canada, for example, sent its managers to a corporate 'wilderness' training centre to learn team-building skills. Success requires the team to learn to communicate with each other, cooperate and work together (Belcourt et al., 2000). If an organization chooses to introduce work teams, managers will have to consider such details as the structure of teams, the actual rewards offered, whether these are contingent upon team or company performance, communication and input from team members (McClurg, 2001).

More recently, it has become fashionable to emphasize the contribution that reconfigured work structures have on the psychological contract. The nature of work and organizational structural features discussed in this chapter – the degree of formal rules and procedures, decision-making and governance processes – are critical factors in the formation and re-formation of reciprocal expectations, aspirations and understandings. In their model of HRM, Beer et al. (1984), for example, envision job design broadening employee responsibilities and resulting in a 'substantial improvement in the 'four Cs' of commitment, competence, cost-effectiveness and congruence. In practice, however, there is much concern and debate over the rupture in the psychological contract resulting from restructuring, particularly 'delayering' and 'downsizing'. According to Edwards (2000, p. 290), downsizing is 'a planned, intentional reduction in personnel'. For those employees 'let go', there is the severing of the explicit employment contract, and for the survivors the psychological contract is adjusted in two ways. First, retained employees become distrustful of committing their energy to an organization that has displayed a lack of loyalty. Second, the survivors are frequently expected to undertake additional duties, with a corresponding increase in work intensification (Thomson and Millar, 2001). In a nutshell, job security has been the quid pro quo for employees' knowledge and skills, commitment and loyalty, and downsizing and the fundamental redesigning of work can result in a less affective emotional attachment to their work organization, lower levels of commitment and loyalty, and the unilateral renegotiation of the psychological contract.

Important though the debate on the psychological contract is in highlighting the complexity of the employment relationship, it would be remiss in a textbook devoted to HRM tensions and paradoxes if it did not draw attention to the rich debate on how differing forms of work organization generate and reflect tension, contradiction and change.

Tension and paradox in job design

As we noted in Chapter 1, contradiction, tension and paradox underscore much of the critical analysis of HRM. Paradox is evident in work design, much of the contemporary literature on organizational and job design placing a great deal of emphasis on a number of paradoxes (Handy, 1994). There are a number of ways in which to think about and conceptualize paradox in work design. Here we use a simple model presented by Jaffee (2001) and illustrated in Figure 5.7. The model shows that paradox stems from what is called 'differentiation–integration tension'. This refers to the inherent tension between the management strategies for achieving a rational division of economic activities and, simultaneously, ensuring that these activities are coordinated and integrated. Differentiation and the division of labour are fundamental management principles that underscore organizational goals to control costs and the quality of their products or services. As organizations increase in size and complexity, integration becomes an issue. How do different workers, departments and managers coordinate and integrate their interdependent activities?

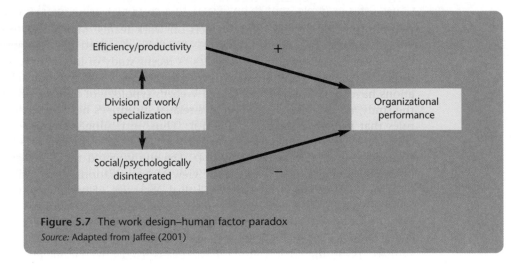

Figure 5.7 The work design–human factor paradox
Source: Adapted from Jaffee (2001)

The tension between differentiation and integration within the organization can be illustrated by a familiar manufacturing strategy: management initially redesigns work involving a rigid division of labour and highly specialized tasks (e.g. Fordism). The *intended* consequence is to rationalize and make the workers more efficient and productive. The *unintended* consequence, however, is the creation of a socially disintegrated work experience that produces low levels of cross-communication, job satisfaction, motivation and commitment to the organization. In other words, the new work arrangement changes people's perceptions of management's commitment and expectations, thereby affecting the psychological contract. This, as we discussed earlier, can limit the positive contribution made by the specialization of labour. Existing views on the implications of JIT production further illustrate such tensions and contradictions. The effects of tighter logistical integration between firms can improve productivity, but a zero inventory can make a firm highly vulnerable to temporary stoppages (Bratton, 1992) and undermine the psychological contract resulting from the 'unrelenting' pressure to meet deadlines:

The brinkmanship of just-in-time production creates *extraordinary pressures* on employees and work organization. Such pressures may drive out HR support activities ... needed to sustain employee motivation and morale. (Scarbrough, 2000, p. 16, emphasis added)

The crux of this problem is managerial 'control'. Management, as Geary and Dobbins (2001, p. 5) remind us, is not simply about controlling the labour process: it is also about enlisting workers' knowledge, creativity and discretionary efforts:

Management remains caught between two opposing imperatives: attempts at regulating employees too tightly run the risk of endangering the employees' creativity and commitment to management goals, while empowering employees runs the risk of reducing management control.

This fundamental paradox at the heart of the employment relationship becomes even more acute when managers redesign organizational structures and arrangements that increase workers' participation and discretionary powers.

The notion of tension and paradox in work design is apparent in the debate on post-bureaucratic design and its effects on work teams. Many mainstream organizational scholars (e.g. Piore and Sabel, 1984) have argued that self-managed teams reverse Tayloristic deskilling tendencies. A recent study of international car manufacturers by Pulignano and Stewart (2006) suggests that new post-bureaucratic organizations have, paradoxically, revitalised Weber's typology of bureaucracy. According to the study, new employee performance-related incentives have generated behavioural rules that *reinforce* bureaucratic control: 'Thus, intriguingly, the use of bureaucratic control emerges as the main element of labour control in this type of workplace' (Pulignano and Stewart, 2006, p. 104). The study would therefore suggest that the binary bureaucratic/post-bureaucratic view of organizational design may be a somewhat misleading analytical device. Critical observers of organizational design have asserted that team-based work regimes are detrimental to workers' interests. They argue that limited 'empowerment' does not reverse the general deskilling trend but has a tendency to increase the intensity of work (L. Clarke, 1997; Rinehart, 2006; Sennett, 1998; Tomaney, 1990) and increases managerial surveillance over the effort bargain (Malloch, 1997; Townley, 1994). Finally, others offer a less pessimistic analysis in which the outcomes of new work regimes are less deterministic (e.g. Geary and Dobbins, 2001; Thompson and McHugh, 2002). Whether post-bureaucratic self-managed work regimes result in the 'upskilling' or 'deskilling' of workers depends on, among other things, factors such as batch size, managerial choice and negotiation (Bratton, 1992). Work team 'empowerment' has not eliminated worker resistance, and managerial control continues to be contested (McKinlay and Taylor, 1998). Similarly, the debate on BPR has focused on whether the empowerment of employees has resulted in work structures that are necessarily less restrictive or repressive than those designed following Taylorist principles. Willmott (1995, p. 96), for example, asserts that, with the assistance of microtechnology, re-engineering is an 'up-dating of Taylor's crusade against custom and practice in which the silicon chip plays an equivalent role in [re-engineering] to that performed by the stop watch in Scientific Management'. The benefits for managers and non-managers of jettisoning the old values and old ways of doing work appear to be mixed in terms of personal growth and empowerment.

Table 5.5 Four approaches to job design

	Motivation assumptions	Critical techniques	Job classification	Issues
Scientific management	Motivation is based on the piecework incentive system of pay. The more pieces the worker produces, the higher the pay	Division of tasks and responsibilities Task analysis 'one best way' Training Rewards	Division of tasks and of 'doing' and 'control' leads to many job classifications	Criteria of motivation may be questioned No role for unions Cooperation costs Product inflexibility
Job enrichment	Motivation is based on social needs and the expectations of workers. To increase performance, focus on achievement, recognition and responsibility	Combine tasks Increase accountability Create natural work units Greater responsibility	Some supervisory tasks are undertaken by workers as the 'control' is shifted downwards	Criteria of motivation may be questioned Undefined union role
Japanese management	Motivation is based on teamwork or 'clan-like' norms and the organizational culture. Performance and motivation are social processes in which some workers try to influence others to work harder	Intensive socialization Lifetime employment Consensual decision-making Non-specialized career paths Seniority-based pay	Requires fewer job classifications because of flexibility and a degree of autonomy	Criteria of motivation may be culture-bound Collaborative union role Work intensification
Re-engineering	Motivation is based on the need to serve the customer. Performance and motivation are social processes in which strong leaders enthuse workers to work harder	Organizational norms and traditions are abandoned Networking Strong top-down leadership Workplace learning Information technology enables change Processes have multiple versions	Multidimensional jobs Workers are organized into process teams Workers are empowered to make decisions	Criteria of motivation may be questioned Market-driven Undefined union role Work intensification

When organizations restructure work and jobs, the changes clearly place HRM centre stage. The precise nature of the impact of these work design strategies is, however, subject to debate. For managers and other employees, job and organizational redesign affects workplace safety, health and wellness (Chapter 13), the need for workplace learning (Chapter 9) and the need to synchronize bundles of better HR practices and employee and collective relations to new work structures (Chapters 12 and 13).

Chapter summary

- We started this chapter by examining the meaning of work in contemporary Western society and then proceeded to evaluate alternative job design strategies, including scientific management, job enrichment, Japanese work structures and re-engineering. These broad job design movements are summarized in Table 5.5.

- The review of the research reported here testifies that, in the early 21st century, flexibility is the management mantra on both sides of the Atlantic. Much of the literature on new organizational designs is couched in the language of 'empowerment' and 'postmodernism'. The postmodern organization has been characterized in the popular and academic management literature as flexible, enabling, innovative, creative, multiskilled and democratic. Despite all the interest in self-managed teams, however, empirical evidence suggests that, in the vast majority of workplaces, the 'quality' of work does not match the rhetoric (Lowe, 2000) and 'non-educative work is systemic' (Bratton, 1999, p. 491).

- For Sewell, and Thompson and McHugh, contemporary work regimes embody neo-Taylorist principles and a technical mode of managerial control. The research on non-standard employment – including freelancers, homeworkers and outworkers – and call centres (see Millward et al., 2000), and the wider debate on the 'McDonaldization' of work and 'electronic sweatshops' suggest both change and continuation in the workplace.

- We have cautioned readers against the tendency to conceptualize new work structures as a smooth transition from one ideal-type model to another. As others have pointed out, the widespread tendency to compress the specific into categories of general trends not only compresses variations in organizational design, but also attaches an apparent coherence to emerging organizational forms that is spurious (Salaman, 1981). The fact that Felstead and Ashton (2000, p. 18) found 'only three out of 10 employees currently work in "modern" organizations' exemplifies Littler's (1982) earlier argument that when it comes to new work designs, change is sporadic, intermittent and slow, and is subject to constant struggle and negotiation.

- The bedrock of emerging organizational forms – self-managed work teams – is a complex 'interlocking' arrangement of technical, government and cultural dimensions. The message of this chapter has been that, in the context of capitalist employment relationships, unintended consequences and tensions will arise with each new organizational form.

- We concluded our discussion on work and work organization by identifying some practical implications for managers and HR professionals. Organizational and job redesign affects both an organization's competitiveness and the experience and motivation of the individual and work group. New work structures typically impact directly on recruitment and selection criteria, performance appraisal, rewards, learning, training and development.

Further studies indicate that work and organizational redesign can cause employees' perceptions of the psychological contract to change.

● The practical implication of changing the way in which work is organized is that managers and HR professionals have not only to develop new HR policies and practices, but also to cope with the tensions, contradictions and paradoxes associated with any new work structure. Finally, managers need to take steps to understand how new forms of work organization can change employees' perception of the content of the psychological contract and from this, when circumstances permit, shape a 'new contract' (Coyle-Shapiro and Kessler, 2000).

Key concepts

- Business process re-engineering
- Job design
- Fordism
- Job enlargement
- Human relations movement

- Job enrichment
- Japanization
- Scientific management
- Job characteristic model
- Work

Chapter review questions

1. Why define 'work' by its social context rather than by the content of the activity?

2. Explain the limits of Taylorism as a job design strategy.

3. 'Job rotation, job enlargement and job enrichment are simply attempts by managers to control individuals at work.' Do you agree or disagree? Discuss.

4. Students often complain about doing group projects; why? Relate your answer to autonomous work teams. Would you want to be a member of such a work group? Discuss your reasons.

5. 'McWork', 'McJobs' or 'McDonaldization' are symbolic terms often used by critics of the 'new economy' to capture the realities of workplace life confronting young people today. What kinds of jobs does 'McWork' refer to? How do the job design concepts discussed in this chapter help you to understand the term 'McWork'? Is it an accurate description of employment today?

Further reading

Albizu, E. and Olazaran, M. (2006) BPR implementation in Europe: the adaptation of a management concept. *New Technology, Work and Employment,* **21**(1): 43–58.

De Menezes, L. and Wood, S. (2006) The reality of flexible work systems in Britain. *International Journal of Human Resource Management,* **17**(1): 106–38.

Geary, J. and Dobbins, A. (2001) Teamworking: A new dynamic in the pursuit of management control. *Human Resource Management,* **11**(1): 3–23.

Grey, C. (2005) *A Very Short, Fairly Interesting and Reasonably Cheap Book about Studying Organizations.* London: Sage.

Sparrow, P. (2000) New employee behaviours, work designs and forms of work organization: What is in store for future work? *Journal of Management Psychology,* **15**(3): 202–18.

Practising human resource management

Searching the web

Log on to the website for the Centre for the Study of Work Teams (www.work-teams.unt.edu) and write a brief report explaining the stereotypical team-based organization as you picture it. What main principles or practices can be identified as a source of efficiency? Can the team-based model be universally applied? What behavioural predictions would you make about people who work in 'post-bureaucratic' organizations? Find three companies that have introduced BPR but were disappointed with the results. What factors led to this disappointment?

HRM group project

Form a study group of three to five people and go to the websites of Daimler-Chrysler AG (www.daimlerchrysler.com), Motorola (www.motorola.ca), Johnson and Johnson (www.johnsonandjohnson.com), Union Carbide (www.unioncarbide.com), Harley-Davidson (www.harley-davidson.com/en/home.asp) or an alternative organization that interests members of the group.

Imagine that your group is a task force established by senior management to investigate the merits of work teams. Write a brief report addressing two aspects:

1. How are the following HRM activities – selection, training and rewards – affected when managers redesign the organization from being a traditional bureaucratic to becoming a team-based structure. One approach is to consider various companies or recruiters on the Internet (see examples in Chapter 7) and compare any differences between the job profiles listed by different organizations or recruiters. Are any patterns visible between team-based and traditionally designed organizations?
2. How is a team-based structure likely to affect employees' psychological contract?

Present this report with the help of PowerPoint so that other members of the management team (class members) can understand the main arguments and reflect on the likely impact that teams would have on HRM.

Chapter case study

WOLDS INSURANCE PLC

Wolds Insurance plc is a large insurance company that employs 1850 people in its branches throughout the UK. The underwriting department at the Newcastle branch consists of 13 clerks, of whom one is a section head and another a head of department. The nature of the work in the department has fundamentally changed over the past 20 years from book-keeping and an accounting process to clerical processing. There are various types of policy, the main difference being between 'commercial' and 'personal'. The vast majority of policies taken out are personal. Until late 1996, the underwriting department was divided into personal and commercial sections, but in January 1997 these were combined. Although clerks vary in the mix of commercial and personal policies they deal with, the variety in the work of each clerk is small.

Before 1993, the processing of policy issue at branch level was manual, the premium being calculated using manuals and charts. Details of the policy were then sent to the head office and issued from there. Head office had introduced a mainframe computer for this process in 1988, but the procedure at branch level remained much the same until mid-1993, when the VDTs were installed in the underwriting department.

At first, the department was not 'online', and premiums still had to be calculated manually. Policy details were, however, to be keyed in directly, and the VDT was used to check the details of any given policy. In 1994, the system went 'online', details of the policy being keyed in directly at branch level. In 1996, the computer was programmed to calculate premiums automatically. Management's aim was to computerize as many policies as possible through complex programming and standardization of the product. This reduced the processing time: for the majority of policies, it was necessary only to transfer details from form to screen and then use

the right classification, as specified in the manual. Before online computerization, a clerk could deal with 35 policies a week, whereas afterwards 80 policies a week could be processed.

Clerical staff numbers were reduced to a third within three years, and the previously separate departments of commercial and personal were combined into one. The division of work in the branch was divided into four functions: underwriting, claims, cash and accounts. In addition, the clerks were divided into two types of employee: those knowledgeable on insurance, capable of answering enquiries and dealing with non-standard cases, and those who processed routine policies. In terms of the knowledge required, standardization had reduced the differences between the policies and had for some reduced the level of knowledge required. Many of the policies are now offered on a 'take it or leave it' basis, and the processing of the policy is routine and repetitive, requiring little knowledge of insurance. Details of the customer and cover required are keyed into the computer in the specified order, and the premium is calculated automatically. Some knowledge of insurance is, however, still required for dealing with enquiries.

The underwriting clerks are beginning to show signs of frustration as much of their working day is spent on routine processing. There is also tension between those clerks doing the routine processing and those working on the non-standard and more interesting cases. This is resulting in serious morale problems, high absenteeism and an increasing number of mistakes in the processing. The manager of the department and the HR manager realize that changes are needed, but they are unsure how to improve the situation.

(The case is based on 'Skill, deskilling and new technology in the non-manual labour process' by Heather Rolfe, in *New Technology, Work and Employment*, 1986, **1**(1): 37–49.)

Assignment

You have recently been appointed HR assistant at Wold Insurance. June Cole, the HR manager, has asked you to consider ways of 'enriching' the work of the underwriting clerks. Prepare a written report focusing on the following questions:

1. What symptoms suggest that something is wrong in the underwriting department?

2. Using the job design concepts discussed in this chapter, suggest how to improve the clerical jobs in the underwriting department.

You may make any assumptions you feel are necessary, providing they are realistic and you make them explicit in your response.

HR-related skill development

Work team meetings are a vital part of the team-building and team performance process. Team meetings can be held for a variety of purposes: informing, collecting opinions and information, resolving conflict, problem-solving and decision-making. Such meetings can, unless properly managed by team leaders, be frustrating and a waste of time. As such, the ability to manage team meetings well is a valuable HR-related skill. To understand what it means to be a designated leader of a work team, and to develop your team leadership skills, go to our website (www.palgrave.com/business/brattonandgold4) and click on 'Team leadership skills'.

Notes

1. Patricia Chisholm (2001) Redesigning Work. *Maclean's*, March 5, p. 36.
2. Tony Clarke and Sarah Dopp (2001) *Challenging McWorld*. Ottawa: Canadian Centre for Policy Alternatives, p. 64.

Part Three

Human resource management practices

Chapter six

Human resource planning

Jeff Gold

Human resource planning is the process of systematically forecasting the future demand and supply for employees and the deployment of their skills within the strategic objectives of the organization.

'People are the primary determinant of business performance. If a firm's people strategy is aligned with a consistent and complementary innovation strategy then there is a high probability of superior business performance.' [1]

'Outsource everything except your soul.' [2]

'Detective agencies rely on human intuition and intelligence, both of which Mma Ramotswe had in abundance. No inventory would ever include those, of course.' [3]

Chapter outline

Chapter objectives

After studying this chapter, you should be able to:

1. Understand the place of planning in human resource management
2. Understand the different approaches to manpower planning
3. Explain the difference between manpower planning and human resource planning
4. Understand key ideas in human resource accounting
5. Give details of developments in e-HR
6. Understand developments in the idea and practice of flexibility
7. Understand the requirements for diversity management
8. Explain the importance of career management

Introduction

At the start of the 21st century, there are increasing claims that the route to competitive advantage is achieved through people (Gratton, 2000). If identical 'non-people' resources, in the form of finance, raw materials, plant, technology, hardware and software, are available to competing organizations, differences in the performance between organizations must be attributed to differences in the performance of people. Further, according the resource-based view of the firm, an organization can derive competitive advantage from its resources through the development of HRM systems and routines that are unique to that organization (Barney et al., 2001). Thus, an organization can apparently plan its deployment and combination of a range of HR practices and achieve high-commitment and enhanced performance (Wall and Wood, 2005).

For senior managers in an organization, whose task it is to plan a response to the pressures of continuous change, the attraction, recruitment, utilization, development and deployment of people of the required quantity and quality for the present and future ought now to rival finance, marketing and production in the construction of strategic plans. Where uncertainty exists, respect is given to those who can claim a degree of knowledge, and control over future events and plans, symbolically at least, is one way of proving this. Thus, the voice of human resource management (HRM) will be heard if it can present a rational and coherent argument for specific human resources (HR) practices that causally contribute to desirable organizational outcomes. This is the reasoning that supports the idea of what Legge (2005, p. 337) calls 'HRM as a modernist project'.

Either explicitly or implicitly, all organizational strategies will contain HR aspects. There is, however, the long-running issue of whether such considerations should play a prominent part in the process of strategy-making. A crucial element in this is the degree to which a link exists between HR practices and the performance of the business, or the so-called 'bottom line'. Thus in recent years, there have been growing efforts to test for or establish a causal link between good HRM and business performance (Cooke, 2000; Guest et al., 2003). Furthermore, it might be argued that the management of people as a strategic asset provides an opportunity to embrace the high-performance paradigm of HRM activity based on high trust, high commitment and high productivity, a view of the employment relationship that has mutual gains for employers, worker and even their unions (Godard, 2004; Godard and Delaney, 2000).

Becoming more strategic represents something of a dilemma. On the one hand, HR inputs might emphasize the importance of integrating policies and procedures with a business strategy in which people are seen as a factor of production who are required to make sure the business plan is implemented. The more business plans are based on figures and mathematical models, however, the greater the need for information about people to be expressed in a similar fashion; the plan for people should 'fit' the plan for the business. The growth of what were called manpower planning techniques through the 1960s, which provided such information, and their incorporation into comprehensive computer models were a key factor in the development of the personnel management role.

By the 1980s, the 'hard' version of HRM (Legge, 2005) was part of a push to address the traditional weakness of personnel managers in making themselves more strategic. This can be contrasted with a 'soft' version that emphasizes people as assets who can be developed and through whose commitment and learning an organization might achieve competitive advantage. It is interesting that the two different orientations, although representing a contrast, are not always incompatible. Indeed, living with ambiguities and conflicting pressures is a common experience for many HR practitioners (Gold and Hamblett, 1999). Tamkin et al. (1997), in a study of UK organizations, showed that although there were many challenges to HR in becoming strategic, HR functions were adopting a variety of approaches to find a strategic role. In some cases, this involved supporting business strategy by developing appropriate policies and procedures. Not all organizations, however, are as effective in developing strategy, and the HR function could develop policy to move the organization in an appropriate direction. In some cases, the HR function is able to be proactive and play a leading role in driving strategy.

The uncertainty and complexity of organization and business conditions in the 2000s has resulted in the employment of varied versions of HRM with concomitant approaches and methods relating to planning. For many years, theoretical development multiplied the number and sophistication of manpower planning techniques, but the activity moved in and out of favour at strategic levels. This was partly because the data and the computer models failed to live up to expectations, with the possibility that personnel departments were unable to make use of the theoretical advances. It was also because the 'people issue' fluctuated in importance. Thus, in times of relatively full employment, people and their skills were important because of their scarcity. During the years of recession in the 1980s and then the 1990s, manpower planning was used to reduce or 'downsize' the workforce. In the 2000s, there is growing evidence that progressive HR practices can enhance a company's sustainability and profitability if there is integration with business purpose (Guest et al., 2003), although there is also evidence of a failure by many senior managers to recognize this (Caulkin, 2001).

This chapter will look at the transition from a traditional manpower planning approach, driven by top-down planning based on numerical techniques, towards **human resource planning** (HRP) as a feature of HRM. The emphasis on quantities, flows and mathematical modelling, which appeared to be the main concern of manpower planning in the 1960s and 70s, is at least complemented by and integrated with a qualitative view of people whose performance lies at the core of business strategy. We have also shown that performance lies at the core of various models of HRM composed of an arrangement of HR practices. HRP will therefore be concerned with the development and provision of a framework that allows an organization to integrate key HR practices so that it may meet the needs of employees, enhance their potential and meet the performance needs of business strategy.

The genesis of human resource planning: manpower planning

Manpower planning owed its primacy to the importance of business strategy and planning in many organizations. It is worth, just for a moment, paying attention to the process of planning at this level. A plan represents one of the outcomes of a process that seeks to find a solution to a defined problem. There have been many attempts to rationalize this process to provide a set of easy-to-follow linear steps so that efficient decisions can be made to formulate a plan from a choice of alternatives prior to implementation. Plans therefore represent the precise and unified articulation of an organization's strategy, produced as the result of a rational consideration of the various issues that affect an organization's future performance before making a choice of the action required. As explained in Chapter 2, during this process senior managers will conduct an appraisal of both internal and external situations using a range of techniques to assess the organization's strengths and weaknesses and the opportunities and threats affecting it – the so-called SWOT analysis. Formally, the emphasis will be on data that can be quantified, which is not surprising since the planning process itself is an organization's attempt to pre-empt and deal with identified problems and uncertainty, and numbers are certain, precise and simple to comprehend. This image of certainty and control is one that gives comfort to many senior managers, although, as argued by Mintzberg et al. (1998) and more recently by McKiernan and Carter (2004), the field of strategic management is filled with division and competing versions of how strategy actually works.

If business strategy and plans find their expression in measurable financial, marketing and production targets with an implicit or explicit demand for people, the manpower plan represents a response by personnel and HR managers to ensure that the necessary supply of people is forthcoming to allow the targets to be met. The rationalized approach to manpower planning and its key stages are shown in Figure 6.1. The manpower plan could therefore be expressed in a way that matches or 'fits' the overall business strategy and plan. In theory at least, a manpower plan could show how the demand for people and their skills within an organization can be balanced by supply.

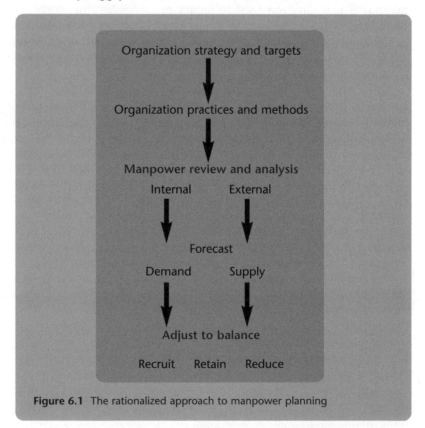

Figure 6.1 The rationalized approach to manpower planning

The rationalized approach leading to a balance between demand and supply can be found in some of the definitions and explanations of manpower planning put forward over the past 30 years. In 1974, the Department of Employment defined manpower planning as:

> strategy for the acquisition, utilisation, improvement and preservation of an organisation's human resources.

This definition was broad and general enough to cover most aspects of personnel management work. Four stages of the planning process were outlined:

1. an evaluation or appreciation of the existing manpower resources
2. an estimation of the proportion of currently employed manpower resources that were likely to be within the firm by the forecast date
3. an assessment or forecast of labour requirements if the organization's overall objectives were to be achieved by the forecast date
4. measures to ensure that the necessary resources were available as and when required, that is, the manpower plan.

Stages 1 and 2 were linked in the 'supply aspect of manpower', with stage 1 being part of 'normal personnel practice' (Department of Employment, 1974). Stage 3 represents the 'demand aspect of manpower'. There were two main reasons for companies to use manpower planning: first, to develop their business objectives and manning levels; and second, to reduce the 'unknown' factor.

For Smith (1980, p. 7), manpower planning meant:

- demand work – analysing, reviewing and attempting to predict the numbers, by kind, of the manpower needed by the organization to achieve its objectives
- supply work – attempting to predict what action was and would be necessary to ensure that the manpower needed was available when required
- designing the interaction between demand and supply so that skills were utilized to the best possible advantage and the legitimate aspirations of the individual were taken into account.

We can see within such definitions and explanations the key influence of the language of labour economics. Thus, the notion of 'equilibrium' serves as an ideal, organizations being composed of a variety of supply and demand problems throughout their structure, which planning will need to bring into an overall balance at an optimum level. The movement towards equilibrium involves a variety of personnel activities such as recruitment, promotion, succession planning, training, reward management, retirement and redundancy.

The complexity of the interaction of these factors within the context of the aims of optimization and overall equilibrium made manpower planning a suitable area of interest for operational research and the application of statistical techniques (Bartholomew, 1971). In this process, organizations could be envisaged as a series of stocks and flows as part of an overall system of resource allocation. Models of behaviour could be formulated in relation to labour turnover, length of service, promotion flow and age distribution. These variables could be expressed as mathematical and statistical formulae and equations allowing the calculation of solutions to manpower decisions. With the growing use of computers, the techniques and models became more ambitious and probably beyond the comprehension of most managers (Parker and Caine, 1996). In large organizations, there was, however, a growth in the number of specialist manpower analysts who were capable of dealing with the complex processes involved.

HRM WEB LINKS

Go to www.informs-cs.org/wsc98papers/088.PDF, where you will find a paper that applies Bayesian forecasting techniques and Markov chain methods to an 'employee scheduling problem' in manufacturing.

In the UK, the Institute of Manpower Studies,[4] based at Sussex University, was a principal advocate of manpower modelling. According to the Institute (Bennison, 1980, p. 2), the manpower planning process involved:

- determining the manpower requirements: how many people
- establishing the supply of manpower
- developing policies to fill the gap between supply and demand.

The Institute favoured a flexible approach in which plans were developed based on an understanding of the whole manpower system. The first step in manpower analysis is to describe the current manpower system and set its expected objectives. The system could be drawn as a 'collection of boxes and flows representing the way that manpower behaves in the organisation' (Bennison, 1980, p. 5). Planners can then assess the critical 'decision points' for manpower policy. Decisions concerning the recruitment and promotion of managers can, for example, occur in a meaningful way using statistical planning techniques in which the 'practical limits of variation' (Bennison, 1980, p. 17) can be defined for factors such as level of labour turnover at particular points, the impact of developments in technology and forecasts of growth. If possible, the relationship of the factors to the decisions will be quantified, allowing the generation of promotion paths under different assumptions of demand and supply.

REFLECTIVE QUESTION

Do you think a manpower system can be adequately represented as a series of stocks and flows?

Emphasizing statistical models of the supply and demand of manpower at the expense of the reality of managing and interacting with people was bound to be greeted with suspicion, certainly by employees and their representatives, as well as by managers 'forced' to act on the results of the calculations. It can be argued that the manpower analysis is there to serve as an aid to decision-making, but the presentation of data and an inability to deal with the ever-increasing complexity of models were always likely to result in the manpower analysis being 'seen' as the plan. The domination of equations that mechanistically provide solutions for problems based on the behaviour of people may actually become divorced from the reality and possess a good chance of missing the real problems; hence, during the 1970s and 80s, manpower planning acquired a poor reputation. For example, Cowling and Walters (1990), reporting on a survey of personnel managers, found that few respondents attributed benefits of planning to increasing job satisfaction/motivation (33.5 per cent), reducing skills shortages (30.2 per cent) and reducing labour turnover (22.4 per cent). Of the respondents at that time who used computers, 3.3 per cent reported a use for job design and 9 per cent one for job analysis. All of these were, and still are, vital areas of concern for any organization, areas that lie at the heart of proving the link between HRM activities and performance (Guest et al., 2003).

There were also a number of doubts about the connection between the business plan and the manpower plan. In a survey of US firms by Nkomo (1988), although 54 per cent of organizations reported the preparation of manpower plans, few reported a strong link between this activity and strategic business planning. Pearson (1991) reported the problem for manpower planners when business objectives might be absent or might not be communicated. Cowling and Walters found that 58.4 per cent of respondents faced a low priority being given to planning compared with immediate management concerns; they concluded, 'Of comprehensive and systematic manpower planning fully integrated into strategic planning there exist few examples at the present time' (1990, p. 6).

During the 1980s, there were a number of attempts to make manpower planning techniques more 'user-friendly' to non-specialists. Thus, the fall-out from theoretical progress in manpower analysis was the application of techniques to help with particular problems in the workplace. Bell (1989) argued that personnel managers understood the concept of manpower planning even if line managers and corporate planners did not, and that they were able to use basic techniques.

Many personnel managers are able to use manpower planning techniques to help them understand and deal with 'real' manpower problems, for example why one department in an organization seems to suffer from a dramatically higher labour turnover rate than others, or why graduate trainees are not retained in sufficient number. At a time when most people employed in most organizations were employed on permanent contracts with defined tasks to perform based on stable skill sets, personnel managers were able to build up a 'toolkit' of key manpower measures such as

- employee turnover
- retention
- stability
- absenteeism.

All could be relatively easily calculated either monthly or quarterly and expressed graphically to reveal trends and future paths.

Through the 1990s, such techniques were incorporated into PC-based computerized personnel information systems. As the software became more user-friendly, personnel departments were able to take advantage of this and make themselves more responsive to business needs. There are now many providers of HR software; we will explore such developments later in this chapter, but you may wish to examine some of the products and the claims made by the suppliers.

HRM WEB LINKS

Go to www.acas.org.uk/index.aspx?articleid=609, a booklet, published in the UK by the Advisory, Conciliation and Arbitration Service. The book on absence and turnover provides assistance to organizations that have labour turnover and absenteeism problems. You will also find examples of formulae used to measure absenteeism and turnover.[5]

Go also to www.softwaresource.co.uk; a site established by the Chartered Institute of Personnel and Development, providing information on and access to many HR software products and suppliers.

The use of manpower planning techniques within computerized personnel information systems can be seen as part of a continuing search by the personnel function to find areas of expertise that would legitimize its position and prove its value by 'adding to the bottom line'. In this approach, manpower plans and policies serve as initiators of operations, and techniques are used to monitor the progress of operations and raise an awareness of problems as they arise. There is an attempt here to use manpower information as a way of understanding problems so that action can be taken as appropriate. The disproportionate influence of the plan as a solution is replaced by an attention to planning as a continuous process of learning about HR problems. In this way, HR managers have been practising what Fyfe (1986, p. 66) referred to as 'the **diagnostic approach** to manpower planning'. This approach built on and broadened the rationalized approach in order to identify problem areas and understand why they were occurring (Figure 6.2). The theoretical idea of a balance between demand and supply, and equilibrium, can occur only on paper or on the computer screen; the more probable real-life situation is one of continuous imbalance as a result of the dynamic conditions facing any organization, the behaviour of people and the imperfections of manpower models. The diagnostic approach was based on the following thesis (Fyfe, 1986, p. 66):

> before any manager seeks to bring about change, or reduce the degree of imbalance, he or she must be fully aware of the reasons behind the imbalance (or the manpower problem) in the first place. Unless managers understand more about the nature of manpower problems, their attempts to control events will suffer from the hit-and-miss syndrome.

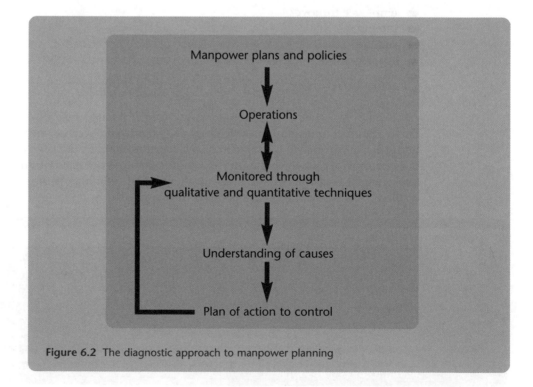

Figure 6.2 The diagnostic approach to manpower planning

In comparison with the rationalized approach, manpower problems using a diagnostic approach are to be identified and explored so that they can be understood, the data being used to help in this process and the speed of the computer providing support at an early stage. The rationalized approach will seek to minimize the time spent on such matters, preferring instead to focus on problems that can be easily defined or that most closely match ready-prepared solutions that may be difficult to challenge. In the rationalized approach, for example, organizational practices and methods – which include the division of labour, the design of work, the technology used, the relationships between departments and groups and the degree of management supervision – will precede the manpower review and be taken as a set of 'givens' in the ensuing calculations. Yet these may be the very factors that lie at the heart of manpower problems. Thus, a telephone sales organization that faces a problem of retaining staff may respond to this imbalance by stepping up recruitment and/or increasing pay.

A diagnostic approach would, however, mean becoming aware of this problem by monitoring manpower statistics such as turnover[6] and stability, and obtaining qualitative data by interviewing staff. The interviews may reveal concerns with job satisfaction and the career paths open to staff, reflecting aspirations they hold that are not being met by current practices. Rather than express these aspirations openly for fear of conflict with management, many staff prefer to seek employment elsewhere. The loss of skilled labour has important cost implications, and, in the face of a continuing shortage of skilled workers, a diagnostic approach to retention can provide a significant pay-off.

Bevan (1991) provides a guide to some of the reasons for high staff turnover. Significantly, but not unexpectedly, pay was not the only issue. Among the main factors identified were:

- the job not matching new employees' expectations
- a lack of attention from line managers and a lack of training
- a lack of autonomy, responsibility, challenge and variety within the work
- disappointment with the promotion and development opportunities
- standards of management, including unapproachable, uncaring and distant behaviour, and a failure to consult.

These are all complex factors reflecting general areas of concern but requiring solutions that are specific to the context of each organization. In the case of the telephone sales example above, the organization could respond to the diagnosis in various ways. Management could, for example, accept the problem and do nothing except lower the quality of recruitment so that new staff would, hopefully, be less likely to have high career aspirations – hardly very progressive and not very complex, but certainly an option. The organization could, however, also attempt to improve the work environment and work practices in order to provide avenues for greater job satisfaction and personal growth. This might have implications for job design, departmental structure and management style, creating a tension that would have to be resolved.

Recent research on employee turnover has sought to explore more closely why voluntary turnover occurs. Morrell et al. (2001) suggest that explanations of employee turnover can be organized into two schools:

1. *economic or labour market* – the emphasis being on external factors such as market conditions (see Local labour markets, 1970–2005 in Chapter 4)

2. *psychological* – the emphasis being on feelings and perceptions relating to job satis-faction, involvement and commitment within the psychological contract.

Research on employee turnover has focused on the latter, seeking to explore more closely why voluntary turnover occurs, which is particularly important given the costs of the replacement and recruitment of new staff as well as the pressure on the remaining staff to cover work. For example, employee turnover may rise in times of organizational change; that is, the 'shock' of changes in patterns of work may lead to decisions to quit (Morrell et al., 2004). A better understanding of the psychological features of turnover can allow for more focused interventions and avoid the unneces-sary costs involved. Morrell et al. (2004, p. 72) suggest the use of measures to mini-mize the effects of change. Such measures include:

- surveys
- consultation processes
- intra- and extra-firm career guidance
- exit interviews
- leaver profiling.

In the 2000s, losing staff is also seen as a loss of intellectual capital, and the replace-ment of 'knowledge workers' can be both expensive and time-consuming (Buck-ingham, 2000). In addition, Des and Shaw (2001) highlight the importance of **social capital** – the value of relationships between people, embedded in network links that facilitate trust and communication vital to overall organizational performance. Social capital is reduced when people leave, with a negative impact on organizational perfor-mance (Shaw et al., 2005).

Human resource planning

In the diagnostic approach to manpower planning, quantitative planning techniques are used in combination with qualitative techniques to identify and understand the causes of manpower problems. This information can then be used to generate solu-tions equal to the complexity of the problems. We have also seen that such an approach has the potential to affect organizational structure, job design and work practices. Organizations can also work out short-term tactics to deal with external manpower issues such as skills shortages. In both the diagnostic approach and the rationalized approach, manpower plans are established with reference to a predeter-mined strategy. HRP, however, seeks to make the links between strategy, structure and people more explicit.

Throughout the 1990s and into the 2000s, the term 'human resource planning' has gradually replaced that of 'manpower planning', but its meaning and practice have been subjected to much discussion and variation. This can be seen to be as a conse-quence of the ongoing debate over what kind of approach to HRM should be adopted in order to provide superior performance at work. As we indicated earlier (see also Chapter 2), there have been a number of efforts to explore the link between HRM prac-tices and organizational performance. Although it is suggested that such efforts may lack consistency in methodology and provide different results, studies in general show that there is some benefit in adopting a 'high road' HRM strategy of high training, high involvement, high rewards and quality commitment (Cooke, 2000). In contrast, 'low road' HRM is characterized by low pay, low job security and work intensification.

In addition to the general view of adopting a high road HRM strategy, further research suggests the importance of introducing HR practices together in a 'bundle' so that they enhance and support each other (Cooke, 2000). Planning to introduce appraisal on its own will, for example, be far less effective without a consideration of training, reward, careers and the attitudes and styles of managers. It is also important to coordinate the implementation (Hoque, 1999), which highlights the importance of a more sophisticated view of HRP.

These moves have received added impetus from findings relating to high-performing organizations. For example, in the UK, a survey of over 3000 organizations combined with 30 case studies found that superior performance came primarily from people working where there was an alignment of 'people strategy' with 'a consistent and complementary innovation strategy' (Department of Trade and Industry, 2005a, p. 74). A crucial finding was the need for an integrated system of HRM covering skills, recruitment, absenteeism, reward and encouragement to be innovative.

A high road HRM strategy linked to a high-performing organization requires a belief by senior management that people represent the key source of competitive advantage because an organization's route to success is based on distinctive product and/or service quality as well as price. Furthermore, the continuing development of those people will be a vital feature of strategy in both its formation and its implementation. In this version, HRP builds on and develops the rationalized and diagnostic approaches to manpower planning that we have already identified in this chapter. It may certainly involve the use of manpower modelling, simulations and statistical techniques, but these will be set within an overall approach to planning that will underpin the bundle of interdependent policies and activities.

HRM WEB LINKS

Go to www.pfdf.org/leaderbooks/l2l/spring98/pfeffer.html#box, an article by Jeffrey Pfeffer, a leading researcher who has shown that managing people using high-performance or high-commitment practices can produce enormous economic returns.

Although there is some evidence for a link between high road HRM and business performance (Wall and Wood, 2005), such evidence may not always convince senior managers in their decision-making. Liff (2000) suggests that HRP implies a link to the resource-based view of firms in which market opportunities are considered against a firm's internal resources when setting strategy. Thus, a consideration of the distinctive expertise and skills of people is held to be a first-order element of making the strategy. There is, however, also significant evidence that many firms in the UK do not view people in this way, preferring to see HRM issues as a third-order issue (Coleman and Keep, 2001). Furthermore, when faced with difficulties, many organizations swiftly move towards a version of HRM in which HR activities are designed to respond to strategy, people being viewed as a resource whose cost must be controlled. Taking the lead from strategy, HRP is in this version concerned more with the right number of people in the right place at the right time who can be utilized in the most cost-effective manner.

Consider, for example, the case of clearing banks in the UK. Whereas clearing banks in the UK could, for much of their history, take a generally reactive approach to a relatively stable environment, by the end of the 1980s and throughout the 1990s, they faced an environment of continuous flux and change in the form of growing competition, deregulation in the markets for products and services, and the introduction of new technology. In the past, clearing banks were considered to be places of employment where loyalty and commitment were rewarded with job security and continuous but slow career progression through a multitiered grading structure. These factors would make traditional banks ripe to adopt a high road HRM strategy, but, at the same time, the banks were forced to adopt a low road version, resulting in branch closures and the loss of many jobs (Storey et al., 1997).

This is a pattern that has been repeated across many organizations. HRP has been used to provide a framework to accommodate 'multifarious practices' of 'pragmatic and opportunistic' organizations (Storey, 1995a). Thus, at the same time as HRP can respond to the direction provided by changes in organizational structure and strategy to cut the cost base by reducing staffing, it can also provide the means by which to achieve desirable HR outcomes such as commitment and high performance. You might be forgiven for thinking that HRP is no different from the use and reputation of manpower planning in this respect. Indeed, those involved in the formation and delivery of HR plans may sometimes feel the conflicts and pressures referred to earlier, requiring an interesting game of words to maintain the appearance of sense.

REFLECTIVE QUESTION

Can an organization claim a high road approach to HRM while adopting low road practices? What are the consequences of this?

Another example can be found in the implementation of business process re-engineering (BPR; Hammer and Champy, 1993) during the 1990s (see also Chapter 5). BPR is based on a radical change of business processes by applying information technology in order to integrate tasks to produce an output of value to the customer. As the change unfolds, unnecessary processes and layers of bureaucracy are identified and removed, and staff become more empowered to deliver high-quality service and products. HRP might focus on the need for skills and learning and other soft HRM practices. Despite the efforts of advocates to disassociate BPR from 'downsizing' (Hammer and Stanton, 1995), BPR has, however, almost always been accompanied by unemployment (Grey and Mitev, 1995), a fact that an HRP plan may attempt, with difficulty, to disguise.

BPR, along with other initiatives to restructure organizations, posed difficulties for HRP in the 1990s. Similarly, in the 2000s, many organizations respond to change and economic difficulties by cutting costs, which is usually translated into making staff redundant. Downsizing by reducing staff numbers is seen by many organizations as a means of improving efficiency, productivity and overall competitiveness (Cross and Travaglione, 2004). Cooke (2000) points out that, in Britain, specific historical, social, political and institutional contextual features have provided a business environment that is incompatible with soft HRM. Thus, with pressure to sustain or increase profits, employees are more likely to be treated as a 'number' in the quest to reduce costs.

This stance has continued despite a realization that losing staff could have negative consequences for organizations as well as for those made unemployed. First, there is the loss of skill, knowledge and wisdom that employees accumulate over years of practice at work. The result of downsizing may thus be a loss of productivity.

Second, there is the effect on those employees who remain at work after a period of downsizing. Where they respond sympathetically towards those made redundant, they may experience effects such as guilt, lower motivation and commitment, mistrust and insecurity (Thornhill et al., 1997); this is referred to as 'survivor syndrome'. A further effect, according to Appelbaum and Donna (2000), is that compromising productivity by downsizing is detrimental to the survivors. Managers may suffer, particularly when 'delayering' occurs. According to research by Littler et al. (2003), managers may suffer from 'burnout' as a consequence of changing workloads and loss of opportunities for progression. There might also be a decline in loyalty and 'even increases in white collar crime' (p. 226).

Third, redundancy is stressful for those made unemployed, possibly through the process of being made redundant itself and then through the experience of unemployment (Pickard, 2001).[7] The general difficulty that HR practitioners face in making people considerations an essential input for business strategy suggests that HRP needs to be considered less as a product, that is, a plan as a written document, and more as a process (Bin Idris and Eldridge, 1998). This echoes Mintzberg's criticisms of strategy as an explicit, rationally predetermined plan as incomplete; for Mintzberg, strategy is a 'pattern in a stream of decisions' (1978, p. 935). The source of such patterns may be formulations of conscious and rational processes expressed by senior managers as intended strategy, but it may also comprise emergent, probably unintentional, learning and discoveries as a result of decisions made gradually over time. Included in this latter process of strategy formation will be the learning of and from employees through their interaction with the organization's structure, work processes and suppliers, clients or customers. Realized strategy will be the result of both intended and emergent processes. Thus, although plans in general suggest prediction, control and relationships that can be expressed in linear terms, it is doubtful whether the world works in this way, making ideas relating to chaos and complexity more attractive (Byrne, 1998).

HRM WEB LINKS

Go to www.brint.com/Systems.htm, which provides links to articles, papers, books and bibliographies on complexity and chaos.

Human resource accounting

To gain credibility and prove the special value of people in organizations, both strategically and competitively, HRM needs to be measured and expressed in financial terms (Toulson and Dewe, 2004). The failure to make a measurable connection between the specific contribution of people and the bottom line has been a key factor in reducing the importance of decisions related to HR. The oft-quoted claims that 'people are our greatest asset' and that people and their knowledge and skills are the one distinctive resource that competitors cannot copy has, however, led to various attempts to state the value of people in the language of accounting and to represent this value in an organization's financial statement. We refer to such efforts as **human resource accounting** (HRA), which we define as the process of identifying, quantifying, accounting and forecasting the value of human resources in order to facilitate effective HRM.

We should, however, be aware that people in organizations differ from other assets in one important respect – unlike capital items and materials, they cannot be owned by an organization. People can be said to 'loan' their abilities to perform in return for rewards from the organization (Mayo, 2002). Organizations will seek to obtain the most from such a loan by combining the knowledge and skills of people with other resources to add value. Furthermore, such value-adding can increase over time through the knowledge and skills that people develop from performing their work and from specific activities such as training and development. An organization might therefore claim that it is important to include such value-adding capability on its balance sheet.

There have for many years been attempts to account for the value of people in organizations, the main focus having been how to develop models to measure the cost and values of people (Flamholz, 1985). One consequence of this was that there was a tendency to treat people in financial terms, 'the dominant image of HRA for many people' (Flamholz, 1985, p. 3) being putting 'people on the balance sheet'. Valid and reliable models of measurement were, however, lacking,[8] and HRA 'progressed at something less than a snail's pace' (Turner, 1996, p. 65).

HRA found more favour in Sweden, where many organizations have used key ideas in decision-making, leading to a 'changed way of thinking' about the management of HR (Gröjer and Johanson, 1998, p. 499). HRA was, for example, integrated into the management control process of three companies researched by Johanson and Nilson (1996). Managers were trained and information systems adjusted. Furthermore, HRA statements were included in the companies' annual reports. It was found that HRA techniques were useful as management tools, but management were also ambivalent towards HRA since the techniques could also be used to assess the efficiency of managers themselves (Johanson, 1999).

HRM WEB LINKS

Go to www.fek.su.se/pei/indexe.html to explore the work of the Personnel Economics Institute at Stockholm University on HR costing and accounting.

As tools for management to control costs, HRA can be accused of contributing to a narrow view of people in organizations as being an expense to be minimized and cut when necessary. This view can significantly underrate the value of people in terms of the accumulation of knowledge and understanding as they learn at work, which makes them difficult to replace as well as difficult to copy. People therefore have a value that is greater than simply the cost of their employment. Although that value is difficult to capture in financial terms, knowledge and understanding in an organization form part of its intangible assets[9] or intellectual capital (Edvinsson and Malone, 1997). What is significant about intellectual capital is that, as the knowledge economy advances, more organizations will need to invest in knowledge-creating activities (Chapter 9), in which the production of new knowledge is a vital differentiator between different organizations (Garvey and Williamson, 2002).

Edvinsson and Malone (1997) suggest that intellectual capital in an organization is composed of two factors. First, there is structural capital, such as hardware and software, trade and brand names, and relationships with customers and suppliers – as Edvinsson and Malone (1997, p. 11) have written, 'everything left at the office when the employees go home'. Second, there is human capital, which is the knowledge and skills of employees at work as well as their values and culture. In combination, human capital plus structural capital equals intellectual capital.

REFLECTIVE QUESTION

What is the intellectual capital of your course? How is this intellectual capital valued?

The factors that comprise intellectual capital are clearly difficult to fit into traditional accounting frameworks. However, the difference between the financial value of the company (its book value) and its value in the capital markets (its market value) has increasingly been recognized as resulting from the assessment of a company's intellectual capital, especially its investment in HR. Such differences have led to a search to find a way of valuing intellectual capital in organizations. The Swedish company Skandia has, for example, developed a set of methods and tools to measure intellectual capital, these being referred to as the Skandia Navigator.[10] Mayo (2002, p. 38) suggests the use of a 'human capital monitor' to calculate the added value of people in an organization. The key idea is that added value, in the form of both financial and non-financial contributions, can be assessed by considering:

People as assets	composed of employment costs, capability, potential, values' alignment and contributions
+	
People's motivation/commitment	affected by factors in the work environment such as leadership, practical support, reward and recognition, and learning and development

Such considerations in HRA can be seen as part of a general move towards values in organizations, although there will still be many difficulties in gathering information to calculate each person's contribution (Mayo, 2002).

Recently in the UK, there have been renewed concerns about the underreporting of an organization's measurement of the quality and effectiveness of people. This led to the appointment by the government of an Accounting For People Task Force in 2003. The task force made its report later in 2003, with a key recommendation that organizations producing annual operating and financial reviews[11] should include information on 'human capital management' (Accounting for People, 2003), although there was an acceptance that the lack of agreed measurements and definitions would require an evolutionary approach. This could, of course, be used as an excuse to avoid any effort to produce human capital management information. In their report for the Chartered Institute of Personnel and Development, Scarbrough and Elias (2002, p. x) suggested that, although no single measure of human capital was available, it was more important, because it was a 'bridging concept' between strategy and HR, to engage in the activity of measurement to gain a greater understanding of 'the productive role of human capital within particular settings'. This is echoed by the findings of Toulson and Dewe (2004), who call for HR managers to become familiar with a range of measurement practices and tools to enhance their understanding of different points of view. The Chartered Institute of Personnel and Development (2005a) has provided a guide on human capital reporting covering a range of measuring tools and methodologies, ranging from simple and subjective anecdotes about the value of people's performance to internal and external benchmarking through to the identification of human capital drivers of performance and models of people strategy interventions.

e-HR

HRP, as an intended and emergent process, and the increasing attention given to intellectual capital in organizations both highlight the need to manage knowledge as an input to decision-making and as an outcome. Human resource information systems (HRIS) seek to support HRP activities through the use of information and communication technology (ICT). It is argued that HRIS can enhance a more systemic consideration of HR activities and their linkage with the organization's vision and goals (Mayfield et al., 2003). Indeed, generating, capturing and disseminating organizational knowledge in all its manifestations are key features of knowledge management and organizational learning (see Chapter 10), and both can be facilitated by HRIS.

According to Broderick and Boudreau (1992), there are three types of ICT application in HRM:

1. transaction processing/reporting/tracking applications, covering operational activities, for example payroll, record-keeping and performance monitoring
2. expert systems to improve decision-making based on an analysis of decisions concerning such issues as sources of new recruits, salaries and training needs
3. decision support systems to improve decision-making through the use of scenario modelling in areas in which there are no clear answers, for example team formation and management development programmes.

Research by Kinnie and Arthurs (1996) found a widespread use of HRIS for transaction applications in operational areas such as employee records, payroll and absence control. There was, however, less use in expert systems and decision support applications, which represent more advanced uses of HRIS. Part of the explanation for the relatively unambiguous use of HRIS lies in the way in which HR departments prove their worth in organizations. A concentration on transaction applications provides a vital flow of data for others to make decisions. The use of HRIS for expert systems and decision support applications that reduce people to numbers might, however, be resisted as representing too much of a clash with people-oriented values (Kinnie and Arthurs, 1996). Therefore, it is argued, a 'halfway position' has been adopted that emphasizes the value of a limited use of HRIS but adds to cost-effectiveness when combined with the professional performance of HR tasks that cannot be performed by ICT. Further research by Ball (2001) supports this position, most HRIS being used mainly for data administration and management rather than manipulation. Ball (2001, p. 690) concluded that 'HRM still seems to be the laggard in running its own systems' to support decision-making and strategy.

A crucial element in any HRIS is how information is used, especially in decisions concerning how people are employed at work. Liff (1997a) outlined three perspectives on the use of an HRIS:

1. An HRIS may provide an objective view of an organization in which the information used is comprehensive and accurate, allowing the best decisions to be made.
2. The design of an HRIS, including the categories and classifications determining the information that should be collected, plays a vital role in constructing the

reality of organization. Of vital importance here is the purpose of one category of data compared with another.

3. The way in which people relate to the information provided will depend on the 'maps' they hold concerning the organization, that is, the store of existing knowledge held by each person to make sense of what happens. Information will be used in making sense of what is going on and what needs to be done, and such information may be accepted or rejected on the basis of how far it accords with a person's map. It is thus quite possible, since each person has a different view of life at work (a different map), that the same information will be interpreted in different ways, leading to different decisions.

In three case studies, Liff (1997a) found that each view could be used to explain managers' use of HRIS. Managers were thus attached to an objective view of an HRIS and the fact that the information it contained was neutral, that is, skills were defined from a 'rational reassessment of current labels' (Liff, 1997a, p. 27). In addition, there was a belief that the HRIS categories could construct a new approach to managing staff and play a role in 'serving dominant business strategy'. The third view could, however, also be found, especially in the way in which apparent discrepancies in information produced by the system could be understood on the basis of existing knowledge of life at work.

In the 2000s, there has been an extension of HRIS towards **e-HR** (Kettley and Reilly, 2003), with many HR departments using the Internet and web-enabled technologies to create an organization network of HR data and information as well as the development of new approaches to HR activities such as e-recruitment, e-learning and e-reward (HRM in Practice 6.1). HR departments are, for example, able to make use of many sources of information available on the Internet. Another approach is to allow staff to access information on HR issues, for example how much holiday they have left for the year, via a business to employee (B2E) portal. Furthermore, making such information available on the Internet allows it to be accessed by staff from a PC anywhere in the world. In addition, other ICT developments provide an opportunity for HR departments to work strategically with other functions. Many large and medium-sized organizations have, for example, attempted to integrate all information flows through enterprise resource planning (ERP) software. One supplier of ERP software claims that it contains tools to integrate resources, machinery, finance and human skills even where operations occur globally using different currencies, languages and legal requirements.

HRM IN PRACTICE 6.1

BT BOOSTS MANAGERS' ROLE IN HR

PEOPLE MANAGEMENT, 14 JULY 2005

BT's implementation of a new PeopleSoft system will give more power to its managers, Margaret Savage, BT's senior vice-president, global services, told delegates at the CIPD's HR Software Show. 'When we talk to our customers we use the phrase "more power to you", which is all about simplicity. We wanted to adopt this in our internal practices', she said.

The system will be rolled out in August, coinciding with the start of BT's new 10-year contract with Accenture, the company that has handled the transactional side of BT's HR function via a service centre for the past five years. This included control of the existing PeopleSoft 7 system – which had started to cause problems. Unable to access HR data on the desktops, managers had to contact the service centre via an 0800 number, which often slowed things down. Overcustomisation also meant the system was unable to adapt as requirements changed.

> **As BT was becoming a more global organisation, it needed a single system that could link everything together.**

As BT was becoming a more global organisation, it needed a single system that could link everything together. But getting the organisation used to the new approach hasn't been easy. Many HR practitioners ques-

tioned the ability of the company's line managers to use the system and take on HR duties via their desktop, while some line managers felt that HR was 'dumping' on them.

So HR business partners have been given the power to view how line managers interact with the system. PeopleSoft was also invited into BT to work through the new system with HR and line managers, encouraging them to give feedback.

HRM WEB LINKS

Find out about ERP's past, present and future at www.erpassist.com/browse.asp?c=ERPPeerPublishing&r=%2Fpub%2Ferp%5Foverview%2Ehtm. You can examine how to 'Transform the role of HR into a strategic business partner' at the following web link: www.lawson.com/WCW.nsf/pub/hcm.

According to Kettley and Reilly (2003), there are three levels of adoption of e-HR:

1. *Project biased e-tools* – basic application of web-enabled tools to key HR processes such as recruitment and training and extending HRIS.
2. *Web-enabled self-service* – a fully integrated organization network of data that can be accessed at any time and place by anyone. Employees can complete a range of transactions, such as booking a training course, without personal contact with HR staff. Workflow technology allows monitoring of absence and overtime payments as well as 'pushing' vital information to key players involved in HR activities.
3. *Advanced B2E solutions* – attempts to influence ways of working and relationships. For example, enhancing e-working by developments in telephony, shared collaboration spaces, online meeting rooms and access to intelligence and knowledge management applications.

REFLECTIVE QUESTION

Do you think that all communications at work can be settled via e-HR and B2E?

It can be argued that e-HR has the potential to transform the influence of HR, enabling a greater participation in strategic decision-making. However, there is at the same time a growing trend to outsource many transactional services to outside HR suppliers. **Outsourcing** is where an organization seeks to source aspects of its production or service processes by setting up a contractual relationship with an external supplier (see below for a more general coverage of outsourcing). The claim in the HR context is that the outsourcing of administrative work will allow HR staff to concentrate more on strategic and high value-added work (HRM in Practice 6.2).

HRM IN PRACTICE 6.2

UNILEVER LOOKS SET TO OUTSOURCE HR

PEOPLE MANAGEMENT, 8 DECEMBER 2005

Unilever is expected to become the next British-based multinational to sign a major HR outsourcing contract. And Royal Mail is considering following suit. Senior HR managers from both organisations revealed their plans at the Human Resources Outsourcing World Europe annual conference in Brussels.

Guy-Joël de Lhoneux, vice-president of HR shared services development at Unilever, said the firm had selected a provider to help commercialise and transform HR but it had not given the final go-ahead. 'There are lots of caveats but, provided these are overcome, we will outsource transactional HR activities,' Lhoneux told *PM*. 'It's about finding a balance between service and cost. We have a change programme and could see outsourcing as a catalyst of change.'

> **'We have to look at outsourcing everything or improving everything internally.'**

Tim Palmer, HR practice lead at advisory firm EquaTerra, which is working with Unilever, said the deal would be one of the biggest ever in terms of annual revenue.

Tony McCarthy, group director of people and organisational development at Royal Mail, said he was considering outsourcing as the HR team needed to keep reducing costs, improving services and building career opportunities as well as simplifying its processes. But he admitted the organisation's HR technology was inadequate. 'We have to look at outsourcing everything or improving everything internally,' he said.

Sako and Tierney (2005) have examined the growth of HR outsourcing, finding that while operations such as payroll administration have been more susceptible to outsourcing, there have recently been more deals that bundle processes together. There are also moves towards a transformational view of HR outsourcing in which an organization seeks consulting and systems integration as part of the bundle. The thinking here is that specialist HR suppliers are able to develop a core competence in HR work and, through their offer of 'robust measurement systems and analytics' (Sako and Tierney, 2005, p. 27), are better able to align HR strategy with business objectives. Furthermore, because HR suppliers are outside the organization, it is argued that they are more accountable, can take a more objective view and gain a more complete understanding of performance. These trends in HR outsourcing will inevitably have a significant impact on the careers of those who enter the HR profession.

Flexibility

Rapid advances in ICT and the pressure exerted to respond to global markets are said to be having a significant effect on work patterns, work location and work times, although some survey evidence suggests such claims may be exaggerated (see Taylor,

2002 and below). In planning how to respond, many organizations invoke the idea of 'flexibility', a term with a variety of different meanings, with a variety of implications for HRP (see also Chapter 5).

REFLECTIVE QUESTION

How many meanings for the idea of flexibility can you think of? As you consider these different meanings, examine the implications for skills, hours and location of work, type of contract and the overall motivation and satisfaction of people at work.

Stredwick and Ellis (2005) suggest some key advantages of **flexible working**. For businesses, there is the chance to exploit the 24-hour economy and open new labour markets that avoid traditional working patterns. Employees seem to like flexible working too, achieving 'far more in the flexible mode' with no 'desire to go back to traditional working patterns' (Stredwick and Ellis, 2005, p. 5).

As a basis of our exploration of flexibility, we will first of all examine a historical but still useful theoretical framework developed in the fields of sociology and labour economics, referred to as **labour market segmentation**. The framework attempted to classify and explain the ways in which organizations were seeking to employ different types of labour. For example, Loveridge (1983) developed a classification based on the following factors:

- the degree to which workers have flexible skills that are specific to an organization
- the degree to which work contains discretionary elements that provide stable earnings.

The classification shown in Figure 6.3 helps to explain how and why some organizations adopt different approaches to the management and planning of the employment relationship for different groups of employees. Thus, workers in the primary internal market include those with important and scarce skills that are specific to a particular organization; an organization would be anxious to retain such workers and develop their potential, and it would be such employees who would form the focus of application of the full range of HR activities. On the other hand, some workers operating in the secondary internal market will be deemed by management to be of less importance, except in terms of their availability at the times required by an organization. This group could include part-time, seasonal and temporary or casual employees. Employers might wish to recruit and retain those employees deemed by management to be the kinds of workers who could be trained to the organization's requirements, but there would be less interest in applying the whole package of HR policies.

Workers operating in the external markets would be considered to be someone else's concern, although there is an important difference between those in the primary external market and those in the secondary external market. The former includes many specialized workers whose skills may be required for specific periods of time or for particular projects, probably as consultants and/or working freelance. The latter includes the range of workers who now work in relatively low-skilled services that have been outsourced to service organizations under contract, for example office cleaning or catering.

Although the idea of labour market segmentation has been recognized for many years, recent times have seen the acceptance of a range of terms and practices that come under the umbrella of the idea of 'flexibility', with all its definitions and implications.

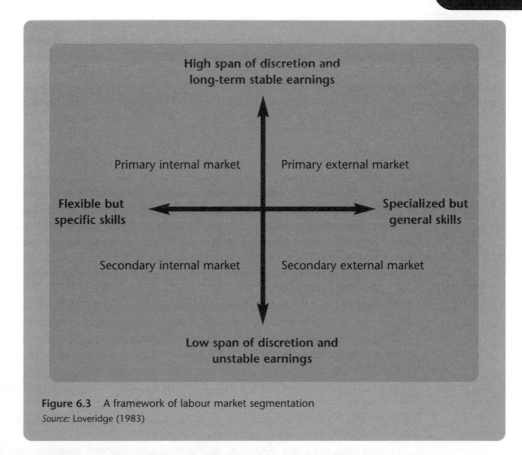

Figure 6.3   A framework of labour market segmentation
Source: Loveridge (1983)

HRM WEB LINKS

Go to www.flexibility.co.uk and use this site to explore different uses of the idea of flexibility.

The 'flexible firm'

The ambiguity of the idea of flexibility has allowed a number of interpretations to justify a variety of organizational activities (see also Chapter 5). Among these is the model of a 'flexible firm' (Atkinson and Meager, 1985, p. 2), which:

> draws into a simple framework the new elements in employers' manpower practices, bringing out the relationships between the various practices and their appropriateness for different companies and groups of workers.

This model identified four types of flexibility:

1. *Functional:* 'a firm's ability to adjust and deploy the skills of its employees to match the tasks required by its changing workload, production methods and/or technology'.
2. *Numerical:* a firm's ability to adjust the level of labour inputs to meet fluctuations in output.

3. *Distancing strategies:* the replacement of internal workers with external subcon-tractors, that is, putting some work, such as running the firm's canteen, out to contract (now referred to as outsourcing).
4. *Financial:* support for the achievement of flexibility through the pay and reward structure.

These flexibilities are achieved through a division of employees into the **core work-force** and the **peripheral workforce**. The core group is composed of those workers expected to deliver functional flexibility and includes those with firm-specific skills and high discretionary elements in their work. The peripheral group is composed of a number of different workers. One category might be directly employed by a firm to perform work with a low discretionary element. Another category might be employed as required on a variety of contracts, for example part-time, temporary and casual workers; this category might also include highly specialized workers such as consult-ants. The final category comprises trainees, some of whom may be prepared for even-tual transfer to the core group. It is important to remember, when considering the issue of flexibility, that organizations do have a choice about the type of flexibility that can be adopted.

This model of the flexible firm has been subjected to much debate. In the late 1980s, the model was criticized as being unsupported by the evidence and as presenting a self-fulfilling prediction of how such a firm should be created (Pollert, 1988). Evidence from the late 1980s suggested that many organizations were adopting flexible working practices in an ad hoc, unplanned and – occasionally – opportunistic manner (Advisory, Conciliation and Arbitration Service, 1988). Thus Pollert (1991, p. xx) could refer to flexibility as a 'panacea of restructuring' as a way of combining different changes in the organization of work, such as multiskilling, job enlargement, labour intensification and cost control.

During much of the 1990s, it was difficult to discern whether the flexible firm remained as an ideal type providing managers with a new set of labels for old practices. During the difficult times of recession, when downsizing was adopted by many organ-izations to reduce costs and intensify the use of labour, flexibility could be presented more positively as way of dealing with change and responding more rapidly to customer requirements, thus securing the future survival of organizations and employ-ment. Thus functional flexibility, as explained in Chapter 5, could be presented as:

- job enlargement
- job enrichment
- job rotation.

Many organizations therefore adopted the language of flexibility and attempted to apply the practices but failed to consider the impact of changes in working practices and arrangements on the employment relationship. Research into the implications of 'lean systems of production', for example, found that multiskilling and more involve-ment in decision-making were offset by greater stress, higher workloads and feelings of blame and isolation (Institute of Personnel and Development, 1996).

Flexible working today

In the late 1990s and into the 2000s, it has been argued that it is the hard HRM approach, with its emphasis on people as numbers within a framework of cost control, that has held most sway in the talk and practice of flexibility (Richbell, 2001). Research by Guest et al. (1998) examined the overall stance of 40 policy-makers in a consortium of companies with an interest in career- and employment-related practices. It was found that there was very little evidence of a coherent policy towards flexible employment, the key factor instead being a desire to reduce and control costs, using short-term and temporary staff when required to circumvent cost constraints.

Thus, the 2004 Workplace Employment Relations Survey (Kersley et al., 2006) revealed that 30 per cent of workplaces had employees on temporary or fixed-term contracts in 2004, a similar proportion to that found in 1998 (32 per cent) (Department of Trade and Industry, 2005b). There has also been a growth in the number of part-time workers, from 21 per cent in 1984 to 25 per cent in 1999. The survey showed that 83 per cent of workplaces had part-time employees, a rise from 79 per cent in 1998 (Department of Trade and Industry, 2005b). Part-time employees made up more than half the workforce in 30 per cent of workplaces, and in 44 per cent of workplaces that employed part-time staff, women made up all the part-time staff. There has also been an increase in the contracting out or outsourcing of services such as cleaning, security, transport and even HR and training, 90 per cent of workplaces with 25 or more employees outsourcing one or more services (Department for Education and Employment, 2000).

In the UK, partly as a response to European Union directives on working time, parental leave and part-time work, and partly as a stimulus to policies on work–life balance, under the 2002 Employment Act and since April 2003, parents of children under the age of six and parents of disabled children have the legal right to request more flexible working with respect to hours worked, time and possibly location. A range of possible 'ways of working' were outlined (Department of Trade and Industry, 2003, p. 12):

- *Annualized hours* – working time organized on the basis of the number of hours to be worked over a year rather than a week; it is usually used to fit in with peaks and troughs of work
- *Compressed hours* – allows individuals to work their total number of agreed hours over a shorter period. For example, employees might work their full weekly hours over four rather than five days.
- *Flexitime* – employees have a choice about their actual working hours, usually outside certain agreed core times.
- *Homeworking* – on a full-time basis, or on a part-time basis where an employee divides time between home and office.
- *Job-sharing* – involves two people employed on a part-time basis, but working together to cover a full-time post.
- *Shift working* – gives employers the scope to have their business open for longer periods than an eight-hour day.
- *Staggered hours* – employees can start and finish their day at different times.
- *Term-time working* – employees can take unpaid leave of absence during the school holidays.

An ongoing survey of responses of adults to these changes has found that there was a 65 per cent awareness of them in 2004, with 14 per cent reporting that they had made a request to alter their working arrangements (Department of Trade and Industry, 2005a).

REFLECTIVE QUESTION

Considering the next 10 years of your working life, which form of flexible working most appeals to you, and how do you expect employers to respond in terms of pay and conditions?

Teleworking, outsourcing and offshoring

One of the significant choices for flexible working has been **teleworking** and/or home-working. Huws (1997) has identified five main types of teleworking:

1. *Multisite:* an alternation between working on an employer's premises and working elsewhere, usually at home but also in a telecottage or telecentre.
2. *Tele-homeworking:* work based at home, usually for a single employer and involving low-skilled work performed by people tied to their homes.
3. *Freelancing:* work for a variety of different clients.
4. *Mobile:* work carried out using communication technology such as mobile phones, fax machines and PC connections via the Internet, often by professional, commercial, technical and managerial staff who work 'on the road'.
5. *Relocated back functions* (call centres): specialist centres carrying out activities such as data entry, airline bookings, telephone banking, telephone sales and helpline services.

According to statistics from the UK's Labour Force Survey (Office for National Statistics, 2005), in 2005 there were 3.1 million people who worked principally at home or used their home as a base, a rise of 0.8 million since 1997. As part of a general increase in the number of teleworkers and people engaging in e-work (8 per cent of the workforce compared with 4 per cent in 1997), most homeworkers (77 per cent) were also teleworkers, requiring a telephone and computer. Another feature of such workers is that they are mainly self-employed. According to Dwelly and Bennion (2003), the trend towards greater homeworking and teleworking is being driven by:

- *technology:* the impact of email, the Internet and cheaper/faster ICT
- *demand:* employees demanding and expecting more flexibility and a better work–life balance
- *employer initiatives:* using homeworking to boost productivity, retention, loyalty and reduction of costs
- EC and UK government *policies* on flexible working.

HRM WEB LINKS

Go to www.flexibility.co.uk/viewers/homeworkers.htm, a site that provides resources for individuals working (or wanting to work) from home. The home page of the Telework Association is www.tca.org.uk, which is this provides advice to workers and managers, and includes an online magazine, job information and a teleworking handbook.

One significant feature of telework has been the growth of call or contact centres, regarded as one of the 'success stories' of the UK economy over the past decade and employing around 800,000 people (Department of Trade and Industry, 2004). The claim is that instead of offering face-to-face personal contact, for example at a bank or an insurance broker, customers can be serviced at lower cost through the use of telephones and other ICT links, with the added possibility of learning about customers in order to enable cross-selling. Korczynski (2002) argues that there are two key but contradictory logics in call centres – the need to be cost efficient but customer-oriented. Thus, customers may appreciate the concern of call centre staff to deal with their needs, while, simultaneously, the length of time taken to respond to customers is being monitored, with pressure to minimize cost. This creates a 'disconnect between customer and organization needs' (Department of Trade and Industry, 2004, p. 3).

It also puts staff under pressure. One view of call centres is, for example, that they provide an opportunity for job intensification in which managers can tightly monitor and control staff performance (Stredwick and Ellis, 2005). One consequence of this is high rates of absenteeism and turnover, with terms such as 'sweatshop' and 'slave labour' frequently being applied (Deery and Kinnie, 2004). A survey by Income Data Services (2003) found attrition rates of 25 per cent in call centres, with pay and intensity of work quoted as primary reasons for this, and a study by Hyman et al. (2003) found that call centre staff suffered stress and fatigue as they attempted to balance working hours with domestic requirements – features of the 'long hours' culture' in the UK. What is important here is that the negative features of call centres can be to some extent minimized by an HR system that provides an integrated bundle of activities supporting high-commitment working.

HRM WEB LINKS

Go to www.bullyonline.org/related/callcntr.htm, which examines the problem of bullying in call centres.

Although call centres have been an apparent success, many organizations have in recent years sought even further cost savings from flexible working by moving their call centres to countries with low wages but similar or even higher skills. Once the customer is used to the lack of face-to-face contact, why not take the process a step further, removing the now irrelevant geographical boundary? This process is referred to as **offshoring**. According to advocates such as the McKinsey Global Institute (Farrell, 2005), offshoring can provide wealth creation even where workers may lose their jobs in the home country. Farrell (2005, p. 68) argues that the 'price' of an organization's ability to cut costs and create new markets is 'continuous change and higher turnover for workers', which can cause 'pain and dislocation'. To avoid this, it is claimed, labour markets need to become more flexible so that workers can benefit from the gains of globalization as well as suffer the costs. Organizations can include training for re-employment, career guidance and reasonable severance packages in their HR plans. One argument is that although jobs may be lost to low-wage economies, displaced workers can retrain and move to higher valued-added jobs.

There is, however, some doubt that highly skilled jobs are safe when economies such as India also aspire to high value-added work (e.g. in ICT development). Levy

(2005) argues that organizations are developing the ability to integrate geographically dispersed operations, which can mean skilled workers in one location competing with skilled workers in different parts of the world.

Offshoring can also be seen as a feature of outsourcing, whereby an organization seeks to source aspects of its production or service processes by setting up a contractual relationship with an external provider. This allows an organization to focus on its core capability and obtain supporting services such as sales, administration (including HR – see above) and ICT at a lower cost from providers who are in turn able to concentrate on their core capability. According to Harland et al. (2005), in addition to focusing on core activities, the principal drivers for outsourcing are freeing up assets, reducing costs and the potential benefits of working with a supplier or partner who is able to exploit advanced technologies. Although organizations have always used a range of subcontracted services, in the last few years there has been a rapid expansion of this, especially in business services, which employ twice as many people as manufacturing; in this area, the global market grew to £126 billion in 2004 and is predicted to grow by 8 per cent a year over the next few years.[12]

Spurred on by rapid developments in ICT, especially web-based infrastructures, outsourcing has become, in the words of *Observer* journalist Simon Caulkin, 'a seemingly unstoppable management bandwagon'.[13] For example, the airline BA is reported to have over 2000 outsourcing contracts in place, including the provision of in-flight catering through the company Gate Gourmet. Among these relationships will be those characterized by a tight specification of contracts, with low trust and pressure to lower costs and compete on price. Colling (2005, p. 95) refers to these as 'distanced' relationships. In contrast, other relationships are more 'engaged', characterized by mutual trust, joint approaches to planning and working via projects and high value-added services in which the outsourced supplier can play a vital role in enhancing decision-making and performance capability – a typical claim of many consultancy and project management service organizations.

The dispute that occurred at Gate Gourmet in 2005 shows, however, the danger of outsourcing. Under pressure to reduce costs in the UK, Gate Gourmet sought to make redundancies and change working conditions. This resulted in a dispute with the trade union, which escalated in August 2005 when the company attempted to bring in 130 temporary workers to cope with the peak travel season. This was followed by an unofficial or 'wildcat' strike by workers and the dismissal of 800 staff. There were a number of consequences for BA: first, they could provide no in-flight food; second, some flights were cancelled; and third, around 1000 BA staff, many of them friends and family members of staff at Gate Gourmet, stopped work in solidarity with them, leading to the delay or cancellation of around 900 flights, at an extra cost of around £45 million.

REFLECTIVE QUESTION

Could the managers at BA have avoided the consequences of outsourcing their catering?

Flexible working, including offshoring and outsourcing, will certainly continue to develop over the next few years. There is, however, still very little evidence on the overall impact on business performance and the motivation and morale of the individuals involved, and what evidence there is tends to reinforce the view that the strategic intention to engage in particular activities will have a crucial impact on HRP processes and the outcomes achieved from workers. Attempts to create flexibility by removing demarcations and boundaries between areas of work can often mean a loss of valued features of work, such as control over the pace of work. Furthermore, extending responsibilities within a job, but removing the prospects of promotion, often as a result of a flattened hierarchy, can easily engender feelings of job insecurity (Burchell et al., 1999). In many outsourced organizations, especially where cost is a crucial feature – and this is the logic of such a process (Colling, 2005) – it is difficult to pursue high road HRM.

Where employees do face seeing their work move from one employer to another, in the UK and the EU as a whole, the Transfer of Undertakings (Protection of Employment) 1981 Regulations provide one source of protection. Revision to the regulations came into force in April 2006; these require transferring organizations to provide information about employees and their contracts, clarify any changing terms and conditions, and make both the organizations involved liable for failing to inform and consult with employees.

HRM WEB LINKS

Go to www.dti.gov.uk/files/file20761.pdf for more information on the Transfer of Undertakings (Protection of Employment) 1981 Regulations.

A backlash may be emerging against the logic of outsourcing and flexibility in general, especially where the business process is subdivided with cost reduction as the main driver, as BA (see above) found to its cost. Its outsourcing of over 2000 of its processes also meant a loss of view of the whole process and, to some extent, a loss of knowledge and control. This raises a crucial point about any argument based on core activities and core competence; according to the resource-based view of the firm that underpins such an argument, it may be difficult for managers to express or understand the processes that produce competitive advantage, which are said to be causally ambiguous. Thus, managers who adopt a mechanistic view of the business may well outsource processes on the basis of cost rather than its systemic value in the business process as a whole.

Attitudes to work

With a growing number of temporary and fixed-term contract workers, there has been some interest in the effect of employment status on motivation and commitment to work.

REFLECTIVE QUESTION

What do you think would be the effect of being given a fixed-term contract? How would it affect your motivation and satisfaction at work?

Research by Guest et al. (1998) into the views of workers in a variety of different settings found that people on fixed-term contracts generally had a positive psychological contract. Reasons given for this were that employees on fixed contracts had more focused work to complete and did not have to engage in organizational politics or complete administrative duties. They might also face lower work demands than permanent staff, avoiding stress and taking less work home. Such employees perhaps benefit from a better work–life balance (Hogarth et al., 2001).

Evans et al. (2004), however, examined the work of highly skilled technical contractors in the USA over a period of two and a half years. It was observed that their work was cyclical, involving periods of contract work on projects, and often involved intense activity and pressures from contracting organizations to use their expertise to solve problems, at any time of day. There were also periods between contracts or 'downtime' – sometimes referred to as 'beach time', 'bench time' or even 'dead time'. They did not consider themselves unemployed at such times – this was normal for contracting (Evans et al., 2004, p. 8). It was found that contractors, even though they were free from the normative pressures for permanent employment, did not necessarily enjoy a desirable flexible lifestyle. The contractors often worked longer hours when contracted, and when they were not, they had to continue working to ensure the next contract, using past work to promote their reputations. They had little time to relax.

The work by Guest et al. (1998) highlights the key significance of the psychological contract, one of the most important findings beings that, irrespective of employment contract, the use of 'progressive' HR practices in combination with an opportunity to innovate within a role resulted in a positive psychological contract, with a positive outcome in terms of organizational commitment and motivation. The overall findings reinforce the view that, in planning to become more flexible, organizations are faced with a choice. Taking an ad hoc approach that is nevertheless driven by cost reduction associated with low road HRM (see above) may produce improved short-term financial results but is likely to have a negative impact on motivation, innovation and commitment. Although the use of outsourcing and temporary and fixed-term contracts may have positive results, a consistent finding in the research is, however, that high road HR practices lead to a positive psychological contract and organizational outcomes. Organizations may be tempted by the 'wrong sort of flexibility' (Michie and Sheehan-Quinn, 2001, p. 302), which does not improve productivity or competitiveness. Sadly, it would seem that many organizations in the UK have given in to such temptation.

Indeed, drawing on an in-depth survey of the attitudes of nearly 2500 employed people towards their jobs and life at work, Taylor (2002, p. 7) suggested that a significant degree of 'hyperbole' surrounded claims about flexibility and dynamic labour markets, with little evidence of a 'coherent HRM agenda'. A key finding was that employees were less satisfied with their work and the number of hours worked. This finding applied to all levels of employee, including higher level professionals and managers, as well as semi-skilled and unskilled manual workers. According to Taylor (2002, p. 10), 'The disgruntled manager has joined the disgruntled manual worker' in complaints about 'the long hours' culture'. In addition, there were trends of a decline in organizational commitment and a sense of obligation to the firms that employed them. The survey cast doubts on many of the claims regarding flexible working in the UK. It was, for example, found that 92 per cent of employees were permanently employed (rather than working part time or on temporary contracts), usually in a specific workplace (rather than home- or teleworking), and that there had been very little change in job tenure.

Diversity management

One of the most important trends in recent years has been the growing interest in the benefits to be achieved by planning for a diverse workforce known as **diversity**

management. This move to diversity can be seen as an extension, but also a contrast, to the promotion of equal opportunities (EO) during the 1970s and 80s. The latter was based on a view that people should be treated equally regardless of race, ethnic origin, gender, sexual orientation and other social categorizations so that 'individuals are enabled freely and equally to compete for social rewards' (Jewson and Mason, 1986, p. 307). Jewson and Mason set equal opportunities within a free-market tradition, and the purpose of legislation and policies was seen as removing obstacles and distortions to the working of markets. They pointed to a liberal approach based on 'positive action' to ensure fair and meritocratic procedures in organizations, underpinned by anti-discrimination legislation. They contrasted this with a more radical view, highlighting the embedded nature of discrimination, which could not be corrected through fair procedures alone. Instead, disadvantaged groups would need 'positive discrimination' to achieve fairness, although this still remains unlawful in the UK.

There has, however, been a general recognition that equal opportunities based on 'sameness' has not fulfilled its promise and that while overt discrimination has been largely removed, there remains embedded prejudice and stereotyping within organizations and society at large. One of the crucial difficulties is that debates on equality are based on ethical arguments, often framed in terms of either social justice or a business case, which Gagnon and Cornelius (2000) suggest tends to produce sterility when it comes to practice.

Diversity, according to Schneider (2001, p. 27) is 'about creating a working culture that seeks, respects, values and harnesses difference'. The basic contrast with equal opportunities is an acceptance that there are differences between people, that such differences can be valued and that they are the source of productive potential within an organization. It is suggested that diversity can provide an organization with a valuable resource in competing both globally and locally. Thus, Singh (2002) highlights a business case for diversity, claiming that inclusion and the development of people 'to the best of their abilities' (p. 3) will result in commitment, creativity and competitive advantage for the organization. For example, Barclays Bank (http://www.personal.barclays.co.uk/BRC1/jsp/brccontrol?task=articlesocial&value=3827&site=pfs) declares the following as part of its strategy:

> Barclays will become a beacon of enlightened equality and diversity policies and practices world-wide and that it will integrate equality and diversity rationale into business, employment, supplier and community practices world-wide.

The relevance of diversity in the group's global strategy is due in part to the importance of cultural factors to the success of future business synergies.

REFLECTIVE QUESTION

How do you think that Barclays can achieve such a vision of diversity?

Like Barclays, many organizations are seeking to manage diversity, and this requires organizations to recognize differences. According to Liff (1997b), there are four approaches to managing diversity based on the degree of commitment to social group equality as an organizational objective and on the perceived relevance of social group differentiation for policy-making. This typology is shown in Figure 6.4.

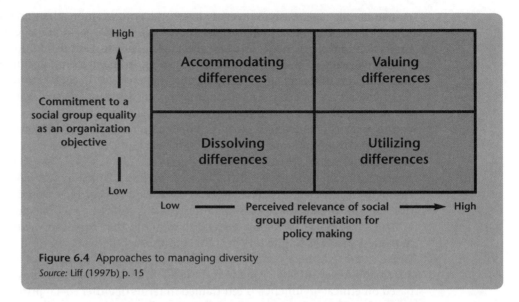

Figure 6.4 Approaches to managing diversity
Source: Liff (1997b) p. 15

The first approach might be to *dissolve differences* in order to 'stress individualism' (Liff, 1997b, p. 13) so that everyone's needs and desires for effective working are recognized. This tends to minimize differences, giving little recognition to the value of difference – rather like traditional equal opportunities approaches. In contrast, a second approach is to *value differences*. Crucial here is the recognition that past practices reinforce inequalities and lead to underrepresentation and disadvantage. This may mean a change of practices to create a culture reinforcing a feeling that everyone has a valued role in an organization. The third approach of *accommodating differences* seeks not to waste talent to ensure everyone has an equal chance. This could mean, for example, targeting recruitment for underrepresented groups that have the necessary qualifications. A fourth approach is to *utilize differences*, recognizing differences and developing policies that value such differences. Liff uses the example of a career track for 'family' women with career breaks, gradual promotion and part-time work. The crucial feature of the policy would be that this track would be valued in the same way as the traditional track.

It might be argued that managing diversity is not a great deal more in advance of traditional approaches to equal opportunities. Indeed, many organizations espouse a commitment to equality *and* diversity, which could easily be translated into a focus on 'sameness', rather than tackle the complexity of 'difference'. However, managing diversity takes a more positive line, in contrast to the preventive stance of equal opportunities (Kirton and Green, 2000). There is also a widening of the coverage beyond traditional concerns with race and gender, and this echoes recent legislative and regulative support on age, sexual orientation and disability. Probably the most important feature is, however, the encouragement to senior management to put diversity at the forefront of its concerns. In recent times, some organizations, for example Ford and BT, have indicated this by the appointment of diversity directors or diversity champions. HRM in Practice 6.3 shows the approach of the BBC.

There is value to be gained from being diverse, in terms of both orientation towards the external context and recognition of the variety within an organization. Diversity needs to be seen strategically and as part of a cultural change process (Singh, 2002). For this to be taken seriously, however, diversity has to be more than checking possible prejudice in recruitment literature or expecting line managers to take responsibility for implementing plans. It needs to be recognized that historical tradition plays a vital role, usually below the surface of consciousness, in maintaining normative value sets that will prevent the advance of the agenda of diversity.[14] There needs to be a challenge to and a critique of the attitudes and background assumptions that are implicitly held by people and also embedded in everyday objects and activities that form the commonality of our lives and to which we are bound (Wood et al., 2004). Thus, greater attention to socialization and the development of a culture of tolerance is required if the positive benefits of diversity are to be gained. There is, however, also the potential for greater conflict based on misunderstandings, which can lead to lower job satisfaction and higher staff turnover (McMillan-Capehart, 2005).

HRM IN PRACTICE 6.3

BBC ANNOUNCES NEW DIVERSITY COUNCIL

PEOPLE MANAGEMENT, 11 AUGUST 2005

The BBC is to set up a diversity leadership council, to be led by director-general Mark Thompson, in the latest phase of its diversity initiative. Diversity at the BBC is currently spread over 17 divisions and more than 200 initiatives, Andrea Callender, the organisation's head of diversity, told delegates at Pearn Kandola's conference, 'Selling diversity in your organisation'.

The council will lead the diversity scheme, with contributions from key stakeholders across the BBC. It will build on work already done, according to Callender, who took up her post in April 2004. She said it was important for diversity practitioners to accept the culture of their organisation and use it to their advantage. 'Whatever the culture, work with it rather than positioning diversity as something to go against. You have to understand the context so that you can understand what really moves people – and it's very rarely the iron-clad business case.'

'No one at the BBC wants to be a manager. They want to be programme makers first.'

At the BBC, the culture is one where employees are articulate, highly-energised and have a positive approach, she said. And they love debate, so Callender exploited this by positioning diversity as something to discuss. She said it was crucial to avoid making diversity a management issue: 'No one at the BBC wants to be a manager. They want to be programme makers first. Anything seen as compromising quality, budgets and deadlines isn't welcome.'

Callender said it was important to find a new definition for diversity so that staff saw it as a positive concept. The BBC definition is now 'a creative opportunity to engage the totality of the UK audience.' She added: 'We're using the BBC's favourite words: creativity, engage and audience.'

HRM WEB LINKS

Go to www.nhsemployers.org/excellence/equality-diversity.cfm, which provides an overview of National Health Service strategy for equality and diversity. The following website sets out the vision for diversity at Barclays Bank in the UK: www.personal.barclays.co.uk/PFS/A/Content/Files/Copy_of_ED_charter_V1.2.pdf.

Check the Employers' Forum on disability at www.employers-forum.co.uk, which provides guidance on recruiting and retaining disabled employees, and the Employers' Forum on Age at www.efa.org.uk.

Career management

One area of HRP that needs to be examined in the light of changes in the workplace is that of **career management** and development. In the past, the term 'career' was one that was usually applied to managerial and professional workers. Many organizations responded to the career aspirations of such employees through HRP policies and processes such as succession planning, secondment, 'fast-track' development for identified 'high-flyers' and a vast array of personal and management development activities. While organizations were structured into a number of hierarchical levels and grades, such employees could look forward to a path of promotion that signified the development of their careers. As Sennett (1998, p. 120) argued, careers provided a 'well-made road' through which individual desires for status and fulfilment could be reached.

Along the way, of course, many employees encountered blocks to their careers, such as a lack of opportunities and support, and, for women, cultural and structural prejudices to career progress referred to as the 'glass ceiling' (Davidson and Cooper, 1992). Graduates too might find their aspirations unsatisfied as they experienced a gap between what they expected and what their organizations provided (Pickard, 1997), and those from ethnic minorities might find themselves 'ghettoed' into certain sectors of work (Singh, 2002). For many employees, however, it was indeed possible to embrace the idea of an organizational career that could be planned for the course of a working life, and theoretical models supported a view that careers could be planned and managed (Grzeda, 1999).

During the 1980s, with the growing influence of ideas relating to people-oriented HRM, many organizations began to see career development for a wider range of employees, the term 'career' being extended to apply not only to a movement through predefined stages such as those found in professional or organizational hierarchies, but also to personal growth and development through employees' interaction with their work environment. This view matched Hirsh's (1990, p. 18) 'developing potential' emergent model of succession planning in which, 'in a person based approach, posts can be considered as ephemeral and may be designed around people'. Furthermore, the responsibility for career management lay with the organization, to 'design and implement processes' that would 'optimize' organizational needs and individual preferences and abilities (Mayo, 1991, p. 69). Verlander (1985), for example, proposed a model of career management based on career counselling between employees and their line managers, with support from the HR development department through training and coaching.

Through the 1990s and into the 2000s, there have been significant changes in the way in which careers are explained, understood and managed. Various tensions, such as competition, recession and short-term financial pressures, a breakdown in functional structures in favour of process structures and even the loss of bureaucratic personnel systems that planned career moves, have combined, in some companies, to 'dump the basic idea of the corporate career' (Hirsh and Jackson, 1997, p. 9), although many employees may still regard their job as a career step (Taylor, 2002). Recently, of course, there has been growing tendency for part-time and temporary contracted relationships with organizations.

Adamson et al. (1998) suggest that there have been three changes in organizational career philosophy:

- an end to the long-term view of employer–employee relationship
- an end to hierarchical movement as being career progression
- an end to logical, ordered and sequential careers.

One of the manifestations of these changes is that fewer organizations would now claim to offer careers for life, with some evidence that employees are unhappy with the ways in which their careers develop (Chartered Institute of Personnel and Development, 2003). If neither individuals nor organizations can plan for the long term, this suggests that the term 'career', with its implication of predictable progression, may have lost its commonly understood meaning. Gibb (1998), for example, suggests that careers and career development are better understood as chaotic systems, characterized by complexity and unpredictability.

Emerging images are that of the portfolio career (Templer and Cawsey, 1999) or boundaryless career (Arthur and Rousseau, 2000). Thus for Arnold (1997, p. 16), a career is the 'sequence of employment-related positions, roles, activities and experiences encountered by a person'. Included in the sequence might be periods of leisure, education and domestic tasks. Over the course of a person's working life, an individual might expect to work for a variety of different organizations in a variety of positions, so each person will need a range of skills, learning new ones as required. This can provide individuals with a chance to gain control over their work and lives, and engage in more meaningful and creative activities (Arthur and Rousseau, 2000). Smeaton (2003, p. 389), for example, in surveys of UK workers, found that those who had become self-employed had higher levels of satisfaction and that 'this form of freedom' enhanced self-esteem.

A contrasting view suggests portfolio work is a threat to work conditions and collective agreements that protect employee conditions, especially where work choice is limited after organizational downsizing (Fenwick, 2003). More recently, Fenwick (2006) examined the stories of the experience of 31 portfolio workers in Canada, that is, individuals who had previously worked in larger organizations, but now contracted their services to different organizations as self-employed workers. It was found that there were dual features of portfolio work. One feature was the creativity and empowerment that came from the challenge of being able to design their own work processes. In contrast, there were the stresses of working with contracts to please clients, the overload of work to hold on to clients and the unpredictability of income. The result of the latter could lead to exhaustion, while workers were at the same time enjoying higher levels of satisfaction, raising 'serious questions about the long-term sustainability of portfolio work' (Fenwick, 2006, p. 76).

For those who still look to their organizations for a career, a crucial issue concerns the responsibility for career development. Hirsh and Jackson (1997, p. 9), for example, refer to a 'pendulum of ownership of career development', in which responsibility swings between the organization and the individual. Their case studies of UK organizations found that this pendulum had swung towards emphasizing individuals as driving the career and development processes, with the provision of career workshops, learning centres and personal development plans (Tamkin et al., 1995). At the same time, as many organizations began to engage in restructuring activities that led to 'delayering' and the removal of grades, the spread of career development initiatives could be seen as way of empowering and motivating staff who remained in place as part of a core workforce. Through HRP, an organization could aim to provide a framework for the integration of career management activities and processes.

REFLECTIVE QUESTION

The notion of careers is subject to change and flux. Who do you think should be responsible for the development of people's working lives? How are you making yourself employable, and what are the skills of employability and lifelong learning?

Examine the HRM web link www.ics.heacademy.ac.uk/Employability/, a site devoted to employability.

What seems to be emerging is a segmented pattern with a rhetoric of career development for everyone at work but with different patterns for different work groups:

- *senior managers and 'high-potential' staff:* careers managed by the organization, not always for life, but with succession planning to fill senior positions
- *highly skilled workers:* attempts to attract and keep key workers by offering career development paths
- *the wider workforce:* more limited development opportunities often caused by and resulting in uncertainty over career paths; there is an expectation that these workers should look after themselves.

In the UK, the Chartered Institute of Personnel and Development (2003) carried out a survey of over 700 organizations relating to their current and emerging practice on career management and found a mixed picture. There was good practice in some organizations, but fewer than one-half had a written strategy for career management, with around a quarter having a strategy for all staff. The survey found a variety of strategic objectives for career management such as growing future senior management/leaders (53 per cent), retaining key staff (50 per cent), supporting changes in the organizational structure/business environment (49 per cent) and producing high-level and specialist skills (21 per cent).

The interesting feature of these findings is a confirmation of the segmented pattern, with most focus on developing and retaining managers and key staff, and only 9 per cent agreeing with the aim of providing employees with a better understanding of career opportunities and expectations. There was, however, an overwhelming espousal of a philosophy of a partnership approach to career management for all employees, even though the reality suggested a focus on particular groups of staff. There was also a variation of emphasis across different sectors, with the focus in the private sector on developing the 'high-potential few' for leadership roles. In the public and voluntary sectors, policy was mainly used to retain and develop staff to make the 'best use of current resources' (Chartered Institute of Personnel and Development, 2003, p. 8).

The survey also found a range of different practices for career management, summarized under the following headings (Chartered Institute of Personnel and Development, 2004, p. 23):

'Doing the basics'

Standard and informal activities
- Informal career support from HR or training function
- Informal career support from boss/other managers/peers
- Development programmes that include work/career experience
- Formal appraisal or development review with manager/boss, including career review.

'Gaining new experiences and skills'

Developmental assignments
- External secondments
- Managed career break schemes
- Internal secondments/project assignments/work shadowing
- Formal mentoring.

'Information and advice'

Information and counselling
- Career counselling by trained individuals
- Career information/advice from staff in a learning centre or career unit
- Career workshops or careers courses
- Career information/tools on the intranet or on paper.

'Developing the élite'

High-potential initiatives
- External secondments
- Managed career break schemes
- Internal secondments/project assignments/work shadowing
- Formal mentoring.

'Job hunting'

Internal job market
- Open internal job market so individuals can apply for an internal job vacancy
- Online vacancy board.

One of the crucial findings was that activities were seldom integrated into a coherent strategy or clearly linked to business strategy. There was a tendency to focus on particular aspects of career management rather than provide a coverage of all areas. This may be detracting from the inclusivity and flexibility of career management provision and the needs of employees. The survey concluded that most organizations were still left attempting to tackle three key issues:

1. making career management a core part of business resourcing and planning
2. ensuring that activities are effective in meeting strategic objectives
3. widening the reach of activities to all staff.

In the midst of the mixed views on responsibility for careers, individuals seeking work in the knowledge economy are exhorted to be more creative in their approach to careers (Hall et al., 2002) and embrace lifelong learning by seeking to update their skills continuously in order to be proactive about careers. There has been a growing emphasis on accepting responsibility for one's own career development through the skills of **employability** and lifelong learning (O'Donoghue and Maguire, 2005; Verhaar and Smulders, 1999), but there is little evidence of adherence to this. For example, Mallon and Walton (2005), in a study of career learning among local government and health workers in the UK and New Zealand, found that few were actively engaging in career learning. Furthermore, most still saw their careers in terms relating to their employment within their organizations (or previous organizations where workers were now working for themselves). It was still very much the case that meanings of careers were organizationally situated and that this affected what was deemed relevant to learn. In addition, and more generally, although there is, as a consequence of the expansion of higher education, a growing number of graduates with higher levels of knowledge and skills, this does not automatically make them employable: employability and a career, skills and knowledge require a valued response from employing organizations (Elias and Purcell, 2003).

REFLECTIVE QUESTION

Do you believe you have the skills required to take control of your career learning?

One model of skills for career self-management has been developed by Ball (1997) and comprises four overlapping competencies[15] (Figure 6.5):

1. *Optimizing the situation*, which involves creating circumstances to support career advances. This requires setting broad goals and anticipating future changes in organizations and one's life, as well as being in a position to respond. Within organizations, it involves spotting and using opportunities for development such as mentoring. Outside organizations, workers can build up a network that can provide them with assistance when required.

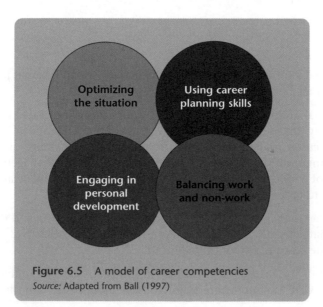

Figure 6.5   A model of career competencies
Source: Adapted from Ball (1997)

2. The importance of the process of *career planning*. In the face of probable changes in work, individuals will need to learn how to review their skills and assess future learning requirements. This process will need to be completed several times throughout a working life.

3. By engaging in *personal development*, workers will become lifelong learners. This involves using development opportunities as they arise, crucial skills here being self-awareness (Stewart and Knowles, 1999) and a consideration of one's transferable skills. This will help in identifying learning needs and making plans to meet them.

4. Finally, there is the *balance between work and non-work*.

HRM WEB LINKS

You might be interested in the student employability profiles of different disciplines at www.heacademy.ac.uk/2174.htm.

Chapter summary

- This chapter has outlined the way in which early approaches to manpower planning were a response to the importance of business strategy and planning in order to ensure the availability of the necessary supply of people, in terms of both number and quality. A rationalized approach, based on the language of economics, was suggested, and the image of organizations as a series of stocks and flows allowed the application of advanced statistics in the construction of manpower models.

- This mechanistic approach, however, often missed the complexity of good manpower management, and manpower planning acquired a poor reputation, few benefits being claimed from the use of manpower planning techniques. There was also little evidence of a link between such plans and business planning.

- Personnel specialists were, however, able to utilize manpower measures of labour turnover, absenteeism and stability to diagnose and solve problems, increasingly aided by PC-based software packages. Manpower information could be used to initiate an understanding of problems such as low employee retention, with a follow-up using qualitative data before solutions were found. Manpower planning could play a vital role in the management of the employment relationship.

- HRP can be seen to be a continuation and extension of this process, which fully recognizes the potential of people and their needs in the development of strategies and plans. Studies have demonstrated the benefit of planning a 'high road' HRM strategy involving training, involvement, high rewards and quality commitment. Integrated systems of HR activities are associated with superior performance in high-performing organizations.

- The evidence of such benefits has not, however, convinced many organizations. In many organizations, HRP uses sophisticated software packages to downsize the workforce, despite a realization that losing staff could have negative consequences for organizations.

- HRA has been advocated as presenting the value of people as assets, but there has been a lack of a valid and reliable model of measurement. Several organizations, especially in

Sweden, have incorporated HRA methods into their management control processes, but research suggests some ambivalence of managers towards their use. Recent years have seen an attempt to value people as part of an organization's intellectual capital.

● HRP activities have recently been supported by HRIS, especially in transaction applications such as employment records, payroll and absence control. Such systems can also be provided over the Internet as a feature of e-HR. Through the use of ERP software, some organizations are attempting an integration of all information flows, but, as with all attempts to portray an organization through an information system, much depends on how the information is interpreted.

● There is a growing trend to outsource many transactional services to outside HR suppliers, with the claim that the transfer of administrative work will allow HR staff to concentrate more on strategic and high value-added work.

● In many organizations, the language of flexibility and a range of different practices have been employed, often without consideration for the effect on employment relations. There has been a growth in the number of part-time and tele-homeworking employees, with government backing for flexible working, as well as in the outsourcing and offshoring of services, but there is little evidence of the overall impact on business performance and people's motivation. Some research suggests growing job insecurity as valued features of work are lost, although other studies have found that a variation in contracts can be used to obtain a better work–life balance.

● There is growing interest in managing diversity at work. Diversity is a means of creating heterogeneity in the workforce where a variety of experiences, backgrounds and networks can enhance an ability to solve complex problems. Managing diversity needs to be seen as part of cultural change.

● Fewer organizations offer careers for life, and career planning has become more difficult. Each person will need a range of skills to develop a portfolio career, and there has been a growing emphasis on people accepting responsibility for developing their own careers and making themselves employable.

Key concepts

- Career management
- Core workforce
- Diversity management
- e-HR
- Employability
- Flexible working
- Human resource accounting
- Human resource planning

- Labour market segmentation
- Manpower planning
- Offshoring
- Outsourcing
- Peripheral workforce
- Social capital
- Teleworking
- Diagnostic approach

Chapter review questions

1. 'When an organization is mapping out its future needs, it is a serious mistake to think primarily in terms of number, flows and economic models.' Discuss.

2. How is HRP linked to corporate planning?

3. What would be your response to the publication of figures that showed an above-average turnover of students in a university/college department?

4. What is meant by 'flexible working'? Explain the implications of flexible working for the management of HR.

5. What are the benefits and costs of outsourcing non-core services?

Further reading

Baruch, Y. (2003) Career systems in transition. *Personnel Review*, **32**(2): 231–51

Daniels, K. and Macdonald, L. (2005) *Equality, Diversity and Discrimination: A Student Text*. London: Chartered Institute of Personnel and Development

McIvor, R. (2005) *The Outsourcing Process: Strategies for Evaluation and Management*. Cambridge: Cambridge University Press.

Marchington, M., Grimshaw, D., Rubery, J. and Willmott, H. (eds) (2005) *Fragmenting Work: Blurring Organizational Boundaries and Disordering Hierarchies*. Oxford: Oxford University Press.

Stredwick, J. and Ellis, S. (2005) *Flexible Working Practices*. London: Institute of Personnel and Development.

Practising human resource management

Searching the web

Forming an HR plan requires a consideration of the requirements at both macro and micro levels. Although figures at the micro level will depend on the effectiveness of HRIS, you will, at the macro level, need a knowledge of figures and trends relating to different labour markets. For the latest labour market trends, in the UK, go to www.statistics.gov.uk/STATBASE/Product.asp?vlnk=550. For trends in education and skills, go to www.dfes.gov.uk/trends and for local area labour force figures, go to www.statistics.gov.uk/StatBase/Product.asp?vlnk=11711. For HR stats elsewhere in the world, see www.unece.org/stats/stats_h.htm (Europe), www.abs.gov.au (Australia), www.statssa.gov.za (South Africa) and www.bls.gov (USA)

HRM group activity

You have been requested to develop a plan for a call centre in the financial services industry that is seeking to move the work of employees to their homes, that is, they will become teleworkers at home.

- What are the HR implications of such a development?
- What difficulties might arise and how should they be overcome?

Try the following web links to begin your study: www.businesslink.gov.uk/bdotg/action/layer?r.s=sl&topicId=1074446319, www.working-at-home.co.uk/ and www.tca.org.uk.

Chapter case study

CDX BANK

For many years, CDX Bank has been one of the UK's major clearing banks. Last year, following a period of intense negotiations amidst a realignment of global financial institutions, the board agreed to recommend a merger with the Singapore-based Eastern Banking Corporation (EBC). Essentially, the merger was a takeover of CDX by EBC, which was considered inevitable in light of the troubled position of CDX in global banking and declining profitability. The troubles for CDX began in the early 1990s, when the bank faced an environment that was increasingly competitive and fast-moving. A series of bad financial decisions, combined with the need to reprocess operations, had led to declining profits and a growing crisis of confidence among shareholders, essentially the institutional investors and pension funds, who exerted pressure to maintain dividends. One result was a pressure on the cost base and a succession of voluntary and compulsory redundancy programmes. In 1992, there were 45,000 employees, but after 'downsizing' there are now around 25,000 staff, over 80 per cent of them employed in the UK.

In the weeks leading up to the merger, staff at CDX became increasingly concerned about their future. Apart from the expectation that a further round of redundancies would be initiated, it was becoming clear that the merger would involve a restructuring and redefinition of roles, including a flattening of the grading structure. Some operations would be 'offshored' – moved overseas where the costs of employment were cheaper. Furthermore, this time redundancy was likely to involve compulsion only. Many employees saw that their careers would become very unsettled and/or would 'plateau'. There were a number of key employees in CDX who were vital to the success of the merger, but many of these employees were beginning to seek work elsewhere, usually with other financial institutions.

Employee representatives within CDX had already expressed their concerns about these fears and the lack of information emerging from management discussions – 'communications about what is happening is a black hole; there seems to be no plan at all'. They also reminded management of earlier difficulties with employee morale among those who had remained following previous rounds of redundancy. Senior managers from CDX and EBC eventually felt they had to respond: they could not afford to lose key employees to the opposition, and they wanted to plan to manage the change so that full information could be provided and employees treated with 'honesty and respect', whatever their fate. Management also wanted to make sure that all actions were based on good principles of HRM. They turned to the HR team for advice.

Discussion questions

1. What advice would you provide to managers on the 'good principles of HRM' during a merger or takeover?

2. What are the key HR problems in 'downsizing' and 'offshoring', and how can these be managed to maintain employee morale?

3. What are the key career issues in CDX, and what advice can you provide to remove or ameliorate employee concerns?

HR-related skill development

It is becoming increasingly evident that many of us will need to learn the skills of career management:

1. What does the term 'career' mean to you, and who is responsible for the development of your career?
2. What skills will you need to manage your career?
3. What issues does the model of career competencies raise for managing your career?

Try the web link: www.cdm.uwaterloo.ca/index2.asp, an online Career Development eManual.

Notes

1. A conclusion from the Work Foundation's report for the Department for Trade and Industry, *People, Strategy and Performance: Results from the Second Work and Enterprise Business Survey*, 2005, p. 74.
2. A quotation from Tom Peters that appeared in the *Observer* on 28 August 2005, at the height of the dispute between Gate Gourmet, an outsourced provider of in-flight meals for BA, and its staff.
3. Alexander McCall Smith's *The No.1 Ladies' Detective Agency*, published by Abacus; 2003, p. 1.
4. The Institute of Manpower Studies is now known as the Institute of Employment Studies; check their website at www.employment-studies.co.uk/.
5. ACAS is a good source of information, with online publications on recruitment and starting work, employment policies and practices, working together for success, communications in the workplace, employment rights, problems between individuals and employers, relations between employers and employee representatives, and codes of practice.
6. You may also find labour turnover analysis referred to as 'wastage analysis'. Consider the source of such language.
7. Read Richard Sennett's *The Corrosion of Character* (1998) for an extensive consideration of the debilitating effects of downsizing and job insecurity.
8. The concepts of validity and reliability will be explored in more detail in Chapter 7.
9. Intangible assets may also include such features as brand names, as well as knowledge and understanding. You may wish to consult Lev Baruch's work on the measurement of intangible assets at http://pages.stern.nyu.edu/~blev/int-research.php.
10. Further details can be found at www.skandia.com/en/sustainability/intellectualcapital.shtml.
11. From 1 April 2005, all quoted companies in the UK are required to produce an operating and financial review (OFR), which provides information relating to development and performance in the financial year, the company's position at the end of the year, and trends and factors that underlie current and future performance and development.

12. Figures quoted in Sako and Tierney (2005).
13. Quoted in the *Observer*, 28 August 2005.
14. It has to be recognized that prejudice is often institutional. That is, there is a declared policy of non-prejudice or even active promotion of diversity but, in practice and often unknowingly, prejudicial action is accepted and regarded as normal. This was a crucial finding of the McPherson Report in the UK in 1999 following the murder of the teenager Stephen Lawrence in 1993. The full report is available at www.archive.official-documents.co.uk/document/cm42/4262/sli-00.htm.
15. Competencies will be explored further in Chapter 8.

Chapter seven

Recruitment and selection

Jeff Gold

> Recruitment is the process of generating a pool of capable people to apply to an organization for employment. Selection is the process by which managers and others use specific instruments to choose from a pool of applicants the person or persons most likely to succeed in the job(s), given management goals and legal requirements.

'Magic radio stations and Heat magazine said recruitment advertising at one of its biggest public-sector titles had been hit by tighter budgets at the NHS and the launch of NHSjobs.com, a free website for healthcare professionals.'[1]

'These tests are a snapshot, but life is a moving picture.'[2]

'HR Directors are largely dissatisfied with the quality of their employees ... they would re-hire less than 60 per cent of current employees.'[3]

Chapter outline

Chapter objectives

After studying this chapter, you should be able to:

1. Understand the place of recruitment and selection as a stage in the formation of the employment relationship
2. Understand the key legal requirements relating to recruitment and selection
3. Explain the nature of attraction in recruitment
4. Explain the effectiveness of the selection interview
5. Understand the value of psychometric testing

Introduction

Recruitment and selection have always been critical processes for organizations. With recent interest in how organizations can achieve high performance (Department of Trade and Industry, 2005), associated with engaged and motivated staff who take a pride in their work, there is growing attention in the form of the bundle of HR practices that lead to a positive psychological contract with employees (see Chapter 1). Recruitment and subsequent selection are vital stages in the formation of the expectations that form such a contract, on the basis of which, with an emphasis on a two-way flow of communication, employees are attracted to and select an organization and the work on offer as much as employers select employees. Thus, employers need to see the attraction and retention of employees as part of the evolving employment relationship, based on a mutual and reciprocal understanding of expectations, as well as an attempt to predict how a potential employee might behave in the future and make a contribution to the organization's requirements. This seems particularly important when the labour market is tight. For example, a survey in the UK by the Chartered Institute of Personnel and Development (2005b) found that 85 per cent of organizations experienced recruitment difficulties, a lack of experience and specialist skills being the most frequent factors. Participants in the survey also identified the importance of branding in recruitment and selection so that the organization stood out as a 'good employer'. Employers are becoming more active and creative in their efforts to recruit new staff (Henkens et al., 2005).

Many approaches to recruitment and selection tend to emphasize the power of employers. For example, traditional approaches attempt to attract a wide choice of candidates for vacancies before screening out those who do not match the criteria set in job descriptions and personnel specifications. Figure 7.1 shows an overall view of the stages of recruitment and selection, and the connection of these processes to human resource planning.

There are wide variations in recruitment and selection practices, reflecting an organization's strategy and its philosophy towards the management of people. Employees seen as part of the *primary internal market* (Chapter 6) become the focus for the bundle of human resources (HR) practices intended to bring about increased motivation, an increased acceptance of responsibility, deepened skills and greater commitment, providing the organization with a competitive edge. Such employees become part of an organization's core workforce, recruitment and selection representing the entry point activities. Seen in this way, emphasis may be placed on admitting only those applicants who are likely to behave, acquire skills and show 'attitudinal commitment' (Guest, 1989, p. 49) in line with the requirements of an organization's strategy; these are the 'right' ones to admit. By implication, an organization needs a way of differentiating between applicants, avoiding the costs of the 'wrong' ones (Newell, 2005, p. 115). To do this, organizations attempt to provide models of psychological and behavioural aspects of people so that judgements can be made about who to admit. At the same time, of course, potential applicants are forming their own 'models' about organizations, and given the tightness of some labour markets, including a high 'quit' rate and competition for staff (Chartered Institute of Personnel and Development, 2005b), this is one feature of recruitment that organizations need to understand better.

As we will explore below, many organizations express their models of employee

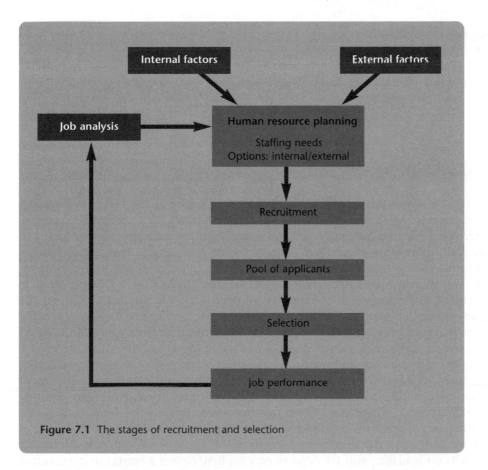

Figure 7.1 The stages of recruitment and selection

characteristics and the behaviour required of potential employees through competency frameworks (Roberts, 1997). Such frameworks have allowed organizations to adopt a range of sophisticated recruitment and selection techniques in order to identify and admit the 'right' people. In this way, as 'organizationally defined critical qualities' (Iles and Salaman, 1995, p. 204), a competency framework augments an organization's power. Once selected, employees may be able to progress and develop a career within that organization. Crucially, however, such models need to work within the constraints of a legal context and a growing interest in diversity management (Daniels and Macdonald, 2005).

Approaches to the recruitment and selection of employees forming the *secondary internal market* could be subject to less screening at the point of entry, attention being paid mainly to possession of the required skills. Such employees might be recruited and selected by cheaper methods but still, perhaps, with a connection to organizational strategy via the specification of competencies. Given the findings relating to studies of workers on fixed-term contracts (Guest, 1998) and the emphasis given by some workers to work–life balance (Hogarth et al., 2001), it would seem, however, that the crucial feature of a positive psychological contract is the use of progressive HR practices whatever the employment contract, and this will include attention to effective recruitment and selection practices. Once again, employers do have a choice relating to the practices they adopt.

REFLECTIVE QUESTION

How would an employer prove to you that it was seeking to develop a positive psychological contract? Go to BP Global Careers at www.bpfutures.com/. Is BP a progressive HRM employer?

Legal context

Variations in recruitment and selection practice are bound by the law of the land. In recent years, UK legislation has had to respond to directives from the European Union. Under the 1998 Data Protection Act, for example, individuals are allowed access to 'specified' information about themselves to ensure its accuracy. This affects application forms and questions that can be asked relating to personal and health information. The Human Rights Act was incorporated into UK law on 1 October 2000 to implement the European Convention on Human Rights in the UK. Although the impact of this Act is still unfolding, a person is guaranteed a right to privacy relating to family, beliefs and freedom of expression. Recruiters thus need to avoid questions about sexual orientation, marital status or age unless these are relevant to the job.

However, recruitment and selection have been notorious areas for demonstrating prejudice and subjective influence, which could well result in infringements under legislation dealing with discrimination. They will also defeat efforts to promote diversity at work. There have been significant changes to the legal context for employment, spurred on by directives from the European Commission. This has made employment law in general something of a minefield and puts increasing emphasis on managers and HR departments to, first, obtain a correct understanding of the legal requirements – from experts where necessary – and second, to ensure that an organization develops and adopts the correct policies, procedures and training in line with its responsibilities under the law.

In the UK, the key legal provisions are contained in the Sex Discrimination Act 1975 (amended in 1986 and 2003), the Race Relations Act 1976 (amended in 2000) and the Disability Discrimination Act 1995 (amended in 2005). The Acts disallow discrimination. In general, there are four forms of discrimination that are against the law:

1. *Direct*, in which workers of a particular sex, race, ethnic or disability group are treated less favourably than other workers, for example in a policy to recruit only men to management posts.
2. *Indirect*, in which a particular requirement apparently treats everyone equally but has a disproportionate effect on a particular group, the requirement not being shown to be justified. A job advert specifying that applicants should be 1.85 m tall might, for example, unjustifiably result in a low proportion of female applicants.
3. *Harassment*, where there is conduct that violates a person's dignity and creates a hostile or degrading environment.
4. *Victimization*, in which individuals are discriminated against because they have exercised their rights under the law.

Since 1995, discrimination against part-time employees can be seen as indirect discrimination against women under the Sex Discrimination Act because most part-time employees are women. The Act is supported by the Equal Pay Act 1970, which sought to eliminate discrimination in pay between men and women. In 1983, this Act was amended to include work 'of equal value'. Under the Act, individuals can claim pay equal to that of a member of the opposite sex when they are doing:

- like work
- work rated as equivalent under a job evaluation scheme
- work of equal value, in terms of demands made under such headings as effort, skill and decision-making.

Further protection is provided by the Part-time Workers (Prevention of Less Favourable Treatment) Regulations 2000 (amended in 2002), which introduced new rights for part-time workers. Basically, part-time workers cannot be treated less favourably than full-time workers unless there are objective reasons for doing so. Part-time workers are entitled to the same hourly rates, pension schemes, leave and maternity/parental leave on a pro rata basis, contractual sick pay and training.[4]

Discrimination on the grounds of race has been extended to religion and beliefs by the Employment Equality (Religion or Belief) Regulations (2003). The law requires everyone to be treated fairly regardless of religion or belief in recruitment and selection and other employment practices such as dress codes. Similarly, the Employment Equality (Sexual Orientation) Regulations (2003) give protection from discrimination on grounds connected with sexual orientation.

In certain circumstances, the laws and regulations allow for discrimination on grounds of genuine occupational requirement for a job. Under Section 7(2) of the Sex Discrimination Act, for example, it is possible to recruit a man only when:

> the essential nature of the job calls for a man for reasons of physiology (excluding physical strength or stamina) or, in dramatic performances or other entertainment, for reasons of authenticity, so that the essential nature of the job would be materially different if carried out by a woman.

In general, HR departments have played a key role in bringing organizational practices relating to recruitment and selection in line with the provisions of the law, although indirect discrimination is more difficult to uncover and eliminate. One obvious process, allowed under the law, is to monitor employees' sex and ethnic origins in order to identify possible forms of hidden discrimination within procedures.

A key area of change in the law relates to disability discrimination. Under the Disability Discrimination Act 1995, it became illegal to discriminate against disabled persons unless discrimination could be justified by the 'circumstances of the particular case'. The Act required organizations employing more than 20 people to remove or make 'reasonable' adjustments to working conditions and procedures that might disadvantage disabled persons, for example selection tests, working hours, the physical features of the premises and special equipment. The Act also widened the definition of disabled persons to include those registered as disabled and those discriminated against because of 'severe' disfigurements such as scars, skin disease and progressive conditions such as HIV and multiple sclerosis. The Act has been amended and extended. For example, from October 2004, organizations have been required to 'take reasonable steps' to deal with physical features that act as a barrier to disabled people who want to access their services. This includes:

- putting in ramps to replace steps
- providing larger, well-defined signs for people with a visual impairment
- improving access to toilet or washing facilities.

In 2005, the Disability Discrimination Act was extended to cover private clubs, rented property and transport operations. There is also now a 'positive duty' for public bodies to eliminate harassment and discrimination against disabled persons, promote positive attitudes and equality of opportunity and encourage participation by disabled persons in public life. This duty also applies to any private sector organizations, such as contractors, who carry out the functions of a public body. HRM in Practice 7.1 provides a creative approach to help visually impaired graduates find job placements.

HRM IN PRACTICE 7.1

BLIND JOBSEEKERS BROUGHT UP TO SPEED

KATIE HOPE, *PEOPLE MANAGEMENT*, 9 MARCH 2006

Speed recruitment days, based on the speed-dating format, are being used to boost the number of visually impaired people in work.

The charity Blind in Business, set up 10 years ago by three blind graduates to make it easier for visually impaired university-leavers to get jobs, believes the events are a way of matching employers and candidates who may otherwise never meet.

'Many companies rely on glossy brochures and websites with flashy technology as a means of attracting graduates. This visual approach can be inaccessible to a lot of visually impaired people,' Gen Herga, employment co-ordinator at Blind in Business, told *PM*.

The charity has recruited 20 employers to meet 20 visually impaired graduates. Each candidate will have a one-on-one interview for seven minutes before moving on to the next employer.

> **Each candidate will have a one-on-one interview for seven minutes before moving on to the next employer.**

Herga says she hopes the event, which is the second the charity has organised, will result in work placements and that the candidates will be motivated to apply to the firm's graduate schemes.

The day is also intended to introduce employers to the practicalities and issues affecting visually impaired graduates and their recruitment managers, including technology that can assist blind employees in the workplace.

Goldman Sachs, which attended the event last year, offered one of the graduates a paid three-month work placement as a result of the day, and has since launched a Visual Impairment Internship Initiative aimed at recruiting more visually impaired people for internships.

Samantha Pirog, executive director at Goldman Sachs, said the day offered a means of tapping into a wider and more varied talent pool.

Perhaps the most noted new area of legal activity relates to age discrimination. There is, apparently, a new demographic time-bomb in the making,[5] with people living longer and having fewer children but requiring support from the working population. According to various projections, people over the age of 65 will form a quarter of the population by 2051 in the UK (Department of Work and Pensions, 2005). There thus needs to be a different approach to considering age and employment because an obvious answer to this difficulty is to allow older people to play a more active role at work. There is, however, also evidence that such people face discrimination because of their age. Thus from 2006, under the Employment Equality (Age) Regulations, age discrimination in employment and vocational training are prohibited, with no quali-fying period. Thus, during recruitment and selection processes, employers need to take care that they do not discriminate on grounds of age. For example, a requirement for five years' driving experience would discriminate against 20-year-old applicants. Adverts for 'young and dynamic' staff would discriminate directly against older applicants. In addition, it will be discriminatory to set a retirement age below 65; indeed, there is a duty on employers to consider requests to work beyond retirement. Older workers have the same rights to claim unfair dismissal or receive redundancy payments as younger workers. As with all other laws and regulations on discrimination, there needs to be justification based on the requirements of the job for discrimination to occur.

The anti-discrimination legislation over the past 25 years provides the foundation for a growing interest in diversity at work. Recruitment is an obvious place to focus on diversity, especially in the context of global operations but also in terms of an increas-ingly diverse workforce. Vodafone, for example, seeks to attract staff from across Europe, recognizing that cultural differences can promote learning and creativity (Tipper, 2004).

Diversity in recruitment is a means of creating heterogeneity in the ability to solve complex problems (McMillan-Capehart, 2005). Tipper (2004, p. 158) argues that it is important to win the 'hearts and minds' of those involved in the recruitment process, including the commercial rationale for diversity. Thus, recent survey evidence (Char-tered Institute of Personnel and Development, 2005b) suggests that more organizations are providing training for interviewers in diversity and that the recruitment teams fit any diversity criteria set by the organization. The survey, of over 600 respondents in the UK, found that various methods are being used to promote diversity in recruitment, for example monitoring recruitment and/or staffing information to gain data on gender, ethnic origin, disability, and so on (70 per cent), training interviewers (69 per cent), operating policies that go beyond the requirements of legislation (40 per cent), checking that any tests used are culture-free and have been tested on diverse norm groups (38 per cent) and ensuring that the recruitment team reflects diversity criteria (35 per cent).

HRM WEB LINKS

ACAS provides a good page of links on equality and diversity laws and regulations at www.acas.org.uk/index/aspx?articleid=337.

A copy of the Disability Discrimination Act can be found at www.opsi.gov.uk/acts/acts1995/1995050.htm. The Act set up a Disability Rights Commission to help secure civil rights for disabled people; visit the website at www.drc.org.uk//.

For more on tackling age discrimination, go the Age Positive website at www.agepositive.gov.uk.

Recruitment and attraction

If high-commitment HRM is concerned with the development of an integrated bundle of policies related to the management of people, **recruitment** and **attraction** represent vital stages in determining which employees will be able to benefit from such policies. Our definition of recruitment is the process of generating a pool of capable people to apply for employment to an organization. Within this definition, we can highlight two crucial issues. First, there is a need to generate people's interest in applying for employment – they need to be attracted to an organization. This implies that people do have a choice about which organizations they wish to work for. Second, people may be capable of fulfilling a role in employment, but the extent to which this will be realized is not totally predictable.

Employees will potentially attempt to retain significant discretion with respect to the effort they are prepared to make and their commitment to the organization. Management will of course seek to influence this process to the advantage of the organization (Watson, 1994), but other parties involved may have different interests. Under different labour market conditions, power in this process will swing towards the buyers or sellers of labour – employers and employees, respectively. It is therefore important to understand that the dimension of power will always be present in recruitment and selection, even in organizations that purport to have a high-commitment HR strategy. Thus, in conditions of tight labour markets, organizations need an active approach to recruitment, recognizing that potential applicants do have choice.

There needs to be an intelligent use of recruitment channels. For example, the ageing profile of the workforce requires an adjustment of polices of recruitment (Lyon and Glover, 1998). Henkens et al. (2005), for example, found that the use of the Internet and agencies for recruitment reflected a bias for younger applicants, whereas older workers were more dependent on formal channels of recruitment. In addition, since the early 1990s, there have been more graduates entering the labour market but the number of 'graduate' jobs has not kept pace, with a consequent reduction in the power of many new graduates to find employment on advantageous terms; also, some employers have reservations about employing graduates for 'nongraduate' jobs (Institute of Personnel and Development, 1997). Stewart and Knowles (2000) suggest, however, that small and medium enterprises are becoming a key source of graduate recruitment, and indeed such firms, which also have less formal and less bureaucratic recruitment practices (Barber et al., 1999), may be becoming more attractive to graduates.

HRM WEB LINKS

Cranfield University provides a Recruitment Confidence Index that measures expectations of future recruitment activity. Go to www.som.cranfield.ac.uk/som/rci.

Fitting the person to the environment, organization and job

Effective recruitment depends on the extent to which overall management philosophy supports and reinforces an approach to HRM that focuses on the utilization and development of new employees once they have gained entry to an organization. Whereas HR policies will be designed to achieve particular organizational targets and goals, those policies will also provide an opportunity for individual needs to emerge and be satisfied. This view assumes that a fit between a person and the environment can be found so that commitment and performance are enhanced (Kristof, 1996). Although some commentators would doubt that such mutuality could ever occur on the basis of equality, and that organizational needs, as determined by senior management, would always take precedence, we have already argued that individual needs may, through HRM activities, influence the perception of the organization's needs.

Recruitment and then selection processes will therefore aim to attract and admit those whom management view as the 'right' people for such an approach. In one sense, an organization already knows who the right people are for its vacancies since they are the very people who are already employed. The survey by the CIPD (2005b) for example, found that 84 per cent of participants had a policy of advertising all vacancies internally, mainly via an intranet and notice boards. Although succession-planning was mainly restricted to larger organizations, there was a clear interest in developing a 'talent pool' for internal promotions.

It is becoming important for organizations to take a strategic view of their recruitment requirements, starting with the strategic plan. Research by Tyson (1995, p. 82) found that although there were many differences between organizations, HRM could help to shape the direction of change, influence culture and 'help bring about the mindset' that decided which strategic issues were considered. HR considerations, including the results of a review of the quantity and quality of people, should thus be integrated into the plan (Chapter 6). The goals, objectives and targets that emerge set the parameters for performance in an organization and for how work is organized into roles and jobs. A key role for HR is to align performance within roles with the strategy, so recruiting the right people for a role depends on how it is defined in terms relating to performance to achieve the strategy (Holbeche, 1999). Increasingly, once a recruitment strategy has been formed, an organization may outsource its implementation, especially where there are large numbers to be recruited (Tulip, 2004).

Traditionally, the specification of the requirements of particular work roles has required the use of job analysis techniques, including a range of interviews, questionnaires and observation processes that provide information about work carried out, the environment in which it occurs and, vitally, the knowledge, skills and attitudes needed to perform well.

In recent years, information derived from the analysis of work performance has been utilized to create a taxonomy of either criterion-related behaviours or standards of performance referred to as **competencies**. Woodruffe (1992, p. 17) has defined competency as 'the set of behaviour patterns that the incumbent needs to bring to a position in order to perform its tasks and functions with competence'.[6] Competency frameworks are concerned with behaviour that is relevant to the job and the effective or competent performance of that job. Such frameworks are usually developed within organizations and are based on the understandings and meanings of behaviour that exist within an organization. It is claimed that competency frameworks 'lie at the heart of all' approaches to HRM (Boam and Sparrow, 1992, p. 13) where the organization's objectives can be aligned with the various HR activities of recruitment and selection, appraisal, training and reward (Holbeche, 1999). It is argued that competencies enhance a common understanding of effective behaviour at work and provide a basis for more consistency in assessment practices (Whiddett and Hollyforde, 2003).

HRM WEB LINKS

SHL is one of the main suppliers of job assessment software that can be used to develop competencies. Details of its work profiling system can be found at www.shlusa.com/selection/sel_workprofilingsys.html. It also provides a useful book on job analysis techniques, which you can download after you complete a short registration requirement. Go to http://www.shl.com/SHL/en-int/Thought_Leadership/Best_Practices_Guides/.

Here is how one large financial services organization in the UK sets out its competencies:

- Self-control
- Self-development
- Personal organization
- Positive approach
- Delivering results
- Providing solutions
- Systemic thinking
- Attention to detail
- Creating customer service
- Delivering customer service
- Continuous improvement
- Developing people
- Working with others
- Influencing
- Leading
- Delivering the vision
- Change and creativity.

Each competency is defined and described by a range of indicators that enables assessment and measurement. The competency of 'creating customer service' is, for example, indicated by:

- anticipating emerging customer needs and planning accordingly
- identifying the customers who will be of value to the company
- recommending changes to current ways of working that will improve customer service
- arranging the collection of customer satisfaction data and acting on them.

The analysis and definition of competencies should allow the identification and isolation of dimensions of behaviour that are distinct and are associated with competent or effective performance. Competencies can therefore be used to provide, at least from an organization's point of view, the behaviours needed at work to achieve the business strategy. On this assumption, the assessment of competencies is one means of selecting employees, as will be discussed below. Competencies will enable organizations to form a model of the kinds of employees it wishes to attract through recruitment.

Whatever the model constructed, an organization's commitment to its HR processes will form part of its evolving value system and make it even more attractive to those seeking employment. Many organizations seek to express their core values within statements of visions and missions. For example, the following can be found on the graduate recruitment pages of Lloyds TSB's website (www.adarkhorse.com/visionValues.php):

> We're a big business. But more importantly, we'd like to be the best – at everything. We already have incredibly high standards. If you join us, it will be your job to help raise them.

> As an organisation we make it our business to be the best company in the financial services industry by being a 'great place for our staff to work'.

For our customers, that means bringing our key CARE values to all our dealings with them.

Customer Understanding – Building stronger relationships with our customers and understanding their individual needs.

Accessibility – Being approachable, honest, straightforward and welcoming whenever, wherever and however our customers want us.

Responsibility – Looking after our customers' best interests, delivering what we promise and respecting the communities we serve.

Expertise – Offering services and products that are right for our customers with the expertise and efficiency they expect.

Such statements form part of the image projected by the company. Projected images, values and information on espoused goals will interact with workers in external labour markets, including both those employed and those unemployed. This interaction will determine the degree of attraction that potential recruits feel towards an organization.

REFLECTIVE QUESTION

Think about an organization you would like to work for. What images, values and information related to that organization come into your mind?

The image projected by an organization and the response from potential employees provide the basis for a compatible person–organization fit, a variant of person–environment fit referred to earlier.[7] Schneider (1987), using a theory of interactional psychology, proposed an attraction–selection–attrition framework to explain the workings of this process and differences between organizations that are caused by the attraction of people to organizational goals, their interaction with the goals and the fact that 'if they don't fit, they leave' (Schneider, 1987, p. 437). The proposed framework is shown in Figure 7.2.

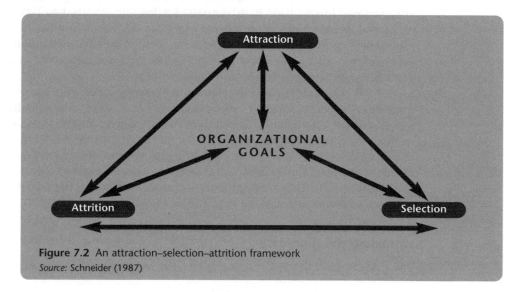

Figure 7.2 An attraction–selection–attrition framework
Source: Schneider (1987)

Schneider used the findings from vocational psychology to argue that people are attracted to an organization on the basis of their own interests and personality. Thus, people of a similar type will be attracted to the same place. Furthermore, the attraction of similar types will begin to determine the place. Following selection, people who do not fit, because of either an error or a misunderstanding of the reality of an organization, will leave, resulting in attrition from that organization.

At the heart of the framework lie organizational goals, originally stated by the founder and/or articulated by top managers, out of which emerge the structures and processes that will form the basis of attraction decisions. This framework has been supported by research conducted by Judge and Cable (1997), who found that applicants seek person–organization fit, attempting to match their values with the reputation of an organization's culture. Furthermore, person–organization fit can be enhanced by an attention to socialization processes once new employees have been selected (Cable and Parsons, 2001). Carless (2005), however, sought to track applicants' perceptions at different moments in time as they moved through the recruitment and selection process to the point of their intention to accept a job offer. In addition to person–organization fit, Carless also examined perceptions of person–job fit, concerned with the extent to which there was a match between an individual's skills, knowledge and abilities and the requirements of a job. It was found that both were positively linked to attraction, the perception that an organization was a desirable place to work. For intention to accept a job offer, however, person–job fit became more important. This suggests that once applicants move toward job acceptance, they become more concerned with how they will use their abilities than with working in an organization that matches their values.

There is also the issue of person–team fit (Hollenbeck, 2000), which considers how people can be matched to variations in organizational structures. For example, in a decentralized structure in which the focus is on self-managing teams, there might be different characteristics required compared with more centralized or departmental structures.

This analysis of attraction, based on images and congruence of values and then use of abilities, is complicated by recent concerns relating to a more diverse workforce. There are also limits on the expression of values set by recent changes in legislation. For example, images used in advertisements for recruits need to take into consideration possible discrimination against older applicants. A number of organizations, especially in the financial services and retail sectors, are seeking to adjust their recruitment to attract an older workforce and retain them for longer by allowing them to work beyond the age of retirement (Trapp, 2004).

There is also some interest in re-attracting ex-employees. This has been particularly important in North America, where some organizations have established alumnus associations or 'talent banks' to maintain contact with former staff and provide opportunities for them to return to work. This has proved to be more cost-effective than using agencies for recruitment. The accounting firm PricewaterhouseCoopers, for example, has an alumnus group of 21,000 members who have access to a website and can attend events. They can also make recommendations to the firm for employment and receive payment for doing so (Carrington, 2005).

Attracting the candidate

The main approaches to attracting applicants can be summarized as follows:

- walk-ins
- employee referrals
- advertising
- websites
- recruitment agencies
- professional associations
- educational associations.

Advertising and other recruitment literature comprise a common means by which values, ethos and the desired image are made manifest, usually in the form of glossy brochures. In recent years, the undoubted expertise that exists within the UK advertising industry has been utilized in company recruitment as they engage in a 'war for talent' (Michaels et al., 2001). The utilitarian approach that focused on specifying job details, terms and conditions is increasingly being superseded by advertising that attempts to communicate a message about the company image, possibly over a long period of time through 'low-involvement' advertisements that seek to create awareness of an organization rather than generate recruits (Collins and Han, 2004). There has been a marked shift towards recruitment advertisements that are creative and reflect the skills normally used in product marketing. Recruitment advertising is now fully established within mainstream advertising.

In recent years, there has been a rapid growth in online recruitment, **e-recruitment** having become another facet of the rapid progression of e-HRM. According to the CIPD (2005b), about one-third of organizations now accept application forms completed online. Like many aspects of the dot.com revolution, e-recruitment has of course been subjected to rapid change with the arrival and departure of companies specializing in recruitment on the web. There are three types of operator online. First, there are general recruitment agents such as Monster and StepStone, providing online job boards that offer a range of services to job-seekers as well as access to job adverts. It is reported that there are over 300 online recruitment providers in the UK and 1400 across Europe, although such figures can never be certain in the flux and change of the dot.com world (Taylor, 2001).

HRM WEB LINKS

Go to the Monster (www.monster.co.uk) and StepStone (www.stepstone.com/) websites and examine the services they offer to job-seekers. What help is offered regarding CVs, learning about salaries and career development?

Second, there are organizations that focus on providing an online recruitment service on behalf of organizations. Such agencies specialize in managing the recruitment process online and claim to provide an automated and cost-effective service. This normally involves working in collaboration with an organization and connecting with its HR information system. For example, Nike in Europe used an agency who designed Nike's website and handled applications from the receipt of CVs through to the offer of jobs. A connect to Nike's HR information system enabled the agency to match applicants to job requirements based on competencies (Pollitt, 2005a).

HRM WEB LINKS

Check the service provided by ActiveRecruiter at www1.jobpartners.com/english/solutions/activerecruiter.

Third, many large companies have established their own websites for recruitment; indeed, most are only accepting online applications via their websites, where all their vacancies are advertised. Such a move assumes that potential applicants have the necessary skills to carry out job-related searches and can find company websites (Feldman and Klass, 2002), and organizations are advised to consider the design of their sites and the terms that applicants might use to carry out job and vacancy searches (Jansen and Jansen, 2005). We might suggest here that online recruitment can discriminate against those still without access to the Internet. It is, however, suggested that companies such as the BBC and British Airways can make large savings in recruitment advertising by such communication through their websites. One result noticed by British Airways was that, by moving to Internet and email recruitment, the number of applicants for their management programme was reduced from 12,000 to 5000, although it was felt that the switch filtered out many who would have been rejected anyway (Merrick, 2001).

While cost saving is clearly a major benefit, some companies see online recruitment more strategically. For example, Whitbread faced a problem of recruiting managers for its 400-site Brewsters and Brewers Fayre restaurant business. It found that agencies could not meet its needs so it developed its own recruitment website (at www.run-a-restaurant.com/). The site was searched over 100,000 times in the first four months, with 1300 applications. This enabled the company to build a database and maintain contact with candidates. Another benefit to the company was establishing consistency with its brand to potential employees (Smethurst, 2004).

REFLECTIVE QUESTION

Go to either the British Airways website at www.britishairwaysjobs.com/baweb1/ or that of Merrill Lynch, an investment company, at www.ml.com/index.asp?id=7695_8199. How do you think these websites filter out those who do and do not wish to work for British Airways or Merrill Lynch? Did you take the interactive challenges? Does online recruitment increase the power of employers in the graduate labour market?

Images presented in recruitment advertisements and brochures, as well as online, can be an important part of the attraction but not the only part. There is not a great deal of evidence that such images are entirely effective, informal 'word-of-mouth' information about jobs often being more accurate and effective (Iles and Salaman, 1995). Sometimes significant events can create interest in an organization – see, for example, HRM in Practice 7.2.

Formal advertising can also be expensive, and an organization will take account of a number of other factors in forming its recruitment plans and choice of media. These might include the following:

- the cost
- the time taken to recruit and select

- the labour market focus, for example skills, profession or occupation
- mobility of labour – geographic and occupational
- retention and labour turnover rates
- legislation and regulations on equal opportunities and diversity.

HRM IN PRACTICE 7.2

BOMBINGS RAISE DEMAND FOR MET JOBS

ANNA CZERNY, *PEOPLE MANAGEMENT*, 15 SEPTEMBER 2005

More and more people are considering joining the police service following the bomb attacks on London, the head of the careers team at the Metropolitan Police has told *PM*.

'We've had a marked increase in the number of telephone enquiries from people asking about a career in the police service since 7 July,' said Superintendent Neil Seabridge. Although the Met doesn't formally record the number of telephone enquiries it gets, Seabridge said they had experienced 'a sharp spike' in interest.

To fuel interest further, the Met held its second faith recruitment event to encourage people from diverse religious backgrounds to join the force. The message from the event was that a person could join the Met without compromising the values of their faith.

> **'I would attribute the groundswell of public support post 7/7 as a significant factor in the increased level of interest.'**

The event attracted over 500 attendees, more than double that of last year. Of the delegates, 346 registered their interest in becoming a police officer. Seabridge said a number of reasons were behind the positive response, including the effect of the bombings. 'I would attribute the groundswell of public support post 7/7 as a significant factor in the increased level of interest,' he said.

Another group eager to work in the police service is retired police officers. According to a recruitment consultancy that places ex-police officers back into police forces, RIG Police Recruit, there has been a 40 per cent increase in demand for such staff since the attacks.

Police forces across the UK, which have been stretched by anti-terrorist investigations, can use former officers to undertake back-office duties, freeing up currently serving officers to work in the field.

Job descriptions

A further manifestation of the image to which recruits will be attracted is a description of the actual work that potential employees will be required to do. The traditional way of providing such information is in the form of a **job description**, usually derived from job analysis and describing the tasks and responsibilities that make up the job. Against each job description, there is normally a specification of the standards of performance. A typical format for a job description is given in Figure 7.3.

In addition to a description of a job, there is, in the form of a **personnel specification**, some attempt to profile the 'ideal' person to fill the job. It is accepted that the ideal person for the job may not actually exist and that the specification will be used only as a framework within which a number of candidates can be assessed. A common format for a personnel specification is the seven-point plan, based on the work of Rodger (1970), shown in Figure 7.4. An alternative to the seven-point plan is Munro-Fraser's fivefold grading system (1971), as in Figure 7.5. In both forms of personnel specification, it is usual to indicate the importance of different requirements. Thus, certain requirements might be expressed as essential and others as desirable.

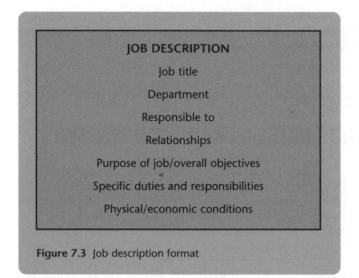

Figure 7.3 Job description format

Both job descriptions and personnel specifications have been key elements in the traditional repertoire of personnel managers. Over the years, various attempts have been made to develop and fine-tune techniques and practices. One such development has been the shift of emphasis in job descriptions away from specifying tasks and responsibilities towards the results to be achieved (Plachy, 1987). There has, however, been a growing awareness of the limitations and problems of such approaches. Watson (1994) noted that job analysis, used to produce job descriptions and personnel specifications, relied too much on the subjective judgement of the analyst to identify the key aspects of a job and derive the qualities that related to successful performance. In addition, the use of frameworks such as the seven-point plan may provide a 'cloak for improper discrimination' (Watson, 1994, p. 189).

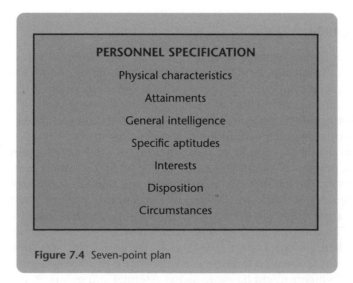

Figure 7.4 Seven-point plan

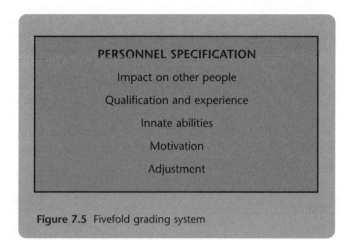

Figure 7.5 Fivefold grading system

HRM WEB LINKS

In the UK, ACAS provides examples of job descriptions and personnel specifications at www.acas.org.uk/index/aspx?articleid=389.

The drive towards flexibility and changing work practices has seen the appearance of new forms of work description. Some organizations have, for example, begun to replace or complement job descriptions with *performance contracts*. These contain details of what a job-holder agrees to accomplish over a period of time, summarizing the purpose of a job, how that purpose will be met over the time specified and how the achievement of objectives will be assessed. This approach allows job requirements to be adjusted by agreement between the job-holder and his or her manager. It also allows a clear link to be established with other HR processes. Performance contracts signal to new recruits the expectation that their jobs will change and that they cannot rely on a job description as the definitive account of their work. Adler (2002b) refers to this reorientation as performance-based recruitment and selection.

Further competencies are, as we have already discussed, increasingly used to create a specification of the characteristics of those sought for particular positions (Roberts, 1997; Industrial Relations Services, 2003a). It has been argued (Feltham, 1992) that the use of competencies allows organizations to free themselves from traditional stereotypes in order to attract applicants from a variety of sources. Stereotypes of the ideal person may be contained within personnel specifications, and organizations may, despite warnings, be reinforcing the stereotype in their recruitment practices. Competencies appear to be more objective, have a variety of uses in attracting applicants and allow an organization to use more reliable and valid selection techniques.

The test of success of a recruitment process is whether it attracts a sufficient number of applicants of the desired quality within the budget set (Connerley et al., 2003). Traditionally, applications are made by a combination of letter, a completed application form and/or a CV. Increasingly, such forms can be submitted by email or completed online – about a third of applications according to the CIPD survey (2005b). Recruiters might reasonably expect a number of applicants per position available, referred to as the *recruitment ratio*, thus allowing a choice to be made. Changes to the recruitment process may affect this ratio. For example, as we have indicated above, e-recruitment via the Internet may reduce the quantity, but not necessarily the quality, of applicants. Too many applicants may reduce the cost per applicant but add further costs in terms of the time taken to screen the applications. Too few applicants may be an indication of a tight labour market but may also be an indication that the values, ethos and image projected by the organization on to the market, including information on the work, as provided by job descriptions and specifications, are poor attractors. Recruiters need to monitor the effect of such factors on the recruitment process. If there are insufficient applicants from particular ethnic groups, too few men or women or disabled applicants, the recruitment process may indirectly discriminate and/or fail to meet legal requirements.

Selection

As we have seen, it is usual for an organization that wishes to recruit new employees to define criteria against which it can measure and assess applicants. Increasingly, however, such criteria are set in the form of competencies composed of *behavioural characteristics* and *attitudes*. Rather than trust to luck, organizations are using more sophisticated selection techniques. Organizations have become increasingly aware of making good selection decisions, since selection involves a number of costs:

- the cost of the selection process itself, including the use of various selection instruments
- the future costs of inducting and training new staff
- the cost of labour turnover if the selected staff are not retained.

The CIPD's research (2005b) on selection methods used in UK organizations showed that interview following the contents of the CV/application form (i.e. biographical) was the most common approach (68 per cent), followed by competency-based interviews (58 per cent) and structured interviews, either panel (56 per cent) and/or one-to-one, and critical incident/behavioural (41 per cent). Other methods being used were references before interviews and tests for specific skills, general abilities, literacy/numeracy and personality; 34 per cent also used an assessment centre.

The configuration of selection techniques chosen will depend on a number of factors. As argued by Wilk and Cappelli (2003, p. 117), it is not simply a case of 'more is better'. Selection methods will depend on the characteristics of the work and the level of pay and training.

It is also crucial to remember that decisions are being made by both employers and potential employees and that the establishment of mutually agreed expectations during selection forms part of the psychological contract (see Chapter 1), which will strongly influence an employee's attitudes and feelings towards the organization (Herriot et al., 1997). As Hausknecht et al. (2004) suggest, there are five reasons why organizations need to consider the reaction of applicants to selection methods:

1. If selection is viewed as invasive, the attraction of the organization may be diminished.
2. Candidates who have a negative experience can dissuade others.
3. A negative selection experience can impact on job acceptance.
4. Selection methods are covered by discrimination legislation and regulations.
5. Mistreatment during selection will put off future applications and may also stop applicants from buying the organization's products or using their services.

REFLECTIVE QUESTION

How would you react to a negative experience in selection?

An important factor is the perception of fair treatment, and this applies to both the methods used and the process as a whole. In addition, there needs to be a clear connection between the methods and the job. Positive reactions to selection can result in greater efforts to perform, which can in turn help organizations to identify the best candidates (Hausknecht et al., 2004).

Underlying the process of selection and the choice of techniques are two key principles:

1. *Individual differences:* Attracting a wide choice of applicants will be of little use unless there is a way of measuring how people differ. People can vary in many ways, for example intelligence, attitudes, social skills, psychological and physical characteristics, experience and so on.
2. *Prediction:* A recognition of the way in which people differ must be extended to a prediction of performance in the workplace.

Selection techniques will, to a varying degree, meet these principles of measuring differences and predicting performance. Organizations may increasingly use a variety of techniques, and statistical theory is used to give credibility to techniques that attempt to measure people's attitudes, attributes, abilities and overall personality.

Some commentators would suggest that this credibility is 'pseudoscientific' and that many limitations remain with selection techniques. Iles and Salaman (1995), for example, claim that this 'psychometric' model appears to value:

- *individualism:* in which individual characteristics are claimed to predict future performance
- *managerialism:* in which top managers define the criteria for performance
- *utility:* in which the costs and benefits, in money terms, of using different selection techniques are assessed.

REFLECTIVE QUESTION

What do you think are the implications and difficulties associated with individualist, managerialist and utilitarian values in selection?

We are once again reminded that power is an important consideration in decision-making on the employment of people. Selection instruments have an image of neutrality and objectivity, but the criteria built into such instruments, which allow the selection and rejection of applicants, make up a knowledge base that provides the organization and its agents with power.

Reliability and validity issues

Two statistical concepts – **reliability** and **validity** – are of particular importance in selection.

Reliability refers to the extent to which a selection technique achieves consistency in what it is measuring over repeated use. If, for example, you were being interviewed by two managers for a job in two separate interviews, you would hope that the interview technique would provide data such that the interviewers agreed with each other about you as an individual. Alternatively, if a number of candidates were given the same selection test, you would want to have some confidence that the test would provide consistent results concerning the individual differences between candidates. The statistical analysis of selection techniques normally provides a *reliability coefficient*, and the higher the coefficient (i.e. the closer it is to 1.0), the more dependable the technique.

Validity refers to the extent to which a selection technique actually measures what it sets out to measure. There are different forms of validity, but the most important in selection is *criterion validity*, which measures the results of a technique against set criteria; this may be the present success of existing employees *(concurrent validity)* or the future performance of new ones *(predictive validity)*.

Validation is in practice a complex process and would require studies involving a large number of candidates in order to allow a correlation coefficient to be calculated – in testing with criteria, this is referred to as a *validity coefficient*. If the coefficient is less than 1.0, an imperfect relationship between test and criterion is indicated. Even if the coefficient indicates such a relationship, a selection technique may, however, still be worth using: that is, you would be better to use the instrument than not use it. In addition, different selection techniques can be assessed in relation to each other according to their validity coefficient results.

One difficulty is that it usually takes a long time to conduct validity studies, and by the time such studies were completed, it would be highly likely that the work from which some of the criteria were derived would have changed. Validity is also related to the particular environment in which performance is carried out and may have different values for different sexes and different ethnic groups. Such problems have not, however, stopped many organizations using tests and other selection techniques that have been validated elsewhere.[8]

Selection interviewing

Of all the techniques used in selection, the interview is the oldest and most widely used, along with application forms and letters of reference, referred to by Cook (1994, p. 15) as 'the classic trio'. Various attempts have been made to classify **selection interviews**, and it may be useful to point out some of the categories that have been developed:

- *Information elicited:* Interviews have a specific focus and require information at different levels:
  - An interview may focus on facts. The style of the interview will be direct, based on a question and answer session.
  - An interview may focus on subjective information once the factual information has been obtained.
  - There may also be a focus on underlying attitudes, requiring intensive probing techniques and usually involving qualified psychologists.
- *Structure:* Interviews may vary from the completely structured, based on planned questions and responses, to the unstructured, allowing complete spontaneity for the applicant and little control for the interviewer. A compromise between the two extremes is most likely, the interviewer maintaining control by the use of guided questions but allowing free expression on relevant topics.

● *Order and involvement:* The need to obtain different kinds of information may mean the involvement of more than one interviewer. Applicants may be interviewed serially or by a panel.

The selection interview has been the subject of much review and research over the past 50 years. During much of that time, the overall results on the validity and reliability of interviews have been disappointing. In 1949, Wagner carried out the first comprehensive review of research associated with the employment interview. Wagner noted that, in the 174 sets of ratings that were reported, the reliability ranged from a correlation coefficient (r) of 0.23 to one of 0.97, with a median value of $r = 0.57$. Validity, from the 222 results obtained, ranged from $r = 0.09$ to $r = 0.94$, with a median of $r = 0.27$ (Wagner, 1949). Wagner considered such results to be unsatisfactory. This pattern of low-validity results continued in other research for the next four decades. In their review, for example, Ulrich and Trumbo (1965) agreed that the interview seemed deficient in terms of reliability and validity, and they were forced to conclude that judgements about overall suitability for employment should be made by other techniques.

HRM WEB LINKS

Each type of employment test (performance, personality and knowledge test) has a different purpose, and many tests have been validated on large populations. Check out www.queendom.com/tests/index.html and www.apa.org/science/testing.html for more information on selection testing instruments. In the UK, tests should be endorsed by the British Psychological Society; go to www.bps.org.uk.

There have been two lines of research to examine the reasons behind such poor results for the selection interview. The first focuses on the processing of information by interviewers that leads to a decision on acceptance or rejection. The second focuses on the skills of effective interviewing. Table 7.1 outlines a summary of this research.

By 1982, Arvey and Campion (1982) were able to report less pessimism about reliability and validity when interviews were conducted by boards (panels) and based on job analysis and job information. In particular, reference was made to the success of *situational interviews* (Latham et al., 1980), in which interview questions are derived from systematic job analysis based on a *critical incident technique*.[9] Questions focus on descriptions of what an applicant would do in a series of situations. Responses are judged against benchmark answers that identify poor, average or excellent employees. In addition to situational interviews, Harris (1989) reported on other new developments in interview format that relied on job analysis. These included *behaviour description interviews*, which assess past behaviour in various situations, and *comprehensive structured interviews*, which contain different types of question, for example situational, job knowledge, job simulation and work requirements. Such developments have resulted in an enhanced effectiveness of the selection interview and improved scores for reliability and validity. To achieve the benefits of such improvements, organizations need to pay more attention to providing formal training on structured selection interviewing (Chapman and Zweig 2005).

The use of questions about past behaviour combined with competencies in selection interviews has enhanced effectiveness even further. Pulakos and Schmitt (1995) compared the validity results in selection of experience-based (or behavioural) questions with situational questions. The former are past-oriented questions and are based on the view that the best predictor of future performance is actual past performance in similar situations. Applicants are asked job-relevant questions about what they did in other situations. This contrasts with situational questions, in which applicants are asked what they would do in response to particular events in particular situations. Responses to both types of question can be scored on behaviour scales, but experience-based questions have shown better results with respect to predictions of job performance, that is, predictive validity. These results can be used by organizations with competency frameworks. An ICT company has, for example, a competency relating to 'managing meetings'. Interviewers could base questions around an applicant's past behaviour in managing meetings by asking the applicant to explain what she or he did in managing a specific meeting. Follow-up questions can be used to reveal further features of the applicant's performance, which can then be assessed against the competency indicators. Research by Campion et al. (1997, p. 655) included such questions as 'better questions' that enhance the effectiveness of the interview.

Table 7.1   Reasons for poor results from selection interviewing

Processing of information

Pre-interview	Use of application forms and photographs to reject on grounds of sex, scholastic standing or physical attractiveness
First impressions	Decisions made quickly lead to a search for the rest of the interview to support the decision. Negative information will be heavily weighted if the decision is rejection, but a positive early decision may lead to warm interviewer behaviour
Stereotypes	Interviewers may hold stereotyped images of a 'good' worker against which applicants are judged. Such images may be personal to each interviewer and potentially based on prejudice
Contrast	Interviewers are influenced by the order in which applicants are interviewed. An average applicant who follows below-average applicants may be rated as above-average. Interviewers may compare applicants against each other rather than against objective criteria
Attraction	Interviewers may be biased towards applicants they 'like'. This attraction may develop where interviewers hold opinions and attitudes similar to those of the applicant

Skills of interviewing

Structure	Variations in interview structure affect reliability, low scores being gained for unstructured interviews
Questions	Interviewers may use multiple, leading, embarrassing and provocative questions
Listening	Interviewers may talk more than listen, especially if they view the applicant favourably. Interviewers may not be 'trained' to listen effectively
Retention and interpretation	Interviewers may have a poor recall of information unless guides are used and notes made. Interviewers have difficulty in interpreting information

Barclay (1999) found a rapid increase in the use of structured techniques as part of a more comprehensive approach to selection. In particular, it was found that *behavioural interviewing* was being used systematically, especially in combination with a competency framework. Further research by Barclay (2001) found that behavioural interviewing was referred to in a variety of ways in organizations, for example competency-based interviewing, criterion-based interviewing, skills-based interviewing, life questioning and behavioural event interviewing. It was claimed that, however referred to, behavioural interviewing had improved the selection process and decisions made, a finding supported by Huffcutt et al. (2001) in their study of the use of interviews for positions of high complexity. However, as Barclay (2001) notes, behavioural interviewing still has some limitations. First, since behavioural questions are based on past behaviour, there is an assumption that behaviour is consistent over time, allowing prediction into the future. This assumption can be challenged on the basis that people do learn from their mistakes and can learn new ways of behaving. Furthermore, it might be suggested that people also tend to behave according to contingent factors such as time, place and especially the presence of others. A second assumption is that behavioural questions allow a fair comparison between different candidates; this might, however, disadvantage those candidates with more limited experience or a poor recall of their experience.

It is interesting at this point to note that much of the progress in interviews as a selection technique has occurred where organizations have sought to identify behaviour and attitudes that match their models of the employees to be selected. This has required an investment in more sophisticated techniques of analysis. Although traditional job analysis techniques allow the production of models of jobs in terms of tasks and responsibilities, organizations faced with change and seeking to employ workers whose potential can be utilized and developed will increasingly turn to techniques of analysis that will produce inventories of characteristics and behaviours, such as competencies, associated with effective performance in the present and the future.

One consequence of more structured approaches to interviewing, including the training of interviewers, is the impact on the reactions of applicants. A review by Posthuma et al. (2002) reported growing research interest in such reactions, generally showing that applicants prefer interviews compared with other selection instruments – the interview had greater face validity. *Face validity* is the reaction of applicants to whether the selection techniques seems connected to the job (Smither et al., 1993). One interesting dilemma, however, emerges for organizations – should the interview focus on establishing a good relationship with an applicant to elicit a positive reaction from the candidate about the selection process, or should the interview be concerned with using good structure and sophisticated questions that have higher predictive validity? In their research, Chapman and Zweig (2005, p. 697) found this tension, some interviewers preferring less structure in favour of building rapport, which 'potentially contaminates an otherwise standardized procedure'.

Organizations need to recognize that the interview is a source of anxiety for applicants, inevitably affecting their performance during interviews. The danger is that an anxiety-affected interview performance may hide an applicant's ability to perform the job (McCarthy and Goffin, 2004). As we have already suggested, discomfort and an unpleasant experience of the selection process will also make the organization less attractive to applicants.

HRM WEB LINKS

Selection interviews can be quite daunting to candidates. To help you to prepare for such interviews, you might read the guides at content.monster.co.uk/section329.asp. For particular guidance on competency-based interviews, try www.allaboutmedical-sales.com/competency.html.

Psychometric testing

Selection based on competencies and attitudes has been one result of the increased attention given to the identification of psychological factors through testing and how such factors predict job performance. Testing, it would seem, offers organizations a cost-effective process in their search for the right people to match the company's personality. For example, during the expansion of the coffee house chain Costa, 1800 new 'team' members were sought. The company worked with a testing house to develop a team-member personality questionnaire based on its values, which would also be simple enough for its managers to use (Dawson, 2005).

We can make the following distinctions between different kinds of tests:

- *Ability tests:* These focus on mental abilities such as verbal reasoning and numerical power but also include physical skills testing such as keyboard speeds. In such tests, there may be right/wrong answers or measurement that allows applicants for a position to be placed in ranked order.
- *Inventories:* These are usually self-report questionnaires about personality, indicating traits, intelligence, values, interests, attitudes and preferences. There are no right/wrong answers but instead a range of choices between possible answers.

Together, tests of personality and ability are referred to as **psychometric tests** and have a good record of reliability and validity. Most people have some fears related to any test, and this has caused some confusion over the meaning, use and value of psychometric tests. The 1990s saw a rapid growth in the number of organizations using such tests, the result of more people, especially HR practitioners, being trained to administer tests (McHenry, 1997a). The CIPD survey (2005b) indicated that 50 per cent of organizations used tests for specific skills, 40 per cent for general ability, 39 per cent for numeracy and literacy and 36 per cent for personality.

Both forms of test provide a set of norms, developed from the scores of a representative group of people (the 'norm' group) of a larger population, for example UK adult men or women in a sales role. Figures are then expressed in *percentiles*, which provides standardization. Thus, a raw score of 120 on a test or a section of a test might be placed in the 60th percentile, indicating that the applicant's result was higher than that of 60 per cent of the norm group but less than the score obtained by 40 per cent. If the test had good predictive validity, this would be a valuable indicator to allow a comparison to be made between different applicants. Inventories would also include some allowance for 'distortions' and 'fake' responses (Dalen et al., 2001) as such tests are generally thought to be less reliable than ability tests. An important issue here is the extent to which a test might discriminate against particular groups of people. Jackson (1996, p. 2) reported that there have been a number of challenges in the US courts relating to unfairness in testing.

REFLECTIVE QUESTION

McHenry (1997a, p. 34) argued that work needed to be done to eliminate and correct tests that contained unfair items. He provided an example of a questionnaire on personality that contained the item, 'I think I would make a good leader.' This was answered 'true' by twice as many men as women, implying that men are twice as likely to become good leaders. What do you think of such an item and its implication?

Ability tests may be of a general kind, for example those relating to general mental ability or abilities such as verbal fluency and numerical ability. In addition, there are also tests for specific abilities, often referred to as *aptitude tests*, for example manual dexterity and spatial ability. There are also tests for specific jobs such as computer aptitude and sales aptitude (Toplis et al., 2005). For many years, there has been a great deal of interest in the extent to which general mental ability and cognitive abilities can be shown to be valid in terms of prediction of performance and can be generalized across a range of occupations (see Schmidt, 2002). For example, Bertua et al. (2005) sought to examine whether general mental ability and cognitive ability tests were valid predictors of job performance and training success in UK organizations. They did this by completing a meta-analysis of 56 papers and books covering 283 samples of testing. The analysis showed that the tests were valid predictors of performance and training success across a range of occupations, including senior managers. This was also the case for changes in the composition of job roles. The authors claimed that the results provided 'unequivocal evidence for the continued and expanded use of general mental ability tests for employee selection in UK organizations' (Bertua et al., 2005, p. 403).

On the personality front, over the past 25 years there has been a growing interest in what has been referred to as the *five-factor model* as an explanation of the factors that determine a person's personality (Wiggins, 1996). The five-factor model[10] proposes that differences between people can be measured in terms of degrees of:

- *emotional stability (neuroticism):* adjustment versus anxiety, level of emotional stability, dependence versus independence
- *extroversion:* sociable versus misanthropic, outgoing versus introverted, confident versus timid
- *openness to experience:* reflection of an enquiring intellect, flexibility versus conformity, rebelliousness versus subduedness
- *agreeableness:* friendliness versus indifference to others, a docile versus a hostile nature, compliance versus hostile non-compliance
- *conscientiousness:* the most ambiguous factor, seen as educational achievement or as will or volition.

Research by Salgado (1997), for example, sought to explore the predictive validity of the five-factor model in relation to job performance through a meta-analysis of 36 studies that related validity measures to personality factors. It was found that conscientiousness and emotional stability showed most validity for job performance, and that openness to experience was valid for training proficiency.

There are, however, doubts about an overreliance on personality tests with respect to their use in predicting future performance, especially in relation to complex tasks such as management. Within the five-factor model, for example, conscientiousness has been highlighted as a predictor of overall job performance. However, a study by Robertson et al. (2000) attempted to test the link between conscientiousness and the performance of 453 managers in five different companies. The results showed no overall statistical relationship, although there was a link with particular performance factors such as being organized and being quality-driven. It was also found that there might be an inverse relationship between conscientiousness and promotability. This result supports the view that suitability for complex work cannot be assessed on the basis of a narrow measurement of a psychological profile.

This situation also applies to the assessment of intelligence. Ceci and Williams (2000) suggest that the measurement of intelligence, although used in various ways by HR departments, does have drawbacks if such measurement is based on the assumption of intelligence as a fixed property of individuals. They argue that intelligent behaviour such as complex thinking is strongly connected to the setting, composed of the task, the location and the other people involved. Limitations on the value of intelligence, as measured by intelligence quotient (IQ) tests, as a predictor have led to a growing interest in the assessment of another kind of intelligence based on feelings, sensing others' feelings and the ability to perform at one's best in relationship with others. This is referred to as *emotional intelligence* (Dulewicz and Higgs, 2000), and there is growing evidence that employers are attempting to utilize this view of intelligence in their competency frameworks (Miller et al., 2001).[11]

Emotional intelligence has been popularized by the work of Daniel Goleman,[11] who divides emotional intelligence into five emotional competencies:

- the ability to identify and name one's emotional states and to understand the link between emotions, thought and action
- the capacity to manage one's emotional states – to control emotions or to shift undesirable emotional states to more adequate ones
- the ability to enter into emotional states (at will) associated with a drive to achieve and be successful
- the capacity to read, be sensitive and influence other people's emotions
- the ability to enter and sustain satisfactory interpersonal relationships.

Online testing

Online testing is also being used for selection and other HR purposes – this being referred to as e-assessment. One feature of testing is to provide a filter for organizations in order to reduce the number of unsuitable candidates (Czerny, 2004), although such a process may screen out good applicants too. Lloyds TSB, for example, has an online application form based on its competency framework; this acts as the first stage in filtering applicants. For the second stage, there is a 20-minute numerical reasoning test also completed online (Pollitt, 2005a). The results of this test are then scored electronically, which then feeds into the bank's recruitment management system.

It is claimed that online testing provides organizations with the ability to test at any time and any place in the world, with the added benefit of a quick processing of applicants. Furthermore, as tests are taken, the results can be accumulated and used to improve the validity of the tests. There might even be a correlation between performance in online tests and successful learning at work, as found in HRM in Practice 7.3.

HRM IN PRACTICE 7.3

ONLINE TESTING GETS TOP SCORE AT DELOITTE

PEOPLE MANAGEMENT, 27 OCTOBER 2005

Graduate recruits at Deloitte who score highly in psychometric tests also perform well in their professional exams, the firm has found.

After adding online verbal and numerical reasoning tests to its recruitment process in spring 2004, Deloitte examined a small group of graduate candidates and found a correlation between scores in the tests and their performance in job-specific exams.

'The verbal and numerical reasoning tests provide evidence of ability and likely performance in professional chartered accountant qualifications,' said Sally Whitman, senior manager in the graduate recruitment team at Deloitte.

> ### 'Online testing has saved us thousands of hours...'

The firm will track the progress of a bigger group this year to validate the findings. It will also look for links between performance in psychometrics and job performance.

Deloitte decided to get rid of paper-based testing to speed up the recruitment process. Paper-based assessment, which used to take 90 minutes and was followed by an interview with a line manager, has been replaced by online testing from PSL, which takes 70 minutes and sifts out unsuccessful applicants after an initial pre-selection stage.

'Online testing has saved us thousands of hours because now line managers only see candidates who have already passed the online assessments,' said Whitman.

One difficulty, however, is that there is a loss of control over the administration of a test; thus, you can take a test at any time and in any place in the world – but also with anyone else to help. Toplis et al. (2005, p. 52) pose the question, 'How do you know who is responding to the test at the end of the line?' There is, however, growing interest in comparing Internet testing with traditional paper and pencil testing. One issue, for example, is whether a person has an understanding of computers. A study by Weichman and Ryan (2003) of student reactions to a computer selection test showed that computer experience did affect the perceptions of the test. Potosky and Bobko (2004) compared the responses of 65 students to Internet and paper and pencil versions of untimed and timed tests. They also assessed the students' understanding of computers in advance of the process and their reactions at the end. One interesting finding was the issue of timing; that is, it was reported that time on the Internet (virtual time) was different from actual time. This affected time to find and read instructions or time to download a test online. The appearance of a test is also affected online, with fewer items seen compared with a full paper test. This may also affect the order in which items are responded to since it is easier to move around a paper test compared with its online counterpart. The results showed interesting differences in test performance between the Internet and paper and pencil versions on the timed test. For the untimed test, there was little difference.

REFLECTION QUESTION

How do you feel about taking a test online?

Whatever developments occur in the use of e-assessment in recruitments, all tests need to conform to the requirements of discrimination laws. In the UK, tests should be endorsed by the British Psychological Society, who will check for any sexual and ethnic bias within the test. In addition to this endorsement, the impact of tests needs to be followed up and monitored to ensure that a test does not result in discrimination in practice against one sex or particular ethnic groups.

HRM WEB LINKS

In recent years, there has been a growth in the availability of online psychometric tests. You can find many tests to take yourself – without applying for a job; go, for example, to www.support4learning.org.uk/jobsearch/assessment_of_your_skills__ abilities__interest_and_values_online_and_assessment_centres.cfm for more information. Try also www.myskillsprofile.com/index.php?partnerid=2221.

Assessment centres

In their examination of organizational selection practices, Wilk and Cappelli (2003) found that as the complexity and demands of work increased, there was a need for a variety of selection methods. Given the weakness of single measures, organizations are increasingly combining techniques and applying them together at an event referred to as an **assessment centre**. Such events may last for one to three days, during which a group of applicants for a post will undergo a variety of techniques. For example, in the case of Lloyds TSB referred to above (Pollitt, 2005a), the last stage of the selection process is attendance at an assessment centre, lasting 24 hours (from 5 pm until 5 pm the following day). Candidates attend in groups of 12 or 24 and are observed by assessors as they complete an interview, a case study presentation, group exercises and a role play. They also complete a numerical reasoning test to verify the online test.

We can make a distinction here between development centres (Chapter 9), which yield information to help to identify development needs, and assessment centres, which are designed to yield information that can be used to make decisions concerning suitability for a job. It is argued that it is the combination of techniques, providing a fuller picture of an applicant's strengths and weaknesses, that makes an assessment centre so valuable. Woodruffe (2000) outlines four generalisations about centres:

1. Participants are observed by assessors who are trained in the use of measurement dimensions such as competencies and the skills of rating.
2. Assessment is by a combination of methods and includes simulations of the key elements of work.
3. Information is brought together from all the methods, usually under competency headings.
4. Participants can be assessed in groups.

Although there may be no such thing as a 'typical' assessment centre (Spychalski et al., 1997), the general methods used are group discussions, role plays and simulations, interviews and tests. The following activities were, for example, used in the assessment centre to select customer service assistants for European Passengers Services Ltd (Mannion and Whittaker, 1996, p. 14):

- Structured Interview
- Perception Exercise
- Communication Exercise
- Structured Interview
- Personality Inventory
- Customer Service Questionnaire
- Tests for clear thinking and numerical estimation.

The objectives for using these methods were to generate information about:

- the ability to work under pressure
- characteristic behaviour when interacting with others
- preferred work styles
- the ability to think quickly
- the ability to make quick and accurate numerical estimates
- experience and aptitude for a customer service role.

The European Passengers Services assessment centre process was judged to be a success, underpinned by the objective and standardized decision-making of the assessors. Candidates attending an assessment centre will be observed by assessors who should be trained to judge candidates' performance against criteria contained within the competency framework used.

REFLECTIVE QUESTION

Have any of your colleagues applying for graduate training programmes been 'through' an assessment centre? What was their reaction to this process?

If your colleagues were to relay negative reactions to you about their experience of selection techniques with one organization, this might affect your image of it. Again, the question of face validity is important – whether the selection techniques seem to the applicants to be connected to the job. Recently, for example, in response to the problem that an assessment centre lacked realism and variety, the accountancy firm Ernst and Young ran its centre in real offices, answering emails and telephone calls. Apparently, this made the expectations of the organizations clearer (Trapp, 2005). Kolk et al. (2003) found that making an assessment centre more transparent to candidates by revealing the dimensions that would be used to make judgements prior to attendance made no difference to the process in terms of validity.

Although not important in a technical sense, face validity could be important in attracting good applicants to an organization. Techniques that may be effective from an organization's perspective may thus be seen as negative and unfair by applicants. In work carried out by Mabey and Iles (1991) on the reactions of MBA students to selection and assessment techniques, interviews were rated fair and useful, whereas tests left many feeling negative. The combination of techniques in an assessment centre was, however, seen as fair and useful in that the event allowed for the use of objective techniques and the opportunity for a dialogue between the applicant and the employer. The findings remind us of the dilemma that faced organizations in the 1990s. That is, although it is increasingly important to select the right kinds of employees using a suitable range of techniques, there is also a danger that, in using such techniques, the organization may simultaneously manage to alienate the very candidates it wants to attract. Bauer et al. (2001) have sought to measure the reactions of applications for jobs using a selection procedural justice scale, in which procedural justice is concerned with the applicants' perceptions with reference to the fairness of the selection procedures. Items in the scale include the job-relatedness of tests, the chance to demonstrate knowledge, skills and abilities, the provision of feedback and treatment with warmth and respect. The scale could be used by organizations to evaluate the fairness of their selection procedures and the correction of problems.

A consideration of procedural justice in selection goes some way towards Herriot and Fletcher's (1990, p. 34) idea of 'front-end' loading processes as a development of the social relationship between applicants and an organization. Both parties in the relationship are making decisions during recruitment and selection, and it is important for an organization to recognize that high-quality applicants, attracted by the image of an organization, could be lost at an early stage unless they were supplied with realistic organization and work information. Applicants have expectations about how the organization will treat them, and recruitment and selection represent an opportunity to clarify these. **Realistic job previews** (RJPs) provide a means of achieving this. RJPs can take the form of case studies of employees and their work, the chance to 'shadow' someone at work, job sampling and videos, the aim being to enable the expectations of applicants to become more realistic. Work by Premack and Wanous (1985) found that RJPs lowered initial expectations about work and an organization, causing some applicants to deselect themselves, but also increase levels of organizational commitment, job satisfaction, performance and job survival among applicants who continue into employment. Phillips (1998) highlights the role of RJPs both before job acceptance, to reduce attrition during recruitment, and afterwards, to improve performance, as part of socialization. Hom et al. (1999) suggest that a key feature of RJPs is their promotion of accurate pre-employment expectations that serve to 'vaccinate' employees when faced with job demands once employed. They also serve to communicate an organization's honesty about such demands.

What is clear is that recruitment and selection provide an arena for engagement between organizations and potential employees within which both parties gain an image of each other. If managers fail to understand the mutuality of this processes, they endanger the attractiveness of the organization and thereby threaten the organization's ability to recruit good applicants (Hausknecht et al., 2004).

STUDY TIP

Most selection techniques are based on the idea that there is a relationship between particular variables such as personality or abilities and future job performance, but attempts to measure the strength of this relationship – the validity – do not show very convincing results. Some studies (e.g. Arthur et al., 2001) suggest that it is important to investigate non-linear relationships between variables and performance. In addition, there is the problem that all performance at work takes place in a situation and that people develop ways of thinking and behaviour according to the situation; this is referred to as *situated cognition and learning*. Check the paper at www.exploratorium.edu/IFI/resources/museumeducation/situated.html.

There are also some doubts about the notion of validity as a real measure of the strength of a relationship. Instead, validity measures play a part in making the reality of the measurement. You can read more about the social construction of validity at www.ped.gu.se/biorn/phgraph/misc/constr/validity.html.

Chapter summary

- This chapter has examined the nature of recruitment and selection for organizations that are pursuing an HRM approach to the management of people. The attraction and retention of employees are crucial to an employment relationship, based on a mutual and reciprocal understanding of expectations. Employers have, however, significant power in recruitment and selection. The overall approach taken will reflect an organization's strategy and its philosophy towards the management of people.

- Recruitment and selection practices are bound by the law of the land, in particular with respect to sex, race and disability discrimination. In addition, there are new regulations relating to discrimination on the grounds of age. Unless exempted by provisions of genuine occupational qualification, discrimination is against the law directly, indirectly or by victimization. In recent years, discrimination legislation has been extended by directives from the European Union, especially the European Convention on Human Rights.

- It is essential that organizations see that, whatever the state of the labour market and their power within it, contact with potential recruits is made through the projection of an image that will impact on and reinforce the expectations of potential recruits.

- Competency frameworks have been developed to link HR practices to the key requirements of an organization's strategy. Competencies can be used to form a model or image of the kinds of employees that an organization seeks to attract and recruit. The response to the image provides the basis for a compatible person–organization fit. Images will feature in recruitment literature and, increasingly, on the Internet via e-recruitment.

- About one-third of organizations use some form of e-recruitment. Large savings in recruitment budgets can be made by advertising through websites. Some organizations use online applications to build a database of applicants for future use.

- Key documents in recruitment and selection are job descriptions and personnel specifications, although there is a growing awareness of the limitations of traditional approaches to their construction. Some organizations have switched to performance contracts, which can be adjusted over time. In addition, personnel specifications may be stated as competencies, which appear more objective.

- Selection techniques seek to measure differences between applicants and provide a prediction of future performance at work. Techniques are chosen on the basis of their consistency in measurement over time – reliability – and the extent to which they measure what they are supposed to measure – validity. An applicant's experience of selection methods strongly influences his or her feelings towards the organization.

- The most common selection technique is the interview, which has been the subject of much research. Recent years have indicated that a structure and the use of behavioural interviewing based on competencies increase the effectiveness of interviews in selection. The use of competencies in selection is a reflection of the interest in assessing personality and abilities by the use of psychometric tests. Techniques of selection may be combined in assessment centres to provide a fuller picture of an applicant's strengths and weaknesses.

- Online testing allows organizations to process applicants more quickly. This may also filter out good applicants as well as unsuitable applicants.

There is growing interest in the perceptions of candidates with respect to the fairness of selection procedures. The use of RJPs can increase commitment and job satisfaction by clarifying expectations and communicating an organization's honesty.

Key concepts

- Assessment centres
- Attraction
- Psychometric tests
- Competencies
- Realistic job previews
- Recruitment
- Reliability

- e-Recruitment
- Selection interviews
- Job description
- Validity
- Online testing
- Personnel specification

Chapter review questions

1. How is an organization's strategy linked to recruitment and selection?

2. Decision-making in selection has become a two-way process. How can applicants' decisions be improved?

3. How can the predictive validity of the employment interview be improved?

4. Should job descriptions be abandoned in recruitment and selection?

5. 'Appeal to their guts instead of just their brains.' How far do you agree with this view of graduate recruitment?

6. Are assessment centres a fair and valid way of selecting employees?

Further reading

Arthur, W., Woehr, D. J. and Graziano, W. G. (2001) Personality testing in employment settings. *Personnel Review*, **30**(6): 657–76.

Cook, M. (2003) *Personnel Selection: Adding Value Through People*. London: John Wiley.

Lievens, F., Highhouse, S. and De Corte, W. (2005) The importance of traits and abilities in supervisors' hirability decisions as a function of method of assessment. *Journal of Occupational and Organizational Psychology*, **78**: 453–470.

Searle, R. (2003) *Selection and Recruitment: A Critical Text*. Basingstoke: Palgrave Macmillan.

Evers, A. N., Anderson, N. and Smit-Voskuyl, O. (eds) (2005) *The Blackwell Handbook of Selection*. Oxford: Blackwell.

Practising human resource management

Searching the web

The significant growth in the number of online recruiters has raised some concerns about standards of service. Go to the website of the Recruitment and Employment Confederation, established to provide a unified voice for those in the recruitment and employment industry; www.rec.uk.com/. Also www.noras.co.uk/ provides independent and audited information on the users of job boards. It provides you with the ability to easily compare online recruitment sites.

HRM group activity

You have been asked to carry out an independent assessment of the approach to online recruitment of different companies. Provide a report that covers the following: (1) an overall impression of the website and ease of navigation for applicants; (2) the image portrayed and the values presented; (3) key information; and (4) how the website attempts to set expectations related to the work. The following sites can be visited:

- Royal Bank of Scotland: www.rbs.com/careers03.asp?id=CAREERS/GRADUATES
- Royal Bank of Canada: www.royalbank.com
- KPMG: www.kpmgcareers.co.uk/
- Sainsbury's: www.sainsburys.co.uk/graduates/
- Microsoft: www.microsoft.com/uk/graduates
- Rolls-Royce: www.rolls-royce.com/careers/default.jsp

Chapter case study

MEISTER SOFTWARE UK

Meister Software UK is the British subsidiary branch of a German-owned worldwide network of software companies. Meister Software is the generic name for a range of software modules that provide a total information solution for manufacturing companies with a turnover of at least £50 million. The British branch is growing rapidly, and during the past year the number of employees has increased from 78 to 108. Most of the employees are graduates with sales, computer or finance backgrounds. The work is highly pressured and

the results focused, in return for which large reward packages are available.

Sales staff in particular need strong presentation and negotiation skills as the market is very competitive and contracts can be worth in excess of £0.5 million. Recently, however, the company has had enormous difficulty in selecting the right calibre of staff for the sales role, even though they are able to attract candidates in sufficient numbers. They recently commissioned an analysis of the role to help to provide a more successful model for the selection of salespeople at Meister. The model should allow the selection process to:

- identify differences between recruits that are important to the role
- carry out the identification of differences in a reliable and consistent manner
- make valid predictions about the future performance of recruits with confidence.

The findings revealed some interesting features of the sales role at Meister relating to the basic skills and attitudes of such a role, as well as indicating how the role was expected to be performed at the company. The first of these Meister factors concerned what was seen as 'professionalism', suggested to be 'an ability to deal sensitively with prospective customers, being 'human' rather than clinical'. References were made to a style of behaviour that was 'non-threatening' and 'non-arrogant' but also 'challenging' when required.

Complementing 'professionalism' was the need to 'make decisions in a complex manner'. This meant that salespeople were expected to be able to use large amounts of information, often simultaneously, to identify patterns and develop several possible alternative actions. Such skills were accompanied by a 'tolerance for ambiguity and a capacity to empathize' with prospective customers. In particular, reference was made to the need to be able 'to understand people and political issues as well as "facts"'.

It was expected that salespeople would 'show pride' in working for Meister and in the Meister product, but it was not expected that a salesperson would sell at all costs. Prospective customers had to be 'right' for Meister. This depended in part on how far sales staff could 'present information in a confident manner' and also in part on how far they could 'adapt their behaviour as they formed relationships with prospective customers'.

The establishment of mutual expectations was seen at Meister as being a core value, and a salesperson had to be able to identify quickly if these could not be formed with a prospective customer. The salesperson's understanding of this would partly be formed by her or his interactions with others at Meister, which highlighted the need for 'peer respect and being a team player' rather than an individualist. It was, however, still expected that a salesperson would be 'self-motivating and be able to work alone'.

Assignment

Using the information about the sales role, you are required to investigate an appropriate selection strategy. You should consider:

1. The preparation of appropriate documentation.

2. Which selection techniques could measure the attributes identified.

3. How an assessment centre would operate for the selection of sales staff.

Include a justification of your results.

HR-related skill development

Choose an organization in your city. Using the information in this chapter as a guide, interview a manager responsible for recruitment (ask, for example, about their current recruitment methods and selection tests). Using the information obtained from your interview and material from this chapter, develop a comprehensive recruitment strategy for the organization based on the position of the person who you interviewed. Prepare an advertisement, including the cost of advertising in appropriate media outlets. Identify appropriate employments instruments to be used and include the rationale behind your choice. Present your findings in the form of a business report or as an oral presentation to your class. You can also develop your interviewing skills by visiting our website (www.palgrave.com/business/brattonand-gold4) and clicking on 'Employment interviews'.

Notes

1. *Guardian*, 28 September 2005.
2. From The Testing of America by Caroline Hsu, 20 September 2004. Available at http://usnews.com/usnews/culture/articles/040920/20test.htm.
3. Robert McHenry in *People Management*, 14 June 2001, p. 37.
4. There are also rights to protect workers on fixed term contracts under the Fixed-term Employees (Prevention of Less Favourable Treatment) Regulations (2002).
5. The notion of the demographic time-bomb was also a frequently referred-to issue in the late 1980s, when the concern was a downturn in the number of young people entering the labour market. It is ironic that in the 1980s and then the 1990s, many experienced staff were made redundant or forced into early retirement, making way for the valued younger staff.
6. This definition, focusing on behaviour patterns, differs from the idea of competence used with National Vocational Qualifications, which concern the performance of activities within an occupation to a prescribed standard. You can read more about the development of National Vocational Qualifications at www.qca.org.uk/610.html.
7. In addition to person–organization fit, organizational psychology literature also identifies person–job fit; see Barber (1998).
8. For a further discussion on reliability and validity, the difference between them and some of the difficulties involved, try http://www.socialresearchmethods.net/kb/rel&val.htm This is a page on Bill Trochim's Research Methods Knowledge Base (www.socialresearchmethods.net/kb/) with some superb references to all aspects of social research.
9. You can find out more about the critical incident technique at www.tiu.edu/psychology/Twelker/critical_incident_technique.htm.
10. You may see the five-factor model referred to as the 'big five' model of personality.
11. See Goleman, D. (1997) *Emotional Intelligence*. New York: Bantam Books.

Chapter eight

Performance management and appraisal

Jeff Gold

Performance management refers to the set of interconnected practices which are designed to ensure that a person's overall capabilities and potential are appraised, so that relevant goals can be set for work and development and, through assessment, data on work behaviour and performance can be collected and reviewed.

'The most important commitment driver we've identified is trust. The second is fairness.'[1]

'Performance appraisal is, in practice, more of an organizational curse than a panacea.'[2]

'Little has been done to unlock the 'black box' of the processes that link HRM (however conceptualized) with organizational performance (however conceptualized).'[3]

Chapter outline

Chapter objectives

After studying this chapter, you should be able to:

1. Explain the purpose and uses of performance management, assessment and appraisal
2. Provide a model of performance management
3. Assess various approaches to understanding performance at work
4. Understand contrasting approaches to assessment and appraisal
5. Explain the use of performance management and appraisal in employee development
6. Understand the use of different performance-rating techniques

Introduction

In recent years, performance management and appraisal have become key features of an organization's drive towards competitive advantage and achieving high performance. This has in many organizations resulted in the development of an integrated **performance management system** (PMS), often based on a competency framework. Indeed, survey evidence has found that discussing and appraising performance is one of the main uses of competencies (Strebler et al., 1997). This is the nub of the strategic link between human resource management (HRM) and organizational performance. The key ideas are that the principal dimensions of a person's work can be defined precisely in performance terms, allowing measurement over agreed periods of time that also take account of particular constraints within the situation of performance (Furnham, 2004). Measurement yields data that become information as they are processed within appraisal, allowing rational, objective and efficient decision-making related to improving performance, identifying training needs, managing careers and setting levels of reward. It is therefore essential to the idea of a 'high road' HRM strategy (Chapter 6). Furthermore, through the use of assessment metrics that connect to business objectives, appraisal and performance management provide the promise of matching human resources (HR) practices with organizational strategy. In the public sector too, in a movement referred to as 'new managerialism' or 'new public management' (Pollitt, 2000), performance management has increasingly been seen as the way to ensure administrative accountability, the meeting of standards and the provision of value-added services.

This chapter will explore the working of PMS, especially appraisal and assessment, and seek to explain some of the contentious features that have, in the past, failed to find respect among employers and employees alike. The chapter will also, however, explore how performance management has the potential to reverse the negative images of the past so that it becomes the source of continuous dialogue between an organization's members.

Performance measurement and human resource management

Significant attention has been paid to setting organizational goals and directions to improve business performance and, importantly, to how such improvements can be measured. Based on the well-known dictum that 'if you can't measure it, you can't manage it', finding ways of measuring performance has become a major preoccupation in many organizations, in both the public and the private sector. All organizations have some means of measuring performance, and whichever methods of measurement are chosen, they are considered to have a key role in the efficient and effective management of the organization (Kennerley and Neely, 2002).

It is argued that measurement of performance is an indication of an organization's culture and the strategic thinking of managers (Pun and White, 2005). Indeed, measurement is a crucial determinant of culture and what managers consider in their thinking. For example, if turnover and costs are the key measures, these will form the indicators used in setting objectives for others and in how achievement is judged. Traditionally, of course, performance measurement has usually been based on accountancy models, with embedded assumptions relating to turnover, costs and especially profit – the bottom line. This provides an underpinning rationale for a control approach to an organization's activities, including performance management and appraisal. It is argued that the control approach is an outcome of the drive towards rationality and efficiency in our organizations. Such beliefs may certainly become part of a set of taken-for-granted assumptions that dominate life in organizations and may also be difficult to challenge.

Organizational leaders, managers and employees are often unaware of the ways in which such beliefs lie behind their actions. Morgan's *Images of Organization* (1997), for example, has provided an examination of the way in which metaphors lie at the foundation of our ideas and explanations about organizations. In this book, Morgan draws on literature highlighting the role of metaphor in explaining complex phenomena, such as organizations, by the crossing of images and language. An organization may thus be crossed with the image of a machine, and this may be very useful in understanding what does and what should happen in organizations. Metaphor, however, provides only a partial view rather than a complete view of a phenomenon: an organization may, for example, be compared with a machine or said to have machine-like qualities, but it is not and never will be a machine.

A danger occurs, however, when the metaphor, in this case a machine, becomes a taken-for-granted assumption. The partial explanatory power of the metaphor may then be taken as a whole, and the organization may be seen literally as a machine. This is not as ridiculous as it sounds because much of the language of organizations, and many of the processes developed, can be related back to such an assumption. Mintzberg (1989, p. 339) argued that the form of structure called 'machine bureaucracy' has dominated thinking on how organizations should be constructed, and that terms such as 'getting organized', 'being rational' and 'achieving efficiency' represent evidence of this domination. As Mintzberg (1990, p. 340) wrote: 'I believe that to most people, what I am calling machine bureaucracy is not just a way to organize, it is the way to organize; it is not one form or structure, it is structure.'

REFLECTION QUESTION

Does the machine metaphor seem to underpin how people talk about work in your organization? What effect does such talk have in terms of how judgements and decisions are made?

As we saw in Chapter 6, there have been growing efforts to prove the special value of people in organizations by measuring and expressing HRM in financial terms (Toulson and Dewe, 2004). This is a partial acceptance of the control approach implied in traditional accountancy models. There has, however, been a trend away from single financial measures, such as return on investment, towards the identification of value-drivers in organizations (Scott, 1998). See for example, HRM in Practice 8.1.

HRM IN PRACTICE 8.1

RBS EXAMINES ITS PEOPLE PRACTICES

RIMA MANOCHA, *PEOPLE MANAGEMENT*, 28 JULY 2005

A project aimed at identifying which people practices drive customer service and business performance has been launched by the Royal Bank of Scotland Group (RBS). The initiative, called Service Excellence through People, will bring together key data on 4,000 of

RBS's retail bank branches worldwide in a bid to take its leading-edge human capital strategy to the next level.

RBS has engaged Harvard Business School and its survey consultants, ISR, to carry out the study, which will analyse people, marketing, customer service and business performance data. Greg Aitken, head of employee research and measurement at RBS, told PM that a key difference between previous work on the service profit chain and the new project was that it would identify causes and actions, not simply highlight change factors.

'This work will identify what aspects of our employee proposition drive superior customer service, sales and business performance. We want to identify actions from this work that will eliminate poor performance. This means line managers in branches will know exactly what they need to do to ensure increased customer service and performance.'

'They believe this study has the potential to be one of the most innovative in the field'

Aitken explained that the RBS study would also encompass data on its call centres. 'Previous studies I have seen are limited in their assessment of call centres. But much of the customer experience at RBS is through call centres, so we need to look at them as well.' The study will examine data on engagement levels, absence and management effectiveness from HR, customer feedback from marketing, and profit and productivity from finance.

'At Harvard, professors Nitin Nohria and Boris Groysberg have expressed a keen interest in working with us. They believe this study has the potential to be one of the most innovative in the field,' said Aitken.

The inclusion of less tangible factors such as customer satisfaction and loyalty, and intellectual capital, can make some value-drivers more difficult to develop. There are, however, measurement models that take a wider view, perhaps more strategic and long term, which encompasses a range of values, not just financial, and can stimulate continuous improvement (Pun and White, 2005). For example, the total quality management (TQM) movement, which emerged in the 1980s and is still prevalent in many organizations, provides tools and measurements to bring about lasting change and a culture of continuous improvement.[4] In the UK, the business excellence model provides a way of understanding how the whole organization works based on nine elements of 'excellence', including people. Each element can be judged on a range of criteria, and improvements planned accordingly. For example, one of the criteria for people is that 'people are involved and empowered'. Another holistic measurement framework is Kaplan and Norton's (2000) balanced scorecard, in which a variety of perspectives are considered under the headings of customer, financial, internal business, and innovation and learning. Measures can be set for each, which can then be aligned with strategy. Managers and employees can then develop their own measures in response.

In the public sector, new managerialism has resulted in a customer-oriented approach to performance measurement (Mwita, 2000). In local government in the UK, for example, a **Best Value** framework was introduced in 1997. Indeed, Best Value now forms part of a statutory framework for performance management in local government and sets five dimensions of performance indicators:

1. *Strategic objectives:* why the service exists and what it seeks to achieve.
2. *Cost/efficiency:* the resources committed to a service and the efficiency with which they are turned into outputs.
3. *Service delivery outcomes:* how well the service is being operated in order to achieve the strategic objectives.

4. *Quality:* the quality of the services delivered, explicitly reflecting users' experience of the services.
5. *Fair access:* ease and equality of access to services.

The overall aim of Best Value is to encourage a reorientation of service delivery towards citizens and customers and produce a quality-driven organization (Sheffield and Coleshill, 2001).

HRM WEB LINKS

There are a variety of approaches and frameworks for setting performance measures. Try www.som.cranfield.ac.uk/som/research/centres/cbp/about.asp, the home page of the Centre for Business Performance, which researches the design and implementation of performance measurement and management systems. The website of the Performance Management Association can be found at www.som.cranfield.ac.uk/som/research/centres/cbp/pma/. You can find out more about the balanced scorecard at www.balancedscorecard.org/. There is more about the business excellence model at www.quality-foundation.co.uk/ex_description.htm. The UK government's local government site covering Best Value can be found at www.bvpi.gov.uk/pages/Index.asp. Finally, check www.innovation.gov.uk/value_added/home.asp?p=home, which provides information about value added, a measurement of wealth, how efficiently wealth is created in an organization and how it is used.

The purpose and processes of performance management

There is considerable pressure on organizations to show that they are organized and systematic in their approach to the management of employee performance and that there is a clear link between such performance and the organization's goals. Activities such as appraisal and assessment have traditionally been completed in isolation and have not always been able to demonstrate their value to organizational performance. Therefore, during the 1990s, there was a growing interest in performance management to ensure that HRM could be seen as vital to an organization's concerns, with performance improvement and competitive advantage (Armstrong and Baron, 2004). The adoption of a PMS represents an attempt by an organization to show a strategic integration of HRM processes, which can together be linked to the goals and direction of an organization. Walters (1995, p. x), for example, saw performance management as being concerned with 'directing and supporting employees to work as effectively and efficiently as possible *in line with the needs of the organization*'. HRM in Practice 8.2 provides an example of one organization's search for a strategic performance management tool.

It is strategic focus that gives performance management its distinctive position in HRM. According to a survey by the Chartered Institute of Personnel and Development (2005c) of over 500 companies in the UK, 87 per cent operated a PMS. The key features of such systems that were reported in the survey were individual annual appraisal (65 per cent), twice-yearly/biannual appraisal (27 per cent) or rolling appraisal (10 per cent). A total of 14 per cent used 360° appraisal (see later in the chapter), but 30 per cent included **self-appraisal**; 62 per cent sought to ensure objective-setting and personal development plans, with 36 per cent providing coaching and/or mentoring, career management and/or succession-planning. In addition, 31 per cent used appraisal to determine performance-related pay.

HRM IN PRACTICE 8.2

PERFORMANCE MANAGEMENT TOOL MAKES COMPANY MORE STRATEGIC

UYEN VU, *CANADIAN HR REPORTER*, 27 FEBRUARY 2006

For many organisations, getting people to rally around a performance management system isn't easy. At Montreal headquartered Aeroplan, a marketing company with about 1,200 employees, the job wasn't as tough. Most of the 220 managers participating in performance management were already sold on the why. It was the how they had trouble with.

The how was a 'very archaic pen-and-paper-based tool,' said Caroline Cyr, manager of organisational performance and development. 'Although we had a formal process per se, we did not have any means to track it. All we had were yearly Excel spreadsheets and graphs to present to senior executives, which were based on aggregated performance management ratings across the company.'

These were ratings used to determine the level of incentive pay each year. At Aeroplan, incentive pay comprised ratings at the corporate level, the team

level and the individual level. The mix of each would vary according to an individual's rank. 'Our people were completely disenchanted with our process. It ticked everybody off. It was not user-friendly. It was a Word document with boxes everywhere and the boxes did not follow the text. They could not track changes they made to their objectives. They could not follow the performance management process adequately. They were completely turned off'.

> '...we're a fast-growing company filled with over-achievers and aggressive targets.'

The need for a performance management tool was urgent, said Cyr, because 'we're a fast-growing company filled with over-achievers and aggressive targets'. Cyr's team came across the Sigal system, a Web-based system that supports a number

of functions under the umbrella of talent management, including performance management, succession planning, competency assessment, recruitment, career management, learning management for all forms of learning, content creation, as well as knowledge management.

With the succession planning and career management tools, 'what we wanted to do was take it to the strategic level. These (processes) are going to help us make strategic decision (such as) who are going to be the future of Aeroplan, what are we going to do as a company to help those individuals grow and become proficient at their jobs. As a company we have a responsibility toward the employee to help them grow.' Once linked to the broader goals of helping employees grow and develop, said Cyr, the performance management process 'becomes much more concrete and much more valuable for the employees'.

The responses indicate the wide variations in activities featured in a PMS, but there is still the crucial issue of how goals and targets are translated and incorporated into the various HRM processes. A key feature of a PMS is the attempt to provide a link between all levels of an organization through goals, critical success factors and performance measures. An organization's goals will thus be derived from business strategy and translated into sector goals, departmental goals, manager goals and employee and/or team goals respectively. At each stage, there will be an attempt to provide measurable performance indicators of the achievement of goals. Furthermore, in response to the dynamic conditions of globalization and technical change, there is a need to review and reset goals and targets through the year (Rose, 2000). Evidence from the CIPD (2005b) survey suggests that organizations can attach a variety of different criteria in performance management, including customer care, quality, flexibility, competence, skills/learning targets, achievement of objectives, business and financial awareness, productivity, working relationships and contribution to the team.

In addition to goals, which provide the direction for performance, a PMS will also provide a means of supporting performance through diagnosing development needs, providing ongoing feedback and review and coaching where required. As we have argued throughout this book, the crucial features of a high road HRM strategy are the coordination of the implementation of HR practices (Hoque, 1999) and the belief by management that people represent the key source of competitive advantage. In a PMS, the attitudes of management are crucial because they are the key actors in the implementation of the various HR processes. The integrated nature of a PMS is outlined in the performance management cycle shown in Figure 8.1.

A PMS might incorporate, especially for managers, **development centres**. Development centres are the same as assessment centres (Chapter 7) in that assessment tests and exercises are used to provide a report on individual strengths and limitations, but they differ in their emphasis on diagnosing development needs, leading to suggested development activities and a **performance and development plan** (PDP). Although a range of activities may be used, a development centre usually involves psychometrics and feedback from a qualified occupational psychologist, multisource feedback and a

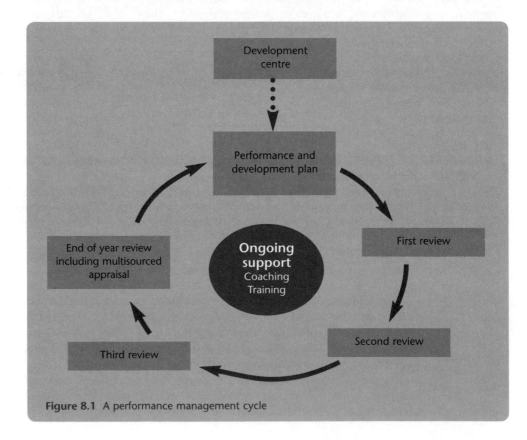

Figure 8.1 A performance management cycle

self-diagnosis against the organization's competency framework. A PDP also includes an attempt to link the overall business aim with key areas of responsibility, the competencies that are expected to be demonstrated in performing a role and **goal-setting** with measurable objectives.

Although development centres are concerned with development needs, their similarity to assessment centres may make it difficult to escape the tension between judgement and development that is a feature of all processes concerned with assessing and appraising people at work. Carrick and Williams (1999) suggest that development centres may, for some participants, result in the diagnosis of many development needs and have a demotivating influence. Because this may be the expected outcome for some potential participants, this may influence their decision to participate and their overall performance if they do. As Woodruffe (2000, p. 32) warns, 'Assessment centres masqerading as development centres are wolves in sheep's clothing.' Overall, there is a need for considerably more research into the value of development centres. However, research carried out by Halman and Fletcher (2000) does highlight some of the tensions inherent in development centres and performance management more generally. This is to do with assessment and performance. In the research, 111 customer services staff attended a development centre. Prior to attending, each person self-assessed his or her performance; they were then rated by assessors as part of the development centre. The research revealed a variety of responses to self-ratings depending on whether participants underrated, overrated or even accurately rated their performance. For example, those who overrated their performance tended to make little adjustment to any feedback provided, possibly due to their view that they did not need to improve their performance. We will consider the issues of ratings, judgement and feedback in performance management in more detail below.

REFLECTION QUESTION

How do you respond to critical feedback when you believe you have performed well?

HRM WEB LINK

Go to www.shl.com/shl/uk, the website of one of the UK's biggest providers of development centre methods.

Once a PDP has been established, according to the performance management cycle, work is carried out to meet the objectives set. There should also be ongoing coaching from the immediate manager and support for any training and development needs identified (Chapter 9). Objectives and performance are reviewed, perhaps every quarter or half-year, to monitor progress and make any adjustments. During the course of the year, feedback might be obtained from different sources, this being used to improve performance as well as being fed into the end-of-year review, at which an overall assessment and appraisal might also be carried out.

Performance, judgements and feedback

As indicated by the CIPD survey (2005c), a PMS can be used for a variety of purposes. Broadly, such purposes can be categorized as follows:

1. The making of administrative decisions concerning pay, promotions and careers, and work responsibilities – the *control* purpose.
2. The improvement of performance through discussing development needs, identifying training opportunities and planning action – the *development* purpose.

Both categories require judgements to be made. In the first category, a manager may be required to make a decision about the value of an employee both in the present and in the future, and this may cause some discomfort. For example, several decades ago, McGregor (1957, p. 89) reported that a key reason why appraisal failed was that managers disliked 'playing God', which involved making judgements about the worth of employees. Levinson (1970) thought that managers experienced the appraisal of others as a hostile and aggressive act against employees that resulted in feelings of guilt related to being critical of employees. Such views highlight the tension between appraisal as a process to control employees and as a supportive development process; it is a tension that has never been resolved and lies at the heart of most debates about the effectiveness of appraisal in particular, as we will explain below, and performance management more generally.

Making judgements about an employee's performance that can lead to decisions about their contribution, value, worth, capability and potential has to be considered as a vital dimension of a manager's relationship with employees. Such decisions will be interpreted by an employee as feedback, and what is particularly interesting is the way in which individuals respond to feedback, because there is no simple formula for how feedback can be used to motivate people, even though managers may be quite convinced, in their own minds, that there is. Managers may not like giving feedback, especially critical feedback (Cannon and Witherspoon, 2005). We do know, however, that feedback has a definite influence in terms of demotivation.

REFLECTIVE QUESTION

What motivates you to work? Make a list of these factors, and then make another list of what demotivates you. It is likely that the latter will be longer, covering a wide range of factors.

Figure 8.2 shows the possibilities of the response by employees to feedback on their performance at work. As suggested, the response to feedback can result in two possibilities: validation if there is agreement with the judgement made or a defensive posture when there is disagreement. The latter is especially likely when feedback is negative or critical, and the impact on subsequent performance can also be negative. DeNisi and Kluger (2000) conducted a review of the research that considered the relationship between feedback and performance. It was found that in one-third of cases, feedback had a negative effect on performance. As DeNisi and Kluger highlighted, while feedback does have the potential to help someone focus on what is to be done in performing a task or learning details, performance usually improves. The main danger, however, occurs with feedback that can have a potentially strong impact on an employee's view of 'self', for example self-belief and self-esteem. The response to feedback, especially critical feedback, is likely to be affective or emotional, which can be detrimental to performance.

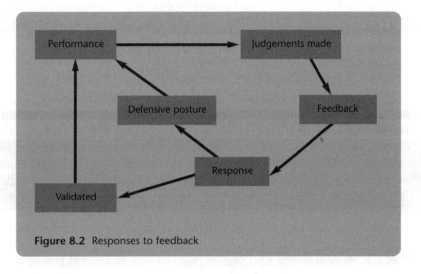

Figure 8.2 Responses to feedback

The requirement for making judgements in the various processes that form a PMS pose particular problems for fostering a diversity agenda. As the survey evidence from CIPD (2005c) suggests, PMSs are used for many purposes, including decisions about people's careers, the development they will undertake, the payment received and their future direction in the organization. There are well-documented patterns in organizations suggesting that some groups suffer disadvantages in these areas. For example, in the UK, around 40 per cent of the workforce, but only around 30 per cent of managers, are women, with far fewer women becoming senior managers or directors of organizations. This is the so-called 'glass ceiling' for women, suggesting that there are limits on their progress in organizations. Female managers are also likely to suffer a 30 per cent shortfall in their earnings compared with men (Office for National Statistics, 2003). Similar problems are faced by those from ethnic minorities, with very few managers being promoted to senior levels (Race for Opportunity, 2002). There are many causes of such difficulties, with biased and stereotyped judgements about performance being key elements. Like selection decisions (see Chapter 7), there are well-known distortions in ratings of people and their performance (Grote, 1996), such as stereotyping and generalizations, similarity bias (rating people who are similar to you more highly) and using first impressions or contrast with others as key data that distort judgement.

One explanation of the biased and potentially prejudiced distortions in judgement in PMS is provided by social role theory (Eagly, 1987); this suggests that social structures influence the roles that people can adopt and the behaviours expected. For example, if it is expected that women will become mothers, this will feed the difference between genders in PMS. As women leave work to care for children, this reinforces the consistent expectation of the social role of women (Diekma and Eagly, 2000), and even when women return to work, it is expected that there will be conflicts between family and work (Benschop and Doorewaard, 1998). As a consequence, women's performance at work may be less highly rated than men's. However, the recent trend of men taking time away from work for family has also been linked to a poor performance rating; that is, both men and women suffer the family care stereotype (Butler and Skattebo, 2004).

REFLECTIVE QUESTION

Have you ever felt your work performance to be judged unfairly against a social stereotype?

HRM WEB LINK

Check www.lboro.ac.uk/admin/personnel/policies/Genderequality.htm to find out how Loughborough University is seeking to promote equality of opportunity in appraisal.

Appraisal and control

We define **appraisal** here as a process that provides an analysis of a person's overall capabilities and potential, allowing informed decisions to be made for particular purposes. An important part of the process is **assessment**, whereby data on an individual's past and current work behaviour and performance are collected and reviewed.

The most usual rationalization and justification for appraisal is to improve individual performance, but there are also a variety of other declared purposes and desired benefits for appraisal, including:

- improving motivation and morale
- clarifying expectations and reducing ambiguity about performance
- determining rewards
- identifying training and development opportunities
- improving communication
- selecting people for promotion
- managing careers
- counselling
- discipline
- planning remedial actions
- setting goals and targets.

The potential list of purposes for appraisal has led to the view that appraisal is something of a 'panacea' in organizations (Taylor, 1998), although expectations and hopes are more often than not confounded.

REFLECTIVE QUESTION

Why do you think it is difficult to meet the hopes and expectations for appraisal systems at work?

When we consider the history of appraisal, it soon becomes apparent that, of all the activities comprising HRM, appraisal is arguably the most contentious and least popular among those who are involved. Managers do not seem to like doing it, employees see no point in it, and HR managers, as guardians of an organization's appraisal policy and procedures, have to stand by and watch their work fall into disrepute. Remarkably, despite the poor record of appraisal within organizations, it is an accepted part of management orthodoxy that there should be some means by which performance can be measured, monitored and controlled (Barlow, 1989). Indeed, a failure to show that management is in control would be regarded as highly ineffective by those with an interest in the affairs of an organization. As a result, appraisal systems have for some time served to prove that the performance of employees is under control, or to give the appearance of its being so. As Barlow (1989, p. 500) has stated: 'Institutionally elaborated systems of management appraisal and development are significant rhetorics in the apparatus of bureaucratic control.'

It might be that the idea of control lies at the heart of the problem of appraisal in organizations, and this stems from the key points we raised above about judgements and feedback. There is always a danger in any situation when a manager has to provide feedback to employees that the outcome will be demotivated employees. The seminal study that highlighted this was carried out by Meyer et al. (1965) at the General Electric Company. Although this work was carried out in the mid-1960s, it is remarkable how the lessons have been forgotten and how the mistakes uncovered at that time have been repeated many times over in many organizations.

The study looked at the appraisal process at a large plant where appraisal was judged to be good. There were 92 appraisees in the study who were appraised by their managers on two occasions over two weeks. The first interview discussed performance and salary, the second performance improvement. The reactions of the appraisees were gathered by interviews, questionnaires and observation. It was discovered that although interviews allowed for general praise, criticism was more specific and prompted defensive reactions. Defensiveness on the part of appraisees involved a denial of shortcomings and blaming others. On average, 13 criticisms were recorded per interview, and the more criticism received, the more defensive the reaction of the appraisee. The study revealed that the defensive behaviour was partly caused by most appraisees rating themselves above average before the interviews – 90 out of 92 appraisees in fact rated themselves as average or above. It was also found that, subsequent to the interviews, criticism had a negative effect on performance. A summary of some of the conclusions from this study is set out in Table 8.1.

Table 8.1 Summary of findings from Meyer et al.'s (1965) study

- Criticism often has a negative effect on motivation and performance
- Praise has little effect – one way or another
- Performance improves with specific goals
- Participation by the employee in goal-setting helps to produce favourable results
- Interviews designed primarily to improve performance should not at the same time weigh salary or promotion in the balance
- Coaching by managers should be day to day rather than just once a year

Since this study, there has in many respects been a long search to find a way of appraising employees that mitigates the negative outcomes. It has, however, to be acknowledged that, given the importance of appraisal in making judgements and decisions that can have a significant bearing on a person's future, it is bound to be perceived as a political process (Poon, 2004). Employees who believe that their appraisal is based on bias and subjects them to unfair punishments are more likely to be less satisfied at work and consider leaving. It is important that appraisal is perceived to be fair (Ilgen et al., 1979).

There is still, however, a tendency to associate feedback with criticism even though most people do their work well most of the time (Swinburne, 2001). One suggestion is that employees may not have realistic expectations about appraisal and perhaps need training on how to use feedback and take action (Cook and Crossman, 2004). Another approach is to widen the sources of feedback. In recent years, for example, there has been a growth in the process of **multisource feedback** (Kettley, 1997), during which individuals receive feedback from different sources, including peers, subordinate staff, customers and themselves. Where feedback is received from 'all round' a job, this is referred to as **360° appraisal or feedback**.[5] The growth in such approaches is based on the view that feedback from different sources allows for more balance and objectivity than does the single view of a line manager. We will examine multisource feedback and 360° appraisal in more detail later in this chapter. Competencies have also been seen as a way of facilitating the review process, linking PDPs to strategy and increasingly, despite many warnings, to pay (Sparrow, 1996).

HRM WEB LINKS

Because of the difficult nature of appraisal, there is a plethora of resources and training programmes available. If you want some basic advice on appraisal interviewing, check the Advisory, Conciliation and Arbitration Service (ACAS), at www.acas.org.uk/index.aspx?articleid=651. ACAS also publishes a booklet on appraisal-related pay, at www.acas.org.uk/index. aspx?articleid=625.

The last conclusion in Table 8.1 emphasizes the role of managers as developers of their employees on a continuous basis. This role is explored in more detail in Chapter 9, but it is worth stating here that assessment and appraisal are likely to occur on both formal and informal occasions, and the latter will occur far more often than the former. Employees are able to accept criticism if it is useful and relevant to them and the work they are doing. Feedback provided in this way has a strong chance of improving performance and, crucially, provides an opportunity for a continuing dialogue between managers and employees out of which will emerge a joint understanding of individual development needs and aspirations. As many managers and employees have found, informal and continuous processes that are operating effectively will make the formal appraisal less isolated and less prone to negativity.

The extent to which employees are able to accept feedback will vary to a considerable degree between employees, and managers will need to be able to cope with such variations. That is, they will need to 'know' their people as individuals, and this in itself will be a reflection of the development of managers. Recent work in understanding what makes people exert effort has shown that a variety of factors, such as clarity of role, recognition, challenge, self-expression and contribution, have a hand in this process. How these factors are combined cannot, however, be generalized, and each person will have his or her own perception of what is important. To understand this, managers are advised to 'get inside the head' of the employee (McHenry, 1997b, p. 29).

The shift towards a more developmental view of appraisal inevitably, however, comes into contention with management orthodoxy, in which it is accepted that there should be some means by which performance can be measured, monitored and controlled (Barlow, 1989). Appraisal systems provide evidence that management is in control, and, as Randell (1994, p. 235) has pointed out, most appraisal schemes in the UK are underpinned by a 'performance control approach'. Figure 8.3 provides the key stages of this approach.

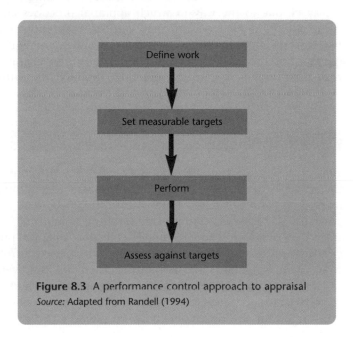

Figure 8.3 A performance control approach to appraisal
Source: Adapted from Randell (1994)

We should not be surprised therefore to find an attachment by many managers to the idea of control in appraisal (Townley, 1994), and the perception by employees that they are being controlled by appraisal systems. Barlow (1989) took the argument further, pointing out that appraisal serves to make rational, simple and static a relationship between managers and employees that is ambiguous, complex and dynamic. Ambiguity, complexity and dynamism cannot be eliminated in reality, and therein lies the falseness of the experience of appraisal. For many employees, appraisal is just not seen as relevant. The following reflects the opinion of one manager about appraisal, gathered in a field study in a sector of the petrochemicals industry (Barlow, 1989, p. 505):

If we were asked for a good man, we certainly wouldn't go hunting through appraisal forms. We'd do it by personal knowledge and I suppose, to some extent, by rule of thumb. Appraisal forms are no use. It's what's left out rather than what's put in that's important.

When an organization seeks to implement strategic changes to improve performance based on principles of learning, communication and involvement of employees, there is an apparent contradiction with appraisal as part of performance management, which is oriented towards control. For example, Soltani et al. (2005) studied a number of organizations that were seeking to utilize principles of TQM. It was found that although there was recognition that appraisal should match the requirements of TQM, there was little evidence of this occurring. Indeed, appraisal was often chararacterized as ineffective, based on high subjectivity that ignored individual objectives, and managers unqualified in providing feedback. These factors tended to work against the changes sought through TQM.

In this section, we have discussed how some of the research evidence has indicated that the reality is that appraisal may be less than effective in achieving its purposes. The problem may be due to the way in which appraisal processes are formulated, based on an explicit or implicit performance control orientation. Organizational leaders and managers will need to ask themselves some fundamental questions on the purpose of appraisal and the nature of organizational control mechanisms if they are to achieve high trust, high commitment and high productivity within the high-performance paradigm of HRM activity (Godard and Delaney, 2000).

From control to development?

It is highly unlikely that the pressure for rationality, efficiency and control in organizations will ease. In the 1990s, the threats of competition and uncertainty, if anything, increased that pressure, and this has continued into the 2000s. The questioning of underlying principles that is required to develop a culture supporting and reinforcing the ideas and practices of a high road HRM approach can be a painful process: it may, for example, be difficult to resist the requirements of financial controllers to show conformity to standardized budgets and accounting. There are, however, other views of reality that challenge the mechanistic view of organizations and its privileged status. Such views need to show an accommodation of the values of control combined with values that argue for the development of people and the gain of employee commitment and trust.

In a seminal paper, Walton (1985) wrote about disillusionment with the apparatus of control that assumed low employee commitment and mere obedience, reporting on a number of organizations that had attempted to move towards a workforce strategy based on commitment. Throughout the 1990s, the drive towards leaner and flatter organizational structures in response to the pressures of globalization, the advance of technology and the requirements of high-quality customer service meant the removal of layers of supervision and an investment, both psychologically and physically, in harnessing the potential of employees (Holbeche, 1998). The crucial contribution towards creating commitment, pride and trust is, however, management's devotion to nurturing a culture that supports the long-term development of people (Gratton, 1997). Performance management and appraisal can serve as the fulcrum of such a process, although considerable difficulties arise (Wilson and Western, 2000). The contrast between control approaches and commitment could not be greater for managers: the former involves a concentration on techniques, the latter a shift towards attitudes, values and beliefs. The skill for HRM practitioners is to acknowledge the importance of the former while arguing for a greater place for the latter.

REFLECTIVE QUESTION

What particular skills are needed by HRM practitioners to argue for two potentially conflicting points of view such as the need for control and the need for commitment?

A developmental PMS that attempts to harness potential would, for many organizations, mean a spread in the coverage to all employees who form the primary internal labour market. For many years, discussions of potential and prospects for development have been confined to managers, providing a strong signal to the rest of the organization that only managers are worthy of such attention – with the implicit assumption that non-managers cannot develop. In the 1990s, however, more organizations attempted to harmonize conditions between different grades of employee and to adopt HRM ideas and practices such as performance management and appraisal. In the 2000s, changes in organizational structure have continued, with increasing efforts to move decision-making to the point of interaction with customers and clients and see such interactions as the source of creativity (see HRM in Practice 8.3).

HRM IN PRACTICE 8.3

DISNEY'S APPROACH TO CREATIVE THINKING

KATIE HOPE, *PEOPLE MANAGEMENT*, 30 JUNE 2005

Companies that fail to tap into their employees' creativity risk extinction, warned Scott Milligan, manager of performance training at the Disney Institute in Florida. During the 1980s and 1990s, 330 companies in the Fortune 500, representing 46 per cent of the largest US firms, disappeared from the index. 'This is probably because they did not react well to change and failed to tap into the creativity that was there,' Milligan told delegates at the Society for Human Resource Management's annual conference.

At Disney it is believed that all employees are creative in some way. The company aims to create a culture that embraces and shares new ideas. It insists that 'Yes and ...' rather than 'Yes, but ....' is used in meetings, and Milligan says this change in language has

contributed to a collaborative culture that encourages people to build on ideas rather than shutting them down.

At Disney it is believed that all employees are creative in some way.

'When I started at Disney this was difficult for me, as I was an executive used to making quick decisions, but by changing the language we have ended up getting more ideas,' he added. It was also important for these creative ideas to be in line with Disney's organisational identity, said Milligan. 'Having parameters provides guidance and distinction on where we are heading as a company; it also avoids wasting resources.' This approach has generated

considerable savings. In one case, staff suggested placing spare pushchairs at internal train stations instead of adapting the trains to take them on board, saving an estimated $1 million.

Disney, which has 55,000 employees in Florida, making it the largest single-site employer in the US, also uses a weekly newsletter to communicate new processes implemented in different business divisions. This led to kitchen staff using the same successful methods to make breakfast pancake batter for guests as the painters used to mix paint to the exact colour required by Disney branding. 'We would never have thought of a connection between these two groups if it wasn't for this means of sharing ideas,' said Milligan.

Line managers, rather than HR specialists who act as guardians of an organization's appraisal policy, have significant responsibility to ensure that effective communication and feedback are given to employees (Industrial Relations Services, 2003b).

In shifting towards a more developmental approach, the suspicion that has surrounded control approaches may remain. This should not be surprising since there has for some time been pressure to shift the orientation. For example, Harper (1983) suggested dropping the word 'appraisal' because it put employees on the defensive. He recommended instead a shift towards future-oriented review and development that actively involved employees in continuously developing ways of improving performance in line with needs. The outcome could be a set of objectives to be achieved by individual employees. Moving in such a direction requires a more flexible consideration by line managers and inevitable tensions, because such objectives might be concerned with immediate performance set against current tasks and standards, but they might also be concerned with a variety of work and personal changes, for example a change of standards, task, job role or even career.

Once employees have been encouraged to pay attention to their progress at work, the organization must be able to respond to their medium- and long-term aspirations (Chapter 6). The manager's role will be to resolve the inevitable tension that will result between individual goals and the manager's interpretation of organizational goals. But how can data about employees be gathered for such purposes? There needs, by necessity, to be a shift in attention towards the performance of work, and this provides a link value for a PMS as means of giving recognition to employees via feedback for what they have done, engaging them in a dialogue about improving performance (Armstrong and Baron, 2004) and, we would argue, identifying how development can help them to meet their needs and aspirations.

The performance of a work task can be presented as a relationship between means and ends (Ouchi, 1979). The means take the form of the attributes, skills, knowledge and attitudes (competencies) of individual employees that are applied to a task in a specific situation. The ends are the outcomes, taking the form of results achieved, which may be measurable either quantitatively or qualitatively against an explicit or implicit standard or target. Between means and ends lies the behaviour of the individual in a **transformation process**, as shown in Figure 8.4.

Although all phases of this process can form the focus of performance management, particular attention to behaviour in the transformation process will reveal how an individual has applied knowledge, skills and attitudes to practice in carrying out a task, taking account of all aspects, including time and place, machinery and equipment, other employees and other circumstances, for example the presence of a manager or a customer. In recent years, there has been significant interest in this part of the transformation process, because it is in practice that new knowledge can be

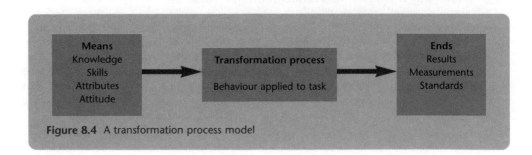

Figure 8.4 A transformation process model

created (Newell et al., 2002). Part of this interest focuses on knowledge that people learn informally in practice, which is acquired intuitively and implicitly through practice, often without intention (Sternberg and Horvath, 1999). Such knowledge is often referred to as *tacit knowledge*, a rather ambiguous term that has nevertheless attracted a great deal of attention in the process of knowledge creation as it emerges from practice (Nonaka et al., 2000). We must also remember that practice occurs in a context, that contextual factors can have a significant bearing on overall performance and these need to be considered in the various PMS processes of managing, measuring, assessing and rewarding performance (Armstrong and Baron, 2004). Thus, attention paid to how an employee performs will provide rich data on current effectiveness and potential for further development.

If, for example, we assume that an employee has been trained to complete a basic task, attention to practice in the transformation process will provide data on a number of issues. The first time she completes the task, an assessment of her behaviour will reveal nervousness until completion, when the results achieved can be compared against a standard. This nervousness can be corrected by adjustments to her skills and practice until confidence has been gained. Further attention reveals that, once confidence has been gained, she performs with some sense of rhythm and flow that achieves a perfect result.

Given static conditions and standards, this is as far as the employee can go in this task. She can continue to perform with confidence, but after some time this becomes too easy. This feeling prompts her to ask for some adjustment, possibly at first to the work targets and then to an extension of tasks within the job. The important point is that ease within the transformation process, assessed by the employee and others, leads to developmental adjustments. Continued attention to process may eventually result in a further range of adjustments, such as increased responsibility through job enlargement and job enrichment, and a reconsideration of the employee's future direction within the organization. On the way, the organization may benefit from rising efficiency and effectiveness, including better standards.

Through attention to the behaviour of an employee in the transformation process, data can thus be provided for a whole gamut of developmental decisions over time, starting with adjustments to reach minimum standards and then addressing career changes and progression. Figure 8.5 shows a representation of this development, starting at the centre with attention to immediate performance and extending outwards to career changes and progression. Individual employees are able to set targets, objectives and goals for each stage through appraisal.

The focus on practice as the starting point for PMS processes is brought into greater prominence when we consider that many people now work in highly skilled jobs requiring significant learning. Such further work often requires a response to unusual or changing situations, where on-the-spot decisions are needed with little time for considered deliberation. This is not untypical of professional work or work requiring high levels of expertise (Beckett, 2000).

A number of techniques have been developed that allow for the consideration of practice with the various stages of the transformation process. The ability to employ various techniques in performance management will depend on a number of contingencies. Ouchi (1979) has provided a framework specifying these and allowing a choice of techniques to be made; Figure 8.6 has been adapted from his work.

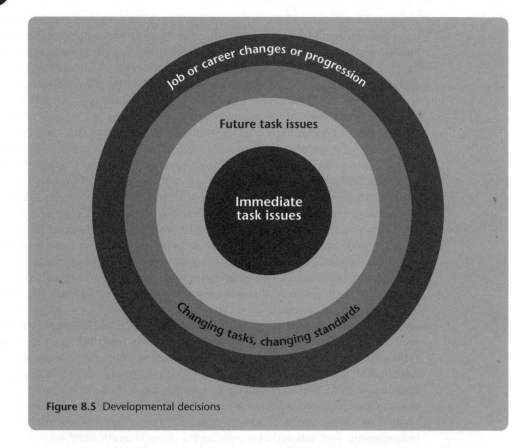

Figure 8.5 Developmental decisions

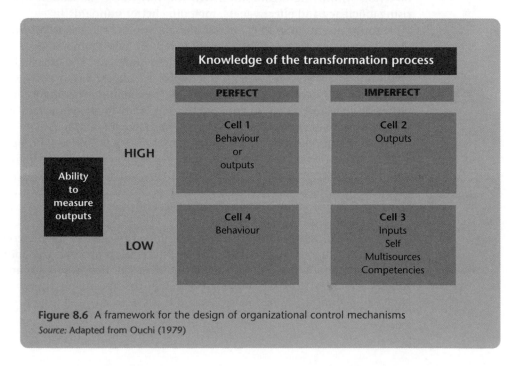

Figure 8.6 A framework for the design of organizational control mechanisms
Source: Adapted from Ouchi (1979)

This framework can be used to reconcile the dilemma that organizations may face in performance management and appraisal, that is, the dilemma between the desire to maintain control and the desire to foster a developmental emphasis. Forms of control depend on the feasibility of measuring desired performance: 'the ability to measure either output or behaviour which is relevant to the desired performance is critical to the "rational" application of ... bureaucratic forms of control' (Ouchi, 1979, p. 843).

In Ouchi's framework, if an organization either has the ability to measure outputs or behaviour or has a high understanding of the transformation process involved in production, the organization could opt for a **bureaucratic control** approach and base appraisal on behaviour, output measurements or both. Thus, in cell 1, typical of traditional manufacturing and service organizations, where work process steps can be clearly stated, both behaviour and output techniques can be used.

In cell 2, only outputs can be successfully measured, perhaps because work processes cannot be observed; this may occur with sales workers. The key issue here seems to be how such outputs are judged and the criteria utilized. Research by Pettijohn et al. (2001), for example, which sought to understand salespersons' perspectives of appraisal, found that although appraisal was a common practice within sales management, there was some dissatisfaction with the criteria used. In particular, sales persons preferred criteria such as customer satisfaction and product knowledge that lay within their control. The failure to include such criteria had implications for the use of appraisal to affect morale, turnover and overall performance.

In cell 4, employees' behaviour can be observed but outputs are more difficult to discern; this may be the result of groups of employees producing group outputs or measurable outputs over a long period of time, for example in research work. Particular difficulties occur when appraisal, which is inherently an individual process, is applied to a group or team; you may already have had experience of groupwork and the problems that occur when a group mark is given for assessed work. In the workplace, there may be variations of effort and variations in the skill required. There is also variability in the life of teams, some teams coming together for a single project, others working together over several tasks. A team may increasingly have to operate over different locations. This suggests that the performance management of teams requires a consideration of relevant circumstances rather than a 'one-size-fits-all' prescription (Scott and Einstein, 2001). For example, van Vijfeijken et al. (2002) suggest that effective group performance management requires a combination of goal-setting and rewards based on group performance. This needs to consider the degree of interdependence between tasks completed by group members, the complexity of tasks and the interdependence of goals, which considers how the goal of one person is affected by or affects the attainment of goals by others.

HRM WEB LINKS

Team appraisal is often a difficult process. You can read about how the problems were tackled at the Smithsonian Institution at www.si.edu/archives/archives/2rmapbackground.html.

In all the above cases, the logic of control may be extended to some form of performance or merit-related pay system (Chapter 10). In cell 3, however, there is an imperfect knowledge of transformation and a low ability to measure outputs, making bureaucratic control virtually impossible. Ouchi refers to this cell as a 'clan' based on a ritualized, ceremonial or 'cultural' form of control arising from shared attitudes, values and beliefs. Cell 3 would include the work of professionals and knowledge workers, most managers and, increasingly, forms of work organization in which higher levels of discretion and autonomy are granted to individual employees or teams. Behaviour, although difficult to observe formally, can be observed by those present at the point of production. A university can, for example, bureaucratically control who becomes a lecturer through its selection processes; hence it is possible to assess 'inputs' through qualifications and other attributes.

Once the lecturer is in place, however, his or her performance is much more difficult to assess and appraise. Some universities are seeking to introduce competency frameworks. For example, one institution is seeking to base performance management on 'an assessment of the outcomes and competence requirements established during the Performance and Development Review'. The difficulty here is the attempt to measure outcomes when the work is non-standardized. Furthermore, the use of competencies has been widely criticized as a reduction and fragmentation of complex work but gives power to those who seek to control such work (Mumford and Gold, 2004).

Consider further the work of professionals in the public sector in recent years, in which performance management and appraisal can be seen as part of a shift towards managerialist language and techniques. In response to deregulation and competition, often sponsored by central government, as part of the trend referred to as new managerialism or new public management (Pollitt, 2000), there have been various attempts to curtail the power of professionals within the public sector and remove or usurp their monopoly (Exworthy and Halford, 1999a). Research so far suggests the emergence of new relationships and a reordering of professions and management: head teachers, for example, require leadership skills, which include the assessment of their staff.[6] In the NHS, with over one million employees, many of whom are professionally qualified, appraisal (referred to as the 'individual performance review') was developed in the 1980s and has been seen as one of the tools necessary to bring a change in culture.

Research by Redman et al. (2000) found that, after several years of experience, appraisal was generally valued, with particular strengths in setting objectives, personal development planning and, where they occurred, quarterly 'mini' reviews. There was, however, also evidence of 'patchy application' (Redman et al., 2000, p. 59). Others have found considerable resentment towards managerial processes in general (Exworthy and Halford, 1999b). The key issue, according to Flynn (1999, p. 26), is the 'concrete internal policies which control and limit professionals'.

Generally, the performance management of people whose work is knowledge-based is difficult to observe and requires a longer time frame for measurement. Reilly (2005) suggests that you cannot impose performance management in such circumstances. Furthermore, such workers tend not to want hierarchical career progression, and many will resist moves into managerial posts. Career-planning tools can help them determine their own career paths.

Referring back to our earlier analysis, we saw that a substantial record had been established to show the problems of appraisal. These stemmed mainly from the way in which systems were established as a way of superiors evaluating employees for a variety of purposes, for example improving performance, pay and promotion. Over the years, a large battery of techniques has been made available to organizations. Some of these techniques, for example psychometric tests and, more recently, assessments made based on competency frameworks, carry validity and reliability scores, suggesting greater 'objectivity'. What cannot be escaped, however, is that all employees have an opinion on how well they are performing, the rewards they desire and deserve, and the training they require. That is, whatever techniques of appraisal are employed, self-appraisal and self-rating will always be there too. When the emphasis of performance management and appraisal is on evaluation and control, it is only to be expected that differences will exist between an individual's self-appraisal and the appraisal of his or her superior. Campbell and Lee (1988) put forward a number of discrepancies between self- and supervisory appraisal:

- *Informational:* There is disagreement over the work to be done, how it is done and the standards to be used in judging the results.
- *Cognitive:* Behaviour and performance are complex, and appraisers attempt to simplify this complexity. Different perceptions will result in disagreement between appraisers and appraisees.
- *Affective:* The evaluative nature of performance control appraisal is threatening to appraisees and triggers defence mechanisms, leading to bias and distortions in interpreting information. Appraisers also may find appraisal threatening.

All this suggests that self-appraisal in an environment of evaluation and control is not effective, which is not surprising. Campbell and Lee (1988, p. 307), however, suggested that 'such pessimistic conclusions did not rule out the possibility that self appraisals can be used as important developmental and motivational tools for individuals'.

We have already shown that employees are able to observe their own performance and obtain data for appraising strengths and weaknesses, and for identifying future goals from the processes of working. We have also demonstrated that such observations may allow the organization to benefit from rising efficiency and effectiveness, including better standards. Allowing employees to appraise themselves for development purposes is an acceptance of the values of such a process for individuals and the organization. The extent to which employees are able to appraise themselves objectively becomes a question of how willing they are to seek and accept feedback from their work behaviour and the environment they are in. Employees can learn to appraise themselves and will treat this as part of their own development if they can see its value for themselves rather than viewing it as a manipulative management tool.

HRM WEB LINK

How good are you at seeking feedback? What are the skills of effective feedback? The following website may help you: www.orgdct.com/feedback%20skills.htm.

Self-appraisal for development will not occur unless it is set in an environment that facilitates and encourages such a process. If a positive experience is gained from self-appraisal, employees may be willing to share their thoughts on the process with others. In recent years, many organizations have sought to increase the amount of feedback received and the number of sources of feedback. Kettley (1997) claims that the growing popularity of multisource feedback has arisen from a number of factors:

- It is a way of empowering employees and promoting teamwork by allowing employees to appraise their managers.
- It increases the reliability of appraisals and balance in flatter organizations.

● It reinforces good management behaviour by allowing people to see themselves as others see them.

Most schemes appear to involve feedback to managers, although there are likely to be increased attempts to extend the process to all employees in the future. The various sources of feedback might include:

● the immediate manager
● staff (**upward appraisal**)
● peers (peer appraisal)
● other parts of the organization (internal customers), external clients and customers
● self-rating.

A scheme providing feedback from all or most of these sources – usually between 8 and 10 – is referred to as 360° appraisal or feedback.

As the number and range of multisource feedback schemes have grown, so too has interest in their impact. The crucial factor is the extent to which self-rating is supported by the ratings of others. What do you think the outcome would be if a manager had a positive perception of his or her performance but was rated less well by others, for example subordinate employees and internal customers? Yammarino and Atwater (1997) have provided an examination of possible HRM outcomes based on the range of agreements between 'self' and 'other' ratings, as shown in Table 8.2.

Table 8.2 Self–other rating agreement and human resource management (HRM)

Type	Ratings	HRM outcomes
Over-estimator	Self-ratings greater than other ratings	Very negative
In agreement/good	High self-ratings similar to other high ratings	Very positive
In agreement/poor	Low self-ratings similar to other ratings	Negative
Under-estimator	Self-ratings less than other ratings	Mixed

Source: Yammarino and Atwater (1997) p. 40

There has been only limited evidence of the impact of multisource feedback. A study by Reilly et al. (1996) on the effect of upward appraisal on management performance showed an improvement where managers started from a low or moderate rating and the feedback process was sustained over time. There was less impact on managers who already had a high performance rating. The study found that the process created an awareness of the behaviours measured, leading to efforts by managers to improve against these measurements, especially in the early phases of the scheme. In addition, the scheme itself provided a powerful message to managers that performance would be assessed and improvement was expected. A further study by Atwater et al. (2000) found that where there were cynical attitudes among managers towards organizational change efforts, there was a low impact of feedback from subordinates on their behaviour. There was also a tendency to reinforce existing commitments to subordinates. Thus, high ratings from subordinates strengthened commitment, whereas low ratings reduced it.

Other studies have shown that there are still dangers in feedback schemes that are used to judge employees and provide information for their development and performance improvement. Handy et al. (1996), in a survey of organizations using 360° feedback, found that whereas most were positive about its use and were confident that it was a stimulus for personal growth, there were also some problems. Individuals could be hurt by too much negative feedback, and there might be confusion over whether the process was for development or for judgement relating to pay or promotion.

More recently, Smither et al. (2005) have sought to explore the impact of multisource feedback on performance over time. To do this, they examined 24 studies but found only small improvements in performance from feedback, suggesting that other factors were also important. The research suggested the following factors were important in determining how much performance improvement might result from multisource feedback:

- the characteristics of the feedback
- initial reactions to the feedback
- personality
- feedback orientation
- the perceived need for change
- beliefs about change
- goal-setting
- taking action.

Each of these factors could have an impact ranging from the nature of the feedback, for example positive or negative, to beliefs about abilities to take action. There are no clear paths to performance improvement from multisource feedback. Instead, the process will benefit some and not others. It will also depend on how the process is positioned in an organization and how support is established. In particular, organizations need to consider the preparation of employees to give and receive feedback and use the various rating techniques. Training programmes for such skills would be crucial before the implementation of multisource feedback schemes. It would also seem that such schemes have more value as development and performance improvement processes than as a judgement mechanism for pay and promotion (McCarthy and Garavan, 2001). In particular, an organization needs to assess the impact of any mulitisource feedback scheme and provide support through developing a coaching culture (DeNisi and Kluger, 2000). HRM in Practice 8.4 shows an example of the use of multisource feedback in a radio company's leadership development programme.

HRM IN PRACTICE 8.4

RADIO COMPANY TUNES INTO MIDDLE MANAGERS FOR SUCCESSION PLANNING

PEOPLE MANAGEMENT, 12 JANUARY 2006

Local commercial radio company UKRD has launched a fast-track management development programme to develop its middle managers.

Together with leadership development consultancy Maximum Performance, the company is seeking to improve its succession planning by training middle managers as well as people with management potential.

...the company is seeking to improve its succession planning...

Ten employees have been selected for the first course, which includes 360-degree feedback, in-house mentoring support, role playing with professional actors and individual coaching.

The company will compare online 360-degree feedback at the beginning and end of the course to evaluate improvement.

It will run the course every six months for 10 employees.

Approaches to performance rating

We can see that, throughout the performance management cycle (see Figure 8.1 above), there are a number of opportunities for **performance rating** to occur. The different approaches to rating can be classified as inputs, results and outcomes, and behaviour.

Inputs

This is a broad and potentially vague category that has traditionally been concerned with listing traits or personality attributes. Typical attributes are dependability, loyalty, decisiveness, resourcefulness and stability. Because such attributes may be difficult to define, there will be little agreement between the different users of lists of measures on their presence in employees. In Chapter 7, we referred to the issue of reliability. The use of personality attributes in performance management and appraisal can lack reliability, giving rise to charges of bias, subjectivity and unfairness. This is normally the case when managers attempt to measure their employees in appraisal interviews. As indicated above, many organizations now prefer to use reliable and valid psychometric instruments as a way of helping employees to diagnose strengths and weaknesses for a development plan.

Results and outcomes

The results and outcomes of work performance provide the most objective technique for collecting data for appraisal. When available, measurements can be taken at different points in time and comparisons made with objectives. Typical measurements might relate to production, sales, the number of satisfied customers or customer complaints. The CIPD (2005c) survey clearly indicated the popularity of such an appoach, with 62 per cent of respondents claiming the use of objective-setting and review as part of their PMS.

We can also include in this section the achievement of standards of competence as contained within, for example, National Vocational Qualifications (England and Wales) and Scottish Vocational Qualifications. Such standards attempt to describe what competent people in a particular occupation are expected to be able to do. Outcomes achieved can be assessed against performance criteria for each standard.[7]

It is not surprising that most measurements are quantifiable, although many organizations will attempt to modify quantification with qualitative measurements or comments. The attractiveness of results and outcomes as objective sources of data makes them a feature of many PMSs, but do such approaches reflect performance control or development approaches? Key questions will relate to how objectives, targets and goals are set, how managers and employees interact in work towards their achievement, and the use made by employees of measurements as feedback in order to develop further.

As Pettijohn et al. (2001) found, it is important that the criteria used to judge performance are controllable by those being judged: a failure to be so affects morale and overall performance. During the 1960s, for example, there was a growth in schemes of *management by objectives*, designed to control the performance of managers and stimulate them in terms of their development. If this could be achieved, the needs of managers and the organization could be integrated. Such schemes soon came under attack, however, and many fell into disrepute. Levinson (1970, p. 134) attacked the practice of management by objectives as self-defeating because it was based on 'reward–punishment psychology', which put pressure on individuals without there being any real choice of objectives. Modern approaches to objectives-setting will face similar charges unless managers pay as much attention to the process by which objectives are set as to the content and quantification of objectives and the environment in which employees work towards their achievement.

Behaviour in performance

We have already examined how attention to the behaviour of employees as practice in the transformation process will reveal how an individual has applied aptitudes, attitudes and competencies to the performance of work and will provide rich data on current effectiveness and the potential for further development. This attention can occur on a continuous basis, taking into account both subjective and objective data. Such an approach forms the foundation of a PMS concerned with the direction of performance and support for the continuing development of employees. Once these processes have been established, employees may be more willing to accept more codified approaches to rating their behaviour. Frameworks of competencies associated with effective performance can, for example, provide the integrating link within a PMS between the identification of key performance factors and setting objectives that can then be reviewed and rated, although there is evidence that the competencies identified are not always included in an appraisal process (Abraham et al., 2001).

In addition to competencies, and closely related, are behaviour-anchored rating scales (BARSs), which provide descriptions of important job behaviour 'anchored' alongside a rating scale. The scales are developed by generating descriptions of effective and ineffective performance from people who know the job; these are then used to develop clusters of performance and scales (Rarick and Baxter, 1986). Each scale describes a dimension of performance that can be used in appraisal. An example from a scale developed for planning is shown as Figure 8.7. Between 'Excellent' and 'Unacceptable' would lie the whole range of possible behaviours of varying degrees of effectiveness.

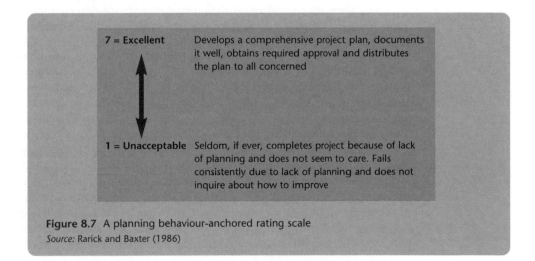

7 = Excellent Develops a comprehensive project plan, documents it well, obtains required approval and distributes the plan to all concerned

1 = Unacceptable Seldom, if ever, completes project because of lack of planning and does not seem to care. Fails consistently due to lack of planning and does not inquire about how to improve

Figure 8.7 A planning behaviour-anchored rating scale
Source: Rarick and Baxter (1986)

An alternative to the BARS is the behavioural observation scale (BOS), on which raters assess the frequency of specific job-related behaviours that are observable. Table 8.3, for example, shows BOSs that have been derived from a financial services company.

Both BARSs and BOSs are based on specific performance and on the descriptions of employees involved in a particular job. What is particularly interesting is the potential for such instruments to enhance self-appraisal and allow a dialogue between employees and others based on more objective criteria. Research by Tziner et al. (2000) provided a comparison between BARSs and BOSs with respect to ratees' satisfaction with their appraisal and setting goals to improve performance. It was found that goals developed by the use of BOSs were more specific than those set using a BARS since they were based on what a rater actually observed rather than on evaluation. Furthermore, since BOSs require a rating of several behaviours rather than the identification of a single 'anchor', as in BARSs, this reduces bias and allows more specific feedback, with the formation of clearer goals.

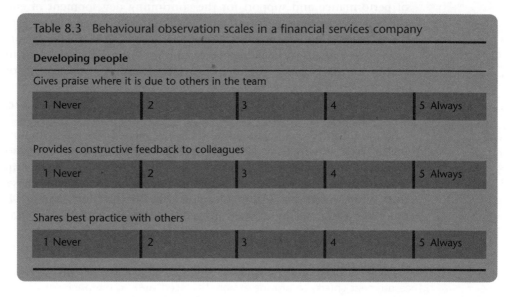

Table 8.3 Behavioural observation scales in a financial services company

Developing people

Gives praise where it is due to others in the team

1 Never	2	3	4	5 Always

Provides constructive feedback to colleagues

1 Never	2	3	4	5 Always

Shares best practice with others

1 Never	2	3	4	5 Always

The recent trend towards performance management and appraisal has gone some way to reconciling the competing uses of judgement and development in organizations. The development of competency frameworks, along with other measurement devices, has improved the reliability and validity of feedback on employees' attitudes, aptitudes and performance. This still, however, does not remove the underlying control emphasis. Indeed, some (Townley, 1994) would claim that the use of the various techniques within a PMS serve to enhance the 'manageability' of employees. PMSs also place a great deal of faith in the support of the management team as the assessors and facilitators of other people's development. There is no guarantee of either, and our understanding of what really happens in performance management and in organizations generally is still limited. Importantly, so much of the literature concerning performance management and appraisal works from the neo-human relations assumption that all employees have an interest in achieving the objectives set or responding to measurements when they have participated in the process (Newton and Findlay, 1996). Employees do, of course, have an interest in what they do at work, but they also have many other interests with only a tangential connection to workplace performance, these possibly including many activities that work against management requirements for performance (Ackroyd and Thompson, 1999).

STUDY TIP

Performance management and appraisal are key HRM activities, but there have been many difficulties in providing effective explanations on how they should be carried out. Part of the reason for this is that there are different interpretations and different meanings relating to performance at work in each organization. Ethnographic research attempts to understand how such interpretations and meanings are made in particular social settings. Check the meaning of ethnography at www.ethnographic-research.com/research.html.

Because ethnographic research attempts to understand the customs, beliefs and behaviour of people, data are usually collected through fieldwork and may include the participation of the researcher. An explanation of ethnographic methods can be found at www.sas.upenn.edu/anthro/CPIA/METHODS/Ethnography.html. You can read about an ongoing ethnographic study of diversity at http://astro.temple.edu/~ruby/opp/.

Chapter summary

- This chapter has examined performance management and appraisal in organizations. The key ideas are that the principal dimensions of a person's work can be defined precisely in performance terms, allowing measurement over agreed periods of time that also takes account of particular constraints within the situation of performance. Data provide the basis for the working of a PMS, essential to the idea of a high road HRM strategy.

- Through its link to measurement, performance management provides evidence that management is rationally, efficiently and effectively controlling an organization. Recent years have seen challenges to a narrow measurement of organization performance with the widening of measurement criteria to provide a more balanced view. In the public sector, new managerialism has resulted in a customer-oriented approach to performance measurement.

- Research evidence shows the importance of performance management, with a wide range of activities featured. Different criteria are used to judge performance and to help diagnose development needs, providing a link to the organization's goals. A performance management cycle integrates various HR processes, including development centres, objective-setting and personal development planning, feedback and reviews.

- Performance management has a control purpose to make decisions about pay, promotion and work responsibility, and a development purpose to improve performance, identify training opportunities and plan action.

- Managers have a vital role to play in providing feedback, both formally as part of a PMS and informally as part of everyday work. The acceptance of feedback as valid will depend on its frequency as part of an ongoing relationship and how well managers understand the perceptions of their staff.

- The performance control approach to appraisal is still seen as evidence of rationality and efficiency at work. Such beliefs often become taken-for-granted assumptions and difficult to challenge. Appraisal as control simplifies relationships but, in the process, makes it less relevant to people's experience of relationships at work and reduces its effectiveness.

- A more developmental approach to performance management and appraisal has been seen as a way of harnessing employees' potential during times of rapid change. This has resulted in the adoption of performance management and appraisal for all employees in many organizations. More attention can be paid to performance at work that provides information on their effectiveness and the potential for further development.

- The contingent factors 'knowledge of the transformation process' and 'ability to measure outputs' need to be considered in approaches measuring performance at work. Whereas the measurement of behaviour and outputs may be suited to typical manufacturing or service work, other approaches increasingly need to be considered. Many professionals and others in the public sector have been subjected to managerialist language and techniques as part of a trend referred to as new managerialism or new public management, although some research suggests considerable resentment towards this.

- Performance might be reviewed and appraised using a variety of multisource feedback processes, including self-appraisal and feedback from managers, peers, subordinates and others as part of a 360° appraisal process. There is only limited evidence of the success of such activities. Cynical attitudes may lead to a low impact of feedback. A key issue here is how people learn to give and receive feedback.

- Performance can be rated in different ways. Inputs in the form of personality attributes or traits may lack reliability and may be seen as subjective and unfair. Results and work outcomes allow quantifiable measurement and are therefore seen as more objective, but research suggests that the criteria used to judge performance need to be controllable by those being judged. Rating behaviour within performance allows the use of such techniques as BARSs and BOSs. Because these are based on people's specific performance at work, they can lead to a relevant dialogue about performance.

- Overall, performance management and appraisal tend to assume that all employees have an interest in achieving the objectives set or responding to measurements set by the organization, although there is much evidence to suggest that people have many other interests, not all of which match the requirements of the organization.

Key concepts

- 360° appraisal or feedback
- Multisource feedback
- Appraisal
- Performance and development plan
- Assessment
- Performance management system
- Best Value

- Performance rating
- Bureaucratic control
- Self-appraisal
- Development centre
- Transformation process
- Goal-setting
- Upward appraisal

Chapter review questions

1. What should be the purpose of performance management and appraisal?

2. Is performance management 'management by objectives' under another name? Will it suffer a similar fate?

3. Does a PMS enhance strategic integration in HRM?

4. Can knowledge workers and/or professionals be performance managed?

5. Do you think that students should have more say in appraising and assessing themselves and each other?

6. Do you think that appraisal and assessment techniques enhance the 'manageability' of employees?

Further reading

Armstrong, M. (2002) *The Performance Management Audit: An Eight-step Audit to Help Analyse, Develop and Improve Performance Management Processes so that the Organisation Achieves its Business Goals.* Cambridge: Cambridge Strategy Publications.

Davenport, T. (2005) *Thinking for a Living. How to get Better Performance and Results from Knowledge Workers.* Boston: Harvard Business School Press.

Fletcher, C. (2004) *Appraisal and Feedback: Making Performance Review Work* (3rd edn). London: Chartered Institute of Personnel and Development.

Halachmi, A. (2002) Performance measurement and government productivity. *Work Study*, **51**(2): 63–73.

Townley, B. (1999) Practical reason and performance appraisal. *Journal of Management Studies*, **36**(3): 287–306.

Practising human resource management

Searching the web

One of the most comprehensive resources for appraisal and performance management on the web is provided by the Zigon Performance Group at www.zigonperf.com/, with links to online resources and articles. There is a performance management library at www.managementhelp.org/emp_perf/emp_perf.htm. Information on a growing trend towards the use of software in appraisal can be found at www.hr-guide.com/data/209.htm. A variety of 'how to' articles can be found at www.zigonperf.com/resources.html.

HRM group activity

During the 1990s, workers in the public sector were increasingly subjected to HRM processes such as performance management and appraisal. You have been asked to examine how these apply to schoolteachers.

First, find out the appraisal and performance management requirements for schoolteachers in England at www.hmso.gov.uk/si/si2001/20012855.htm and www.teachernet.gov.uk/performancemanagement.

Second, examine the view of the General Teaching Council at www.gtce.org.uk/. Use the search facility to find papers on performance management and appraisal.

Now find out the response of some of the teaching unions. The National Union of Teachers website is www.teachers.org.uk/, and the National Association of Schoolmasters and Union of Women Teachers is at www.teachersunion.org.uk/.

Finally, read Brown, A. (2005) Implementing performance management in England's primary schools. *International Journal of Productivity and Performance Management*, **54**(5/6): 468–81.

Chapter case study

INSIGHT COMMUNICATIONS

Insight Communications is a major telecommunications company. After a recent restructuring activity, the marketing and solutions department was reorganized into 12 virtual teams, each working in a different location across Europe. A key change was an increased focus on selling, in which teams had previously worked with sales units as consultants. The new role demanded that staff work in virtual cross-functional teams to deliver a complete solution to customers' needs, the idea being to reduce customers' need.

Halfway through the financial year, it was becoming evident that most teams were failing to achieve their targets. Of the 12 teams, 7 had low overall sales, 3 were significantly short of the expected achievement, and only 2 teams were meeting or ahead of the target. Furthermore, it

was becoming increasingly difficult for the head of department to manage the performance of the teams, and, as the manager responsible for the achievement of an overall target, he was beginning to feel that the restructuring was a step too far. The monthly financial and performance reports showed an increasing variance against targets, and this made the head of department feel very uneasy about the future. The company was downsizing again, and this was a bad time to be failing to deliver.

In addition, team members were often expected to establish and lead the virtual cross-functional teams but had indicated that they often felt unable to meet this requirement and were disappointed about how their performance was judged. The large distances involved often resulted in isolation and a lack of communication.

Discussion questions

1. What are the key skills for a virtual cross-functional solutions sales team?

2. How can their performance be managed effectively?

3. What methods can be employed to achieve short-, medium- and long-term performance improvement?

4. What approaches to effective communication with virtual teams can be employed? What feedback skills are necessary?

HR-related skill development

Performance appraisal is not a precise science but a subjective judgement. There are some guidelines that may, however, increase an employee's acceptance of the appraisal process and intention to improve performance in the future. Using the information in this chapter, and the following websites which contain sample performance assessment tools and guidelines (www.businessballs.com/performanceappraisals.htm, www.cipd.co.uk/subjects/perfmangmt/perfapprsl/, www.performancereview.com, www.zigonperf.com/freeresources.asp), pair up with another student and review and appraise each other's work. Identify realistic measurements and dates of completion.

Also go to our website (www.palgrave.com/business/brattonandgold4) and click on 'The appraisal interview'. After completing the appraisal interview, ask:

1. Is the appraisal process effective and fair?
2. Did the activity illustrate the problems of appraisal?
3. How might you suggest improving the appraisal process?

Notes

1. Kevin Hogarth, HR director at Capital One; as quoted in *People Management,* 27 January 2005, p. 33.
2. Taylor (1998, p. 185).
3. Legge (2005, p. 30).
4. The idea of continuous improvement in TQM is referred to as kaizen. There is a close connection to another system of continuous improvement and measure called six sigma. Find out more at www.isixsigma.com/.
5. You might consider other variations such as 180°, 270° and 540° feedback (see McCarthy and Garavan, 2001).
6. In the UK, the National College for School Leadership has been established with the aim of ensuring 'that school leaders have the skills, recognition, capacity and ambition to transform the school education system into the best in the world'. You can find further details on its website: www.ncsl.org.uk/. There has been a growing interest in the role of leadership in the public sector as a vital feature of meeting the challenges of the 21st century. Check the report from the Cabinet Office at www.strategy.gov.uk/work_areas/leadership/index.asp.
7. National Vocational Qualifications and Scottish Vocational Qualifications will be covered in more detail in Chapter 9, but you may wish to examine the websites at www.qca.org.uk/14-19/qualifications/index_nvqs.htm and www.sqa.org.uk/SVQ/.

Chapter nine

Human resource development
Jeff Gold

> Human resource development comprises the procedures and processes that purposely seek to provide learning activities to enhance the skills, knowledge and capabilities of people, teams and the organization so that there is a change in action to achieve the desired outcomes.

'Skills matter. They help business to compete, and they help individuals to raise their employability and to provide a route to a better life. The success of the country depends on its skill base.'[1]

'We must firmly convince our line managers of the benefits of training. We must concentrate more on evaluating our results and demonstrating the benefits to the business.'[2]

'The critical task for government policymakers and leaders in organisations is to maximise the learning ability of people by encouraging and supporting individual and collective learning.'[3]

Chapter outline

Chapter objectives

After studying this chapter, you should be able to:

1. Discuss the place of human resource development (HRD) within human resource management (HRM)
2. Understand the connections between HRD and strategy
3. Discuss the effectiveness of a national infrastructure for HRD
4. Explain how HRD may be implemented
5. Explain key ideas of workplace learning
6. Understand developments in knowledge management and e-learning

Introduction

Human resource development (HRD), as an organization's investment in the learning of its people, acts as a powerful signal of its intentions:

1. By replacing the words 'training cost' with 'investment', there is an indication that a longer term view is being taken, particularly with respect to the outcomes of HRD. There is a significant contrast with the view of training as a short-term cost, which has persistently acted as a powerful break on many training strategies. HRD implies that learning will be a strategic consideration in an organization.
2. HRD acts as a triggering mechanism for the progression of other human resource management (HRM) policies that are aimed at recruiting, retaining and rewarding employees, who are recognized as the qualitative difference between organizations. The investment in employee learning is a way of creating a primary internal market, and policies aimed at progressively upgrading skills reduce an organization's dependency on external sources of skill.
3. If an organization is seeking to adopt a 'high road' HRM strategy (Cooke, 2000), engendering the conditions whereby loyalty and commitment towards an organization's aims can be encouraged, HRD carries the prospect of unleashing the potential that lies within all people, allowing employees to contribute to and indeed transform strategy.

In recent years, ideas and practices relating to HRD have moved beyond a narrow conception of training and development. Many organizations now claim to take a holistic view that embraces the idea of learning at individual and organizational levels as a crucial source of competitive advantage. HRD has attempted to move out of training departments into every aspect of organizational life as many organizations claim attraction to the idea of a learning organization, with increasing moves towards finding ways to integrate work and learning.

Technology, global markets, customer expectations and competition have all contributed to the view that organizations need to achieve 'high-performance working', leading to the generation of high value-added products and services for customers, and trust and commitment from enthusiastic employees (International Labour Organization, 2000). Key features of such an approach are the attention paid to learning throughout the organization and the fact that learning is the only strategy to cope with change. There is a growing emphasis on viewing an organization as a total learning system and finding its 'core competencies', which reveal its 'collective learning' (Prahalad and Hamel, 1990, p. 82). In addition, continuing advances in information and communication technology (ICT) have fostered an e-learning movement, and accelerating change has stimulated a growing interest in organization learning and knowledge management, the development of an organization's intellectual capital (Edvinsson and Malone, 1997) and the potential for learning between organizations. These are indeed powerful ideas that feed the message that learning is an obvious 'good thing', although some doubt whether this is always the case (Contu et al., 2003).

One important consequence is a growing interest in the profession of HRD and its theoretical development. After many years of low oganizational awareness for their expertise (Gold et al., 2003a), HRD practitioners now form a significant section of the Chartered Institute of Personnel and Development (CIPD) in the UK, where they are able to present themselves as the experts in the development of knowledge, skills and learning, and as proactive in their approach to change (Mankin, 2001). Accompanying this growth, there has been more focus on the theoretical basis of HRD (Woodall, 2001), new journals and conferences being devoted to HRD as a separate discipline rather than a subdiscipline of HRM.

As we will examine below, however, not all organizations have responded positively to the message of the virtues of HRD. In particular, in the UK, there continues to be a concern over the degree to which skills gaps and skill deficiencies continue to prevent UK organizations from improving productivity to compete in the global economy. The problem appears to be inherently 'systemic and cultural' (Bloom et al., 2004, p. 3). Thus, even though recent survey evidence suggests that more organizations are including training plans in their business plans (Learning and Skills Council, 2005), some of the assumptions that underpin an organization's investment in people are being questioned, especially if they are framed in terms of the mutual interest of employees and employers in the benefits of learning at work (Rainbird, 2000).

Strategy and human resource development

In most formulations of HRM, training, employee development and any other learning activities that form an organization's HRD provision represent significant if not pivotal components. Ashton and Felstead (1995, p. 235), for example, regard the investment by an organization in the skills of employees as a 'litmus test' for a change in the way in which they are managed. Of the bundle of HR practices required for a high road HRM strategy (Cooke, 2000, p. 5), HRD has a pivotal role in the integration of practices to create an internal labour market with links to organizational structure and strategy. A key image, as mentioned above, is that of high-performance working (International Labour Organization, 2000), in which high-level skills and high discretion in the performance of work allow a decentralization of decision-making to those people closest to customers. Associated with such a view is the importance attached to learning, especially within self-managed teams; team members are able to define their own learning needs (Stern and Sommerlad, 1999).

It has, however, long been recognized that there are some key elements of organizational context that will limit and constrain the design of HRM policies and their implementation, what Guest (1989, p. 50) referred to as the 'cement' that binds the system to ensure a successful outcome to HRM policies. Included in the cement are both the support of leaders and senior managers and a culture that reinforces HRM.

Two important implications arise from this view. First, employees are recruited for a skilled working role that will require learning and change, rather than for a job that might soon become obsolete. Employees are expected to retrain, and indeed many employees undertake courses of self-study in order to continue their learning and remain 'employable'. Employees are therefore carefully selected as much for their ability to learn as for their current repertoire of skills. Once recruited, employees become worth investing in, although the form of this investment may be subtler than simply possessing a large training budget. That is, learning becomes embedded into workplace practice as an ongoing process.

Second, line managers are fully involved in the development of their subordinates, to such an extent that the differentiation between learning and working becomes virtually impossible to discern (and include in a budget). There is an emphasis on informal learning and an appreciation of its value, which line managers regard as part of their job and a responsibility on which they will be assessed. It is the acceptance of this responsibility, more than any other within HRM, by line managers, that carries the potential to produce the outcomes of loyalty, flexibility, quality and commitment. Not least of these outcomes is that more formal HRD activities, such as training courses, are likely to prove their value, but the transfer of learning into the workplace can also alter the nature of work itself and the relationships between managers and employees. Thus, the processes linking performance, appraisal and development would be carried out effectively by line managers as part of their normal work, resulting in the assessment of the need for job improvement and career development.

REFLECTIVE QUESTION

Do you recognize the image of line managers portrayed above? What factors might prevent its realization?

McGoldrick and Stewart (1996) have identified leadership as a key variable in linking strategy, culture and the commitment of employees. The view of leadership employed draws upon Bass's (1985) idea of transformational leadership, made up of four components:

- charisma
- inspiration
- individualized consideration
- intellectual stimulation.

The International Labour Organization (2000, p. 1) model of high-performance working also sees leadership as a 'starting point' for providing vision and a 'sense of momentum and direction'. The Department of Trade and Industry (2005) survey of 3000 organizations suggested that high performance was associated with leadership that was visible and accessible, and enacted by those who set high expectations. Such views of leadership are particularly important when strategy is considered, although we should also note that there is, in the UK, general dissatisfaction with the spread of leadership skills (Council for Excellence in Management and Leadership, 2002). Leadership is particularly important when organizational values are challenged through initiatives such as the promotion of diversity.

Over the years, particularly in the West, managers in organizations and writers have viewed the process of planning strategy as deliberate and purposeful. This has been labelled by Mintzberg (1990) as the 'design school' model of strategic work. The key features of this approach are a prescription to assess external and internal situations, uncovering threats and opportunities, strengths and weaknesses, and the declaration of an intent incorporating the values and visions of the strategy-makers. This is followed by an attempt to formulate strategies that simply and clearly reconcile the gap between perceptions of current reality and desires for the future.

It would thus seem that the extent to which HRD becomes a feature of strategy depends on the ability of senior managers to sense important environmental trends and signals in HRD terms, that is, learning for employees. Pettigrew et al. (1988), in a model of factors that trigger and drive training activity, identified the external forces that may begin the process. Technological and market changes may signal a skills gap, government requirements on health and safety may force training to be considered, or financial support from external agencies may become available. Crucially, Pettigrew et al.'s model recognized the importance of a positive culture for training and the existence of training 'champions' among leaders and senior managers who contribute to a company philosophy that supports training, at least in espoused terms. Although crucial, this view of strategy places a great reliance on the ability of senior managers to deliberate on the factors mentioned above, which include HRD action through plans and policy.

Another view of strategy-making is provided by Mintzberg (1987), who suggested that learning can emerge within an organization if senior managers allow it. Strategies can emerge from the actions of employees, as exemplified by the following quotation (Mintzberg, 1987, p. 68):

> A salesman visits a customer. The product isn't quite right, and together they work out some modifications. The salesman returns to the company and puts the changes through; after two or three more rounds, they finally get it right. A new product emerges, which eventually opens up a new market. The company has changed strategic course.

Through employees' interaction with production processes, customers, suppliers and clients, both internal and external to their organization, employees can monitor, respond to and learn from evolving situations. Through such interactions, employees develop what Yanow (2004) refers to as 'local knowledge', and if senior managers can value it more carefully, it can flow to create knowledge that will inform the organization's strategy. Such a process requires the reconciliation of emergent learning with deliberate control. Leaders and senior managers must be able to use the tension between the two processes of deliberate and emerging strategy-making, and resolve the dilemma, in order to craft a strategy for the real world. If they can see strategies only in deliberate planning terms, they not only run the risk of such strategies becoming unrealized, but also waste the learning that can emerge from their employees.

Integrating HRD into strategy therefore requires the development of the senior management team so that the dilemma to be resolved between control through planning and emergent learning becomes an acceptable form of their thinking. Recent years have seen increased attention being paid to the view of managers as strategic learners who are able to appreciate the complexity of the issues that impact on organizations and the groups and individuals within them. Managers are encouraged to debate and discuss the key issues that emerge, set them in a wider context and utilize the learning gained in order to bring competitive advantage (Grundy, 1994). This may also involve a greater degree of involvement and transparency in decision-making.

HRM WEB LINK

Read more about the work of Henry Mintzberg at www.onepine.info/pminz.htm.

Strategic human resource development

These thoughts on the making of organizational strategy are mirrored in recent deliberations on **strategic human resource development**. An orthodox view makes HRD entirely responsive to organizational strategy. It is for others to define the needs relating to the work to be carried out and the skills and knowledge necessary for implementation. For example, Mayo (2004) provides a view of developing an HRD strategy, arguing that it must be business-led in order to create value. This requires a recognition of the drivers in terms of:

- the medium- to long-term goals of the business, covering mission, vision and values, principles and beliefs about people and their development, maintaining core competencies
- current goals and objectives relating to the strategies of various business units, manpower plans and change programmes
- problems and issues that require an HRD response, such as waste, ineffectiveness, compliance with regulations and the needs of individuals and teams

HRD specialists thus respond by providing solutions (Garavan et al., 1999) through the development of a training system involving the identification of training needs by employees. This view is very much tied to the idea that skills are quantifiable and measurable, allowing tasks to be defined in terms of the skills and people assessed against such definitions (Thursfield, 2000). An extension of this view is to incorporate competencies, expressed as either criterion-related behaviours or standards of performance (Chapter 7). Organizational goals can be cascaded through to employees and expressed as performance expectations. Line managers work with employees to set performance targets and identify the competencies required for effectiveness. HRD is tied to the performance management system (Chapter 8), and its contribution will be judged on the benefits it brings in achieving performance targets.

Alternative versions of strategic HRD provide for a more reciprocal and proactive influence on organizational strategy. Boxall and Purcell (2003, p. 245) suggest that recruitment and selection should complement training and development: 'it is important to learn how to balance HR practices that reinforce the execution of a given strategy with practices that help the firm to conceive of a completely different one'. HRD specialists could play an important role by developing new ideas that both match strategy and take it forward. They can also develop facilitating and change management skills (McCracken and Wallace, 2000), which they are able to do because managers themselves appreciate the emergent features of strategy-making and provide support for learning activities.

Gold and Smith (2003) highlight the various ways in which senior managers can respond to external pressures for change. One such response is to see learning as the way forward. That is, the need for change includes HRD as a principal component in the formation of a strategic plan. This is accompanied by managers acting as key advocates of HRD, recognizing that people are more likely to be productive when they feel that their work is personally meaningful and not simply a means to another end (Boud and Garrick, 1999). One important effect is that management become more accepting of ideas from others within the organization, a culture that supports learning thus being developed. Although such ideas can feature in any organization, they seem to have particular relevance to knowledge-based organizations, in which the production of new knowledge is a vital differentiator (Garvey and Williamson, 2002; Newell et al., 2002).

When we consider the evidence on strategic HRD, there are mixed views. In the UK, the results from the National Employers Skills Survey (Learning and Skills Council, 2005)[4] indicated that, compared with the last survey in 2003, there had been rises in the proportion of employers with formal business plans (from 56 per cent to 58 per cent) and with training plans (from 39 per cent to 44 per cent). The results suggested that there was a correlation between the existence of a business plan, a training plan and a training budget.

There are, however, doubts about the extent to which such progress can be called strategic HRD. Thus, even where strategic management is taken seriously, the focus in the UK is in most cases on profit maximization and cost minimization, which makes HRD and skills a fourth-order consideration (Coleman and Keep, 2001). Training is seldom considered either as an input or a direct outcome of strategic considerations, and this confounds the drive towards high-performance working and high road HRM. Indeed, Guest (2000) found, in a survey of over 1000 managers and chief executives, that although those who adopted 'high-commitment' HRM practices showed a link to business performance, most respondents (90 per cent) did not put people issues as a top priority: marketing and financial matters had much greater importance.

This highlights a key point about strategy-making: even when strategy is given full consideration, there are a number of possible paths that may be taken – for example cost, mergers, information technology and marketing – and using the skills and learning of the workforce is only one of them (Coleman and Keep, 2001). Choosing a path other than skills and learning lies at the core of a UK problem of low-priced, low-quality production and a low demand for skills. Thus, if an organization chooses a production process that implies a low product specification[5] in terms of skills, this has a corresponding impact on the demand for skill (Green et al., 2003), maintaining what Keep (2004, p. 16) refers to as an organization's 'low skills trajectory'. It is a problem with which governments, especially in the UK, have been increasingly concerned.

Diversity and human resource development

The issue of diversity is prompting many organizations to find a training response, and it is one which needs to be considered strategically (Home Office, 2003). As we have already identified, a number of changes in the legal context (see Chapter 6) are widening the coverage of anti-discrimination legislation, and this is coinciding with a broadening of philosophies that seek equal opportunities at work towards diversity, often emphasizing business benefits. In addition, in the UK, especially in the public sector, there has been a growing awareness of the embedded nature of discrimination following the publication of the report of the Stephen Lawrence Inquiry (Macpherson, 1999).[6]

This is inevitably a difficult issue, but a common view is that HRD and training activities have an important part to play. A survey of over 850 organizations across the public sector in the UK (Institute of Employment Studies, 2002, p. 29) found that over 70 per cent had HRD activities focusing on discrimination and diversity with the 'hope' of raising awareness and changing behaviour that would 'eliminate' discrimination. It was also found that, although there were variations in the priority given to the training, priority was increasing. One of the crucial findings was that the shift towards diversity meant a recognition of the need to take a long-term view of cultural change – it is not a 'one-size-fits-all' or a 'one-off' effort but has to be continuous. The Home Office (2003, p. 4) suggests a strategic approach, based on a philosophy that 'embraces diversity'. The strategy needs to be problem-oriented by identifying the issues that need to be confronted and 'be explicit about them' so that it is clear what is being tackled in order that any learning can be matched to the need. Crucially, for such learning to have any chance of being effective, it requires a supportive learning climate (see below). It remains to be seen whether diversity training will bring about real changes in attitudes and behaviour. Wood et al. (2004) argue that a critical confrontation of deeply embedded prejudices is required if the aspirations of the diversity agenda are to be seriously considered.

Establishing human resource development

A principal and underlying assumption within HRD is that, through the provision of learning activities in whatever form, employees are worth investing in, and there will be benefits for the individuals involved, the organization, the economy and society as whole. A recent survey by the CIPD (2005d) suggests that many organizations will value employees, believing that the future will be more demanding in terms of higher-level skills or different kinds of skills. There are, however, disparate and usually competing ways of presenting the case for HRD, which carry significantly different implications for how HRD is provided, delivered and measured.

In the UK, decisions about HRD are taken principally by those in organizations in what is referred to as a **voluntarist approach**. The role of government in this approach is to encourage organizations to take responsibility for their own training and development and its finance. This can be contrasted with a more **interventionist approach** in which the government or its agents seek to influence decision-making in organizations and make decisions in the interests of the economy as a whole.

There is in France, for example, a system of training levies supported by a range of other interventions that form a 'social partnership' between the government and organizations (Noble, 1997, p. 9). The levy is an annual sum of money set by the government as a proportion of payroll, which is then used as a grant to organizations to fund training. If an organization does not provide training, it pays the levy but does not receive any grant. In the UK, however, the voluntarist approach relies heavily on market forces for skills, and in particular on the views of decision-makers in organizations.

> ### REFLECTIVE QUESTION
>
> Do you think a levy system is a fair approach to encouraging organizations to devote resources to HRD?

One view, probably the dominant one, is that people are worth investing in as a form of capital. People's performance and the results achieved can then be considered as a return on investment and assessed in terms of costs and benefits. This view is referred to as **human capital theory** (Garrick, 1999). Although the theory may be dominant, it may also obscure key processes such as how management can ensure successful performance and how costs and benefits can be measured. Furthermore, it can present HRD in fairly narrow terms based on tangible and measurable benefits (Heyes, 2000), which may place a restriction on activities that have an uncertain pay-off over a longer time period. Investment can therefore become reduced to a cost.

Nowhere in the industrialized West is the restriction on development more in evidence than in the UK, where Taylorist–Fordist approaches to control (Chapter 5), through job design and the deskilling of jobs in order to reduce training costs, continue to hold sway in many organizations. In Chapter 8, we referred to the role of metaphor in understanding organizations and how the machine may come to be seen as the ideal way of organizing. Marsick and Watkins (1999) suggest that the machine metaphor[7] causes jobs to be seen as parts coordinated by a rational control system, in which performance can be measured as observable behaviour that is quantifiable and criterion referenced. A number of other implications can be drawn:

● Attitudes are important only insofar as they can be manipulated to reinforce the desired performance.
● Each individual has a responsibility for his or her part, but no more, and has to work against a set standard.
● Learning is based on a deficit model, which assesses the gap between the behaviour of employees and the set standard.
● Training attempts to close the gap by bringing employees up to, but not beyond, the desired standard or competence.
● There is little place for a consideration of attitudes, feelings and personal development.

A further implication of the above ideal is a subservience of HRD to accounting procedures that measure the cause-and-effect relationships between programmes and output and profit in the short term. If a relationship cannot be shown, there will be pressure to provide the proof or cut the cost of the training. Even where organizations espouse an HRD approach, sufficient amounts of the machine ideal all too often remain in place, and hidden from view, to present an effective and powerful barrier to organization learning. For example, many HRD professionals come under pressure to prove the 'bottom line value' of their work and show a return on investment (ROI) in evaluation (see below; Burkett, 2005).

REFLECTIVE QUESTION

To what extent do the above features of the machine metaphor influence the learning programmes in which you are involved?

Human capital theory (and the implied machine image) may be dominant in HRD but can be contrasted with a softer and more developmental view of people and their potential. Gold and Smith (2003), for example, found that some managers who were strong advocates of HRD took a **developmental humanistic approach** based on the personal empowerment of the workforce through learning. The achievement of results is still important, but the key argument is that individuals are most productive when they feel that their work is personally meaningful rather than simply a means to an end. Furthermore, learning provides a way of coping with change and fulfilling ambitions. HRD can therefore move beyond the technical limitations of training and embrace key ideas of learning and development implied in such concepts as the learning organization and lifelong learning. The tensions between human capital theory and the developmental humanist view still, however, require those involved in HRD to present arguments in appropriate terms.

These tensions perhaps become most evident when the issue for learning is diversity. This issue can be presented as a business case that promotes effective resource use and creativity, but it can also lead to an exploration of values, assumptions and deeply held opinions that are not always easy to discuss.

These views provide a background against which the case for HRD is made at the different levels of individuals, the organization and the economy/society. In recent years, there have been various attempts to do just this. At the individual level, for example, evidence is presented that there is a close relationship between learning in all its forms and job prospects, especially in terms of avoiding unemployment and increasing overall earnings (Campbell, 1999). In the UK, findings from the quarterly Labour Force Survey consistently show higher weekly earnings for graduates than those with A levels or equivalent. For example, in August 2005, graduate weekly earnings up to the age of 34 were £507 per week, compared with £307 for those with A levels or equivalent.[8] For training at work, there are difficulties in making precise measurements, but the effect of training is overall to provide a positive wage effect (Machin and Vignoles, 2001). In addition, those who are more qualified tend to receive more training, which in turn increases their earnings potential (Blundell et al., 1999).

At the level of the organization, there have been many attempts to prove that HRD has an effect on performance, but, as Machin and Vignoles (2001) suggest, this link is difficult to show. This is partly because research tends to examine the impact on inter- mediate factors such as labour turnover and productivity rather than on profitability. There is also the 'endogeneity problem' (Machin and Vignoles, 2001, p. 11), which means that the direction of causality may be reversed: instead of HRD being the cause of an improvement in production and profitability, it may be that more productive and profitable firms do more HRD. Others have, however, argued that HRD serves a variety of purposes other than profitability (Green, 1999), for example attracting good-quality staff, indicating the values of the firm and engendering commitment in times of change. HRD is, of course, as we have argued above, a central feature of the bundle of HR practices that have been shown to impact on corporate performance. Nevertheless, it has become a crucial feature of the case for HRD that there needs to be an association between skills and organizational performance (Tamkin et al., 2004). For example, the survey by Green et al. (2003), which investigated over 1000 senior managers, on the relationship between product specification and skill requirements found an association between managers' perceptions of higher levels of product spec- ifications and higher levels of skills, and this was often connected with technical changes and computerization.

Probably the most significant areas of recent research in this field concern the oper- ation of high-performing firms (Tamkin et al., 2004). According to the Department of Trade and Industry (2005a), the crucial features of a high-performing firm are:

- informality and dialogue that allow faster decision-making
- an open sharing of information between peers and networks of managers
- visible and accessible leadership and management
- a focus on the long term and on outcomes
- culture and employee relations characterized by pride, innovation and strong interpersonal relations.

These features are supported by a bundle of HR practices, including workforce devel- opment and skill levels, which relate to the overall direction of the organization and work changes. Further case investigations of high-performing firms (Sung and Ashton, 2005) suggest that skill development is focused on performance and is continuous. In addition, it is not just a matter of technical skills but of 'creating a work environment in which employees can learn all the time as part of their normal work and where they can take advantage of the system for performance and innovation' (Sung and Ashton, 2005, p. 26).

At the level of the national economy and society as a whole, there are inevitable difficulties in separating out the linkages. At a most basic level, there is a connection between school enrolment, the proportion of the labour force in higher education and the size and rate of growth of a country's gross domestic product (Sianesi and Van Reenan, 2000). There is, however, a lack of systematic evidence to support a link between training and economic growth (Machin and Vignoles, 2001), although this has not prevented an identification of the importance of skills for national competitiveness and the negative phenomenon of social exclusion (National Skills Task Force, 2000).

If these are the arguments used to support HRD, why is there continuing concern about skills levels and overall commitment to HRD in the UK? There has been a large effort to examine the causes of low commitment to HRD and significant responses by the government and others to create an infrastructure of support for HRD.

Skills and commitment

The examination of skills and the commitment to HRD have been long-standing issues in the UK. Recent concerns relating to global competition, change and the impact of ICT have, however, provided an impetus for a more strategic consideration, particularly in the context of a view that there is a transformation from industrial production to a knowledge-based society. The attention to skills and commitment to HRD can therefore be seen as part of a broader agenda pursued by UK governments during the 1990s, starting with the White Paper *Education and Training for the 21st Century* (Department for Education and Employment, 1991) and moving on to the 1998 Green Paper *The Learning Age* (Department for Education and Employment, 1998), with visions of a 'learning revolution' incorporating 'lifelong learning' and the 'learning society'.

In relation to the general supply of skills to the economy, the National Skills Task Force was set up in 1998 by the government to develop a national skills agenda to 'ensure that Britain has the skills needed to sustain high levels of employment, compete in the global marketplace and provide opportunity for all' (National Skills Task Force, 1998, p. 38). There then followed one of the most rigorous investigations of skills and commitment to HRD ever conducted, with 18 commissioned research reports, two major skills surveys to examine skill needs, shortages and recruitment difficulties, and an exploration of the link between business strategy and HRD. In addition, there were detailed case studies from such key sectors as engineering, telecommunications and banking and finance.

One of the key findings of the final report of the National Skills Task Force (2000) was that there was a mismatch between skill supply and demand, especially in technical jobs such as craft and professional work. Many employers seemed, however, to underestimate or not recognize their skills gaps, or not consider future needs. It was also found that training tended to be concentrated among managers and senior staff, whereas unskilled, 'flexible' workers and those in small organizations received very little – a finding confirmed in a survey by the CIPD (Cannell, 2002). The Task Force established skill priorities relating to basic skills, generic skills, intermediate skills, ICT specialist skills and mathematics. There was also concern about the number of qualified adults in the workforce, especially when compared with countries such as France and Germany (National Skills Task Force, 2000). In addition, concerns about management and leadership development in the UK led to the formation of the Council for Excellence in Management and Leadership in April 2000 to develop a strategy ensuring that the UK had the managers and leaders of the future to match the best in the world. A report was published in May 2002 (Council for Excellence in Management and Leadership, 2002).

As a result of all this investigatory work, in July 2003, the UK government launched its skills strategy White Paper, *21st Century Skills – Realising our Potential: Individuals, Employers, Nation* (Department for Education and Skills, 2003). This set out the continuing difficulty of skills gaps in the UK, which was linked to an inferior output per hour performance in relation to competitor nations such as France, Germany and the USA.[9] The strategy set out the route to ensure that people could develop skills and become more adaptable and employable, although this would also require a response from employers. The White Paper thus sought to encourage employers to invest in training by improved support services to organizations, and to provide better advice. A move towards a statutory approach was avoided, raising concerns that public funding might be used to support organizations that might carry out training anyway and not necessarily impact on organizations that did not. In March 2005, the government updated the strategy with a new White Paper, *Skills: Getting on in Business, Getting on at Work* (Department for Education and Skills, 2005).

This set out proposals to:

- put employers' needs centre stage in the design and delivery of training
- support individuals in gaining the skills and qualifications they needed to achieve the quality of life they wanted
- reform supply.

HRM WEB LINKS

One consequence of the 'learning revolution' in the UK has been a very rapid development of web resources. Check the Department for Education and Skills website at www.dfes.gov.uk/, where you can find links to latest research commissioned by the UK government. The skills strategy and progress reports can be found www.dfes.gov.uk/skillsstrategy/. You can access the 2005 White Paper at www.dfes.gov.uk/publications/skillsgettingon/. In addition, you can access a range of documents that clarify and support the strategy at www.lsc.gov.uk/National/Partners/SENET/Guide2/skills.htm.cfm#geton. www.lifelonglearning.co.uk/ provides access to a site established to promote the idea of lifelong learning.

The website of the Council for Excellence in Management and Leadership is www.managementandleadershipcouncil.org/index.htm.

Overall, research on skills in the UK has supported a pattern suggesting the continuation of the findings of Finegold and Soskice (1988), who presented the idea of a self-reinforcing cycle of low-quality products and low skills. They argued that, as a nation, the UK's failure to educate and train its workforce to the same level as its competitors was both a cause and a consequence of its relatively poor economic performance – a cause because the absence of a well-educated and trained workforce restrained the response of UK organizations to changing world economic conditions, and a consequence because the production techniques of UK organizations for many years signalled a demand for a low-skilled workforce. In the 1990s, it was argued that employers, expecting low skills among their workforce, aimed to compete in low-skilled product and service markets (Keep, 1999). Furthermore, if a narrow human capital view is taken, employers seek a return from training with a demonstration of a contribution to profits; if this cannot be shown, the investment may be curtailed and seen as a cost that can be cut.

There are certainly many examples of organizations in the UK that do not take a restricted view, and attempts have been made to show the effect of HRD activities not just on the bottom line, but also on the climate of work and willingness to change (Johnson et al., 2000).[10] However, in many organizations within the voluntarist environment of the UK, that is, where employers have a choice about how much they can invest in HRD, many choose to minimize, leaving those outside organizations (government and its agents) with little option but to offer a range of supply-side measures and an 'exhortation' to employers to provide more activities (Keep, 1999).

Working on the basis of a voluntarist approach to HRD, successive governments in the UK have framed their policies around the idea of a market-led system for skills in which demand and supply determine the amount of training provided. In particular, the demand for skills must come from decision-makers in organizations, although, as we have already suggested above, there is a tendency to make HRD a fourth-order consideration strategically, and pressures to meet financial targets in the short term can lead to a low level of demand for HRD. This seems in particular to affect the large number of the workforce who have low or no qualifications, whereas those who are well qualified may receive an unequal share of HRD resources (National Skills Task Force, 2000). For those outside work, low qualifications may prevent entry into the labour market and contribute to the emerging difficulties of social exclusion; as we will see, this issue has become a crucial feature of policy-making in recent years.

Given the difficulties outlined above, the role of government and its agents within a market-led approach has been to improve the UK's training infrastructure and provide funding for interventions to support the smooth working of the system where markets fail. It should be noted here that overall policy is essentially an English policy, with policies for Scotland and Wales now largely decentralized among the devolved authorities. There are, however, common links between all parts of the UK.

HRM WEB LINKS

Details of Scotland's skills strategy and labour market information can be found at www.futureskillsscotland.org.uk/web/site/home/home.asp?. For Wales, try www.learning.wales.gov.uk/, and for Northern Ireland, go to www.delni.gov.uk/.

Broadly, the efforts to stimulate the demand for skills within organizations has been based on an improvement in the supply of skills and the fact that higher skills can be indicated by the achievement of higher levels of qualification. It thus seems to be argued that skills can persuade organizations to change their requirements for producing goods and services in the economy (Keep, 2005). For example, an important area of policy is support for small and medium-sized enterprises (SMEs).[11] Such organizations have been notoriously difficult to influence with respect to formal training initiatives such as Investors in People, even when funding is available (Matlay, 2004). To stimulate demand, a small business action plan was established in January 2004, focusing on the importance of informal approaches to learning in which brokers would provide independent and impartial advice to match the needs of small and medium-sized enterprises with training provision (Mole, 2004).

Important foundations in the supply infrastructure have been the establishment of a framework of vocational qualifications based on national standards, that is, national vocational qualifications (NVQs, in England, Northern Ireland and Wales) and Scottish vocational qualifications (SVQs), and a national network of regional and sector institutions to coordinate national HRD initiatives aimed at improving the functioning of the markets. NVQs and SVQs have been developed to provide a national framework of vocational qualifications in the UK. The framework, covering most occupations, provides qualifications based on the required outcomes expected from the performance of a task in a work role, expressed as performance standards with criteria. These describe what competent people in a particular occupation are expected to be able to do and are usually referred to as 'competences'.[12] The qualifications are organized into five levels, with definitions of the requirements for each level. Table 9.1 shows the general definitions of the levels.

Table 9.1   The national framework for NVQs and SVQs

Levels	Description
Level 1	Competence that involves the application of knowledge in the performance of a range of varied work activities, most of which are routine and predictable
Level 2	Competence that involves the application of knowledge in a significant range of varied work activities, performed in a variety of contexts. Some of these activities are complex or non-routine, and there is some individual responsibility or autonomy. Collaboration with others, perhaps through membership of a work group or team, is often a requirement
Level 3	Competence that involves the application of knowledge in a broad range of varied work activities performed in a wide variety of contexts, most of which are complex and non-routine. There is considerable responsibility and autonomy and control or guidance of others is often required
Level 4	Competence that involves the application of knowledge in a broad range of complex, technical or professional work activities performed in a variety of contexts and with a substantial degree of personal responsibility and autonomy. Responsibility for the work of others and the allocation of resources is often present
Level 5	Competence that involves the application of a range of fundamental principles across a wide and often unpredictable variety of contexts. Very substantial personal autonomy and often significant responsibility for the work of others and for the allocation of substantial resources features strongly, as do personal accountabilities for analysis, diagnosis, design, planning, execution and evaluation

Source: www.qca.org.uk/14-19/qualifications/index_nvqs.htm

It is claimed that NVQs and SVQs are directly relevant to employers' needs since they are based on standards set by employer-led standard-setting bodies. There has recently been an attempt to align the levels of vocational qualifications with higher education qualifications. From January 2006, there has been a national qualifications framework (NQF); Table 9.2 shows this framework with examples.

Table 9.2 The national qualifications framework

Revised levels	Vocational qualifications (original level)	Higher education
8 Specialist awards 7 Level 7 Diploma in Translation	5 Level 5 NVQ in Construction Project Management Level 5 Diploma in Translation	D (doctoral) Doctorates M (masters) Masters degrees, postgraduate certificates and diplomas
6 Level 6 Diploma in Management 5 Level 5 BTEC Higher National Diploma in 3D Design 4 Level 4 Certificate in Early Years Practice	4 Level 4 NVQ in Advice and Guidance Level 4 Diploma in Management Level 4 BTEC Higher National Diploma in 3D Design Level 4 Certificate in Early Years Practice	H (honours) Bachelors degrees, graduate certificates and diplomas I (intermediate) Diplomas of higher education and further education, foundation degrees, higher national diplomas C (certificate) Certificates of higher education
3 Level 3 Certificate in Small Animal Care Level 3 NVQ in Aeronautical Engineering A levels		
2 Level 2 Diploma for Beauty Specialists Level 2 NVQ in Agricultural Crop Production GCSEs Grades A*–C		
1 Level 1 Certificate in Motor Vehicle Studies, Level 1 NVQ in Bakery GCSEs Grades D–G		
Entry Entry Level Certificate in Adult Literacy		

Source: Qualifications and Curriculum Authority

There has undoubtedly been an increase in the number of people gaining qualifications in the UK. According to the Qualifications and Curriculum Authority (QCA),[13] which is the agency acting as the guardian for all standards in education and training, 4,033,465 NVQ certificates were awarded up to 31 March 2003, an increase of 11 per cent on the number awarded up to 2002.

Competence-based NVQs and SVQs have not, however, been without their critics. There have been concerns over the meaning of competence, with its emphasis on achievement of outcomes and assessment measured against standards in preference to attention to knowledge and understanding. In addition, short-term political pressures have, throughout the history of NVQs, tended to influence and distort their development (Williams, 1999), and there are doubts whether NVQs and SVQs provide a more effective framework for training than other approaches (Grugulis, 2002; Hillier, 1997). Keep (1999) suggested that NVQs have added to the number of vocational qualifications on offer rather than rationalizing them: according to the QCA, for example, there were 743 NVQ titles in the framework at the end of September 2001, accessible via a national database. Despite the criticisms, however, NVQs and SVQs have become an important feature of the training infrastructure and are used by governments to set targets and by some organizations to build and implement training plans, as shown in HRM in Practice 9.1.

HRM IN PRACTICE 9.1

GETTING THE VALUE FROM NVQs AT THE NORTHERN SNOOKER CENTRE

JUNE WILLIAMSON, COMPANY SECRETARY

The Northern Snooker Centre Ltd (NSC) is a long-established family business in Leeds. With over 33 staff, the company has developed from having 9 snooker tables to over 27, plus 16 pool tables and three bar and lounge areas that are open 24 hours a day and 365 days a year. The family owners have consistently worked towards developing a customer-focused culture and ethos based on staff training and development, teamwork and leadership. The company regards the 'team' as the whole workforce and has therefore sought to provide learning opportunities for everyone, using NVQs as a key mechanism.

NVQs offer added value to NSC, particularly through training employees as assessors. In-house assessment has provided bonding opportunities by allowing time to be set aside for training and discussion. Morale, communication and recognition have all been boosted. NVQs also offer convenience and flexibility. Staff have been able to set their own pace and most learning is at work.

> **Morale, communication and recognition have all been boosted.**

Recent revisions of NVQs have been a breath of fresh air. There was previously a lot of repetition in providing evidence against the performance criteria for each unit. This led to huge evidence portfolios that were monotonous to compile and assess. Now, we can use different kinds of evidence, like taped discussions between students and assessors, for a cross-section of units.

In NSC, NVQs have been confidence-builders, with no exams and no feeling inadequate in front of a class of people. Staff who have not studied for many years have felt a great sense of achievement in completing their NVQ work.

The company covers the cost and offers wage increases, with a celebratory night out on completion. NVQs benefit everyone – company and employees alike.

One criticism of the UK's vocational education system, based as it is on competence-based NVQs, is that, in contrast with other countries such as Germany, there is a lack of rigour. The German apprenticeship system is based on combining academic and technical skills with guidance from workplace experience, which results in workers of a higher status (Grugulis, 2002). It is partly to counter such criticisms that the government introduced a framework of work-based training that leads to apprenticeship status. The Apprenticeship[14] system is composed of:

- *Entry to employment:* a programme for school leavers not yet ready to take up apprenticeship or employment
- *Apprenticeships:* one-year programmes leading to an NVQ at level 2, key skills and a technical certificate
- *Advanced Apprenticeships:* two-year programmes leading to an NVQ at level 3, key skills and a technical certificate.

It is not clear whether this attempt to return to quality-driven, work-based learning has succeeded. There are concerns about completion rates and, as argued by Fuller and Unwin (2003), the quality of the learning depends on the culture of the organization, including the learning opportunities made available, the degree to which there is breadth in the opportunities and how far apprentices are allowed to participate in skilled practices. In 2005, however, the final report from the Apprenticeship Task Force (2005) argued that apprenticeships improved business performance and represented cost-effectiveness in terms of training in that apprentices were more productive over time. Furthermore, apprentices were more likely to stay with the organization and reinforce company values.

HRM WEB LINK

Find out more about Apprenticeships at www.apprenticeships.org.uk/. There is more on work-based qualifications at www.qca.org.uk/14-19/qualifications/116_brief-guides-work-based.htm.

In terms of institutions to support the delivery of the government's strategy, from 1990 until 2001 this was principally the responsibility of locally based Training and Enterprise Councils (TECs; Local Enterprise Companies, or LECs, in Scotland). TECs and LECs undertook a wide variety of activities, including the finance and administration of the various programmes designed to improve the position of young people in the training market and enhance their employability. Such programmes included Youth Training (now called the New Deal) and Modern Apprenticeships, which aimed to improve the number of those qualified in technical, craft and junior management skills. Importantly, NVQs and SVQs were a required component of such schemes and were used by TECs and LECs to measure the success of programmes and to meet targets set by government.

A key strength of the TECs was that, as locally based institutions, they formed key links with local bodies such as local authorities, careers services, chambers of commerce and so on. However, whereas TECs could point to significant achievements in providing business support and increasing the number of qualifications, there were concerns about a variability in performance between TECs and the clarity of focus in achieving government objectives (Department for Education and Employment, 1998). There were also difficulties relating to boundaries, many TECs focusing on narrowly defined business areas such as a city or a town (Coulson, 1999). During the late 1990s, UK government policy was increasingly influenced by what has been referred to as 'new regionalism' (Webb and Collis, 2000). The basic idea here was that a region should form the basis of thinking and policy relating to development, competitiveness and growth. This could be augmented by the notion of a 'learning region' in which local knowledge and relationships across a region provided a context that supported learning between institutions.

In the UK, particularly in England, these arguments were used, in 2000, to create Regional Development Agencies (RDAs) in order to develop regional strategies and action plans and, from 2001, to replace TECs with Learning and Skills Councils (LSCs) with delivery units set at a subregional level, for example West Yorkshire or North Yorkshire. The LSCs oversee all education and training for those over 16 years of age, including further education colleges, and a network of training providers who focus on the delivery of Apprenticeships and related programmes. Forty-seven local LSCs replaced 82 TECs, a key difference being that the national LSC set the guidelines on the achievement of targets relating to its vision, as its website describes: 'by 2010, young people and adults in England will have the knowledge and productive skills matching the best in the world'. LSCs also provide contracts for the delivery of services to small businesses, usually called Business Link (although officially called the Small Business Service). From June 2006, LSCs will be organized on a regional basis to more closely reflect the stance of the RDAs.

Through the LSC and Business Link, a National Employer Training Programme, available throughout England from April 2006, is attempting to stimulate skills for adult learners. This provides free tuition for everyone for a level 2 qualification and support for achieving level 3. Furthermore, in an attempt to give employers a forum to consider skills needs, the government also established a Skills for Business network composed of 25 Sector Skills Councils (SSCs; employer-led organizations that cover a specific sector – for example Cogent covers the chemical, nuclear, oil and gas, petroleum and polymer industries). The goals of Sector Skills Councils are:

- to reduce skills gaps and shortages
- to improve productivity, business and public service performance
- to increase opportunities to boost the skills and productivity of everyone in the sector's workforce
- to improve learning supply, including apprenticeships, higher education and National Occupational Standards.

HRM WEB LINKS

You can find up-to-date information about strategies, plans and services from the various websites. Try www.lsc.gov.uk/National/default.htm for the LSC home page. Details of the National Employer Training Programme can be found at http://readingroom.lsc.gov.uk/LSC/2005/internaladmin/procurement/netp-design-framework-2006-07.pdf. Go to www.consumer.gov.uk/rda/info/for information about the formation of Regional Development Agencies. Other agencies forming the infrastructure include the Learning and Skills Development Agency at www.lsda.org.uk/home.asp, with a Learning and Skills Research Centre at www.lsrc.ac.uk/; Sector Skills Councils at www.ssda.org.uk/; and the Small Business Service at www.sbs.gov.uk/. The website for Cogent is www.cogent-ssc.com/.

The demand for skills

It would appear that radical changes in the HRD infrastructure are being sought by the UK government in order to stimulate the acquisition of skills. As the prime minister stated in the Foreword to the 2003 skills strategy White Paper (Department for Education and Skills, 2003):

> The skills of our people are a vital national asset. Skills help businesses achieve the productivity, innovation and profitability needed to compete. They help our public services provide the quality and choice that people want. They help individuals raise their employability, and achieve their ambitions for themselves, their families and their communities.

There is, however, continued reliance on a market-led approach, and for a market-led approach to operate to ensure a high demand for skills, action is required principally from within organizations. But, as we have already indicated, many organizations may not regard HRD as being central to their requirements other than to keep production in shape. There is thus continuing concern that the UK, having enjoyed a sustained period of relative full employment, is not making intelligent use of the workforce, who will in time to come be unable to rise to the challenges of future demands (Stanfield et al., 2004). The result is a skills gap, defined by Bloom et al. (2004, p. 12) as 'deficiencies between the skills of the current workforce and those required to meet business objectives'. Perhaps of even greater concern are 'latent skills gaps' (Bloom et al., 2004, p. 12), when an organization accepts and adjusts to low skill requirements for production and loses awareness that this is holding it back. In such circumstances, it may not always be clear whether HRD has a direct causal impact on improvements in organizational measurements such as profitability. As Green (1997) reported, the benefit to employers of training is established through 'intermediate' variables such as labour turnover and organizational commitment, although evidence to support this is not robust.

Most important is probably the definition of the firm-specific skills required for the specific production requirements of an organization. If tasks are designed as requiring a high level of skill, this will trigger a requirement for a highly trained workforce and for investment in that workforce if skilled labour is not available in the external market. Furthermore, the presence of skilled employees is likely to contribute to the interpretation by managers that any changes, particularly in technology, can be dealt with by their employees, so they are able to take advantage of any benefits that the changes may bring (Green and Ashton, 1992).

The recognition of trade unions may also lead to more effective HRD strategies (Green et al., 1998). Under provisions in the 2002 Employment Act, recognition can be granted to union learning representatives (ULRs), who can have paid time off to arrange learning for members. Several particular purposes are allowed, the first being to promote the value of training and learning, including the analysis of training needs, advice to members and arrangement of events for training and learning. Second, ULRs consult with employers on issues concerning members' training and learning. ULRs are entitled to receive paid time off so they can be trained to carry out their role, attending courses with their union in order to have the skills to analyse needs and negotiate with employers (Lee and Cassell, 2004). ULRs can also seek to codify arrangements for learning and training at work through learning agreements and learning committees. This may cover the rights of individuals to learning, and resources for ULRs to their complete duties. From April 2006, a union academy is seeking to offer guidance to employers and employees on learning at work and to provide courses.

HRM WEB LINKS

Check the ULR page of the RMT Union at www.rul.org.uk/rulrs.asp. The Association of University Teachers provides an extensive range of booklets to support ULRs at www.aut.org.uk/index.cfm?articleid=834. The home page of the Union Learning Fund, which provides support to unions for learning at work, is at www.unionlearningfund.org.uk/about.htm. A guide on the role of ULRs and learning agreements can be downloaded at www.dfes.gov.uk/learning&skills/pdf/GUIDE.pdf.

Considering technological change specifically, it is possible to foresee two scenarios as a response to technological change:

1. On the basis of pressures to meet short-term targets and with a poor HRD infrastructure, investment in skills is considered too risky. The consequence is the use of new technology to deskill employees and reduce cost.

2. On the basis of an established skill base that meets the situational requirements of production, and with belief and trust in the ability of employees to learn, any change is used to take advantage of human talents and 'upskill' employees.

In other words, an organization does have a choice about whether the goods and services it produces meet a high specification, requiring high-level skills to provide high value-added, or meet a low specification, requiring lower level skills that provide low value-added (Bloom et al., 2004). However, for organizations that opt for the latter, as argued by Wilson and Hogarth (2003), this may be entirely rational, reflecting the conditions of such factors as the structure of domestic markets, short-term financial pressure, models of competitive advantage based on economies of scale, central control, cost containment and standardization. This may also explain why even the idea or vision of high-performance working may not necessarily be equated with high skills.

Lloyd and Payne (2004) have suggested that there is still limited evidence of such a link and confusion between idealized views of high-performance work and how work is actually performed. For example, production could still be organized around neo-Fordist principles of job design, so even if workers had high skills, they might not be utilized. Lloyd and Payne argue that there remain many institutional limitations preventing long-term investment in skills that have not been addressed by governments. Although some organizations have been able to avoid such difficulties and take the high skills route, many have not, with the consequence that the workforce is becoming 'polarized' (Lloyd and Payne, 2004, p. 18) between extremes of high and low skill.

One aspect of policy that has sought to encourage organizations to consider how skills and training can be considered strategically, and even pursue a high skills vision (Bell et al., 2004), is the Investors in People (IiP) initiative (see HRM in Practice 9.2). Established in October 1991, IiP provides a set of standards for training and development requiring organizations to develop business plans that include schemes to develop all employees and evaluate the results. There is some evidence that this initiative has had a degree of success. First, it has survived since 1991 and over 37,000 organizations in the UK have achieved the standard. Second, through partnership arrangements, the IiP standard has been adopted by organizations in Australia and South Africa, with pilots in Germany, France and the Netherlands (Bell et al., 2004).

HRM IN PRACTICE 9.2

NTP AND INVESTORS IN PEOPLE

JOANNE ASKIN AND ANDREA STEPHENSON, NTP

NTP Limited (NTP) is a successful learning and skills consultancy based in Sheffield. The company has recognised that the Investors in People Standard has a sound theoretical and practical base, largely relating to motivation theories. It provides a framework for ensuring that people feel involved in planning for the future of the business, that they are encouraged to take responsibility for the way they do their work and that they feel valued and recognised for doing a good job. One of NTP's core values, agreed at a recent whole company meeting, is that people will enjoy working for the company.

NTP has also recognised the value of having a regular review of the organisation from an experienced assessor to confirm its good practice and to provide suggestions that feed into the company's continuous improvement strategy. Moreover, the Standard provides an external recognition of the investment the company makes in its staff through effective planning and through learning and development. We believe that this attracts potential customers and employees.

NTP has a culture of consultation, which helps to ensure that people can contribute to its continuous improvement activities. There is an active staff forum, a member of which represents staff interests on the NTP board of directors. In addi-

tion a group has been set up, which includes representatives from each area of the business, to champion Investors in People. This group has been asked to review the company against the current version of the Standard, which was introduced in January 2005, in preparation for the review in January 2007.

Our customers benefit from working with a company whose staff enjoy their work...

The group consisted of Joanne Askin (project manager and representative for core functions), Sharon White (ITC training), Linda Hartle (managing) and Kath Walker (IiP consultant and representative for the consulting division). The group met for the first time on 30 September 2005 to agree the way forward. The group has undertaken a gap analysis against the IiP standard and produced a detailed action plan to achieve re-recognition in

January 2007, which all areas of the business are working towards. This information has been cascaded throughout the business by the group and discussions will have taken place by the end of June 2006 at all team meetings throughout the business.

We believe the standard benefits all of those who work for and with the company. NTP has four divisions, three of which deliver services to businesses, which entail working on-site with the customer. A large percentage of the staff work from home with remote access to head office. Using the framework helps the company to ensure that staff from each division feel that they belong to one company and that they feel part of the company's continued success, contributing to its strategy and vision. Our customers benefit from working with a company whose staff enjoy their work and which can provide innovative solutions through the way the divisions work together.

Until 2001, the IiP initiative was managed by the TECs, but it is now delivered by LSCs and Business Link, and is a feature of their targets in terms of both the number of organizations that commit to IiP and the number that achieve the standard. Although the processes involved proved for some organizations, even those committed to IiP, to be too difficult, or circumstances such as restructuring caused a delay in reaching the standard, the main result appears to be an improvement in training practice (Hillage and Moralee, 1996). Furthermore, a study examining organizations that had already gained IiP found that the main benefits of IiP came if it was used as a way to assess performance and implement continuous improvement (Alberga, 1997). It could, however, be argued that IiP represents something of a spurious means of stimulating the demand for HRD within an organization. Down and Smith (1998), for example, found that many organizations achieving IiP had least to change because they were already doing what was required to achieve the award. There are also concerns of uneven coverage of training, with a greater concentration at managerial and professional level and low rates of accreditation among small businesses (Hoque et al., 2005). Furthermore, once the award has been gained, an organization may revert its commitment on training provision (Hoque, 2003), leading to staff cynicism. As Bell et al. (2002, p. 1077) found, employees can easily be critical of management motives for implementing IiP – 'all managers wanted was a laurel wreath on the paperwork'.

Alternatively, as Gold and Smith (2003) argue, IiP can play a special role in providing a rationale, a process and a positive language for HRD where managers are already convinced of its virtues. They suggest that the recommendations, ideas and exhortations relating to HRD and learning at work, plus the structures to support these, are a feature of what they term the **learning movement**. The key point is that even though the learning movement provides the resources to support HRD, decision-makers still have a choice and can remain oblivious to pressures for more HRD, or sceptical about the benefits. Gold and Smith found that making a decision in favour of HRD was related to a recognition of the need to change and the fact that this could be achieved through HRD. A further factor was, however, the background orientations of the decision-makers, which made them favourably disposed towards HRD; that is, the managers themselves had had positive experiences of HRD or espoused values of openness, trust and commitment, which they believed could be achieved through HRD. It was also found that, once a decision to pursue HRD had been made, it was usually then necessary to persuade others, which often required a great deal of discussion and action to keep HRD alive, especially where more sceptical views might block progress.

The implications here are clear. Pursuing a policy of HRD has to reflect the strategy of senior managers who are able to view their organizations in a variety of ways. Seeing people as being worth investing in means being able to ward off the competing pressures that might challenge this view, while providing the support for a value system that we might call a learning environment. In such an environment, key participants are able to respond to calls for the spread of HRD activities throughout the workforce, and to ensure their success. Of particular importance are the actions of managers at all levels in supporting learning and turning an aversion to risk-taking into opportunity-spotting.

HRM WEB LINKS

The home page of Investors in People is www.investorsinpeople.co.uk/IIP/Web/default.htm. Other initiatives aimed at stimulating demand for learning include the Union Learning Fund at www.unionlearningfund.org.uk/, and more online information about courses at www.learndirect.co.uk/ and www.learndirectscotland.com/ in Scotland.

Implementing human resource development

Although there are many recommendations to adopt a more strategic approach to HRD and make it more business-driven, there remains the crucial factor of how HRD is implemented. A number of uncertainties and tensions arise here. Who, for example, should take responsibility for HRD? Should it be HRD specialists, with their sophisticated repertoire of interventions and techniques, or line managers, who are close to work performance and are able to influence the way in which people learn and develop, and the environment in which this occurs? How should needs be identified, and whose interests should they serve: those of employees seeking opportunity and reward for the sacrifice of their effort, or those of the organization in the pursuit of goals and targets? What activities should be used, and do the activities add value? How does HRD relate to business goals? A crucial feature of HRD, given the claims made for its connection with high-performance working and knowledge creation, is the measurement and assessment of learning. In any organization, there is a range of factors that influence learning, and HRD practitioners may not be the best people to make judgements about its impact (Clarke, 2004).

Overall, there may be still insufficient evidence about what is happening inside organizations when HRD is considered, which is compounded when we consider both formal and informal approaches to learning at work. For example, line managers seem to offer low support for formal training (Chartered Institute of Personnel and Development, 2005d) but play a crucial role in what is learnt informally on an everyday basis. So although it is becoming clearer that formal aspects of HRD, such as plans, policies and activities, can have a crucial impact, informal features may be of even greater importance. In particular, we might consider the impact of work groups on learning or how line managers really inhibit or support HRD processes. These aspects of HRD are certainly significant, although they are also more difficult to examine and measure.

REFLECTIVE QUESTION

How do your peers, colleagues and/or managers influence everyday learning where you are?

Formal models of implementation have shown a remarkable tendency to match the conventional wisdom of how organizations should be run. Depending on the resources committed to their activities, trainers have had to justify the commitment by an adherence to prescriptive approaches. Employees traditionally learnt their jobs by exposure to experienced workers who would show them what to do ('sitting by Nellie'). Much learning undoubtedly did occur in this way, but as a learning system it was haphazard and lengthy, and bad habits as well as good could be passed on. In some cases, reinforced by employers' tendencies to deskill work, employees were unwilling to give away their 'secrets' for fear of losing their jobs. Most importantly, line managers did not see it as their responsibility to become involved in training, thus adding to forces that served to prohibit any consideration of valuing employee potential.

A systematic training model

The preferred routine is to adopt a **systematic training model**, an approach that emerged during the 1960s under the encouragement of the industrial training boards.[15] The approach was based on a four-stage process, shown in Figure 9.1, and was widely adopted, becoming ingrained in the thinking of most training practitioners.

This model neatly matches the conception of what most organizations would regard as rationality and efficiency, a consistent theme in many HRM processes. There is an emphasis on cost-effectiveness throughout: training needs are identified so that wasteful expenditure can be avoided, objectives involving standards are set, programmes are designed and implemented based on the objectives, and outcomes are evaluated or, more precisely, validated to ensure that the programme meets the objectives originally specified and the organizational criteria. There is a preference for off-the-job learning, partly because of the weaknesses identified in the 'sitting by Nellie' approach, and partly to formalize training so that it is standardized, measurable and

Identify training needs
and specify objectives

↓

Design activities

↓

Implement activities

↓

Evaluate activities

Figure 9.1 A four-stage training model

undertaken by specialist trainers. The trainer can focus on the provision of separate training activities that avoid the complexity of day-to-day work activities and make evaluation all the easier.

In this systematic model, the assessment and analysis of training needs is concerned with identifying gaps between work performance and standards of work or performance criteria that have a training solution. Once these have been identified, clear and specific objectives can be established that can be used to design learning events and evaluate the outcomes. Training needs can exist and be identified throughout an organization. Boydell (1976) identified three possible levels; organization, job or occupation, and individual. Needs are in theory identified at corporate or organizational level and fed through to the individual level. The approach reflects a mechanistic view of organizations and the people within them. In particular, there is an emphasis on the flow of information down the hierarchy to individuals, whose training needs are assessed against standards defined by others. Each person has a responsibility to perform against the standard and to receive appropriate training if they are unable to meet the standard.

Emerging from a consideration of needs will be plans for development activities. These may take the form of on-the-job or work-based opportunities supported by line managers and others, or off-the-job courses run by specialists and, increasingly, open and distance learning or e-learning (see below) activities. **Evaluation** occurs as the last stage of the model. Although a number of writers have pointed out the value of evaluation at each stage (Donnelly, 1987), the image of evaluation encompassed by many trainers is that of a final stage added on at the end of a training course. In such cases, evaluation serves to provide feedback to trainers, so that small adjustments and improvements may be made to activities, or to provide data to prove that the training meets the objectives set, so that expenditure on training may be justified.

REFLECTIVE QUESTION

The four-stage model may be rational and efficient, but is it a model of HRD?

Over the years, the basic elements of the four-stage training model have remained, and most organizations that claim to have a systematic and planned approach to training would have some representation of it. There have also been a number of refinements by advocates of a more realistic and more sophisticated model. Donnelly (1987) argued that senior management may, in reality, abdicate responsibility for training policy to training departments, with a consequent potential for widening the gap between training and organizational requirements. Essential prerequisites for any effort to implement a training model are a consideration of budgets, attitudes, abilities and culture or climate. A key requirement of training activity is that it should be relevant and 'reflect the real world'.

We can, however, easily see how training could become either isolated from organizational strategy or reactive to it. Garavan et al. (1999, p. 171) suggest that a 'jug and mug' metaphor may be suited to the trainer role here, with a very passive involvement of learners at any stage. Bramley (1989) argued that the training subsystem may become independent of the organizational context. He advocated turning the four stages into a cycle that is open to the context by involving managers in analysing work situations to identify desirable changes, and designing and delivering the training to bring the changes about. Evaluation occurs throughout the process, with an emphasis on managers taking responsibility for encouraging the **transfer of learning** that occurs during training into workplace performance. In this way, the model is made effective rather than mechanistically efficient.

Refinements to the basic form of the systematic model imply that a more sophisticated view of training is taken. This essentially involves taking account of reality and organizational context. Implicit in such a view are the inherent limitations of organizational reality, which may prevent the basic model operating or may maintain training activity at a low level. The reality may thus be little consideration for training in relation to organizational strategy and a culture that emphasizes short-term results against set standards. Organizational politics may interfere with decisions on training needs (Clarke, 2003), or managers may simply refuse to accept responsibility for supporting the transfer of learning where training is undertaken. These are all features of an organization's learning climate, a consideration of which is essential for the implementation of an HRD approach.

Taylor (1991) argued that it is possible to present two views of why systematic training models may not match organizational reality. In the first, referred to as the *rehabilitative critique*, it is argued that the concepts of the systematic model are sound and can be used as an approximation of reality, serving to highlight the problems to be overcome at each stage by refining techniques. In identifying training needs, for example, trainers may not have access to the 'real' learning needs of the organization because of a lack of access to information and low credibility with senior managers. The refinement would be for trainers to raise the profile of training. However, the second view – the *radical critique* – argues that the systematic model is based on flawed assumptions and is merely a 'legitimising myth' (Taylor, 1991, p. 270) to establish the role of the trainer and allow management's right to define skill within the employment relationship. It is often assumed, for example, that training is in everyone's best interest. In times of rapid change, however, the definition of skill and the redesign of work, which determine and are determined by employee learning, may lead to a divergence of interest between employees and management and unbalance the employment relationship between them.

Taylor (1991) concluded that although systematic models may have helped to professionalize the training activity and provide a simple and easily understood explanation of training procedures, such models were incomplete and really only suitable for organizations operating in stable environments where goals could be clearly set, outcomes measured and mere compliance obtained from employees. According to Taylor (1991, p. 273), however:

> Continued adherence towards what is still essentially a mechanistic procedure may well prevent trainers tapping into the more nebulous but powerful organizational forces such as mission, creativity, culture and values.

Thus, in recent years, there has been greater interest in considering some of the key contextual issues that make training, and learning generally, more effective. This may include factors such as the motivation and interests of learners, the support from managers and supervisors and the overall learning culture. Instead of being systematic, trainers need to become *systemic* in their thinking about the learning process at work (Chiaburu and Tekleab, 2005), that is, understanding the various factors that have an impact on HRD, the interdependence and tensions between the factors and how they combine to produce (or not) training, learning and development in all parts of the organization.

HRM WEB LINKS

There are many HRD resources available on the web. For a closer look at needs analysis, try www.trainingneedsanalysis.co.uk/index.htm. This is the site of a company specializing in needs assessment, but it provides a great deal of information about various processes and the selection of different methods.

If you are looking for activities, try www.trainingzone.co.uk/. You will have to join the site, but once you are logged on, it is an amazing collection of resources and news.

www.mapnp.org/library/trng_dev/trng_dev.htm is the training and development page of the Free Management Library. If you are prepared to explore a little, you will find links to many HRD resources.

An integrated and systemic approach

In contrast to the mechanistic view of training implied by the systematic approach above, many organizations, especially those facing uncertain environments and the expectation of rapid and continuous change, have sought a more integrated and systemic approach in recent years. It is an approach that highlights key interdependencies within organizations, such as the link to strategy, the role of line managers, the link to team-based learning and knowledge transfer (Hirsh and Tamkin, 2005). It is therefore an approach to which the label 'human resource development' seems more suited.

Because change may occur frequently, it is important the people are able and prepared to adapt and move beyond their existing skills, knowledge and abilities. In Chapter 6, we highlighted the fact that there were significant tensions in the idea of making workers more flexible and multiskilled. For example, *total productive maintenance* is a feature of what is referred to as *lean manufacturing* and focuses on improving production and the integration of maintenance of equipment with production. The aim is to prevent costly downtime in production through break-downs, accidents and defects by involving everyone in improvement. This puts an emphasis on training machine operators so that they have a deeper knowledge of the equipment and become multiskilled in order that repairs can be completed as they arise. The total productive maintenance path is one possible path that brings the developmental potential of people to the fore, and this allows HRD specialists to play a more proactive role.[16] Sloman (2005) suggests a shift from training, which is principally instructor-led and content-based interventions, to learning based on the self-direction of staff and learning from work, with managers taking responsibility to support this process.

As we have already indicated, the development of competency frameworks (Chapter 7) purports to link business objectives and employee performance, although as recent work has suggested, such frameworks may not reflect skills gaps (Hirsh and Tamkin, 2005). As we explained in Chapter 8, competencies can be utilized within a performance management system to provide a performance and development plan that will include an identification of training needs and a plan to meet such needs. Instead of being driven by trainers, training needs in principle are demand-led (Chiu et al., 1999), relating to business needs, the requirement for change or the results of self-assessment. Research into the use of competencies has found that the main uses are the discussion and rating of job performance, and identifying training needs (Strebler et al., 1997). It is interesting to note that overall satisfaction with competencies depended on the way in which they were introduced and the provision of training for those who would be required to use them. It was, however, also found that where competencies were used in performance review, identifying training and development needs might actually be detrimental to confidence when using competencies. It seemed that some respondents were sceptical that actions agreed in performance reviews would actually be carried out. As one manager observed, 'I am convinced that unless the system is undertaken professionally, it has negative value and becomes a cynics' charter. It is therefore all or nothing' (quoted in Strebler et al., 1997, p. 76). This difficulty highlights the importance of the line manager's role in the assessment and development of others.

Whatever the quality of the assessment of needs and the HRD activities undertaken, the context in which these occur has a vital impact on their value. A policy of HRD has to be translated into the structures, systems and processes that might be called a **learning climate or environment**. The learning climate in an organization is composed of subjectively perceived physical and psychosocial variables that will fashion an employee's effectiveness in realizing his or her learning potential (Temporal, 1978). Such variables may also act as a block to learning. Physical variables cover the jobs and tasks that an employee is asked to undertake, the structure within which these are set, and factors such as noise and the amount of working space. Of particular significance is the extent to which the work carried out can be adjusted in line with employee learning, for example following the completion of an HRD activity.

Psychosocial variables may be more powerful; these include the norms, attitudes, processes, systems and procedures operating in the workplace. They appear within the relationships in which an employee is involved, for example with managers, work colleagues, customers and suppliers. More recently, Fuller and Unwin (2003, p. 46), drawing on their research of apprenticeship learning, have suggested that an organiz-ation's *learning environment* can be considered as *expansive* or *restrictive*, as two ends of a continuum. At the more expansive end, an organization is characterized by such factors as access to learning and a range of qualifications, a vision of workplace learning and career progression, the valuation of skills and knowledge and managers as facilitators of development. By contrast, a restricted environment is characterized as little or no access to qualifications, a lack of vision, recognition and support for learning and managers as controllers of development.

REFLECTIVE QUESTION

Consider any organization you have worked in. Which end of the expansive–restrictive continuum most accurately describes its stand on learning?

At the heart of the learning climate or learning environment lies the line manager–employee relationship. HRD requires the integration of the various activities, the key to achieving this lying in the thoughts, feelings and actions of line managers. Some organizations have recognized this and have included 'developing others' within their competency frameworks for managers (Industrial Relations Services, 2001). Gibb (2003) provides a number of advantages from the greater involvement by line managers in HRD:

- It will mean that development becomes possible for a wider range of staff and encourages a proactive approach to lifelong learning.
- There is likely to be a better link between organizational and individual needs because line managers are more likely to understand the requirements of work as well as the organizational goals.
- Helping the learning of others is a learning process for line managers too.
- It can lead to better relations and help to support change in organizations.

Of course, as identified by Gibb, there might also be some difficulties. For example, pressures of work may reduce the opportunities for HRD, and managers may not have the skills or positive attitudes for developing others. In addition, by giving responsibility to line managers, the role of specialist HRD practitioners may be reduced and the provision of resources outsourced. Nevertheless, there has been growing interest in how a line manager can support HRD, including **coaching and mentoring**.

Coaching was, of course, originally a development within the sporting field aimed at improving performance (Evered and Selman, 1989), but during the 1970s and 80s it was adapted as a management activity to enhance the development of employees, with particular emphasis on the transfer of learning from formal training courses into workplace activity. Coaching is now one of a range of activities within organizations concerned with helping both managers and staff. The CIPD (2005d) survey of over 750 organizations found that 88 per cent used coaching by line managers. The particular focus of attention in coaching is combining performance improvement with HRD (Megginson and Pedler, 1992). This focus is not, however, without tension, and the quandary of being accountable for performance and HRD could lead to a regression into stereotyped management behaviour (Phillips, 1995). That is, managers may find it difficult to develop their staff when there is need to meet performance targets, the latter usually taking precedence.

Recent times have nevertheless seen the emergence of coaching in a variety of contexts, with calls to create a 'coaching culture' (Clutterbuck and Megginson, 2005, p. 44) in which 'coaching is the predominant style of managing and working together'. For example, BP recently incorporated coaching as a key element of its development programme for new first-level leaders. Each participant was paired with a more experienced colleague who was able to provide support through the programme and further learning once the programme had finished (Priestland and Hanig, 2005).

For managers working at senior levels within organizations, there has been a growing interest in *executive coaching*, which, according to Carter (2001), has arisen because more traditional approaches to management development do not provide sufficient feedback to senior managers. Smither et al. (2003) found that working with an executive coach improved a manager's overall ratings from staff and led to more specific goals. It also seems particularly useful when a manager makes a transition from one level of responsibility to another (Kaufman, 2006).

Mentoring in organizations can be understood as help given by one person to another to find new meanings in work and/or life (Megginson and Clutterbuck, 1995). The distinctive feature of mentoring, and in contrast to coaching, is the focus on longer term learning and development. To ensure that this focus is maintained, mentoring is therefore more likely to be carried out by a more senior or experienced manager who is not the line manager, although the line manager may fulfil this role in some organizations. Over the past 30 years, there has been a great deal of interest in mentoring. Recent attention has examined the matching of mentor and mentee (Hale, 2000), the delivery of mentoring, including tele-mentoring (Stokes, 2001), and mentoring change managers during projects of change (Rix and Gold, 2000). However, because mentoring is a process usually involving conversations between two or more people held in private, there remain gaps in understanding related to what happens, the experience of the participants and the value gained (Megginson, 2000). Nevertheless, there is a growing body of research, especially in the USA, that points to the benefits of mentoring. For example, the work of Payne and Huffman (2005) suggests that mentoring can enhance positive commitment and reduce labour turnover.

Coaching and mentoring are both processes that feature HRD as a management responsibility. In particular, they are processes that can provide a link between HRD activities, transfer to work and evaluation. Figure 9.2 shows a model of the transfer within HRD adapted from the work of Baldwin and Ford (1988, p. 65).

The model specifies six crucial linkages, indicated by arrows in Figure 9.2. We can, for example, see that new skills can be learnt and retained, but support and opportunity to use the learning must be provided in the work environment. Key support activities comprise coaching and mentoring by managers to include goal-setting, reinforcement activities, encouragement to attend and modelling of behaviours. Billett (2001, p. 213), for example, suggests that the successful development of workplace knowledge, particularly after HRD input, is underpinned by the degree to which 'affordances' are provided within the workplace, that is, opportunities for learners to engage with learning at work and be supported by managers as mentors and coaches. A culture of learning and support from managers has a direct effect on the motivation of staff for training and learning (Chiaburu and Tekleab, 2005). The activities of managers to support transfer within HRD are a key feature of the evaluation of HRD. As we indicated above, within the mechanistic view of training, evaluation often appears as the final stage. The key purpose of evaluation is to show how training input leads to particular outputs and outcomes. In a well-known model of evaluation (Kirkpatrick, 1983), for example, measurements could be taken at four stages to show a chain of causality in order to prove a result. Figure 9.3 shows the stages.

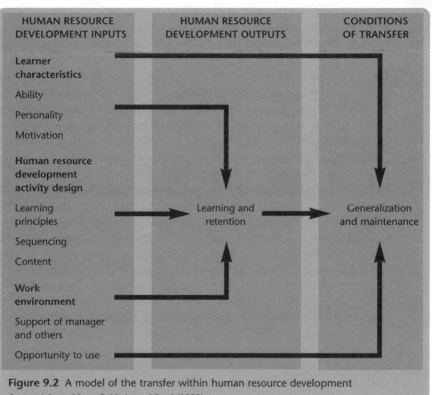

Figure 9.2 A model of the transfer within human resource development
Source: Adapted from Baldwin and Ford (1988)

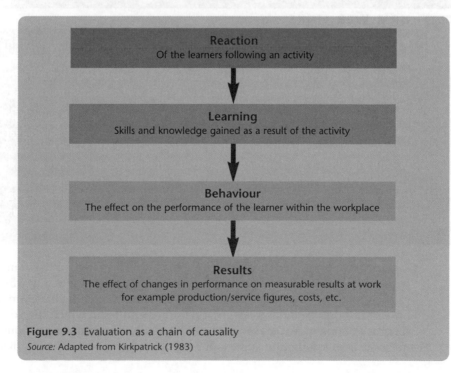

Figure 9.3 Evaluation as a chain of causality
Source: Adapted from Kirkpatrick (1983)

This view of evaluation matched the mechanistic view of training and became the orthodoxy for many years, with a number of adaptations to improve its working. For example, Phillips (1996a) added another stage beyond results. This would require an effort to assess costs and benefits to enable the measurement of net programme benefits or what is usually called the 'return on investment' (ROI), calculated by the ratio of programme benefits to programme costs, expressed as a percentage (Phillips 2005).[17] Phillips points to the use of doing this calculation as evidence to prove the value of HRD and as a key part of the process of communicating to different audiences. Although HRD staff may not have the time to devote to data collection, it is increasingly possible to complete the process leading to the calculation of ROI by using specialized software (Burkett, 2005).

Proving the worth of HRD by producing an acceptable ROI is certainly growing in importance,[18] but there have been persistent doubts about its efficacy and value when applied to many training and development activities (Guba and Lincoln, 1989), especially the idea that the outcomes of training can be quantified and measured as if in a chain of causality. As we have indicated above, there are key factors in the organizational context, such as the support of others and opportunities for application, that affect the ability to use new skills and knowledge and affect overall work performance. Thus, whereas the mechanistic view of training will seek to use evaluation to prove the worth of training, ultimately to the organization in terms of cost savings and profit improvement, an HRD approach will seek to use evaluation to improve the quality of HRD activities and enhance the learning of participants in activities. It will do this by providing data for feedback and review discussions, especially between participants and their managers or peers, so that opportunities for application and continued learning can be identified. In this way, evaluation can play a key role in workplace learning (see below).

HRM WEB LINKS

If you would like more information about mentoring and coaching, visit the European Mentoring and Coaching Council at www.emccouncil.org/. This includes access to research about mentoring and coaching from its annual conference. Further material can found at www.mentoring-australia.com and www.coachingnetwork.org.uk/.

If you would like to explore an organization's learning climate, an online questionnaire can be found at www.psych.rochester.edu/SDT/measures/auton_learn.html. Go to www.orau.gov/pbm/training.html for a set of links on evaluation and the impact of training, but if you wish to explore the technique of reviewing in learning, try www.reviewing.co.uk/. This site also has a section on evaluation and transfer at reviewing.co.uk/reviews/evaluation-transfer.htm. For a broad view of evaluation and the latest ideas for practice, www.evaluation.org.uk/ is the site of the UK Evaluation Society.

The move from mechanistic training towards integrated and systemic HRD is not without its difficulties and problems. Chief among these, especially where there is an explicit link with organizational strategy, is that it is becoming increasingly difficult to understand organizations as single and unified entities in which the voice of management is dominant. As Garavan et al. (1999) argue, most comments about HRD tend to make such an assumption and adopt a top-down perspective. Typical of such a view is the idea that competency frameworks, working as a link between strategy and performance, provide descriptions of a 'one-best-way' approach to fulfil work tasks; they also work prescriptively to state corporate values for everyone (Industrial Relations Services, 2001). There is, however, also the potential of such frameworks to restrict creativity and retreat to narrow and mechanistic training activities that serve short-term needs (Garavan and McGuire, 2001). Further difficulties arise from the generalized and abstracted presentation of a skill as a combination of different competencies. As Holman (2000) argues, the root problem is the belief that there are definitive meanings of skill. Instead, skill is often dependent on the situation and context, which are highly varied.

A further manifestation of the unified view is the notion of learning as a 'good thing', but such an assumption should also beg the question, good for whom? It is increasingly being recognized that, rather than seeing organizations as single, unified and stable entities, a more pluralist and dynamic view needs to be adopted, composed of a set of ongoing activities and processes. It is within such activities and processes that people make sense of what they do and how work should occur, including what should and should not be learnt. As Bratton (2001) argues, where management presents HRD to pursue policies of 'lean' production, employees may be reluctant to learn new skills. In the context of a change to the employment relationship during restructuring, an employee may be required to learn but may also become aware that such learning has a cost and could undermine her or his collective relations with other employees. Employees may realize that the learning agenda belongs to management and that talk of corporate values, strategy and competencies is not neutral but rests on a dominant management ideology. The past few years have seen a burgeoning debate within HRD over whether HRD is about improving the performance of the organization or enhancing the ability of individuals and groups to learn (Clarke, 2004). There is growing interest, at least among academics, of a more critical approach to HRD (Fenwick, 2004; Turnbull and Elliot, 2005).[19]

Based on the contested possibilities of HRD, Gold and Smith (2003) have presented an image[20] of how learning activities may or may not become accepted features of ongoing life at work. This is shown in Figure 9.4. A number of features of this image have already been referred to above, for example the idea of the learning movement as the recommendations, ideas and exhortations relating to HRD and learning at work plus the structures to support these, the strategic management responses to change and the learning movement based on background orientations that made them favourably disposed towards HRD. A significant feature of the image is the jagged arrows; these indicate that HRD does not proceed in a linear or unproblematic manner but on the basis of meanings that have to be made between different people. There may thus be an HRD plan developed to respond to changes in the market, but how such a plan is implemented will depend on the interests of various individuals and groups. The image suggests that such people may need to be persuaded of the value of HRD and convinced to engage in various activities. A key group to be convinced might, for example, be the managers, who would need to coach others and support their learning. Persuading other employees may not always be as easy.

Given that some employees may undertake HRD activities, the image in Figure 9.4 indicates that particular outputs and outcomes may be achieved, although it can never be assured that training automatically becomes learning (Antonacopoulou, 2001). Even where systematic evaluation is undertaken, it may not always be

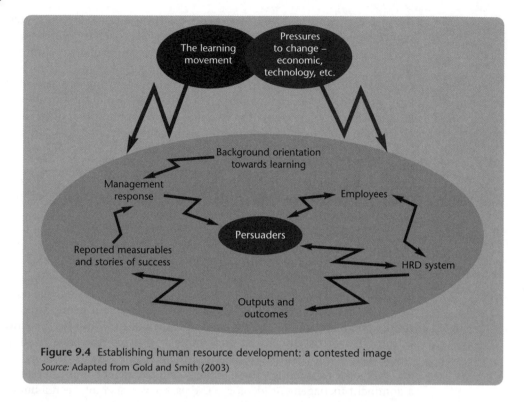

Figure 9.4 Establishing human resource development: a contested image
Source: Adapted from Gold and Smith (2003)

possible to attribute cause and effect. Precise bottom line pay-offs from HRD may be difficult to show (Johnson et al., 2000). Given the need for some evidence of effectiveness of HRD for further decisions, what may, however, be provided is indirect measurable outcomes and anecdotal evidence in the form of people telling stories to each other about their experiences (Gold et al., 2003b). The latter are a particularly interesting form of evidence, and stories are an important source of making sense of work, allowing people to explain HRD events in a meaningful and memorable way (Gabriel, 2000).

REFLECTIVE QUESTIONS

Do you think the image (Figure 9.4) helps to explain why HRD becomes more established in some organizations than others? Have you told stories to explain the value of any learning you have done?

The image in Figure 9.4 goes some way towards explaining the variegated establishment of HRD and movement beyond the notion of mechanistic and linear training. It brings out the inherent uncertainty and the importance of talk and persuasion at work to make HRD happen. There are, however, still some important issues to consider, such as the importance of informal learning, especially the learning that occurs within working practice, and how learning can become organizational. We will consider such issues in the next section.

Workplace learning

If there is a single theme that has in recent years widened and transformed the idea of HRD, from a subset of HRM into a matter of strategic concern, and is central to organizational survival, renewal and progress, it is the theme of learning. Learning in the workplace is seen as the crucial contributor to dealing with change, coping with uncertainty and complexity in the environment and creating opportunities for sustainable competitive advantage (Antonacopoulou et al., 2005; Bratton et al., 2004). Workplace learning has therefore become a key idea in recent years.

First, it casts a whole organization as a unit of learning, allowing managers to take a strategic view and others to think in terms of how their learning impacts on the wider context. Second, it is an idea that unifies an increasingly diverse set of influences and disciplines within HRD (McCormack, 2000), such as training and organization development, knowledge and information systems. Some writers have extended the influences further. Swanson (2001), for example, talks about HRD as an octopus that draws on a variety of different influences – anthropology, sociology, speech communications, music, philosophy and, in the future, chaos theory. McGoldrick et al. (2001, p. 346), accepting the multidisciplinary character of HRD, argue that there is 'no single lens for viewing HRD research', that a variety of perspectives are being employed and that this is leading to increasing sophistication in theorizing about and understanding learning at work. Third, workplace learning highlights the significance of HRD practitioners as people with specialist knowledge and skills, and contributes to the advancement of their professional status (Gold et al., 2003a). Key ideas for application include, for example:

- the **learning organization** and **organization learning**
- **knowledge management** and production
- **e-learning**.

We will first of all consider the idea of the learning organization.

Many managers and leaders have been attracted by the idea that their organization should become a learning organization (sometimes referred to as a learning company). This was an idea that had a significant impact during the 1990s, a large number of conferences, books and journals being devoted to it. Although there has been significant ambiguity surrounding the meaning of the term, there is little doubt about its impact – it became the vision of many organizational leaders and managers. A survey in 1996 of chief executives (KPMG, 1996) found that respondents believed that:

- learning and adaptation must be accelerated through innovative and creative means
- learning must at least keep pace with the change in their organization's environment
- learning and innovation were the key to their organization's survival and success
- building a learning organization is a way of challenging and moving away from their current culture.

In the UK, the idea of the learning organization was developed by Pedler et al.'s (1988) learning company project report, which provided the following definition: an organization which facilitates the learning of all its members and continuously transforms itself. Pedler et al. (1991) went on to provide a list of dimensions of a learning company that could be used to differentiate it from a non-learning company. Among these were a learning approach to strategy, participative policy-making, 'informating' (i.e. the use of information technology to inform and empower people), reward flexibility and self-development opportunities for all. Another source of encouragement for the learning organizations was Senge's (1990) idea of five disciplines that were required as a foundation:

- personal mastery
- a shared vision
- team learning
- mental models
- systems thinking.

What became clear was that such models represented an ideal of a learning organization but became difficult to implement. The KPMG survey (1996, p. 2), for example, found that even where managers were in favour of learning organizations, they often faced difficulties in finding support for the idea: 'I have been trying to foster the learning concept for some time but with little success as the resistance to change is too great.'

REFLECTIVE QUESTION

Why do you think the learning organization idea has been difficult to implement?

Part of the difficulty, as explained by Garavan (1997), was the idea that a learning organization was an ideal rather than a reality that could be achieved. In recent years, the idea has been compared to a journey, possibly one that is never completed. Learning organizations have nevertheless retained some of their persuasive appeal as an influence on thinking about workplace learning. For Örtenblad (2004), the vagueness of the idea of the learning organization can also be a source of creativity, although he argues that there is need for some clarity to avoid the concept of the learning organization becoming a mere fashion. He does suggest that overly bureaucratic organization structures might pose particular difficulties, so some have suggested that smaller organizations might be more suited to the idea because their structures are relatively organic and flexible with less bureaucracy (Birdthistle and Fleming, 2005). Larger organizations can, however, also benefit through project-based learning (see below).

Understanding learning

How we understand and explain learning in organizations is, of course, crucial. Throughout the 20th century, there have been many ideas concerning learning, and a traditional distinction is usually made between 'associative learning' (or behavourism) and 'cognitive learning', the main differences between the two traditions being summarized in Table 9.3.

We can see how the nature of the work that employees are required to perform will lead to the acceptance of a particular view of learning. It will also underpin much of a manager's understanding of human behaviour and motivation. The reduction of work into low-skilled and repetitive tasks will therefore favour associative and behaviourist views of learning even where, in the initial phases of learning, knowledge and understanding are required. The main thrust of the learning is to produce behaviour that can be repeated time after time in relatively unchanging conditions. More complex work favours the need for knowledge, understanding and higher-order cognitive skills, underpinned by cognitive learning theories. The work of writers such as Anderson (1981), for example, considers learning from an information-processing perspective in which learners seek to solve problems by seeking relevant information, matching and processing the information into a solution to provide knowledge and understanding before execution through action.

Table 9.3 Traditions of learning

Associative learning or behaviourism	Cognitive learning
Learning in terms of responses to stimuli: 'automatic' learning	Insightful learning
Classical conditioning (Pavlov's dogs)	Thinking, discovering, understanding, seeing relationships and meaning
Operant or instrumental conditioning	New arrangements of previously learned concepts and principles

Behaviourist and cognitive theories of learning are viewed by Beckett and Hager (2002, p. 98) as representing a 'standard paradigm of learning'. The basic assumption here is that the 'human mind' is viewed as a 'stock room' that is at first empty but gradually becomes filled with knowledge. The 'best learning' occurs when it is true or 'more or less certain'.

Some theories of learning contain elements of both associative and cognitive learning but most importantly emphasize the process of learning and its continuity. This has resulted in a great deal of attraction to such theories in organizations pursuing HRD policies. Kolb (1984), for example, provided an integrated theory of experiential learning in which learning is prompted through the interaction of a learner and her or his environment. The theory stresses the central role of individual needs and goals in determining the type of experience sought and the extent to which all stages of learning are completed. For learning to occur, all stages of a learning cycle should be completed. Individual learners will, however, have an established pattern of assumptions, attitudes and aptitudes that will determine effectiveness in learning.[21] Kolb's learning cycle is shown in Figure 9.5.

According to Kolb, learning occurs through grasping an experience and transforming it. The transformation of the impact of experience on the senses (CE), through internal reflection (RO), allows the emergence of ideas (AC) that can be extended into the external world through new actions (AE). Unless the process can be completed in full, learning does not occur, and individuals may not begin the journey to qualitatively finer and higher forms of awareness, which may be called development.

Kolb's model has been very influential for many HRD practitioners and has also heightened awareness of the factors that contribute to learning or prevent learning at work. Learning activities at work could thus be designed on the basis of individual and group learning preferences. Learners might also attempt to overcome their blocks to learning. Individuals might, for example, lack the belief that they can take action in

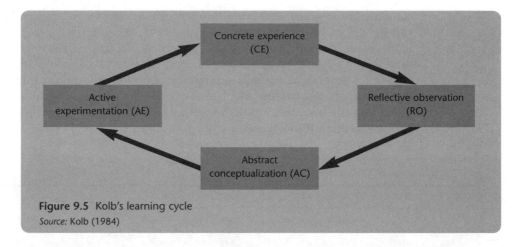

Figure 9.5 Kolb's learning cycle
Source: Kolb (1984)

certain situations or believe that certain activities should not be carried out because this would cause offence to their values. The important point about such blocks is that they are based on personal meanings, feelings and emotions towards learning, and this connects with other models of learning such as neurolinguistic programming (NLP), for example, which examines the way in which learners represent the world in their brains and order their thoughts by language to produce largely automatic actions (Dowlen, 1996). Learners can examine how such processes occur and how they can model themselves on the processes of others whom they see as more effective. Harri-Augstein and Webb (1995) presented an approach to learning based on uncovering personal meanings and myths that produce 'robot-like' performance and appear very difficult to change. It is suggested that, through critical awareness, learners can begin to experiment and change. Such views of learning link to a growing interest in adult learning and development and the importance of reflection to examine behaviour, and assumptions and premises about learning (Mezirow, 1991).

HRM WEB LINKS

If you want to explore connections between various theories of learning, try www.learningandteaching.info/learning/. www.anlp.org/ is the home page of the Association of Neuro-linguistic Programming, but if you want to read a critical examination, try http://skepdic.com/neurolin.html.

A key writer in adult learning has been Stephen Brookfield. If you want to read more about his views, go to www.geocities.com/stephenbrookfield/. This site includes access to key articles on self-directed learning and critical reflection.

The idea that learners construct meanings as they learn is referred to as *constructivism*; you can find more about this view and its implications at http://carbon.cudenver.edu/~mryder/itc_data/constructivism.html.

Although models of learning such as Kolb's cycle have been influential, they are not without criticism for being overly focused on individuals at the expense of their interaction and involvement with others (Holman et al., 1997). In addition, there has been growing interest in how people learn on an everyday basis, mostly with others on an informal basis, through their participation in practice. There has been a growing influence of the work of Russian psychologist Lev Vygotsky and his sociocultural theory of human development (Wells, 1999). Vygotsky (1978) suggested that learning occurs through participation in actions and interaction with others. The result of what happens socially is an internalization of understanding within the individual. This process from the outside to within is mediated, principally through the use of 'tools' such as language and other social symbols. Vygotsky's work underpins much of the recent interest in social approaches to learning, especially in what are referred to as *communities of practice* (CoPs; see below). Beckett and Hager (2002) see such interest as part of an 'emerging paradigm' of learning, which:

- is organic/holistic
- is contextual
- is activity- and experience-based
- arises in situations in which learning is not the main aim
- is activated by individual learners rather than by teachers/trainers
- is often collaborative/collegial.

As we will see below, this view is particularly pertinent to the idea of organization learning.

Organization learning

Although many organizations have attempted to pursue the vision of a *learning organization*, which by necessity requires attention to individual and group or team learning, there has also been significant interest in the idea of *organization learning*. The difference between learning organization and organization learning is subtle but important: whereas the former is concerned with ideas and practices to enhance the learning of groups and individuals so that the organization can benefit, organization learning is an attempt to use the ideas of learning at an organizational level; that is, it relates to how learning occurs organizationally and collectively. Much of the interest in organization learning has occurred in academic circles, and it now constitutes a field of interest in its own right, with journals and conferences, along with a diverse body of knowledge, devoted to it (Easterby-Smith et al., 1999). It is not just, however, academics who have an interest: organization learning is also invoked as a response to cope with the challenges of global competition and technological change.

The key idea is that if current ways of working (the organization's routines), which are the result of an accumulation of experience over time, are insufficient to remain or become competitive, the organization must change its practices and learn new ways of doing things (Antonacopoulou et al., 2005; Easterby-Smith et al., 1998). This may not, however, always be possible or even identified. The organization may accept its current ways of working and resist any attempts to change, apart from slight modifications to keep things as they are. This what is referred to as *single-loop learning* (Argyris and Schön, 1978). By contrast, an organization needs to challenge its current principles of work so that it can respond to changes in the environment and understand the reasons why it may fail to do so. Such a critical approach by the organization is referred to as *double-loop learning*.

However, as we have indicated above, this immediately raises questions about the status and view of the term 'organization'. Much of the organization learning literature works from the assumpion that an organization is a single and unified entity with the ability to learn. The difficulty here is that learning is clearly a human attribute, whereas the term 'organization' is used to understand a set of activities and processes carried out by people working with other resources. As pointed out by Weick and Westley (1996), organizations cannot be directly perceived, so explaining learning at an organizational level requires the invocation of particular metaphors, which is not equal to direct experience. A biological metaphor of organization might, for example, suggest that organizations learn very much like humans – hence Dixon (1994) turns Kolb's learning cycle, an explanation of individual learning, into an organizational learning cycle. A computer metaphor might explain learning for individuals and organization as information-processing in which data are taken in, made sensible, stored in memory to be called upon as required and corrected for errors if these are found. Whatever the metaphor employed, there still remains the problem of how learning by individuals and groups becomes a property of the organization.

One view of organization learning that has gained popularity in recent years is the cultural view (Yanow, 2000). The importance of this view is that it focuses attention on what groups practise and on the values, beliefs and norms that are shared through talk, rituals, myths and stories between members of a group. Thus, in any place we refer to as an organization, there will be a variety of groups, all practising or 'organizing' according to the meanings they have made within the group. Organization learning is therefore concerned with what people do in their local situation. This also means that organization learning is not only concerned with change, innovation or finding new ways to compete. Because organization learning is based on the meanings made within groups, it can also be concerned with sustaining the group and its practices – which those outside the group may call 'resistance' to change and learning. Furthermore, most collective learning takes place informally within relationships that are to be found in the 'dark side' of organizations (Pedler and Aspinall, 1996). This is difficult territory for researchers to access.

The cultural view supports some of the research that has been carried out, indicating that organization learning is mostly informal and improvisational, 'situated' in a particular context, and is a function of the activity that occurs at a local level (Lave and Wenger, 1991) within CoPs. Furthermore, learning within CoPs is likely to be at variance with what is supposed to happen, at least in the eyes of managers, who will have formed and espoused abstract versions of what should be learnt but will miss vital details in the process. Brown and Duguid (1991) used the ideas of CoPs and situated learning to make a distinction between canonical practice and non-canonical practice, the former referring to what is supposed to be learnt and the latter to what is actually learnt and practised in the working context. Learning is strongly related to becoming a practitioner within a CoP, with its own norms, stories and views about what is effective. This makes the task of achieving the benefits of organization learning even more complex. It also explains how so much insight and understanding remains hidden in organizations and how the downsizing trends of the early 1990s often resulted in the break up of CoPs and the loss of core knowledge. Brown and Duguid (1991, p. 53) argued that an organization needs to be conceived as a 'community-of-communities' and to 'see beyond its canonical abstractions of practice to the rich, full-bloodied activities themselves'. Recent years have seen some attempt to harness the creative potential of CoPs. Thus, although they are informal and self-organizing around the demands of the situation (Wenger and Snyder, 2000), it is argued that managers can identify potential CoPs and provide an infrastructure of support so that they can be made 'a central part of their companies' success' (Wenger and Snyder, 2000, p. 145).

REFLECTIVE QUESTION

How far are students members of a CoP? Do they practice 'non-canonically'? What difficulties does this cause?

Given the essentially informal nature of CoPs, it is interesting how they have become recognized as contributors to company success; this might be understood as the human capital version of informal learning (Garrick, 1998). We would, however, suggest that the ongoing and everyday processes that make up life within CoPs are not amenable to easy control by managers. Nevertheless, there is a desire to utilize informal learning to underpin improvements in organizational performance (Fuller et al., 2003). Hager (2003), for example, while acknowledging the value of the role of participation in learning, also highlights the fact that participation might produce values that resist change and closed boundaries. He presents a contrasting metaphor of construction that brings together learners, their context and the articulation of learning.

An example of this is the study of lawyers completed by Gold et al. (2006). This focused on the situations in practice when lawyers had to perform under pressure, for example in court, or with clients.[22] Individual professionals were able to present their views of the events and derive learning, which they validated with others. The study showed that there were considerable opportunities for practice-based learning, which was shared with others, and that this stood in contrast to more formal and individualized approaches to learning. The process also revealed the importance of practice for knowledge production.

Knowledge management

The recent interest in organization learning and informal learning within CoPs has been stimulated by the view that the economy has become knowledge-based (Organisation for Economic Co-operation and Development, 1996), the basic idea being that knowledge becomes the key ingredient of products and services. Differences between organizations and nations will therefore depend on the extent to which information can be obtained, turned into knowledge and applied to production. The emphasis on knowledge has resulted in a plethora of new concepts, such as knowledge workers, knowledge-intensive organizations, knowledge networks and knowledge societies. There is also an emphasis on the skills of employees who are recast as knowledge workers. They are the owners of intellectual capital since it is people who are able to construct, manipulate and apply new knowledge, adding value to what is produced. Human capital accumulation has therefore become one of the new reasons for an investment in HRD (Garavan et al., 2001) and a contrast to the previous narrow conceptions implied by human capital theory (see Chapter 2, The resource-based model).

The key reason for such developments has of course been the advances made in the application of ICT, especially in combination with the Internet. ICT can be used to store, retrieve, analyse and communicate information involving a convergence of microtechnologies, computing, telecommunications, broadcasting and optical electronics in a revolutionary way (Castells, 1996). An important characteristic of the revolution is how knowledge is applied to knowledge-generating and information-processing/communication devices with a feedback loop that enables knowledge and information to be viably accumulated and transferred. Not all knowledge can, however, be captured by ICT, and this highlights the never-ending value of people.

In considering knowledge, it is common to distinguish between 'knowing-that' and 'knowing-how'. The former is concerned with knowledge about facts and explanations for facts that are explicit and communicable, and the latter refers to the ability to do something in a particular situation. Knowing-that is based on knowledge that has been *codified*, for example written into books, journals or papers on the Internet, and therefore becomes communicable. It is this knowledge that lies at the heart of the digital revolution.

Knowing-how is, however, particularly important in the performance of skilled work. Whereas performance may require knowing-that, dealing with the particulars of a situation, a new or unexpected situation in particular 'cannot be accomplished by procedural knowledge alone or by following a manual' (Eraut, 2000 p. 128). Such knowledge is personal, based on the requirements of the situation and the understanding of the person carrying out the performance. This is referred to as *tacit knowledge*; it is the ability to deal with different situations, known and unknown, often responding spontaneously to surprise through improvisation and without thought (Schön, 1983). To work out the difference between codified and tacit knowledge, think about riding a bike. Could you codify the explanation into a manual for riding bikes? It is more likely that it will be very difficult to explain the skill of riding a bike because the understanding is tacit. Tacit knowing is needed to maximize the benefit accrued from the rapid accumulation of codified knowledge generated by advances in ICT. It is also crucial to the development of new knowledge.

One of the most well-known knowledge-based approaches to organization learning is Nonaka and Takeuchi's (1995) knowledge-creating model. According to this model, organization learning and the creation of knowledge have to start with an individual's tacit knowledge. This first has to be expressed to the individual using diagrams, metaphors and drawings. Because it is tacit, the knowledge is difficult to codify in words. Second, there is an attempt to express the knowledge to others. Third, this knowledge is combined with that of other members of the group. In the final stage, the knowledge becomes tacit again but in a new form. It is accepted by the group and becomes part of their accepted behaviour. And so the process begins again. One limitation of the model is that it is based on a number of case studies and presents a rather idealized version of the processes.

Making tacit knowledge explicit is, however, also a feature of other versions of organization learning. Crossan's (1999) framework is, for example, composed of the four subprocesses of *intuiting, interpreting, integrating* and *institionalizing*. Nevertheless, as Crossan acknowledges, the subprocesses are unlikely to flow without inhibition. Factors that may prevent flow include institutionalized features such as reward systems, planning systems and structures; there is also an influence from group dynamics and other relationships between people.

There may be difficulties in applying models of organization learning and knowledge-creating, particularly with reference to tacit knowledge, but this has not prevented the rapid growth of attempts to capture the knowledge that is generated by learning. This is one of the key factors that is driving the interest in knowledge management, which Mayo (1998, p. 36) defines as:

the management of the information, knowledge and experience available to an organization – its creation, capture, storage, availability and utilization – in order that organizational activities build on what is already known and extend it further.

Many organizations have attempted to introduce *knowledge management*, including appointing managers as learning officers or knowledge officers and installing networked software to accentuate the process (Lank, 2002). Other roles include company librarians, webmasters and designers, and information consultants. The basic argument is that if knowledge is, in the knowledge economy, the source of competitive advantage, its capture and storage will form an essential resource; it is the organization's intellectual capital. In some respects, following a point made by Scarbrough and Swan (2001), knowledge management superseded the learning organization phenomenon from the late 1990s, although there has increasingly been more attention paid to the systems and technologies of knowledge management than to learning within the workplace, thereby 'glossing over the complex and intangible aspects of human behaviour' (Scarbrough and Swan, 2001, p. 8).

HRM WEB LINKS

Go to www.brint.com/km/; this site provides access to many resources relating to knowledge management, including The Online Book on Knowledge Management, at www.kmbook.com. The knowledge management server at the University of Texas has links to resources and publications on knowledge management at www.kmresource. com/exp_university.htm. See also the Knowledge Management magazine at www. kmmagazine.com/. In addition, try www.knowledge.sai-global.com/ in Australia and www.kmssa.org.za/html/ in South Africa.

One attempt to restore the link with learning has been the work of Kessels (1996, 2001) and others on *knowledge productivity*. According to Garvey and Williamson (2002), successful knowledge-productive organizations are proactive in learning new ways of doing things. They do this by going beyond formal knowledge management systems and attempting to work also with informal and tacit knowledge. There are clearly multiple opportunities for the sharing of knowledge between individuals and team members, across departments and even within networks of different organizations. This means creating a climate of trust whereby people can share ideas informally and formally. There is an acceptance that learning is a social activity, and this may not always be productive. Competition between units can have a negative impact (Hansen et al., 2005). To promote knowledge-sharing, Von Krogh (2003) argues that three factors are necessary:

1. *Opportunity structures*, which provide occasions for knowledge-sharing and depend on cues and interactions between members of the community. It is, however, acknowledged that a community of workers may not always have the same interest.
2. *Care*, involving empathy, help and trust.
3. *Authenticity*, involving the sharing of accurate and reliable knowledge.

Some organizations are now seeking to exploit social learning by becoming project-based (HRM in Practice 9.3). Consider, for example, the work of professional services in law, architecture or advertising, the work of the culture industries such as fashion, film-making or videos and the work of those producing software and multimedia products (Sydow et al., 2004). These all require a project-based approach to enable a response to customer demand that expects differentiated goods and services that meet their particular requirements; such products need to be customized through negotiation rather than standardized. Although many organizations have some degree of project work, project-based firms do most of their work in projects and organize support for such work in response to project requirements rather than through traditional functional arrangements (Lindkvist, 2004).

HRM IN PRACTICE 9.3

PROJECT-BASED LEARNING AT LBBC

ROBERT PICKARD AND JIM ALEXANDER, LBBC

LBBC Technologies is a Yorkshire-based small and medium-sized enterprise (SME) that was formed in 2004 out of a 125-year-old, traditional, family-owned manufacturing company. We were experiencing all the typical problems of a hierarchical, departmentally based organization, the main one being the lack of ownership and the prevalence of a blame culture. These problems resulted in poor service delivery, poor financial performance and low morale.

A major reason we decided therefore to establish LBBC Technologies as a project-based organization was to develop a structure that would encourage the continuous ownership of a project from conception through to completion by a project manager and a small team. More fundamentally than this, we wanted to create a dynamic organization that had the flexibility to rapidly respond and adapt to the changing markets we serve.

We now have a flatter structure and run our operations as much as possible as individual projects. Each project has a project manager and a small team. We generate high levels of commitment to fulfil the deliverables of projects by ensuring a significant involvement of team members throughout its execution. Once this level of commitment has been achieved, we find that the benefits of people 'not wanting to let their colleagues down' comes into play.

> ...we find that the benefits of people 'not wanting to let their colleagues down' comes into play.

From a practical aspect, a project team will gain a commitment from the required resources to complete the project. If insufficient resources are available, a conflict arises; this is resolved by the interested parties sitting down and agreeing a compromise.

How project learning is adding to the company's future

By increasing involvement and exposing people to new areas of the business, we are finding that new pairs of eyes frequently produce opportunities for process or product improvements. The system is increasing job satisfaction and removing many of the sources of frustration created by a departmental structure. This in turn is generating increased job satisfaction, greater motivation and better performance.

Increased individual performance, in conjunction with the breakdown of departmental barriers, has enabled a greater use of human resources, reflected by an increased turnover per employee. By creating greater ownership and increased commitment to fulfilling project deliverables, we are realizing improved product/service delivery and improved relationships with our customers. By tapping into everyone in the business, we are beginning to see the increased knowledge base we are creating begin to emerge into new opportunities for us.

REFLECTIVE QUESTION

How do you think such functions as finance, marketing and HRD are affected by project-based working?

Because many projects are concerned with developing new or different products, they contain the potential to create new knowledge and learning. Taking advantage of this so that it can be shared elsewhere in the organization requires a range of learning devices, such as project reviews, logs of critical incidents and the informal sharing of ideas. In project-based organizations, there is need to explore learning within projects and to exploit learning between projects and within the organization as a whole (Brady and Davies, 2004).

e-Learning

One area in which the technology revolution is having a massive impact in HRD is the provision of e-learning. Until very recently, the term 'e-learning' would have been covered by a range of different activities involving the delivery of HRD activities, including computer-based training, web-based training and online learning. Preceding these terms were those of 'distance learning' and 'flexible learning'. Through the rapid investment in web facilities, all these terms have now been incorporated under the heading 'e-learning'.[23] It is difficult to define e-learning precisely, and any attempt to pin it down is likely to be superseded by events. The CIPD, however, uses the following (Sloman and Reynolds, 2002, p. 3):

> Learning that is delivered, enabled or mediated by electronic technology for the explicit purpose of training in organizations. It does not include stand-alone technology-based training such as the use of CD-ROMs in isolation.

The distinction between e-learning and other technologically based delivery lies in the use of networked ICT and the Internet. This includes the delivery of learning materials via the web in a way similar to that of flexible learning packages. In addition, supported learning can be provided over the Internet within 'virtual communities'. There are also many ways to support learning informally across the Internet, for example Microsoft Groups (http://groups.msn.com/) or Community Zero (www.communityzero.com/).

Research has suggested a number of benefits of e-learning (Pollard and Hillage, 2001), including the ability to learn 'just in time' at the learner's pace and convenience, the provision of updateable materials and a reduction in delivery costs. There is also the possibility of collaborative working, sometimes with learners spread over large distances, with tutor support, the flexibility of access from anywhere at any time and the monitoring of learner progress. Most computer-mediated conferencing systems enable a moderator to track participation and adjust provision as required. On the downside, a learner clearly needs access to ICT with an Internet or network connection. This can be expensive to set up and requires collaboration between information technology and HRD/learning specialists. Furthermore, the material has to be digital, and this is far from the only way to deliver learning.

The CIPD survey (2005d) found that 54 per cent of respondents reported the use of e-learning, with a further 39 per cent claiming that they had plans to introduce it over the next year. It was also found that e-learning accounted for less than 10 per cent of training time, but there were expectations that this would rise over the next few years, in some cases to as high as 50 per cent. e-Learning was principally being used for IT training and technical training. It was less suited to 'people skills' and interpersonal skills such as team-building and diversity training. The suggestion was that e-learning would be targeted mostly at technical or knowledge-based training. One important finding was that 94 per cent of respondents felt that e-learning was more effective when combined with other forms of learning. This supports Sloman's (2002) view that e-learning needs to be part of a strategy that includes on-the-job learning and class-room activities. He refers to this as 'blended learning'.

Several larger organizations have attempted to use e-learning to recast central HRD provision. There is an emphasis on employee self-service via company intranets, allowing staff to take responsibility for their choice of training. For example, at the Spanish company Telefonica, as part of a new training policy to increase participation and interaction (Gascó et al., 2004), a distance learning system was installed to provide geographical and time flexibility; this was composed of self-study, technical and video-conferencing provision. An extension of this policy is the creation of corporate universities. The university for Lloyds TSB, for example, provides computer-based facilities for all its staff and access to learning materials as well as career information. It claims more than 2000 computers in branches and departments to complement the existing facilities at the group's central and local training centres, and there is also a call centre facility to provide support (www.lloydstsbjobs.com/visit_the_university.asp).

Cunningham et al. (2000) suggest that most corporate universities are simply re-badged training departments but that they may over time develop into significant suppliers of HRD activities, going beyond the boundaries of their initiating organizations. There are also likely to be growing links between corporate universities and more traditional universities in a variety of strategic alliances (Clarke and Hermens, 2001).

HRM WEB LINKS

The e-Learning Centre provides links to articles and resources relating to e-learning; you can find it at www.e-learningcentre.co.uk/. The eLearning Network acts as a source of information and best practice at www.elearningnetwork.org/frameset.htm. www.unext.com/about.htm shows an attempt between leading universities to provide online programmes. www.capella.edu/ provides access to Cappella University, which offers 500 online undergraduate and postgraduate courses. If you are interested in speculations on the effect of technology on the future, you can read the work of BT's futurologist at www.bt.com/sphere/insights/pearson/.

There are clearly more developments to come in e-learning, and technological developments, including improved access possibilities, will certainly continue apace. The role of HRD specialists will inescapably be affected as learners move from being present in training rooms to being members of virtual communities. A key issue will be how learning theories can be used in different aspects of e-learning environments. For example, behaviourist theories might be incorporated into staged learning and social learning theories for the development of support processes and communities online (Gillani, 2003). There will be many opportunities for knowledge-sharing through a variety of modes of contact and timings of interaction. Much will, however, depend, as we indicated earlier, on the nature of the demand for skills within organizations, which will have a knock-on effect on the supply of e-learning materials and activities. As recent research on training in the knowledge economy shows, many barriers to learning at work still exist, and these have a negative impact on willingness to learn (Schramm, 2002). Learners can, however, increasingly bypass organizational barriers by joining informal learning communities online.

STUDY TIP

HRD is, as has been shown in this chapter, a wide-ranging concept that has not yet established a distinctive position in organizations or the academic world. A key issue concerns the purpose of HRD, and it would be easy to respond in a relatively instrumental fashion – that is, to improve and enhance an individual's, organization's or nation's productive capability. This would, however, represent too narrow a view. In this chapter, we have argued that, by adopting a pluralist view of organizations, there are bound to be different views on the purpose of HRD and the way in which learning is valued.

One approach to studying different perspectives in HRD and projects of learning has been to use learning histories, in which, through access to events and documents, a researcher attempts to understand what is happening and facilitate individual and organizational reflection. You can read about learning histories at www.ccs.mit.edu/LH/. Within a learning history, different values can be studied through the use of narratives and storytelling, which allow people to express their versions of events, incorporating what they value and how they feel. Data from storytelling can then be used in narrative analysis. You can read more about this in Riesman (1993).

Chapter summary

- This chapter has examined the idea and practice of HRD as investment in people's learning at work. The idea incorporates traditional views of training and development but seeks to extend attention to learning throughout an organization as a strategy to cope with change. The message of learning at work has become an obvious 'good thing', and this has led to growing interest in HRD as a profession and its theoretical development, although there are continuing debates about the meaning of HRD.

- For HRD to become a feature of organizational strategy, senior managers must incorporate the need for learning within their consideration of trends and signals in the environment, such as changes in markets and technology. A strategy for HRD can often respond to organizational strategy by the use of competencies to set performance expectations and targets. Strategic HRD can also influence organizational strategy through the development of new ideas, especially where senior managers appreciate that learning is a way of responding to external pressures for change.

- In the UK, there is little evidence that HRD is a key consideration in strategic management. People are not usually a top priority, marketing and financial matters having greater importance.

- There is, broadly speaking, a 'voluntarist' approach to HRD in the UK, contrasted with a more 'interventionist' approach in some other countries. Decision-makers in organizations determine the demand for skills, taking a broadly human capital view that may lead to a restricted approach to HRD. In contrast, some organizations adopt a developmental humanist approach, which can lead to a greater focus on the potential of people for learning.

- There is evidence to suggest that learning has an impact on an individual's earning power and employment prospects. For organizations, HRD is a key element of the bundle of HR practices that impact on performance. For nations, investment in skills has implications for competitiveness and social inclusion. The UK government has given significant attention to supporting progress towards a learning society. Low skill levels among many workers remain a problem in the UK, but there have been developments to improve the HRD infrastructure through a national framework of qualifications and institutions to administer national programmes and encourage a demand-led approach.

- A systematic approach to training is still the preference in many organizations; this emphasizes the need for cost-effective provision. Recent years have seen attempts to develop a more integrated approach that recognizes interdependencies with organizations and the importance of line managers in HRD. This often involves the use of competency frameworks and performance management systems.

- The learning climate or learning environment in an organization greatly influences the effectiveness of HRD policies, especially the relationships between managers and employees. To support HRD, managers have been encouraged to become mentors and coaches. Both roles can provide a link between HRD activities, evaluation and the transfer of learning.

- HRD makes a unitarist assumption about organizations, leading to top-down approaches. Competency frameworks describe a 'one best way' to perform work, which may restrict creativity. There is likely to be a variety of views on work and learning.

- Workplace learning is a more recent notion that takes a broad organizational perspective on learning and allows a range of influences on HRD, including ideas relating to the learning organization. The importance of learning at work has increased attention to learning theories, especially experiential learning and models that examine personal meanings and encourage reflection.

- Organization learning has become a key field of interest. Some explanations assume that organizations learn like people, but there are also attempts to provide different explanations by focusing on the culture of groups and how learning occurs in the context of their practice.

- Advances in ICT have resulted in a greater interest in knowledge production and knowledge management. Knowledge can be concerned with facts and explanations that can be codified and easily communicated. There is also knowledge that is tacit, more indeterminate, difficult to express and concerned with responding to difficult problems.

- Technology is creating an e-learning revolution, leading to a new alliance between providers, new methods of delivery and the formation of virtual communities of learners. HRD specialists are learning new skills to support e-learning provision.

Key concepts

- Coaching and mentoring
- Learning climate or environment
- Developmental humanistic approach
- Learning organization
- e-Learning
- Organization learning
- Evaluation

- Strategic human resource development
- Human capital theory
- Learning movement
- Interventionist approach
- Transfer of learning
- Knowledge management
- Voluntarist approach
- Systematic training model

Chapter review questions

1. What is meant by strategic HRD and how is it connected with organizational strategy?

2. What should be the role of government in HRD?

3. How can graduate skills be better employed by organizations?

4. Learning is a 'good thing' for everyone. Discuss.

5. What should be the role of managers in HRD?

6. Can organizations gain benefits from the work of projects?

Further reading

Amin, A. and Cohendet, P. (2004) *Architectures of Knowledge: Firms, Capabilities, and Communities.* Oxford: Oxford University Press

Clutterbuck, D. and Megginson, D. (2005) *Making Coaching Work: Creating a Coaching Culture.* London: Chartered Institute of Personnel and Development.

Ellinger, A. and Bostrom, R. (2002) An examination of managers' beliefs about their roles as facilitators of learning. *Management Learning*, **33**(2): 147–79.

Evans, K., Unwin, L., Rainbird, H. and Hodkinson, P. (2006) *Improving Workplace Learning.* London: Routledge.

Home Office (2003) *Training in Racism and Cultural Diversity.* London: Home Office.

Institute of Employment Studies (2002) *A Review of Training in Racism Awareness and Valuing Cultural Diversity.* Brighton: IES.

Macpherson, W. (1999) *The Stephen Lawrence Inquiry.* London: Stationery Office.

Örtenblad, A. (2002) Organizational learning: a radical perspective. *International Journal of Management Reviews*, **4**(1): 87–100.

Sadler-Smith, E. (2006) *Learning and Development for Managers: Perspectives from Research and Practice.* Oxford: Blackwell.

Wood, I., Rodgers, H. and Gold, J. (2004) Picturing prejudice: learning to see diversity. Paper presented to the European HRD Conference, Limerick, May.

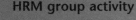

Practising human resource management

Searching the web

HRD is increasingly being seen as a separate discipline in its own right rather than a subdiscipline of HRM. As a consequence, more attention is being paid to HRD research by academics, and more interest has arisen in the results of research by HRD professionals. You can find more details about the 'academic' study of HRD at the following websites:

- www.ahrd.org/, the site of the Academy of HRD in the USA
- www.b.shuttle.de/wifo/ehrd/=portal.htm, the European HRD portal, providing research-based information on HRD in Europe
- www.ufhrd.co.uk/ the site of the university forum for HRD in the UK.

For other HRD sites, see the list at the beginning of the book.

HRM group activity

You are the HRD manager of a large consultancy that employs a wide range of professionally qualified staff and have been tasked with developing a continuous professional development (CPD) policy for different professional groups employed.

Visit the Professional Associations Research Network at www.parn.org.uk/parn.cfm?sct=100&content=homepage2.cfm. This has a CPD centre providing access to case studies, guides and publications on CPD.

A key group within the consultancy are the engineers. www.iie.org.uk/devcareer/index.asp?page=8 provides access to the professional development page of the Institution of Incorporated Engineers, and www.iee.org/oncomms/sector/ provides information on professional networks for electrical engineers.

There are also qualified surveyors (CPD information at www.rics.org/Careerseducationandtraining/), chartered accountants (see www.icaew.co.uk/) and architects (visit www.riba.org/go/RIBA/Member/CPD_495.html).

Make a presentation on the key features of a CPD policy and the specific requirements for the different professional groups.

Chapter case study

ATKINSON GENERATION

Atkinson Generation (AG) is a leading distributor of engines and equipment. The company has main dealer status with Watson Engines, the UK's principal producer of power engines. There are 35 staff based at its location in Banbury, Oxfordshire.

After several years of profitable trading, the company has, for the past two years, been faced with a significant loss. There is a sense of 'lack of direction' and a need to change quickly and dramatically in order to survive. A recent meeting with Watson Engines has presented AG with a stark choice: it had to 'shape up or ship out'. As the dealer status with Watson Engines accounted for 80 per cent of its business, managers at AG realized that radical changes were needed. A shared purpose and vision, combined with training that met a nationally recognized benchmark, was required.

The four AG managers attended a series of workshops organized by the local chamber of commerce, where they could share experiences and learn from other companies. They were then able to produce a strategic plan incorporating key performance indicators and a breakdown of the skills necessary for its delivery. More important would be the style of managing change and the provision of learning opportunities for all staff to meet their desires. As indicated by the Managing Director John Atkinson: 'I fundamentally believe that everyone at AG should be able to identify what they need to learn and get on and do it.'

The following were considered to be key elements:

- A learning and development-oriented appraisal system needs to be established for everyone in the company so that individual needs can be identified.
- All managers must become 'learning managers' so that they can coach and support others.
- Communication needs to provide full information on company results and the budget, as well as allow feedback from staff.
- The company should seek support from its local business advisory service regarding a national benchmark for training and development, qualifications and financial support.

Discussion questions

1. How can appraisal be utilized to identify individual learning needs, and how can the company ensure that such needs link to the strategic plan and key performance indicators?

2. What are the skills required by 'learning managers'? What training do such managers need?

3. What are the requirements for effective two-way communication?

4. What help can be provided for this small company regarding benchmarking, qualifications for its workforce and finance for its training?

HR-related skill development

HRD is an important HRM function in terms of both implementing organizational strategy and facilitating organizational effectiveness. After learning needs have been determined and learning objectives set, formal learning programmes must be designed. Designing a formal learning session or workshop involves a number of critical activities and decisions, including those related to content, learning methods, materials and equipment, and site. All managers should be effective coaches and teachers. To help you to develop teaching and coaching skills, we have developed an activity that requires you to design and deliver a segment of a learning module. To gain knowledge of the 10 steps of programme design and be able to identify the skills of effective trainers, go to our website www.palgrave.com/business/brattonandgold4 and click on 'Coaching'.

Notes

1. Charles Clarke who was the education secretary at the launch of the UK government's skills strategy White Paper, *21st Century Skills.*

2. James, R. (2005) Gaining manager buy-in to training and development. In CIPD (2005) *Latest Trends In Learning, Training and Development.* London: CIPD.

3. A line taken from 'A Declaration on Learning: A Call to Action', available at www.peterhoney. com/main/declaration.

4. The survey is based on telephone interviews, 27,172 interviews being conducted with the most senior person at sites with responsibility for human resources and personnel issues.

5. Products with a high product specification tend to be more complex and entail frequent updating and/or alteration of the specification.

6. You can find out more about the Stephen Lawrence Inquiry and what became known as 'institutional racism' at www.cre.gov.uk/gdpract/cj_sli.html.

7. You might be interested to consider the implications of other metaphors referred to by Marsick and Watkins, that is, open systems, brain, chaos and complexity.

8. More information about the Labour Force Survey can be obtained from www.statistics.gov.uk/ StatBase/Source.asp?vlnk=358&More=Y#general.

9. The White Paper suggested that output per hour worked is around 25 per cent higher in the USA and Germany, and more than 30 per cent higher in France, than in the UK.

10. In the UK, the National Training Awards have been established since 1987 as annual awards for organizations, groups and individuals who demonstrate that an investment in HRD brings about value-added benefits, in order to identify excellence in HRD and to celebrate and promote exemplars. The objectives have more recently been extended to encompass the broadened scope of government policy. Thus, current objectives include the encouragement of a greater commitment to lifelong learning, training and self-development, and the identification and promotion of the contribution of performance improvements by various learning routes. More details can be obtained from the website at www.nationaltrainingawards.com/.

11. A small and medium-sized enterprise is usually understood as an organization employing between 10 and 249 employees. Organizations employing fewer than 10 are referred to as microbusinesses. These two categories together comprise over 95 per cent of organizations in the UK.

12. It is worth noting that NVQ competence refers to standards or outcomes to be achieved that can be assessed against performance criteria. This approach to competence contrasts with that considered in Chapter 6, which was concerned with behaviours.

13. In Scotland, this function is performed by the Scottish Qualifications Authority.

14. Previously referred to as Modern Apprenticeships: there are slight variations in Scotland, Wales and Northern Ireland. See http://www.scottish-enterprise.com/modernapprenticeships for Scotland, http://www.elwa.ac.uk/ElwaWeb/elwa.aspx?pageid=645 in Wales and http://www.bconstructive.co.uk/apprenticeships/nireland.asp for Northern Ireland.

15. Industrial training boards were set up under the Industrial Training Act of 1964 to administer the collection of a training levy and the distribution of training grants within particular sectors of the economy, for example construction and engineering. As a highly interventionist approach, most were eventually abolished during the 1980s, but they left a significant legacy in their propagation of training ideas. Industrial training boards that still exist operate under strict regulations, see, for example, the Engineering Construction Industry Training Board at www.ecitb.org.uk/.

16. Read more about total productive maintenance at www.productivityeurope.org/content/view/ 15/58/.

17. Phillips (2005) gives the following example of ROI calculations:
   Programme cost = £35,000
   Benefits = £105,000
   Net benefit = £70,000
   ROI = (£70,000/£35,000) x 100 = 200 per cent.

18. ROI is particularly important in the USA; see the ROI Network at www.astd.org/astd/ Education/roi_network/roi_home.htm .

19. Among other possibilities, a more critical HRD might consider issues of power imbalances and social justice, for example the experience of women, disadvantaged ethnic and sexual groups. Issues that are normally suppressed such as violence, bullying, sexism and racism might be more fully considered.

20. The image works with what is referred as the *sociology of translation*, drawn from actor network theory. Further understanding can be gained from the Actor Network resource at www.lancs.ac.uk/fss/sociology/css/antres/antres.htm. You might also like to consult John Law's home page at www.lancs.ac.uk/fss/sociology/staff/law/law.htm.

21. Kolb's experiential learning model is one of a number that have led to the popularity of assessing our approach to learning through learning style questionnaires. If you would like to examine your style of learning, try www.cdtl.nus.edu.sg/success/sl8.htm, which includes links to various online instruments. You could also try www.support4learning.org.uk/education/learning_styles.cfm. But take care: recent research by Coffield et al. (2004) examined 69 learning style instruments but found that many had psychometric drawbacks and were not recommended for use in education or training.

22. Such moments were labelled 'hot action' following the work of Beckett (2000).

23. On 5 January 2006, a search for 'e-learning' on Google returned 63,900,000 hits.

Chapter ten

Reward management

John Bratton

> Reward refers to all of the monetary, non-monetary and psychological payments that an organization provides for its employees in exchange for the work they perform.

'Although economic rewards play an important part in securing adherence to organizational goals and management authority, they are limited in their effectiveness. Organizations would be far less effective systems than they actually are if such rewards were the only means, or even the principal means, of motivation available.'[1]

'There is no such thing as a good pay system; there is only a series of bad ones. The trick is to choose the least bad one.'[2]

Chapter outline

Chapter objectives

After studying this chapter, you should be able to:

1. Explain the key functions and role of reward management
2. Describe the notion of aligning business strategy with reward practices
3. Describe three key employee behaviours desired by organizations and the role that economic rewards play in shaping such behaviours
4. Define and evaluate different rewards options, including base pay, performance pay and indirect pay
5. Describe and evaluate reward techniques such as job analysis, job evaluation and appraisal
6. Explain how governments intervene in the pay determination process
7. Explain the paradoxes and tensions in rewards systems in relation to managing the employment relationship

Introduction

In the context of managing people, the reward system emphasizes a core facet of the employment relationship: that it constitutes an economic exchange or relationship. That is, an employee undertakes a certain amount of physical and/or mental effort and accepts the instructions of others, in return receiving a level of payment or reward. Reward is one of the four human resource management (HRM) policy areas incorporated into Beer et al.'s (1984) and Fombrun et al.'s (1984) conceptual models and is identified as a key management 'lever' in Storey's model of HRM (see Chapter 1). As the quotations at the head of the chapter attest, reward practices engender debate among academics and organizational leaders on the role that reward plays in achieving such substantive employee behaviours as task performance, flexibility, quality and commitment. According to Beer et al. (1984, p. 113), 'The design and management of reward systems constitute one of the most difficult HRM tasks for the general manager.'

Economic and social factors shape the design of reward systems. Global forces at work today compel managers to improve labour productivity and the quality of their organization's products and services, while satisfying local consumer tastes and preferences in diverse local markets (see Chapter 3). Authors taking a multifaceted perspective to the concept of 'high-commitment–high-performance' work systems link reward practices positively to the performance of the firm, a better social climate between management and other employees, and employeee trust and organizational commitment (see, for example, Paauwe, 2004). Research interest has also focused on the role that reward, particularly performance-related pay, plays in controlling the workforce (Kessler, 2001). In addition, social and psychological factors impinge on reward management. Reward is critically important in bringing about a system of 'distributive justice', according to Paauwe (2004, p. 68), and forming an employee's notion of 'fairness' and 'trust' in decision-making (Boselie et al., 2001). The concept of the psychological contract (see Chapter 1) would also suggest that any 'incongruence' of expectation concerning the rewards employees receive when they join the organization can lead to a perceived violation of the contract, resulting in decreased motivation and less trust in the employer (Morrison and Robinson, 1997; Rousseau and Ho, 2000). Given the problematic nature of pay, it is, however, not surprising that Brown (1989, p. 25) states, 'The satisfactory management of employment requires the satisfactory management of remuneration as a necessary, if not a sufficient, precondition.'

Over the past decade, the way in which managers and other employees have been rewarded has undergone significant change. The 'old pay' of reward by hours worked or years served in the organization – seniority – has given way to fashionable 'new pay' practices designed to make reward contingent upon individual effort and performance. The old pay systems, it is argued, were designed to suit extensive specialization and hierarchical and static organizational forms. In contrast, good new pay practices go hand in hand with a more uncertain business environment and new organizational and work configurations, which demand more flexibility (see Chapters 4, 5 and 6). Some writers have described these changes in reward practice as 'revolutionary' because they overthrow the traditional job-evaluated grade structures associated with Taylorism and the collective manner of setting rewards favoured by trade unions (Paauwe, 2004). Other writers have been more critical and have interpreted these developments as attempts to exclude trade unions in order to construct a more individualized employment relationship (Gunnigle et al., 1998), as a way of creating an organizational culture driven by 'ideology' (Sisson and Storey, 2000), a so-called 'enterprise culture' (Smith, 1992), globalization and corporate downsizing (Sebbens, 2000), and as inherently 'ethically deficient' (Heery, 2000).

Every work organization has to decide how to design a reward system. Regardless of any other rewards it offers to its employees, it must make three basic decisions about monetary reward: how much to pay, whether monetary rewards should be paid on an individual, group or collective basis, and how much emphasis should be placed on monetary reward as part of the total employment relationship. Decisions must be consistent with the organization's goals, with society's values on notions of fairness and with government legislation. The literature suggests that there is no single reward system that fits all organizations. To help in understanding this complex area, we provide a conceptual model for studying reward management. This model identifies major reward concepts and processes. We also examine the role of government in reward management. On a more theoretical level, we conclude with a critical analysis of the position of rewards in the prescriptive HRM model, which reveals tensions, contradictions and ethical concerns.

The nature of reward management

In reward literature, the term 'compensation' is used as an alternative to 'reward'. Both are problematic, and we consider that the new vocabulary of 'reward management' best captures the current changes in management thinking on pay, which emphasizes employee flexibility and performance (Armstrong, 1998). Managers typically define reward as the package of monetary rewards (wages, salaries and benefits), but employees generally define reward even more narrowly, as the wage or salary received from the employer for their work. To understand reward and comprehend its crucial role in managing the employment relationship, it is, however, necessary to conceptualize reward in its broadest sense.

An organization can provide two types of reward: extrinsic and intrinsic. *Extrinsic rewards* satisfy an employee's basic needs for survival, security and recognition, and derive from factors associated with the job context. This includes financial payments, working conditions and managerial behaviour. *Intrinsic rewards* refer to psychological 'enjoyment' and the satisfaction of 'challenge' (Bartol and Locke, 2000; Caruth and Handlogten, 2001), sometimes called 'psychic income', that a worker derives from her or his paid work, and that satisfy 'higher-level' needs for self-esteem and personal development. These rewards derive from factors inherent in the way in which the work is designed, that is, the job content. This includes design features, such as the degree of variety of the work and the extent of autonomy, as well as the significance attributed to the work. Consequently, for our purposes, we will define reward in the following terms:

> Reward refers to all the monetary, non-monetary and psychological payments that an organization provides for its employees in exchange for the work they perform.

The mix of extrinsic and intrinsic rewards provided by the employer is termed its *reward system*, the monetary or economic element of the reward system being called the *pay system*. A reward system also consists of the integrated policies, processes, practices and administrative procedures for implementing the system within the framework of the human resources (HR) strategy and the total organizational system. The management of rewards must meet numerous economic and behavioural objectives (Figure 10.1).

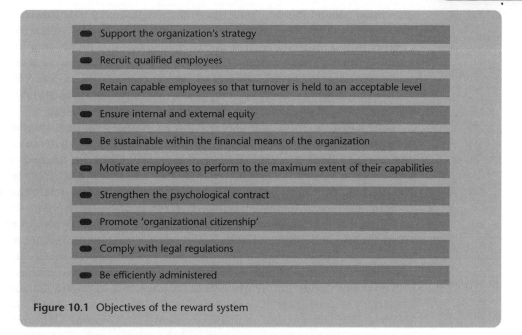

- Support the organization's strategy
- Recruit qualified employees
- Retain capable employees so that turnover is held to an acceptable level
- Ensure internal and external equity
- Be sustainable within the financial means of the organization
- Motivate employees to perform to the maximum extent of their capabilities
- Strengthen the psychological contract
- Promote 'organizational citizenship'
- Comply with legal regulations
- Be efficiently administered

Figure 10.1 Objectives of the reward system

A pay or reward strategy comprises an organization's plan and actions pertaining to the mix and total amount of direct pay (e.g. salary) and indirect monetary payments (benefits) paid to various categories of worker. In other words, the two key questions for pay strategy are 'How should monetary payments be paid?' and 'How much should be paid?' The optimal choice relating to these two aspects of pay strategy ultimately depends on the organizational and reward system. At one extreme, the reward system may include direct pay only, at the other extreme, no pay whatsoever. It is easy to think, 'Who works for nothing?', but many voluntary organizations, such as Oxfam and the Salvation Army, rely upon thousands of hours of unpaid labour. These examples illustrate the importance of intrinsic rewards derived from the work. The volunteers receive intrinsic rewards derived from the significance attributed to the work: they are not 'serving customers', they are 'feeding the destitute'. Similarly, highly qualified professionals may choose to work for organizations such as Médicins Sans Frontières or Amnesty International, at a much lower salary than they could earn in a private hospital or law practice, because of the meaning attached to the work. The key point is that the amount of pay needed to recruit and retain qualified workers will vary with the other rewards that the organization offers (Long, 2002).

To fully understand the conceptual analysis of the place of rewards within an HR strategy, it is first necessary to recall the nature of the employment relationship discussed in Chapter 1. We noted there that the way in which workers are rewarded for their work, as part of the wage–effort bargain, is central to the capitalist employment relationship. All pay systems contain two elements that are in contradiction with each other:

1. *Cooperation* between worker and employer or manager is an essential ingredient of the employment relationship if anything is to be produced and is fostered through the logic of financial gain for the worker.
2. *Tensions* and *conflict* are engendered through the logic that makes the 'buying' of labour power the reward for one group and the cost for the other.

This fundamental tension underlying the employment relationship makes for an unstable contract between the two parties, which, in the context of global price competition and technological change, is constantly being adjusted. To increase market 'viability', for example, employers attempt to increase performance through pay incentives or pay cuts to reduce labour costs. Furthermore, 'effort' itself is 'a highly unstable phenomenon' and payment systems form part of an array of managerial strategies designed as 'effort controllers' (Baldamus, 1961).

The nature of the employment contract means that the employee and those responsible for reward management have different objectives when it comes to monetary rewards. For the individual employee, the pay cheque at the end of the month is typically the major source of personal income and hence a critical determinant of an individual's purchasing power. The absolute level of earnings determines the standard of living and social well-being of the recipient and will therefore be the most important consideration for most employees. Employees constantly seek to maximize their financial reward because of inflation and rising expectations. Furthermore, the axiom of 'a fair day's pay for a fair day's work' raises the question of relative income. In most cases, what is seen to be 'fair' will be a very rough personalized evaluation.

The organization, on the other hand, is interested in reward management for two important reasons. First, it is interested in the absolute cost of the financial rewards because of its bearing on profitability or cost-effectiveness. The importance of this varies with the type of organization and the relative cost of employees, so that in a refinery labour costs are minimal, whereas in education or health they are substantial. Second, the organization views a reward system as a determinant of employees' work attitudes and behaviours. A reward system affects an individual's decision to join an organization, to work at her or his maximum potential, to undertake special behaviours beneficial to the organization that extend beyond contractual obligations – referred to as 'organizational citizenship behaviour' – to undertake training, to accept additional responsibilities and to remain with the organization. Employee dissatisfaction with the reward system may cause a variety of consequences, including high labour turnover, low task performance, low commitment and unionization of the workforce (HRM in Practice 10.1).

HRM IN PRACTICE 10.1

WATER FIRM WIDENS SCOPE OF PERFORMANCE-RELATED PAY

KATIE HOPE, *PEOPLE MANAGEMENT*, OCTOBER 13 2005

Severn Trent Water has introduced performance-related pay for all front-line staff so they are assessed in the same way as managers and directors.

The water company, which has 5,000 employees, has agreed a two-year deal linking total award to overall company performance based on profit, safety and attendance records. The new pay structure will be introduced in 2006.

> 'In the first year we had more people rated above average as managers were reluctant to say staff were average.'

'This is an important step in terms of alignment and marks a shift in culture, pay practice and trade union partnership by enabling genuine pay progression linked to performance,' said David Akers, HR operations manager for Severn Trent Water.

As part of the deal, Severn Trent Water would be sharing

the books detailing company performance with the unions, Akers said.

The new deal follows a two-year agreement introduced in 2004. This standardized pay across the company and, for the first time, allocated a performance-related award based on individual employees' performance, in addition to a basic award applied to all who qualified for a pay increase.

Akers said the new pay matrix required training so that line managers who were responsible for determining the award became comfortable with rating their staff. 'In the first year we had more people rated above average as managers were reluctant to say staff were average. HR had to stay close to the process to check managers were being consistent,' he said.

Since the new pay structure was introduced there has been a 20 per cent increase in the number of employees who say that they feel fairly rewarded and recognized for what they do, according to an internal employee survey.

Akers said the driver to introduce performance-related pay came from a changing regulatory environment which meant performance was increasingly important. Previously, the company also had mixed pay practices, with staff on different rates and outdated practices including a 'sheepdog allowance' paid to staff who had to look after reservoirs.

An attempt to introduce performance-related pay in 1998 had been rejected by trade unions.

REFLECTIVE QUESTION

Think about the reward system at your most recent job in terms of conflict and tension, workplace behaviour and equity. Did the reward system cause conflict or tension among the workforce? If so, why? What impact did the reward system have on your behaviour in the workplace? Do you believe that it was equitable? Share your experience with members of your class. Of the reward systems described by class members, which appear to generate most conflict, which appear to be most effective or most equitable, and why?

A model of reward management

To help us examine the complexities and principles underpinning new pay systems, we have developed a **pay model** that serves as both a framework for studying reward management and a guide for the chapter (Figure 10.2). The model contains five basic building blocks:

1. a strategic perspective
2. reward objectives
3. reward options
4. reward techniques
5. reward competitiveness.

Our model shows first that reward management is linked to organizational strategy. A *strategic perspective* focuses on those reward choices that support the organization's strategic goals. Going back to our discussion on business strategy (see Chapter 2), this means that each business strategy – and in this example we used Porter's (1980) typology of cost leadership and differentiation – should be supported by a different

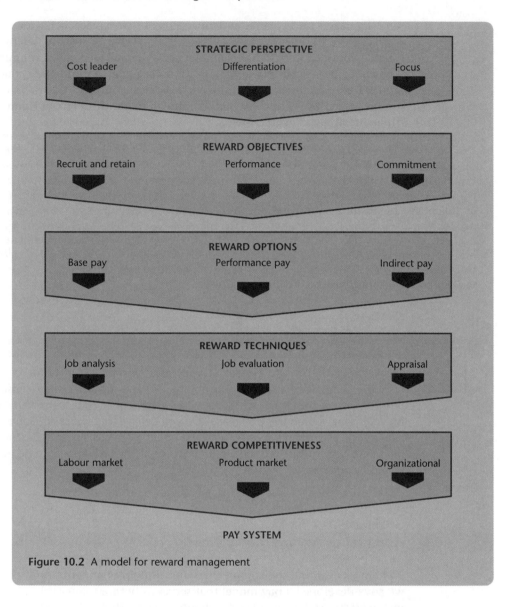

Figure 10.2 A model for reward management

HR strategy, including employee rewards. The underlying premise here is that the design of the employee reward system should flow from and seek to execute the organization's business strategy: the principle of *strategic pay*.

The *reward objectives* emphasize the linkage between a reward system and human behaviour. There are three principal behaviours that are desired by management – membership behaviour, task behaviour and commitment behaviour – and the reward system can play a central role in eliciting all three behaviours (Long, 2002). The reward system is an important consideration when the organization is trying to attract suitable employees, and once workers are members of the organization, their task behaviour and levels of performance are influenced by the reward system. The employment relationship is more than an economic exchange: it embraces a social and a psychological relationship. Employees typically interact with other employees and managers. Acceptable and unacceptable workplace behaviour on the part of workers and notions of 'fairness' are inevitably partly socially determined. Commitment behaviour occurs when employees and managers alike voluntarily undertake behaviour beneficial to the organization that goes beyond the economic exchange and is linked to the notion of the psychological contract.

Every employer has *reward options*, shown in the third box of Figure 10.2. There are three broad reward components:

- *base pay*, which is the level of pay (wage or fixed salary) that constitutes the rate for the job and is generally based on some unit of time – an hour, a week, a month or a year
- *performance pay*
- *indirect pay* or 'benefits' consisting of non-cash items or services (for example, life insurance).

These and other alternative monetary rewards explained later in the chapter offer managers a choice of components and elements that can be included in the reward system that best fits their organization.

The fourth component of our reward model in Figure 10.2 shows *reward techniques*. Three techniques are examined:

- job analysis
- job evaluation
- appraisal.

Internal equity refers to the pay relationships between jobs within a single organization, this policy being translated into practice by reward techniques. The focus here is on comparing jobs and individuals in terms of their relative contributions to the organization's objectives. How, for example, does the work of the chef compare with the work of the receptionist or the waiter? Job evaluation is the most common method used to compare the relative values of different jobs inside the organization. Of course, not all these reward techniques may be relevant to an organization, and in a unionized workplace there may be strong resistance to such techniques as appraisal.

Reward competitiveness is the fifth component of the model, referring to comparisons between the organization's pay and that of competitive organizations. Competitiveness is important if the organization is going to attract, retain and motivate its employees while achieving the other objectives of controlling labour costs and complying with pay legislation. Rewards that are perceived by prospective members to be inadequate or inequitable will make it difficult for the organization to attract the type of people necessary for success. There are also constraints that define the parameters within which reward choices can be made, including:

- labour market constraints
- product/service market constraints
- organizational constraints, including internal financial constraints and external legal constraints.

In terms of the latter, we should remind readers that the employment relationship involves a legal relationship, another objective of a reward system being compliance with employment legislation and regulations. We will now examine in more detail each of the five basic components of the reward management model.

HRM WEB LINKS

For the latest information on employment income in Britain, go to the National Statistics website at www.statistics.gov.uk. For information on employment income in North America, go to Statistics Canada's website at www.statcan.ca; for the USA go to the Bureau of Labor Statistics at www.bls.gov; for South Africa try www.statssa.gov. za and for Australia www.abs.gov.au. To obtain general information on reward management, go to www.rewardstrategies.com, www.employersinc.com/content.aspx?cid=104, www.worldatwork.org and www.hrreporter.ca and click on 'Compensation'.

Strategic perspective

Contingency theory suggests that an organization's reward system should be dependent on its external and internal contexts. The external context is globalization, compelling business organizations to downsize and become more cost-effective (Sebbens, 2000). The external environment also consists of the national context, which is strongly influenced by international developments. Some key national developments that affect the reward system include structural change in the labour market, restructuring in industry, shifts from traditional work to knowledge work, and social and political trends (Chapter 4). The significant internal context affecting reward management comprises organizational strategy, organizational restructuring, organizational culture and psychological contract issues.

Hill and Jones (2004, p. 3) define strategy as 'a specific pattern of decisions and actions that managers take to achieve an organization's goals'. As the hierarchy of established goals is translated from one level to the next, the reward for their satisfactory implementation constitutes critical elements of managerial control within the organization. A reward system is thus a key mechanism that can influence each step of the strategy process (Gerhart, 2000). In addition to its importance in influencing employee goal behaviours, a reward system influences at least two other important behaviours. The first is *membership behaviour*, which happens when qualified people join and remain with the organization. Thus, reward moulds the composition of the organization in terms of its competencies and intellectual capital. The second is *conflict behaviour*, which may derive from employee dissatisfaction with the reward system and is expressed through formal disputes, absenteeism or sabotage. This type of employee behaviour can undermine organizational strategy.

Taken together, fashionable new pay concepts routinely suggest that an organization's approach to reward management design starts with business strategy and work design. It argues that an 'effective' reward system requires employees' pay to fit or be aligned with the organization's strategy. Furthermore, the closer the alignment or 'fit' between the reward system and the strategic context, the more effective the organization (Gomez-Mejia and Balkin, 1992; Lawler, 1990, 1995; Mintzberg et al., 1998; Pfeffer, 1998). The notion of alignment is explained by Pfeffer (1998, p. 99):

> The diagnostic framework is premised on the idea of alignment, that is, that an organization does specific things to manage the employment relationship and these practices need to be first, internally consistent or aligned with one another, and second, externally consistent, in the sense that the organization's procedures produce behaviors and competencies required for it to compete successfully given its chosen marketplace and way of differentiating itself in that marketplace.

Let us illustrate this contingency theory with an example of two business organizations with two different business strategies and completely different reward systems. Precision Engineering produces high-quality, customized machine tools for the aerospace industry. The manufacturing process is organized around self-managed work teams, and workers rotate through the various jobs within the teams that they are qualified to perform. Rather than pay an hourly wage rate to the skilled machine operators, which is the industry norm, the company pays a base salary, additional pay being awarded if the workers learn new skills. All employees receive an excellent benefits package and profit-sharing bonuses based on company profits. Labour costs at Precision Engineering are above the industry average. The culture at Precision Engineering encourages informal workplace learning, and, not surprisingly, labour turnover is extremely low.

Seafresh Foods operates a plant that produces fish fingers. The work is organized around a conveyor belt with workers stationed along the assembly line performing each step in the process, from gutting the fish to packaging. The work requires little training and is monotonous. In contrast to Precision Engineering, workers at Seafresh Foods are paid an hourly wage rate that is 10 per cent above the minimum wage, and there are no additional payments or benefits. Labour turnover exceeds 100 per cent a year.

REFLECTIVE QUESTION

Think about the business strategy and reward systems at these two companies. How can Precision Engineering compete when it pays above the industry average? And how can Seafresh Foods survive with such a high turnover? Go back to Chapter 2 and look again at the 'integrative model'.

The contingency approach would suggest that, despite the two completely different reward systems at Precision Engineering and Seafresh Foods, both are effective (Long, 2002). Going back to our discussion on business strategy (Chapter 2), each reward system is aligned with the firm's business strategy. Using Porter's (1980) typology – differentiation and cost leadership – Precision Engineering is following a differentiation competitive strategy, with a focus on high-quality machine tools. Owing to the complexity of the production process, high-skilled workers are employed and are given a considerable amount of autonomy. The reward system (salary, benefits and pay-for-knowledge) supports the 'high-commitment' HR strategy. But to answer the question we posed above – 'How can Precision Engineering compete when it pays above the industry average?' – the firm competes with lower paying competitors for the following reasons:

1. There is higher productivity resulting from increased functional flexibility.
2. A highly skilled and flexible workforce reduces machine downtime and scrap rates.
3. The use of self-managed work teams eliminates the amount paid to supervisors and quality control inspectors as team members undertake these tasks.
4. Low turnover means that recruitment and training costs are reduced.

In contrast, Seafresh Foods depends on its survival by following a cost leadership strategy (in which low-cost production is essential). This competitive strategy requires low-skilled employees and little employee commitment because managers exert control using technology (the speed of the assembly line). Labour turnover is high, but unskilled workers are easy to recruit and training costs are low. At Seafresh Foods, the reward system (near-minimum wage only) supports a 'traditional low-commitment' HR strategy (see HRM in Practice 2.4 for a real-life example of business strategy and reward practice alignment).

At both macro- and micro-level, the contingency approach has been used as an analytical tool for explaining developments and the factors influencing the choice of reward systems over time. The macroeconomic exigencies of the past decade, for example deregulation, privatization and the need for flexibility and innovation, explain why managers chose a payment system based on a combination of individual performance, pay-for-knowledge and profit-sharing to meet the needs of a high-quality manufacturing strategy. The innovations seek to encourage entrepreneurial behaviour and encourage workers to take commercial risks in order to encourage employee flexibility and behavioural traits that promote both learning and quality, and also to meet the perceived needs of 'post-Fordist' production models (Chapter 5).

Recent prescriptive strategic management and new pay literature has emphasized the need for companies to adopt 'good' reward practices that encourage a constellation of behaviours and attitudes from managers and other employees that supports the organization's business strategy and design, as illustrated in Table 10.1.

Table 10.1 Alignment of business strategy, organizational design and reward practices

Bureaucratic 'old' pay model	Post-bureaucratic 'new' pay model
Base wage or salary	Variable pay
Based on cost of living and labour market	Based on business performance
Evenly distributed between employees	Differentiated
Correlated with seniority	Based on individual performance
Based on individual performance	Based on team (unit) and organizational performance
Viewed as a result of behaviour	Used as a means of communicating values

Source: Adapted from Pfeffer (1998)

The debate concerns whether the current managerial drive to establish a close relationship between individual pay and individual performance constitutes a qualitative change from past management strategies. In other words, is the shift an ad hoc, reactive response to contextual changes, or do the reported changes surrounding new pay systems represent a more proactive and strategic HRM approach (Kessler, 1995)? Prescriptive management literature on the perennial managerial concern of motivation suggests that payment systems directly linking pay to individual or group performance are certainly not new. In the 1960s, it was advocated that an individual performance-based payment system – regulated through productivity bargaining – be adopted to increase labour productivity. The current trend towards variable or contingency pay arrangements can best be understood in terms of the dominant political ideology over the past two decades in many developed countries, particularly Britain and North America. A concerted ideological campaign against automatic annual pay increases and 'artificially inflated' public sector pay by the Thatcher government in the UK encouraged a movement towards linking pay to individual performance and local labour markets (Curnow, 1986; Pendleton, 1997b; Sisson and Storey, 2000).

Whether current pay practices conform to the historical pattern and can be judged as reactive, or as more proactive and strategic, is debatable. A recent study (Chartered Institute for Personnel and Development, 2006b) found that only 35 per cent of UK organizations surveyed actually had a reward strategy. Recognizing the difficulty of identifying the strategic intent of managers, Kessler (1995) argues that there is insufficient evidence to support the hypothesis that the selection of payment systems is based upon the theoretical principle of 'fit' commonly cited in the literature. Furthermore, to depict recent developments in reward systems as evidence that pay is a 'key lever' in pursuit of the HRM goals of commitment, flexibility and quality is to ignore historical data. The alternative pay systems currently gaining popularity with managers indicate that they are selecting reward options to deal with new versions of traditional managerial problems. What might be qualitatively different and would indicate attempts to use reward in a strategic way, argues Kessler, would be the use of variable pay systems to facilitate cultural change. As we discuss below, reward research indeed suggests that current reward practices aim to bring about a fundamental change in organizational culture. On the specific question of the concept of strategy–reward fit, however, there is evidence of an alignment between reward and business strategy (Rynes and Gerhart, 2000). Whether a fit between business strategy and pay influences organizational performance remains open to debate, but we shall leave this question until Chapter 14, turning now instead to the second component of the reward management model outlined in Figure 10.2 above.

Reward objectives

The new reward model has three behavioural objectives:

1. *Membership behaviour* to recruit and retain a sufficient number of qualified workers
2. *Task behaviour* to motivate employees to be flexible and perform to the fullest extent of their capabilities
3. *Compliance behaviour* to encourage employees to follow workplace rules and undertake special behaviours beneficial to the organization without direct supervision or instructions, including high levels of employee commitment.

Recruit and retain

The reward system enables an organization to attract and retain suitably qualified employees to perform the work of the organization. According to the neoclassical economic model, which is concerned with using demand and supply analysis but incorporates psychological factors to explain human behaviour, people choose work organizations that maximize their utility, meaning that they consider not only pay, but also non-monetary factors such as job security, prestige, work environment and other aspects that matter to them. This hedonic theory of pay holds that jobs with less desirable non-monetary characteristics should command positive compensatory pay differentials, whereas jobs and organizations with more favourable characteristics should command a lower rate of pay. This market theory of pay is only partially true as there are many jobs that have undesirable non-monetary characteristics (e.g. dangerous and unhealthy work) but do not command positive compensatory pay differentials. Other 'post-institutional' economists (Rynes and Gerhart, 2000) point out that firms within an industry often have different enduring pay levels for the same occupations because of factors such as equity beliefs, ability to pay and HR strategy (Pfeffer, 1998).

A reward system that is out of touch with what the market is paying for a particular job, or one that is inequitable, may therefore demand constant recruitment just to secure the necessary workers. Furthermore, if employees, once recruited, perceive any internal inequity – for example, with another individual or group performing identical work – the organization may have difficulty retaining them for long. Constant recruitment and high turnover increase both recruitment and training costs. Caruth and Handlogten (2001, p. 4) suggest that 'equitable pay, a sound benefits program, and a psychologically supportive organizational climate' may reduce employee turnover costs. Empirical research on how reward influences recruitment and retention is, however, limited, and we have much to learn about how, why and when reward influences employees' attraction to and retention within an organization (Barber and Bretz, 2000).

Performance

Can money motivate people to work? This question has been a concern of employers and managers since the Industrial Revolution, the fact that the question is intensely debated being a reflection of its complexity (Bartol and Locke, 2000). Much of current management thinking on this question comes from theories of motivation. 'Needs' theories of motivation emphasize what motivates people rather than how they are motivated. The two most well-known needs theories are those of Maslow (1954) and Herzberg (1966). Maslow argued that higher-order needs become progressively more important once lower-order ones have been satisfied, whereas Herzberg demonstrated that pay takes on significance as a source of satisfaction when it is perceived as a form of recognition or reward. Monetary variables are a key component of the more recent 'process' theories of motivation, Vroom's (1964) expectancy theory, for example, granting a prominent role to rewards (see below).

As most prescriptive texts on employee behaviour affirm, understanding the nature of the relationship between pay, commitment and motivation is complex and requires, at the very least, a knowledge of both the individual and the context. From this perspective, it is not surprising therefore to find disagreement over the strength or effectiveness of the reward–commitment link. Locke et al. (1980, pp. 379–81) assert that 'Money is the crucial incentive because … it is related to all of man's needs.' In contrast, Pfeffer (1998, p. 112) argues, 'People do work for money – but they work even more for meaning in their lives.' Caruth and Handlogten (2001, p. 4) express the received wisdom on the pay–motivation link: 'A compensation system that rewards employees fairly according to efforts expended and results produced creates a motivating work environment.' In the debate on the rewards–motivation link, there is a tendency for writers to view workers through a management lens, at the expense of analysing management per se – what managers do and how well they do it. Blinder's (1990, quoted by Kessler, 1995, p. 261) insightful conclusion is particularly helpful in understanding the complexity of the reward–commitment link: 'Changing the way workers are treated may boost productivity more than changing the way they are paid.'

An increasing number of North American and British companies have adopted individual performance-related pay (IPRP; see below). One survey, for example, found, in a poll of 316 Canadian companies, that 74 per cent of employers offered performance-related pay arrangements, up 8 per cent from the 1996 figure.[3] Since the mid-1980s, the proportion of workplaces in Britain with some form of performance-related pay arrangement has been on the increase. In 2004, two-fifths – 40 per cent – of all workplaces in Britain operated a performance-related payment system, in which the level of pay is determined by the amount of work completed or is related to a subjective assessment of performance by a manager. Data from the Workplace Employment Relations Survey reveal that the use of performance-related pay is more prevalent in the private sector – 44 per cent – than the public sector – 19 per cent (Kersley et al., 2006, p. 21).

Numerous writers have made the observation that variable or contingent reward systems are linked to the rhetoric of the 'enterprise culture', the enterprise culture in turn being the context for substituting performance-related pay for more traditional time-related or seniority-based pay systems (see, for example, Heery, 2000; Smith, 1992). Performance-related pay is said to underpin a more purposeful and 'objective-achieving' strategy for managing workers. As Smith (1992, p. 178) states, the apparent change to performance-related pay represents 'a move away from the traditional view of rewards as incentives aimed at generating short-term improvements in employee performance, and towards rewards or total pay systems aimed at improving organizational performance'.

Commitment

As we have noted, the employment relationship is more than just an economic exchange, embracing instead a psychological relationship. The new HRM practices imply a change in the commitment of parties to one another at the psychological level. Indeed, it is argued (Guest, 1998, p. 42) that the 'whole rationale for introducing HRM policies is to increase levels of commitment so that other positive outcomes can ensue'. Depending on the writer's perspective, the notion of commitment is discussed in terms of 'organizational citizenship behaviour' (Long, 2002) or 'compliance' and 'control of meaning', psychosocial factors subject to management manipulation (Thompson and McHugh, 2002). The reward system aims to promote commitment behaviours, but employee commitment is an elusive construct because reward practices do not directly affect behaviour. Within the structured environment of the workplace, reward first affects employee attitudes, perceptions and perceived obligations rooted in the cultural environment in which paid work is performed, which in turn drives behaviour. These processes help to develop organizational commitment through a reference to shared goals and values, a sense of 'belonging', conformity and an intention to remain a member of the organization.

The fashionable argument that reward is one of the most noticeable HR practices through which the psychological contract can be 'created, fulfilled, changed, or violated' (Rousseau and Ho, 2000, p. 274) reflects the fact that financial reward lies at the heart of the employment relationship. A perceived breach involves perceptual and cognitive processes that convince the employee that the organization has 'reneged' on the contract. So how does reward shape the psychological contract, and how does a breach of contract occur? According to Rousseau and Ho (2000), reward plays two important roles in shaping the psychological contract. The first is to signal to workers, through monetary incentives, the behaviour that the organization values. The second role is to promote a particular form of employment relationship 'based on what the compensation system signals, in conjunction with other human resource practices, regarding the attachment between workers and the firm' (Rousseau and Ho, 2000, p. 305). Violation refers to the feelings of anger and betrayal experienced when the employee perceives that a breach of contract has occurred. A violation may occur when communication on the nature of the contract turns out to be different from (less favourable than) what the worker expected (Morrison and Robinson, 1997).

The perceptual and idiosyncratic nature of psychological contracts means that what others have received from the organization does matter: an employee may perceive a contract breach even if co-workers have received the same reward. Thus, the breach process is more complex than the process underlying equity judgements; it is 'a reciprocal relationship based on *perceived* obligations' between the employee and the organization (Morrison and Robinson, 1997, p. 242, emphasis added). In practice, every employee will put a somewhat different valuation on the rewards provided and on the value of their contribution, and may or may not perceive a contract breach depending on their individual traits and circumstances. The importance of a perceived breach of the psychological contract and subsequent employee behaviours will, however, vary for different organizations. Those practising a high-commitment HR strategy and knowledge-based organizations will find behaviour caused by perceived violation of the contract to be of particular importance, whereas those practising a traditional HR strategy will be concerned primarily with measurable pay–task behaviour outcomes.

Reward options

Turning to the third heading in Figure 10.2 above, reward options – base pay, performance pay and indirect pay – can be seen. The purpose of this section is to provide a foundation for answering the question 'What role should each of the three reward components play in the reward mix?' The mix of components to be included in the reward package will depend on the organizational and HR strategy and on reward objectives. Managers are particularly interested in effort-related behaviours, those behaviours which directly or indirectly influence the achievement of the organization's objectives. Table 10.2 classifies some of these behaviours into five groups:

- time
- energy
- competence
- cooperation
- commitment.

To be efficient, managers must ensure that employees turn up for work at the scheduled times; absenteeism and lateness must be minimized. In addition, employees must put into the job sufficient energy to complete their allotted tasks within set time limits. Job incumbents must also be competent so that the tasks are completed without error and above minimum performance standards (minimum acceptable levels of performance, typically set by management unless they are jointly negotiated). Changes in job design (Chapter 5) require employees to work cooperatively with their co-workers in order to improve the organization's effectiveness.

Table 10.2 Types of employee reward

Type of reward	Examples	Type of behaviour
Individual rewards	Basic wage Overtime Piece rate Commission Bonuses Merit Paid leave Benefits	Time: maintaining work attendance Energy: performing tasks Competence: completing tasks without errors
Team rewards	Team bonuses Gain-sharing	Cooperation: with co-workers
Organizational rewards	Profit-sharing Share ownership Gain-sharing	Commitment to institutional goals

Three different types of reward – individual, team and organizational – are shown in Table 10.2:

- *Individual rewards* are paid directly to the individual employee and are based on a commitment of time, energy or a combination of both.
- *Team reward* systems have become more prevalent in Europe and North America as organizations have reconfigured work systems that emphasize self-managed teams.
- *Organizational rewards*, such as profit-sharing, have also grown in popularity as a way of motivating employees and gaining employee commitment to customer-driven work cultures (Pryce and Nicholson, 1988).

Let us now look at different types of pay in more detail in terms of the reward options headings in Figure 10.2.

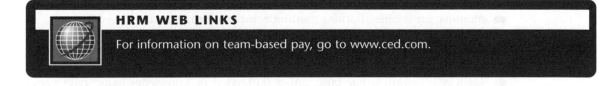

HRM WEB LINKS

For information on team-based pay, go to www.ced.com.

Base pay

Base (or basic) pay is the irreducible minimum rate of pay for the job. It is calculated on time worked, rather than on results achieved, and tends to reflect the value of the job itself as measured by some form of job evaluation. In many organizations, base pay is the basis on which earnings are built by the addition of one or more of the other types of reward. The base wage for a skilled machine operator, for example, may be £9.85 an hour for a 35-hour week, but operators may receive more because of additional incentive and overtime payments. Base pay can be selected for at least two important reasons:

- *Simplicity:* It is easier to implement and administer than a performance-related system.
- *Psychological reasons:* It demonstrates a commitment on the part of the organization, thereby creating a greater likelihood of employee commitment to the organization (Long, 2002).

A distinction is often made between a salary and a wage. A *salary* is a fixed periodical payment to a non-manual employee; it is usually expressed in annual terms, and salaried staff typically do not receive overtime pay. A *wage*, however, is the payment made to manual workers, nearly always being calculated as an hourly rate. In North America and Britain, an increasing number of employers have lessened the divide between salaries and wages by introducing 'single-status' payment schemes. This type of reward system is designed to harmonize the terms and conditions of employment between manual and white-collar employees (e.g. so that manual and non-manual employees receive the same number of holidays, amount of sickness benefit and pension).

Two main methods are used to establish the level of base pay. The first method – *market pricing* – may be based on the 'going industry rate' for a particular job and on traditional structures whose origins 'are shrouded in the mists of time' (Armstrong, 1998, p. 5). According to a CIPD (2006b) study, the most popular way of establishing a link between an organization's internal system of rewards and external market rates is to use pay surveys and job adverts. The second method – *job evaluation* – involves a systematic determination of the relative value or worth of all the jobs in the organization before correlating this system to the labour market. Both of these reward processes are discussed in detail later in the chapter.

Performance pay

Financial rewards added to base pay are related to certain work-related behaviours: performance, learning or experience. If these payments are not consolidated into base pay, they are known as 'performance pay,' 'variable pay,' 'contingency pay' or 'at-risk pay'. The main types of performance pay are as follows:

- *Performance-related pay* ties additional payments directly to performance, either of an individual or a team of employees.
- *Incentive pay* is offered prior to setting actual performance targets.
- *Merit pay* is offered for outstanding past performance.
- *Commission* is a financial incentive typically offered to sales representatives on the basis of a percentage of the sales value they generate.
- *Knowledge-contingent pay* (also called skill-based or knowledge-based pay) varies according to the level and value of the skills and competencies achieved by the individual.
- *Team-based pay* provides rewards to employees based on their contribution to the work team.
- *Organization performance pay* provides additional income to employees based on the profitability of the firm.

Individual performance-related pay (IPRP) is a system that directly ties pay to the level of performance rather than the fact of employment. For advocates of new pay systems, it is axiomatic that reward be contingent on individual employee effort and performance. The prescriptive new pay literature suggests that correctly designed IPRP systems have numerous advantages. First, they signal key task behaviours and provide information about current performance levels. Second, they reduce the need for other types of managerial control (e.g. direct supervision, technology or peer pressure) over the labour process. Third, the practice helps to change the culture of the organization and promote an 'entrepreneurial' type of behaviour. It is no coincidence, for example, that some of the most publicized IPRP programmes have been introduced in newly privatized public utilities. This has led some commentators to suggest that IPRP has been adopted in many organizations for largely 'ideological' reasons (Sisson and Storey, 2000).

The premise underpinning IPRP is the oversimplistic assumption that pay alone motivates workers. Psychological theory and empirical research suggest, however, that the link between incentives and individual motivation is a more complex process. One of the most widely accepted explanations of motivation is Vroom's (1964) expectancy theory, touched on earlier in the chapter. This approach to worker motivation argues that managers must have an understanding of their subordinates' goals and the link between effort and performance, between performance and rewards, and between the rewards and individual goal satisfaction. The theory recognizes that there is no universal principle for explaining everyone's motivation, which means that a successful link between performance and reward is difficult to accomplish in practice.

It is difficult to generalize about the limitations of IPRP systems because the types of system involved differ so widely (Long, 2002). IPRP systems can undermine teamwork, but, according to Pfeffer (1998, p. 223), the major problem with individual performance-related pay is the 'symbolic message' that variable pay sends to employees:

> A system ... rewarding myriad micro behaviors, sends the message that management believes people won't do what is necessary unless they are rewarded for every little thing. A system of micro-level behavioral and outcome incentives also tends to convey an absence of trust, implying that people must be measured and rewarded for everything or they won't do what is expected of them.

The upshot is that the more an organization emphasizes financial rewards above all else, the more intrinsic motivation diminishes. The extent to which an organization emphasizes performance pay will depend upon whether this type of reward supports the organization's strategy.

Before we leave this topic, we should note that much of the theory and research on reward–performance links and management reward practices is North American. In contrast, a cross-cultural study found that Chinese and American managers differed in the importance they attached to reward decisions. Chinese managers in the study, for example, placed more emphasis on work-based relationship needs and less emphasis on employee task performance when making a monetary recognition decision than did American managers (Zhou and Martocchio, 2001).

REFLECTIVE QUESTION

If you are an employer, paying employees only when the desired performance takes place sounds like 'common sense'. Can you think of any circumstances in which individual-based performance pay would be advantageous or disadvantageous for a particular organization?

The next three types of pay in the list above – *incentive pay*, *merit pay* and *commission* – need no further explanation.

Knowledge-contingent pay systems tie pay to work-related learning. From a management perspective, it is argued that, by encouraging functional flexibility, pay-for-knowledge systems reverse the trend towards increased specialization. From a trade union perspective, pay-for-knowledge arrangements individualize the employment relationship because they sever the link between increased pay and collective bargaining (Bacon and Storey, 1993).

Survey evidence indicates that many organizations are placing less emphasis on individual incentives and more emphasis on group or *team-based* and *organization-based performance rewards* (e.g. Guthrie and Hollensbe, 2004; Long, 2002). This trend mirrors changes in organizational design and the current enthusiasm for work-based organizational structures. McClurg (2001) found that team-based reward systems are limited in number and often operate in a fashion similar to that of gain-sharing programmes, in which additional payment is made to employees when profits increase or costs to the firm decrease. Guthrie and Hollensbe's (2004) study of group incentives found that when a significant amount of employee pay was at risk, group or team incentives prompted employees to set higher performance goals.

HRM IN PRACTICE 10.2

STOCK OPTIONS STILL THE PREFERRED INCENTIVE

RAY MURRILL, *CANADIAN HR REPORTER*, 21 JUNE 2005

Stock options have long been one of the cornerstones of a competitive executive compensation package. But new accounting rules and growing scrutiny from institutional investors are prompting organizations to revisit – and perhaps rethink – how stock options are designed and implemented.

Stock options continue to be among the most prevalent types of long-term incentives in Canada. In fact, according to a recent Watson Wyatt study, 98.6 per cent of the 214 companies that form the S&P/TSX Composite Index reported having stock option plans in 2003.

While few dispute the need for fair, competitive and performance-linked executive compensation, Canadian institutional investors are calling on organizations to review how they use stock options. Some of the guiding principles being advocated by institutional investors include:

- having a large portion of an executive's compensation package based on performance, with pay and performance linked through meaningful and measurable performance targets

> **Stock options continue to be among the most prevalent types of long-term incentives in Canada.**

- ensuring executives are significant shareholders in the companies they lead – with an emphasis on owning shares versus holding options

- ensuring complete disclosure of executive compensation arrangements
- ensuring board compensation committees seek independent executive compensation advice
- limiting the number of stock options granted, and ensuring those that are granted are focused on the achievement of long-term business objectives and subject to appropriate vesting criteria.

In the United States, major institutional investors are also quite vocal about the need for change. Specifically, they hold the view that traditional time-vested stock options are not 'performance-based,' and that grant levels and vesting criteria should be linked to performance criteria other than share price. U.S. institutional investors have also expressed a lack of confidence in companies' use of 'earnings per share' as a performance measure because of the potential for manipulation of results.

The move towards more performance-based long-term incentive plans is further complicated by the challenge of determining what performance measures should be used. Should these measures be relative measures or absolute measures? Should they be externally focused against a peer group or internally focused? If a peer group comparison is selected, how does one define an appropriate peer group and will it be stable over the performance period? How does one define threshold, target and maximum performance? And what role will board discretion play with a plan that utilizes rigidly defined metrics?

Profit-related pay is a form of contingent performance pay that involves the employer paying current or deferred sums based on company profits in addition to established base pay (HRM in Practice 10.2). Payment can be in the form of current distribution (paid quarterly or annually), deferred plans (paid at retirement and/or upon disability) or combination plans. With encouragement from Conservative governments, profit-related pay has become more widespread for some employees in Britain since the early 1990s. The 2004 Workplace Employee Relations Survey found that 37 per cent of private sector workplaces had some form of profit-related payment scheme. The financial services sector reported the highest incidence of profit-related payments, at 67 per cent, followed by the electricity, gas and water sector at 59 per cent. Interestingly, foreign-owned establishments had a greater tendency than UK-owned establishments to use profit-related payments: 50 per cent and 34 per cent, respectively (Kersley et al., 2006, pp. 192–3). Advocates of profit-sharing contend that it can increase performance, result in greater employment stability and form a 'win–win' situation for both employees and employers (Tyson, 1996). The capacity for profit-related payments to motivate employees may, however, depend on gender (HRM in Practice 10.3). Profit-sharing is seen by managers as a way of increasing organizational performance through employee involvement in decision-making (Pendleton, 1997b) and stronger employee identification with the business (Long, 2002).

HRM IN PRACTICE 10.3

GERMAN WOMEN PREFER FIXED SALARIES, MEN PERFORMANCE-RELATED PAY

HRM GUIDE, APRIL 2006

The fact that on average women earn less than men is not necessarily the result of discrimination: when given a choice between a fixed salary and performance-related pay, women choose the former far more often than men, even if they could earn more by opting for the latter. This is the result of a study carried out by the Institute for the Study of Labor and the University of Bonn.

> **'Men, for example, are more prepared to take risks.'**

'In our experiment only 44 per cent of all women taking part chose the performance-related options, although many of them could have earned more if they had,' is how the Bonn economist Professor Armin Falk summarizes the results. 'By contrast 68 per cent of the men chose this option.' The results correspond to the statistical data of the socioeconomic panel, a survey which the German Institute of Economic Research carries out each year. According to this, 33 per cent of all women work in the public sector, a field in which fixed (though relatively low) pay is the norm. In contrast, only 21 per cent of men are employed in this field.

Professor Falk carries out research at the prestigious Institute for the Study of Labor (IZA, i.e. Institut zur Zukunft der Arbeit), at the same time working as the head of the University of Bonn's Laboratory for Experimental Economic Research. In the study he and a member of his team, Dr. Thomas Dohmen, wanted to investigate what effect the choice of a pay incentive scheme could have on the composition of the workforce. 'We have also got our participants to do experiments which enable us to draw conclusions about specific traits of their character,' Dr. Dohmen explains. These include, for example, risk affinity, egoism and assessment of one's own abilities. 'Men, for example, are more prepared to take risks,' is how Thomas Dohmen sums up the conclusions. 'Our results show this quite clearly. These findings should at least partly explain why women tend to opt for fixed pay.'

The method of payment therefore seems to have a big influence on determining for what type of person a company is attractive. 'If, for example, a bank pays its managers on the competitive principle, it risks attracting above-average financial experts who assess their own abilities too positively,' Professor Falk explains, for the customer this could be a dangerous combination.

An employee stock plan is any type of financial arrangement through which employees acquire shares in the company that employs them. Stock ownership, it is alleged, encourages employees 'to think like owners' (Long, 2002). In Britain, the 2004 Workplace Employment Relations Survey found that 21 per cent of private sector workplaces operated an employee share scheme (Kersley et al., 2006). A litany of ethical lapses and financial fraud in some North American and European corporations, together with the high-profile collapse of Enron Corp., the US corporate giant, has tended to diminish the popularity of employee stock plans, most notably in North America and South Korea (see Chapter 3).

HRM WEB LINKS

Go to www.fed.org/programs.html for information on the role of employee stock options. For more information on profit-related pay and share-ownership schemes in Britain, go to the 2004 Workplace Employee Relations Survey website at www.dti.gov.uk/employment/research-evaluation/wers-2004/index.html.

Indirect pay

Indirect pay (often known as 'employee benefits') refers to that part of the total reward package provided to employees in addition to base or performance pay. There are three main types of indirect pay:

1. health and life insurance
2. deferred income plans, often known as retirement or pension plans
3. miscellaneous benefits, which may range from the provision of a company car to the purchase of club memberships.

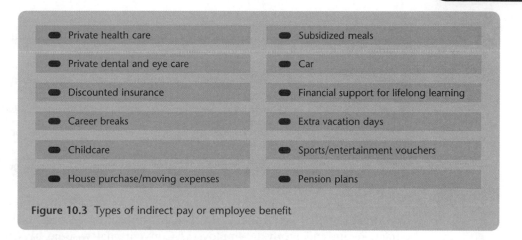

● Private health care	● Subsidized meals
● Private dental and eye care	● Car
● Discounted insurance	● Financial support for lifelong learning
● Career breaks	● Extra vacation days
● Childcare	● Sports/entertainment vouchers
● House purchase/moving expenses	● Pension plans

Figure 10.3 Types of indirect pay or employee benefit

Figure 10.3 lists some of the various types of indirect pay or employee benefits.

As with other aspects of new pay policies, proponents of new reward models recommend, with regard to benefit provision, greater differentiation and flexibility through the introduction of individualized benefits. One innovation is 'cafeteria' benefit programmes, which allow employees to select benefits that match their individual needs (HRM in Practice 10.4). Employees are provided with a benefit account containing a specified payment, the types and prices of benefits being provided to each employee in the form of a printout. This programme creates additional administrative costs, but advocates claim that employees, through participation, come to understand the value of benefits that the organization is offering. Young employees might, for example, select dental and medical benefits, whereas older employees might select a pension. Table 10.3 lists the most commonly cited advantages and disadvantages of cafeteria or flexible benefits schemes.

HRM IN PRACTICE 10.4

PICK UP A GOOD BENEFIT PACKAGE AT PENGUIN

PEOPLE MANAGEMENT, 23 FEBRUARY 2006

Penguin Books' imaginative use of benefits has helped it to manage 1,500 redundancies in the past six and a half years without any industrial tribunals. Susan Taylor, former HR director of Penguin Books, said its range of benefits had helped it to maintain the vital psychological contract with staff despite a period of rapid change.

'I would urge you to think creatively about things you can do in your business that don't cost a lot of money but mean a lot to employees,' Taylor told delegates.

> 'I would urge you to think creatively about things you can do in your business that don't cost a lot of money but mean a lot to employees.'

The publishing company, which now has 1,000 employees, offers a range of unusual staff benefits, including the 'Rough Guide Holiday Club', which allows staff to book holidays at industry rates; an offer of two free books a day; and a summertime working option that allows employees to work longer hours from Monday to Thursday so that they can leave at lunchtime on Fridays in July and August. The company also has individual merit pay awards, worth between £300 and £1,000, which one in 10 employees receives annually to mark special contributions to work.

Table 10.3 Advantages and disadvantages of flexible benefits

Advantages	Disadvantages
Employees select benefits to match their individual needs	Poor selection creates unwanted costs
Benefits target the needs of a diverse workforce	Additional administrative costs arise
Maximizes the psychological value of benefits because paying only for most desired benefits	Encourages the cost of popular benefits to be marked up

There is, however, some debate over employee benefits. Do they, for example, facilitate organizational performance? Do benefits impact on an organization's ability to attract, retain and motivate employees? Conventional wisdom says that employee benefits can affect recruitment and retention, but there is little research to support this conclusion (Milkovitch and Newman, 2004). Given the absence of empirical evidence on the relationship between employee benefits and performance, and the escalating cost of benefits, benefits are under constant scrutiny by managers.

HRM WEB LINKS

Go to www.ifebp.org, www.benefitslinks.com and www.benefits.org for information on benefits.

Reward techniques

Returning to Figure 10.2 above, let us consider the fourth reward management heading, that of reward techniques.

Traditional or 'old' pay writers emphasized the importance of **internal equity**, which refers to comparisons between jobs or skill levels inside the organization. The process involves comparing jobs and employees' skills and competencies in terms of their relative contributions to the organization's goals (Milkovitch and Newman, 2004). Internal reward relationships, it is argued, affect employee behaviour in terms of staying with the organization, becoming more flexible by investing in more work-related learning or determining whether there is a breach in the psychological contract. Internal equity is established through three reward techniques:

1. job analysis
2. job evaluation
3. appraisal.

New pay writers, such as Lawler (1990, 1995), stress that reward should not be job but person-based, such that the position of employees within the pay structure is determined less by the formal job description and more by the skills and performance they bring to that job. Thus, job analysis and job evaluation are techniques associated with old pay structures developed to meet the needs of bureaucratic Fordist-type organizations. Not surprisingly, Lawler (1990) inveighs against traditional job evaluation and instead advocates 'skill-based pay' (see Heery, 2000).

Job analysis

If financial reward is to be based on work performed, a technique is needed to iden-tify the differences and similarities between different jobs in the organization. Knowledge on jobs and their requirements is collected through **job analysis**, which can be defined as:

> The systematic process of collecting and evaluating information about the tasks, respon-sibilities and the context of a specific job.

Job analysis information informs the manager about the nature of a specific job, in particular the major tasks undertaken by the incumbent, the outcomes that are expected, the job's relationships to other jobs in the organizational hierarchy and job-holder characteristics. The basic premise underlying job analysis is that jobs are more likely to be described, differentiated and evaluated consistently if accurate informa-tion is available to reward managers (Milkovitch and Newman, 2004). Figure 10.4 shows that job analysis information is a prerequisite for preparing job descriptions and for job evaluation.

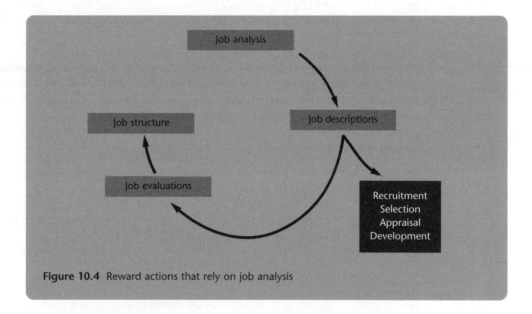

Figure 10.4 Reward actions that rely on job analysis

The process of job analysis consists of two main stages (Figure 10.5):

1. data collection
2. the application of data by the preparation of job descriptions, job specifications and job standards.

Collecting the information involves three tasks: identifying the jobs to be analysed, developing a job analysis questionnaire and collecting the data. In job identification, analysts first identify the jobs within the organization; in stable organizations, this can be accomplished by reading previous job analysis reports or the organization chart, or by interviewing workers. Questionnaires help analysts to gather information

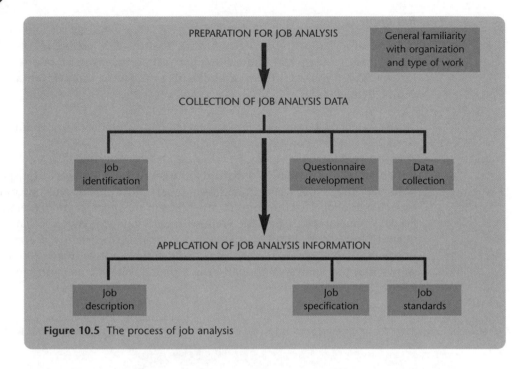

Figure 10.5 The process of job analysis

on the duties, responsibilities, human abilities and performance standards of the jobs investigated, but there is no one best way to collect the data as analysts need to make trade-offs between accuracy, time and cost. Figure 10.6 illustrates five different methods of gathering job analysis data.

Job analysis information is then used to develop job descriptions, job specifications and job performance standards:

- A *job description* is a written statement that explains the purpose, scope, duties, and responsibilities of a specified job.
- A *job specification* is a detailed statement of the human characteristics involved in the job, including aptitudes, skills, knowledge, physical demands, mental demands and the experience required to perform the job.
- A *job performance standard* is a minimum acceptable level of performance.

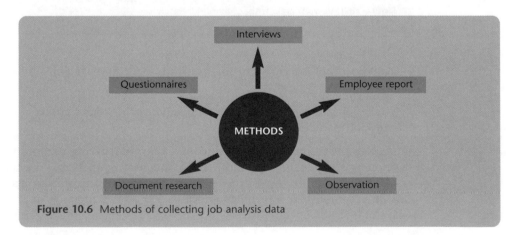

Figure 10.6 Methods of collecting job analysis data

Job evaluation

Job evaluation is a generic label for a variety of processes used to establish pay structures inside an organization. Formal job evaluation can be defined as:

> A systematic process designed to determine the relative worth of jobs within a single work organization.

The goal of job evaluation is to achieve internal equity by determining a hierarchy of jobs that is based on the relative contribution of each job to the organization. This hierarchy is then used to allocate rates of pay to jobs regardless of the incumbent. The importance of job evaluation to managers has increased because of equal pay legislation, which requires, either implicitly or explicitly, that gender-neutral job evaluation schemes be adopted and used to determine and compare the value of jobs within the organization.

Job evaluation is often misunderstood so the following three characteristics of all formal job evaluation methods need to be emphasized:

1. The technique is systematic rather than scientific, the process depending on a series of subjective judgements.
2. The premise that job evaluation is based on the worth of the job rather than on the worth of its incumbent is fundamental (Risher, 1978; Welbourne and Trevor, 2000).
3. The validity of the job evaluation process, or how accurately the method assesses job worth, is suspect (Collins and Muchinsky, 1993).

Studies have suggested that formal job evaluation offers an opportunity for discretionary decision-making, 'departmental power' thus affecting the outcome (Welbourne and Trevor, 2000). A political perspective on job evaluation also emphasizes the fact that job evaluation ratings are often gender biased through the gender linkage of job titles. In one study, for example, evaluators assigned significantly lower ratings to jobs with a female-stereotyped title, such as 'secretary–accounting', than to the same job with a more gender-neutral title, for example 'assistant–accounting' (McShane, 1990). Furthermore, the presence of job evaluation might inhibit the development of a flexible 'high-involvement' workplace. The study by McNabb and Whitfield (2001) suggests that formal job evaluation may be incompatible with a 'commitment' HR strategy because the process adds 'rigidity' to the job and the pay structure and imparts a 'top-down' ethos to decision-making.

The job evaluation process itself comprises four steps:

1. Gather the data.
2. Select compensable factors.
3. Evaluate the job.
4. Assign pay to the job.

Let us look at each of these in turn.

Gather the job analysis data

Information must be collected via a method of job analysis, and validity should be a guiding principle in this first step. The job analyser must accurately capture all the job's content, as ambiguous, incomplete or inaccurate job descriptions can result in jobs being incorrectly evaluated.

Select compensable factors
Compensable factors are the factors the organization chooses to reward through differential pay. The most typical compensable factors are skill, effort, knowledge, responsibility and working conditions.

Evaluate the job
There are four fundamental methods of job evaluation:

- ranking
- job-grading
- factor comparison
- the **point method**.

The latter is the most commonly used evaluation technique. For comparison purposes, we will provide brief descriptions of the other methods but will focus on the point method.

In *ranking*, jobs are ordered from the least to the most valued in the organization, this rank order or hierarchy of jobs being based on a subjective evaluation of relative value. In a typical factory, we might finish up with the rank order shown in Table 10.4; in this example, the evaluators have agreed that the job of inspector is the most valued of the six jobs listed. Rates of pay will then reflect this simple hierarchy. This method has a number of advantages: it is simple, fast and inexpensive. The ranking method will be attractive for small organizations and for those with a limited number of jobs. Obvious disadvantages are that it is crude and entirely subjective; the results are therefore difficult to defend, and legal challenges might make the approach costly.

Table 10.4 Typical job-ranking

Job title	Rank
	Most valued
1. Forklift driver	1. Inspector
2. Machinist	2. Machinist
3. Inspector	3. Secretary
4. Secretary	4. Forklift driver
5. File clerk	5. Labourer
6. Labourer	6. File clerk
	Least valued

Job-grading, or job classification, works by placing jobs in a hierarchy or series of job grades. It is decided in advance how many grades of pay will be created, the jobs falling into each grade based on the degree to which the jobs possess a set of compensable factors. The lowest grade will be defined as containing those jobs that require little skill and are closely supervised. With each successive grade, skills, knowledge and responsibilities increase. Grade A will, for example, include jobs that require no previous experience, are under immediate supervision and need no independent judgement. Grade F will contain jobs that require apprenticeship training under general supervision with some independent judgement. In our example in Table 10.4, the file clerk and the machinist might be slotted into grades A and F respectively. The advantage of this method is that it is relatively simple, quick and inexpensive. A disadvantage is that complex jobs are difficult to fit into the system as a job may seem to have the characteristics of two or more grades.

Factor comparison is a quantitative method that evaluates jobs on the basis of a set of compensable factors. Jobs in the organization are compared with each other across several factors, such as skill, mental effort, responsibility, physical effort and working conditions. For each job, the compensable factors are ranked according to their relative importance in each job. Once each benchmark job has been ranked on each factor, the job evaluator(s) allocate a monetary value to each factor. This is done by deciding how much of the pay rate for each benchmark job is associated with skill requirement, how much with mental effort and so on across all the compensable factors. The main disadvantage of this approach is that it is complex, and translating factor comparison into actual pay rates is a cumbersome exercise. Because of its complexity, it is used less frequently than the other methods.

The *point method* is also a quantitative method and is the most frequently used of the four techniques. Like the factor comparison method, the point method develops separate scales for each compensable factor in order to establish a hierarchy of jobs, but instead of using monetary values, points are used. Each job's relative value, and hence its location in the pay structure, is determined by adding up the points assigned to each compensable factor.

The exercise starts with the allocation of a range of points to each compensable factor. Any number between 1 and 100 points might be assigned to each factor. Next, each of the factors is given a weighting, which is an assessment of how important one factor is in relation to another. In the case of the machinist, for example, if skill is felt to be twice as important as working conditions, it is assigned twice as many points (20 versus 10). The results of the evaluation might look like those displayed in Table 10.5.

The point values allocated to each compensable factor are then added up across factors, allowing jobs to be placed in a hierarchy according to their total point value. In our example, this would mean that the machinist's wage rate would be twice that of the labourer. Such a differential might be unacceptable, but this difficulty can be overcome by tailoring the job evaluation scheme to the organization's pay policy and practical objectives.

Table 10.5 Point system matrixes

Job title	Factor					
	Skill	Mental effort	Responsibility	Physical effort	Working conditions	Total
Forklift driver	10	10	10	10	5	45
Machinist	20	15	17	8	10	70
Inspector	20	20	40	5	5	90
Secretary	20	20	35	5	5	85
File clerk	10	5	5	5	5	30
Labourer	5	2	2	17	9	35

The point system has the advantages that it is relatively stable over time and, because of its comprehensiveness, is more acceptable to interested parties. Its short-comings include a high administrative cost, which might be too high to justify its use in small organizations. A variation of the point system is the widely used 'Hay plan', which employs a standard points matrix applicable across organizational and national boundaries. Managers should, however, be aware that, as far as job evaluation is concerned, there is no perfect system because the process involves subjective judgement. Moreover, if women are employed, care needs to be taken to ensure that there is no gender bias in the job evaluation ratings, for example by giving a higher weighting to physical demands and continuous service in the organization, which tend to favour men. Aspects of the Equal Pay Act are discussed later in this chapter, the focus here having been on job evaluation as a technique to achieve internal equity in pay within the organization (HRM in Practice 10.5).

HRM IN PRACTICE 10.5

WORKERS SUE FORD FOR BIAS

N. SHIROUZU, *GLOBE AND MAIL*, 15 FEBRUARY 2001

A group of salaried workers at Ford Motor Co. has sued the auto maker, charging that it used an employee-evaluation system to weed out older workers.

The complaint comes against the backdrop of unease inside Ford about the new review policy, which marks a sharp change from the company's previous practices and is a highly visible symbol of chief executive officer Jacques Nasser's crusade to overhaul the 98-year-old company culture. The policy, a merit-based review system, was instituted at the beginning of last year. Under Mr. Nasser's evaluation system, which affects some 18,000 Ford salaried workers around the world, employees are graded A, B or C. Last year, 10 per cent of salaried workers received A grades, 80 per cent got Bs and

10 per cent received Cs.

The auto maker altered the system, analogous to the grading system on a curve used in school, for this year's evaluation so that only 5 per cent of the affected workers would receive Cs, and 85 per cent Bs

> ### Ford is committed to becoming 'a diverse company...'

and 10 per cent As. According to the company, those workers who receive Cs are not eligible for pay raises or bonuses, and those who get a C ranking for two years straight may be asked to accept demotion or leave the company.

Ford spokesman Ed Miller declined to comment specifically on the age discrimination

case, but noted that the new evaluation system is not biased against older executives and engineers. 'This suit attacks diversity, but we see diversity as being race, gender, and age,' he said. Ford is committed to becoming 'a diverse company, racially, ethnically and along gender lines, age and sexual orientation.' The suit highlights the obstacles that corporations face when they use personnel policies to affect culture.

But lawyers for the plaintiffs in the age discrimination complaint say Ford is using the evaluation system to systematically pluck out older managers. 'We believe the new evaluation system was deliberately designed to reduce Ford's workforce based on age,' said Sue Eisenberg, one of the three principal lawyers for the plaintiffs.

Assign pay to the job

The end product of a job evaluation exercise is a hierarchy of jobs in terms of their relative value to the organization. Assigning pay to this hierarchy of jobs is referred to as 'pricing the pay structure', this practice requiring a policy decision on how the organization's pay levels relate to those of their competitors.

Appraisal

Performance appraisal is the process of evaluating individuals in terms of their job performance and is examined in detail in Chapter 8. The appraisal process has come under much critical scrutiny in recent years. It is argued, for example, that the technique is designed to make employees 'known' to the organizational controllers and to assist in the process of managerial control. As such, 'appraisal remains inextricably linked to the contested terrain of control and thus lies at the heart of the management of the employment relationship' (Newton and Findlay, 1996, p. 56). It is suggested that the growing use of performance appraisal is symbolic of the desire by managers to change their organizational culture to 'a system of shared meaning' (Robbins, 1990, p. 438). The appraisal process provides a 'disciplinary matrix' with which to communicate and reinforce organizational values and inculcate employee loyalty, commitment and dependency (Legge, 2005; Townley, 1989, 1994).

Reward competitiveness

The final component of the reward management system in Figure 10.2 above is reward competitiveness, which refers to reward relationships external to the organization – comparisons with competitors (Milkovitch and Newman, 2004). How should an organization position its pay relative to what competitors are paying? The organization has three options: to be a pay leader, to match the market rate or to lag behind what competitive organizations are paying. The constraints defining the parameters within which reward choices can be made include those relating to:

- the labour market
- the product/service market
- the organization.

Labour market

Managers may typically be heard saying, 'Our pay levels are based upon the market.' Understanding markets requires an analysis of the demand for and supply of labour. The demand for people focuses on organizations' hiring behaviour and how much they are able and willing to pay their employees. The demand for HR is a derived demand in that employers require people not for their own sake but because they can help to provide goods and services, the sale of which provides revenue. The supply of HR focuses on many factors, including the wage rate for that particular occupation, its status, employees' qualifications and the preferences of people regarding paid work and leisure (see Chapter 4).

Economists inform us that, in a perfectly 'free market', the pay level of a particular occupation in a certain geographic area is determined by the interaction between demand and supply. Most markets, including labour, are not, however, free but have what economists call 'imperfections' on both the demand (e.g. discrimination) and the supply (e.g. membership of a professional body) side. The labour market provides a context for reward management and can set limits within which it operates.

Product market

Competitive pressures, both national and global, are major factors affecting levels of pay. An employer's ability to pay is constrained by her or his ability to compete, so the nature of the product market affects external competitiveness and the pay level that the organization sets. The degree of competition between producers and the level of the demand for products are the two key product market factors, both affecting the ability of the firm to change the prices of its products and services. If prices cannot be changed without suffering a loss of revenue from decreased sales, the ability of the organization to pay higher rates is constrained. The product market factors set the limits within which the pay level can be established.

Organization

Conditions in the labour market and product market set the upper limits within which the pay level can be established. Within the European Union and in many industrialized countries, the floor, or minimum, is set by minimum wage legislation. The conditions in both the labour and product markets offer managers a choice; the pay level can be set within a range of possibilities. The concept of strategic choice emphasizes the role of managerial choice in determining the pay level to be established within an organization. A general model of the factors influencing the determination of external competitiveness and pay level is presented in Figure 10.7.

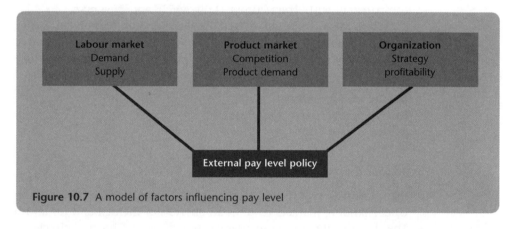

Figure 10.7 A model of factors influencing pay level

Establishing pay levels

Having considered each of the components of reward management, let us now look at how pay levels are established in practice.

The appropriate pay level for any job reflects its relative and absolute worth. A job's relative worth to the organization is determined by its ranking through the job evaluation process, whereas its absolute worth is influenced by what the labour market pays similar jobs. What is the 'going rate'? To answer this question, most organizations rely on pay surveys of key or 'benchmark' jobs; the data are used to anchor the organization's pay scale, other jobs then being slotted in on the basis of their relative worth to the organization.

HRM WEB LINKS

Go to www.statistics.gov.uk (UK New Earnings Survey), www.salariesreview.com/surveys/index.cfm, www.bls.gov, www.watsonwyatt.com, www.kpmg.com (KPMG), www.haygroup.com (Hay Management Consultants USA), www.abs.gov.au (Australia) and www.kelly.co.za (South Africa) for published pay surveys.

Determining the right pay level means combining the results of the job analysis and evaluation process (internal equity criteria) and market pay data (external competitiveness criteria) on a graph, as depicted in Figure 10.8. The horizontal axis depicts an internally consistent job structure based on job evaluation, each grade being made up of a number of jobs (A–O) within the organization. The jobs in each category are considered equal for pay purposes – they have about the same number of points. Each grade has its own pay range defining the lower and upper limits of pay for jobs in that grade, and all the jobs within the grade have the same range. Jobs in grade 1 (i.e. jobs A, B and C), for example, have lower points and pay range than jobs in grade 2 (D, E and F). The actual minimum and maximum pay rates paid by the organization's competitors are established by survey data.

Individual levels of pay within the range may reflect differences in performance or seniority. As depicted, organizations can structure their rate ranges to overlap a little with adjacent ranges so that an employee with experience or seniority might earn more than an entry-level person in the pay grade above.

Each dot on the graph in Figure 10.8 represents the intersection of the going pay rate (the vertical axis), as determined by the pay survey, and the point value (horizontal axis) for a particular benchmark job. Key jobs B, E and L are, for example, worth 100, 375 and 750 points respectively and are paid £5.50, £7.00, and £9.80 an hour. A pay trend line is drawn through the dots, as close to as many points as possible, using

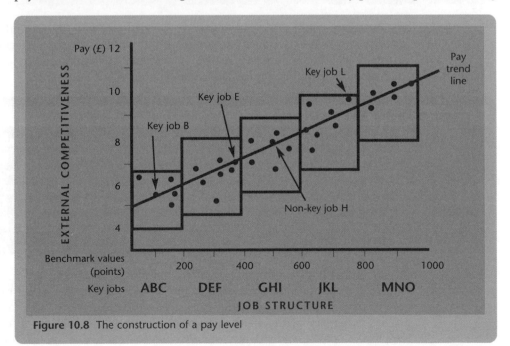

Figure 10.8 The construction of a pay level

a statistical technique called the least squares method. The pay trend line serves as a reference line around which pay structures and rates are established for non-benchmark jobs in the organization. There are two steps in this process. The first step is to locate the point value for the non-benchmark job on the horizontal axis; the second is to trace the line vertically to the pay trend line and then horizontally to the pay scale. The amount on the vertical axis is then the appropriate pay rate for the non-benchmark job. Non-benchmark job H is, for example, worth 500 points. By tracing a vertical line up to the paytrend line and then horizontally to the vertical pay scale in Figure 10.8, it can be seen that the appropriate pay rate for job H is £8.00 per hour. Thus, both market survey information and job evaluation translate the concepts of external competitiveness and internal equity into pay practices.

Once a pay trend line has been established, management has three choices – to lead the competition, to match what other organizations are paying or to lag behind what competitors are paying their employees – establishing a lag or lead policy by shifting the pay trend line down or up. The least risk approach is to set the pay level to match that of the competition, although some organizations may set different pay policies for different categories of employee with different skill sets. The company could, for example, adopt a 'lead' policy for critical skills, such as computer design engineers, a 'match' policy for less critical skill sets and a 'lag' policy for jobs that could be easily filled in the local labour market. A variety of pay policies may thus exist within organizations. Although the pay levels within an organization reflect external competitiveness and internal equity considerations, the decision on the final pay level – the organization's pay policy – will be determined by many factors, including competitive strategy, HR strategy, reward objectives, organizational design and culture.

Government and pay

In European states and North America, government has a profound impact, both directly and indirectly, on employees' reward. In Britain, the *direct* effect on pay occurs through legislation and pay control plans, the key legislation related to reward management being shown in Table 10.6.

HRM WEB LINKS

Go to the following websites to compare employment standards legislation relating to reward: www.hmso.gov.uk/acts.htm provides Acts of Parliament for the UK in full; www.labour-travail.hrdc-drhc.gc.ca/sfmc_fmcs/index.cfm?fuseaction=english gives information on Canadian employment standards and legislation. When there, click on the 'Employment law' button. For other countries, see a list of links at the beginning of this book. Are there any major differences in the statutory provision provided by your jurisdiction and that of others?

Government can also directly affect reward management by introducing pay control programmes, which typically aim to maintain low inflation by limiting the size of pay increases. Pay controls can vary in the broadness of their application and in the stringency of the standard applied. Broadness of application can include all employees, public and private, or focus on one particular group, for example the government's own employees. The standard for allowable pay increases can range from zero to increases equal to some change in the consumer price index or a measure of labour productivity. Over the past two decades, numerous governments have used a tight control of public sector pay to influence pay trends in their economies. In Britain, the Conservative government's approach to public sector pay was summarized over a decade ago by Norman Lamont, then chief secretary to the Treasury, when he said that the government had used a 'combination of pressures' to 'reproduce the discipline which markets exert in the private sector'.[4]

Table 10.6 Key UK legislation relating to reward management

Act	Date	Coverage
Equal Pay Act	1970	Male and female employees to receive equal pay for like work, equivalent work and work of equal value
Sex Discrimination Act	1986	Removal from the employer's pay structure, wage regulations, collective agreement, and so on, of any term that is discriminatory
Social Security and Contribution and Benefits Act	1992	Enforcement of statutory maternity pay for a maximum of 18 weeks Employer responsible for sick pay for the first 28 weeks of absence through sickness
Employment Rights Act	1996	Restricts unauthorized deductions and payments from the wages of employees Guaranteed payment for a whole day Right to an itemized pay statement Notice pay if the employer becomes insolvent
National Minimum Wage Act	1999	Enforcement of a statutory minimum wage Written statement on wage calculations
Employment Act	2002	Enforcement of statutory paternity and maternity pay Details of rate of statutory pay
National Minimum Wage Act	2003	Enforcement notice requiring an employer to pay the minimum wage to an employee amended in relation to past periods and termination of employment

In addition, government has an *indirect* influence on the pay-setting process, as depicted in Figure 10.9. Government actions affect both the demand and supply of labour, and consequently pay levels. First, legislation can restrict the *supply* of labour in an occupation: a statute setting minimum age limits would, for example, restrict the supply of young people. Second, government also affects the *demand* for labour. The government is a major employer and therefore a dominant force in determining pay levels in and beyond the public sector. Another indirect influence on pay levels, by affecting the markets and in turn pay, comprises government fiscal and monetary policies. Reward techniques (performance appraisal and job evaluation) and outcomes (pay levels and pay structures) must also comply with the laws passed by Parliament. This responsibility usually falls on the HR specialist. Given the importance of equal pay legislation for reward management, the next section examines the important issue of pay equity.

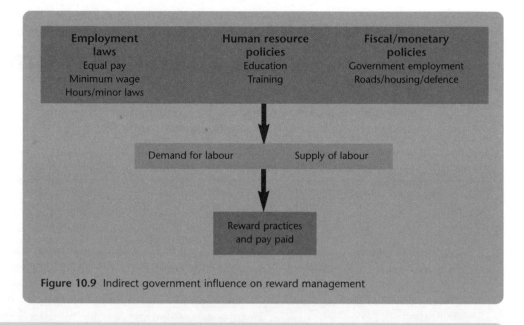

Figure 10.9 Indirect government influence on reward management

REFLECTIVE QUESTION

It has been pointed out by some that minimum wage regulations increase the cost of doing business and cause unemployment. What do you think of this argument? Go to www.fraserinstitute.ca and www.clc-ctc.ca for contrasting views on this issue.

Equal pay legislation

Discriminatory employment practices are a manifestation of prejudicial patterns of behaviour in society generally.[5]

Pay equity is important to all workers and thus has implications for satisfaction with the level of pay (Brown, 2001). The concept of pay equity is in conflict with the view that employees' pay should be dictated by the supply and demand of labour. Equal pay legislation has existed in the UK for three decades, but its origins can be traced back to 1919 when the International Labour Organization made the concept of equal pay for work of equal value one of its founding principles. Then, in 1951, the International Labour Organization passed Convention 100: 'Each member shall ... ensure the application to all workers of the principle of equal remuneration for men and women workers for work of equal value.' In 1972, the UK became bound to Article 19 of the EEC's Treaty of Rome, which stated that 'Each member state shall ... maintain the application of the principle that men and women should receive equal pay for equal work.' The Equal Pay Act 1970 inserted into contracts of employment an implied term, the 'equality clause'. This enforced equal terms in the contract of employment for women in the same employment, requiring the elimination of less favourable terms where men and women were employed on like work, and where a job evaluation assessor had rated the work as equivalent in the same employment (HRM in Practice 10.6).

HRM IN PRACTICE 10.6

PART-TIME LECTURER WINS PRECEDENT-SETTING VICTORY

CAUT BULLETIN, 53(2) FEBRUARY 2006

A university lecturer has won an important settlement which may ensure that part-time British academic staff are paid a pro-rata equivalent to their full-time colleagues.

Susan Birch, who was employed on a part-time basis at Leeds Metropolitan University, challenged her inadequate pay and precarious job status using the European Union's Part Time Workers (Less Favourable Treatment) Regulations 2000. The regulations put in place minimum standards for rates of pay, access to pension and other benefits, training opportunities and other working conditions.

Birch worked as a teacher trainer and taught English as a second language for seven years, teaching more hours than her full-time colleagues for less pay.

She took the university to court after reading about new laws regulating the use of part-time workers. The lecturers' union, NATFHE, supported her through the three-year employment tribunal process, viewing it as a landmark case that could represent major gains for thousands of hourly-paid employees.

> ‘Many experience poverty pay, job insecurity and poor working conditions...’

The university agreed to a settlement just before the case was due to go to a final hearing, Birch received £25,000 in compensation and was transferred to a full-time position.

NATFHE General Secretary Paul Mackney said the case establishes that part-time lecturers are entitled to equal, pro-rata pay rates to full-time colleagues.

‘This will bring confidence and hope to thousands of badly paid lecturers in further and high education. More than 40 per cent of university teaching staff are on hourly-paid contracts. Many experience poverty pay, job insecurity and poor working conditions – often not even having a desk’.

NATFHE is continuing to work on the long-term goal of a fully pro-rata system, where part-time staff are employed with equivalent rates of pay and working conditions to full-time colleagues.

Despite the existence of equal pay legislation in the UK since 1975, the income disparity between men and women is widely acknowledged (Figure 10.10). In Britain, although the gender pay gap narrowed a little between 2003 and 2004, women's median hourly pay was still 85.7 per cent of men's pay. On the internationally comparable measure, women's average hourly pay (excluding overtime) was 81.8 per cent of men's pay (New Earnings Survey, 2005).

Equal pay legislation has failed to address the problem of *occupational segregation*, that is, the gap between the types of job performed by men and those performed by women, which is acknowledged to be an important source of lower earnings for women relative to men. Research suggests that the percentage of women employed in an occupation is negatively associated with earnings: ‘In sum, being a woman has a negative effect on income’, conclude Gattiker and Cohen (1997, p. 523). One commentator has also suggested that equal pay for women will not be guaranteed by legislation alone but will be secured ‘only when its justice is adequately understood and practised by men’ (Wedderburn, 1986, p. 503).

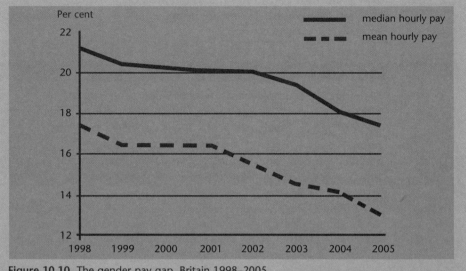

Figure 10.10 The gender pay gap, Britain 1998–2005

Source: New Earnings Survey (2005) National Statistics Online www.statistics.gov.uk/cci/

HRM WEB LINKS

Go to the following websites to compare men's and women's pay levels: www.statistics.gov.uk, www.ilo.org, www.clc.ca, www.tom.quack.net/wagegap.html, www.statssa.gov.za and www.abs.gov.au. How does pay for women compare with that for men in your jurisdiction?

In 1982, the European Court held that the UK's Equal Pay Act did not comply with Article 119 of the Treaty of Rome because equal pay was available for work of equal value only when the employer had chosen to conduct a job evaluation study, which a woman could in fact compel her employer to do. Consequently, the Equal Pay Act was amended by the 1983 Equal Pay (Amendment) Regulations; this means that even where there is no 'like work' or non-discriminatory job evaluation, the equality clause entitles a woman to conditions corresponding to those of a man if her work is of 'equal value'. The new Regulations were first tested in the case of *Hayward* v. *Cammell Laird Shipbuilders Ltd* [1987], in which a cook – supported by her trade union and the Equal Opportunities Commission – established her work as being of equal value to that of men working in the shipyard as insulation engineers, painters and joiners. Conway (1987) argues that 'The equal value concept recognizes that occupational segregation persists and that the concomitant under-valuation of "women's" work is responsible for a large part of the earning s gap.' The European Commission further expanded the provision for equal opportunities within the European Union with the Fourth Medium-Term Action Programme on Equal Opportunities, which came into operation on 1 January 1996 (see Singh, 1997).

All legislation requires, either implicitly or explicitly, that gender-neutral job evaluation schemes be adopted or developed and used to determine and compare the value of female-dominated and male-dominated jobs. Formal job evaluation can be seen as important in generating a feeling of equity in the workplace (McNabb and Whitfield,

2001) and thus constitutes the foundation of pay equity (Conway, 1987). It is critical that job evaluation schemes are designed and applied with the least possible amount of bias, particularly gender bias.

Paradox and reward

Let us finish our discussion of reward management by examining some of the fallacies and inconsistencies inherent in reward systems and, through the work of Edmund Heery (2000), some ethical concerns with new pay models.

The objectives of the new reward model are identified in normative models of HRM, including employee commitment and functional flexibility. Managers' attempts to foster worker commitment through variable or contingency pay arrangements, however, might be undermined if reward to superior performers could not be paid because of the poor financial performance of the company. Disappointment resulting from unfulfilled expectations might be a source of dissatisfaction with the organization, leading to a breach of the psychological contract rather than increased commitment. Betcherman et al. (1994), for example, note that most variable reward systems fail to 'stick' for economic reasons: there are no profits or productivity gains to share. We should note Beer et al.'s (1984) and Pfeffer's (1998) argument that IPRP creates tensions that can undermine workers' 'intrinsic motivation'. Furthermore, IPRP is prone to the 'twin vices of subjectivity and inconsistency' (Kessler, 1994) and might become discredited in the eyes of subordinates because of perceived 'procedural injustices' caused by subjective and inconsistent appraisals by managers. The literature would suggest that if this occurred, the psychological contract would be breached and employee commitment weakened.

The goal of flexibility through a pay-for-knowledge system might also not be achieved because of economic reasons, especially if the high cost of paying for additional skills, which is not directly relevant to increasing productivity, leads to the 'capping' of skill or knowledge acquisition. Again, in the context of raised employee expectations, disappointment is likely to impact negatively on the psychological contract and the commitment goal.

Heery's (2000) criticism of the new pay is based on its 'ethical deficiencies'. He argues that ethicists interested in HRM should be concerned about new reward practices for two reasons:

- increased employee risk
- diminished collective representation in reward systems.

The movement towards variable or contingency pay and benefits represents a dramatic growth in pay-at-risk for employees, a characteristic of other 'innovative' management practices such as outsourcing. New reward practices cause *employee risk* by increasing the proportion of pay that is contingent on individual, team or organizational performance. The link between pay and working time, for instance, which offers more predictable earnings for employees, will be progressively reduced. Another major ethical concern with the new reward model is the decline of *collective representation* in the effort–reward process. New reward systems have been adopted at a time when trade union membership and collective bargaining power have declined in Britain and the USA. The absence of a strong collective voice in the reward process arguably means that the new reward 'is potentially unjust in both procedural and distributive senses; and that it affords little scope for the exercise of democratic rights by citizens at the place of work' (Heery, 2000, pp. 182–3).

Finally, we should appreciate the relationship between the choice of payment system and managerial power. The selection of the reward system does not operate in a vacuum, reward practices being dictated by perceptions of power between labour and management. The implication is that we can predict that pay systems will change according to their effectiveness, vis-à-vis the relationship of effort to wages (Baldamus, 1961) and the balance of power (Nichols, 1980). In the context of a neutered, politically weak labour movement (e.g. Australia, Britain, New Zealand and the USA), it seems that managers' interests have focused on reward systems that link pay to individual performance. The balance of power between workers and management is a strategic factor that helps to explain the selection of pay arrangements within any HR strategy.

Chapter summary

- This chapter has emphasized that reward management is central to the effective management of the employment relationship. A reward system influences at least two important employee behaviours: membership behaviour and conflict behaviour, which may derive from employee dissatisfaction with the reward system.

- A reward system is a key mechanism that can influence each step of the strategy process. Current new pay literature stresses that an 'effective' pay system is one that is aligned with the organization's business strategy.

- We discussed in the chapter why no single best pay system exists. A pay system that may seem highly appropriate in one period, with a particular organization and work design supporting a management strategy, can be highly inappropriate in the next, when the business strategy and organizational design has changed.

- We explained that changes in reward systems reflect shifts in management thinking. The adoption of more IPRP systems is ideologically driven to encourage entrepreneurial behaviour, although there is an apparent lack of consensus on the type of reward system that might encourage such attitudinal and behavioural change (Kessler, 2001).

- We have examined the complex argument that reward practices create, fulfil, change or violate the psychological contract, explaining how this phenomenon involves perceptual and cognitive processes that convince the employee that the organization has 'reneged' on the contract.

- The pay model we have developed shows that reward is multidimensional, incorporating such aspects as pay structures, pay levels, incentives and benefits. It emphasizes two fundamental policy issues: internal equity and external competitiveness.

- We have also examined how government intervenes both directly and indirectly in the pay determination process. Keeping up to date and complying with pay legislation is a prime responsibility of HRM specialists.

- We have explored some of the tension in reward systems. Under the logic of political economy, pay systems – whether associated with 'hard' or 'soft' HRM models – cannot obviate the contradictory tensions that bedevil employment relations.

- Finally, we focused on some 'ethical deficiencies' associated with the new reward model. We explained that the movement towards variable or contingency pay and benefits generates employee risk in remuneration. We also discussed how, with the absence of a strong collective representation in the reward process, the new reward practices potentially undermine democratic rights in the workplace.

Key concepts

- **Job evaluation**
- **Pay equity**
- **Internal equity**
- **Pay model**
- **Job analysis**
- **Point method**

Chapter review questions

1. Explain the statement 'The design of reward systems is contingent upon the organizational context in which they must operate.'

2. How does reward affect and shape the psychological contract?

3. Is money the prime driver of employee performance?

4. 'New payment systems generate greater employee risk and diminish democratic rights in the workplace.' Discuss.

5. 'Equal pay for women will be secure only when its justice is adequately understood and practised by men' (Wedderburn, 1986). Do you agree or disagree? Discuss.

Further reading

Beer, M. and Cannon, M. (2004) Promise and peril in implementing pay-for-performance. *Human Resource Management*, **43**(1): 3–48.

Chartered Institute of Personnel and Development (2006b) *Reward Management: Survey Report*. London: CIPD.

Guthrie, J. P. and Hollensbe, E. C. (2004) Group incentives and performance: a study of spontaneous goal setting, goal choice and commitment. *Journal of Management*, **30**(2): 263–84.

Heery, E. (2000) The new pay: risk and representation at work. In D. Winstanley and J. Woodall (eds) *Ethical Issues in Contemporary Human Resource Management* (pp. 172–88). Basingstoke: Palgrave Macmillan.

Kersley, B., Alpin, C., Forth, J., Bryson, A., Bewley, H. Dix, G. and Oxenbridge, S. (2006) The determinants of pay and other terms and conditions. In Kersley et al. (eds) *Inside the Workplace: Findings from the 2004 Workplace Employment Relations Survey* (pp. 178–206). London: Routledge.

Kessler, I. (2001) Reward system choices. In J. Storey (ed.) *Human Resource Management: A Critical Text* (2nd edn) (pp. 206–31). London: Thomson Learning.

Morrison, E. and Robinson, S. (1997) When employees feel betrayed: a model of how psychological contract violation develops. *Academy of Management Review*, **22**(1): 226–56.

Paauwe, J. (2004) *HRM and Performance*. New York: Oxford University Press.

Rynes, S. and Gerhart, B. (eds) (2000) *Compensation in Organizations: Current Research and Practice*. San Francisco: Jossey-Bass.

Singh, R. (1997) Equal opportunities for men and women in the EU: a commentary. *Industrial Relations Journal*, **28**(1): 68–71.

Practising human resource management

Searching the web

On an individual basis, or working in a small group, pick two or three online HR-related websites (e.g. www.rewardstrategies.com, www.evanomics.com, www.remuneration.org, www.shrm.org/hrlinks, www.compensationcanada.com, www.bizcenter.com/designing.htm, www.hkihrm.org, www.ahri.com.au and www.ipm.co.za) and explore 'Rewards/compensation and benefits'. Also enter the website of an organization you or the group are familiar with, or one you have studied (e.g. www.britishairways.com). From the information in this chapter and from your research, develop two or three reward objectives and decide what types of reward you would include in a reward system. Explain the reasons for your choice. Bring this information to class and present your findings and recommendation in an oral report.

HRM group project

Form a group of three or four students. The purpose of this group assignment is to allow you to apply your knowledge of reward theory to a business organization. Specifically, students will:

- Carry out research on secondary and primary sources related to reward management
- Apply key principles and theories to a case
- Demonstrate academic writing skills.

Each group member should take responsibility for researching the various aspects of the assignment.

One team member(s) should interview at least one manager or an HR professional responsible for rewards. The interviewer(s) should probe the nature of the organization's reward strategy and system: What is the organization's reward strategy? How does the reward strategy relate to business strategy? In addition, ask about reward options: What is the mix between base, performance and indirect pay? What new reward systems have been introduced, and why?

CITY BANK

The past decade has been a watershed for the UK banking industry, particularly for City Bank, a medium-sized clearing bank. Following the deregulation of the financial sector in 1986, City Bank has faced increased competition from other financial institutions, for example building societies, an intense squeeze on profit margins and the need to make considerable provisions for bad debts. Under such pressure, City Bank introduced new technology, new financial products and a new reward system for bank managers and staff. Information and communication technologies enabled the bank to process much larger volumes of business, and, just as importantly, these new technologies themselves facilitated the development of new, technically based, products and services (such as home banking, smart cards and debit cards) that City Bank started to market to its customers.

Running parallel with these technical changes was the dismantling of the paternalistic personnel management system. In essence, City Bank's bureaucratic culture and its associated belief system for managers and staff of appropriate behaviour being rewarded by steady promotion through the ranks was swept aside. The new culture in the fast-changing environment emphasized customer service and the importance of measuring and rewarding staff according to their performance. Other features of the new culture were the widening gulf between career and non-career staff, the segmentation of recruitment and training, growing occupational specialization and a declining employment level.

The new performance-related reward system was introduced at a senior management meeting in January 1996. Addressing the meeting, Elizabeth Mulberry, director of human resources, said that the proposed reward system would be a key strategy to 'maintain our share of the high street business'. She went on to outline that the salary of bank managers would in future be tied to their 'leadership skills and the quality of customer service'. The CEO of City Bank explained the new direction as follows.

City Bank's culture has entered a new phase, and the climate is favourable for a shift in emphasis from management by paternalism to management by leadership. It is essential that bank managers ensure that the broad picture is known, understood and reflected in measurable personal objectives for those in their management team. Branch leadership also requires the ability to discriminate in the reward given to the exceptional compared with the standard performance.

Under the new reward system, the pay of each branch manager would be linked to her or his leadership skills and the quality of customer service. The reward system would link managers' pay to behaviour traits relating to leadership and customer service. Central to the drive for quality customer service, explained Elizabeth Mulberry, would be the way in which bank managers and their staff treated their customers. A questionnaire would be periodically sent out to a sample of the branch's customers, and the branch manager and staff would be evaluated for base salary on such variables as the length of time that customers queued for service, customer focus and the ability to communicate bank products and services. In turn, each bank manager would be rated on bank revenue variables (e.g. the number of new mortgages, employee development and leadership).

According to the interoffice memorandum that was to be sent out to the 400 branch managers, variable pay for both managers and staff was to be based on what was accomplished: 'because customer service is central to City Bank's strategic plan, a three category rating system that involves "not meeting" customer expectations, "meeting" them or "far exceeding" them is the essence of the new reward system.'

Assignment

As a research assistant for Right Consulting Services, a large consulting firm that specializes in management development in the finance and banking sector, you have been given the task of drafting a report to one of the firm's associates, Dr Perry.

Your report to Dr Perry should:

1. Outline the merits and limitations of City Bank's proposed reward system for the managers and staff

2. Identify an alternative reward system for City Bank's employees congruent with their strategic plan.

HR-related skill development

The formal job evaluation process is concerned with assessing the relative worth of different jobs in an organization rather than the performance of the individual employee occupying the position. As we have emphasized in this chapter, the process is systematic rather than scientific, depending on the judgement of people. To give you experience of the job evaluation process using the point method, we have devised a fairly realistic simulation of what would go on in a job evaluation committee. You can participate in the simulation and develop an important HR skill by going to our website, www.palgrave.com/business/brattonandgold4 and clicking on 'Job evaluation exercise'.

Notes

1. Herbert, S. (1991) Organizations and markets. *Journal of Economic Perspectives* **5**(33); quoted in Pfeffer (1998, p. 215).
2. Richard Johnston, human resources director of Flowpak Engineering; quoted by Bratton (1992, p. 171).
3. *Globe and Mail*, 1997, August 26, p. B12.
4. Quoted in *Future Uncertain for Public Sector Pay*. Bargaining Report, Labour Research Department, May 1991.
5. Smith, A., Craver, C. and Clark, L. (1982) *Employment Discrimination Law* (2nd edn) (p. 1); quoted in Lord Wedderburn (1986, p. 447).

Chapter eleven

Union–management relations

John Bratton

Union–management relations address the collective aspects
of the employment relationship and focus on the relations between
organized employees (represented by a union) and management, as well
as on the processes within which a union and an employer interact
to regulate the employment contract.

'The increasingly powerful "new economy" seems to offer little role or place for trade unions.'[1]

*'Pay, the principal component of any employment contract, is now fixed by formal collective
bargaining for no more than one-third of the employed population.'*[2]

*'"New record high for employers recognizing unions in 2001." This report confirms that unions
are very much back in business and that employers want to do business with them. Sensible
employers understand that today's unions seek partnership and good working relationships.
They can be good for business, as well as good for staff.'*[3]

*'During the past half century the rights of workers have been diminishing: so too has
been their ability to exercise their dwindling rights.'*[4]

Chapter outline

Chapter objectives

After studying this chapter, you should be able to:

1. Describe contemporary trends in union–management relations
2. Explain and critically evaluate different types of union–management strategy
3. Explain the pattern of trade union membership and union structure
4. Understand the nature and importance of collective bargaining
5. Describe the core legal principles relating to union–management relations
6. Critically evaluate the importance of 'new unionism' and 'partnership' for
   union–management relations

Introduction

Union–management relations address the collective dimension of the employment relationship. Over the past two decades, part of Anglo-American management parlance has insisted that trade unions in a postindustrial era represent little more than dinosaurs from the past. We disagree with this. The management of work and people includes both individual and collective relations (Boxall and Purcell, 2003; Kelly, 2005). As a field of study, however, academics differ over the use of the terms 'industrial relations', 'labour relations', 'employment relations' and 'union–management relations' (see Godard, 2005; Kelly, 2005; Wajcman, 2000; Wood, 2000), but in this chapter we use the terms interchangeably. In so doing, we focus upon the relationship between organized labour and management, the balance of power between the two parties, the amount of conflict underlying this relationship, and the extent to which pay and conditions of employment relationship are determined by collective bargaining.

Trade unions and union–management relations remain important in understanding the contexts that affect and shape human resource management (HRM) and, more importantly, in providing a workers' collective voice in managerial decision-making in the workplace (Gollan, 2006; Purcell, 2004). It should also be noted that some employment policies – pay and benefits, employee involvement schemes and joint consultation – can result from employee relations policies, union–management policies or both, and in the workplace the policies may be virtually indistinguishable between union and non-union settings (Gunderson et al., 2001).

Over the past two decades, British union–management relations have been substantially modified by a combination of economic, political and social factors. Indeed, the new economic and legal climate has changed the landscape of union–management relations so much as to cause one industrial relations scholar to state: 'It is difficult to believe that such a world existed less than twenty years ago' (Hyman, 1997b, p. 317). In Chapter 4, we provided a survey of these economic and political developments and discussed the beginning of a process of change and adaptation on the part of management and labour. With the election of the Conservative government in 1979, many observers consider the period 1983–87 to be a 'watershed' in British union–management relations. In addition, although the history of British union–management relations can cite a number of watersheds, what is not in doubt is that the past three decades have witnessed major contextual changes, including the shift from manufacturing to service employment, the ascendency of neoconservative and neoliberal ideologies that make the market supreme, the promotion of individualism over employment decisions, the creation of laws hostile to trade unions and collective bargaining (Cully et al., 1999; Kersley et al., 2006; Marginson and Wood, 2000; Millward et al., 2000; Smith and Morton, 2006).

The experience of fundamental change in the context, institutions and processes of union–management relations has not been unique to the UK. In the rest of the European Union (EU), the traditional pattern of union–management relations also underwent profound modifications. Throughout Europe, the drive for competitive advantage has been pursued consistently and universally, and employers and managers have demonstrated initiative and determination in remodelling their national industrial relations systems. European employers have, for example, increasingly exercised their prerogative over key business decisions and enhanced management legitimacy, with government help, by popularizing the ideological argument for the veneration of the 'marketplace'. European trade unions have been weakened both numerically and politically, and have been forced, in general, to retreat. The trade unions' participation in the collective bargaining process has similarly been marked by retreat and action to defend living standards, working conditions and rules governing the use of human resources (Baglioni and Crouch, 1991). The response to intensified global competition has not, however, been the same in every EU member state (Morley et al., 2000). Thus, in some respects, the pattern of European industrial relations systems remains sharply diversified, as it was in the 1970s. In other respects, however, comparative analysis reveals similarities between member states, pointing to what writers refer to as a 'transnational convergence' (Baglioni and Crouch, 1991; Morley et al., 2000; Streeck and Visser, 1997).

In North America, global competition over the past two decades has resulted in changes in the USA that have prompted some writers to describe the 'transformation of American industrial relations' (Kochan et al., 1986). Although the transformation thesis might be an exaggeration of the perceived changes in that country, and although the thesis is not universally accepted in the USA, US companies have, with government indulgence, persuaded or compelled a weakened trade union movement to accept significant changes in collective agreements and working practices. Furthermore, US companies have increasingly turned to a union-free environment, what is referred to as a 'union replacement' strategy. This management response to unions includes relocating the business to a rural region where unionization is less well developed (e.g. southern states such as Kentucky) and/or using consultants to run employee programmes to induce the workforce to consider withdrawing from their union. Industrial relations in different parts of North America have not, however, all followed identical routes. As numerous Canadian scholars have pointed out, Canadian unions have, in terms of legal support for unions, membership trends and bargaining strength, enjoyed relative success compared with unions in the USA and Britain (Murray, 2001).

Running parallel with (and not unrelated to) these contextual and union–management changes has, of course, been the ascendancy of the HRM model. Much of the critical literature presents the HRM model as being inconsistent with traditional union–management relations and collective bargaining, albeit for very different reasons (Godard, 1991; Guest, 1995; Wells, 1993). Critics argue not only that HRM policies and practices shift the mode of regulating the employment contract from the collective towards the individual, but also that the HRM paradigm is designed with the object of weakening or avoiding union presence in the workplace (Godard, 2005).

Others, however, have argued that independent trade unions and variants of the HRM model can not only coexist, but are even necessary to its successful implementation and development. They argue that trade unions should become proactive or change 'champions', actively promoting the more positive elements of the soft HRM model (Betcherman et al., 1994; Guest, 1995; Verma, 1995). Part of this discourse is the idea of **social partnership**, which has recently moved to the centre stage of British union–management relations (Bacon and Storey, 2000). The social partnership model is conceptualized in terms of 'mutual gains' for both unions and the organization. For the unions, partnership offers union representatives 'a place at the table' and the potential opportunity to revitalize union influence and membership in the workplace (Coupar and Stevens, 1998). For the employer, partnership can offer flexible working, employee commitment and the opportunity to undertake major restructuring with union support (Heery, 2002). Not surprisingly, the notion of social partnership and its potential benefits to the stakeholders is subject to considerable debate in the HRM/industrial relations literature.

The HRM/industrial relations discourse poses some interesting questions for academics and practitioners. Can, for example, a worker be simultaneously committed to the goals of both the organization and the trade union? How does the HRM concept of 'high worker commitment' present a threat to unions? Is 'dual commitment' possible? Can HRM-inspired initiatives, such as work teams, coexist with seniority and 'job control' unionism? In terms of the individualization of the employment relationship, can the HRM model function alongside traditional collective bargaining? Is the social partnership model compatible with the traditional role of unions, which is to defend their members' interests? Some industrial relations scholars suggest that trade unions face strategic choices: they can either simply oppose the changes or opt for a proactive interventionist strategy that will embrace the more positive elements of the HRM model. Others, meanwhile, cogently argue that HRM and strong unions are incompatible.

This chapter examines these interrelated questions by providing an analysis of management and union strategies. After defining union–management relations and the scope of this interdisciplinary field of study, we deal with a number of strategic decisions that management must take with regard to trade unions. The chapter then proceeds to discuss trends in union membership and structure, collective bargaining and the legal context of union–management relations. Finally, the chapter turns to the issue of social partnership, 'worker commitment' and an assessment of the unions' response to the HRM model and union contraction.

REFLECTIVE QUESTION

Look again at the quotations at the start of this chapter. Do you think that unions have a role to play in the new so-called 'knowledge-based' economy?

Union–management relations

As we mentioned above, there is controversy among the academic community over the precise meaning and relevance of the term 'industrial relations'. Much of the debate concerns reappraising the significance of industrial relations in the light of declining union membership, the contraction of collective bargaining and the apparent marginalization of traditional industrial relations, in the research and academic community as well as in the workplace. As Wood (2000, p. 1) suggests, the 'lifeblood' of industrial relations – unions and collective bargaining – 'once so central … seem to have ceased to be of such consuming interest'. It has therefore become widely accepted that union–management or industrial relations must be reconceptualized and extend its focus beyond unions, collective bargaining and strikes to a broader concern with the employment relationship (Taras et al., 2001; Wood, 2000). Furthermore, it is acknowledged that any reconceptualization of modern union–management relations must focus sufficient attention on the fact that these principal institutions and processes are not gender-neutral but reflect 'masculine priorities and privilege' in work organizations (Wajcman, 2000, p. 183).

In a non-unionized workplace, managers have flexibility in designing work, selecting, promoting and training people, and determining rewards and other HRM practices, but much of this can change when workers join a union. After recognizing the union, representatives from union and management negotiate a collective agreement that spells out details of the employment relationship that will be *jointly* determined. This can typically include establishing some control over each of the four key HR policies and practices of the HRM model shown in Figure 1.4:

- First and foremost, unions seek to control *rewards* and attempt to maximize the pay side of the wage–effort contract.
- In the area of *recruitment and selection*, unions have, in some industries at least (e.g. construction, film and theatre), had some control over external recruiting.
- Unions also take an active interest in work-related learning and *employee development*, trying to ensure that training opportunities are distributed equitably and that the employer adheres to the principle of maintained earnings during training.
- Perhaps most controversially, the whole practice of *employee appraisal* poses challenges to the unions. The central tenet of traditional unionism has been the collectivist culture, namely the insistence on rewards according to the same definite standard and its application in the workplace. Such collectivist goals have resulted in unions strongly resisting all forms of performance appraisal based on individual performance.

These examples illustrate that 'control over work relations' (Hyman, 1975, p. 31) is a central feature of union–management relations. Union–management relations, for current purposes, refers to:

- the *relations* between organized employees (represented by a union) and management
- the *processes* that regulate the employment contract
- the *context* within which a union and an employer interact.

Let us briefly expand on the components of this definition. The 'relations' between the workforce and management are both economic and social: it is an economic relation because employers buy employees' physical and mental abilities, and it is a social relation because when employees enter into a contract they agree to comply with the employer's standards and rules. These relationships between the workforce and management may be played out in different arenas – at the workplace level, at the industry level and at the national level – where union, employer and government representatives participate in a social dialogue on economic and employment-related issues.

The term 'processes' refers to collective bargaining, by which unions represent their members' interests through formal negotiations with management representatives. 'Context' refers to the economic, legal and political conditions and constraints within which union–management relations take place. Our definition of union–management relations recognizes the fluidity of contexts and the processes of control over the employment relationship. This dynamic mix means that, in a unionized environment, managing the interactions between union and management representatives can be a significant area of HRM activity.

HRM WEB LINKS

Go to www.eiro.eurofound.ie/ for information on economic, political and collective bargaining developments in the EU. For information on industrial relations in North America, go to the website at Cornell University (www.workindex.com/) and click on 'Labour relations'. See also www.ir-net.co.za (S. Africa) and the list at the beginning of the book.

Management strategies

Management plays a predominant role in constructing collective relations in the workplace, managers shaping the options and largely determining the outcomes (Hyman, 1997a), and employees and their unions generally reacting to management initiatives (HRM in Practice 11.1). Over the past two decades, British scholars have shown a much greater interest in the study of management and **management strategy**, and there is a large body of literature that examines the links between 'new' management organizational practices (Chapter 5) and management behaviour. A number of empirical studies have investigated how British managers have reorganized the conduct of workplace union–management relations (see, for example, Cully et al., 1999; Gollan, 2002; Guest, 1995; Kersley et al., 2006; Millward and Stevens, 1986; Millward et al., 1992, 2000).

HRM IN PRACTICE 11.1

WAL-MART WORKERS VOTE FOR UNION
Retail giant vows to appeal the decision by tire and lube employees in Surrey store

PETER KENNEDY, *GLOBE AND MAIL*, 10 MARCH 2006, P.S3

A small group of Wal-Mart Canada employees in Surrey touched off a war of words yesterday by voting to be certified as members of the United Food and Commercial Works Union.

Andy Neufeld, a spokesman for the UFCWU, called the decision a 'big, big step to take,' and said the Lube Express shop workers deserve praise for their courage in deciding to join the union by a margin of seven to two. In reaching the decision, they have joined tire and lube workers in Cranbrook, B.C., who elected to join the UFCWU last September.

'It is a positive signal to other Wal-Mart employees, that despite the company's drastic efforts to keep unions out, the logic of joining a union is pretty powerful,' Mr. Neufeld said. The next step, he said, will be to try to reach a collective agreement with the retail giant, which has 70,000 employees in Canada, at 256 stores across the country.

But if Wal-Mart's previous labour practices in Canada are any indication, the union clearly faces an uphill struggle. 'This decision will be appealed,' Wal-Mart Canada spokesman Andrew Pelletier said.

> **So far, the UFCWU has been unable to implement a collective agreement in Canada.**

Mr. Pelletier said Wal-Mart store employees, known as associates, typically work as a cohesive unit.

'Therefore we think it is complexly unrepresentative and frankly undemocratic to try to carve out from a store of about 250–300, seven to 10 workers, and say they should be a separate bargaining unit'. In cases where Wal-Mart associates were allowed to hold storewide votes on whether to be certified, they have always voted against joining a union. So far, the UFCWU has been unable to implement a collective agreement in Canada.

Mr. Neufeld said he is well aware of the challenges that lie ahead. 'Wal-Mart pours a phenomenal amount of money and resources and lawyers as part of their effort to just litigate and delay and deny their employees the right to join a union,' he said. 'To be sure, it is an uphill struggle.' Wal-Mart is appealing a certification vote by the Cranbrook workers.

The company closed its store in Jonquière, Que., in April of 2005 after it became the first in North America to unionize. Wal-Mart said the store was unprofitable. But last September, the Quebec Labour Board ruled that the closing of the Wal-Mart store amounted to a reprisal against unionized workers and ordered the company to compensate former employees.

Still, Mr. Pelletier said the company is not anti-union. 'We are a big generator of union construction jobs and many of our customers are union members,' he said. 'We are pro-workplace democracy.'

The management of an organization involves choices and constraints. On the one hand, management may seek to maintain unilateral control of the organization by retaining or extending its managerial prerogative or the right to manage. Alternatively, management may accept the legitimacy of trade unions in the decision-making process – management by agreement. In the 1970s, public policy and managers were strongly influenced by the recommendations of the 1968 Donovan Commission. From 1979 to 1997, as part of the neoconservative and neoliberal movement, employers changed and shifted more towards individualistic approaches to managing the employment relationship. In essence, the early debates on HRM/industrial relations centred on the belief that globalization and the unstoppable force of market energy would release human energy and productivity providing that the maze of social regulation was removed (Saul, 2005). Within this dominant discourse, management introduced new initiatives, found new confidence and changed the emphasis in its union–management relations policies (Sisson, 1994). Recent survey and case study data suggest, however, that this trend has again shifted somewhat to embrace the 'social partnership' model (Bacon and Storey, 2000; Heery, 2002; Sparrow and Marchington, 1998). To examine management's strategic decisions and actions towards trade unions, we need to examine industrial relations strategies.

Strategies towards unions

An industrial relations strategy refers to the plans and policies chosen by management to deal with trade unions (Gospel and Littler, 1983). The idea of choice among alternative industrial relations strategies is closely linked to the concept of 'business strategy' and 'human resources (HR) strategy' (Chapter 2). In recent years, however, thought-provoking contributions to the debate on globalization have highlighted the increasing global dominance of the neoliberal, Protestant, Anglo-American model of capitalism in various areas, including union representation (see Jacoby, 2005). Even when an organization has a simple business strategy, its HR and industrial relations strategies may be very complex and often suggest different and contradictory directions (Anderson et al., 1989). The choice of a strategy towards unions involves managers in considering a number of complex factors: labour market conditions, national legal and business systems, the history of the organization, management philosophy or values, and the union and bargaining structures facing the management (Anderson et al., 1989; Cappelli, 1984; Hyman, 1999; Thompson, 2001).

The relationship between the business strategy, the economic environment and the union–management strategy is perhaps the easiest to establish. The outcome of union–management pay bargaining will have a direct impact on the organization's ability to implement the business strategy. Under the EU monetary system, for example, British managers have to ensure that local pay and productivity movements correspond with those of other EU competitors. It is therefore much less likely in 2007 than in 1973 that the industrial relations manager will enter the negotiations with a 'do your best' mandate from senior management. The following quotation, taken from a case study, illustrates the constraints:[5]

> Previously we would have a management meeting. I would then do the negotiating. If at the end of the day I had to go two or three per cent more than we intended, that would be it ... Now, if I want to go outside the budget I have to get permission from head office.

These internal constraints at the bargaining table reflect external constraints caused by competition. Global price competition and privatization have thus caused organizations to search for alternative business strategies and, at the same time, to re-evaluate their relationships with trade unions.

Although it is simplifying a complex phenomenon, the various strategic alternatives can, for analytical purposes, be classified into three broad industrial relations strategies (Anderson et al., 1989; Thompson, 2001):

- union acceptance
- union replacement
- union avoidance.

The *union acceptance* strategy is defined here as a decision by top managers to accept the legitimacy of the union role and, in turn, of collective bargaining as a process for regulating the employment relationship to support their corporate strategy. The reform and restructuring of workplace bargaining arrangements during the 1960s and 70s have been characterized as an industrial relations strategy designed to engender 'a degree of order, regulation and control' (Nichols and Beynon, 1977, p. 129). Survey evidence indicates that, even in the inimical environment of the 1980s, a number of important Japanese companies chose a union acceptance strategy, albeit in a modified form, to achieve their employment objectives (Bassett, 1987; Wickens, 1987). In Britain, between 1984 and 2004, survey data from the Workplace Employment Relations Survey (WERS, 2004) indicate a sharp decline in the adoption of a union acceptance strategy. In the private sector, for example, the proportion of workplaces adopting a union acceptance/recognition strategy fell from 48 per cent to 16 per cent (Kersley et al., 2006; Millward et al., 2000). The incidence of union recognition for the purposes of negotiating pay and conditions was much higher among larger private sector establishments (500 or more employees) than small ones (10–24 employees): 52 per cent and 11 per cent, respectively (Kersley et al., 2006).

The *union replacement* strategy means that top management have decided to achieve their strategic goals, whether this involves introducing new technology, relocating to another part of the UK or European Community or subcontracting out work, without any consultation or agreement with trade unions. Derecognition refers to a decision by senior management to withdraw from collective bargaining in favour of unilateral arrangements for the governance of employment relations. Douglas Smith, chair of the Advisory, Conciliation and Arbitration Service (ACAS), said in his 1987 address to the Institute of Personnel Management conference that 'across the spectrum there were now managements whose intention was increasingly to marginalize trade unions'.

Several studies over the past two decades provide convincing evidence of derecognition practices in Britain (Claydon, 1989; Smith and Morton, 1993). Similarly, US corporations in the 1980s adopted a union replacement strategy, and an increasing number of top management decided to decertify (derecognize) the existing unions (Cappelli and Chalykoff, 1985). Opposition to unions is said to be so intense in US business organizations that 'American employers are willing to engage in almost any form of legal or *illegal* action to create and maintain a union-free environment' (Deery, 1995, p. 538, emphasis added). Among North American industrial relations theorists, there is a popular view that Canadian employers are less willing to oppose unionization than are their US counterparts. Bentham's (2002, p. 181) recent study suggests, however, that this may be a misconception because the vast majority of Canadian workplaces studied 'engaged in actions that can only be characterized as overt and active resistance' to unions.

HRM WEB LINKS

For information on how union–management strategies in Britain have changed over the past two decades, go to the WERS 2004 website: www.dti.gov.uk/employment/research–evaluation/wers–2004/dissemination–results/page25904.html.

Derecognition continued in UK workplaces during the 1990s. The WERS 98 results showed that 6 per cent of all established workplaces derecognized unions between 1990 and 1998 (Millward et al., 2000). Bacon and Storey's (2000) analysis of management action reveals a 'disjuncture between unions and "new" corporate thinking'. One manager (quoted in Bacon and Storey, 2000, p. 412) expressed the new management thinking towards unions like this:

> Collectivism via trade unions is something we want to remove ... We are not anti-union, it is just that they are incompatible with our current direction. I think we can win by edict in the current climate and drive through changes against any opposition and hope that in the end people will see there is no choice.

One interesting aspect of Bacon and Storey's study is the evidence suggesting that British management did not take full advantage of its power. Two reasons are given for this. First, the 'heavy threats' to the unions contributed to higher levels of employee apprehension, dissatisfaction and mistrust of management. This observation can be linked to the importance of the psychological contract discussed in Chapter 1. It is highlighted here because it would appear that the adoption of a union replacement strategy, particularly in a period of major organizational restructuring and potential downsizing, can rupture the contract, with subsequent decreases in employee loyalty and commitment. With this in mind, Bacon and Storey's (2000, p. 423) comment that managers were 'reluctant to sacrifice employee trust' is important. The second reason managers did not use their power and push through with derecognizing the unions was because the very threat of such action alone 'allowed managers to introduce many of the changes they had wanted to drive through' in the workplace (Bacon and Storey, 2000, pp. 413–14). Overall, then, although most managers have an enduring preference for non-union relations (what is referred to as 'unitarism'), pragmatic considerations in these cases deterred the adoption of a union replacement strategy.

The *union avoidance* strategy is defined here as a decision to maintain the status quo of a non-union workforce by pursuing HR policies such as non-union grievance and discipline procedures, employee participation schemes, work teams and the active countering of union recruitment campaigns. Given that the majority of business organizations are not unionized, we can assume that the union avoidance strategy is the most prevalent industrial relations strategy in Britain and North America, although, as Gollan (2002) has recently stated, research on management strategies towards non-union employee representation is limited. Researchers argue that individual employee involvement schemes increase employees' motivation and commitment to organizational goals and therefore reduce the need for a trade union (Chapter 12). Management also establishes consultative councils to give non-union employees a 'voice', and 'independent' staff associations as a substitute for unions in determining pay to keep the worksite union-free. In addition, the selection process can be used to screen out applicants likely to be prone to joining a union, and training can be used to build commitment to the organization. The retail giant Marks & Spencer exemplifies the union avoidance strategy; the company's chairman and chief executive put it like this:[6]

> Human relations in industry should cover the problems of the individual at work ... the contribution people can make, given encouragement – these are the foundations of an effective policy and a major contribution to a successful operation.

The choice of an industrial relations strategy for a particular organization will depend upon a complex set of interrelationships between constraints and strategic choices and between management's objectives, as delineated by the business strategy, HR strategy, ideological norms and beliefs, and the national institutional system in which the organization is embedded (Clark and Almond, 2004; Maurice and Sorge, 2000). Whatever industrial relations strategy is chosen, it must also be evaluated in order to identify where objectives have been achieved and where they have not. Comparative measures of industrial conflict, cooperation and grievance rates can, for example, be used to evaluate an industrial relations strategy. A recent study by Gollan (2002) of the union avoidance strategy at News International Newspapers (UK) evaluated the effectiveness of the company's non-union Employee Consultative Council and News International Staff Association. The results revealed 'widespread dissatisfaction with management' and a 'perceived lack of effective voice' among employees (Gollan, 2002, p. 329). Moreover, the benefits to the company of a union avoidance strategy were 'questionable': the management's strategy 'could result in greater indirect union influence in workplace issues and greater employee dissatisfaction at the workplace' (Gollan, 2002, p. 330).

Finally, the academic and public discourse on 'varieties of capitalism', thereby challenging the convergence or takeover thesis, dispels the idea that employers and managers adopt a single strategy: management can choose from a variety of strategies. Empirical evidence suggests that union avoidance tactics often appear to be used alongside union acceptance and union replacement tactics (Anderson et al., 1989). Recent studies evince a considerable variation in HR and industrial relations practices within different countries and emphasize the persistence of national differences in union–management relations.

Ferner et al.'s (2005) study is a thought-provoking contribution in that it provides an in-depth analysis of the multifaceted reality of union–management relations in US multinationals operating in the UK. The authors of the study argue that although there are obvious demonstrations of a distinctive American anti-unionism, the case study data present a complex picture. Based on the results of their study, Ferner et al. (2005, p. 723) conclude that the industrial relations strategy adopted by US subsidiaries operating in the UK is the 'complex outcome of the interaction of US ideological norms [anti-unionism] with the UK institutional system' (political and legal support for voluntary collective relationships). As Gospel and Littler (1983, p. 12) prophetically conclude, 'The combination of strategies has been highly complex, and employers have searched in a zig-zag backwards and forwards movement between them'. Perhaps a similar judgement is warranted with regard to management's response to trade unions in diversified global markets and national institutional systems.

In Britain, for example, since the election of the New Labour government in 1997, political and legal contexts have encouraged both management and unions to reassess their strategies. Evidence of this is the growing interest in the notion of 'social partnership', which is part of a broader strategy to improve productivity and organizational performance. These valedictory words from Prime Minister Tony Blair's address to the 1999 Trades Union Congress (TUC) conference (quoted in Brown, 2000, p. 305) sent a strong signal to organizations that they should reassess their union–management strategies:

> I see trade unions as a force for good, an essential part of our democracy, but as more than that, potentially, as a force for economic success. They are part of the solution to achieving business success and not an obstacle to it.

We examine the notion of 'partnership' in more detail below, but at this point we should also note examples of workplace partnership outside the EU. In post-apartheid South Africa, for example, trade unions have shifted from confrontation with employers to participation in newly created 'tripartite forums' in order to encourage private investment and further the economic interests of working people (Barrett, 1996). In Canada, Betcherman et al. (1994) note some interest in tripartite collaboration between management, labour and government to create 'high-performance work systems' (see also Streeck, 1996; Terry, 1995).

HRM WEB LINKS

Go to www.ipa-involve.com and www.acas.org.uk for information on how many work organizations have negotiated partnership agreements in the UK.

The significance of this debate on union–management strategies is this: the HRM model is not restricted to a 'union exclusion' environment. Guest (1995) analyses the strategic union–management relations options available to management, the 'new realism' option appearing to illustrate the case of HRM and union–management relations operating in tandem. With support from New Labour and EU legislation on European works councils (see Chapter 12), British managers are beginning to take a more proactive approach towards union involvement in decision-making, workplace partnerships and the more positive developmental elements of the HRM model. With the current enthusiasm for partnership, it is easy to forget that management strategies can and do change depending on the economic and political climate, and that different strategies can be applied to different firms within the same industrial sector and to different groups of employees within the same organization. With this caveat in mind, the implications of the growing globalization of corporate structures will compel top management to make strategic choices about their business processes and how they will arrange related aspects of HR practices and union–management relations.

STUDY TIP

The importance of business strategy to the development and implementation of union–management strategy cannot be overstated. In order to understand alternative union–management strategies, one must first understand business strategy. Before reading on, go back to Chapter 2 and reread the section containing Figure 2.8. If you are writing an assignment on union–management strategies, you may wish also to obtain a copy of Gospel's (1994) book *Markets, Firms and the Management of Labour in Modern Britain*. Thinking about the different business strategies, how are business strategies and union–management strategies related? Can we predict that one type of business strategy will be more likely to encourage the adoption of a workplace partnership?

Trade unions

Most students using this textbook will be probably be surprised to learn that, three decades ago, British trade unions were considered to be powerful social institutions that merited close study. Indeed, one scholar referred to trade unions as 'one of the most powerful forces shaping our society' (Clegg, 1976, p. 1). Between 1968 and 1979, trade union membership increased by 3.2 million to 13.2 million, and **trade union density** exceeded 50 per cent. The sheer scale of union organization represented a 'decade of exceptional union growth' (Bain and Price, 1983, p. 6).

In contrast, between 1979 and 2000, union membership in Britain dropped sharply: in 1979, 53 per cent of workers were union members; by 2000, this had fallen to 29 per cent. The 1980s were referred to as the 'decade of non-unionism', and the 1990s as the decade of 'renewal' or 'revitalization' (Heery et al., 2004). This section examines trends in union membership over the past two decades and goes on to examine trade union structure and bargaining power, in the belief that a knowledge of these developments is important for understanding the debate on HRM and unions.

Union membership

The decline in aggregate membership of British trade unions is well documented and is shown in Table 11.1. In 1979, when Margaret Thatcher was first elected prime minister of Britain, union membership was over 12 million. Since then, membership has fallen by over 4 million, or 38 per cent. From the peak years of 1976–80, union density fell from 55 per cent, to stand at 33 per cent in 2001–05. Although union membership appears to be relatively stable in a few North European countries and Canada, union decline is a worldwide phenomenon (Verma et al., 2002).

Table 11.2 describes the pattern of union decline across major sectors of the British economy from 1980 to 1998. Drawing on WERS 98 data, union presence at workplace level remained stable in the early 1980s at 73 per cent but then fell sharply to 64 per cent in 1990, continuing to fall to 54 per cent in 1998 (Millward et al., 2000). The survey also showed that union presence differed significantly across the broad sectors of the economy. The decline in union presence was most marked in private manufacturing – down from 77 per cent in 1980 to 42 per cent of workplaces in 1998. Although trade union presence in the public sector remained almost ubiquitous over the two decades, it fell from 50 per cent of establishments in 1980 to 35 per cent in 1998. Furthermore, in both private manufacturing and services, the decline was 'more substantial in small workplaces' and among traditionally 'male-dominated' worksites (Millward et al., 2000, p. 86).

Table 11.1 Union membership in the UK, 1971–2005

5-year annual average	Members (000s)	% of employed
1971–75	11,548 (+1.5)	50.0
1976–80	12,916 (+1.5)	55.9
1981–85	11,350 (–3.5)	49.1
1986–90	10,299 (–1.7)	44.6
1991–95	8,740 (–4.0)	37.8
1996–2000	7,910 (–9.5)	34.2
2001–05	7,772 (–1.7)	33.6

Source: Data from Sneade (2001) and the EIRO website

Table 11.2 Union presence by broad sector, 1980–2004

	Percentages				
	1980	1984	1990	1998	2004
All establishments	73	73	64	54	34
Sector of ownership					
Private manufacturing	77	67	58	42	na
Private services	50	53	46	35	22[1]
Public sector	99	100	99	97	64

Note:
1. WERS 2004 data do not differentiate between private manufacturing and private services, this figure only refers to the 'private' sector
Source: Adapted with permission from Millward et al. (2000) p. 85 and Kersley et al. (2006) p. 12

REFLECTIVE QUESTION

Can you think of any environmental factors (e.g. new legislation) that may lead workers to join unions? What internal factors (e.g. perceived violation of the employment contract) may affect unionization?

It is helpful to situate Britain's trade union experience in an international perspective by comparing the proportion of those in employment who are members of a trade union, that is, union density (Table 11.3). A word of caution: because of differing definitions, union density is a notoriously problematic area of international comparison. This is due to differences in how countries calculate the total number of union members and the total number of eligible members in the equation. Given this caveat, trade union density in the EU and North America over the past decade has been highly variable. In four EU member states – Spain, the Netherlands, Germany and France – trade union density in 2005 represented less than 30 per cent of the workforce. In the three EU member states of Sweden, Finland and Denmark, union density in 2000 came close to 80 per cent of the workforce. In North America, trade union density in Canada stood at 32 per cent, and that in the USA at 13 per cent, in 2005. There are difficulties in interpreting absolute differences in union membership between countries, but the trend is clear: many have experienced a substantial decline in union membership over the past two decades (Brown et al., 1997).

Table 11.3 Union membership in selected countries as a percentage of all employees, 1970–2005

	1970	1980	1990	1995	2000	2005
Australia	50	48	40	33	35	40
Belgium	45	56	51	53	69	69
Canada	31	36	36	34	32	31[1]
Denmark	60	76	71	82	80	88
Finland	51	70	72	81	79	71
France	22	17	10	9	9	9
Germany	33	36	33	29[2]	29[2]	30[2]
Ireland	53	57	50	38	44	45
Italy	36	49	39	38	35c	35
Japan	35	31	25	24	22	20
Netherlands	38	35	25	26	27	25
New Zealand	41	56	45	22	24	24[3]
Norway	51	57	56	56	56	57
Portugal	61	61	32	32	30	30
Spain	27	25	11	15	15	15
Sweden	68	80	82	83	79	79
UK	45	50	39	32	29	32
USA	23	22	16	15	14	13

Notes: Unweighted average of 15 'old' EU member states, 43%; unweighted average of 25 'new' EU states, 39%
1. 2003 figure
2. Post-East–West unification figure
3. 2000 figure
Source: Brown et al. (1997); OECD, International Labour Organization and the EIRO website (2006)

HRM WEB LINKS

For further information on union presence in the workplace in different countries, go to the International Labour Organization website (www.ilo.org), and for the figure for EU member states go to www.eiro.eurofound.ie.

Interpreting union decline

Although the general pattern clearly indicates that union membership and density have fallen sharply and continually since 1979, there is a debate over the precise scale of the trend, its cause and its likely duration. Part of the problem is measurement. Estimates of the decline in union density range from as few as 8.3 percentage points to as many as 12.1. These strikingly different estimates occur because the key statistic of union density can be measured in nine different ways depending on which of three different data series for potential membership and trade union membership is used (see Kelly and Bailey, 1989).

One influential explanation of variations in the rate of unionization over time categorizes the determinants under the following headings (Bain and Price, 1983):

- business cycle
- public policy
- work and organizational design
- industrial restructuring
- employer policies
- union leadership.

Although Bain and Price's approach is comprehensive, it is difficult to disentangle the relative importance of each of the six determinants in interpreting aggregate union decline in the UK since 1979. Within the *business cycle* framework, Disney (1990) suggests that the downturn in union density in the 1980s was caused by macroeconomic factors. Trade unions' traditional difficulties in recruiting and gaining recognition in the private services sector, smaller establishments, foreign-owned plants and newly established greenfield sites have intensified. Proponents of the business cycle explanation also assume that high levels of unemployment have eroded the constituencies of manual workers, from which unions have traditionally recruited (Waddington, 1992).

Following the election of a Conservative government in 1979, *public policy* towards trade unions shifted away from a positive encouragement of trade union recognition. The suggested determinant – government action – clearly can affect unionization. Public policies that create a favourable environment for union recognition will initiate a virtuous circle of recognition and increase in membership, a circle that can be put into reverse by adverse policies and government 'example-setting' or role model (Towers, 1989). Freeman and Pelletier (1990), using a quantitative analysis of changes in union density, estimate that the Thatcher government's industrial relations laws reduced British trade union density by 1–1.7 percentage points per year from 1980 to 1986. This type of analysis is, however, fraught with problems: it is difficult to disentangle cause and effect when dealing with trade union law (Disney, 1990).

Others argue that employers have used the fear of unemployment and a hostile trade union to redesign the nature of work and organizations, which has impacted negatively on union–management relations. The studies by Millward et al. (1992, 2000) offer several explanations for the pervasive decrease in union density between 1980 and 1998. The variation is explained by *work and organizational design* characteristics, such as changes in establishment size and the age of the workplace: 'older workplaces have higher densities', argue Millward et al. (1992, p. 63). Similarly, Machin (2000, pp. 631–4) has identified the negative association of unionization in the workplace with the age of the establishment: the sharp fall was 'driven by the failure to organize in the newer workplaces' – defined as those less than 10 years old at the time of the survey. Comparing the WERS 2004 results with those of earlier workplace surveys, Kersley et al. (2006, pp. 12–13) provide evidence that only in the public sector, where management support for union membership is much more prevalent, is union membership widespread.

The continual *industrial restructuring* from manufacturing to service employment also affects union membership. Millward et al. (2000) conclude that a union presence continues to be widespread in the public sector and concentrated in large workplaces in the private sector. There is, however, evidence of 'a general withering of enthusiasm' for union representation within continuing workplaces, especially in the private sector, and 'a lack of recruitment among new workplaces in both private and public sectors' (Millward et al., 2000, p. 136). Another significant development is the collapse of compulsory unionism – the 'closed shop' – among non-manual workers in highly unionized British companies (Wright, 1996).

The restructuring of British industry and labour market factors are clearly critical in determining whether workers decide to become and remain union members, but *employer policies* and behaviour will significantly influence workers' support for unionization. If managers are openly hostile or less supportive of unions in their workplace, workers will be more likely to perceive union membership to be an act of 'disloyalty' to the organization and, more importantly, as jeopardizing their employment prospects. As we noted when we discussed union–management strategies, the strategic derecognition of unions is a small but growing trend (Bassett, 1988; Brown et al., 1997), which has been associated with the growing adoption of the HRM model. Undy et al. (1981) have argued that union leadership has a positive effect on union growth as leaders act as catalysts in union recruitment campaigns. Isolating and measuring the independent effect of union leadership on union growth from the other variables is, however, problematic for researchers (Bain and Price, 1983). As has already been mentioned, the inclusion of the union 'voice' in workplace governance was not part of the management mantra during the 1980s and 90s.

With New Labour's 1999 Employment Relations Act, the climate for union recognition became more favourable. In broad terms, this Act offers a number of measures, including a procedure to achieve recognition in the face of employer opposition, to encourage union membership and recognition (Wood and Godard, 1999; Wood et al., 2002). Moreover, the whole rhetoric of New Labour towards the trade unions, and social partnership in particular, encourages employers and workers to reassess the benefits of unionization. The TUC's annual survey, *Focus on Recognition* (Trades Union Congress, 2000), reported that unions won 470 new recognition agreements with employers in 2001, compared with 159 in 2000. The result encouraged the TUC to refer to a 'union renaissance'. The analysis of trade union development over the past two decades emphasizes the interplay between long-term economic developments, the shift towards the service sector, the increasing number of peripheral workers, the adverse political and legal environments and the growing number of firms adopting a union exclusion strategy.

HRM WEB LINKS

For further information on the union renaissance report and the latest figures for union recognition agreements, go to the TUC website at www.tuc.org.uk and follow the headings to 'Organization and recruitment'.

Union structure

The word 'structure' in relation to trade unions denotes the 'external shape' of trade unions (Hyman, 1975) or job territories, the areas of the labour market from which the union aims to recruit. A union's internal structure, the relationship between its parts, is referred to as 'trade union government'. There are many variants of **union structure** within countries, traditionally expressed in terms of the four classic ideal types within British union structures: craft, industrial, general and white-collar unions. In practice, however, most of these classical union structures have never existed in their true forms (Ebbinghaus and Waddington, 2000). The British union movement is associated with multiunionism as craft and general unions cross the boundaries of workplaces and industries (Visser and Waddington, 1996). Technological change has both undermined the traditional craft unions and created new occupations, thus blurring the distinction between manual and non-manual. The wave of union mergers over the past two decades reflects the 'deep crisis' in unionization and has resulted in the formation of 'super-unions' (Ebbinghaus and Waddington, 2000).

Table 11.4 illustrates the wave of mergers and amalgamations in the British union system since 1979. It reveals that the number of trade unions affiliated to the TUC has fallen from 109 to 67, almost entirely as a result of mergers. Over the period 1986–95, there were 99 mergers, and the overall number of British unions fell by 142 (Willman, 1996). By 2005, the proportion of total union members represented by the TUC was 86.2 per cent. Table 11.4 also reveals a philosophy of 'big is best' to encourage 'natural growth', and an 'industrial logic' (Waddington, 1988) in order to avoid the duplication of administrative costs. In January 2002, for example, the formation of AMICUS joined the largely manual Amalgamated Engineering and Electrical Union (AEEU) with the white-collar and blue-collar Manufacturing, Science and Finance Union. In explaining merger activity, formal union links to the British Labour Party, what is called a 'political logic', are also influential (Waddington and Whitston, 1994).

The structure of British trade unions is recognized to be complex, diverse and 'chaotic' (Hyman, 1997b), and the competitive scramble to seek membership anywhere has created trade union structures that are even more bewildering and incomprehensible. The membership distribution between individual trade unions is skewed. At one extreme, there is a relatively small number of trade unions with a disproportionate share of the total union membership, whereas at the other, there is a large number of unions with very small memberships. As the data in Table 11.4 show, the 10 largest TUC-affiliated unions have a total membership of over 6 million, 85 per cent of all TUC membership. The major structural characteristic of British trade unions in 2005 was the predominance of horizontal or 'conglomerate' unions, that is, large individual unions whose members are distributed over a wide range of different industries. In the past decade, parallel trends of restructuring have become evident among trade unions in other developed capitalist economies (see, for example, Ebbinghaus and Waddington, 2000; Streeck and Visser, 1997; Visser and Waddington, 1996).

Table 11.4 Largest Trades Union Congress (TUC) affiliated unions, 1979–2005

| Ranking union (size) | Affiliated membership | | | |
	Membership (000s) 1979	2005	% change 1979–2005	Website (www)
1. UNISON[1]	1,697	1,301	(–)23.3	unison.org.uk
2. AMICUS[2]	2,196	1,179	(–)46.3	amicustheunion.org
3. Transport and General Workers' Union (TGWU)	2,862	820	(–)71.3	tgwu.org.uk
4. General, Municipal Boilermakers' Union (GMB)	967	600	(–)37.9	gmb.org.uk
5. Union of Shop, Distributive and Allied Workers (USDAW)	470	331	(–)29.6	usdaw.org.uk
6. Public and Commercial Services Union (PCS)	n.d.	295		pcs.org.uk
7. Communication Workers Union (CWU)[3]	197	258	(+)30.9	cwu.org.uk
8. National Union of Teachers (NUT)	291	239	(–)17.9	teachers.org.uk
9. National Association of Schoolmasters and Union of Women Teachers (NASUWT)	124	223	(+)79.8	nasuwt.org.uk
10. Union of Construction, Allied Trades and Technicians	320	110	(–)65.6	ucatt.org.uk
Total TUC membership	12,175	6,416	(–)47.3	tuc.org.uk
Number of TUC unions	109	67	(–)38.5	

Notes:
1. Merger in 1992 of NALGO, NUPE and COHSE
2. Merger in 2002 of AEEU and the MSF
3. Growth is caused by merger activity within the communications industry
Source: TUC website (2006)

HRM WEB LINKS

For further information on union membership, governance, services and policies, go to any of the websites listed in Table 11.4.

Union bargaining power

There has been considerable debate over the effects of the decline in union membership and density on unions' bargaining power. The contraction of employment in the unionized manufacturing sector is widely assumed to undermine union bargaining strength. One indicator of union bargaining power is the propensity of strike activity, and the most noticeable feature of Figure 11.1 is the substantial fall in the number of officially recorded stoppages over the last quarter of the 20th century. In the period

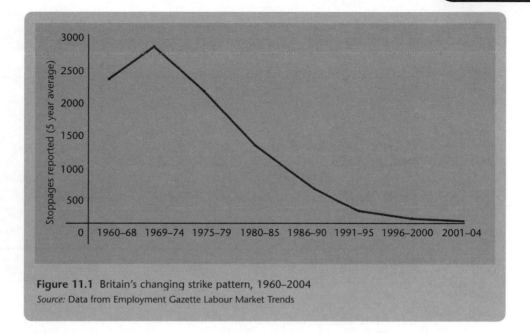

Figure 11.1 Britain's changing strike pattern, 1960–2004
Source: Data from Employment Gazette Labour Market Trends

1960–79, with both Conservative and Labour administrations, the number of stoppages each year never fell below 2000, whereas throughout the 1990s, the number of reported stoppages never rose above 500.

Although any comparison between time periods and between countries involving the number of strikes must be made with caution because of the exclusion of some of the smallest stoppages from the statistics, the trend is nonetheless unequivocally downward, and the strike has virtually disappeared as a union tactic. Between 1990 and 1998, the incidence of both strike and non-strike industrial action declined sharply, from 13 per cent to just 2 per cent of workplaces. In addition, strike action affected only 2 per cent of unionized workplaces in 1998, compared with 16 per cent in 1990 (Millward et al., 2000). In 2004, official statistics show 103 strikes, the lowest total since records began in 1891. As others have observed, collective forms of industrial disputes have virtually disappeared from British workplaces (Cully et al., 1999).

The definition of industrial strikes in the EU statistics varies considerably between member states. For example, in the UK, official figures are from the Office for National Statistics and exclude industrial stoppages involving fewer than 10 employees, those lasting less than one day, and those not directly related to terms and conditions of employment (e.g., a 'political' protest). In Germany, the statistics are based on reports from employers, and in Denmark from larger public and private employers' associations; in Italy, statistics on industrial stoppages are collated by the local police offices. Table 11.5 provides information on the number of industrial stoppages in selective EU member states from 2000 to 2004. The figures reveal considerable differences between the selected countries, with Norway, Poland and Sweden being least strike-prone and Denmark, Spain and Italy most strike-prone, and a higher average level of disputes in the 'old' than the 'new' EU member states.

Table 11.5 Number of industrial disputes in selected EU member states, 2000–04

	2000	2001	2002	2003	2004
Denmark	1,081	954	1,349	681	804
Finland	96	84	76	112	82
France	1,563	1,089	nd	nd	nd
Ireland	39	26	27	24	8
Italy	966	746	616	708	nd
Netherlands	23	16	16	14	nd
Norway	29	3	16	5	12
Poland	44	11	1	24	11
Spain	727	729	684	674	457
Sweden	2	20	10	11	9
UK	212	194	146	133	130

Source: EIRO website, www.eiro.eurofound.ie/ (2006)

The reasons for the downward trend in industrial stoppages in the UK are numerous, and their exploration lies beyond the scope of this chapter. Several studies identify new industrial relations law, the pre-strike ballot provisions of the Trade Union Act 1984, and the draconian fines meted out to miltiant unions (see, for example, Bassett, 1987; Brown et al., 1997; Kelly, 1988). All earlier evidence suggests that the strike pattern is strongly cyclical: the propensity to strike rises during an economic boom and falls during a recession. Furthermore, the decline in strike activity over the past two decades occurred in all Organization for Economic Co-operation and Development countries (Kessler and Bayliss, 1995). Moreover, strike patterns cannot be used as an unambiguous index of union power, nor do they mean that strikes are a thing of the past (Kelly, 1988).

Collective bargaining

The previous sections have examined the principal 'actors' in industrial relations: management and the unions. We now focus our attention on a central employment relations process that regulates employment relations: **collective bargaining**. The freedom for workers to bargain collectively is a core human right (Adams, 2006). We define collective bargaining as:

> an institutional system of negotiation in which the making, interpretation and administration of rules, as well as the application of statutory controls affecting the employment relationship, are decided within union–management negotiating committees.

Several important points arise from this definition:

1. Collective bargaining is a process through which representatives of the union and management jointly determine some rules appertaining to the employment contract. As such, collective bargaining establishes a form of workplace democracy, which has been well articulated by Chamberlain and Kuhn (1965, p. 135; quoted in Adams, 2006, p. 17):

The ethical principle underlying the concept of collective bargaining as a process of industrial governance is that those who are integral to the conduct of the enterprise should have a voice in decisions of concern to them. Collctive bargaining is a correlation of political democracy.

2. There are two types of rule: *substantive* and *procedural*. Substantive rules establish terms and conditions of employment, such as pay, working hours and holidays, whereas procedural rules regulate the way in which substantive rules are made and interpreted, and indicate how workplace conflicts are to be resolved.
3. The parties that negotiate the collective agreement also enforce the agreement. The British system of collective bargaining is perhaps most noted for its lack of legal regulation. Collective agreements are, with a few exceptions, not regarded as contracts of legal enforcement between the parties.[7]

Collective bargaining structure

The structure of collective bargaining is the framework within which negotiations take place and defines the scope of employers and employees covered by the collective agreement. There is in Britain no single uniform structure of collective bargaining, the major structural characteristic of the system being wide variety. Thus, collective bargaining is conducted at several levels: at the workplace, corporate or industry level. The term 'multiemployer bargaining' refers to an arrangement whereby a number of employers reach a central collective agreement on pay and conditions with a trade union(s). The multiemployer agreement therefore covers all those companies that are signatories to the agreement. Single-employer bargaining, particularly in large multi-plant businesses (e.g. the motor industry), can be either centralized or decentralized. Where a holding company covers a group of companies, bargaining can be conducted at the level of the subsidiary companies or below – at the divisional level or at the level of the individual plant. Some multiplant companies have a single-company agreement applying to all their plants, whereas other similar companies have a separate agreement at each plant.

In practice, survey evidence shows that collective bargaining structures are closely linked with business structures and 'profit centres'. Union recognition and the coverage of collective bargaining are mutually dependent, and both have been contracting. This is best charted by considering bargaining over rewards (Brown et al., 2000). Table 11.6 reveals the changes in the pattern of pay determination since 1984. Based upon WERS survey data, the table shows that the proportion of British workplaces (with 25 or more employees) in which collective bargaining was the dominant method of pay determination fell from 60 per cent in 1984 to 26 per cent in 2004.

Subsequent WERS survey results revealed changes in the level at which the pay bargaining has occurred in Britain. There has been a marked decline in the influence of national or industry-wide collective agreements. In 1984, multiemployer agreements featured in 41 per cent of workplaces, whereas by 2004 multiemployer arrangements had contracted to only 7 per cent. Table 11.6 also indicates that bargaining over pay is no longer the norm in Britain: the proportion of all workplaces in which pay was not subject to negotiation increased from 40 per cent in 1984 to 70 per cent in 2004, although the aggregate data mask variations in pay bargaining. The proportion of workers covered by collective agreements broadly reflects the pattern of union density, workers employed in the public sector and in workplaces employing 25 or more individuals being more likely to have their pay determined by collective bargaining (Brown et al., 2000; Cully et al., 1999; Kersley et al., 2006). It should be noted that the fall in the proportion of workers who are union members – union density – and covered by collective bargaining over the past 20 years also occurred in Australia, Japan and the USA (Brown et al., 1997; O'Hagan et al., 2005).

Table 11.6 Basis for pay determination in Britain, 1984–2004

	Percentages			
	1984	1990	1998	2004
Collective bargaining	60	42	29	26
Level of negotiations				
Multiemployer bargaining	41	23	13	7
Single-employer, multisite	12	14	12	5
Workplace/establishment	5	4	3	1
Not the result of bargaining	40	58	71	70

Source: Millward et al. (2000) p. 186 and Kersley et al. (2006) p. 20. Used with permission

Bargaining over pay, effort level and the control of work is the raison d'être of trade unionism, but the WERS surveys descriptive statistics underscore how little involved union shop stewards (elected representatives of union members in the workplace where they are themselves employed) are in pay bargaining and how shop steward influence over work organization issues is 'minimal'. In workplaces where shop stewards were reported to be involved in pay bargaining, over one-third of the managers engaged in the process indicated that the 'negotiations' amounted to 'no more than consultation' (Brown et al., 2000, p. 616). Brown et al.'s (2000) analysis of earlier WERS data suggest that, in many instances, the term 'bargaining' is an inappropriate choice of language for the way in which pay decisions are reached because the essential ingredients of bargaining, that is, discussion and agreement, may both be absent.

The steep decline in the proportion of workplaces determining pay and conditions of employment through collective bargaining appears to be largely confined to Germany and the UK. The coverage rate is as high as 90 per cent or more in Belgium, Finland, France, Italy and Sweden. In the 'old' EU member states, the coverage rate is two-thirds or more. In Japan and the USA, the coverage rate is 20 and 15 per cent, respectively (Table 11.7).

Demonstrating any change in bargaining coverage is more problematic because of inconsistencies in the questions posed by researchers, so only a crude indicator is gained by comparing earlier studies. Whereas, in 1966, for example, it was reported that shop stewards exercised influence over recruitment and selection in 46 per cent of workplaces, union influence in this key area of HR activity had collapsed by 1998. In addition, apart from the handling of grievances, union influence in the regulation of work design aspects of the employment contract had, overall, 'very substantially' declined (Brown et al., 2000, p. 617). In summary, union influence over pay and work organization aspects of the employment contract is not the norm in the modern workplace.

Table 11.7 Direct collective bargaining coverage in selected countries, 2002

	Coverage (%)
Austria	78
Belgium	90
Denmark	83
Finland	90
France	92
Germany	67
Ireland	66
Italy	90
Japan	20
Netherlands	88
Spain	68
UK	36
USA	15
Sweden	90

Source: EIRO website, www.eiro.eurofound.ie/ (2004)

HRM WEB LINKS

The WERS 2004 survey *First Findings* is available at www.dti.gov.uk/employment/ research–evaluation/wers–2004/dissemination–results/page25904.html. For EU data, see www.eiro.eurofound.ie/.

The collective agreement

The outcome of union–management negotiations is a **collective agreement** (in North America also referred to as a 'contract'). The collective agreement provides for the terms and conditions of employment of those covered by the agreement, also specifying the procedure that will govern the relationship between the signatories. In Britain, the terms of the collective agreement are binding in law on the parties if they are incorporated into the individual contract of employment (see Selwyn, 2004, for a legal discussion on incorporation). The content of the collective agreements varies widely. Generally speaking, the greater the level of aggregation (e.g. industry-based agreements), the fewer the subjects that can be covered in detail. The following provisions are typically found in a collective agreement: pay rates, benefits, hours of work, working arrangements and workload (referred to as 'substantives rules'), and guidelines dealing with discipline, grievances, technological change and redundancy (referred to as 'procedural rules').

Trade unions and human resource management

The literature presents the HRM model as being inconsistent with traditional stereotyped union–management relations in North America and Britain. As Adams (1995) points out, the adversarial traditions of Anglo-Saxon industrial relations systems elicit 'low trust' and non-cooperation between labour and management rather than a propensity towards 'high trust' and cooperation. Guest (1987, 1990) suggests there is a prima facie case that the 'collectivist' traditions of trade unions must be at odds with the 'individualistic' goal in the normative HRM model: 'there is no recognition of any broader concept of pluralism within society giving rise to solidaristic collective orientation' (Guest, 1987, p. 519). The HRM model poses a threat to trade unions in at least four ways:

1. individualization of the employment contract
2. the demise of union representation
3. intensification of work
4. the undermining of union solidarity through organizational commitment.

First, the 'web of rules' that regulates the modern employment relationship is being increasingly established, argue management critics, unilaterally by employers rather than through bilateral – union–management negotiations – processes. Although appraisal has been characterized as being an explicit HRM technique to 'control' workers' activity (Townley, 1994), it also, when used to determine reward for individual performance, undermines the raison d'être of unions: bargaining the effort–wage contract. As Bacon and Storey (1993, pp. 9–10) correctly argue, 'Performance-related pay individualizes the employment relationship because it isolates employees and personalizes issues such as design and evaluation of work'. Moreover, by reducing the role of unions in pay determination, performance appraisal severs the link between increased rewards and collective action. In effect, the HRM reward system offers formal and psychological contracts for hourly workers that have been the norm for many managers (Guest, 1989). Individual performance-related pay and pay-for-knowledge are the paradigm individualistic HRM techniques that symbolize attempts by management to move towards an 'individually oriented' rather than union-oriented organizational culture (Bacon and Storey, 1993).

Second, the collective logic of trade union representation is challenged by other HRM high-commitment practices. HRM advocates call for the 'socialization of the workforce' (Champy, 1996, p. 155). Work-based learning programmes that potentially strengthen support for corporate culture and 'socialize' workers to accept the hegemony of managerial authority can undermine workplace unionism (Bratton, 2001). At the company Xerox, for example, Wells (1993, p. 67) argues that training attempted 'to shape the workers' attitudes to management as well as to provide job skills'. Promotion based on individual performance and 'competencies', rather than seniority, inevitably removes an area of the internal labour market from union influence. The HRM practice of communicating directly to the workforce information on quality and business operations can weaken the position and authority of union stewards. Furthermore, team-based work regimes, closely associated with the new HRM model, can undermine collective union consciousness. Team practices try to engender a new corporate culture in which workers identify with the symbols and values that managers communicate directly to them (Bacon and Storey, 1993), in which deviant behaviour is managed by the workers themselves (Bratton, 1992; Wells, 1993) and in which team members create a culture that reproduces the conditions of their own subordination, a new organizational culture (Burawoy, 1979).

Third, critical writers on the labour process have plausibly argued that new HRM work structures are a sophisticated form of labour intensification and therefore have largely negative implications for workers (Sayer, 1986; Thompson and McHugh, 2002; Tomaney, 1990). If we accept the tenor of this research, we can plausibly argue that new HRM-inspired work initiatives will fulfil a historic role of creating working conditions that encourage rather than weaken workplace unionism. The ability of work teams to mortally weaken workplace unionism is contingent upon the context in which they are utilized and upon the union strategies adopted. Management's goal of labour flexibility and adaptability is akin to management demands for the removal of 'restrictive working practices' in the 1960s. On this issue, the unions demonstrate a willingness, and have the capacity, to bargain.

Fourth, the HRM goal of worker commitment is potentially the 'main challenge to the union' (Guest, 1989, p. 43). The importance of 'commitment' to the development and implementation of HR strategy has been stressed in recent years, but the notion of worker commitment is complex. It implies a social psychological state of deep identification with a work organization and an acceptance of its goals and values (Guest, 1995). One variant of the HRM model explicitly contrasts the relative advantages of two approaches to workplace control systems: *compliance* and *commitment* (see Table 1.1). Compliance demands a control system based on formally established rules and procedures; it is 'bureaucratic control' (Edwards, 1979). Bureaucratic control generates 'reactive' behaviour patterns such as working to contract. In contrast, the HRM model seeks to elicit high commitment from workers and thereby cultivate 'proactive' behaviour with committed workers expending their effort 'beyond contract' for the enterprise (Guest, 1995, p. 113).

The idea of worker commitment as a powerful, cost-effective mechanism of control is a common theme in critical industrial sociology literature (see, for example, Burawoy, 1979; Edwards, 1979; Friedman, 1977). The rationale behind the goal of worker commitment is explained by the tensions inherent in the capitalist employment relationship: the need to achieve both the control and the consent of workers in order to maximize profits. As Lincoln and Kalleberg (1992, pp. 23–4) put it:

> The problem of control in organizations is in large measure solved when the commitment of its members is high. Committed workers are self-directed and motivated actors whose inducement to participation and compliance is their moral bond to the organization.

The case for eliciting the commitment of workers seems plausible, but literature on the topic suggests that the concept of commitment is problematic. As Guest (1987) argues, the first issue is 'commitment to what?' Writers taking a managerial perspective are interested in commitment to values that drive business strategy, but Guest (1987, 1995) points out that workers can have multiple and perhaps competing commitments to a profession, a career, a craft, a union and a family. Arguably, the higher the level of commitment to a particular set of skills or professional standards, the greater the likelihood of resistance to multiskilling and flexible job designs. The goal of commitment might thus contradict the goal of flexibility.

Closely associated with the debate on HRM and union–management relations is the related notion of 'dual commitment'. Theorists and practitioners have posed the question of whether workers can be simultaneously committed to the goals and values of both the work organization and their trade union. The argument goes something like this. If US-style HRM models underscore 'individualism' and commitment, this approach to managing people must be incompatible with the core ideologies of workplace trade unionism – 'collectivism' and representation. Using a simple matrix model, Guest (1995) argues that, logically, if commitment to company and union are caused by the same variable, they operate from competing ends of the same continuum and dual commitment is not possible. On the other hand, if they are caused by different variables, dual commitment is possible because a change in a variable affecting company commitment need not influence union commitment.

Murphy and Olthuis (1995) found support for the idea of dual commitment. Their Canadian study reported that 'many workers are attached to both the union and the company and have a type of "dual commitment" [and] attachment to the company does not necessarily lessen attachment to the union, and vice versa' (Murphy and Olthuis, 1995, p. 77). This, and the body of research that Guest (1995) reviewed, appears to support the hypothesis that dual commitment is possible where the union–management relations climate is characterized as being cooperative and non-adversarial.

REFLECTIVE QUESTION

How does the research on commitment help you to understand the HRM/union–management relations discourse?

The logic of the HRM model is (at least in theory) that workplace unionism will eventually 'wither and die'. This interpretation of HRM is expressed by trade union leaders thus: 'In the wrong hands HRM becomes both a sharp weapon to prise workers apart from their union, and a blunt instrument to bully employees' (Monks, 1998, p. xiii). The new corporate culture certainly aims to encourage workers to identify with their company's ideals and their work team rather than with the union collective. The argument that unions and HRM cannot coexist does not, however, appear to be consistent with the empirical evidence (Wood, 1995).

HRM IN PRACTICE 11.2

BEWARE THE DAMAGE ONE CANNOT SEE
Strikes and lockouts feed the 'us versus them' mentality that HR tries so hard to break down

JAMIE KNIGHT, *CANADIAN HR REPORTER*, 27 FEBRUARY 2006

Is a labour disruption in your future?

If an organization is involved in collective bargaining, and it is not subject to binding arbitration (such as would be the case for healthcare providers, for example), it may be subject to strike action or, less often, an employer-initiated lockout. Each provincial and federal jurisdiction has a clearly delineated procedure that requires some kind of formal conciliation before the parties get to the point of a labour disruption. But sooner or later, without a resolution, the organization will make its way to one minute past midnight.

A strike may last only a few days if the organization is lucky. More typically, a strike will continue for the better part of two months, perhaps longer, and hopefully not forever. Strikes are often nasty affairs. Like an iceberg, what one sees may be only a small part of the destructive force of a strike. It is what one cannot see that may cause lasting damage to the organization. From a human resources standpoint, there are three major problems created by a labour disruption that have their largest impact below the surface.

First, a labour dispute breaks up the family. Human resources professionals spend a great deal of time and energy striving against an 'us versus them' kind of mindset and getting all employees to focus on organization objectives and to pull together as one unified team. All of that goes out the window as soon as the strike or lockout starts. A work stoppage is entirely us versus them: there are two opposing sides and there is a clear dividing line, symbolized by the picket line. The striking employees want what management is not prepared to give them, usually money. The point of the strike is to try to harm the company to the point where the company 'surrenders' to the union's demands. The company is trying to 'break' the strike, by putting monetary and ethical pressure on employees to cross the line. The obvious analogy is no longer teamwork, but warfare; people have ceased working together, but have turned on each other to fight over dwindling treasure.

> Like an iceberg, what one sees may be only a small part of the destructive force of a strike. It is what one cannot see that may cause lasting damage to the organization.

Second, a labour dispute reveals character flaws and deficiencies. It is exciting to be part of a group of strikers. Mob mentality takes over and a person may act in a way he would never act if alone or in another context. He may damage property, threaten people, even hurt people. He chants aggressive insults, even though he would never harm a fly or degrade another human being. He is motivated by greed, even though his job may give him everything he needs.

For management's part a sense of superiority and hypocrisy may preside when managers are dismissive of employee demands, forgetting that their own compensation is measurably higher. A spirit of meanness enters into the mindset of both sides, so that there is self-justification and self-congratulation for conduct that is really just an unsavoury means to an end.

Third, a labour dispute breeds disloyalty, a sense of betrayal on both sides and a loss of security. This works both ways, so that management no longer feels it can count on its employees and, for their part, the employees wonder if the company they have always found reliable actually views them as nothing more than part of the machinery. If a strike persists to the point where employees 'cross the line' or if the employer tries to use replacement workers, there will be vile bitterness within employee ranks.

Union strategies: partnership and paradox?

The debate on trade unions and HRM provides the backcloth to examining union strategies. The actual formulation of a strategy depends to a large extent on the external conditions facing trade unions, employers' HR actions, and the internal politics of the union. In his study of the sources of change in British trade unions, Heery (2005, p. 103) argues that union strategy is not simply a pragmatic adjustment to changing national business system: 'It is also an expression of internal politics, dialogue and power ... [thus] union politics matter.' In recent publications, it has been stressed that trade unions are 'strategic actors' and as such generate different strategic responses to environmental and organizational change.

Several reasons can explain this diversity of responses. Trade unions are complex organizations that have developed with different ideologies and associated strategies. 'Business unionism' – dealing with bread-and-butter issues – is, for example, the dominant ideology in the USA and has also played a large part in union development in Britain, Canada and Japan (Adams, 1995). The unions' response will also be partly conditioned by their experience of management-initiated HRM policies. Furthermore, the response will be different depending on whether the union perceives management to be adopting different versions of the HRM model (Legge, 2005). Several industrial relations theorists have sought to clarify the types of response made by European, Canadian and US unions (Beaumont, 1991; Heery, 2002, 2004, 2005; Martinez Lucio and Weston, 1992). It would be misleading to develop a typology of union strategies – one with mutually exclusive categories – but, for our purposes, we have identified two dominant strategic approaches for the renewal of British trade unions:

- organizing strategy
- partnership strategy.

Organizing strategy

The organizing strategy, also referred to as **new unionism**, is internally focused and places a renewed emphasis on 'organizing the unorganized'. A sustained attempt is made to recruit those workers outside the traditional white male norm of full-time employment. The union 'organization model' developed in North America has informed the strategy, which embraces a number of basic principles and union tactics: a change in union priorities, such that they accommodate a more diverse workforce, a strategy of 'field enlargement' through 'targeted' recruitment campaigns – such as agency work – person-to-person recruitment and 'issue-based' organizing, for example focusing on 'justice, dignity and respect' issues in the workplace (Heery, 2002, 2004, 2005).

The purpose of this strategy is, despite the novelty of the language, rather traditional: it is to establish an effective workplace union organization that can be self-sustaining in terms of recruitment and service to members. Union recruitment drives will be supported by the statutory union recognition procedure introduced by the UK Labour government in 2000. The Employment Relations Act 1999 union recognition procedure is, however, likely to help union recruitment campaigns only in sectors of the economy 'where unions already have a presence' (Wood et al., 2002, p. 233). In analysing the nature of this union strategy, Heery (2002, pp. 27–8) has noted that it focuses on the 'qualitative interests' of workers and is built on the assumption of 'opposed interests' between workers and the organization.

To be successful, the organizing strategy for union renewal requires five broad conditions to be present in the workplace (Kelly, 1998):

- a perceived sense of injustice or violation of the contract
- attribution of the injustice to managerial behaviour
- the presence of effective workplace unionism through which the collective action can occur
- confidence that collective action will have the desired effect, that is, it will remove the injustice
- charismatic union leaders who can mobilize the membership and legitimize collective action.

Of these five influences on non-union employees to unionize, perceived union 'instrumentality' – a belief that a union will improve working conditions – apparently has the greatest effect (Charlwood, 2002). According to Heery (2005), conditions for regenerative change require that unions become more responsive to the needs of women in paid employment and workers in non-traditional, precarious employment. A renewal strategy requires increased investment in internal structures that facilitate the cross-subsidy of union activities that diminishes the risks of organizing. Furthermore, 'union renewal' strategies will need to include more 'open' institutions, increase rank-and-file participation, especially among women and visible minorities in paid employment, reform internal union structures to increase democratic decision-making, and develop a worker-centred societal vision (Kumar and Schenk, 2006). Any study of the trade union movement strategic response to the formidable challenges of adjustment and confrontation resulting from globalization and HRM policies and practices of employers has to be cognizant of the possible difference between trade union rhetoric and labour's actual response in the workplace.

Partnership strategy

The second dominant strategy for the renewal of unions is the 'social partnership' strategy. This strategy is externally focused, with its emphasis on union–management relations embedded in 'union-friendly' employment law. Central to the argument is the belief that renewal requires unions to take advantage of the facilitating effect of employment law and European social policy to develop a new form of workplace governance around the notion of partnership. The theoretical basis of the approach can be traced back to North American literature on 'strategic partnerships', 'mutual gains' and 'win–win' rewards coming to labour by cooperating with employers to develop high-performance work systems (Betcherman et al., 1994; Guest, 1995; Kochan et al., 1986; Verma, 1995).

In the early 1990s, it was argued that, rather than viewing the soft HRM model as a threat, 'unions should champion it, becoming more enthusiastic than management' (Guest, 1995, p. 134). The premise here is that the policies and practices inherent in the soft HRM model include many to which trade unions could subscribe. With the election of New Labour in the UK in 1997, and the 1999 Employment Relations Act, union leaders and managers were challenged to reappraise collective relations in the workplace (Bacon and Storey, 2000). In 1999, the TUC published *Partners for Progress: New Unionism at the Workplace*, which advocated workplace partnership between local union representatives and managers. In the context of a continuing contraction of members and collective bargaining coverage, the unions presented themselves to potential members and employers alike as 'facilitators of cooperative collective relationships' that would have mutual economic benefits (Brown, 2000, p. 303).

The term 'partnership' is used in a variety of ways. At the European level, it can refer to union involvement in the European Social Dialogue. At the national level, partnership can be applied to tripartite discussions between employer and union representatives and the government, for example between the Confederation of British Industry, the TUC and the UK government. At workplace level, partnership is the term applied to agreements to promote flexibility in working practices in exchange for employee involvement mechanisms. Partnership agreements seek to give unions a place at the 'strategy table' by portraying themselves as an authoritative partner in economic and business management, hence (Industrial Relations Services, 1998, p. 12; quoted in Munro and Rainbird, 2000, p. 225):

> Partnership provides a clear workplace philosophy based on employer and union working together to achieve common goals such as fairness and competitiveness, and recognizing that although they have different constituencies, and at times different interests, these can best be served by making common cause wherever possible.

By embracing partnership, the trade unions seek to improve union influence and membership by building long-term partnerships with employers. The TUC document *Partners for Progress: New Unionism at the Workplace* outlined six principles of workplace partnerships (Figure 11.2).

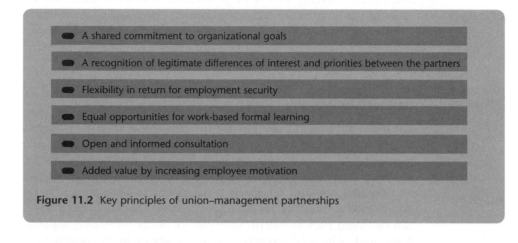

- A shared commitment to organizational goals
- A recognition of legitimate differences of interest and priorities between the partners
- Flexibility in return for employment security
- Equal opportunities for work-based formal learning
- Open and informed consultation
- Added value by increasing employee motivation

Figure 11.2 Key principles of union–management partnerships

HRM IN PRACTICE 11.3

RELATIONSHIPS THE KEY TO CORPORATE SUCCESS IN 2020

Companies of the future to harness knowledge workers for competitive advantage

HRM GUIDE, APRIL 2006

Knowledge workers will be companies' most valuable source of competitive advantage in 2020, whether in outward-facing functions such as sales or inward-facing ones such as knowledge management. According to respondents to a major new survey on the company of the future, the value of price competitiveness to customers is expected to decline relative to other factors, such as personalisation of products and quality of customer service.

This is one highlight of Foresight 2020, a far-reaching new research report launched today by the Economist Intelligence Unit, sponsored by Cisco

Systems. The research is based on a survey of more than 1,650 executives and a series of in-depth interviews with senior executives, and includes essays on eight key industries.

> **'Customers are looking for a high level of interactivity...'**

Respondents to the survey believe that employees' ability to communicate, to solve problems and to lead will be more important to their organisations' future success than functional and technical capabilities. 'The focus of manage-

ment attention will be on the areas of the business, from innovation to customer service, where personal chemistry or creative insight matter more than rules and processes', says Andrew Palmer, the editor of the report.

'Customers are looking for a high level of interactivity and personalisation,' said Rob Lloyd, Senior Vice President of Cisco U.S. and Canada Operations. 'To be successful, companies have to invest in works and technologies that can drive collaboration and interactions inside and outside the company across the entire value chain of customers, partners and suppliers.'

HRM WEB LINKS

John Lewis Partnership is one of the UK's top 10 retail businesses, employing over 63,000 employees. It is also the largest example of worker co-ownership in Great Britain. For further information on the John Lewis Partnership, go to www.johnlewis-partnership.co.uk. For further information on the TUC's position on workplace partnership, go to the TUC website at www.tuc.org.uk.

By 2001, more than 50 partnership agreements had been negotiated, including agreements between the Co-operative Bank and the union BIFU, Tesco and the Union of Shop, Distributive and Allied Workers, and Legal and General and AMICUS–MSF. Partnership agreements typically provide a commitment to employment security in exchange for flexible working. Other features address 'dignity' at work, employee 'voice' and work-related learning and employee development issues. UNISON's proactive workplace learning partnerships, for example, 'represent both continuity and change in relation to traditional collectivist approaches to servicing members' needs' (Munro and Rainbird, 2000, p. 227) and suggest that the initiatives have been mutually beneficial for the management and workers concerned (Munro and Rainbird, 2004). Workplace learning researchers have identified trade union 'learning representatives' as an important innovation in British trade unions (see Forrester, 2005; Wallis et al., 2005). From an employer's perspective, partnership can facilitate major restructuring with the support of the union, de-emphasize costly distributive collective bargaining over innovation and change, reduce costs, improve customer service standards, improve quality and strengthen employee commitment to organizational goals (Thomas and Wallis, 1998). As Heery (2005) notes, in a 'post-voluntarist' UK context, increasingly regulated European labour market, employment law is a key explanatory variable encouraging unions towards engagement in new recruitment issues and renewal activity.

REFLECTIVE QUESTION

What do you think of workplace partnerships? How does the partnership strategy reframe employment relations? What are the advantages and disadvantages of partnership?

Partnership agreements also have their detractors (e.g. Bacon and Storey, 2000; Clayton, 1998; Kelly, 1996). Clayton (1998), for example, remains sceptical about the likelihood of workplace partnership developing as a vehicle for reconstituting trade union power in response to long-term decline. To paraphrase Guest (2001), UK management is currently driving the bus, and although the unions may be invited along for the ride, they will remain in the passenger seats to offer guidance only; they will not be trusted to do any driving. Kelly (1996, p. 101) argues that, rather than strengthening the unionization process, partnership can potentially 'weaken or inhibit the growth of workplace union organization', and partnership agreements may form part of 'a longer term *non-union* strategy' (Bacon and Storey, 2000, p. 410). Moreover, an analysis of the characteristics of British corporate governance – a preference for short-term financial performance and the maintenance of shareholder values (Purcell, 1995) – suggests that British business is an infertile environment for social partnership (Heery, 2002).

Statutory provisions, in particular the European Works Council Directive of 1994, will help to override potential employer opposition to partnership, but whether partnership is, however, capable of delivering the benefits for unions and employers will depend upon a balanced assessment of the arrangement. In the long run, partnership is likely to be sustained if it holds the promise of real benefits for employer, employees and unions. The interests of employers and labour are not identical so an effective approach to partnership must involve acceptable trade-offs, the trade-offs associated with the partnership model being shown in Table 11.8. It is hard to disentangle the effects of partnership; with this in mind, the challenge for trade unions is to transcend the polarized positions of outright opposition to partnership and cooperation, and focus on a strategy to extract the potential from partnership without eschewing traditional union-building activities. The outcome is indeterminate and will depend upon the ongoing interaction between union and management, and, as Heery (2002) concludes, upon whether the 'qualitative' gains (e.g. 'voice', dignity and respect) are not heavily outweighed by 'quantitative' losses (e.g. job loss, work intensification and lower income growth).

Table 11.8 The benefits and costs of a partnership strategy

	Benefits	Costs
For organizations	● Efficiency gains ● Lower absenteeism/turnover ● Better union–management relations ● Potential for improved performance	● Greater investment in work-related learning and other human resource programmes ● Having to share information ● Having to share decision-making
For workers	● Access to work-related learning ● Potential increased skills ● Discretion over the work process	● A need for greater commitment to the firm ● Job loss and lower income growth ● Greater work intensification and job-related stress
For unions	● Participation in decision-making ● Affirmation of an independent voice for workers ● Access to information ● Improved status	● A move away from job control unionism ● Isolation from union members ● Union polices work changes ● Leaders challenge

Source: Adapted from Betcherman et al. (1994)

We should note the apparent contradiction between the two union strategy alternatives. The organizing strategy is predicated on the assumption that workers' and employers' interests are different, whereas partnership assumes the reverse. This seemingly contradictory mix of union positions may be justified because of a growing divergence in business and HR strategies within national economies. Just as an HR strategy is contingent upon the business strategy, the argument is that union strategies differentiate between 'good' and 'bad' employers. Partnership can thrive and deliver the benefits for all stakeholders where the 'acceptance of unions remains high and there is a commitment to value-added competition' (Heery, 2002, p. 31). Elsewhere, however, a traditional organizing strategy might be required. This perspective recognizes the links between business, HR and union strategies, as well as the role of power in organization decision-making; as such, it brings a certain 'realism' to the study of HRM and union–management relations that is frequently lost in the rhetoric and in the prescriptive HRM texts.

Finally, several writers have noted the relatively small number of partnership agreements in British workplaces. If the partnership strategy has not been extensively adopted, there are at least three possible explanations:

- Employers might be too preoccupied with downsizing rather than introducing the relatively costly partnership alternative.
- The investment cost associated with partnership is high, as are the risks, given that any social partnership arrangement will experience the underlying conflicts inherent in employment relations.
- Employers might also be reluctant to invest in partnership because the effect on the bottom line is unclear (Chapter 14).

Legal context of union–management relations

Management and union strategies, collective bargaining processes and outcomes (e.g. pay levels, labour productivity and industrial disputes) are influenced by economic, political and legal factors. The state, which is normally thought of as comprising the executive, Parliament, the judiciary, the civil service and the police and armed forces, has considerable influence on union–management relations in two major areas: through legislation and through **third-party intervention** (e.g. ACAS).

Collective labour law is an aspect of union–management relations that interacts with the institutions, processes and behaviour of the key actors in the system. Union organization and governance, relations between different unions, union recognition by employers, collective bargaining and manifestations of collective workplace conflict, such as strikes, are the main concerns. Whereas individual labour law governs the relation between individual employees and their employer, collective labour law governs the collective aspects of the employment relationship. The Employment Relations Act 1999, for example, provides a statutory framework for union organization and governance and collective bargaining, including statutory union recognition provision, changed balloting procedures and increased protection for union members when participating in official industrial action (see Chapter 4 for a discussion of industrial relations legislation over the past 20 years; Wood and Godard, 1999; Wood et al., 2002, for an analysis of the Employment Relations Act 1999). Reviewing trade union rights under New Labour, from 1997, Smith and Morton (2006, p. 414) argue that partnership agreements 'entrench employers' power'. They also contend that, to strengthen workers' power, New Labour needs to establish 'a statutory right of trade unions to have access to, and assembly at, the workplace'. Some of the key UK legislative provisions related to unions and union–management relations, including New Labour legislation, are shown in Table 11.9.

Table 11.9 Main UK legislative provisions related to union–management relations, 1980–2004

Act	Date	Coverage
Employment Act	1980	Public funds for union ballots (since repealed) Provision for codes on picketing and closed shop
Employment Act	1982	New definition of a 'trade dispute'
Trade Union Act	1984	Compulsory secret ballots for union positions and before industrial action; otherwise no immunity
Employment Act	1988	Greater control to members of union governance
Employment Act	1990	Abolished the closed shop and immunity in respect of secondary industrial action
Trade Union and Labour (Consolidation) Act	1992	Consolidated all relevant law on unions and labour relations together with Advisory, Conciliation and Arbitration Service (ACAS). Code provides for disclosure of information to unions for collective bargaining purposes
Trade Union Reform and Employment Rights Act	1993	Independent scrutineer of union elections given more powers. Voting fully postal
Employment Relations Act	1999	New statutory framework for collective bargaining, including statutory union recognition provision, changed balloting procedures and increased protection for union members when participating in official industrial action
Employment Relations Act	2004	Union recognition rights for the purpose of conducting collective bargaining. Outlines additional responsibilities of the Central Arbitration Committee (CAC) to facilitate collective bargaining

HRM WEB LINKS

Go to the following websites to compare collective labour law relating to unions and union–management relations: www.hmso.gov.uk/acts.htm provides the full text of UK Acts of Parliament, www.labour-travail.hrdc-drhc.gc.ca//index.cfm/doc/english and www.law-lib.utoronto.ca/ give information on Canadian laws, and www.labor-link.org and www.dol.gov/elaws/aud_gen_emp.asp outline the US information.

ACAS, the UK third-party intervention institution, was established in 1974 in order to promote orderly union–management relations and to intervene in those industrial disputes which the government viewed as particularly damaging to the national economy. ACAS is a state mechanism and is funded by the government. In 1993, legislation removed ACAS's responsibility for the promotion of collective bargaining. The role of ACAS as an arbitrator and mediator is less significant today, given the decline in official industrial stoppages, but recent ACAS figures reveal that requests for individual conciliation are increasing each year.

HRM WEB LINKS

For information on ACAS, go to www.acas.org.uk.

Chapter summary

- This chapter recognizes that managing work and people in the workplace includes a collective dimension. In so doing, we examined three alternative union–management strategies: union acceptance, union replacement and union avoidance. Research on management strategies indicates that a union avoidance strategy is the one most frequently adopted by UK and US companies. We have emphasized that the selection of an industrial relations strategy involves managers considering a number of complex economic, political, legal and historical factors. Given the different conditions, culture and leadership philosophy and styles in organizations, each union–management strategy is likely to be unique and display contradictory practices.

- We have also examined union membership, structure, collective bargaining and union strategies. In a nutshell, the dramatic reduction in union membership, the significant decline in the number of strikes and the trajectory of decentralized bargaining has led to a shift in power towards management. Where the preferences of management and unions differ, as they often do, the party with the perceived power will dictate the outcome nearer to its preferences. The argument here is that this shift in bargaining power makes it more likely that employers will be tempted to take a short-term view and choose traditional cost-cutting HR measures that can potentially violate the psychological contract.

- Although long-term economic forces played a part in such developments, the politics of the New Right of Thatcher in Britain and Reagan in the USA in the 1980s and much of the 1990s played a critical role in management resurgence, the decline of unionization and power, and the demise of multiemployer collective bargaining. In Britain, the politics of New Labour appear to be encouraging a renewal of union growth and influence in the workplace.

- Analysing four fundamental factors influencing union–management relations – the state of the labour market, management's strategic capacity, labour's strategic capacity and the legal and political context of union–management relations – we can say that the jury is still out on whether New Labour's policies will reverse industrial relations trends in the foreseeable future.

- This chapter examined two dominant union strategies: organizing strategy and partnership strategy. We noted that the long-term success of the partnership strategy will depend upon ongoing union–management relations and on whether or not the qualitative gains are heavily outweighed by quantitative losses. We also emphasized the apparent contradiction in the two union strategy alternatives. Finally, we concluded that partnership can thrive and deliver the benefits for employers, employees and unions where a union acceptance strategy is the norm and there is a commitment to value-added competition. In other worksites, an organizing strategy might be required.

Key concepts

- Collective agreement
- Social partnership
- Collective bargaining
- Third-party intervention

- Management strategy
- Trade union density
- New unionism
- Union structure

Chapter review questions

1. What is meant by the term 'union–management relations'?

2. Why are union–management strategies said to be the result of strategic choices?

3. To what extent, and why, can some variants of the HRM model be viewed as a union exclusion strategy?

4. How can contextual factors explain the development of British trade unions?

5. To what extent is collective bargaining in Britain too fragmented to function effectively in an enlarged European market?

6. What contradictions might be found in the twin goals of new unionism and social partnership?

Further reading

Benson, J. (2006) Japanese management, enterprise unions and company performance. *Industrial Relations Journal*, **37**(3): 242–58.

Charlwood, A. (2002) Why do non-union employees want to unionize? Evidence from Britain. *British Journal of Industrial Relations*, **40**(3): 463–91.

Danford, A. (2005) New union strategies and forms of work organization in UK manufacturing. In B. Harley, J. Hyman and P. Thompson, P. (eds) *Participation and Democracy at Work* (pp. 166–85). Basingstoke: Palgrave Macmillan.

Delsen, L., Benders, J. and Smits, J. (2006) Choices within collective labour agreements à la carte in the Netherlands. *British Journal of Industrial Relations*, **44**(1): 51–72.

Ferner, A., Almond, P., Colling, T. and Edwards, T. (2005) Policies on union representation in US multi-nationals in the UK: between micro-politics and macro-institutions. *British Journal of Industrial Relations*, **43**(4): 703–28.

Forrester, K. (2005) Learning for revival: British trade unions and workplace learning. *Studies in Continuing Education*, **27**(3): 257–70.

Gollan, P. J. (2002) So what's new? Management strategies towards non-union employee representation at News International. *Industrial Relations Journal*, **33**(4): 316–31.

Guest, D. (2001) Industrial relations and human resource management. In J. Storey (ed.) *Human Resource Management: A Critical Text* (2nd edn) (pp. 96–113). London: Thomson Learning.

Heery, E. (2005) Sources of change in trade unions. *Work, Employment and Society*, **19**(1): 91–106.

Heery, E., Conley, H., Delridge, R., Simms, M. and Stewart, P. (2004) Trade union responses to non-standard work. In G. Healy, E. Heery, P. Taylor and W. Brown (eds) *The Future of Worker Representation* (pp. 127–50). Basingstoke: Palgrave Macmillan.

Kumar, P. and Schenk, C. (2006) *Paths to Union Renewal*. Peterborough, Ontario: Broadview Press.

Roche, W. and Geary, J. (2002) Advocates, critics and union involvement in workplace partnerships: Irish airports. *British Journal of Industrial Relations*, **40**(4): 659–88.

Smith, P. and Morton, G. (2006) Nine years of New Labour: neoliberalism and workers' rights. *British Journal of Industrial Relations*, **44**(3): 401–20.

Wood, S., Moore, S. and Willman, P. (2002) Third time lucky for statutory recognition in the UK. *Industrial Relations Journal*, **33**(3): 215–33.

Practising human resource management

Searching the web

On an individual basis, or working in a small group, pick two or three online union-related websites, for example www.tuc.org.uk (UK), www.ilo.org (the International Labour Organization in Geneva), www.clc-cta.ca (Canada) or www.aflcio.org/home.htm (USA). What are some of the major issues affecting workers around the world? What identifiable strategies have the unions developed, and how do they compare with the union approaches discussed in this chapter? Bring this information to class and present your findings in an oral report.

HRM group project

Form a group of three or four students. The purpose of this group assignment is to allow you to apply your knowledge of union–management strategies in the workplace. Specifically, your task is to examine how two selected organizations have formulated and implemented a union–management strategy.

First, enter the websites of two organizations, for example Barclays Bank (www.barclays.co.uk/) and Tesco (www.tesco.co.uk/). Then compare the partnership agreements negotiated between the different managements and unions:

- How are the agreements similar and different?
- Do the partnership agreements contain the TUC's six principles (see Figure 12.2 above)?
- What kinds of change or external business pressure did the organizations face, and how does a partnership help the organizations to manage change?
- Given the nature of your selected organizations' business strategy and structure, is conflict a likely obstacle to change in the organizations?
- How does the union–management strategy relate to business strategy?
- Is there any evidence that union–management relations facilitate or hinder change?
- How well do you think managers have managed union–management relations in these organizations?
- What other changes do you think that the organizations should make to their HR/industrial relations strategy and why?

Each group member should take responsibility for researching the various aspects of the assignment. Present your findings in a written report.

EAST YORKSHIRE CITY COUNCIL

Rose Peller, the newly appointed chief executive of East Yorkshire City Council, had a mandate to restructure the city's local government. One of her first tasks was to set up a quality committee of senior managers to transform the council's culture, employee attitudes and performance, her objective being to introduce total quality management throughout the council's administration. Workshops on total quality management started with the senior management team and department managers, some of the workshops on leadership aiming to turn old-fashioned local government managers into 'active leaders', trying to enthuse instead of dictate.

The proposed changes are both physical and cultural. Part of the restructuring is to introduce open-plan working areas throughout the council's buildings, in terms of both dismantling the counters between staff and customers and getting managers out of their offices. It is envisaged that the manager's role will become one of facilitator, and employees, after they have been organized into quality teams, will have greater autonomy and no longer hand problem-solving automatically to managers. In addition, Ms Peller, with support from the Conservative-controlled council, is planning to introduce performance-related pay, which will be linked to personal goals rather than office targets. Together with total quality management, it is expected that this will contribute to the new culture in local government.

At a planning meeting, Rose Peller expressed her views in a forceful manner: 'Since the department managers will be working in teams, they should know more about the people they are working with, which should make the appraisal system fairer. The more people work together and get rid of these hierarchical barriers the better', she said.

East Yorkshire City Council employs 620 manual and non-manual employees, and 85 per cent are in UNISON, the recently created public sector union.

Assignment

As an assistant HR officer at East Yorkshire City Council, you have been asked to produce a report for the planning committee on the industrial relations and negotiating issues associated with the introduction of total quality management and performance-related pay. Your report should include the anticipated reaction of the trade union UNISON and the union's objectives in future negotiations between senior management and the union.

HR-related skill development

The grievance process is an integral part of administering the collective agreement, a grievance being a formal dispute between an employee (or the union) and management involving the interpretation, application or alleged violation of the collective agreement. The union files most grievances, and once they have been filed, management should seek to resolve them fairly and quickly. Handling a grievance is a key skill for managers in a unionized (and non unionized, if there is a grievance process in place) workplace, but many lack the basic knowledge and skills to conduct a formal grievance investigation and interview.

To help you to develop grievance management skills and to give you experience of the grievance process, we have devised a grievance case with supporting information. You can participate, either at individual or group level, in the simulation and develop an important HR skill by going to our website www.palgrave.com/business/brattonandgold4 and clicking on 'Handling grievances'.

Notes

1. Machin (2000, p. 643).
2. Brown et al. (2000, p. 616).
3. John Monks, TUC general secretary, commenting on the new annual TUC survey on union recognition, www.tuc.org.uk, January 2002.
4. Adams (2006, p. 11).
5. Richard Johnson, personnel manager of Flowpak Engineering, quoted in Bratton (1992, p. 162).
6. Lord Sieff (1981), chairman and chief executive of Marks & Spencer; quoted by J. Purcell and K. Sisson (1983) Strategies and practice in the management of industrial relations. In G. Bain (ed.) *Industrial Relations in Britain* (p. 114). Oxford: Blackwell.
7. See *Ford Motor Co.* v. *Amalgamated Union of Engineering and Foundry Workers* (1969). For a discussion of this important judgement, see Davies, P., and Freedland, M. (1984) *Labour Law: Text and Materials* (p. 779). London: Weidenfeld & Nicolson.

Chapter twelve

Employee involvement and relations

John Bratton

Employee relations are a complex set of human resource practices and organizational cultures that seek to secure commitment and compliance with organizational goals and standards through effective communications, employee involvement, employee rights and managerial disciplinary action.

'The demand for instant communication is increasing workplace stress, causing anger among colleagues and generally distracting people from getting things done.'[1]

'The pressures leading firms to explore the introduction of employment involvement practices have a great deal to do with productivity, flexibility, and competition – management's agenda – and less relationship to workers' desire for a stronger voice in the operations of the worksite.'[2]

'Collective voice achieves what the lone voice could never do: it humanizes and civilizes the workplace.'[3]

Chapter outline

Chapter objectives

After studying this chapter, you should be able to:

1. Explain why managers might want to increase employee involvement (EI) and describe the different dimensions of EI

2. Appreciate the importance of employee communication in the human resource management paradigm

3. Identify some ethical issues and their relevance to employee relations

4. Describe the major issues relating to sexual harassment in the workplace and the implications for managing employee relations

5. Explain the concepts, values and legal framework that underline the disciplinary process in employment

Introduction

Whereas 'labour relations' addresses the 'collectivist' dimension of the employment relationship (Chapter 11), 'employee relations', on the other hand, primarily addresses individual aspects of employer–employee relations. The term 'employee relations' needs further explanation. In recent years, various labels to cover the multiple aspects of the employment relationship have fallen in and out of fashion. As we noted in Chapter 1, some authors interchangeably use the terms 'personnel management' and 'human resource management' (HRM), and for one particular aspect of employment relations, they use 'industrial relations', 'labour relations' and 'employee relations'. Each of these terms has its own particular set of meanings among the academic community. As we discussed in Chapter 11, 'industrial relations' and 'labour relations' have, for example, been associated with industrial trade unions, collective bargaining and strikes.

The term 'employee relations' became popular among some British academics during the 1980s and was used to reflect the emergence of a 'new industrial order' (see Blyton and Turnbull, 1998). As Mabey et al. (1998b, p. 278) comment, each label has 'its own connotations [and] none of them succeeds entirely in capturing the essence of the numerous unfolding types of relations associated with work'. Although we are concerned to include 'traditional' union representatives in our analysis of HRM, we use the label 'employee relations' in a restricted manner as a way of addressing some individual and collective aspects of employment relations in the workplace. Within this perspective, employee relations denotes an assortment of employer and government initiatives for providing or improving two-way communications between management and employees, for engaging employees either directly or indirectly in decision-making in matters that affect them, for protecting employee rights and for securing employee compliance with management rules through disciplinary action. We will seek to demonstrate that these complex employee relations practices constitute important social technologies that aim to improve both employee voice and organizational performance through communication and employee commitment.

In this chapter, we explain key issues related to communication in the workplace. We then go on to explain the terms and the various forms of employee involvement (EI) before presenting a theory of EI. Different mechanisms of 'employee voice', such as joint consultative committees (JCCs) and European works councils (EWCs), are also examined, along with some paradoxes associated with EI. Ethical issues, equity and harassment in the workplace are discussed in some detail before we conclude the chapter with an overview of the process and rules governing employee discipline.

The nature of employee relations

The assortment of employer initiatives and human resources (HR) policies and practices that constitute employee relations – communication, involvement, rights and discipline – is shown in Figure 12.1. As in other areas of HRM, the ethical dimension of employee relations policy and practice has tended to be downplayed in most HRM texts, where the focus in recent years has been on 'best fit' and 'best HR practices' (Winstanley and Woodall, 2000). Ethical considerations inevitably require managers to reflect on what constitutes ethical employee relations practice in an increasingly globalized and diversified workplace. Empirical data and legal cases continue to reveal in detail problems of discrimination, inequality, harassment and inequitable managerial behaviour.

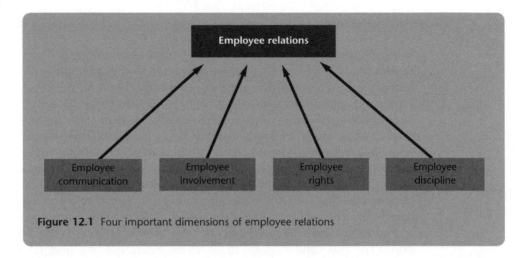

Figure 12.1 Four important dimensions of employee relations

REFLECTIVE QUESTION

Looking at the four key dimensions of employee relations, how can HR practices in each area impact positively and negatively on employee relations? Try to think about your own work experience of 'good' and 'poor' employee relations.

Over the past decade, interest in the various aspects of employee voice has grown considerably in Europe and North America (Dundon et al., 2004; Gollan, 2006; Marchington, 2001; Mayrhofer et al., 2000; Verma and Taras, 2001). Some writers define employee voice in terms of two-way communication between management and employees (Bryson, 2004), whereas others suggest that it is best understood as a complex set of HR practices that are dialectically fashioned by internal management choice, on the one hand, and external regulation, on the other (Dundon et al., 2004). Processes that provide for employee voice include direct EI in workplace decision-making, whether via upward quality control techniques or indirect participative arrangements such as a **works council** or JCC, with trade union representation. It is suggested that employee voice plays a critical role in constructing and maintaining a strong organizational culture and improves organizational performance. Taras and Kaufman (2006) rightly observe that management expects the employee voice mechanism to encourage cooperative and productive modes of employment interaction, while workers expect that any meaningful employee voice forum will provide a capacity to influence managerial decision-making. Dundon et al. (2004) posit that employee voice can be viewed as:

- a form of *contribution to decision-making*
- an articulation of *individual dissatisfaction* (or satisfaction)
- a demonstration of *collective organization.*

Arguably, interpersonal communication is the most important work activity, especially in high-commitment work systems, which seek to enlist the creativity, expertise and knowledge of all workers (Guirdham, 2005). The central role of interpersonal communication is also acknowledged in the 'transformational' leadership literature (Trethewey, 1997). The link to leadership and change, which comes from interpersonal communications theory, emphasizes the different ways in which managers communicate the content of a message and how those ways affect relationships between managers and subordinates. Witherspoon (1997, p. x), a specialist in leadership and communication, argues that 'leadership is to a great extent a communication process', and in our three-dimensional model of management (see Figure 1.3), communication is part of the process of influence by which managers accomplish their work.

EI is another key dimension of voice and employee relations that is regarded as playing a central role in the development of high-performance work systems (Dundon et al., 2004; Marchington, 2001). In Britain, successive Workplace Employee Relations Surveys (WERSs) have documented the growth of EI initiatives (Cully et al., 1999; Kersley et al., 2006; Millward et al., 1992, 2000). The European Works Council (EWC) Directive of 1994 (see later in the chapter for a description of EWCs) also stimulated academics and practitioners to examine in even greater depth the participation and communications debate (Mayrhofer et al., 2000). The call for greater worker involvement in decision-making and work itself has a long history (Brannen et al., 1976), but the current unprecedented interest appears to be associated with globalization, the exigencies of knowledge-based work and the need for managers to share information and decision-making in order to achieve a competitive advantage. Much of the academic literature characterizes EI and two-way communications by being 'management rather than union driven' (Marchington and Wilkinson, 2000; Sisson and Storey, 2000) and part of a sophisticated management strategy designed to increase profitability through consultation and communication: employee voice (Gollan, 2006; Verma and Taras, 2001; Wall and Wood, 2005). EI is therefore closely associated with a high-trust, high-commitment HR strategy (see Chapter 2).

The contemporary debate on employee relations practices emphasizes, from a managerialist perspective, the fact that such HR practices fundamentally transform the climate of employee relations because they lead to long-term changes in workers' attitudes and commitment; as such, communication and EI practices shape 'organizational citizenship'. A violation of an employee's psychological contract (see Chapter 1) may be prevented by communication (Guest and Conway, 2002; Morrison and Robinson, 1997). As Morrison and Robinson (1997, p. 237) argue, 'Communication ... will help to minimize the "false consensus effect," whereby people assume that they share the same perceptions.'

Another aspect of the debate, from a critical perspective, is the argument that employee relations initiatives, such as EI, by promoting individual employees rather than employees' collective bodies, deliberately undermine the role of the trade unions and moreover increase managerial control over the labour process (Thompson and McHugh, 2002; Wells, 1993). In terms of public policy, recent interest in EI and partnership deals between unions and management has been encouraged by UK and European Union (EU) legislation, in particular, the 1994 EWC Directive. A set of individual employment rights affects the nature of employee relations. The right to be treated fairly and equitably is embedded in UK and EU legislation, which attempts to regulate the behaviour of employers and employees in the workplace.

When employee relations practices fail to create, or reinforce, desirable employee behaviours, managers may resort to disciplinary action to encourage compliance with organizational rules and standards. Employee discipline, the fourth key dimension in employee relations, is the regulation of human activity to produce predictable and effective performance (Torrington, 1998). It ranges from the threat of being dismissed to the subtle persuasions of mentoring. Maintaining discipline is one of managers' central activities. A framework of legal rules and procedures surrounds the disciplinary process to provide a fair and consistent method of dealing with alleged inappropriate or unacceptable behaviour. We will now examine in more detail each of the key dimensions of employee relations.

Employee communication

Downward communication patterns from managers to non-managers need to be explored within the wider context of organizational culture and management practices. The exchange of information and the transmission of meaning form the very essence of organizational life. Information about the organization – its production, its products and services, its external environment and its people – is a prerequisite for effective EI in decision-making. A strong advocate of high-performance work systems, Pfeffer (1998, p. 93), not surprisingly, argues that 'the sharing of information on such things as financial performance, strategy, and operational measures conveys to the organization's people that they are trusted'. Employee communications can be simply viewed as the process by which information is exchanged between a sender and a receiver, but the communication process is complicated by organizational characteristics such as hierarchy and power relations, and by the fact that managers and non-managers all have idiosyncrasies, abilities and biases.

We need to begin with a notion of what is meant by **employee communication**. One simple definition focuses on information disclosure: 'The systematic provision of information to employees concerning all aspects of their employment and the wider issues relating to the organization in which they work' (Advisory, Conciliation and Arbitration Service, 1987, p. 3). Meaning is a core concept in communication, and researchers in this field of study define their discipline in complex behavioural and contextual terms. Byers, for example, brings together three ideas associated with communications – *behaviour*, *meaning* and *context* – and defines communication in the workplace (Byers, 1997, p. 4) as:

> both behaviours and symbols, generated either intentionally or unintentionally, occurring between and among people who assign meaning to them, within an organizational setting.

Communication is symbolic, which means that the words managers and workers speak or the gestures they make have no inherent meaning. Symbolic meanings, conveyed both verbally and non-verbally, only 'gain their significance from an agreed-upon meaning' (Martin and Nakayama, 2000, p. 61). To make it more complicated, people communicate differently depending on the context in which communication occurs, each message may have multiple layers of meaning, and culture influences communication, by which the perception of reality is created, sustained and transformed: 'All communities in all places at all times manifest their own view of reality in what they do. The entire culture reflects the contemporary model of reality' (Burke, 1985, quoted in Martin and Nakayama, 2000, p. 62).

The role of employee communication can be seen in studies of managers and their work. Writers (e.g. Mintzberg, 1973) have found that managers spend a vast proportion of their working time on interpersonal communications; indeed, the business of managers is communications. In our discussion of management, communication is an important skill for 'getting things done' (see Figure 1.3), but our model of management also suggests that various contingencies, for example the internal characteristics of an organization, such as structure, impact on the communication process. The size of the organization will generally affect how sophisticated the communication system is. In small organizations, the system might be informal and subject to frequent management intervention. In large organizations, on the other hand, specialists may serve as employee communications managers. Most organizations use a mixture of formal and informal ad hoc arrangements to communicate to their employees. Furthermore, communications will be determined by the organization's business and HR strategy: for example, the more the company's manufacturing and HRM strategies empower people and are knowledge- and innovative-oriented, the more important communications become.

All managers engage in downward communication in one form or another, but communication scholars emphasize that, to be effective, employee communication must be a two-way process to give employees the opportunity to participate, and it should also take place regularly. Researchers, academics and practitioners have also stressed some key issues related to communications in the workplace (Figure 12.2).

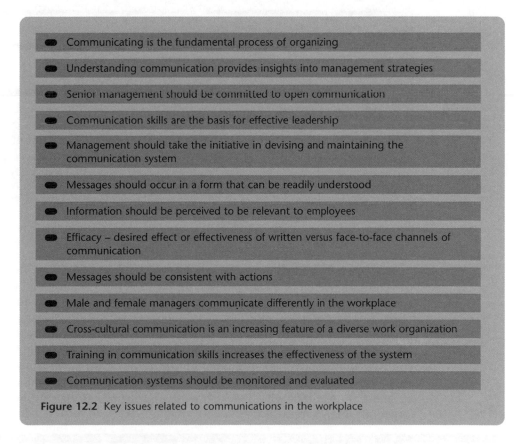

- Communicating is the fundamental process of organizing
- Understanding communication provides insights into management strategies
- Senior management should be committed to open communication
- Communication skills are the basis for effective leadership
- Management should take the initiative in devising and maintaining the communication system
- Messages should occur in a form that can be readily understood
- Information should be perceived to be relevant to employees
- Efficacy – desired effect or effectiveness of written versus face-to-face channels of communication
- Messages should be consistent with actions
- Male and female managers communicate differently in the workplace
- Cross-cultural communication is an increasing feature of a diverse work organization
- Training in communication skills increases the effectiveness of the system
- Communication systems should be monitored and evaluated

Figure 12.2 Key issues related to communications in the workplace

A communications model

The communications model in Figure 12.3 depicts employee communication as a process by which information is exchanged between a sender and a receiver. Employees have three basic methods of transmitting information:

- verbal
- non-verbal
- written.

Verbal communication ranges from a casual conversation between two employees to a formal speech by the managing director. In face-to-face meetings, the meaning of the information being conveyed by the sender can be expressed through gesture or facial expressions, which is referred to as **non-verbal communication**. *Written* communication ranges from a casual note to a co-worker to an annual report. *Electronically mediated* methods of communication, such as email and videoconferencing systems, are an increasingly popular form of communication within and across organizations and have revolutionized written and verbal business communications (although not without some cost to employee stress; see Chapter 13). The content of any message consists of what is being communicated; the way in which content is communicated – through the various channels – describes the sender's communication style. And different communication styles affect the perception of a message or set of messages.

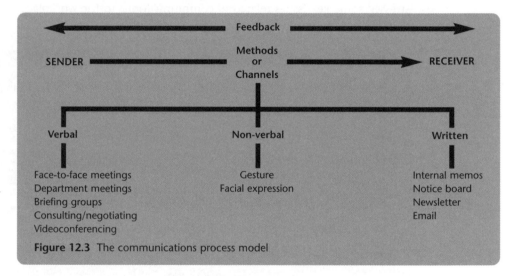

Figure 12.3 The communications process model

This interpersonal communications model has its limitations in that it characterizes communication as a linear process and ignores different cultures and subcultures and organizational hierarchies and power relationships (Rees, T. 1998; Tan, 1998; Thompson and McHugh, 2002). These limitations are particularly significant to international HRM, in which managers have to be aware of, and sensitive to, the cultural situation in which the organization is embedded (see Chapter 3). Arguably, this contextually impoverished model of employee communication needs to be augmented by a sensitivity to cross-cultural norms, as well as to the overall organizational contexts that give rise to the shared meanings that allow interpersonal communication to occur.

HRM WEB LINKS

For more information on electronic business communication, go to www.idm.internet.com/ix/, www.intrack.com/intranet/ and www.internetjournal.earth.

Developing an effective communication system

Communication theorists adopting a functionalist perspective have identified a number of challenges that must be taken into account when managers try to devise a communication system that will enable the organization to run more efficiently, and some of these are now discussed.

Disparate geographical locations

In a large organization, for example a hospital, university or electricity company, there may be multiple sites or plants that create a problem of contact and consistency in the communication system. Videoconferencing technology may be used to communicate between worksites when dealing with routine, non-controversial information and simple issues. Panteli and Dawson's (2001) study on the use of videoconferencing questioned, however, the appropriateness of videoconferencing systems to all forms of multi-site workplace meeting. Contrary to earlier research, they found that videoconferencing systems were not a rich communication medium and were not appropriate for meetings requiring complex decision-making activities or 'more creative discussions'.

Large variety of skill groups

A large public organization such as a local government is responsible for different types of employee: refuse collectors, fire-fighters, librarians, social workers, environmental officers. This might mean that there is no community of interest and no common corporate objective, which normally binds employees together. Considerable time and effort may have to be spent on identifying relevant information for each of the skill groups and in disseminating this to them. It also indicates that there are challenges in centralizing and coordinating the communication system in such organizations.

Cross-cultural communications

As we discussed in Chapter 3, there is, in our globalized world, a growing recognition that managers should, in order to communicate effectively, understand the importance of culturally sensitive communications (Blum, 1997; Tan, 1998). Culture can be defined as a community's shared attitudes, values, behaviour and acts of communicating or 'mental programmes' that are passed from one generation to the next (Hofstede, 1980). Communication both outside and inside the workplace is therefore a culture-bound activity (Martin and Nakayama, 2000; Tan, 1998).

According to cross-cultural studies, managers in different cultures place more or less emphasis on written rather than oral communication and can be more or less direct when communicating perceived good or neutral news. Researchers have, for example, observed that Japanese managers prefer oral communication to written communication and can be more indirect and circular; they can therefore go off at a tangent when discussing an issue. In contrast, North American managers display the opposite communication traits; they tend to prefer written communications and expect messages to be explicit and to the point. Although we should be cautious of the dangers of stereotyping cultural or national characteristics, the literature suggests that misunderstanding and conflicts may arise when managers from an Asian culture interact with those from a Western culture, as the former may consider the direct approach to communicating preferred by the other party to be offensive (Tan, 1998). One practical application of the insights obtained from studies on the West–East cultural divide is cultural diversity training.

Gendered communications

If communication is culture-bound, there is evidence to suggest that it is also gender-bound. Gender can be defined as the characteristics associated with being a man or a woman, which are shaped by cultural ideas and have to be learned. A number of academics have written about gender differences in the way in which men and women communicate in work organizations. Current psychological research on leadership and team dynamics suggests that men and women exhibit different interpersonal communication styles (Crawford, 1995; Tannen, 1993; Winter et al., 2001). Studies suggest that male managers tend to be loud, direct, dominant and aggressive. Women, on the other hand, tend to be more open, self-revealing and polite when they speak (Aries, 1996), are superior at decoding non-verbal communication and possess 'softer', more 'feminine' skills of communication, which are valued in post-bureaucratic organizations (Hawkins, 1995; Helgesen, 1995; Wajcman, 1998). In other words, communication is a context-bound exchange of meaning between organizational people and is a gender-bound activity.

Employment arrangements and financial constraints

The growing tendency to employ part-time workers creates challenges in ensuring that face-to-face communication takes place with all employees. Added to this is the fact that certain groups of employees, for example sales representatives, can spend a large proportion of their time away from their office. In a highly cost-conscious business environment, managers may face a challenge in justifying the cost of practising effective communication, for example an employee news bulletin.

REFLECTIVE QUESTION

Thinking about your own work experience or the experience of a friend, relative or family member, can you cite a situation in which you have perceived differences in communication style between men and women? How important is it to recognize that communication is 'culture-bound'?

Two-way communication

The prescriptive literature on communication provides guidance on what constitutes good practice. It is emphasized that communication can flow in three directions – downwards, upwards and horizontally. Communication that flows from one level of the organization to a lower level is *downward* communication. When we think of managers communicating with subordinates, the downward pattern is the one we usually think of. *Upward* communication flows to a higher level in the organization; it keeps managers aware of how employees feel about their jobs and the organization in general. Communication that flows between employees at the same level in the organization is *horizontal* communication. This type of communication includes communication between co-workers in different departments or divisions of the organization, and between co-workers in the same team.

This formal communication follows the organization's chain of command or hierarchy, but the organization's informal communication network – the **grapevine** – is based not on hierarchy but on social relationships. The grapevine is an important means through which employees fulfil their need to know about the organization.

New employees generally digest more information about the company informally from their co-workers than they do from formal orientation programmes, and 75 per cent of employees claim that the grapevine is their first source of important information in the workplace (McShane, 2006).

It is also emphasized that communication is a two-way process, with both upward and downward communication flows. The most common forms of two-way communication are 'suggestion schemes', attitude surveys and employee appraisals. Two-way communication should not, however, be confused with consultation. The aim of the two-way communication process is often only to ensure that employees have understood the message; it does not necessarily imply that employees' reactions, feelings and criticisms will have any effect upon the decision-making process. In post-bureaucratic organizations (see Chapter 5 for a discussion on bureaucracy and organizational design), in which employee participation is essential, there will be other structures and processes that enable employees to be involved more directly in decision-making (HRM in Practice 12.1). Thus, information disclosure and two-way communication are essential prerequisites, given the rise of knowledge work and job redesign that puts a premium on work-related learning, flexibility and commitment.

HRM IN PRACTICE 12.1

COMMUNICATION OVERLOAD SPREADING

S. PHELPS AND R. SPENCE, *GLOBE AND MAIL*, 2 SEPTEMBER 2005, P. C1.

So you can talk on your cell phone while driving or answering email. You can type text messages on your BlackBerry while contributing to a meeting. You are a true warrior of the technological age. But you may also be suffering from battle fatigue.

Though many people celebrate their ability to multitask, if you're feeling high levels of stress, anger and impatience, or find it difficult to focus, you may be suffering from communication overload. It's a growing problem. A study last year found that the demand for instant, almost constant, communication is increasing workplace

stress, causing anger among colleagues and generally distracting people from getting things done, in meetings and elsewhere.

> ...communication overload... is a growing problem.

The study, led by the University of Surrey's Digital Research Centre, and commissioned by Siemens Communications Inc., was originally conducted to identify whether new technology had changed patterns of acceptable business etiquette. What it uncovered, however, was the rise of the SAD – stressed, angry, dis-

tracted – workforce. It also found a growing resentment of 'communication intrusion' – becoming constantly contacted by others for help with their projects while you're trying to finish your own.

The answer to communication overload is not simply to multitask. While you think you're getting two or three things done at once, you're probably not doing a good job at any one of them – and this will reduce your overall productivity.

Communication overload will break you down if you don't take control and find a better approach. How? You have to bite the bullet and prioritize.

REFLECTIVE QUESTION

Do you think that web-based, online chat systems will improve cross-cultural communication? How does this new communications technology impact on international HRM?

Direct communication methods

Survey evidence indicates that managers use a variety of arrangements for communicating with their subordinates, including regular meetings, management chain newsletters, notice boards, email, suggestion schemes and employee surveys (Kersley et al., 2006; Millward et al., 1992, 2000). Table 12.1 lists the most frequently discussed direct communication methods and shows the proportion of workplaces operating such schemes.

Table 12.1 Use of direct communication methods, 1998–2004, by sector ownership

| | % of all workplaces | | | | | |
| | 1998 | | | 2004 | | |
	Private	Public	All	Private	Public	All
Regular meetings between management and workforce or team briefings	82	96	85	90	97	91
Management chain newsletters	46	75	52	60	81	64
Regular newsletters	35	59	40	41	63	45
Notice boards	–	–	–	72	86	74
Employee surveys[1]	–	–	–	37	66	42
Suggestion schemes[1]	29	35	31	30	30	30
Email[1]	–	–	–	36	48	38
Intranet[1]	–	–	–	31	48	34

Note:
1. No comparable data for 1998
Source: Adapted from Kersley et al. (2006) p. 135

The survey data offer support to the argument that organizations are using combinations or clusters of certain EI practices associated with new organizational designs, such as team briefings. Formally designated work teams were reported in 72 per cent of workplaces. The incidence and use of workforce meetings or team briefings to transmit information from managers to employees increased in the private sector from 82 to 90 per cent. The issues commonly discussed at these two types of meeting included production issues, planning, training, and health and safety. When there is time for employees to raise questions or make comments, team briefings are considered to be an effective way of passing information downwards and upwards through the hierarchy – that is, of increasing the two-way communication flow. Mechanisms designed specifically to elicit information from employees about workplace issues include suggestion schemes and employee surveys. Close to one-third (30 per cent) of all workplaces operated an employee suggestion scheme, and 42 per cent of the respondents reported conducting an employee attitude survey within the previous two years.

HRM WEB LINKS

Further details on the research methods used and outcome of the surveys, including information on how managers communicate with their subordinates, can be found at the website of WERS 2004: see www.dti.gov.uk/employment/research–evaluation/wers–2004/dissemination–results/page25904.html and www.data-archive.ac.uk.

Information disclosed by management

What type of information is communicated through the various communication activities? The kinds of information most likely to be regularly disclosed by managers are staffing plans, the financial position of the workplace and the company, and investment plans (Table 12.2). Since 1998, the incidence of information disclosed on each of these issues, apart from staffing plans, has decreased. Managers in organizations with recognized unions give more information on all topics than do managers in non-unionized workplaces, and UK-owned establishments are less likely than their foreign-owned counterparts to disclose information to their employees (Millward and Stevens, 1986). Several observers have emphasized the importance of information disclosure for creating effective employee relations. For example, information-sharing is positively related to employee satisfaction and trust in workplace decision-making (see Paauwe, 2004, p. 77).

Table 12.2 Information disclosed by management, 1998–2004, by sector ownership

| | % of all workplaces | | | | | |
| | 1998 | | | 2004 | | |
	Private	Public	All	Private	Public	All
Investment plans	47	59	50	40	50	41
Financial position of workplace	56	82	62	51	76	55
Financial position of company	66	67	66	51	53	51
Staffing plans	55	81	61	61	81	64

Source: Adapted from Kersley et al. (2005) p. 18

Employee involvement

The second key dimension of employee relations is EI. A review of the literature reveals that the terms 'employee participation' and **employee involvement** have different meanings. In essence, *employee participation* involves workers exerting a countervailing and upward pressure on management control, which need not imply unity of purpose between managers and non-managers. *Employee involvement* is, in contrast, perceived to be a softer form of participation, implying a commonality of interest between employees and management, and stressing that involvement should be directed at the workforce as a whole rather than being restricted to trade union channels. As Guest (1986, p. 687) states: 'involvement is considered to be more flexible and better geared to the goal of securing commitment and shared interest'.

When people talk about participation or involvement, they are reflecting their own attitudes and work experiences, as well as their own hopes for the future. Managers tend to talk about participation when in fact they mean consultation. In this context, consultation, which is explored more fully later in the chapter, usually means a structure for improving communications, either top-down, or upward in the form of problem-solving. When offered consultation, employees and, in unionized workplaces, union representatives tend to believe, however, that they are about to be given participation. Differing expectations among employees will affect their attitude, their propensity to participate and ultimately the success of participation techniques in the organization. A vital first step, if there is to be any meeting of minds, is therefore to create a common language and conceptual model.

Definitions of EI or participation do not always reflect the range of possibilities – from having some say over how work is designed and executed to exerting a significant influence over strategic decisions. Strauss maintains that meaningful employee participation in decision-making demands that workers are able to exert influence over their working environment. He defines participation as 'a process which allows employees to exert some influence over their work and the conditions under which they work' (Strauss, 1998, p. 15). If we take the literal meaning of the term 'employee participation', the process should provide workers or their representatives with the opportunity to take part in and influence decisions that affect their working lives. As such, an employee participation environment creates an alternative network to traditional hierarchical patterns (Stohl and Cheney, 2001).

There are two types of participation:

- direct
- indirect.

Direct participation refers to those forms of participation in which individual employees, albeit often in a very limited way, are involved in decision-making processes that affect their everyday work routines. Examples of direct EI include **briefing groups**, quality circles, problem-solving teams, self-managed teams (see Chapter 5 for a discussion on work teams) and financial involvement. As a direct form of EI, financial involvement, which includes profit-related rewards, aims to improve competitiveness by educating employees on the operation of the business. Financial participation initiatives are therefore predicated on the belief that workers with a financial stake in the enterprise are more likely to be better 'corporate citizens' and work more productively for the company (Marchington, 2001). For a discussion on profit-related rewards, see Chapter 10.

Indirect participation refers to those forms of participation in which representatives or delegates of the main body of employees participate in the decision-making process. Examples of indirect participation include JCCs, EWCs and 'worker directors', all forms that are associated with the broader notion of 'industrial democracy' (Bullock, 1977). It is clear from the WERS data that indirect EI has become less extensive in the period between 1980 and 1998 (Cully et al., 1999; Millward et al., 2000).

Management theorists have provided conceptual models of EI (see Daft, 2001; Salamon, 1987). Figure 12.4 depicts an adaptation of such models and shows the relationship between three constituent elements:

1. the forms of involvement – direct and indirect
2. the level of involvement in the organizational hierarchy
3. the degree of involvement.

Figure 12.4 shows a continuum of EI from a situation in which employees have no autonomy (e.g. a traditionally designed assembly line) to full involvement, in which workers participate in strategic decision-making. Current methods of EI fall along this continuum. Those methods are based on involvement through the communication of information, financial involvement, upward problem-solving, quality circles, extended consultation, cross-functional teams, self-directed teams, collective bargaining, worker directors and works councils.

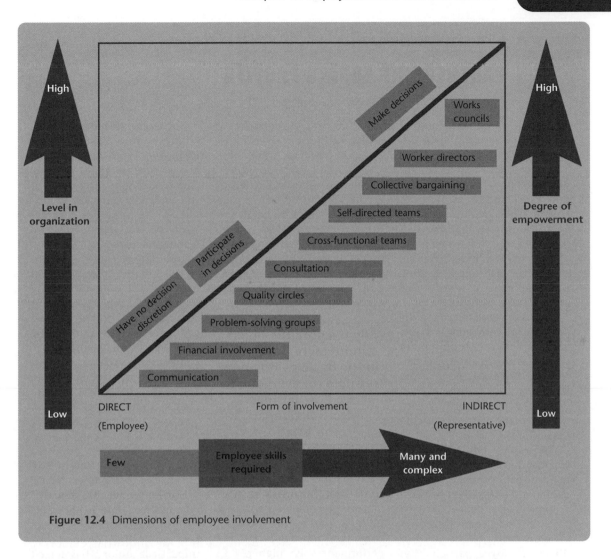

Figure 12.4 Dimensions of employee involvement

These different forms of EI are evident in North America and Europe. As we discussed in Chapter 5, many US and Canadian companies have introduced quality circles, briefing groups and various forms of work teams; in Chapter 10, we examined the growth of financial participation schemes, such as profit-sharing and stock options (see HRM in Practice 10.2). In the EU, EWCs are a common feature of the corporate governance landscape, although it is outside the scope of this chapter to examine the wider debate on works councils, worker directors and European-style industrial democracy. Similarly, EI through the process of collective bargaining was examined in Chapter 11. Before examining EI techniques in detail, however, let us address the question, 'Why the enthusiasm for EI?'

HRM WEB LINKS

For general information on EI schemes, go to www.acas.org.uk (Britain), www. hrdc-drhc.gc.ca (Canada), www.clc-ctc.ca (Canada) or www.workindex.com/(USA).

HRM IN PRACTICE 12.2

PARTNERSHIP EQUALS PROFITS

JENNIE WALSH, *PEOPLE MANAGEMENT*, 19 MARCH 1998

Companies that continue to resist any form of employee participation risk losing business advantage, according to a report published by the Involvement and Participation Association.

More than 65 per cent of organizations that allow their workforce full involvement in all business activities, including long-range planning and product development, believe they are gaining a competitive edge.

The study, Benchmarking the partnership company, is based on a survey to benchmark key principles at work in firms committed to partnership, and includes case studies from Rover, Remploy, ScottishPower, the John Lewis Partnership and HP Bulmer.

The report concludes that successful partnership operates within a set of mutual commitments and obligations between an organization and its people. These include commitment to business goals, job security and direct employee participation in training, development and job design.

Although 70 per cent of companies in the survey were unionized, partnership operated in the same organizations on both a representative level (using formal bargaining structures) and through individual participation (such as self-managed teams).

The report's authors, David Guest, professor of occupational psychology at Birkbeck College, and Riccardo Peccei, lecturer in industrial relations at the London School of Economics, admitted to being surprised by the survey results.

'By opening the books and involving everyone in the business it is now possible for everyone to see how business decisions impact on us all.'

> **'By opening the books and involving everyone in the business it is now possible for everyone to see how business decisions impact on us all.'**

'The most striking thing is that partnership pays off,' Guest said. 'Organizations have a better psychological contract, there is greater trust between employees and employers and performance is higher.' To ensure that these positive results were not simply employer propaganda, the survey cross-matched managers' responses with those of employee representatives – and achieved the same results. But although employee involvement is clearly beneficial to 'partnership' companies, the practice is not widespread.

'Some organizations still have relatively low trust in their employees and in employee bodies such as trade unions,' Guest said. 'But, according to the evidence, this view is misplaced. Organizations that are prepared to take risks are reaping the benefits.'

According to Guest, the principles of shared obligations that underpin the benchmarks are important in making them an accepted part of the overall culture of the organization. The most successful examples are companies, such as Rover, where the partnership culture continues to exist despite changes in the leadership of the company and the unions.

Stephen Dunn, head of group HR at ScottishPower, admitted that partnership is not an easy option for companies facing shrinking profits and increased competition. But he believes that partnership arrangements between ScottishPower and its three trade unions has forced all parties to think in new ways and to work for business advantage.

'It is about looking for solutions to things that, in the past, may have led to conflict,' he said. 'By opening the books and involving everyone in the business it is now possible for everyone to see how business decisions impact on us all.'

REFLECTIVE QUESTION

Thinking about the different HR strategies and their rationale, what is the connection between business strategy, HR strategy, EI and two-way communications? These different forms of EI need to be understood as part of an HR strategy. Before reading on, go back and look at Figure 2.8, rereading that section of the text.

A general theory of employee involvement

Management has continually to address two interlinked problems – those of *control* and *commitment* – with regard to managing the employment relationship. Fox (1985) argues that, faced with the management problem of securing employee compliance, identification and commitment, management has adopted a range of employment strategies including EI. The current enthusiasm for improved EI needs to be viewed within the context of changing business and concomitant HR strategies in which the purpose of the latter is to secure EI support and commitment to high-performance work systems. EI aims to support management's goals either directly through performance improvements, or indirectly through organizational commitment (Marchington, 2001). The commitment–performance link is predicated on a number of assumptions, the first being that giving workers more autonomy over work tasks will strengthen organizational citizenship. Moreover, it will increase workers' commitment to the organization's goals, which will in turn result in enhanced individual and organizational performance. The involvement–commitment cycle is depicted in Figure 12.5 and is the reverse of the vicious circle of control discussed by Clegg and Dunkerley (1980) and Huczynski and Buchanan (2001). Lubricating the whole commitment–performance process is a communication style that attempts to build an internal culture encouraging initiative, learning, creativity and greater employee identification with the organization.

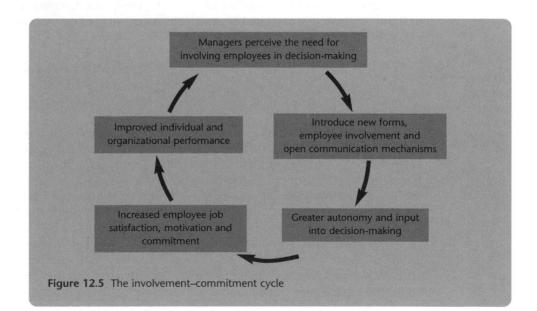

Figure 12.5 The involvement–commitment cycle

REFLECTIVE QUESTION

What do you think of the assumptions underpinning the involvement–commitment cycle? Can the growth of EI be explained by employer 'needs', or are there other forces determining this employee relations practice?

Management theorists have put forward three main reasons why senior management introduces EI schemes (Verma, 1995):

- moral
- economic
- behavioural.

The first reason for introducing EI is derived from an ethical, political and moral base, the argument being that, in a democratic society, workers should be involved in the decision-making process when the outcomes of those decisions impact on their lives. EI therefore presents a socially acceptable management style. The development of EI and communications will be encouraged because companies generally desire to project 'a socially responsible stance on such issues' (Marchington and Wilding, 1983, p. 32).

The second reason for introducing EI, championed by the 'model of excellence' school in North America, derives from the utilitarian principle that EI improves the quality of decision-making and productivity. Marchington (1982) argues that EI potentially improves the quality of a decision and its chances of successful implementation on the factory floor. Similarly, it is asserted that EI improves productivity and energizes workers (Verma and Taras, 2001), as well as increasing employees' trust in management (Mabey et al., 1998b) and reducing work stress (Mackie et al., 2001). Research on the EI–firm performance link suggests that giving employees a voice on a range of organizational decisions yields benefits to both the organization and the workforce (Heller et al., 1998).

The third justification for EI derives from the perennial managerial problems associated with perceived dysfunctional behaviour: resistance to change, strikes, absenteeism and other forms of conflict (Beer et al., 1984; Guest, 1986). EI is seen as a solution to these dysfunctional human behaviours. According to Beer et al. (1984, p. 53), by introducing EI schemes:

> Employers hope that participative mechanisms will create a greater coincidence of interests between employers and employees, thereby increasing trust, reducing the potential for conflict, and increasing the potential for an effective mutual influence process.

Surveys of managers have shown that EI is typically management-initiated, with the objective of enhancing employee commitment to organizational goals (see Delbridge and Whitfield, 2001; Marchington, 1995, 2001; Marchington et al., 1992). The most frequently cited reason for introducing financial participation (e.g. profit-sharing schemes) was, for example, to promote worker identification and commitment (Marchington, 1995, 2001). In addition, EI arrangements might be introduced in order to avert union organization. As Beer et al. (1984, p. 153) posit, 'Some companies introduce participative methods at the shop floor in the hope that a greater congruence of interest will make it less likely that workers will organize.' Thus, EI practices might go hand in hand with changes in an organization's culture away from a collective trade union focus and towards an individual-oriented focus, by promoting a direct relationship between worker and management (Batstone and Gourlay, 1986). EI practices can also, according to Townley (1994), be used to 'educate' and 'reconstitute the individual', thereby making workers' behaviour and performance more manageable.

HRM WEB LINKS

For more examples of companies introducing EI practices, go to the websites of the following companies: General Electric (www.ge.com), Wal-Mart (www.walmart.com), IBM (www.ibm.com), ICI (www.ici.com) or a company you are studying. Once there, go to 'Employee participation' or/and 'Communications' or a similar prompt.

Indirect employee participation

Let us turn to another dimension of EI, that of consultation and indirect employee participation. In its simplest form, consultation may take the form of an informal exchange of views between a group of workers and their manager on an incoming piece of machinery or a reorganization of the office. When, however, the size of the organization makes it difficult for workers to access management and there is a trade union present, a more formal and indirect employee participation network needs to be established. Such a body is a joint or 'labour–management' committee (LMC):

> Involving employees through their representatives in discussion and consideration of relevant matters which affect or concern those they represent, thereby allowing employees to influence the proposals *before* the final management decision is made. (Institute of Personnel Management, 1981, emphasis added)

LMCs are voluntary workplace institutions negotiated between management and employee representatives. Consultation through an LMC differs from joint regulation or collective bargaining because the latter forms of indirect participation utilize the processes of negotiation and agreement between representatives from management and employees. We can develop the difference between **joint consultation** and collective bargaining further. The difference rests on the idea that both conflict and a common interest are inherent elements of the employment relationship that need to be handled in different ways. *Consultation* is viewed as a means of promoting action when there are no obvious conflicts of interest, whereas *collective bargaining* is a means of reconciling divergent interests, although we should stress that every aspect of the employment relationship has the potential for conflict. The distinction between the two approaches to participation is concerned with the 'formal identification of those aspects of the employment relationship in which this conflict should be legitimized and subject to joint agreement by inclusion within the process of collective bargaining' (Salamon, 1987, p. 259).

The balance between joint consultation and collective bargaining will depend upon the power of trade unions. Daniel and Millward (1983, p. 135) found that the existence of LMCs or JCCs was closely allied to the relative bargaining power of the unions:

> Consultative committees may tend to become an adjunct to the institutes of collective bargaining where workplace trade union organization is well established, but provide an alternative channel of representation where it is weak.

Models of joint consultation

Academics have put forward two different models of consultation. The *revitalization model* suggests that recent support for consultation has coincided with the increased use of direct EI approaches by employers. This, it is argued, has the effect, whether planned or not, of undermining collective bargaining and consequently weakening workplace trade unionism (Batstone, 1984; Edwards, 1985). In contrast, the *marginality model* suggests an increased trivialization and marginalization of joint consultation in the early 1980s, particularly in organizations confronted by deteriorating economic conditions (MacInnes, 1987).

Marchington (1987) has challenged the conceptualization of these two models, arguing that the two consultative models do not describe the full range of processes that may take place in the consultative arena. Instead, Marchington proposed a third model, the *complementary model*, in which joint consultation complements rather than competes with joint regulation or collective bargaining. The argument is that 'consultation acts as an adjunct to the bargaining machinery' (Marchington, 1987, p. 340). With this model, collective bargaining is used to determine pay and conditions of employment, whereas joint consultation focuses on issues of an integrative nature and helps to lubricate employment relationships; both processes can provide benefits for employees and the organization. Millward and Stevens' (1986) study found support for Marchington's complementary model, reporting that 'complex consultative structures co-exist with complex collective bargaining arrangements in the public sector in particular' (Millward and Stevens, 1986, p. 143).

Extent of joint consultation

Evidence has been collected from a number of surveys on the extent of joint consultation (e.g. Cully et al., 1998; Millward et al., 1992; Kersley et al., 2006). The 1998 WERS of private sector, multinational companies in the UK found that the overall proportion of the workplaces with LMCs fell between 1984 and 1998 from 34 per cent to 28 per cent. WERS 2004 data reveal the extent to which managers normally inform, consult or negotiate with employee representatives (union or non-union) on key aspects of the employment relationship (Table 12.3). In 67 per cent of workplaces, management did not engage with employee representatives on any of the 12 terms and conditions of employment listed. Management were most likely to negotiate over pay with union employee representatives (61 per cent) and non-union employee representatives (18 per cent), and least likely to engage employee representatives with respect to staff selection.

In all cases, the presence of a trade union in the workplace significantly increased the likelihood that managers would engage in some form of joint regulation of the employment relationship. WERS 2004 data appear to corroborate Dundon et al.'s findings that, in the majority of unionized workplaces, joint consultation and collective bargaining operated alongside non-union employee voice channels. Moreover, they found that 'shop stewards appeared more willing than they did a decade ago to participate in such dual representative channels' (Dundon et al., 2004, p. 1160). MacInnes (1985) reminds us that the separation of joint consultation from collective negotiations is often attempted by simply excluding from the negotiating agenda any item that normally is the subject of joint regulation. The result can be the creation of the 'canteen, car park, toilet paper syndrome' and has prompted some observers to characterize the subject matter of JCCs as a 'diet of anodyne trivia and old hat' (MacInnes, 1985, pp. 103–4).

Table 12.3 Incidence of joint regulation of terms and conditions, 2004

	% of all workplaces					
	Nothing		Consult		Negotiate	
	Non-union	Union[1]	Non-union	Union	Non-union	Union
Staff selection	78	42	9	23	3	9
Staffing plans	75	33	12	34	3	7
Performance appraisal	75	33	12	33	4	14
Training	75	36	13	31	3	9
Pensions	73	22	6	16	10	36
Equal opportunities	72	22	14	40	5	15
Hours	71	18	8	20	16	53
Holidays	71	19	5	13	15	52
Pay	70	16	5	13	18	61
Health and safety	69	17	17	49	5	15
Grievance procedure	69	15	14	36	9	28
Discipline procedure	69	15	13	35	8	9

Note:
1. Relates to workplaces with recognized trade unions
Source: Adapted from Kersley et al. (2005) p. 22

Although we have always to be careful when making international comparisons – because, for example, researchers define HR practices differently – survey studies show that, across Western Europe between 1997 and 2000, EI practices and downward and upward communication increased by an average of 52 per cent (Mayrhofer et al., 2000). In Canada, 43 per cent of workplaces reported some form of EI in decision-making (Verma and Taras, 2001). These findings need to be contrasted with more critical studies suggesting that EI in decision-making has not shown any sign of substantive improvement (Thompson and McHugh, 2002).

The structure and operation of joint consultation committees

When choosing a joint consultative structure or developing an existing one, it is necessary for managers to make a number of decisions guided by its aims, philosophy and strategy. Joint consultation requires a high-trust relationship and regular information disclosure to all participating parties. Managers have to decide how much information will be disclosed, by whom and how. Management's role in a consultative structure is generally to communicate information and be fully involved in the process; anything less than this will result in decisions being made or agreed upon without their knowledge or support. Managers may adopt either of two broad approaches: they can integrate the two processes of consultation and negotiation within the collective bargaining machinery, or they can agree to maintain a separate machinery of joint consultation and regulation.

Three main reasons have been identified for the *integration* of consultative and negotiating machinery:

1. Communicating, consulting and negotiating are integrally linked together in the handling of employee relations.

2. Union representatives need to be fully involved in the consultative process, if only as a prelude to negotiations.
3. As the scope of collective bargaining expands, the issues left are otherwise allocated to what may be viewed as an irrelevant process.

On the other hand, substantive reasons have been cited for establishing *separate* consultative and collective bargaining structures:

1. Separation may help to overcome organizational complexity.
2. The fact that collective bargaining deals with substantive or procedural matters, and consultation addresses other matters of common interest, forces the two structures apart.
3. Regular JCC or LMC meetings and the publication of minutes ensure that joint consultation is accorded a proper place in the organizational system and confirms management's commitment and responsibility to consultation with its employees.

An example of a joint consultation and collective bargaining structure in the public sector is shown in Figure 12.6.

When there are two sets of arrangements, the terms of reference of the LMC need to be specified by defining both its subject matter and the nature of its authority. The subject matter may be defined in terms of:

- excluding from its deliberation anything that is subject to joint regulation, that is, substantive (e.g. pay and vacation time) and procedural (e.g. discipline and grievance processes) matters
- enumerating the items that are to be regarded as matters for joint consultation (e.g. a corporate plan, HR trends, education and training)
- items chosen on an ad hoc basis, deciding whether or not an issue should be dealt with in the joint regulation machinery.

HRM WEB LINKS

For more information on JCCs, go to the websites of ACAS (www.acas.org.uk) and the Trades Union Congress (www.tuc.org.uk). See also www.ccma.org.za (South Africa) and www.airc.gov.au (Australia).

European works councils

EWCs have been part of the German industrial relations landscape since the end of the Second World War. Much of the early research on works councils was focused on German 'codetermination' (*Mitbestimmung*) and worker participation in decision-making, manifested in the Works Constitution Act. EWCs are not the same as LMCs or JCCs: whereas LMCs are voluntary committees, the term 'European works council' is used to describe only *mandatory* consultative committees. Accordingly, works councils can be defined as 'Institutionalized bodies of collective worker participation at the workplace level, with specific informatory, consultative and codetermination rights in personnel, social and economic affairs' (Frege, 2002, p. 223).

Works councils are legally independent of trade unions, and their members are elected in a ballot of all employees rather than just union members. The key functions of EWCs are:

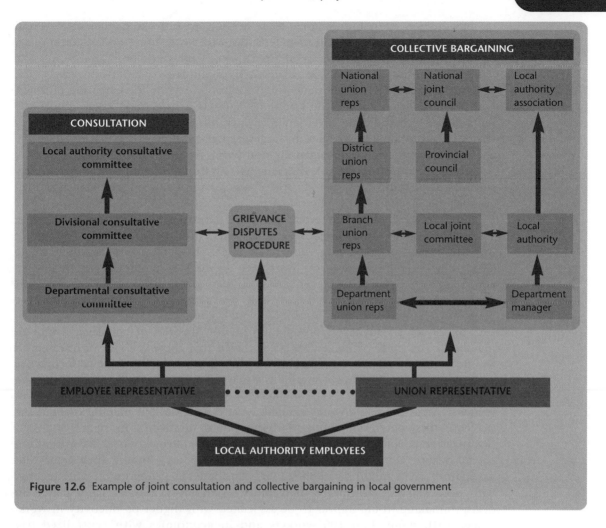

Figure 12.6 Example of joint consultation and collective bargaining in local government

- establishing two-way communication between employees and management and union and management
- maintaining peaceful and cooperative employment relations (as EWCs are not allowed to initiate a stoppage of work)
- providing training for representatives.

Since the early 1990s, UK managers, trade unions and academics have become more interested in the EWC model, this renewed interest having come about for three principal reasons. First, EU legislation has focused attention on EWCs. As mentioned earlier, the 1994 EWC Directive required organizations employing more than 1000 employees in the EU (excluding the UK) and at least two establishments in different member states, with at least 150 employees (again excluding the UK), to set up works councils. The EWC Directive's principal objective is to induce organizations across the EU to set up an EWC system for the purpose of informing and consulting employees. In December 1999, the 1994 EWC Directive became law in the UK. To date, agreements between management and unions to establish EWCs have been concluded in over 600 European companies (Gilman and Marginson, 2002). The new EU Directive on Information and Consultation (2001) is likely to provoke further interest and academic research, especially in member states without a strong EWC tradition (e.g. Britain and Ireland).

Second, the decline of union membership in Britain and bargaining power over the past two decades has induced trade union leaders to explore the extension of union and workers' rights outside the traditional collective bargaining arena, under the umbrella of EU employee governance law. Third, the introduction of mandatory EWCs in 'transitional economies' in Central Europe has evoked a debate about the conditions for successful implementation of EWCs (Frege, 2002). Although the EWC system is still in its infancy, at least in the UK, EWCs are 'the most prominent, widespread and powerful form of industrial democracy in contemporary capitalist societies' (Frege, 2002, p. 221).

The 1998 WERS of private sector, multinational companies in the UK found that 19 per cent of the workplaces operated an EWC (Cully et al., 1998). EWCs have differing degrees of power (Mayrhofer et al., 2000): in Germany, for example, where EWCs have been a feature of the workplace for decades, employee representatives can resort to the courts to prevent or delay managerial decisions in areas such as changing working practices and dismissals. The range of issues discussed and the degree of legislative support for EWCs would, comment Mayrhofer et al. (2000, p. 226), 'shock US managers brought up on the theories of "manager's right to manage"'. The study by Frege (2002) concluded that there is a lack of research on the determinants of different employment relations, how EWCs work in practice and the specific relation between unions and works councils. Evaluating the existing literature, Frege (2002, p. 241) concludes, 'we know much about the ontology of works councils (what is a works council, what does it do) but much less about the determinants, outcomes and underlying causal relations'. In terms of EWC–organization performance links, Addison et al. (2000) have also made a contribution to the debate. Using economic data from Germany and Britain, they argue that mandatory EWCs might be a policy to be considered in strong union work regimes with decentralized 'distributive bargaining'. Mandatory indirect participation in decision-making would appear to be associated with higher productivity in workplaces with more than 100 workers and in economies with centralized pay bargaining (e.g. Germany).

Obstacles to employee involvement

Two major impediments to the introduction of effective EI – so-called 'double blockage' – have been identified in the literature: the attitude of workplace union representatives and the attitude of line managers (Dundon et al., 2004).

Trade unions traditionally prefer bargaining to consultation and have characterized consultative processes as a potential managerial strategy for 'incorporating' union representatives into management forms of control or as a union avoidance strategy (Clarke, 1977; Gilson and Wager, 2000). In essence, joint consultation is viewed as an inadequate expedient, preventing unions from defending their members through 'free' collective bargaining. As one industrial relations theorist has asserted, 'increasing the involvement only of employees … appears to be part of a strategy aimed at reducing the role and influence of stewards' (Batstone, 1984, pp. 264–5). More recently, the dominance of US thinking on HRM, the use of non-union organizations as 'exemplars of good practice' and the individualization of organizational communication have partly explained union hostility to innovations in EI (Mayrhofer et al., 2000). However, although this is a plausible interpretation for events in US/UK contexts, non-union EI regimes sit uncomfortably with the history and circumstances of employee relations in Western EU member states (Brewster et al., 1999).

Managerial philosophy and HR strategy might be another major obstacle to EI. Managers seek to construct an organizational culture that reflects their own ideologies and styles of management and will reinforce their strategies and control (Gospel and Palmer, 1993). It is therefore not surprising to find evidence that the major obstacle to EI is resistance to change by middle and junior management (see, for example, Marchington, 1980; Rendall, 1986). What is clearly apparent in the debate is that EI activities are a critical component of the 'high-performance–high-commitment' work system. EI is characterized by a high-trust employment relationship, one of operating by consent rather than coercion (Champy, 1996). As is the case with all HR policies, the effective implementation of EI necessitates commitment at the most senior level of the organization: anything less might mean indirect and direct EI arrangements being 'squeezed out' because of pressure of work.

Employee involvement and paradox

The types of EI scheme initiated by management to improve organizational performance contain contradictions and paradoxes. Contemporary forms of EI also contain ethical concerns (Clayton, 2000). Stohl and Cheney (2001) analyse four main types of EI paradox:

- structure
- agency
- identity
- power.

They posit that paradox is inherent in EI processes and that these paradoxes set limits that constrain the effectiveness of EI networks.

Organizational *structures* are created to govern EI, but most organizations eliminate workers from the most influential network: the executive. Strauss (1998) explains this potential paradox. Most EI initiatives involve direct participation (e.g. briefing groups), but this form of EI can make only limited changes to the way in which work is designed because 'really important decisions', for example investment in new technology, are made by senior management. It is not surprising, then, that although EI is 'often intended to enhance productivity by empowering workers to make decisions, the system's very design prevents workers having a say in how they might become more involved' (Stohl and Cheney, 2001, p. 362). Put another way, 'Learn, innovate and voice your opinions as I have planned!'

The idea of *agency* relates to an individual's sense of being and a feeling that she or he can or does make a difference (Giddens, 1984). EI is rooted in the beliefs that workers can have an effect and that their knowledge and skills are fundamental to organizational success. The notion of agency helps us to examine the psychological contract within a frame of interpretation that calls for substantial individual expression and contribution. One paradox of agency references the tensions and contradictions present in self-managed work teams in which teams may rely on the active subordination of team members to the will of the team. Thus, 'Do things our way but in a way that is still distinctively your own!' Not surprisingly, workers may become ambivalent and hesitant about participating in such a regime.

The paradox of *identity* addresses issues of boundaries, space and the divide between the in-group and the out-group (Stohl and Cheney, 2001). The paradox of identity is linked to the notion of employee commitment. At one level, EI implies commitment to the processes of learning and discussion, and to diversity and difference. At another level, however, 'commitment is expected to equal agreement' (Stohl and Cheney, 2001, p. 380). Within the context of EI and work-based learning networks, voicing an alternative view is interpreted by managers and non-managers alike as a means of resistance, as lack of commitment or even as evidence of 'sabotage' (Zorn et al., 1999). In a so-called 'learning organization', the paradox of identity may be expressed as 'Be a self-directed learner to meet organizational priorities.'

The fourth paradox is that of *power*, which centres on issues of leadership, access to resources, opportunities for independent voice and the shaping of employee behaviour. The popular EI literature emphasizes the importance of 'strong leaders' to facilitate and lead participatory efforts. Stohl and Cheney (2001, p. 388) provide persuasive evidence of EI regimes 'getting workers to make decisions that management would have made themselves'. In other words, 'Be an independent thinker, just as I have commanded you!'

Paradox is an integral part of the EI paradigm, but the contemporary forms of EI also raise ethical concerns. As Clayton (2000) points out, the growing interest in the ethics of EI might reflect a degree of unease over the shift in power towards employers and management resulting from the decline in trade union density and influence, the growth of precarious employment, and exorbitant salary increases for corporate executives. Moreover, any ethical concerns relating to EI are based on the recognition that the employment relationship is inherently conflictual and, as such, the benefits of employees engaging in management-designed 'employee voice mechanisms' may be offset by the unwitting effects of greater exploitation, work intensification and stress (Clayton, 2000). These alleged negative effects partly account for the continued scepticism towards EI on the part of some observers (see also Thompson and McHugh, 2002). The dynamics of the employment relationship, together with the power and ethical issues it generates, affirm the support for independent collective voice mechanisms and acceptance that cooperation between managers and managed can only be partial and qualified (Clayton, 2000). As discussed in Chapter 1, the challenge for both managers and workers is whether creativity and innovation can emerge from these paradoxes.

Employee rights

The third key dimension of employee relations is a set of individual employment rights. The equality of employee relations is a function of organizational values and culture, but, in addition, it is shaped by individual legal rights that protect employees against inequitable behaviour by managers or other co-workers. A fundamental tenet underpinning effective employee relations is that employees must have confidence in management's intention to be fair and equitable. The right to be treated fairly and equitably, with its links to concepts of rights, obligations and 'social justice', has, of course, an ethical dimension (Winstanley and Woodall, 2000). As Liff and Dickens (2000) persuasively argue, treating people fairly on merit is a fundamental 'moral value', which has widespread legitimacy as an approach to managing the employment relationship. The premise underlying the approach is that men and women are fundamentally alike (Liff and Dickens, 2000, p. 87).

The case for equitable managerial behaviour is made on both legal and economic grounds. As we have explained elsewhere (see, for example, Chapter 4), individual employment rights, embodied in UK and EU legislation, regulate the behaviour of employers and employees. The Sex Discrimination Acts of 1975 and 1986, the Race Relations Act 1976 and more recently the Disability Discrimination Act 2005 address issues of discrimination and harassment with regards to an employee's gender, disability, ethnicity, race or sexual orientation. To comply with the legislation, HR professionals have developed codes of practice as a guide to better HR practices.

The debate on the merits of equality managerial action emphasizes the economic or 'business case' argument. Rather than being an appeal to social justice and/or 'ethical behaviour', equality managerial behaviour is argued for as a means to an end – meeting a strategic goal of improved performance. The benefits of diversity management, the ability to manage effectively a workforce consisting of a human mosaic in which people with different beliefs, values and behaviour patterns are employed, are similarly assessed on economic merits (see, for example, Paauwe, 2004). In the context of market-driven capitalism, the increased emphasis on economic utilitarian goals rather than individual legal rights reflects the limited achievements in practice of legal compliance and the forces of globalization (Liff and Dickens, 2000).

Sexual harassment as a employee relations issue

Different forms of hostility and misogyny towards women in the workplace, in particular **sexual harassment**, have received considerable attention from researchers, policy-makers and practitioners over the past few decades. Research suggests that the negative consequencies of sexual harassment and a misogynistic workplace extend beyond individual targets to include co-workers, work groups and whole organizations (Miner-Rubino and Cortina, 2004). As Keith (2000, p. 287) points out, sexual harassment 'poisons the atmosphere in the workplace'. In the 21st century, sexual harassment in the workplace is an important issue in HRM, centring as it does around issues of social justice and efficiency. First, workplace sexual harassment is unlawful, and the courts have increasingly viewed its prevention as the responsibility of the employer. The legal concept of 'detriment' is important here. Sexual harassment is a 'detriment' per se; it can lead to an employment-related detriment to the female employee and, as such, has serious implications for management. In 1986, the European Parliament passed a resolution on violence against women, commissioning a report on the dignity of women at work, which led to the adoption of the EU code of practice (Figure 12.7).

In 1998, the allegations of sexual impropriety against US President Bill Clinton highlighted some difficult aspects raised by cases of sexual harassment in the workplace. The first issue is credibility because there is seldom a witness to support whether the conduct being complained about actually happened. There are, for example, no witnesses to the alleged conduct of Mr Clinton and the White House employee Monica Lewinsky. Credibility and circumstantial evidence are under scrutiny here. Who has more credibility? Is there indirect evidence that might support or dismiss the allegations?

The EU code of practice defines sexual harassment as 'unwanted conduct of a sexual nature' affecting 'the dignity of women and men at work'. It defines harassment as largely subjective, in that it is for the individual to decide whether the conduct is acceptable or offensive.

The code says that member states should take action in the public sector and that employers should be encouraged to:

- issue a policy statement
- communicate it effectively to all employees
- designate someone to provide advice to employees subjected to harassment
- adopt a formal complaints procedure
- treat sexual harassment as a disciplinary offence.

Figure 12.7 The European Union code on sexual harassment

The Clinton case raises another issue that often applies to workplace investigations, the question of containment. In the presidential investigation, the public prosecutor apparently had no interest in limiting the scope of the investigation, but for many HR professionals, containment, in addition to what is legitimate and necessary in terms of conducting a sexual harassment complaint, is also an issue. The aim will be to contain the allegation and limit knowledge about the complaint to those who need to know. Managers have to take appropriate action to prevent sexual harassment and to inform employees of the consequences of sexual harassment.

Workplace sexual harassment is 'the most intimate manifestation of employment discrimination faced by women' (Keith, 2000, p. 277), and legal protection against it is complex and sensitive. There is concern expressed by some authors about how women are treated in law (e.g. Debono, 2001), contending that women are disadvantaged because of a patriarchal or sexist jurisprudence. Debono (2001) found that there are sexist elements to the jurisprudence related to workplace sexual harassment decisions in the UK, the USA and New Zealand. Although the legislation is progressive, it is argued that, 'sexist attitudes still remain with those who have the power to use the legislation to compensate the victims' (Debono, 2001, p. 338).

Returning to the economic implications of workplace sexual harassment, research on consequences has identified a host of negative work outcomes, including a loss of commitment to work, decreased job satisfaction, increased absenteeism and decreased job performance (see, for example, Montgomery and Kelloway, 2002; Mueller et al., 2001), findings consistent with research on workplace violence. Less well researched are possible links between victimization and the psychological contract. The stress caused by sexual harassment affects the expectations that employees and employers have of each other. It is highlighted because the victim's commitment and loyalty to the organization decreases and the intent to leave the organization increases. In addition, with increased focus on international HRM, sexual harassment in the workplace has profound implications for multinational corporations (see Chapter 3). Based on data from several countries, Luthar and Luthar (2002) conclude that the likelihood of female expatriates being sexually harassed is greater in some cultures than others. Studies tend to emphasize that exposure to workplace sexual harassment impacts negatively on the quality of employee relations and is, moreover, associated with impaired employee well-being and individual and organizational performance.

Employee discipline

So far, we have looked at communication practices, management-initiated EI and employee rights. To complete the discussion on employee relations, we must examine a fourth set of HR policies and practices that affect the quality of employee relations: **employee discipline**.

When employee voice mechanisms fail to create or reinforce desirable employee attitudes and behaviours, managers may resort to disciplinary action. Indeed, there is evidence that there has been an increased use of formal disciplinary measures since EI practices were introduced. Bratton's (1992, p. 197) analysis of work teams, for example, showed that when a payment-by-results scheme was withdrawn, it 'increased the propensity of management to invoke formal disciplinary procedures'. Similarly, Mabey et al. (1998b) found a disjuncture between the rhetoric of empowerment and the practical reality of total quality management. Their study found that workers had 'negative perceptions' of total quality management because of a culture incorporating the 'excessive use of disciplinary actions against individuals' (Mabey et al., 1998b, p. 66). In recent years, rates of disciplinary sanctions and dismissals have increased, providing further evidence of the general UK movement from collective relations towards the *individualization* of the employment relationship (Knight and Latreille, 2000).

The modern workplace is pervaded by rules established by management to regulate the behaviour of workers. Indeed, it is argued that obedience underscores the relationship between the employer and employee: 'There is certainly nothing more essential to the contractual relation between master and servant than the duty of obedience' (Cairns, 1974, quoted in Wedderburn, 1986, p. 187). Disciplinary practices, ranging from oral warnings to termination of the employment relationship, aim to make workers' behaviour predictable. As discussed elsewhere in this text, the employment relationship involves a legal relationship, and for those employers and managers who share a less-than-sophisticated management style known as 'my way or the highway', there is a framework of legal rights regulating the disciplinary process. The purpose of these laws and standards is to provide a fair and consistent method of dealing with alleged inappropriate or unacceptable work behaviour, but they vary widely between national legal systems. In addition to legal rules, collective agreements in unionized workplaces generally grant management the power to 'institute rules of behaviour and to mete out punishment, subject to the employees' right to grieve' (Giles and Starkman, 2001, p. 308).

The purpose of this section is modest: to provide an overview of the disciplinary concepts, practices, procedures and statutory rights found in the workplace. UK students and practitioners requiring a detailed knowledge of employment law relating to discipline and dismissal are advised to refer to Selwyn's *Law of Employment* (2004) or a similar text.

HRM WEB LINKS

Go to the following websites to compare employment standards legislation relating to discipline at work: www.hmso.gov.uk/acts.htm, which provides full texts of UK Acts of Parliament; and www.sdc.gc.ca/en/gateways/topics/lzl-lal.shtml for a comparative study of Canadian employment standards. See also the list at the beginning of this book.

Disciplinary concepts

Discipline can be defined as the process maintaining compliance with the rules that regulate employment in order to produce a controlled and effective performance. The purpose of discipline is:

- *improvement:* the disciplinary process is seen as one of counselling the disobedient employee back to acceptable behaviour
- *punishment:* the disciplinary process is seen as being about imposing penalties
- *deterrent:* the process is seen as educational to deter others.

Corrective discipline refers to management action that follows the infraction of a rule. In North America, the 'hot-stove rule' is used to guide correct discipline. This states that disciplinary action (e.g. warnings or suspension from work) should have the same characteristics as the penalty an individual receives from touching a hot stove. These characteristics are that discipline should be, with warning, immediate, consistent and impersonal. Most modern workplaces apply a policy of *progressive discipline*, which means that the employer notifies employees of unacceptable conduct and provides them with an adequate opportunity to correct their behaviour.

Disciplinary rules and procedures are necessary for promoting orderly employment relations as well as fairness and consistency in the treatment of individuals. *Rules* set standards of conduct and performance in the workplace, whereas *procedures* help to ensure that the standards are adhered to and also provide a fair method of dealing with alleged failures to observe them. A disciplinary process should incorporate the requirements of natural justice, which means that employees should be informed in advance of any disciplinary hearing of the alleged misconduct, be given the right to challenge the alleged evidence, have the right to representation and to have witnesses, and be given the right to appeal against any decisions taken by management (Selwyn, 2004).

Rules of behaviour

Every organization has rules, for example rules about time-keeping, quality standards, safety and personal hygiene. Rules of behaviour in the workplace should be clear, readily understood and no more than are sufficient to cover all obvious and usual disciplinary matters. The UK Employment Rights Act 1996 requires employers to provide written information for their employees about certain aspects of their disciplinary rules and procedures. In particular, employees should be given a clear indication of the type of conduct, often referred to as 'gross misconduct', that may warrant summary dismissal, that is, dismissal without notice (Selwyn, 2004). Workplace rules will be shaped by national cultures and subcultures. Behaviours considered acts of 'gross misconduct' are shown in Figure 12.8.

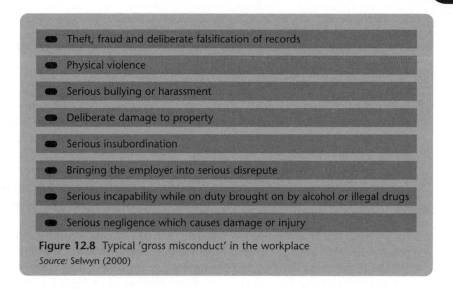

- Theft, fraud and deliberate falsification of records
- Physical violence
- Serious bullying or harassment
- Deliberate damage to property
- Serious insubordination
- Bringing the employer into serious disrepute
- Serious incapability while on duty brought on by alcohol or illegal drugs
- Serious negligence which causes damage or injury

Figure 12.8 Typical 'gross misconduct' in the workplace
Source: Selwyn (2000)

Penalties

The employer can impose a number of penalties for infractions, such as:

- rebuke
- warnings
- transfer or demotion
- suspension
- dismissal.

A *rebuke* may be, for example, a simple 'Don't do that.' For most employees, the rebuke may be sufficient to change behaviour. Formal *warnings* should not be given lightly because the manager is making some sort of commitment to action if the behaviour is repeated. Furthermore, the legislation on dismissal in Western countries has made the system of warnings an integral part of disciplinary practice, which has to be followed if the employer is to succeed in defending a dismissal decision. All written warnings should be dated, signed and kept on record for a period agreed by rules known to both sides. Disciplinary *transfer* or *demotion* is a penalty that is substantial but falls short of dismissal. *Suspension* involves a penalty that is serious but avoids the disadvantage of being longlasting. If all other penalties fail to modify the employee's behaviour, the employee may be *dismissed* with 'just cause'. There is an array of legal statute and precedent intended to safeguard the individual employee against unreasonable dismissal, the point of legal intervention varying from one country to another (Torrington, 1998).

Procedures in discipline

Across Britain, formal disciplinary procedures are the norm even in the smallest workplaces. A formal procedure provides a framework that avoids the risk of inconsistent ad hoc decisions. Torrington (1998) identifies four key features of a disciplinary procedure:

1. fairness
2. facilities for representation
3. procedural steps
4. management rules.

The disciplinary process must be conducted in a fair manner, *fairness* being best ensured by even-handedness in the disciplinary hearing. The employee should be entitled to know the nature of the charge in sufficient detail to enable her or him to prepare a case (*Hutchins* v. *British Railways Board* [1974]). Employees should always be given an opportunity to state their case (*Tesco (Holdings) Ltd* v. *Hill* [1977]) no matter what the circumstances are. Fairness will also be enhanced if there is an appeal stage. Due process should allow for the employee to be informed of her or his right to appeal to a higher level of management that has not previously been involved in the disciplinary decision or to an independent arbitrator (Selwyn, 2004).

To help the errant employee explain her or his case, the disciplinary procedure should allow *facilities for representation*, which means that another employee or representative should be allowed to accompany the employee (*Rank Xerox (UK) Ltd* v. *Goodchild* [1979]). In the UK, Section 10 of the Employment Relations Act 1999 creates a new right for a worker, when invited by the employer to attend a disciplinary hearing, to make a reasonable request to be accompanied by a single companion. The representative can be either an official of an independent trade union or a co-worker (Selwyn, 2004).

Procedural steps should be limited so that there are sufficient for justice to be done but not so many that matters become long and drawn-out. The steps are typically associated with progressive discipline, which means that the employer notifies the employee of unacceptable conduct and provides her or him with an adequate opportunity to correct the behaviour. A typical progressive discipline procedure is shown in Figure 12.9.

An employee who has committed an infraction is verbally warned and informed that if the same infraction is repeated (within some specified time period), the degree

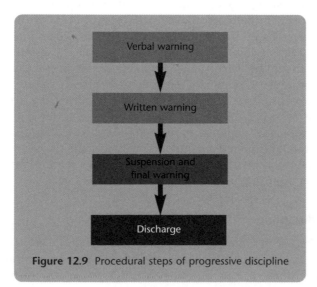

Figure 12.9 Procedural steps of progressive discipline

of disciplinary action will be increased. If the employee commits the same or a similar violation (or possibly an unrelated infraction) within the specified period, the employee will then be given a written warning, which will be placed in her or his personnel file. An employee who again transgresses will be suspended from employment for a period of time without pay and will be given a final warning. This warning will normally specify termination of the employment contract as a result of another such infraction (see HRM in Practice 12.3). If the employee is again guilty of misconduct, the employee may be discharged for 'just cause'. The legal notion of just cause means that there is a factual basis to warrant the dismissal, and/or the nature of the penalty was justified, taking into account all the relevant circumstances (Centre for Labour–Management Development, 2001).

HRM IN PRACTICE 12.3

TWO CO-WORKERS KILLED AFTER EMPLOYEE RECEIVES A DISCIPLINARY LETTER

JILL MAHONEY, *GLOBE AND MAIL*, 17 OCTOBER 2002, P. A20B; KATHERINE HARDING, *GLOBE AND MAIL*, 23 OCTOBER 2002, P. C1

In Kamloops, British Columbia, Canada, long-time government employee Richard Anderson killed two co-workers before turning his gun on himself after receiving a disciplinary letter that could have brought dismissal. According to police, it took the 55-year-old married father of two grown children only two minutes to kill his boss and co-worker. Mr. Anderson then killed himself. The crime scene was the boardroom of the Ministry of Water, Land and Air Protection's one-storey office.

Experts say reprimanding or firing an employee with potential rage issues can be especially dicey, especially within organizations facing mass lay-offs, which is the case in the British Columbia civil service. 'Typically, somebody doesn't just snap,' said Steve Kaufer, co-founder of the Workplace Violence Research Institute in Palm Springs, California. 'There's a whole succession of behaviours and things that are leading up to a serious incident of workplace violence.'

> **'There's a whole succession of behaviours and things that are leading up to a serious incident of workplace violence.'**

When employers suspect a dismissal will go badly, Mr. Kaufer said it should be done away from the worker's colleagues, in a room with more than one exit. The area should be clear of objects that could be workplace weapons: coffee cups, scissors and chairs. Extra security should be posted nearby. 'It's important to maintain a sense of dignity for the employee, so that they understand that there's a future ahead of them at another place of employment,' Mr Kaufer added.

Workplace violence experts agree that such acts as this rarely happen in a vacuum. 'They are always as a result of long difficulties an individual has had either at work or at home,' said Glenn French, a research director at the Canadian Initiative on Workplace Violence. Employers and employees should be alert for some of the dozens of signals that can be sent out by a person who's not coping well. Gerry Smith, a human resources consultant, highlighted several changes in normal day-to-day behaviour patterns, a history of addictive behaviour, alcohol, drug and substance abuse, paranoid thinking, and a history of confrontational behaviour, or increased argumentativeness. Employers should take seriously potential threats among their workforce and try to talk to the employee or bring in outside help.

Management rules pervade every workplace. Rules underscore management's prerogative to design work, to make decisions and to take actions to manage the workplace. Management rules typically cover six aspects of workplace activity and behaviour: insubordination, negligence, safety, theft, unacceptable behaviour at work (e.g. the harassment of co-workers or fighting) and unreliability. Management rules provide guidelines on employee behaviour as long as the rules are clear, understood and supervised.

In the UK, the ACAS code of practice on disciplinary and grievance procedures (Figure 12.10) provides practical guidance on how employers and managers should deal with disciplinary issues in the workplace. In Britain, the Employment Act 2002 created a new prescribed procedure for handling discipline in the workplace. The so-called 'three-step' disciplinary procedure requires:

1. the employer to specify the concerns in writing
2. the employee to attend a formal meeting with the manager
3. a right to appeal on the part of the employee.

WERS 2004 survey data show that 71 per cent of workplaces in Britain had implemented this three-step statutory procedure for handling discipline, and these formal procedures were more prevalent in larger workplaces, in the public sector and in workplaces with a recognized trade union (Kersley et al., 2006).

'Good' disciplinary procedures should:

- Be in writing

- Specify to whom they apply

- Be non-discriminatory

- Provide for matters to be dealt with without undue delay

- Provide for proceedings, witness statements and records to be kept confidential

- Indicate the disciplinary actions that may be taken

- Specify the levels of management that have the authority to take the various forms of disciplinary action

- Provide for workers to be informed of the complaints against them and where possible all relevant evidence before any hearing

- Provide workers with an opportunity to state their case before decisions are reached

- Provide workers with the right to be accompanied by a co-worker or trade union official

- Ensure that, except for gross misconduct, no employee is dismissed for a first breach of discipline

- Ensure that disciplinary action is not taken until the case has been carefully investigated

- Ensure that workers are given an explanation for any penalty imposed

- Provide a right of appeal – normally to a more senior manager – and specify the procedure to be followed

Figure 12.10 Advisory, Conciliation and Arbitration Service guide to disciplinary action
Source: Selwyn (2000)

STUDY TIP

Most medium and large organizations have a disciplinary framework within which managers administer rules and conduct disciplinary interviewing, and to protect employee rights, most jurisdictions have a framework of law to administer the disciplinary process. In order to avoid unfair dismissal charges or grievances, a manager should have an understanding of the law relating to discipline and dismissal. Obtain a copy of Selwyn's *Law of Employment* (2004) and, using the index, list the statutes and any principal legal judgements that impact on discipline and dismissal. Here are some questions you may wish to seek the answers to:

- What is meant by the term 'rules of natural justice'?
- What is meant by 'just cause'?
- Who has the burden of proof in discipline cases?
- When is dismissal appropriate for a first offence?

REFLECTIVE QUESTION

What do you think of the ACAS guidelines in Figure 12.10? How important is it for an organization's disciplinary process to be seen to be 'equitable'?

Chapter summary

- Communicating is the fundamental process of organizing and leading in the workplace. It includes written, verbal and non-verbal communication, each of which encompasses several methods of transmitting information. Communication flows downwards, upwards and horizontally in organizations. Prescriptive texts emphasize that the role of the HRM department is to ensure that there are no deviations or blockages in that flow that can cause communication problems.

- The fewer obstacles that occur in communication, the more goals, feedback and other management messages to employees will be received as they were intended. Employee communications can also be interpreted as a strategy to build a strong corporate culture in order to exert more control over the workforce.

- EI occurs when employees take an active role in the decision-making process within the organization. EI may be formal or informal, direct or indirect, voluntary or legislated; it may range from a manager exchanging information with an employee or an employee representative on a specific issue, to complete participation in a major investment decision.

- Greater participation has been identified with high-performance work systems and the commitment HR strategy. As many companies attempt to draw upon their employees' skills and knowledge more fully, EI and two-way communication can be seen to be a logical development in employee relations to enlist employees' skills and cooperation.

- The terms 'employee participation', 'employee involvement' and 'employee empowerment' have different meanings. Differing expectations among employees and union representatives therefore tend to affect the attitudes of the key players in the industrial relations system, the propensity to participate and ultimately the success of any experiments in EI. Hence, a vital first step, if there is to be any meeting of minds, is to create a common language and conceptual framework.

- Data available from WERS studies provide evidence that British managers are adopting EI techniques. There is, however, a deep scepticism that EI schemes might be used by managers to circumvent established collective bargaining machinery and thereby marginalize the role of the workplace union representatives. It would thus strengthen individualism in the management of the employment relationship. We also noted that the 1994 EWC Directive and the 2001 EU Directive on Information and Consultation are likely to provoke further interest in and research on indirect EI, especially in member states without a strong EWC tradition, such as Britain.

- EI innovations are more likely to succeed if management is aware of the concerns and potential problems confronting union representatives. Ethical concerns relating to EI are based on the recognition that the employment relationship is inherently conflictual and, as such, the benefits of EI in decision-making may be offset by the effects of work intensification and stress (Clayton, 2000).

- This chapter explained how the equality of employee relations is a function of organizational values and culture, but also that individual legal rights protecting employees against inequitable behaviour by managers or other co-workers shape it and provide support for independent employee voice processes. As such, choices and restrictions underlie HR interventions to promote effective employee relations. We also explored the arguments that equitable behaviour is based on legal, social justice and economic positions.

- Discipline is a key feature of employee relations in the workplace. Disciplinary practices vary between national legal systems, but to command support among the workforce and avoid violations of the psychological contract, managers should design and apply disciplinary practices with due regard to the requirements of natural justice.

Key concepts

- Briefing groups
- Grapevine
- Employee communication
- Joint consultation
- Non-verbal communication

- Employee involvement
- Sexual harassment
- Employee discipline
- Works council

Chapter review questions

1.   What are the links between HR strategies and EI and communication practices?

2.   Identify and discuss different schemes that the HR department manages in order to improve employee communications.

3.   'EI is a central component of high-performance work systems.' Do you agree or disagree? Discuss.

4.   Explain the difference between participation and involvement in the workplace.

5.   'Collective voice achieves what the lone voice could never do: it humanizes and civilizes the workplace.' Do you agree or disagree? Why?

6.   What is meant by 'sexual discrimination'? Explain why an effective response to incidents of sexual harassment in the workplace is important for the employer and manager.

Further reading

Dundon, T., Wilkinson, A., Marchington, M. and Ackers, P. (2004) The meaning and purpose of employee voice. *International Journal of Human Resource Management*, **15**(6): 1149–70.

Frege, C. (2002) A critical assessment of the theoretical and empirical research on works councils. *British Journal of Industrial Relations*, **40**(2): 221–48.

Gollan, P. J. (2006) Editorial: consultation and non-union employee representation. *Industrial Relations Journal*, **37**(5): 428–37.

Guirdham, M. (2005) *Communicating Across Cultures at Work*. Basingstoke: Palgrave Macmillan.

Hall, M. and Marginson, P. (2005) Trojan horse or paper tigers? Assessing the significance of European Works Councils. In B. Harley, J. Hyman, and P. Thompson (eds) *Participation and Democracy at Work* (pp. 204–21). Basingstoke: Palgrave Macmillan.

Kamenou, N. and Fearfull, A. (2006) Ethnic minority women: a lost voice in HRM. *Human Resource Management Journal*, **16**(2): 154–72.

Liff, S. and Dickens, L. (2000) Ethics and equality: reconciling false dilemmas. In D. Winstanley and J. Woodall (eds) *Ethical Issues in Contemporary Human Resource Management* (pp. 85–101). Basingstoke: Palgrave Macmillan.

Marchington, M. (2001) Employee involvement at work. In J. Storey (ed.) *Human Resource Management: A Critical Text* (2nd edn) (pp. 232–52). London: Routledge.

Wall, T. D. and Wood, S. J. (2005) The romance of human resource management and business performance, and the case for big science. *Human Resources*, **58**(4): 429–61.

Woodhams, C. and Lipton, B. (2006) Gender-based equal opportunities policy and practice in small firms: the impact of HR professionals, *Human Resource Management Journal* **16**(1): 74–97.

Practising human resource management

Searching the web

On an individual basis, or working in a small group, pick two or three online HR-related websites (e.g. www.jiscmail.ac.uk/lists/industrial-relations-research.html, www. shrm.org/hrlinks, www.sdc.gc.ca/en/gateways/topics/lzl-lal.shtml or www.fdmmag.com/articles/03aco.htm) and the Employee Involvement Association (www.eia.com), and explore 'Employee involvement'. Enter the website of an organization you or the group are familiar with or one you have studied (e.g. www.rolls-royce.com, www.microsoft.com, www.thebodyshop.com or www.royalbankscot.co.uk/). From the information in this chapter and from your research, select a cluster of EI-type practices and explain the reasons for your choice. (Hint: make some assumptions about your business and HR strategies.) Bring this information to class, and present your findings and recommendation in an oral report.

 ### HRM group project

Form a group of three or four students. The purpose of this group assignment is to allow you to apply your knowledge of EI and information disclosure in the workplace to an organization. Specifically:

1. Carry out web-based research of the law relating to EI and the disclosure of corporate information in at least two countries, for example Australia, Britain, Canada or the USA, and other EU member states.
2. Compare the laws and write a brief management report on the major provisions covering EI and information disclosure.

How are the laws similar and different? A team member(s) should interview at least one manager or HR professional. The interviewer(s) should probe the nature of the organization's EI arrangements: What EI arrangements does the organization use? How does the EI system relate to the business strategy? What EI initiatives have been introduced and why? Each group member should take responsibility for researching the various aspects of the assignment.

Chapter case study

COMMUNICATIONS AT FORRESTER COMPUTER SERVICES

In this age of 'flatter' management structures, Forrest Computer Services (FCS) must have one of the flattest. Last year, it reduced its management hierarchy to almost pancake proportions when it introduced self-managed teams and abolished all but the most senior management jobs.

FCS has a business team of 14 senior managers reporting to the three people who make up the board. Below this are a host of client teams, each with about 15 members, operating as separate commercial units without a manager. Teams have to be able to provide a full client support service and draw on all the technical, financial and administrative skills that this requires. Within this framework, employees can decide whom they want to team up with, and teams can elect whether or not they want a leader. Those which have opted for a team leader have not necessarily chosen the person most senior under the older organization.

This was a radical reorganization brought about by necessity. The decision followed a massive deficit of £72 million on a turnover of £726.5 million in 2001; this shocked the company, which had been growing steadily. This initially meant slashing costs and therefore staff, so the workforce shrank from 750 to fewer than 500 employees.

But FCS senior management knew they had to do more than cut costs: they had to improve productivity and competitiveness if the company was to remain in an ever-tightening market. 'We introduced self-managed teams to build up our client service because that is where we must have the edge', said Forrest's HR director, Carolyn Oliver. 'Every software house can provide the software and systems the clients want: it is the efficiency with which the client is handled that makes the difference and that comes down to the way we are organized', she said.

Reorganization put a tremendous burden on the HR department, the way in which it had to work and the communication system. On top of the reorganization, working practices – recruitment processes, reward strategies, training and development, and employee participation – were completely reassessed. On the one hand, this created a free-flowing organization with the flexibility and motivation to react to changes in the market. On the other hand, it bolstered the need for watertight HR systems to keep this motivated mass from running out of control.

Oliver said that the implementation of the plan proved to be a massive employee participation exercise, and in the early weeks, there was much misleading and irrelevant information being communicated through the grapevine. 'Top management wanted the ideas to come from the shop floor. So we brought together 20 people from all levels of the organization bar the most senior, put them into two teams and sent them away for the weekend to thrash out their own ideas of how the company should be organized', explained Oliver.

This was, however, only the beginning of the consultation process. The next step involved setting up employee task forces to look at the different issues implied by reorganization. FCS's senior managers disseminated information from the two working parties around the company and asked people to apply for one of the 70 places available on the 10 task forces. About 200 people applied from the spectrum of jobs and locations in the company. Six weeks later, the task forces presented their findings to the board. 'They ranged from one extreme to the other. Some liked the way things were and simply wanted to stay put. Others wanted to do away with all senior managers right to the top', remarked Oliver. FCS opted for something in the middle – a senior business team with many client teams reporting in.

The HR department had to make the system work. Carolyn Oliver admitted frankly that she had underestimated the reaction of managers to their sudden loss of power. 'They felt threatened and believed that their services would no longer be required by the company', she said. It was a 'hard slog' convincing them that the new-style FCS was for them too, Oliver said. 'You cannot reassure managers by writing to them or making promises in a company newsletter', she went on to explain.

As all the teams were essentially operating in the same computer services market, there was a danger that they would all end up competing against each other instead of against company competitors. Oliver admitted there has to be a tight coordination of client service teams, a close control of the standards they worked to and effective organizational communication. Introducing multiskilled, self-managed teams also highlighted demands from employees for a more permanent system of employee participation in the company.

Discussion questions

1. What methods could the company have adopted to convince the managers that they had a future at FCS?

2. Should managers try to eliminate the organizational grapevine?

3. Discuss the alternative channels of communication that FCS could have used to disseminate information from the first two working parties to employees.

4. What recommendations would you make for establishing a permanent system of employee participation at FCS? Justify your case.

HR-related skill development

The formal disciplinary process is concerned with regulating employee behaviour to produce controlled and effective behaviour. The disciplinary interview is a central part of the disciplinary process, but most managers use the formal disciplinary interview as the last resort. Many managers also lack the basic knowledge and skills to conduct such a legally bound activity. To help you develop this important management skill and to give you experience of the disciplinary process, we have devised a disciplinary case with supporting information. You can participate, at either an individual or a group level, in the simulation and develop an important HR skill by going to www.palgrave.com/business/brattonandgold4 and clicking on 'Disciplinary interview exercise'.

Notes

1. Shawn Phelps and Rick Spence, Communication overload spreading. *Globe and Mail*, September 2, 2005, p. C1.
2. Anvil Verma and Daphne Taras (2001, p. 454).
3. Margaret Prosser (2001) Speaking up for the collective voice. *IPA Bulletin*, 7, p. 1; quoted by Dundon et al. (2004, p. 1151).

Chapter thirteen

Health and wellness management

John Bratton

Health and wellness management is concerned with the design and maintenance of a work environment that supports the organization's objectives, creates a safe and healthy workplace and promotes the well-being of employees.

'Long before you reach the Russian city, Norilsk announces itself with mounds of dirty blackened snow on the fragile grass of the summer tundra. Then comes the hellish vision of the world's most polluted Arctic metropolis. Looming at the end of the road is a horizon of massive smokestacks … and thousands of denuded trees as lifeless as blackened matchsticks. Inside malodorous smelters, Russian workers wear respirators as they trudge through the hot suffocating air, heavy with clouds of dust and gases. … Pollutants from this factory have drifted as far as the Canadian Arctic. Traces of heavy metals have been found in the breast milk of Inuit mothers.'[1]

'Workplace wellness is a key success factor in supporting a business to achieve its desired results.'[2]

Chapter outline

Chapter objectives

After studying this chapter, you should be able to:

1. Explain the benefits of a health and wellness strategy
2. Discuss some key developments in occupational safety, health and wellness
3. Describe the components of a workplace wellness programme
4. Outline the regulatory framework for workplace health and safety
5. Describe some physical and psychosocial hazards in the modern workplace
6. Critique management strategies for health and wellness in the workplace

Introduction

Most mornings, we turn the door handle and set off to work in factories, steel mills, offices, banks, schools, hospitals, universities and other workplaces. Most of us assume that we will return home safely at the end of the working day, but many workers unfortunately will not. In 2003–04, 235 British workers lost their lives through a workplace fatality, another 30,666 suffered a major work-related injury, and a further 129,143 employees suffered a work-related injury serious enough to warrant having more than three days' absence from work. In a survey conducted in 2003, 2.2 million workers also reported that they suffered from an illness they believed was work-related (Health and Safety Statistics, 2003/04). In the European Union (EU), there are around 6000 fatalities and 10 million workers suffer work-induced injury or ill-health (Walters, 2004). The data underscore an important reality about paid work: it can be an unhealthy, even deadly, experience.

The World Health Organization (WHO) defines 'health' as 'a state of complete physical, mental and social well-being, not merely an absence of disease and infirmity'.[3] According to this definition, managers are immersed in one of society's greatest challenges – the design and maintenance of a work organization that both supports the organization's objectives and provides an environment that is safe and healthy for its employees. Occupational health and safety encapsulate quite distinct yet intrinsically related concepts concerned with the identification and control of work-induced ill-health and accidents. Whereas *accidents* are visible or measurable, not without cause and largely preventable, work-induced *ill-health* is largely invisible and can develop over a long period of time, for example asbestosis (Cullen, 2002). Although workplace health and safety have long been legitimate areas for regulation, as evidenced by health and safety legislation, occupational safety has typically been given precedence over more general workplace health concerns. The concept of workplace wellness goes beyond the regulation and management of work-related health and safety, to focus on shaping employees' entire lifestyle and well-being. What is important to recognize is that concerns about health and wellness are no longer limited to areas of industrial work. Front-line office workers, managers and professionals are demanding to work in a 'healthy organization', and employers are increasingly acknowledging the negative economic consequences of employee ill-health (see HRM in Practice 13.3 below).

The growing recognition that health and wellness form an important subgroup of organizational contingencies affecting HRM underscores the need to develop a proactive strategy that manages health- and wellness-related risks. In what follows, we begin by considering the importance of health and wellness in the human resource management (HRM) model, and why a working knowledge of workplace health, safety and wellness is important for every manager. After giving a brief history of occupational health and safety legislation, we identify some hazards in the modern workplace. The chapter goes on to examine what managers can do to minimize work-induced injuries and ill-health. Finally, we seek to examine the paradoxes surrounding the issue of health and wellness so that there can be a better understanding of the complexities of the employment relationship.

REFLECTIVE QUESTION

Read the chapter's opening quotation again. Who are the stakeholders in health and wellness? What are the responsibilities of employers and government to ensure that work is conducted in a safe and healthy environment? Consider an organization that you have worked in. Critically review its health and safety record and training.

Health and wellness and human resource management

Although there has been a significant growth in empirical research on HRM problems and issues, it is unfortunately true that workplace health and safety is under-researched by HRM scholars, partly because it has entered HRM discourse in only a marginal way. Rising costs associated with work-induced injuries and ill-health, psychological contract issues and new laws are important reasons why workplace health, safety and wellness should be part of any introduction to the field of HRM. But there is another important reason why HRM scholars and practitioners need to pay more attention to health and wellness: if strategic HRM means anything, it must encompass the development and promotion of a set of health and wellness policies to protect the organization's most valued asset, its employees.

The employer has a legal duty to maintain a healthy and safe workplace, the health and safety function being directly related to key HRM activities such as selection, appraisal, rewards and learning, and development. Health and safety considerations and policy can affect the selection process in two ways. First, it is safe to assume that, during the recruitment process, potential applicants will be more attracted to an organization that has a reputation for offering a healthy and safe work environment for its employees. Second, the maintenance of a healthy and safe workplace can be facilitated in the selection process by choosing applicants with personality traits that decrease the likelihood of an accident. The appraisal of a manager's performance that incorporates the safety record of a department or section can also facilitate health and safety. Research suggests that safety management programmes are more effective when the accident rates of their sections are an important criterion of managerial performance.

Safe work behaviour can be encouraged by a reward system that ties bonus payments to the safety record of a work group or section. Some organizations also provide prizes to their employees for safe work behaviour, a good safety record or suggestions for improving health and safety. Training and human resources (HR) development play a critical role in promoting health and safety awareness among employees, and indeed the Health and Safety at Work etc. Act (HASAWA) 1974 requires employers to provide instruction and training to ensure the health and safety of their employees. Studies indicate that safety training for new employees is particularly beneficial because accidents are highest during the early months in a new job.

On the question of the importance of occupational health and safety, although economic cost and HR considerations will always be predominant for the organization, the costs of ill-health and work-related accidents are not only borne by the victims, the families and their employers: the costs of occupational ill-health and accidents are also clearly borne by the taxpayer and public sector services. The health care sector, for example, bears the costs of workplace ill-health and accidents. Reliable estimates of the total cost of occupational ill-health and accidents are incomplete, which is perhaps symptomatic of the low priority given to this area of work. The Health and Safety Executive (HSE) has admitted that although occupational diseases kill more people in the UK each year than industrial accidents, there is only limited information on the former. An official survey in 1993 put the cost to society for deaths and accidents (excluding occupational disease) in British workplaces at £10–15 billion, or 1.75–2.75 per cent of the gross domestic product.[4] In Canada, compensation for victims of workplace accidents exceeds US$3 billion, this figure excluding the cost to the public health care system resulting from long-term work-related illnesses.

The changing approach to workplace health and safety

The traditional approach to safety in the workplace used the **careless worker model**. It was assumed by most employers, the courts and accident prevention bodies that most accidents resulted from an employee's failure to take safety seriously or protect herself or himself. The implication of this is that work can be made safe simply by changing the behaviour of employees by poster campaigns and accident prevention training. In the past, the attitudes of trade unions often paralleled those of the employers and managers. Early trade union activity tended to focus on basic wage and job security issues rather than safety: trade union representatives used their negotiating skill to 'win' wage increases, and health and safety often came rather low down in their bargaining priorities. If union representatives did include health and safety as part of their activities, it was often so that they could negotiate the payment of 'danger' or 'dirt' money over and above the regular wage rate. According to Eva and Oswald (1981, p. 33), the tendency for union officials was 'to put the onus on to inspectors and government rather than to see health and safety as part of the everyday activity of local union representatives'. Among employees, dangerous and hazardous work systems were accepted as part of the risk of working. Lost fingers and deafness, for example, were viewed as a matter of 'luck' or the 'inevitable' outcome of work. In the early 1970s, a major investigation into occupational health and safety concluded that 'the most important single reason for accidents at work is apathy' (Robens, 1972, p. 1). So there is a paradox here. When there are major disasters on land, air or sea involving fatalities, society as a whole takes a keen interest, yet society's reaction towards the fact that hundreds of employees die and thousands receive serious injuries every year in the workplace tends to be muted.

In the 1960s, approximately 1000 employees were killed at work in the UK and 23 million working days were lost annually on account of industrial injury and disease. Such statistics led investigators to argue that 'for both humanitarian and economic reasons, no society can accept with complacency that such levels of death, injury, disease and waste must be regarded as the inevitable price of meeting its needs for goods and services' (Robens, 1972, p. 1). Since the Robens Report, there has been a growing interest in health affairs as well as safety in the workplace. Importantly, regulatory bodies and many organizations reached a developmental stage in which the careless worker model no longer effectively addressed work-induced ill-health caused by toxic substances, noise, stress, and badly designed and unsafe systems of work. A new approach to occupational health and safety, the *shared responsibility model*, assumes that the best way to reduce levels of occupational accidents and disease relies on the cooperation of both employers and employees, a 'self-generating effort' between 'those who create the risks and those who work with them' (Robens, 1972, p. 7).

In the late 1970s, the British Trades Union Congress (TUC) articulated a 'trade union approach' to health and safety emphasizing that the basic problem of accidents stemmed from the hazards and risks that were built into the workplace. The trade union approach argued that the way to improve occupational health and safety was through redesigning organizations and work systems in order to 'remove hazards and risks at source'.[5] An HSE document[6] would seem to support this approach, stating that most accidents involve an element of failure in control – in other words a failure in managerial skill. A guiding principle when drawing up arrangements for securing health and safety should be that work should, as far as possible, be adapted to people and not vice versa. The trade union approach to health and safety, which draws attention to potential hazards in the labour process, is depicted in Figure 13.1.

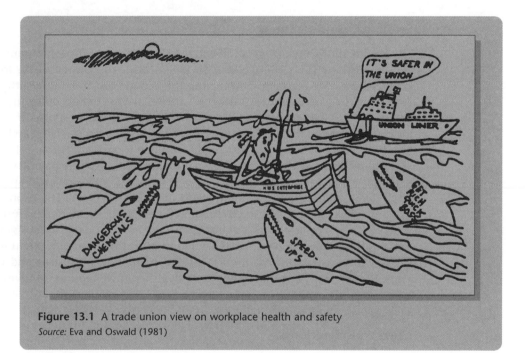

Figure 13.1 A trade union view on workplace health and safety
Source: Eva and Oswald (1981)

In an effort to effectively leverage HR to improve competitiveness and encourage a readiness for organizational change (Madsen, 2003), many work organizations introduced a *wellness model* in the 1990s. Wellness is the 'process of living at one's highest possible level as a whole person' (Schafer, 1996, p. 33). It is a general philosophy or holistic approach taken by top management to enhance the overall well-being of the workforce through a combination of voluntary diagnostic and educational health programmes. Whereas workplace 'health' manages the tension between organizational goals and employee health, the intrinsically related concept of 'wellness' endeavours to 'improve' emotional, intellectual, physical, social and spiritual health (Madsen, 2003, p. 48). Just as safety is regulated and typically given primacy over workplace health issues, wellness is far less likely to be monitored and managed than general health in the workplace (Mearns and Hope, 2005). Workplace wellness encourages the view that both the employer and the employee benefit from wellness management activities. A common metaphor to underlie the approach is the 'healthy organization' (Haunschild, 2003). The performance arguments – that is, that wellness interventions reduce employee absenteeism, improve the bottom line and encourage workers to accept change – provides the ideological basis of wellness management (Haunschild, 2003). A 2003 survey of Canadian workplaces reported that 83.4 per cent of employers offered some form of wellness programming (Bentley, 2005).

The importance of health and wellness

There are strong economic, legal, psychological and moral reasons why managers should take health and safety seriously and these are discussed in turn.

Economic considerations

The Health and Safety Commission and the Department of the Environment, Transport and the Regions (HSC/DETR) (2000) document made the 'business case' for health and safety in the workplace. In considering the economics of an unhealthy and unsafe workplace, it is necessary to distinguish between costs falling upon the organization and costs falling upon government-funded bodies such as hospitals. It is not difficult for an organization to calculate the economic costs of a work-related accident. In addition to direct costs related to lost production due to an accident and illness, there are also indirect costs. The indirect costs can include the overtime payments necessary to make up for lost production, the cost of retaining a replacement employee and the legal cost associated with court hearings in contested cases. The economic costs of work-related accidents, and the techniques for assessing them, require further research.

A safe and healthy work environment can reduce operating costs and improve organizational effectiveness. It has been long argued that an investment in health and wellness improves worker commitment and performance (Mearns and Hope, 2005). Thus, top management should approach health and wellness as an investment rather than a cost (Dyck, 2002).

Legal considerations

With respect to workplace health and safety, the legal rights of employees can be categorized into two broad categories: individual and collective. The first source of *individual* rights evolves from common law. Every employer has a vicarious common law duty to provide a safe working environment for her or his employees. The primary source of individual rights arises from statute law; in Britain, an example is the HASAWA 1974. Within the EU, individual rights stemming from directives under Article 189 of the Treaty of Rome are a second important source of legislated protection standards promoting safe working environments.

The main source of *collective* health and safety rights arises from the negotiated collective agreements between union and management. In current labour law, Canadian, American and New Zealand workers have legal rights to refuse to perform unsafe or unhealthy work (Pye et al., 2001). In 1974, a Royal Commission on the Health and Safety of Workers first articulated the three principal rights of Canadian workers: the right to refuse dangerous work without penalty, the right to participate in identifying and correcting health and safety problems and the right to know about hazards in the workplace. These three fundamental rights continue to be enshrined in current Canadian legislation (Montgomery and Kelloway, 2002). In the EU and the USA, failure to provide a safe working environment may result in the employer being prosecuted for **corporate manslaughter**. Health and safety legislation is discussed more fully in the next section.

HRM WEB LINKS

Visit the websites of any of the following occupational health and safety organizations for detailed information on health and safety legislation: Britain (www.open.gov.uk/hse), Canada (www.hrdc.gc.ca, www.canoshweb.org.en and www.ccohs.ca), Finland (www.occuphealth.fi), Australia (www.nohsc.gov.au), Hong Kong (www. hkosha.org.hk) and Europe (www.osha.eu.int).

Psychological considerations

Apart from economic and legal considerations, a healthy and safe work environment helps to facilitate employee commitment and improve industrial relations. In Beer et al.'s (1984) HRM model, it is recognized that, going beyond the legal requirement of 'due diligence', a healthy organization can have a strong positive effect on the psychological contract by strengthening employee commitment, motivation and loyalty: 'there is some evidence to indicate that work system design may have effects on physical health, mental health, and longevity of life itself' (Beer et al., 1984, p. 153). Similarly, at a collective level, it is argued that union–management relations are improved when employers satisfy their employees' health and safety needs. When organizations accept greater responsibility for the health, wellness and safety of their employees, it can change workplace behaviour, and employees may take a less militant stance during wage bargaining if management pays attention to housekeeping.

Moral considerations

Do employers have a moral responsibility to provide employees and their dependants with a safe and healthy working environment? Health and wellness issues have implications for corporate responsibility and managerial ethics. In this regard, Gewirth (1991) argues that those individuals who contribute to the causation of work-related diseases (e.g. asbestosis, lung cancer and exposure to second-hand smoke) and who do so knowingly can be held to be both causally and morally responsible for their action. Dohery and Tyson (2000) argue persuasively that managers are not innocent bystanders with regard to employee health and well-being: their actions – such as choice of production processes and substances, work speed-up, extra work hours and performance-based pay – have adverse effects on employees' work–life balance, and their physical and mental well-being.

A major challenge to managers is clearly to provide a safe and healthy work environment for their employees. Economic and moral reasons dictate such a policy, but, as we have already stated, there is also a pervasive portfolio of legislation, regulations, codes of practice and guidance notes dealing with occupational health and safety, and, as with other employment law, the HR practitioner has taken on the role of advising managers on the content and legal obligations of this.

Health and safety legislation

The history of occupational safety legislation can be traced back to the Industrial Revolution in the 18th century. The conditions of employment in the new factories were appalling, as indicated by this 1833 testimony:

> I can bear witness that the factory system in Bradford has engendered a multitude of cripples, and that the effect of long continued labour upon the physique is apparent not only in actual deformity, but also, and much more generally, in stunted growth, relaxation of the muscles, and delicacy of the whole frame.[7]

The early conditions of employment have, however, to be related to their context before they can be evaluated historically. It must be remembered that employment standards were low before the process of industrialization began: comparisons of conditions of employment and health and safety provisions must begin from here rather than from late 20th-century standards. Many employment practices in the early factories were inherited from the preindustrial era, an example being child labour. In the new factories, children worked for their parents and were necessarily involved in the same hours of work as the adults for whom they worked. Family labour was a bridge between the conditions of employment in the pre-factory world and the new factory system, and the early Factory Acts did not automatically abolish family labour.

Pioneering legislation

The 1802 Health and Morals of Apprentices Act was designed to curb some of the abuses of child labour. This Act applied only to pauper apprentices in the factories; it restricted hours of work to 12, prohibited night work and provided for instruction in the 'three Rs'. Enforcement of the Act was ineffective, however, because the inspectors were 'generally well disposed to the mill-owner' (Gregg, 1973, p. 55). The 1833 Factory Act outlawed the employment of children under nine years old, limited the hours of work of children aged between 9 and 13 to eight per day and appointed four government factory inspectors to enforce the legal requirements. Early safety legislation was confined to textile factories and affected only the conditions of employment of women and children.

The 1867 Factory Act extended safety laws beyond the textile mills and even began to abandon the myth that safety law's only purpose was to protect women and children: adult male employees had been considered, theoretically at least, to be capable of protecting themselves (Hobsbawm, 1968). The 1901 Factories and Workshops Consolidation Act introduced a more comprehensive health and safety code for industrial workplaces. This Act remained the governing Act until the Factories Act 1937. During the period 1850–1901, the Factory Acts were strengthened, due to a combination of factors, including social reformers, the inspectorate and, more significantly, campaigning by a growing and more militant trade union movement (Eva and Oswald, 1981). Nonetheless, progress was painfully slow, hindered by consistent opposition from the majority of employers, who claimed that the Factory Acts would make British industry uncompetitive.

The Factories Act 1961

The Factories Act 1961 consolidated industrial safety law. The Act defined a 'factory' as any premise in which two or more persons were employed in manual labour in any process for the purpose of economic gain. Part I of the Act was concerned with general provisions affecting the health of the factory employee. The Act established minimum standards in factories for cleanliness, space for employees to work in, temperature, ventilation and lighting. For example, the temperature of the defined workplace was not to be less than 60°F (15.5°C) in rooms where much of the work was done sitting and did not involve serious physical effort. Part II of the Act laid down general requirements aimed to promote the safety of factory employees. For example, Section 14(1) specified that 'Every dangerous part of any machinery ... shall be securely fenced.' The Act also contained general welfare provisions, such as the adequate supply and maintenance of washroom facilities and a statutory reporting system for accidents and industrial diseases.

The Offices, Shops and Railway Premises Act 1963

The rise in employment in the service sector, together with the growth of white-collar trade unionism, helped to explain the extension of legal protection to non-industrial workers and the growing concern for general occupational health issues. The Act gave protection similar to that provided for factories. The general provisions followed those of the Factories Act 1961, dealing with cleanliness, ventilation, lighting, temperature and so on.

The Robens Report and the Health and Safety at Work etc. Act 1974

Occupational health and safety came under detailed scrutiny in the 1970s. Trade unions representing white-collar workers pressed for health and safety legislation to be extended to employees in laboratories, education, hospitals and local government, who were not covered by any of the earlier statutes. Thus, the Labour government set up a Committee on Safety and Health at Work, chaired by Lord Robens, to review the whole field and make recommendations. The committee's findings can be summarized thus:

- Despite a wide range of legal regulation, work was continuing to kill, maim and sicken tens of thousands of employees each year. The committee considered that the most important reason for this unacceptable state of affairs was apathy.
- There was too much law. The committee identified 11 major statutes, supported by nearly 500 supplementary statutory instruments. The committee believed that the sheer volume of law had become counterproductive.
- Much of the law was obscure, haphazard and out of date, many laws regulating obsolete production processes. Furthermore, the law focused on physical safeguards rather than preventive measures such as training and joint consultation.
- The provision for enforcement of the existing legislation was fragmented and ineffective. The committee felt that the pattern of control was one of 'bewildering complexity'.
- Existing health and safety law ignored a large number of employees: statutes prior to 1974 excluded over 8 million workers in communication, education, hospitals and local government.

The committee made four main proposals to improve occupational health and safety:

1. The law should be rationalized. A unified framework of legislation should be based upon the employment relationship (rather than on a factory or mine), and all employers involved with work or affected by work activities (except for domestic servants in private homes) would be covered by the new legislation.
2. A self-regulating system involving employers, employees and union representatives should be created to encourage organizational decision-makers to design and maintain safe work systems and help employees to take more responsibility for health and safety. The basic concept was to be the employer's duty towards her or his employees – employers being bound to design and maintain safe and healthy systems of work – and the concomitant duty of the employees was to behave in a manner safeguarding their own health and that of their co-workers.
3. A new unified statutory framework setting out general principles should be enacted.
4. A new unified enforcement agency headed by a national body with overall responsibility should be established and should provide new, stronger powers of sanction.

In 1972, the Robens committee published its report, and the Conservative government introduced a new Bill in Parliament. Two years later, the Conservatives lost the general election, but in 1974 the Labour government reintroduced a similar Bill, which became the **Health and Safety at Work etc. Act 1974**, examined in more detail in the next section.

The Health and Safety at Work etc. Act 1974

This Act vested trade unions with significant powers related to workplace health and safety matters. As Nichols (1990, p. 366) points out, compared with the 1980s and 90s, the HASAWA was 'a product of a different politics and philosophy'. The complete coverage of this complex Act is outside the scope of this chapter, but we will highlight its salient features so that readers can become familiar with some important principles and terminology. The main duties on employers are contained within Section 2 of the Act (Figure 13.2).

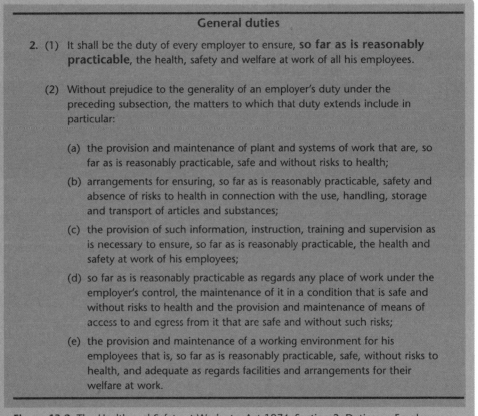

General duties

2. (1) It shall be the duty of every employer to ensure, **so far as is reasonably practicable**, the health, safety and welfare at work of all his employees.

(2) Without prejudice to the generality of an employer's duty under the preceding subsection, the matters to which that duty extends include in particular:

(a) the provision and maintenance of plant and systems of work that are, so far as is reasonably practicable, safe and without risks to health;

(b) arrangements for ensuring, so far as is reasonably practicable, safety and absence of risks to health in connection with the use, handling, storage and transport of articles and substances;

(c) the provision of such information, instruction, training and supervision as is necessary to ensure, so far as is reasonably practicable, the health and safety at work of his employees;

(d) so far as is reasonably practicable as regards any place of work under the employer's control, the maintenance of it in a condition that is safe and without risks to health and the provision and maintenance of means of access to and egress from it that are safe and without such risks;

(e) the provision and maintenance of a working environment for his employees that is, so far as is reasonably practicable, safe, without risks to health, and adequate as regards facilities and arrangements for their welfare at work.

Figure 13.2 The Health and Safety at Work etc. Act 1974, Section 2: Duties on Employers

HRM WEB LINKS

Go to www.hmso.gov.uk/acts.htm for the full text of UK Acts of Parliament. For sites in other countries consult the list at the beginning of this book.

European Union health and safety legislation

In addition to health and safety legislation from their national governments, employers within EU member countries have EU directives to follow, which adds to the complexity of the situation. EU law affects the health and safety legislation of the

UK as it overrides domestic law. The Social Charter (see Appendix A) gives added weight to occupational health and safety, stating that workers have the 'right to health protection and safety at the workplace'. EU directives under Article 189 of the Treaty of Rome are also an important source of health and safety legislation. They cover a wide range of health and safety issues, such as the use of asbestos, the control of major industrial accident hazards, risk assessment, equipment regulations and the prevention of repetitive strain injuries. Directives are binding, although member states can decide upon the means of giving them legal and administrative effect. In the UK, this is usually in the form of regulations, which are normally published with associated approved codes of practice and guidance notes. Teague and Grahl (1992, p. 136) optimistically argue that the new EU health and safety legislation will 'not be of the "lowest common denominator" type but "maximalist" in nature'.

HRM WEB LINKS

Visit the websites of any of the following occupational health and safety organizations – Australia (www.safetyline.wa.gov.au), Britain (www.open.gov.uk/hse), Finland (www.occuphealth.fi). or other countries (consult the list at the beginning of this book) – for more information on how health and safety regulations impact on the design of work and the management of the employment relationship.

The UK's New Labour government has recently expressed a commitment to improving occupational health and safety. The Revitalising Health and Safety statement, launched by the deputy prime minister and chair of the HSC in June 2000, set national targets for improving health and safety performance:

- to reduce the number of working days lost from work-related injury by 30 per cent
- to reduce work-related ill-health by 20 per cent
- to reduce fatalities by 10 per cent by 2010 (Health and Safety Statistics, 2000/01).

Research on health and safety legislation in France and Germany demonstrates, however, the importance of joint safety committees for improving health and safety performance in the workplace (Reilly et al., 1995; Walters, 2004).

The implications of health and safety legislation for managers and HR professionals are formidable. As safety experts rightly point out, workplace accidents and and ill-health are not without cause, are largely preventable and often arise from failures in control and management (Cullen, 2002). Hazard prevention and control requires managers to undertake risk assessment in order to help the organization decide what health and safety measures need to be implemented.

If the ensuing debate on the Social Charter results in the EU adopting the 'maximalist' model, joint consultative health and safety committees will play a key role in determining strategic approaches to workplace health and safety. As Legge (2005) points out, however, the track record of the EU in the area of health and safety has been 'modest', and, particularly during economic recession, employers, unions and governments tend to 'water down' directives and fail to comply with health and safety regulations. Similarly, Bain (1997) provides a pessimistic analysis of trends in workplace health and safety. He persuasively argues that, in Europe and the USA, powerful business lobbies and governments have mounted an offensive against health and safety legislation. The source of the current campaign for the 'deregulation' of health and safety safeguards is market-driven and can be located in growing competitive pressures (Bain, 1997).

The perceptive reader will have noticed similarities between the argument opposing factory legislation in the 19th century and the 21st-century debate on the 1997 Kyoto Protocol, a pact for reducing greenhouse gas emissions linked to warming of the planet. Many Canadian and US corporations are opposed to the Kyoto Protocol because meeting the Kyoto targets would, they argue, make North American industry uncompetitive.

REFLECTIVE QUESTION

Henry Ford once said, 'History is bunk.' Consider the current debate on the 1997 Kyoto Protocol. Can the stakeholders – employers, employees, governments, communities – of today learn anything from the history of factory safety legislation in the 19th century? What are your views? What role, if any, should employers and governments play in meeting the Kyoto targets?

Workplace health and wellness issues

This section examines several health issues of special concern to today's managers and explains the meaning of workplace wellness.

Health issues

The dynamics of the modern workplace and the changes in the way in which organizations manage employment relations have been linked to numerous health problems. For example, precarious employment, unequal power distribution, work intensification and role conflicts have been associated with negative physiological changes, somatic complaints and psychological stress. This section examines several health and wellness issues: sick building syndrome (SBS), workplace stress, alcohol abuse, smoking and acquired immune deficiency syndrome (AIDS).

Sick building syndrome

Interest in the physical aspects of the work building, as a factor affecting employee performance, goes back to at least the 1930s with the Hawthorne experiments in the USA (see Chapter 5). In the 1980s, the construction of 'tight' office buildings with no openable windows in Europe and North America and building-related ill-health problems focused attention on the working conditions of office workers (HRM in Practice 13.1). In 1982, sick building syndrome (SBS) was recognized by the WHO as occurring where a cluster of work-related symptoms of unknown cause were significantly more prevalent among the occupants of certain buildings in comparison to others. Typical symptoms of SBS listed by WHO include eye/nose/throat irritation, a sensation of dry mucous membranes and skin, a skin rash, mental fatigue, headaches, a high frequency of airway infection and cough, nausea, dizziness, hoarseness and wheezing (Bain and Baldry, 1995). In 1992, the HSC calculated that the staff of 30–50 per cent of newly 'remodelled' buildings in Britain suffered a high incidence of illness. In Canada, it has been estimated that there are 1800 'sick' buildings affecting 250,000 workers. Based on such data, Bain and Baldry (1995, p. 21) argue that the problem of SBS has been 'severely underestimated'.

HRM IN PRACTICE 13.1

CAPITAL'S GLASS GLOBE FAILS GREEN TEST

DAVID HENCKE, *GUARDIAN*, 30 JULY 2001

London's new city hall – the glass globe designed by world-renowned architect Norman Foster – has been criticized in an official commissioned confidential report for falling 'well short' of 'an exemplar building' for the capital. The report warns that the building ... could leave the London authority's new employees open to absenteeism through sick building syndrome, glare and having to work in high humidity in summer and sudden chills in winter.

The report says the building fails to meet best energy use standards by setting carbon emissions of 70 kg per square

> **'...the building fails to meet best energy use standards...'**

metre per year. ... It claims the building 'has a standard that is 16% poorer than if a standard naturally ventilated building had been chosen'. The report is critical of the use of air conditioning – even though it will use ecologically sound recycled water from boreholes – saying that naturally ventilated build-

ings have fewer instances of absenteeism by staff. 'Employees can lose more than a week per person per year through this problem' – known as sick building syndrome. Other criticisms cover the ... dangers of condensation and high humidity in the summer.

The official GLA [Greater London Assembly] website says the 50-metre-high building 'incorporates features designed to make the building as green as possible'. Victor Anderson, a Green party member of the GLA, said: 'The public website is propaganda.'

The causes of SBS have concentrated on possible structural or technical factors such as inadequate ventilation. The UK HSE suggests that SBS may be caused by a lack of fresh air supply, inadequate ventilation, unsuitable lighting, airborne pollutants and, at a more general level, low morale. Bain and Baldry propose, in the context of global price competition, recession and high energy costs, that SBS is related also to an emphasis on cost reduction and the intensification of office work. They conclude that 'Changes in the balance of power in the office environment have undoubtedly made it easier for management to gain employee acceptance of much more demanding practices and patterns of work' (Bain and Baldry, 1995, p. 30).

The growing incidence of SBS is a major challenge for the HR professional. SBS increases labour costs via absenteeism, which may in turn undermine the empowerment approach associated with the soft HRM model as managers resort to disciplinary measures to reduce time taken off work.

HRM WEB LINKS

Visit the website www.iea.cc/ergonomics for information on ergonomics, the study of relationships between the physical attributes of workers and their work environment.

Workplace stress

The term 'stress' in now part of the regular vocabulary of managers and other employees. Although a certain degree of stress is normal in life, if stress is repeated or prolonged, individuals experience physical and psychological discomfort. The changing nature of work (see Chapter 5), work experience, changes in technology, for example the BlackBerry and mobile phone-buzzing, a 24/7, on-demand lifestyle, and new types of working such as call centres (see Chapter 4), may lead to increased stress and stress-related ill-health. Stress at work can also impact negatively on job performance. Figure 13.3 illustrates some common symptoms of stress.

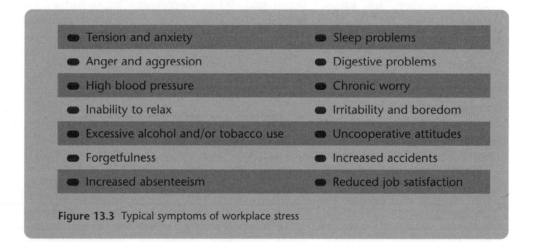

Tension and anxiety	Sleep problems
Anger and aggression	Digestive problems
High blood pressure	Chronic worry
Inability to relax	Irritability and boredom
Excessive alcohol and/or tobacco use	Uncooperative attitudes
Forgetfulness	Increased accidents
Increased absenteeism	Reduced job satisfaction

Figure 13.3 Typical symptoms of workplace stress

HRM WEB LINKS

Go to the websites www.tuc.org.uk/search/searches/20060814-113716-Stress/page1.cfm, www.hse.gov.uk, www.res.bham.ac.uk/publications/researchpubs/1988%20data/OCCHEALT.htm and www.hrreporter.com for more information on workplace stress.

Much research into job stress has tended to focus on 'executive burnout' and individuals in the higher echelons of the organizational hierarchy, but stress can affect employees at lower levels too. One US study found that the two most stressful jobs were a manual labourer and a secretary. In another US study, researchers reported that the incidence of a first heart attack was 2.5 times greater among skilled manual employees than among senior management grades, the rate in fact increasing the lower the occupational grade.[8] In a further report, a US health organization discovered that women in clerical occupations suffered twice the incidence rate of heart disease of all other female employees.[9] In addition to the physical and psychological disabilities it causes, occupational stress costs individuals and business considerable sums of money (HRM in Practice 13.2). The Conference Board of Canada has, for example, estimated that workplace stress costs the Canadian economy $12 billion annually (Montgomery and Kelloway, 2002).

HRM IN PRACTICE 13.2

WORKPLACE STRESS MORE PREVALENT THAN ILLNESS, INJURY

National survey finds Canadians more likely to suffer emotional, mental woes from jobs

JANE COUTTS, *GLOBE AND MAIL*, 8 APRIL 1998

Toronto workers are almost three times more likely to complain of health problems arising from workplace stress than from work-related illness or injuries, a Canadian survey shows.

The survey, conducted by Canada Health Monitor, found that 25 per cent of workers reported stress, mental or emotional health problems arising from work, compared with 9 per cent reporting workplace injury and another 9 per cent who said they suffered from work-related physical illness (such as headaches from bad air or noise).

'People aren't acknowledging workplace ill-health as a major health issue, when it's a really big drag on healthcare budgets and productivity,' said Earl Berger, managing director of the Health Monitor, which is a national, semi-annual survey on health issues.

The tendency has been to focus on more tangible health problems than stress, an emphasis that is costing employers and employees a lot in the long run, Dr Berger said.

'People are staying away from work and they are staying away for long periods of time and somebody is paying for it,' Dr

Berger said. While employees suffer from the stress they are feeling, employers lose productivity, insurance companies pay in disability claims and drug expenses, and the health system pays for care.

'It's not necessarily change people have difficulty with, it's the uncertainty and loss associated with change.'

The research released to the *Globe and Mail*, based on random national telephone interviews of 1515 people done in 1996, shows that while 20 per cent of white-collar workers report health problems because of workplace stress, compared with 25 per cent of blue-collar workers, it is blue-collar workers who are more likely to report being absent from work because of stress and who, when they are sick, stay off longer. More than one-third of blue-collar workers said they stayed off work because of stress: 59 per cent of those who missed work were absent 13 days or more. In comparison, 24 per cent of

white-collar workers with stress-related health problems stayed home from work: 35 per cent of them were absent more than 13 days.

Rick Lash, a consultant at the Hay Group in Toronto, which specializes in human resources issues, said in an interview that there are multiple messages for employers in the Health Monitor study. 'They have to deal with the culture they've created that's causing such a level of stress and anxiety for people on the job, right back to reassessing their strategy and looking at the impact of that strategy on workers,' he said. Companies should also look at their managers' skills and their ability to help people handle change and manage their emotions on the job, he said. Employers also need to look for ways to support workers in times of change.

'It's not necessarily change people have difficulty with, it's the uncertainty and loss associated with change,' he said. Today's unstable work environments are demanding from workers a flexibility many have not developed, coupled with increasing job expectations, Dr Lash said.

REFLECTIVE QUESTION

Think about a time when you felt under considerable stress. What were the causes of that stress? Could any of the work-related stressors be eliminated or reduced? If not, explain why. Go to www.hse.gov.uk for an example of a stress audit questionnaire.

Causes of workplace stress

Workplace stress occurs when some element of work has a negative impact on an employee's physical and mental well-being. Work overload and unrealistic time deadlines will, for example, put an employee under pressure, and stress may result. Workplace sexual harassment is another source of stress. In addition, occupational stress cannot be separated from personal life: illness in the family or divorce puts an employee under pressure and leads to stress. Factors that cause stress are numerous, and their relationships are complex, but researchers have identified two major types of stressor: work-related factors and individual factors.

Work-related factors

A variety of work-related factors – role ambiguity, frustration, conflict, job design, violence and harassment – can lead to stress.

Role ambiguity exists when the job is poorly defined, when uncertainty surrounds job expectations and when supervisory staff and their subordinates have different expectations of an employee's responsibilities. Individuals experiencing role ambiguity will be uncertain how their performance will be evaluated and will therefore experience stress.

Frustration, a result of a motivation being blocked to prevent an individual achieving a desired goal, has a major effect. A clerical employee trying to finish a major report before the end of the day is likely to become frustrated by repeated computer breakdowns that prevent the goal being reached. Huczynski and Buchanan (2001) draw on Swedish research to illustrate the frustration of information technology:

> Office workers who used to wait happily for hours while folders were retrieved from filing cabinets now complain when their computer terminals do not give them instant information on request ... Stress arose mainly from computer breakdowns and telephone calls which interrupted their work. The employees never knew how long these interruptions would last, and had to watch helplessly while their work piled up. So they worked rapidly in the mornings in case something stopped them later.

Conflicts, both interpersonal and inter-team, are another problem. When employees with different social experiences, personalities, needs and points of view interact with their co-workers, disagreements may cause stress.

Job design is a further factor. Jobs that have a limited variety of tasks and low discretion (see Figure 5.4), may cause stress. Contrary to stories about executive burnout, several studies report that the most stressful jobs are those which combine work intensification and low discretion. Craig (1981, p. 10) identified job design as a stressor for office workers: 'Countless office staff work in high bureaucracies which have been described as "honeycombs of depression"...Work that "drives you crazy" because it's so boring'. In the same genre, Mann and Holdsworth (2003, p. 208) found that 'teleworking' – paid work carried out in a location where the worker has no personal contact with co-workers – generates significant negative emotions and, overall, 'tele-workers experience more mental ill-health than office-workers'.

Workplace violence is a critical safety issue facing many organizations. There are three major types of workplace violence:

- *Type 1:* the perpetrator of the violence has no legitimate relationship with the targeted employee and enters the workplace to commit a criminal act (e.g. robbery). Retail and service industry employees and taxi drivers are those most exposed to this type of workplace violence.
- *Type 2:* the perpetrator is an employee or former employee of the organization, typically a 'disgruntled employee' who commits a violent act against a co-worker or supervisor for what is perceived to be unfair treatment.
- *Type 3:* the perpetrator is a recipient of a service provided by the targeted employee. Social workers, health care providers and teachers are particularly vulnerable to this type of workplace violence (HRM in Practice 13.3).

HRM IN PRACTICE 13.3

BEATEN UP – JUST FOR DOING YOUR JOB

COLIN COTTELL, *GUARDIAN*, 28 JULY 2001

A commonly held view is that the public sector offers a quiet life, safe and secure, well away from the cut and thrust of business. Everyday reality can be rather different. 'Someone was banging on the window and giving a member of my staff racial abuse', says Jason Humphreys, a station supervisor on the East London line of London Underground. 'I told him, "Don't talk to my staff like that". He turned round, punched me in the stomach, and kicked me in the leg. Though it only lasted 20 seconds it seemed like it went on forever.' Mr Humphreys says that the attack, the fifth made on him in his 16 years on the Underground, led him to reconsider his career. 'I did think of leaving. I had had enough. I thought, I can't do it any more. It was only the support of colleagues at work that convinced me to stay.'

David Cassells, a former nurse, has first-hand experience of the problem. 'There has always been a problem in the National Health Service, but in recent times it has become more serious.

'Nurses are by far the most vulnerable to attacks from members of the public … '

Now it's everywhere, not just one hospital, not just A&E, every ward, every department, even short stay wards', he says. … Former social worker Christine Eales knows about abuse. She's had more than her fair share. 'During my seven years in the job, I was held hostage twice, shot at twice, and nearly stabbed' she says. 'I finally said "No, I have had enough" after a 14-year-old boy with a ball bearing gun shot at nine members of staff. You expect to

be attacked in a client's house, or in the car park, but not sitting at your desk.'

Evidence of the threat to those delivering frontline public services is not just anecdotal. The TUC report *Violent Times*, found that: 'Nurses are by far the most vulnerable to attacks from members of the public; more than one in three had been physically attacked at work in the previous year. Other high risk jobs include care workers (21%), and those working in education and welfare (14%).'

'It puts people off coming into the profession. With unemployment so low, why be a nurse, with all that responsibility, a low salary, no back up and left so vulnerable, and to get abuse on top of all that? Not a good career move.' It's not just a question of more money, Cassells says. 'It's about bringing back control; having enough staff so they feel secure.'

Montgomery and Kelloway (2002) identify three groups of employee at particular risk of experiencing workplace violence:

1. those who interact with the public
2. those making decisions that influence other people's lives
3. those denying the public a request or a service.

The consequences of workplace violence go beyond immediate physical injury or death; research studies (see, for example, Montgomery and Kelloway, 2002) suggest that the trauma caused by the violence has negative results for both the individual employee (i.e. impaired mental and physical health) and the organization (i.e. decreased commitment, retention and performance).

Harassment (racial and sexual) is another workplace stressor of increasing importance. Racial harassment can range from racist jokes or verbal abuse to racist graffiti in the workplace or physical attacks on black or other racial minority employees. No matter how subtle it is, racial harassment is extremely stressful; it can damage the health of ethnic minority group employees and presents managers with a major challenge.

Sexual harassment can take two forms. The first is a hostile environment involving behaviour that is unwelcome and undesirable or offensive. This kind of sexual harassment includes, for example, unwanted propositions and sexual innuendo. It can be difficult for an HR manager to convince employees and other managers to take this kind of sexual harassment seriously as it is often viewed as a 'joke', something to do with 'chatting up' attractive female co-workers or bottom-pinching. Evidence of behaviour that is sufficiently severe or pervasive as to cause changes in the conditions of employment can, however, lead to a legal case.

The second form of sexual harassment is quid pro quo harassment, which is essentially a kind of sex-for-promotion blackmail. The alleged perpetrator is normally a superior, and the blackmail is either 'give in to my sexual desires and I'll give you promotion' or 'give in or your job prospects will suffer'. Both forms of sexual harassment relate to power relationships, harassment aimed at women by men who occupy positions of power. It is, as one writer put it, 'a new, formal title for an age-old predicament, the boss-man with anything from a lascivious line of chat, to wandering hands, to explicit demands for sex as a reward for giving you, the women, work'.[10]

Individual-related factors

Individual factors causing stress are equally varied and complex; they include financial worries, marital problems, pregnancy, problems with children and the death of a spouse. A record number of mortgages, for example, were foreclosed in Britain in the early 1990s, doubtless causing considerable individual stress. A major personal factor that can cause stress among working women is the *dual-role* syndrome – the additional burden of coping with two jobs: the paid job and the unwaged 'job' at home (cooking, housework, shopping and so on; Figure 13.4). As Craig (1981, p. 18) puts it:

> The pressures on working mothers are enormous. Feeling guilty because you're not an ideal stay-at-home mum ... get the breakfasts, get the shopping done, go to the launderette, fetch the kids from school, do the ironing, clean the house. A carefully worked out timetable can be upset and life thrown into chaos when your lunch hour is switched or you're required to do overtime without notice.

Figure 13.4 Stress caused by the 'dual-role' syndrome
Source: Personnel Management Plus (1992) April

Research appears to support the dual-role syndrome as an explanation of work-related stress. A Canadian study among bank employees reported that 22 per cent of the respondents said their stress was triggered by balancing family and work.[11]

Huczynski and Buchanan (2004) draw attention to research demonstrating a relationship between personality and stress. Individual factors include difficulty in coping with change, a lack of confidence and assertiveness in relationships, and poor stress management. 'Type A' personalities – those individuals who are highly competitive, set high standards, place considerable emphasis on meeting deadlines and are workaholics – tend to have a higher propensity to exhibit symptoms of stress (McShane, 2006).

In summary, Figure 13.5 illustrates examples of work-related and individual causes of stress.

Until recently, job stress was considered to be a personal problem, but it is now recognized that stress is a major health problem at work and that it is a responsibility of general management to provide the initiative to eliminate or reduce the causes of stress. At an organizational level, attention to basic job design principles can alleviate the conditions that may cause stress. At the individual level, HR professionals have conducted workshops on stress management to help individual employees cope with stress and avoid an overexposure to stress-causing situations. Workshops designed to change lifestyles by promoting healthy eating and fitness, while helping employees to relieve the strains caused by job stress, cannot eliminate the source of the problem. Like other occupational hazards, stress needs to be controlled at source; as discussed above, stress arises from a variety of sources, and it is important for HR managers to identify priorities and investigate ways of dealing with the problem. Management should look at the job design (see Chapter 5) and organizational structure, and conduct detailed surveys to identify priorities for action. Table 13.1 shows some of the specific actions that individuals and HR practitioners can take to alleviate occupational stress.

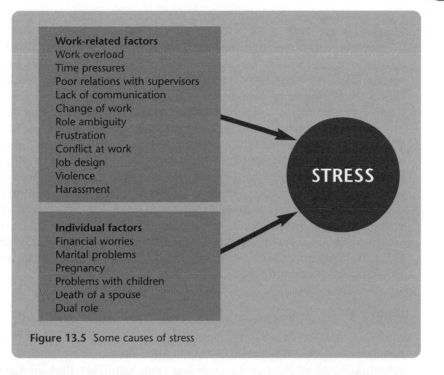

Figure 13.5 Some causes of stress

Table 13.1 Action to reduce workplace stress

Individual strategies	Organizational strategies
Physical exercise	Meeting with employees to discuss the extent of stress
Hobbies	Conduct a survey and inspect the workplace for stress-causing factors
Meditation	Improve job and organizational design
Group discussions	Improve communication
Assertiveness training	Develop a stress policy and monitor its effectiveness
	Train managers to be sensitive to the causes and early symptoms of stress

Alcohol and drug abuse

A recent estimate indicates that there are, in England and Wales, approximately 3 million excessive drinkers and 850,000 problem and dependent drinkers. About 1 in 25 of the population in England and Wales, and possibly as high as 1 in 10 in Scotland, may be personally affected by severe alcohol-related problems.[12]

The excessive consumption of alcohol is both a health problem and a job performance problem in every occupational category, be it manual, white collar or managerial. In alcohol abuse, behavioural problems range from tardiness in the early stages to prolonged absenteeism in the later ones. A US study estimated that problem drinkers are absent from work for, on average, 22 days per year and are at least twice as likely as non-drinkers to have an accident.[13] The direct and indirect costs of alcohol abuse to employers include the costs of accidents, lower productivity, poor-quality work, bad decisions, absenteeism and managers' lost time in dealing with employees with an alcohol problem.

Employers have been advised to have a written statement of policy regarding alcohol abuse, which can be discussed and agreed with employees and, where applicable, union representatives. The policy should recognize that alcohol abuse is an illness, and it should be supportive rather than punitive or employees will hide their drink problem for as long as possible. The HSE advocates that a policy should encourage any employee who believes that she or he has a drink problem to seek help voluntarily, and should, subject to certain provisions, give the same protection of employment and pension rights as those granted to an employee with problems that are related to other forms of ill-health. Research in Scotland estimated that 20 per cent of employers had a policy to deal with problem drinkers. In addition to preparing a policy, management can devise a procedure for dealing with alcohol abuse; to encourage employees to seek advice, it is suggested that this procedure should be separate from the disciplinary procedure. Finally, the HRM department is advised to establish links with an external voluntary organization to obtain help and develop an employee assistance programme.

Smoking

The tragic death of non-smoker Dana Reeve, the 44-year-old widow of *Superman* actor Christopher Reeve, in March 2006, highlighted the dangers of both active and passive smoking (HRM in Practice 13.4). It has been estimated that, in England, 364,000 patients are admitted to hospital each year owing to diseases caused by smoking, and around 114,000 people in the UK are killed by smoking every year. Most die from one of three main diseases associated with cigarette smoking: lung cancer, chronic obstructive lung disease (bronchitis and emphysema) and coronary heart disease.[14] Passive or 'second-hand' smoking (inhaling other people's smoke) is estimated to kill more than 11,000 people in the UK every year, 600 of whom die from exposure to second-hand smoke in the workplace. It is estimated that, between 1950 and 2000, 6 million Britons have died from tobacco-related diseases (ASH, 2005, p. 1).

HRM IN PRACTICE 13.4

BUT SHE DIDN'T EVEN SMOKE

ROBERT BUCKMAN, *GLOBE AND MAIL*, 11 MARCH 2006

Behind the human tragedy of non-smoker Dana Reeve's death at the age of 44 from lung cancer, there is also a widespread sense of genuine bewilderment. We thought that of all the cancers, lung cancer was the one that seemed pretty well sorted out. If you were a smoker, you had a high risk of getting it; if you were a non-smoker, you didn't.

It did seem relatively straightforward. Of course, many people knew someone – or knew of someone – who had never smoked a cigarette in their lifetime and, despite that, developed lung cancer. But cases like those were supposed to be incredibly rare, weren't they?

There are differences between genders directly related to smoking habits. As most people realize, lung cancer in women has continued to increase and became the leading cause of cancer deaths in women – exceeding deaths due to breast cancer – more than six years ago. That change was large-scale and progressive, and clearly mirrored the increase in smoking among women that started accelerating 20 years ago. So the overall figures clearly show the direct relationship between smoking and lung cancer, as we have all known since the 1960s.

What has also been known – but not discussed in great detail – is the number of lung-cancer cases that occur in non-smokers. It is difficult to be very accurate, but in general terms about 90 per cent of all lung cancers occur in active smokers, and 10 per cent in non-smokers, among whom the greatest contributory risk comes from second-hand smoke (passive smoking).

This used to be a big problem in the workplace because non-smokers sat next to smokers for many hours a day, five or more days a week, inhaling their smoke (and incidentally inhaling their carbon monoxide in large quantities, increasing the risk of heart disease as well). Smoking is now illegal in the office and the only place where a smoker can jeopardize a non-smoker is at home.

When it comes to smoking ... we are right to take it seriously.

But the risk comes from continued exposure – if you simply walk past a group of smokers outside an office building, you may be able to smell tobacco smoke, but a fleeting whiff is not a serious health risk for you. To put everything in perspective, if all cigarette smoking miraculously stopped today, then in about 20 years there would be a big decline in the incidence of lung cancer and the other smoking-related cancers including, unexpectedly, some cases of pre-menopausal breast cancer (which is 1½ times more common among women who smoked or were exposed to second-hand smoke as teenagers).

When it comes to smoking (both active and passive), we are right to take it seriously.

In many countries, smoking in the workplace is a major problem because active smoking may be a fire hazard or hygiene risk. In addition, the estimated cost attributable to absenteeism and lost productivity associated with active smoking is said to be approximately US$825 per employee per year (Montgomery and Kelloway, 2002). Figure 13.6 shows employers' costs associated with workplace smoking (money that 'goes up in smoke'). Passive smoking in the workplace is also a problem because non-smokers work or live next to or among smokers (in office environments and also in pubs, clubs, aeroplanes, trains and so on) for their full working week, inhaling their smoke and carbon monoxide in large quantities. A decade ago, the first second-hand smoke case against the USA tobacco industry, filed on behalf of thousands of US-based flight attendants in 1991,[15] resulted in a settlement of US$300 million. As we saw in HRM in Practice 13.4, smoking is unlawful in the workplace in the USA and Canada, and the only place where a smoker can jeopardize the health of a non-smoker is at home. In the past, managers in Britain agreed that successful non-smoking policies required consultation with employees and, in a unionized workplace, a joint approach by management and trade union. From February 2006, following the historic vote in the British House of Commons, there will be no scope for negotiation: smoking will be banned in all workplaces starting in the summer 2007.

HRM WEB LINKS

Go to the website www.ash.org.uk for factsheets on smoking statistics: illness and death. Fact Sheet No. 2 lists both non-lethal illnesses and deaths caused by smoking.

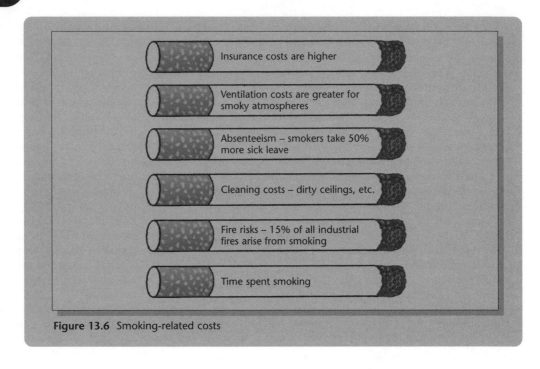

Figure 13.6 Smoking-related costs

Acquired immune deficiency syndrome

> I was not trained to manage fear, discrimination, and dying in the workplace.[16]

A textbook on HRM for this new millennium would be incomplete if no reference were made to society's most recent menace – AIDS – caused by the human immuno-deficiency virus (HIV), which attacks the body's immune system. In 2002, over 14 million people were estimated to be infected with AIDS in the three continents of Africa, Europe and the Americas. In South Africa, an estimated 4.7 million citizens were infected, equivalent to about 1 in 4 of the adult population.[17] Data from studies in Tanzania and Uganda show that, between the ages of 25 and 35, 4 in 5 deaths are HIV-related,[18] and in India, the WHO has estimated the number of people affected with AIDS to lie between 3 and 5 million.[19] In the USA, AIDS was the leading cause of death among 25–44-year-olds between 1992 and 1996; to date, 343,000 Americans have died of AIDS and another 900,000 are HIV-infected – about 1 in 250 people.[20]

In Canada, mandatory testing for AIDS is regarded as a serious intrusion on individual rights, and employers are prohibited from subjecting job applicants to any type of medical testing for the presence of the HIV virus. Furthermore, the employer is obligated to accommodate the needs of an employee with a disability such as AIDS by, for example, redefining work assignments. The fear of catching HIV can, however, create problems for HR managers. Employees might refuse to work with a person with AIDS; as one North American HR manager explained, 'No matter how sophisticated or educated you are, AIDS can trigger irrational things in people … There's a big potential for disruption. It could close a plant down.'[21] A North American chain store manager, one of whose employees developed AIDS and died, had to call in the Red Cross to explain to distraught employees that AIDS cannot be transmitted through normal contact in the workplace. Six months later, some employees were still refusing to use the drinking fountain or the toilet.

Green (1998) reported that few US firms surveyed had a policy regarding AIDS and that larger firms were more likely to have HIV-specific policies, over 50 per cent of companies with more than 100 employees holding a specific AIDS policy. More worrying perhaps is the finding that there is, among employers, a 'declining interest' in AIDS education in the workplace. In 1997, 18 per cent of US companies surveyed provided HIV education for their employees, compared with 28 per cent in 1992 (Green, 1998). Companies that have encountered the problem of managing AIDS in the workplace have found that it is better to expect a problem and be proactive in educating employees on the issues raised by AIDS. As with any HRM policy, this requires a clear endorsement from top management down. The chairman of Levi Strauss, Robert Hass, confirms the need for senior management support: 'This [AIDS] is frequently viewed as something that the personnel department should take care of, but there has to be support from the top. You can't do it with one flyer.'[16] As attitudes and legal considerations change, AIDS has important implications for HRM policy and practices.

HRM WEB LINKS

Visit the following websites for information on AIDS and HRM: UK (www.tht.org.uk), Canada (www.cdnaids.ca), South Africa (www.aidslink.org.za) and Australia (www.acsa.org.au).

Workplace wellness

Workplace wellness models typically focus on individual behaviour and the programmes and activities promoting individual behaviour change. Smoking, binge-drinking patterns, poor diet and lack of physical exercise have all been identified as lifestyle problems impacting on the health of the workforce. Here, consistent with the literature, workplace wellness will refer to any voluntary health improving programme and activity instigated by the employer to effect changes in non-occupational health behaviours. Smoking cessation, personal fitness programmes, and employee assistance programmes are early examples of workplace health-improvement initiatives. A wide variety of initiatives that fall under the wellness promotion strategy have been instigated in establishments with 500 or more employees, including part or all the following:

- a smoke-free workplace
- employer-sponsored sports
- discounted gym facilities
- health examinations offered to employees
- 'health fairs' hosted on the premises
- wellness newsletters
- smoking cessation incentives
- weight loss incentives
- blood pressure and cholesterol testing

- energy-based therapy seminars
- **employee assistance programme (EAP).**

An employee assistance programme provides confidential professional assistance to employees and their families to help resolve problems affecting their personal lives and, in some cases, their job performance. Typically, an EAP provides services such as alcohol and drug abuse, legal, financial, marriage and crisis counselling. These various workplace wellness initiatives tend to operate independently and focus on individual employee goals. Few organizations integrate wellness programmes and initiatives into an overall HR strategy with concrete measures and expected targets (Dyck, 2002). See Chapter 14 for evaluating HR programmes.

REFLECTIVE QUESTION

Haunschild (2003) posits that characterizing wellness management merely as a 'healthy' philanthropic act is naïve and neglects intended control strategies. Can you think how wellness programmes can act against the interests of the employee?

HRM WEB LINKS

Go to the websites www.nqi.ca/newsevents/details.aspx?ID=422, www.health-works.ca and www.healthworkandwellness.com for more information on workplace wellness.

HRM IN PRACTICE 13.5

UNIONS, MANAGEMENT SEE WELLNESS THROUGH DIFFERENT PRISMS

UYEN VU, *CANADIAN HR REPORTER*, 9 MAY 2005

Think of a wellness program, and an image of workers in gym clothes out together for a walk might come to mind. Or it's a roomful of employees learning from the experts how to eat right, monitor their hearts or quit bad habits. Many people see in these images a picture of good health. The way Lydia Makrides puts it, it should be a slam-dunk for unions to support such programs.

'The unions are there to look after the well-being of their employees. So they can't possibly be against anything that helps their members become healthy,' said Makrides, director of the Atlantic Health and Wellness Institute, a Halifax-based wellness provider.

But the view from the union's side isn't as rosy. Despite being vigilant advocates for health and safety, many union leaders are at best grudgingly silent on wellness programs. At worst, some even oppose them outright. Part of the blame, said Makrides, has to fall on wellness providers such as herself.

'What happens is when we approach the employer, the union is often ignored. The union finds out (about the initiative) after the fact, and therefore there's no buy-in.' And because program providers often emphasize the business case to pitch wellness to employers, it's natural for unions to take from that message: The employer is doing this to save money. This is not about employees.

Now, 'Is the union on board?' is one of the first questions Makrides asks when an employer brings her in to implement wellness initiatives. 'I've learned from my previous experiences.' In her current project to measure health outcomes over four years at the Nova Scotia Department of Justice, that crucial question led to the inclusion of a Nova Scotia government employee union representative on the steering committee.

Rory Hancey, manager of labour relations at the Department of Justice, said one of the biggest concerns the union had was that workers' health information being gathered and tracked would be used in connection to attendance management. With that concern addressed, the union has expressed just as much interest as the employer in seeing health costs reduced as a long-term outcome of the project, said Hancey.

The failure of many employers to consult with unions and representatives of joint health and safety committees is indeed one of the reasons some unions don't support wellness programs, said Denis St-Jean, national health and safety office at the Public Service Alliance of Canada. But on a deeper level, there's the enduring suspicion unions have that employers are bringing in wellness programs for the wrong reasons, said St-Jean.

> ## 'As far as the union is concerned, most CEOs or senior managers don't see employee health as a huge issue'

'As far as the union is concerned, most CEOs or senior managers don't see employee health as a huge issue,' said St-Jean. Pointing to the prevalence of contract, part-time and seasonal employees within the federal public service, he said, 'if one of them becomes ill, that person is weeded out of the system anyway.'

Wellness programs often appear at a workplace almost as an afterthought, said St-Jean. They're usually brought in on the heel of other cost containment measures, such as greater monitoring of absenteeism, reduction of drug plans, and increased appeals of workers' compensation claims, said St-Jean.

'During the recent negotiation (at Canada Post) there was a reduction in prescription drug payment,' said St-Jean. 'Meanwhile (the organization) goes ahead with wellness programs to improve employee efficiency and productivity. And that's a typical approach.'

At the Canadian Union of Postal Workers (CUPW), national health representative Gayle Bossenberry said there is a high potential for subtle forms of reprisals against workers for lifestyle choices deemed unhealthy.

'Some parts of these programs really encroach into workers' personal lives, and we don't think the employer has any business going into these areas,' said Bossenberry. 'Instead, they should just deal with the workplace hazards.' She added, however, that the CUPW would consider teaming up with management to tackle certain organizational issues, such as stress, harassment and violence in the workplace.

Managing health and wellness

The message presented in various national statistics is that occupational health and safety programmes prevent work-induced injuries and illness. Moreover, the effective management of health, safety and wellness can result in zero tolerance for workplace illness and injuries (Dyck, 2002). Health, in the broadest sense, perhaps more than any other HR activity, offers the manager an opportunity to be more proactive than reactive. It must be emphasized, however, that top management's involvement in developing and implementing health, wellness and safety policies and programmes is essential. A number of strategies can be used by organizations to ensure a

1.	**Design**	safe and healthy systems of work
2.	**Exhibit**	strong management commitment to programmes
3.	**Inspect**	the workplace for health and safety hazards
4.	**Establish**	procedures and controls for dealing with health, wellness and safety risks
5.	**Promote**	a workplace wellness strategy
6.	**Develop**	a safety training programmes
7.	**Set up**	a health, wellness and safety committee
8.	**Monitor**	health, wellness and safety policies and programmes
9.	**Integrate**	to form a comprehensive wellness system that supports strategy
10.	**Draw up**	an action plan and checklist

Figure 13.7 Strategies to improve workplace health and wellness

healthy workplace and ensure compliance with legal requirements. This section does not aim to be prescriptive, offering advice on what managers should be doing. Instead, the strategies summarized in Figure 13.7 are intended primarily to generate discussion on the implications of health and safety for management practices, and on how health, safety and wellness interventions can be reconciled with broader management objectives.

Design safer systems of work

The most direct approach to ensuring a safe and healthy workplace is to design systems of work that are safe and without risk to health. This can often be done satisfactorily only at the design, planning and/or purchasing stage. Simply trying to persuade employees, for example by poster campaigns, to adapt their behaviour to unsafe systems of work does not usually lead to reflection and learning on the causes of work-induced injuries and ill-health. The HSE maintains[6] that (emphasis added):

> Most accidents involve an element of failure in control – in other words *failure in managerial skill*. A guiding principle when drawing up arrangements for securing health and safety should be that, so far as possible, work would be adapted to people and not vice versa.

As managers identify processes, machines and substances that are hazardous to the health and well-being of employees, they must modify the process to eliminate or reduce the hazard and risk 'at source'.

Exhibit commitment

Top management carries the prime responsibility under the HASAWA 1974 for ensuring a safe and healthy workplace. The Robens Report believed that 'apathy' was a major cause of workplace accidents. No matter how much activity related to health and safety is initiated by HR professionals, health and safety should be an integral part of every manager's responsibility, from the chief executive officer down to the lowest level supervisor. Anything less than total support from top management raises questions about the sincerity of the organization's commitment in the eyes of employees, government agencies and the public at large. To exhibit commitment, managers' salary and promotion might be tied to a satisfactory safety record and compliance. If safety officers are to be effective, they must be given adequate authority in the management hierarchy to make changes and implement changes.

Inspect the workplace

Another proactive approach to the management of health and safety is regular formal inspections of the workplace: regular monitoring of the work environment and regular physical examination of the employees. Construction sites and manufacturing plants, for example, require regular inspections to check the application of safety standards and relevant laws. In some manufacturing processes, frequent monitoring of air quality and levels of dust and noise is needed. Organizations may also monitor a wide range of matters relating to employees' health, from routine eye tests and chest X-rays to screening for breast/cervical cancer and the incidence of infertility and abnormal childbirths. A 'health' survey of employees can also help to identify hazardous and unhealthy processes.

We can identify three main types of formal inspection:

1. accident
2. special
3. general.

Accident inspections will follow an accident or dangerous incident (a 'near miss') in the workplace. *Special* inspections might concentrate on a particular workstation, system of work or hazard, for example the training of forklift truck operators on dust problems; this would then be the first step in a plan of action. *General* inspections involve a comprehensive survey of the entire workplace. In a unionized workplace, these are frequently conducted jointly with the union safety representative. Thorough preparation, including the design of a comprehensive checklist covering all aspects of the workplace, is essential if managers are to discover all health hazards.

Establish procedures and controls

A health and **safety policy** is likely to fail unless effective procedures and controls are established. The procedures for handling health and safety problems need to meet some basic requirements:

- to allow employees' representatives to talk directly to the managers who can make decisions
- to operate without undue delay
- to be able to handle emergency problems
- to permit discussion about long-term decisions affecting health, wellness and safety.

These recommendations clearly have important implications for HR policy and action, so let us briefly examine these considerations. Problems might occur if line managers were expected by senior management to be responsible for safe working practices but were at the same time denied the authority to make decisions and implement changes. In principle, organizational procedures should ensure that the authority of a particular level of management to make decisions matches the responsibility of each level of management for health and safety.

The consensus on better practice suggests that health and safety committees include key departmental managers, employees and, in unionized workplaces, union representatives. At best, committees can be a vehicle for discussion and the strategic planning of health and wellness. At worst, they can degenerate into a 'talking shop' that will draw scepticism from the rest of the workforce. Managers must perceive their rewards, or a significant proportion of them, as contingent upon the success of a health and wellness programme. To evaluate that success, monthly, quarterly and annual statistics need to be reported directly to the senior management team.

Promote a wellness strategy

The challenge for HR professionals is to develop and implement a workplace wellness strategy that is explicitly linked to the organization's HRM strategy. Wellness programmes and initiatives should be developed through a partnership approach involving all stakeholders. HR professionals can promote wellness intiatives by developing a business case for workplace wellness.

Research on the efficacy of workplace wellness has typically attempted to use various objective outcome measures to demonstrate the benefit of such programmes for employers. These measures typically include employee job satisafaction surveys, rates of programme utilization/participation, employee absenteeism rates, employee turnover rates, productivity rates, benefit plan costs, insurance costs, organizational 'climate' surveys and decreased workplace accidents. Establishing the causal links between performance or behaviour variables and wellness initiatives is, however, sometimes problematic (Mearns and Hope, 2005; see also Chapter 14). A review of literature would appear to indicate significant tangible benefits to employers of workplace wellness initiatives. These benefits may include favourable changes to the psychological contract. An employee's perception of the 'wellness climate' – the shared perceptions of the importance of health and wellness in the workplace – affects safety and wellness behaviours. Thus, individuals who perceive a positive wellness climate in the organization are more likely to adopt safe working behaviours, perform better and engage in a healthy lifestyle (Dyck, 2002; Mearns and Hope, 2005).

Develop safety training programmes

One way to obtain compliance with health and safety regulations is through enhancing employees' knowledge, understanding and commitment, which can be achieved through health and safety programmes. The purpose of safety training is generally the same as that of any other training programme: to improve job knowledge and skills, and to ensure optimum employee performance at the specified level. In health and safety training, specified performance standards include attention to safety rules and regulations regarding safe work behaviour. Like any other training, health and safety training should be developed systematically. First, problems or training needs will be identified by inspection, by accident reports and through discussion during health and safety committee meetings. Next, the planning, execution and evaluation of the training will take place (see Chapter 9).

The HASAWA 1974 imposes a duty on employers to provide training to ensure a healthy and safe workplace. Research suggests that safety awareness training programmes only have a short-term effect on employees' behaviour, which suggests that, after employees have completed their safety training at the orientation stage, management should organize regular refresher courses. Experience suggests that line managers, supervisors and safety representatives also need to be exposed to regular training. Top management support is a key ingredient in the availability and success of health and safety training, but studies indicate that the number of representatives attending TUC health and safety courses has fallen (Booth, 1985).

Set up health and safety committees

Health and safety is one area of working life in which there has been statutory support for employee representation for over three decades. The HASAWA requires employers to establish a **safety committee** if a safety representative requests this. The 1998 Workplace Employee Relations Survey found that 68 per cent of all workplaces reported the presence of at least one employee representative on health and safety matters (Millward et al., 2000). As already noted, joint health and safety committees may, under the EU Social Charter, represent the future shape of European health and safety legislation (Reilly et al., 1995), and there is a substantial body of evidence to suggest that union health and safety representatives can make an important contribution to the improvement of health and safety at work (James and Walters, 2002). It is management's responsibility to prevent a safety committee developing into a talking shop with ineffective decision-making.

HRM WEB LINKS

For more information on health and safety representation in Britain over the past two decades, go to the 1998 Workplace Employee Relations Survey website: www.dti.gov.uk/employment/research-evaulation/wers-98/index.html. For the most recent survey (results being finalized as the book goes to press), go to www.dti.gov.uk/employment/research–evaluation/wers–2004/dissemination–results/page25904.html.

The functions of the committees and their terms of reference depend on individual company policy, relevant safety legislation and the situation regarding employee–union relations. The Safety Representatives and Safety Committees (SRSC) Guidance Notes suggest the following terms of reference (Regulation 9, pp. 37–8):

(a) The study of accident and notifiable diseases statistics and trends, so that reports can be made to management on unsafe and unhealthy conditions and practices, together with recommendations for corrective action.
(b) Examination of safety audit reports on a similar basis.
(c) Consideration of reports and factual information provided by inspectors of the enforcing authority appointed under the Health and Safety at Work etc. Act.
(d) Consideration of reports which safety representatives may wish to submit.

(e) Assistance in the development of works safety rules and safe systems of work.

(f) A watch on the effectiveness of the safety content of employee training.

(g) A watch on the adequacy of safety and health communication and publicity in the workplace.

(h) The provision of a link with the appropriate inspectorates of the enforcing authority.

Employers or their representatives are primarily responsible for compliance with health and safety laws, but the existence of these committees does not diminish the employer's duty to ensure a healthy and safe workplace. The work of the safety committees should supplement management's arrangements for regular and effective monitoring for health and safety precautions – but it cannot be a substitute for management action. All forms of safety arrangements that encourage employee participation in workplace health and safety matters reduce the incidence of accidents. The studies by Reilly et al. (1995) and James and Walters (2002) show, however, strong support for union–management health and safety committees as an important variable for promoting a safer workplace. Reilly et al.'s study found that establishments with joint health and safety committees – and with all the employee representatives chosen by the union – had, 'on average, 5.7 fewer injuries per 1000 employees compared with establishments where management deals with health and safety matters without any form of worker consultation' (Reilly et al., 1995, p. 283).

Walters (1987) has undertaken a study of the implementation of the SRSC Regulations. The findings from his small sample of cases in the print industry suggest that the joint regulation of health and safety is based on an assumption of trade union organization and power in the workplace. With a hostile economic and political environment in the 1980s and much of the 1990s, this power diminished, and the SRSC Regulations have had a very limited direct effect on the joint regulation of health and safety in the workplace: 'It is only in the large workplaces that any significant application of the SRSC Regulations with regard to joint inspections, provision of information and time off for training seems to have been made' (Walters, 1987, p. 48). The authoritative study by Millward et al. (1992) indicates, however, that, in spite of the hostile industrial relations climate of the 1980s, the propensity for joint health and safety committees to exist in the British workplace is still high.

Monitor policy

Safety specialists argue that the safety policy should reflect the employer's commitment to developing safe systems of work and pursuing a healthy work environment. Apart from giving details of the specialist safety services provided by the organization, the safety policy also outlines the safety responsibilities of all levels of management within the hierarchy. This part of the safety policy is particularly important for identifying which member of the management hierarchy should be involved when a health and safety problem arises in the workplace.

In practice, many employers are 'turning a blind eye' to health and safety requirements. Furthermore, many safety policies are unhelpful in practice because of a failure to monitor their relevance to reconfigured work arrangements. Critics have argued that 'many safety policies are just pious blueprints which look good but are either ignored or unworkable' (Trades Union Congress, 1986, p. 163). A proactive approach would involve managers regularly checking to ensure that safety policy and practices are changed to suit new developments in the workplace.

Integrate

Workplace wellness programmes and activities should be integrated to form a comprehensive safety, health and wellness strategy that is explicitly linked to the organization's HRM strategy. The role of management is to:

- determine the current status of health and wellness initiatives in the organization
- develop a business case for workplace wellness
- encourage a shared responsibility approach to employee well-being
- shape policies and practices
- collect outcome data
- evaluate workplace wellness programme outcomes.

Draw up an action plan

Managers can be more proactive in the area of safety, health and wellness by developing an 'action plan' and checklist (Figure 13.8).

Paradox in workplace health and wellness

The notion of paradox and tension that we have discussed in other areas of HRM is also apparent in occupational health and wellness. The model in Figure 5.7 shows that paradox stems from the multiple consequences of a single management action, which seem to conflict with those of another. The abstraction presented in Figure 5.7 can be illuminated using a concrete health and wellness case. Portable computers, cell phones and email have enabled us all to be connected to the Internet and the organization 7 days a week, 24 hours a day. These high-tech instruments have, however, produced negative results, causing some observers to describe them as 'electronic versions of a ball and chain, keeping us in work mode around the clock' (Drohan, 2000, p. B15). The intended consequence of these high-tech instruments is improved productivity, but the unanticipated consequence of high-tech communications has yielded a major problem of stress and burnout caused by the inability of individuals to maintain the boundary between work and home. This unintended consequence of the high-tech revolution can counteract the positive consequences.

Health and wellness form an important part of the HRM context, but it is not simply a technical issue of, for example, supplying hard hats and goggles. Above all, occupational health and safety highlights the fact that employment relations involves an economic and power relationship. In terms of economics, 'pure market' ideology panders to the shareholder and 'profitability over safety' is favoured (Glasbeek, 1991, p. 196). With regard to power, it is argued that: 'In all technical questions pertaining to workplace health and safety there is the *social element*. That is ...the power relations in production: who tells whom to do what and how fast' (Sass, 1982, p. 52; quoted in Giles and Iain, 1989). Wellness management also contains a social element. It is arguably about organizations attempting to appropriate the employee's whole body as a matter of surveillance and control (Haunschild, 2003; Townley, 1994). Using

HSE OHS checklist for employers
Preventing occupational ill health

Yes/No/Uncertain

- Do I know whether any of my operations involve a health risk? ☐ ☐ ☐
  For example exposure to skin irritants such as solvents, poor working practices when using harmful materials, exposure to excessive noise, exposure to harmful dusts, fumes or gases, frequent heaving lifting or carrying
- Do I take account of any specific regulations or recommendations applying to these risks? ☐ ☐ ☐
  For example specific regulations covering work with lead and asbestos
- Are all the risks that have been identified adequately controlled? ☐ ☐ ☐
  For example through improved workplace design engineering controls or by using personal protection
- Is the effectiveness of controls being assessed and monitored? ☐ ☐ ☐
  For example by regular environmental monitoring, possibly backed up with health checks

Placement and rehabilitation

Yes/No/Uncertain

- Do I know whether any of my operations carry specific health requirements? ☐ ☐ ☐
  For example good eyesight or colour vision
- Do I know whether any of my operations present a hazard to people with a particular problem? ☐ ☐ ☐
  For example dusty conditions may be unsuitable for some workers with chest problems
- Do I take these factors into consideration in a clear and fair way at recruitment and subsequently? ☐ ☐ ☐
  For example by ensuring that the specific health requirements for a job are assessed and people are not turned down because of irrelevant health conditions
- Am I prepared to modify working arrangements where practicable to accommodate employees with health problems? ☐ ☐ ☐
  For example by rearranging working hours, adjusting the height of work surfaces

First aid and treatment

Yes/No/Uncertain

- Do my first aid procedures comply with the First Aid at Work Regulations? ☐ ☐ ☐
  See HSE guidance booklet HS (R)11
- Have I considered my first aid needs for coping with illness at work, and made appropriate arrangements? ☐ ☐ ☐
  For example emergency on call arrangements with a local doctor or nurse
- Have I considered whether any additional treatment services would be cost-effective in my operation and if so, made suitable arrangements? ☐ ☐ ☐
  For example regular visits to the workplace by physiotherapists or dentists to avoid workers having to take time off for appointments

Health promotion

Yes/No/Uncertain

- Have I considered whether the benefits of health education, employee assistance or counselling programmes would justify their introduction, and have I introduced such programmes? ☐ ☐ ☐
  For example programmes aimed at improving diet and reducing smoking and problem drinking. The workplace can be an ideal location in which to encourage employees towards healthier living
- Do I know whether screening tests are available that could improve the health of my staff by detecting treatable illness at an earlier stage, and if so, have I arranged for them to be carried out? ☐ ☐ ☐
  For example arrangements with local health authorities or others for cervical smears to be carried out at the workplace

Information, instruction and training

Yes/No/Uncertain

- Do my employees understand any health risks involved in their work and how to minimise them? ☐ ☐ ☐
- Have my employees received sufficient instruction and training in how to avoid ill health? ☐ ☐ ☐
  For example hygiene procedures and correct use of personal protective equipment

If you answered NO or UNCERTAIN to any of these questions you need help.

Figure 13.8 Checklist for health and safety
Source: Health and Safety Executive

Foucault's power analysis, wellness management represents a process of discipline since activities such as medical screening, fitness programmes and lifestyle counselling are connected to selection, promotion and production processes (Haunschild, 2003). It is interesting to note that interest in wellness management has increased rapidly in the USA at a time when the regulatory power of the official health and safety agency, the Occupational Safety and Health Administration, has allegedly been curtailed under the Clinton and Bush junior administration (Cullen, 2002).

Studies undertaken in UK call centres illustrate how economic imperatives impose on health and wellness management. Taylor et al. (2003, p. 452), for example, conclude that highly competitive market conditions compel managers to design work-place norms in which work intensification is 'a habitual and inescapable necessity'. Although the heterogeneity of small firms makes generalization suspect, others have noted that the level of work-induced injuries and ill-health is proportionally worse in small European firms (Walters, 2004). Whereas large establishments are more likely to be regulated and inspected and have worker representatives, small establishments, especially small companies, are less likely to be unionized, and the employment relationship and the design of work are such that health and safety are, 'at best, easily overlooked and at worst deliberately avoided' (Walters, 2004, p. 171).

Most obviously, the economic cost of workplace health, safety and wellness is a double-edged sword for the organization. On the one hand, health and safety measures that protect individuals from physical or chemical hazards can conflict with management's objective of containing production costs. On the other, as we have explained, effective health and wellness interventions can improve the performance of employees and the organization by reducing the cost associated with accidents, disabilities, absenteeism and illness.

To manage the employment relationship effectively, it also needs to be recognized that the employer's perspective on health and wellness issues can affect an individual's beliefs and levels of trust. Talk of a reciprocal commitment and a psychological contract has a hollow ring for many manual workers: more pressing may be malodorous processes and dangerous work systems. Critical, too, is the ability of global companies to relocate to other parts of the world to avoid stringent health and safety laws and regulations (see HRM in Practice 4.2). Creating a level playing field in terms of health and safety legislation within major economic trading blocs may partly ameliorate this problem; since the passing of the Single European Act in 1987, for example, a company's health and safety policies have been influenced by EU directives and the Social Charter.

Growing public awareness and concern about 'green' and environmental issues has had an effect on occupational health and wellness. Organizations have had to become more sensitive to workers' health and general environmental concerns. Manufacturing 'environmentally friendly' products and services, and using ecologically sustainable processes, presents a continuing challenge to all managers in the early 21st century. Running parallel with these social developments is the growing demand from powerful business lobbies to 'deregulate' business operations, including dismantling health and safety legislation (Bain, 1997). Deregulation and the growth of outsourcing (Mayhew and Quinlan, 1997) may operate to reduce protection of the organization's 'human assets'. If organizations adopt an HRM model that is 'union free', it might, given the research evidence (see, for example, James and Walters, 2002; Reilly et al., 1995; Walters, 2004), expose employees to greater work-induced hazards, thereby offering a further paradox in the HRM paradigm.

In this chapter, we have placed occupational health and wellness into the HRM context so that there can be a better understanding of managing the employment relationship. The discussion on paradox goes back to basics in reminding us of some of the complexities – economic, legal, social and psychological – and tensions inherent in the employment relationship. The key point is that health and wellness policies and practices must, as with other aspects of the HR strategy, be properly integrated in the sense that they are both complementary to and compatible with business strategy.

Chapter summary

- Employee health and wellness should be an important aspect of managing the employment relationship. To follow the logic of the HRM model, organizations need to protect their investment in their human assets. This chapter established the importance of workplace health and wellness from an economic, legal, psychological and moral perspective.

- As in other aspects of the employment relationship, government legislation and health and safety regulations influence the management of health and safety. The HASAWA 1974, for example, requires employers to ensure the health, safety and wellness at work of all employees. Furthermore, in Britain, the HSC has overall responsibility for workplace health and safety.

- EU directives and the Social Charter are an important source of health and safety regulations and counter 'pure market' ideology. With such developments in the law, and a growing awareness of safety hazards and wellness issues, it is likely that HRM professionals will face challenges and greater responsibilities in this area during the foreseeable future.

- In this chapter, we have examined some contemporary health issues, such as SBS, workplace stress, alcoholism, smoking, workplace violence and AIDS, and key elements of a workplace wellness programme.

- Trade unions have attempted to secure improvements in health and wellness at work through collective bargaining and have pressed for some stringent health and safety legislation. Under New Labour, the HSC/DETR strategy document gives support for the development of voluntaristic partnership activity between employers and workers (James and Walters, 2002). See Chapter 11 for an extended discussion on 'partnerships' in the workplace.

- A broad array of policies and actions has been discussed to ensure a healthy and safe workplace and ensure compliance with legal requirements. It has been emphasized that senior management involvement is essential for developing and implementing health and wellness policies and programmes.

- Critical analysis of health and wellness management draws attention to the fact that employment relations involves an economic and power relationship. Shareholder interests and return on investment may come before workers' health and safety. Wellness management arguably is a distraction because it manages the consequences rather than causes of ill-health.

Key concepts

- 'Careless worker' model
- Safety committee
- Safety policy
- Corporate manslaughter
- Workplace wellness
- Employee assistance programme
- Health and Safety at Work etc. Act 1974
- 'So far as is reasonably practicable'

Chapter review questions

1. Explain the careless worker model. 'Spending money on health and wellness programmes is a luxury most small organizations cannot afford.' Build an argument to support this statement, and an argument to negate it.

2. Explain the role of an HRM specialist in providing a safe and healthy environment for employees.

3. Explain the symptoms and causes of job stress and what an organization can do to alleviate them.

4. Explain how an HR professional can justify a workplace wellness programme.

5. 'Stress on women both inside and outside the work organization is a huge challenge.' Discuss.

Further reading

ASH (2005) Smoking statistics: illness and death. www.ash.org.uk

Bain, P. (1997) Human resource malpractice: the deregulation of health and safety at work in the USA and Britain. *Industrial Relations Journal*, **28**(3): 176–91.

Dohery, N. and Tyson, S. (2000) HRM and employee well-being: raising the ethical stakes. In D. Winstanley and J. Woodall (eds) *Ethical Issues in Contemporary Human Resource Management* (pp. 102–15), Basingstoke: Palgrave Macmillan.

Haunschild, A. (2003) Humanization through discipline? Foucault and the goodness of employee health programmes. *Journal of Critical Postmodern Organization Science*, **2**(3): 46–59.

James, P. and Walters, D. (2002) Worker representation in health and safety: options for regulatory reform. *Industrial Relations Journal*, **33**(2): 141–56.

Mueller, C., De Coster, S. and Estes, S. (2001) Sexual harassment in the workplace. *Work and Occupations*, **28**(4): 411–46.

Walters, D. (2004) Worker representation and health and safety in small enterprises in Europe. *Industrial Relations Journal*, **35**(2):169–86.

Practising human resource management

Searching the web

Government health and safety legislation provides for regulations to deal with various types of workplace health and safety hazard. A key element of these laws in Britain and Canada, for example, is the health and safety committee, which has a broad range of responsibilities. Go to the websites of the following occupational health and wellness organizations: Australia (www.nohsc.gov.au), Britain (www.hse.gov.uk), Canada (http://lmi-imt.hrdc-drhc.ga.ca and www.ccohs.ca), Finland (www.occuphealth.fi), South Africa (www.asosh.org) or a country you are studying. Examine the relevant sections of the health and safety legislation that deal with health and safety committees. What information is given on the role of occupational health and safety committees? How can these committees help managers to provide a safer and healthier workplace?

HRM group project

Form a study group of three to five people, and visit the websites of any of the following organizations, one that a member has worked in or one that interests members of the group: Sainsbury's (www.sainsburys.co.uk), the Body Shop (www.bodyshop.co.uk), the Royal Bank of Canada (www.royalbank.com) or Lexus (USA) (www.lexususa.com). Critically review the organization's health and safety policies and training in terms of workplace violence and sexual harassment. Go also to the website of the American Institute of Stress (www.stress.org). Using other websites, define what a 'healthy organization' is. How do organizations go about achieving this status?

Chapter case study

MANAGING WORKPLACE WELLNESS AT THE CITY OF KAMLOOPS[22]

Setting

In 1999, Canadian local governments spent more than $43 billion on providing services and managing the assets of local communities across the country. Typical municipal services included police, fire protection, road management, public transit, utility services, land use planning and development, taxation and local economic development (The Governance Network, 2002). Local governments provide more jobs than any other level of government in Canada, employing 350,717 in 1999. In that year, local governments in British Columbia employed approximately 10per cent of that total (The Governance Network, 2002).

In its 2002 study on the Canadian municipal sector and HR entitled *At the Crossroads of Change*, the Federation of Canadian Municipalities identified a number of the challenges facing local governments. These included remaining competitive in terms of attracting people and investment in a global economy, considering citizen demands for approaches to economic development that are environmentally sustainable, and responding to increasingly sophisticated taxpayer expectations relating to accountability and performance. In addition, the transfer of service responsibility from other levels of government and fiscal realities has put immense pressure on local governments to review their corporate management. The consideration of innovative and alternative service delivery has also created a requirement for organizational change and staff development to meet the needs of local governments in this new environment (The Governance Network, 2002).

Kamloops is one of the largest cities in the central interior of British Columbia, Canada, with a city population base of 80,000. The local government, or what is known as the City of Kamloops, has over 500 full-time equivalent employees. Approximately 60 per cent of the staff are represented by the Canadian Union of Public Employees, the rest being divided between firefighters represented by the International Association of Firefighters, and management, who are non-unionized. In the past 2 years, the organization had experienced a major change in its senior management staffing, with a new City mayor, new Chief Administrative Officer and new Human Resources Director taking over the helm from long-standing incumbents. With its new leadership, the City of Kamloops embarked on a quality improvement initiative labelled Quest for Quality, with the goal of becoming an employer of choice in Canada and improving its capability of facing both external and internal challenges. One of the main objectives of Quest for Quality was to provide employees with the most enjoyable and fulfilling working environment as possible and help them to balance this with their home and personal lives.

Challenges for the HR department

Shortly after these changes, a disability management programme was also introduced. The programme provided managers with consistent attendance data through bi-weekly payroll reports, showing details on when staff were absent and the status of their leave banks. In addition, training on attendance management and a coaching process were offered to managers to help them deal with staff who had consistently high absenteeism rates. The Canadian Union of Public Employees outside workers, such as labourers and equipment operators, historically had higher rates of absenteeism compared with the other employee groups at the City of Kamloops, and emphasis was made, particularly by the Occupational Health and Safety Division, on decreasing the number of days on which these employees missed work.

As a proactive measure within the disability management programme and in line with the Quest for Quality undertaking, the City also implemented a wellness initiative. The Human Resources Department approached wellness as one piece of a healthy workplace approach, which also included developing a safer physical environment and a positive organizational culture. The wellness initiative itself focused on increasing and recognizing staff involvement in both mental and physical health activities, and supporting healthy lifestyles, behaviours and coping skills for employees. As a result, the organization provided two company gyms at the worksite, as well as educational workshops on such topics as nicotine cessation, diabetes and osteoporosis. An employee assistance programme providing short-term counselling and health testing for blood sugar, cholesterol and bone density were also offered to staff on a regular basis. A walking programme, which supplied staff with pedometers and incentives for individual participation, was used to encourage employee involvement in physical activity.

Human Resources Department Meeting

At the monthly meeting of the Human Resources Department, the wellness initiative was item 3 on the agenda. When the issue was reached, the HR Coordinator, Lori Brown, explained how it was expected that, over time, the wellness initiative would contribute to general staff morale. George Brotherton, who had been sceptical about the wellness efforts, said, 'I'm not sure whether the City can continue with this initiative; there are more pressing matters that we must address.'

Lori responded that the employees had continually expressed a high level of satisfaction with the wellness events and offerings, and senior management was pleased with the positive feedback it had received about the initiative. The Human Resources Director, who was chairing the meeting, asked Lori whether she could prepare a report for the next meeting to justify the portion of the Human Resources Department's budget that was being spent on the wellness initiative.

Assignment

Working either alone or in a small group, prepare a report drawing on the material from this case study and addressing the following:

1. What challenges does the Human Resources Department face in identifying the contribution that the wellness initiative has provided towards the City's goals?

2. What benefits could the organization see as a result of this wellness initiative?

3. What recommendations would you make with regard to a process for evaluation?

Additional Information

*   Health Canada (1998) *Influencing Employee Health. Workplace Health System.* Ottawa: Canadian Fitness and Lifestyle Research Institute.

*   Governance Network (2002) *At the Crossroads of Change: Human Resources and the Municipal Sector.* Ottawa: Federation of Canadian Municipalities.

*   Go to the City of Kamloops website at www.kamloops.ca.

*   Visit the Canadian Healthy Workplace Week website at http://www.nqi.ca/chww/index.htm.

*   To find out about how to implement a healthy workplace through the National Quality Institute in Canada, go to http://www.nqi.ca/HealthyWorkplace/default.aspx.

HR-related skill development

In recent years, many organizations have implemented stop smoking programmes. Research has documented that smokers are absent approximately 40 per cent more than non-smokers, providing employers with an economic incentive to introduce smoking cessation policies. For more information, go to our website www. palgrave.com/business/brattonandgold4 and click on 'Smoking cessation poli-cies'. Choose an organization in your city. Using the information from our website as a guide, interview a manager responsible for health and safety (asking, for example, whether the company has a policy on smoking). Using the information obtained from your interview, material from this chapter and Internet sources, write a report outlining the benefits and costs you would expect to see after implementing a smoking cessation programme.

Notes

1. Geoffrey York (2001) Russian city ravaging Arctic land. *Globe and Mail*, July 25, p. A1.
2. David Knudson, Editorial, *Network*, Summer 2005, p. 7. Human Resources Institute of Alberta, Canada.
3. Quoted in Kinnersley, P. (1987) *The Hazards of Work* (p. 1). London: Pluto Press.
4. Institute of Professional and Managerial Staffs (1993) *Health and Safety: Keep it Together*, pp. 5–6; quoted by Bain (1997, p. 177).
5 Trades Union Congress (1979) *The Safety Rep and Union Organization* (p. 10). London: TUC Education.
6. Trades Union Congress (1989) *Workplace Health: A Trade Unionists' Guide* (p. 2). London: Labour Research Department.
7. Witness to the Factories' Inquiry Commission, 1833, and quoted in F. Engels (1973), *The Condi-tions of the Working Class in England* (English edn) (p. 194). London: Progress.
8. See Fletcher, B. et al. (1979) Exploring the myth of executive stress. *Personnel Management*, May; quoted in Craig (1981, p. 10).
9. Haynes, S. G. and Feinleils, M. (1980) Women, work and coronary heart disease, prospective find-ings from the Framingham Heart Study. *American Journal of Public Health*, 70; quoted in Craig (1981, p. 10).
10. Anna Raeburn (1980) *Cosmopolitan*, August; quoted in Craig (1981, p. 19).
11. Ijeoma Ross and Gayle MacDonald (1997) Scars from stress cut deep in workplace, *Globe and Mail*, October 9, p. B16.
12. Quoted in Bargaining Report. London: Labour Research Department, 1983.
13. Filipowicz, C. A. (1979) The troubled employee: whose responsibility? *The Personnel Administrator*, June; quoted in Stone, T. H. and Meltz, N. M. (1988) *Human Resource Management in Canada* (2nd edn) (p. 529). Toronto: HRW.
14. ASH Factsheet No. 2: Smoking Statistics: Illness and Death.
15. Tobacco firms agree to pay in secondhand-smoke case, *Globe and Mail*, 1997, October 11, p. A12.
16. Lee Smith, a former executive of Levi Strauss and Co., quoted in: Managing AIDS: How one boss struggled to cope, *Business Week*, 1993, February 1, p. 48.
17. *Globe and Mail* (2002), April 8, p. A2.
18. Anonymous (1998) International: Serial killer at large. *The Economist*, February 7.
19. Anonymous (1998) India wakes up to AIDS. *The Economist*, Dec 20–Jan 2.
20. Greene, J. (1998) Employers learn to live with AIDS, *HR Magazine*, February.
21. *Business Week*, 1993, February 1, pp. 53–4.zz
22. The case study author, Lori Rilkoff, MSc in HRM, CHRP, is a graduate of the University of Leicester and Thompson Rivers University, where she now lectures in HRM, and is employee relations manager at the City of Kamloops, Kamloops, British Columbia, Canada, lrilkoff@kamloops.ca.

Part Four

The evaluation context

Chapter fourteen

Evaluating human resource management

John Bratton

Human resource management evaluation refers to the processes
that measure, evaluate and communicate the value added of
human resource management practices.

'HR measurement ... a practice that is central to the future growth and success of our profession.'[1]

'HR used to be the feel-good department. Now the focus is on value added. We are in the midst
of a fundamental shift from being a cost item on the balance sheet to being, if not a profit centre,
then to at least being able to justify return on investment.'[2]

'HR must become bottom-line valid. It must demonstrate its validity to the business, its ability to
accomplish business objectives and its ability to speak of accomplishments in business language.'[3]

Chapter outline

Chapter objectives

After studying this chapter, you should be able to:

1. Explain the importance of measuring the human resource management (HRM)
   contribution
2. Describe some variables used to measure the value added of HRM
3. Understand some techniques for evaluating the HRM function
4. Critically evaluate research on the HRM–performance link

Introduction

In recent years, the human resource (HR) function has undergone an unprecedented change in its role, status and influence. Observers of the human resource management (HRM) arena have emphasized the change in focus of the HR specialist from that of an 'employee advocate' to being a 'member of the management team' (Schuler, 1990), or have emphasized the ways in which strategic HRM affects organizational performance (Boxall and Purcell, 2003). The message is that the HR specialist is involved in both the operational – recruitment and selection, rewards, training and development, and employee relations – and strategic dimensions of the business. The quotations opening this chapter reveal something of the debate and research focus that managers and HR professionals have become increasingly concerned with, demonstrating the financial contribution – the 'value added', the 'bottom line contribution', the **return on investment** (ROI) – that the HR function makes to the organization's performance. The debate has focused largely on the competing merits of two schools of thought: the 'best fit' (contingency) school (see Chapter 2) and, the focus here, the 'best HR practice' school. The best HR practice approach seeks to identify a set of universal HR practices for organizations to implement if they wish to achieve above-average performance.

As we first mentioned in Chapter 2, demonstrating statistically significant relationships between measures of best HR practice and organizational performance has become the dominant research issue in HRM. This research raises a number of pertinent questions: What types of performance data are available to measure the HRM–performance link? What best HR practices produce superior performance results? How exactly do HR practices create value – the so-called 'black box problem'? To answer such questions, researchers and HR professionals have to be able to measure, evaluate and communicate the value added of HR practices. As Ulrich and Beatty (2001, p. 306) argue, 'The objective of HR professionals is to ensure that HR adds value to strategic planning and business results of the organization.' When, however, only 23 per cent of workplaces with 25 or more employees have HR specialists (Millward et al., 2000), our focus here on the value-added approach to HRM must be directed to all managers.

In this chapter, we review the literature advocating the need for a value-added approach to HRM. The first section draws upon Phillips' (1996b) work and identifies management trends that connect organizational performance and the HR function's role in the process. As a preliminary step towards understanding the impact of HR activities on organizational performance, the chapter discusses a variety of fundamental concepts and issues before focusing on specific ways by which to evaluate the HR contribution; it includes a discussion of statistical evaluation and HR accounting and auditing. The final section reviews studies that seek to demonstrate a relationship between HR strategy and organizational performance.

Rationale for human resource management evaluation

The notion that the HR function should move beyond its administrative and controlling roles and add value has been popular in US management texts for over a decade. Drucker, the American management guru, suggested, for example, that the HR department should behave differently and demonstrate its strategic capabilities, needing to 'redirect itself away from concern with the cost of employees to concern with their *yield*' (emphasis added).[4] Developments in the role of HRM derive from changing business demands and trends (Boxall and Purcell, 2003; Fitz-enz, 2000; Fitz-enz and Davison, 2002; Nutley, 2000; Phillips, 1996b; Ulrich and Beatty, 2001), most of which we have examined throughout this text. According to Phillips (1996b), there are seven compelling trends in management thinking and practices that have changed the role of HR (Figure 14.1):

1. organizational change
2. flexibility and productivity improvements
3. the adoption of HR strategies
4. the increased importance of human capital
5. increased accountability
6. partnership relationships
7. the growing use of HR information systems.

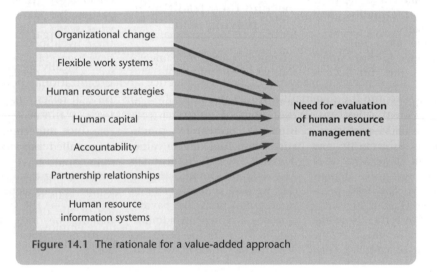

Figure 14.1 The rationale for a value-added approach

One development we discussed in Chapter 5 is *organizational* change and restructuring, which includes teamworking and re-engineering. Alongside these structural changes are increased employee involvement (EI) arrangements. The role of HR in this change process is to become a 'change agent' and be consultative rather than administrative. The second trend – increasing labour *flexibility* and productivity – envisions the role of HR as that of an initiator, enabler and evaluator of these work-restructuring regimes. The adoption of *HR strategies* by organizations underscores the importance of measuring the contribution of individual, team and organizational variables towards organizational performance (HRM in Practice 14.1). The resource-based view of strategic HRM draws attention to the increased importance of employees or *human capital* as a strategy for sustainable competitiveness. Phillips (1996b, p. 6) suggests that the contribution of human capital to the organization's bottom line is 'sometimes subtle, occasionally mysterious, and at times very convincing'. Whether the evidence is convincing, we shall explore later in this chapter.

HRM IN PRACTICE 14.1

HR FOCUSING ON HOW IT CAN ADD VALUE

TERRENCE BELFORD, *GLOBE AND MAIL*, 25 MARCH 2002

Human resources professionals are in the midst of reinventing themselves – changing what they do for the companies that employ them and how they relate to those on the operations side. Their goal is to shoot for the corporate gold – a seat around the senior management table right alongside decision makers like the chief operating, information and finance officers.

The single most important tool they have in their uphill struggle is the intellectual capital held within any corporation. In the past, the profession has focused on winning the hearts of employees. Today their aim is to quantify and harness their minds. 'HR used to be the feel-good department,' says Michael Ford, president of the Human Resources Institute of Alberta. 'Now the focus is on value added. We are in the midst of a fundamental shift from being a cost item on the balance sheet to being, if not a profit centre, then to at least being able to justify return on investment.'

> **Success and a seat at the senior management table will depend on HR professionals looking beyond their traditional playing field.**

Granted, such a fundamental shift takes time and brings with it a certain measure of confusion. 'The main problem right now is figuring out just what HR is going to do within a corporation,' says Paul Juniper, president of the HR Professionals Association of Ontario. 'Historically we have performed administrative functions like payroll, pensions and benefits administration. We were the personnel department. We hired, we fired, and we took care of the details. We never added a lot of value to the company.'

That role changed with the advent of the technological age. In the past decade, many employers found that they could first automate most of those traditional functions and then become more effective by outsourcing them to third parties. For HR professionals, what seemed like a threat to their livelihood may actually have been a blessing. 'Suddenly, we were relieved of these humdrum tasks ... That left the HR department free to devote its time to developing a new role, one that could help the company reach its strategic objectives.'

Success and a seat at the senior management table will depend on HR professionals looking beyond their traditional playing field, Mr. Juniper adds.

The *accountability* issue is illustrated by examples of strategic HR practices that present their successes in measurable improvements. The premise behind this concept can be illustrated by Fitz-enz's (2000, p. 4) blunt statement that 'if we don't know how to measure our primary value-producing asset, we can't manage it'. The sixth trend relates to power and politics within organizations. Partly in response to the development and adoption of HR strategies, and to the development of outsourcing the HR function, the HR profession is 'desperately trying to collaborate with line management' (Phillips, 1996b, p. 20) by building *partnership relationships* with other managers. And an important part of this is being able to demonstrate to line management the bottom line contribution of the HRM function. Ulrich and Beatty (2001, p. 294) put it like this:

> HR professionals must be more than partners; they must be players. Players contribute. They are engaged. They add value. They are in the game, not at the game. They deliver results. They do things that make a difference.

The seventh important development encouraging accountability in the HRM function is the growing use of *HR information systems*. The capability of IT systems allows greater amounts of data to be collected, analysed and reported, and potentially leads to more accurate measures of the economic value of worker performance. These seven changes are closely integrated and relate to greater demands for accountability and value-added HR practices and systems.

REFLECTIVE QUESTION

According to Peter Drucker, 'You can't manage what you can't measure.' At a time when so many people are engaged in so-called knowledge work, how valid is this maxim when strictly applied to managing people?

Human resource management–performance model

For **HR measurement**, demonstrating the link between HRM strategy and organizational performance requires the measurement of some set of variables. The methodology for ensuring high internal validity would ideally permit a calculation of how different HRM strategies or individual practices affect economic performance while controlling the other factors that might influence those performance outcomes. *High internal validity* refers to the extent to which the results can be generalized to infer the likely impacts of HRM practices, were they to be introduced elsewhere. Figure 14.2

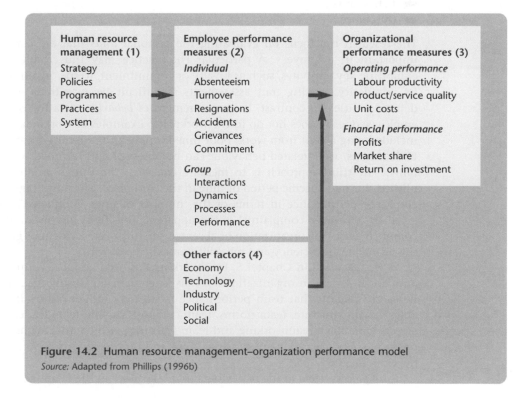

Figure 14.2 Human resource management–organization performance model
Source: Adapted from Phillips (1996b)

presents a basic model showing the relationship between HRM practices and organizational performance. The HRM added-value model indicates the overall relationship between three major elements:

- HRM
- HR performance measures, at both individual employee and work team levels
- organizational performance measures.

Human resource management

The HRM element in Figure 14.2 includes the HR strategy, policies, programmes, practices and system that exist in work organizations and have an impact on employee and group performance, which in turn affects individual and organizational performance. Much of the recent research has focused on how 'innovative' bundles of HRM practices, such as selection, training and learning, appraisal and rewards, impact on employee performance. It is worth emphasizing Fitz-enz's (2000, p. xii) point that 'people are the only element with the inherent power to generate value'.

Employee performance measures

The second element in Figure 14.2 depicts the performance effects of HRM, estimated in part by employee performance measures. Researchers have a number of options when it comes to measuring individual employees and teams. Saks (2000) outlines three measurements:

- traits
- behaviours
- outcomes.

The research can focus on evaluating the personal *traits* that are considered to be important in employees. A particular HR practice may thus result in employees exhibiting key attributes, such as loyalty or commitment, to the organization. Despite its popularity, making trait assessments is difficult because traits are not clearly defined entities. In contrast, the measurement of *behaviour* data focuses on what an employee does or does not do in the workplace. Examples of work-related behaviours include being absent from work, poor time-keeping and resigning from employment. Unlike traits, work-related behaviour can be observed and recorded with some reliability. The third approach is to measure *outcomes*, the things produced or accomplished during a specific period of time in the workplace. The advantage of measuring employee performance in terms of the 'number of units completed', the 'accident level' or 'customer complaints' is the apparent objectivity involved. Whether it is commitment to the organization or absenteeism, turnover, accident or grievance rates, the problem of deficiency and reliability must be dealt with.

As we discussed in Chapter 5, teamworking has become more common in British and North American organizations, as has interest in measuring team performance. Research suggests that team performance is strongly influenced by four *input* variables – team structure, team norms, team composition and team leadership – and by *process* variables – teamworking and team learning – which affect team performance outcomes. The measurement of these input and process factors is not, however, well developed (Saks, 2000).

Team process refers to the behaviours that take place in the team (across individuals and across time). Although a review of all team process theory is outside the scope of this chapter, we should highlight two important concepts that help to clarify potential process indicators of team effectiveness. There seems to be ample evidence that how the team approaches the job to be done has important consequences for ultimate team performance, this being referred to as *work team strategies* (Kline, 1999). The second concept is that of *team learning*, as the amount of informal learning that takes place within a team appears to affect team outcomes (Kasl et al., 1997).

When defining *team performance*, researchers and practitioners are usually thinking in terms of how well the team has been able to accomplish certain team outcomes. In work organizations, team performance is conceptualized in terms of efficiency, that is, accomplishment relative to the resources utilized, efficiency thus being an output to input ratio. Banker et al. (1996), for example, studied the impact of work teams on labour productivity, which was measured as a ratio of the number of units produced to the total number of production hours. Their results indicated that labour productivity improved following the formation of work teams. Finally, when undertaking research on work team performance, or when team data are to be analysed, it is important to remember that the unit of analysis is the team, the sample size therefore being the number of teams involved in the investigation (Saks, 2000).

Organizational performance measures

Individual employee and work team measures affect organizational performance, the third element in the model shown in Figure 14.2 above. Researchers and practitioners have used a number of organizational performance measures, including labour productivity ratios, product and service quality, unit cost ratios, revenue productivity and ROI. Saks (2000) also points out that researchers frequently tend to rely on single indicators of performance, ignore the relationships between 'multiple measures', tend to ignore the fact that some measures of organizational performance, for example change in market share, take longer to materialize than, say, a change in employee behaviour, and use performance indicators across dissimilar workplaces with no regard for their appropriateness, thus rendering comparisons meaningless.

Given that work organizations exist in order to accomplish a goal(s), researchers have often conceptualized organizational performance in terms of *goal attainment*, four specific indicators reflecting this approach:

- profit-related indices
- productivity
- quality
- perceptual measures of goal attainment.

Profit-related indices or financial variables include percentage ROI. Labour *productivity*, a popular indicator, is usually defined as the quantity or volume of the major product or service that the organization provides and is expressed as a rate, that is, productivity per worker or per unit of time. Huselid (1995), for example, measured productivity in terms of sales per employee. Another indicator is *quality*, which usually refers to the attributes of the primary service or product provided by the firm. Other examples include the airline industry, which conducts random surveys of passengers to obtain data on perceptions of the quality of in-flight service. The monitoring of performance data can of course be used as a surveillance tool – 'a modern-day Panopticon' (Cully et al., 1999, p. 114). Finally, although hard financial data are often used to measure organizational outcomes, researchers also use *perceptual measures* to quantify performance. Both Cully et al. (1999) and Den Hartog and Verburg (2004), for example, measured perceived economic outcomes by asking managers to compare their own organizations in a particular area (e.g. productivity) relative to other organizations in the same industry, using a subjective scale ranging from 'a lot above average' to 'a lot below average'.

The organizational outcome measures discussed here are important for at least three reasons:

1. These are employee-related outcomes, and as such they are most directly influenced by HR practices. Different rewards and training programmes are, for example, likely to have some influence on most, if not all, of the outcomes.
2. These outcomes (e.g. productivity, quality and employee unit cost) can influence the organization's financial operational goals.
3. The outcomes can influence the individual psychological contract (Chapter 1) as well as aspects of individual behaviour and/or outputs.

Other factors

Disentangling the HRM–organizational performance equation is complicated by the fact that employee performance measures are only one set of variables that impact on organizational performance. Other variables, such as changes in the economy, technology, industry, government policies and social trends, the fourth element in Figure 14.2 above, also affect organizational performance. A company that exports its products can, for example, experience a substantial rise or fall in revenue productivity as a result of a sustained strengthening or weakening of a nation's currency. Further support for the other factors caveat is the financial implosion of many companies following the 11 September 2001 attack on the World Trade Center in New York: the financial performance and subsequent collapse of Canada's second largest airline, Canada 3000, was, for example, the result of the sharp fall in passenger traffic after the attack rather than of HRM practices or employee performance.

HRM WEB LINKS

Go to www.bbk.ac.uk/manop/man/mgesrc.htm for information on carrying out research on the relationship between HRM and organizational performance.

Measurement issues

Measurement is central to the HRM–organization performance model, but there are a number of challenges in selecting and using measurement. First, what mix of best HR practices should be selected in order to achieve performance improvement? While US academic Jeffrey Pfeffer (1994, 1998) identified 16 best practices in successful organizations, later consolidated into seven key HR practices, European researchers Den Hartog and Verburg (2004) isolated eight key practices to test the HR practices–organizational performance link (Table 14.1).

Table 14.1 Selective human resource practices for performance improvement according to Pfeffer and Den Hartog and Verburg

Pfeffer's (1998) seven practices	Den Hartog and Verburg's (2004) eight practices
1. Employment security	1. Employment skills
2. Selective hiring	2. Autonomy
3. Self-managed work teams	3. Pay-for-performance
4. High pay contingent on company performance	4. Profit-sharing
5. Extensive training	5. Performance appraisal
6. Reduction of status differences	6. Team performance
7. Sharing information	7. Information-sharing
	8. Job evaluation

A second challenge facing researchers when selecting measurements, and one not unrelated to the first challenge, is operationalizing the variables under scrutiny. Suppose the researchers select 'training' as a key best HR practice. How will they determine whether sample organizations undertake 'extensive training'? They might decide to ask respondents, 'Does your establishment undertake intensive training?' The response to the question 'Does your establishment undertake intensive training?' will thus become the operational definition of the concept of training in their research. Training can, however, also be operationalized as management development, formal workplace learning or skills training (Den Hartog and Verburg, 2004). In addition, respondents' interpretation of 'extensive' might be inconsistent.

Similarly, a further challenge arises because the concept of 'best HR practices' is based on subjective judgements. Researchers and respondents might, for example, define a 'self-managed team' in different ways, with or without a 'supervisor' or team 'leader', or define an 'employee involvement' practice as employee 'participation' or as 'involvement' in corporate governance – the proverbial 'apples and oranges'. Subjective judgements of HR practice may be especially problematic when comparing multiple workplaces or work units within a single company. If the respondents to a questionnaire share a different meaning and definition of a 'best HR practice', estimates of the effects of the new strategic HR practices will be biased.

A third challenge relates to the performance variables in the HRM–performance equation. The measurements, often regarded as objective and accurate reflections of an organization's financial performance, can be based on measures that are inaccurate and in some cases fraudulently misleading. The wave of corporate accounting scandals that implicated top US executives at Enron, Adelphia Communications and WorldCom in 2002, and Parmalat Finanziaria SpA in 2004, has, for example, severely shaken the trust of investors, employees and market-watchers in reported financial statements. In June 2002, for instance, WorldCom Inc. revealed one of the largest accounting scandals in management history, admitting that it had overstated its profits by US$3.85 billion. An accurate measurement of the HRM contribution to the organization's financial bottom line obviously becomes entirely misleading with such fraudulent accounting practices.

A fourth challenge facing researchers when using measurements, and one not unrelated to the third identifiable challenge, is that research into the outcomes of new HR strategies requires management participation and, moreover, a disclosure of commercially sensitive information on performance indicators that many managers are unwilling or unable to provide to an independent researcher. The researcher therefore has to use intermediate performance indicators such as accidents/injuries, absenteeism rates, voluntary resignations, and formal grievance and complaints rates (see, for example, Betcherman et al., 1994).

A fifth challenge is how to isolate external variables. Exchange rates can, for example, significantly affect the financial bottom line, which makes it difficult to measure accurately the impact of HRM practices. Guest (1997, p. 268) recognizes this problem when he states, 'We also need a theory about how much of the variance can be explained by the human factor.' Even if relevant indicators are made available to the researcher and the external variables are isolated, the problem of identifying the causal links remains a challenge. Do certain best or better HR practices lead to better performing firms, or do better performing firms adopt certain HRM practices? Given the current state of affairs, it appears that there is no single conceptual model of organizational performance – but there is no shortage of possibilities either. In short, the implications of HR strategic choices for organizational performance are difficult to measure with complete confidence. With this in mind, Ichniowski et al. (1996, p. 312) argue that, 'The key to credible results is creating a collage of studies that use different designs with their own particular strengths and limitations.'

Overall, these measurement challenges may raise questions concerning the appropriateness of HR and organizational measures, questions that underscore the importance of the statistical concepts of reliability and validity. When evaluating the HRM contribution to the organization's performance, all measures, whatever the level of measurement (individual, team or organization), must be of high quality, that is, they must be reliable and valid. *Reliability* refers to the degree to which a measure results in the same values when it is repeated. *Validity* refers to the appropriateness of the inferences we draw from a test score. In using employment tests (e.g. ability tests; see Chapter 7) to make selection decisions, we are, for example, making an inference from a test score about an applicant's future job performance. If the measures have poor reliability and validity, the results of the HRM–organizational performance research will therefore be at best difficult to interpret, and at worst lack credibility (Saks, 2000). The various measurement options described here reflect a mixture of objective and subjective data. Each has its own strengths and weaknesses with regard to reliability and validity.

REFLECTIVE QUESTION

What do you think of these measurement issues? Can the measurement of the HRM contribution be truly objective?

Researching human resource management: designs and methods

Both the academic researcher and the HR professional must make choices about how to handle the most important HR variables and how to study them; these choices demand an overall **research design**. According to Palys (1997, pp. 76–7, emphasis added), '*research design* involves stating a game plan through which one can gather information that addresses one's research purpose in a simple, elegant, and systematic way'. The 'game plan' through which researchers gather information on the contribution of HRM strategy usually takes the form of one of the following four research designs:

1. survey
2. case studies
3. experimental
4. meta-analysis.

Here we offer a brief summary of each design.

Survey research

Of all the data-gathering techniques available to the academic and the practitioner, the survey, either written or oral, is the one used most extensively. In its most basic form, a survey elicits information on people's opinions of or attitudes towards a certain topic by asking people specific questions. The large-scale surveys of changing employment relations in Britain in the past decade by Millward et al. (2000) and Kersley et al. (2006) are good examples of this type of research design. Surveys have been used to gather information on employment relations since the beginning of large-scale industrial capitalism. In 1880, a survey of French workers to study employer pay practices (Bottomore and Rubel, 1956, quoted in Gray and Guppy, 1999, p. 4) asked:

> (1) Does your employer or his representative resort to trickery in order to defraud you of part of your earnings? And; (2) If you are paid piece rates, is the quality of the article made a pretext for fraudulent deductions from your wages?

In this case, the researcher using the survey to elicit information was Karl Marx.

Survey research is most appropriate when the researcher wants to learn about the relationship between variables and to be able to predict the level of one variable with knowledge of another, for example 'What makes women (or men) managers prefer one style of workplace leader over another?' Survey research designs are also used for assessing the impact of change (Kraut, 1996), such as the impact of introducing a specific recruitment and selection practice on long-term team cohesiveness and performance. HR practitioners use employee attitude surveys to evaluate the effectiveness of their HR department (Phillips, 1996b).

HRM WEB LINKS

Go to any of the following websites for information on the purpose of the survey: www.lpsos-reid.com (the Angus Reid Group), www.gallup.com (the Gallup Poll) or www.norc.org (the National Opinion Research Centre).

Qualitative case study research

Qualitative research refers to the gathering and sorting of information through a variety of techniques, including interviews, focus groups, observations and the use of archival data in organizational files, records or reports. A case study is an intensive description and analysis of a phenomenon or workplace unit such as an employee, team or organization. The case study researcher seeks holistic description and interpretation, and uses a wide range of qualitative research techniques.

In an attempt to differentiate between quantitative and qualitative approaches to serious inquiry, Berg (2007) explains that 'quantity' is an amount of something whereas 'quality' refers to the what, how, when and where of a thing. Qualitative research thus refers 'to the meanings, concepts, definitions, characteristics, metaphors, symbols, and descriptions of things' (Berg, 2007, p. 3). Qualitative inquiry is a process that locates the researcher in the workplace, studying people in their natural settings, attempting to make sense of, or interpret, social phenomena in terms of the meanings people attach to them (Denzin and Lincoln, 2005). Quantitative research, however, emphasizes the measurement and analysis of causal relationships between variables rather than of processes – that is, how things happen.

Qualitative researchers stress the socially constructed nature of the workplace and employment relations, and the situational constraints that shape the research (Denzin and Lincoln, 2005). Qualitative case study research is most useful when the researcher wants to obtain a rich, in-depth description of some event or process. Qualitative data obtained from interviewing employees and/or managers, coupled with actual results on a work-related issue, create a very convincing case study (Phillips, 1996b).

Experimental research

The origin of **experimental research** can be traced back to the work of John Stuart Mill and his treatise entitled *A System of Logic*, first published in 1873. Mill proposed a number of principles, in the form of canons or laws, which he argued were a requirement for establishing order among controlled events. One law, the method of difference (quoted in Merriam and Simpson, 1995, p. 52), stated:

> If an instance in which the phenomenon under investigation occurs, and an instance in which it does not occur have every circumstances in common save one, that one occurring only in the former, the circumstances in which alone the two instances differ is the effect, or the cause, or an indispensable part of the cause of the phenomenon.

Merriam and Simpson (1995) interpret Mill's law as meaning that if two sets of events are alike and something is either added to or taken from the event, causing a difference between those two events, the difference can be attributed to what was added or withdrawn. Isolating and observing single variables in this way is common in the natural sciences but less useful in the social sciences because of the multivariate nature of human activity.

Although the conditions required for true 'classical' experimental designs are lacking, the approach is, however, used to conduct research in the workplace. Experimental research designs are used to provide evidence regarding cause-and-effect relationships with as much control as possible. An experimental design can, for example, test the effects of a HR practice such as a training workshop or a pay system on employee attitudes and behaviours.

Take the training workshop. Two work teams are given training on problem-solving and team leadership skills, some measure of achievement (e.g. quality or productivity) then being administered at the end of the month. The measurement of achievement for those teams exposed to the training is compared with that of another similar team deprived of the training. Experimental research therefore incorporates two important features: an *experimental group* and a *control group*. The experimental group is exposed to, or deprived of, some particular HR intervention (manipulation), whereas the control group is part of the research study but does not receive the HR intervention (Figure 14.3). The pre- and post-measures for the control group are the same as those collected from the experimental group. By comparing and contrasting the scores on these measures, the expectation is that there will be an increase or improvement in scores (from pre-test to post-test) for those in the experimental group who received the HR intervention but not for participants in the control group.

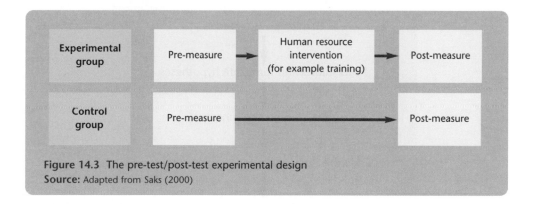

Figure 14.3 The pre-test/post-test experimental design
Source: Adapted from Saks (2000)

Although 'true' experimental research designs provide the means of testing the causal effects of HR interventions in the workplace, there are a number of ethical concerns facing the researcher who conducts experimental research, the most important of which are participants' freedom of choice to participate, the right to receive beneficial interventions and the deception of participants (Saks, 2000).

REFLECTIVE QUESTION

Given the number of external and internal variables affecting work and employment relations, do you think that experimental research designs provide a reliable means of measuring the contribution of HR interventions in the workplace?

Existing research and meta-analysis

In recent years, a new technique called *meta-analysis* has been used to study the impact of HR practices. This technique allows the researcher or HRM professional to combine the results of existing research in a particular area and to calculate the overall effect of an HR intervention. Meta-analyses of selection tests, for example, provide information on the usefulness of the various tests for predicting job performance. The results of a meta-analysis can be particularly useful to small organizations that do not have the ability to conduct the large-scale research studies that are often required to test the validity of a selection test or the impact of a particular HR practice (Saks, 2000).

The defining feature of meta-analysis is the statistical analysis of the results of many empirical studies. Drawing upon the work of Saks (2000), the meta-analysis review process is depicted in Figure 14.4. The meta-analysis review process begins with a compilation of all the relevant empirical studies on the HRM topic under investigation. After reading the papers, the researcher formulates hypotheses about the potential study characteristics that might affect the relationship between the variables being investigated. The results of meta-analyses in HRM can help HR professionals to decide whether an HR intervention will add value. An organization can, for example, use meta-analysis to measure the value added of a training programme (see, for example, Alliger et al., 1997).

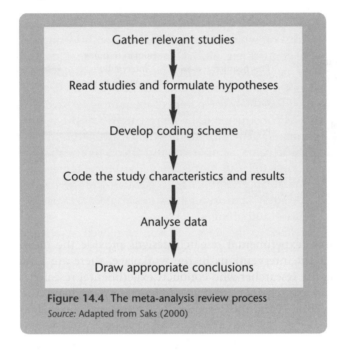

Figure 14.4 The meta-analysis review process
Source: Adapted from Saks (2000)

Research design issues

Whichever of the research designs discussed above we choose to adopt, a number of common issues cut across them all.

When academics conduct research in the workplace, at issue is the question of how knowledge is constructed. The study of knowledge and the justification of belief (Dancy, 1985) is referred to as **epistemology**, and at the heart of epistemology lie such questions as, 'Which beliefs are justified and which are not?', 'What is the relationship between seeing and knowing?' and, in management studies, 'Whose knowledge is produced in the research interview?' This has practical implications in terms of:

- the research context
- the nature and size of the sample
- the sources of data employed.

First – considering the *research context* – the investigator has to decide how important it is for the purposes of the research to conduct the inquiry in an actual organization. This might involve one organization, such as in an experiment to test the effects of an

HR practice, or several, allowing the researcher to study differences between particular HR strategies. The issue of the research context is illustrated by the academic debate on quantitative survey versus qualitative case study. It is argued, for example, that workplace surveys generate a vast amount of quantitative data that can test theories and permit a statistical analysis of HRM practices and performance. Critics of this research design point out that the researcher is 'outside looking in', and, given the nature of the research instrument – a mail questionnaire – the results cannot hope to provide an accurate picture of the subtleties and intricacy of the way in which work is structured and *actually* performed, and the dynamics of the employment relationship. Case studies, on the other hand, involve the researcher being 'inside', and qualitative methods can provide rich data on workplace HR activities.

The second issue relates to the *nature and size of the sample* under investigation. There will be occasions on which the researcher may wish to study all the people in a particular workplace context (e.g. all the employees of a small company), but in most cases, research may be carried out with a sample of employees. Two particularly important features of the sample are its characteristics and its size. The phrase 'sample characteristics' is used to convey the nature of the sample relative to the population of interest. The sample is constructed to be representative of the population so that the researcher can legitimately generalize to the whole population from the data obtained from the research participants. Sample size also affects representativeness, that is, it is harder for a small sample (relative to the population) to be representative. Thus, larger samples allow for the greatest confidence in generalizing the results of a study. One limitation of the case study approach relates to sample size: how far can a researcher generalize from the case study results?

The third issue relates to the *sources of data* employed. A research design usually implies just who (or what) is going to be measured, assessed, tested or monitored. In management research, it is quite common to make use of mail questionnaires or self-reports compiled by managers. With self-reported data, there is always the potential for bias (Saks, 2000), the obvious concern being that if only one response is received per establishment, 'any idiosyncratic opinions or interpretations of the questions can distort the results' (Ichniowski et al., 1996, p. 309). Thompson and McHugh (2002) argue that researchers often do not appreciate the important limitations of self-completed questionnaires. In particular, they point out potential problems when investigators rely on managerial informants for data on HR interventions and their effects when the informants themselves have a role or stake in the practice. The data are less than accurate because such informants may, rather than reporting the reality (what *is*), fall into a normative (what *ought to be*) mode (Guest, 1999; Thompson and McHugh, 2002).

In other words, self-completed mail questionnaires have the potential to induce 'socially desirable responses', responses that are intended to make the respondent look good in the eyes of the investigator or society at large (Saks, 2000). Thus, asking a manager in a survey if she or he 'values employee voice' is likely to produce an affirmative answer; most people will reason that they will look unreasonable if they do not answer 'Yes' to this question. The investigator can check on the possibility of distortion in self-reports by surveying the views of relevant others. The value of talking to both managers and workers is emphasized by Nichols (1986; quoted in Bratton, 1992, p. 14):

> A study which systematically samples both managers and workers is always likely to provide at least some snippets of information that rarely surface in other accounts and to suggest different lines of interpretation.

There is another issue related to data collection that we should also note: the notion that we can ever have an objective account of the phenomenon under investigation, because all such accounts are 'linguistic reconstructions'. This is called the 'constructivist model'. A constructivist or formative approach recognizes that the researcher and those being researched create the data and ensuing analysis through an interactive process. The researcher's data do not *discover* social reality; rather, what is 'discovered' arises from the interactive process and its political, cultural and structural contexts (Charmaz, 2000). The interview is traditionally viewed as an opportunity for knowledge to be transmitted between, for example, a manager and a researcher, yet, through the interactional process, the viewed and the viewer are active makers of meaning, assembling and modifying their questions and answers in response to the dynamics of the interview. The researcher is not simply a conduit for information but is instead deeply implicated in the production of knowledge (Schneider, 1999).

The constructivist approach suggests that what the manager and the situation actually are is a consequence of various accounts and interpretations. From this perspective, managers act as 'practical authors' of their own identities (Shotter, 1993). This does not mean that knowledge is impossible: 'No one *does* know, because no one *can* know' (Dancy, 1985, p. 7). It does mean, however, that the knowledge that is produced on what managers and HR specialists allegedly do cannot be an objective narrative about their workplace activities, and we must maintain a healthy scepticism as we journey through the HRM discourse (Grint, 1995).

The key point arising from this overview of research design is that there is no one best way to do HR research: each research design seeks to make the workplace and HR practices transparent in a different way (HRMI in Practice 14.2). Of course, we all have our biases, but our intention in this chapter is not to privilege one methodological approach over another – quantitative survey research versus qualitative case study research, for example.

HRM IN PRACTICE 14.2

PRODUCTIVITY IS A TIME BOMB

HENRY MINTZBERG, *GLOBE AND MAIL*, 13 JUNE 2002

Some economists have been issuing dire warnings about the Canadian economy recently. 'Economists are concerned that Canadian companies have been adding too many workers – and therefore expenses – without showing a corresponding increase in output,' wrote a reporter in the *Globe and Mail* recently. The implication, almost in so many words, is that these foolish Canadian managers are running around hiring people they don't need.

These economists know better: they have statistics.

Since I am not an economist, and am suspicious of statistics in any event, but work in the world of managers and organizations, let me venture another hypothesis: Productivity is killing the American economy. What is productivity, exactly? In fact nothing exactly. You take some measure of output, some gross product or other, and divide it by the number of declared hours of work and the

like. The result, I assure you, is gross. It represents what can be measured and ignores all sorts of interesting things that cannot.

Ideas are outputs too, but they don't figure because they can't be measured, even if they may show up much later in the form of better products and processes. So if a company emasculates its new product development activity, or closes research laboratories that looks good to the economists because the hours of declared work go down while the measured output remains the same.

Hours worked show up as long as they can be counted – a worker who spends 37.5 paid hours on the job, for example, even his or her 2.1 hours paid overtime. But what about the manager on a monthly salary who now works 60 hours instead of 50? That doesn't count in these statistics – burning out doesn't count.

I received an email recently from someone I had been working with in the US. He said, 'Henry, you won't believe what's going on here. More cost cutting. We have hardly anyone left to make things work.' A sizeable portion of American business is now rotting from within, while the economy becomes astonishingly more productive. Well, maybe it is not all that astonishing.

Thanks to 'shareholder value' – no human values in this, just an obsession with short-term stock price – workers and managers get 'downsized' regularly so that

---

> **But as workers and managers depart, out goes commitment, out goes respect, out goes the social glue that binds people together in a healthy social system.**

---

those who are left have to do that much more. And often they have to do it with less, because of the enhanced bargaining power of their employers. This, too, drives up productivity, alongside the living standards of those who own the stock, for a while at least.

But as workers and managers depart, out goes commitment, out goes respect, out goes the social glue that binds people together in a healthy social system. Indeed, out goes the database of the company, which is in the heads of the managers more than in the computers. And with the managers goes much of the potential for innovation, because that comes from the grounded initiatives of middle managers far more than the ethereal 'strategies' of senior executives. America does have one great hope. That is to convince its major trading partners to imitate this nonsense. 'Shareholder value' is sweeping across this so-called globe, although the Germans, Japanese, and some others remain a bit reticent. The Canadians, too, apparently. But economists are working on that.

Approaches to evaluating human resource strategy

Previous sections of this chapter have described the measurement of individual, team and organizational variables, as well as the different approaches to researching HR practices. Once the data have been collected, the emphasis shifts to evaluation – the ways in which the data are used and analysed to interpret the HRM–organizational performance link. Evaluating the effects of labour practices and economic performance is well established in the field of industrial relations: numerous empirical studies have, for example, monitored the impact of unions on wages and productivity. Although the 1960s and 70s saw research on the effects of such management initiatives as EI schemes on various outcomes (attitudes, job satisfaction and productivity), Purcell (1989, pp. 72–3) suggested that if it were possible to prove that 'enlightened or progressive' HRM were invariably associated with higher productivity and lower costs, 'life for the … HRM executive would be easier. As it is, there is little conclusive evidence.' Similarly, Legge (2005, p. 230) makes the point that there are 'few, if any, systematic evaluations' of 'high-commitment' management practices on organizational performance.

With regard to the HRM–performance link, there are still gaps in our knowledge, but there have, over the past two decades, been 'considerable advancements' in the evaluation of HR strategy on organization performance (Phillips, 1996b). Much of this research has been spurred on by debates surrounding the relative merits of high-performance work systems and the new HRM paradigm. There are a number of ways of evaluating HRM practices and the HRM system, three of which will be described here:

- statistical evaluation
- financial evaluation
- system evaluation.

Statistical evaluation of human resource strategy

The statistical evaluation of HR strategy includes basic descriptive indices, such as measures of central tendency, as well as statistics that allow us to make statements about the relationship or correlation between HR practices and outcome variables. It is outside the scope of this chapter to cover statistical analysis, but regression analysis is a statistical method for evaluating the relationships between variables. For example, a researcher can use data to demonstrate a positive link between clusters of 'participative' HR practices and performance outcomes. Table 14.2 illustrates how regression analysis is used to present research findings. This table reports the correlations between HR practices, measures associated with high-performance work systems and the culture orientation. Den Hartog and Verburg's study (2004, p. 69) found that employee skill and direction correlated positively with three out of the four culture measures, especially 'innovation' and 'goal'.

Table 14.2 Correlations between human resource practices, outcomes and cultural orientations

	Firm performance	Beyond contract	Economic outcome	Employee turnover	Manager/specialist turnover	Employee absenteeism	Manager/specialist absenteeism	Supportive	Innovative	Rules	Goal
Employee skill/direction	.12	.31 **	.25 **	−.15	.03	−.20 **	−.24 **	.23 **	.41 **	.15	.42 **
Autonomy	.04	.27 **	.09	−.10	.02	−.04	−.05	.15	.06	−.30 **	.08
Reward	−.02	.10	.22 **	.11	−.02	−.09	−.19 **	.09	.21 **	−.03	.33 **
Profit-sharing	.07	.06	.17 *	−.08	−.03	.06	−.08	.00	.18	.01	.27 **
Performance evaluation	.03	.13	.15	−.15	−.17 *	.03	.12	.08	.16 *	.04	.11
Team performance	−.02	.14	.07	.02	−.08	−.10	−.04	.12	.12	−.05	.22 **
Information-sharing	−.02	.08	.01	−.17 *	−.02	−.14	−.01	.01	.04	.02	.06
Job evaluation	.14	−.02	.13	−.03	.09	−.03	−.10	.06	.21 **	.10	.11

Note: *p < .05; ** p < .01 (two-tailed)
Source: Adapted from Den Hartog and Verburg (2004) p. 69

HRM WEB LINKS

Go to the 2005 Workplace Employee Relations Survey website www.dti.gov.uk/
employment/research-evaluation/grants/wers/index.html for more examples of statistical techniques used to compute the mean differences and measures of association
between variables.

Financial evaluation of the human resource strategy

In recent years, HR professionals have had to demonstrate the value added of their
programmes and departments. They have also had to develop the skill to communicate with other managers, in the language of business, the HR contribution to the
financial bottom line (Fitz-enz, 2000; Pfeffer, 1994; Phillips, 1996b). As Pfeffer (1994,
p. 57) argues, 'In a world in which financial results are measured, a failure to measure
human resource policy and practice implementation dooms this to second-class
status, oversight, neglect, and potential failure.' It has thus become apparent that HR
specialists need to be able to evaluate in financial terms the costs and benefits of
different HR strategies and individual HRM practices. A production manager, for
example, proposes investing in new technology and incorporates into the proposal
projected increases in productivity and resultant decreases in unit production cost.
With this in mind, HR professionals must compete for scarce organizational resources
in the same language as their colleagues and present credible information on the relative costs and benefits of HR interventions. This section describes one approach to
evaluating HR strategies in financial terms: ROI.

The basic approach here is to calculate the cost of a HR intervention, such as
training or an employee participation arrangement, and to determine the benefit in
monetary terms of results such as improved productivity or a reduction in absenteeism, accidents and grievances. For example, a food-processing plant was considering implementing a training programme to improve the quality of the meat-cutting
and housekeeping, as well as the number of preventable accidents. The cost of the
training intervention was calculated in terms of direct costs, indirect costs, development costs, overhead costs and pay, the total cost of the training intervention being
calculated to be £18,475. The benefits of the training intervention were calculated in
terms of the improvement in the quality of the meat packaging and the reduction in
the number of accidents. After training, there were 330 fewer meat portions rejected
per shift, which was calculated as saving £74,250 per year. The investigators also
reported a decrease of nine accidents per year, at a cost saving of £8,213 per year. The
total saving to the organization was thus £82,463.

To calculate the ROI of an HR intervention programme, the manager needs to
calculate the total costs and benefits of the programme using the following formula
(Saks, 2000):

$$ROI = \frac{\text{Net benefits}}{\text{Intervention costs}}$$

The return on the investment for the training programme in the above example is
therefore £82,463/£18,475 = 4.5 (45 per cent), or £63,988 per year (£82,463–£18,475).

The method of calculating the ROI involves estimating the costs and benefits of an HR intervention, but in reality it can be more difficult to calculate the full benefits. This is because 'soft' measures such as communication, learning, interpersonal skills and so on are much more difficult to quantify in monetary terms than are 'hard' measures such as absenteeism, productivity and labour productivity. Although the calculation of ROI in the evaluation of HR practices is a powerful way to demonstrate the value added of HR interventions, very few organizations actually use the technique in practice (Saks, 2000). For more detailed and complex examples of calculating the ROI of HR practices, the reader should refer to readings devoted to these topics (Fitz-enz, 1995, 2000; Phillips, 1996b).

Evaluating human resource management systems

Statistical and financial evaluations of the HR contribution are best suited to evaluating particular HR practices or programmes. When evaluating an entire HRM system, managers have used two methods in recent years (Nutley, 2000; Saks, 2000):

- HRM auditing
- HRM benchmarking.

HRM auditing

The term 'HRM audit' can be interpreted in different ways, but, as in a financial audit, there are a number of generally accepted elements of audit practice (Nutley, 2000, p. 22):

1. independence from the subject being audited
2. technical work in the form of a systematic gathering and analysis of data
3. an evaluation of HR activities, policies and systems based on the evidence
4. a clearly defined object of the process
5. action in response to audit findings.

In other words, an HRM audit is a process of evaluating the effectiveness of the entire HR function. According to Phillips (1996b), the use of HR audits has been increasing in North American workplaces. A number of benefits result from an HR audit (Figure 14.5).

The HR audit process consists of five sequential steps. *Step one* involves the HRM auditor determining the scope of the audit. The audit may be comprehensive and

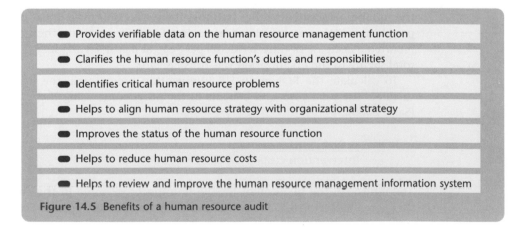

- Provides verifiable data on the human resource management function
- Clarifies the human resource function's duties and responsibilities
- Identifies critical human resource problems
- Helps to align human resource strategy with organizational strategy
- Improves the status of the human resource function
- Helps to reduce human resource costs
- Helps to review and improve the human resource management information system

Figure 14.5 Benefits of a human resource audit

focus on the entire HR function, or programmatic and focus on a specific HR practice. *Step two* requires the HRM auditor to decide how to conduct the audit. During this phase, the auditor will need to gather information on state-of-the art practices in each area of HRM and on ratios or measures for absenteeism, turnover, grievances and workplace accidents. *Step three* requires the audit team to collect the information through a variety of methods, including interviews, surveys and organizational data, the survey being the commonly preferred method (Phillips, 1996b). *Step four* involves the team analysing the data and comparing statistics, noting discrepancies and corrective actions. *Step five*, the final stage of the HRM audit process, involves the audit team writing a report on the results of the audit. The report typically provides a summary of the strengths and weaknesses of the HRM function, explains the deficiencies and provides suggestions for corrective action to address these deficiencies. Phillips (1996b) contends that the HR audit is an important exercise that can help to improve the efficiency of the HR function, but it falls short of a valid approach to measuring the HRM contribution to the organization's bottom line performance.

HRM benchmarking

Arguably, benchmarking occupies a central role in the 'best HR practice' (universalism) models of strategic HRM. Benchmarking involves managers learning and adopting best or at least better HR practices by comparing their HR practices with those of other (more successful) organizations. It is thus a form of auditing (Phillips, 1996b). Benchmarking HRM practices serves a number of important purposes. First, organizations can gauge their own practices against those in excellent organizations and can get an idea of how they compare and how well they are doing. Second, benchmarking enables managers to learn from other organizations about effective HR strategies. Third, benchmarking can help to create and initiate the need for change because it identifies what an organization needs to do to improve relative to the HR strategy in excellent companies.

The benchmarking process for HRM evaluation purposes consists of seven key phases (Phillips, 1996b), shown in Figure 14.6:

1. Identify exactly which HR practice managers wish to benchmark. An organization might, for example, wish to benchmark HR training, HRM performance measures or HR reward systems. Obviously, the HR practices that are chosen for benchmarking should be those considered to be most critical for an organization's overall viability, but, as already discussed above, what actually constitutes best practice and how it is measured are problematic.
2. Establish a project team because of the amount of work required to conduct a benchmarking evaluation.
3. Identify the benchmark partners. These partners should be those prepared to participate in the exercise and with so-called 'best practices'. They may include internal units, competitors and non-competitors in the same industry, organizations or international organizations.
4. Collect data from each of the benchmarking partners (e.g. firms A, B and C).
5. Analyse and interpret the data.
6. Following analysis of the data, prepare the major findings from the benchmarking partners in the form of a written report.
7. Develop action plans to improve HR strategy and practices.

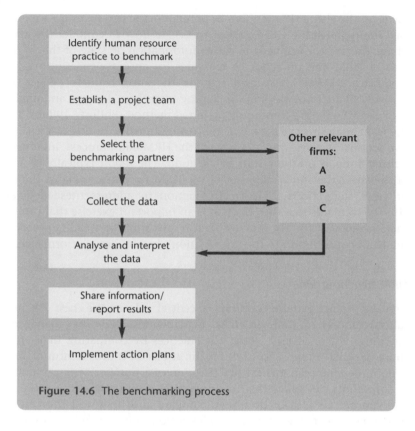

Figure 14.6 The benchmarking process

This final step in the benchmarking process involves calculating performance gaps between the way things are and the desired or best practice, the best practices that are most important for a particular organization depending on its business strategy and technology. The linear diagram underestimates the challenges of identifying best HR practices and measuring the performance gaps. As Pfeffer (1994, p. 65) rightly argues, 'The specific implementation of the practices, and the form they may take, are obviously contingent not only on strategy but also on other contextual factors such as location, nature and interdependence of the work, and so forth.' Performance gaps should be identified for every benchmarked item. Action plans are then developed to address the performance gaps and to implement the best practices in each area for which a performance gap has been identified. A report should be prepared for members of the organization, indicating the benchmarking process, the major findings, performance gaps and action plans.

Benchmarking can be used as a tool for evaluating an organization's HRM strategy and HRM practices, for setting new standards and for constantly improving HR practices that can impact on an organization's financial performance (Saks, 2000). Cully et al.'s large-scale survey of British workplaces found that, in 48 per cent of all workplaces, managers reported that their establishment had, at some stage during the past five years, undertaken a benchmarking process. Interestingly, the greater the degree of competition faced by the organization, the more likely managers were to have engaged in competitive benchmarking (Table 14.3).

Table 14.3 Benchmarking, by degree of competition

	Workplaces benchmarked against in the past five years		
	Any other workplaces (%)	Other workplaces in same industry (%)	Other workplaces located overseas (%)
Degree of competition			
Very high	57	48	11
Average or low	39	36	3
All workplaces	**48**	**42**	**7**

Source: Adapted from Cully et al. (1999) p. 118

With research design issues and the available evaluation techniques in mind, the rest of the chapter focuses on selected studies that have explored the association between HR strategy and organizational performance.

REFLECTIVE QUESTION

Identifying best practices is a critical issue in HRM benchmarking. If you were involved in an HRM benchmarking exercise, how would you define or identify what constitutes 'best' or 'better' practices'?

Demonstrating the human resource strategy–organization performance link

Reflecting on the past decade, we can affirm that demonstrating a positive relationship between HRM and performance became the dominant research issue in the HRM field. Academics have been interested in understanding the effect of specific HRM practices for a long time. For example, in the mid-1920s, the famous Hawthorne studies identified job design practices that could improve worker performance. What is different in the renewed interest in understanding the link between HRM practices and performance, however, is that contemporary debate has focused on the competing merits of various clusters or bundles of best HR practices (universalistic prescriptions) impacting on bottom line outcomes (see, for example, Arthur, 1994; Ashton and Sung, 2002; Becker and Gerhart, 1996; Betcherman et al., 1994; Boxall, 2003; Buyens and De Vos, 2001; Delaney and Huselid, 1996; Den Hartog and Verburg, 2004; Frege, 2002; Guest, 1997; Huselid, 1995; Hutchinson et al., 2000; Ichniowski et al., 1996; Konzelmann et al., 2006; Paauwe and Boselie, 2003; Pfeffer, 1998; Wright et al., 2003; Youndt et al., 1996) (see also HRM in Practice 14.3). The review of studies informed by the universalistic thesis was undertaken in 1996 by Ichniowski and his colleagues and suggested there were potentially 'large pay-offs' when 'bundles' of best HR practices were adopted. In this section, we review key studies to gain an understanding of the nature of the **HRM–performance link** and to assess the degree to which HR strategy may predict economic performance.

In the USA and Canada, studies have found that superior firm performance is associated with coherent clusters of HR practices in the way in which organizations manage people. Arthur (1994), for example, investigated the performance effects of two labour management taxonomies: 'control' (traditional personnel management) and 'commitment' (new HRM) in US mini-steel mills. His statistical regression results indicated that commitment-type HR practices were associated with both lower scrap rates (an indicator of production quality) and a significantly lower number of labour hours per ton of steel (an indicator of labour efficiency) than were control-type HRM practices. In addition, Arthur found that integrated, and sets of, best HR practices had a greater impact than individual HR practices. Arthur's research, however, left major questions unanswered: What is the magnitude of the effect of HR strategy on economic outcomes? And how generalizable are the findings?

MacDuffie's (1995) study suggested that Arthur's (1994) findings could be generalizable, at least to other manufacturing workplaces. In a later publication, Frits and MacDuffie (1996) provided further support for the 'internal fit' perspective, suggesting that when teamworking and complementary HR practices are introduced simultaneously, 'not only does new work practice induce an incremental improvement in performance, but so do the complementary practices' (Frits and MacDuffie, 1996, p. 428). This is shown in Figure 14.7. When a new work practice, such as self-managed work teams, is introduced, the greatest impact on performance over a period of time will occur when a complementary bundle of HR practices accompanies the new work regime (line B).

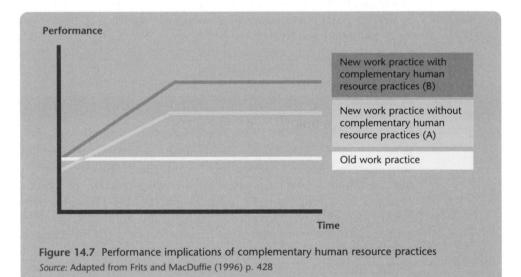

Figure 14.7 Performance implications of complementary human resource practices
Source: Adapted from Frits and MacDuffie (1996) p. 428

The studies by MacDuffie (1995) and Frits and MacDuffie (1996) were limited in that they focused on intermediate variables such as productivity and quality rather than on overall financial outcomes, and were unable to measure the magnitude of the effect of HR strategy on the firm's financial bottom line (Bamberger and Meshoulam, 2000). Huselid's (1995) study responded to these limitations and attempted to estimate how greatly the HR strategy impacted on the organization's financial bottom line outcome. In his study, Huselid (1995) determined that so-called 'high-performance' HR practices had two major dimensions. The first dimension referred to worker skills, which included various practices to enhance workers' knowledge, skills and abilities. The second dimension referred to worker motivation, which included practices recognizing and reinforcing desirable worker workplace behaviours (Table 14.4).

HRM IN PRACTICE 14.3

HR 'CAN LOWER NHS DEATH RATES'

ZOE ROBERTS, *PEOPLE MANAGEMENT*, 11 OCTOBER 2001

There is a direct link between the quality of HR practices and patient mortality in the health service according to a startling research report, *Organization, Management and Effectiveness in NHS Trusts.*

The research, which is completed but not yet published, found that the quality of HR initiatives had a significant impact on the level of patient care and mortality in hospitals.

'Our analysis found a strong relationship between aspects of HR management and death rates,' said Carol Borrill, researcher at the Aston Centre for Health Services Organisation Research, who carried out the report with colleague Michael West. 'The higher the levels of staff teamworking, training, development and appraisals, the lower the patient mortality.'

Andrew Foster, HR director for the NHS Executive, flagged up the importance of the results when he spoke at the AHHRM conference.

'Until now there has been no research that links current HR practices with a bottom-line output like patient mortality,' he told *PM.* 'The overall challenge for anyone involved in HR is to convince general man-

> **'We were pleased to find that ... staff working in teams experienced higher levels of innovation and lower levels of stress.'**

agement of the value of people management. This study shows a demonstrable link between HR and output in the NHS and I consider it to be the strongest weapon in my locker.'

Foster is compiling a five-year plan for HR in the NHS that will have a high-profile launch next year on the 54th anniversary of the service.

'The plan will have a significant section that relates to evidence-based cases for HR in the boardroom – so research into HR and patient mortality will be included in this,' Foster said. 'With a fixed budget you need an evidence-based case for investment in people issues.'

Despite research linking people management and productivity, the range of outputs from the NHS has proved hard to measure. The researchers surveyed 81 hospitals over a period of two years and gathered information on the quality of HR initiatives and on performance data.

'We were pleased to find that the results were consistent with an earlier teamwork survey, which found that staff working in teams experienced higher levels of innovation and lower levels of stress,' Borrill said.

Drawing data from a sample of nearly 1000 establishments, Huselid found strong support for the positive effects of commitment or high-performance HR practices on both intermediate individual worker outcomes (e.g. turnover and productivity) and organizational financial outcomes. In particular, HR practices were significantly related to lower employee turnover and higher productivity and corporate financial performance. Huselid's study also provides some insight into the 'best fit' perspective. His findings suggest that although internal fit – the degree to which complementary HR practices are implemented as a cluster – does have a significant and positive effect on financial outcomes, external fit – the degree to which HR strategy is aligned with business strategy – does not (Bamberger and Meshoulam, 2000).

In another study of the HRM–performance link, Delery and Doty (1996) identified seven strategic HR practices that have been linked to organizational performance: internal career opportunities, training, results-oriented appraisals, profit-sharing, employment security, participation and job descriptions. They found that 'differences in HR practices are associated with rather large differences in financial performance' (Delery and Doty, 1996, p. 825). Youndt et al.'s (1996) research combined a cluster of

HR practices into two indexes – labelled the 'administrative HR system' and the 'human-capital-enhancing HR system' – and found that these impacted positively on organizational performance when the HR practices were aligned with the organization's business strategy. Delaney and Huselid (1996, p. 965) pointed out the effect of a mix of HR practices on perceptions of organizational performance, their findings suggesting that:

> progressive HRM practices, including selectivity in staffing, training, and incentive compensation, are positively related to perceptual measures of organizational performance.

Table 14.4 The two dimensions of high-performance human resource practices

Worker skills and internal processes	Employee motivation
Information-sharing	Performance appraisals to determine pay
Job analysis	Performance to determine promotion
Internal hiring	Qualified applicants per positions
Regular attitude surveys	
Quality of work–life programs	
Participation teams	
Profit-sharing	
Training	
Formal grievance procedures	
Employment tests for hiring	

Source: Huselid (1995)

Betcherman et al. (1994), using data generated from Canadian companies, discovered a statistically significant association between the 'new' HR practices and lower unit costs. Interestingly, the authors provided evidence that 'innovative' HR practices operate best in certain workplace 'environments'. The more intangible variables, such as 'progressive decision-making' and 'social responsibility', impacted more significantly on performance outcomes than did more tangible incentive-pay plans. The results suggest that 'innovative [HRM] practices and programs on their own are not enough to substantially improve performance. What seems more important is that they be introduced into a supportive work environment' (Betcherman et al., 1994, p. 72).

A study of business enterprises in the US and Canada by Wright et al. (2003) found evidence that 'progressive' HR practices improve operational performance and profitability at least in part through enhanced employee commitment to the organization. It is noteworthy that Wright et al.'s (2003, p. 32) results were based on data garnered from employees: 'using employees as the source of the HR practice measures ensures that the measure represents the actual practices rather than the espoused policies of the business'. Similarly, the recent study by Konzelmann et al. (2006) argues that although securing full cooperation from employees is required if a cluster of better HR practices is to increase organizational performance, the form of corporate governance under which managers operate might actually inhibit their ability to secure and maintain a high-commitment-based HRM regime. Organizations that have a dominant external stakeholder, such as public limited companies, might have to give priority to external shareholders' demands rather than employees' demands for greater consultation and progressive HR practices. The implications are profound: 'What secures positive HRM outcomes are, for workers, the quality of consultation and personnel policy [and] securing these objectives corporate governance has an important part to play' (Konzelmann et al., 2006, p. 560).

Reviewing some of the seminal studies on the HRM–organization performance link, Ichniowski et al. (1996) concluded that the empirical evidence of intra-industry studies showed that high-performance work configurations and complementary bundles of HRM practices gave rise to superior output and quality performances, and that the magnitude of these performance effects was 'large'. Moreover, Ichniowski et al. (1996, p. 32, emphasis added) concluded that:

> There are no one or two 'magic bullets' that are *the* work practices that will stimulate worker and business performance. Work teams or quality circles alone are not enough. Rather, *whole systems* need to be changed.

As we have emphasized in earlier chapters, organizations are deeply 'embedded' in the wider national institutional environments in which they operate. Based on the work of Paauwe and Boselie (2003) and Den Hartog and Verburg. (2004), the findings from seminal US studies on the HRM–organization performance link may not be generalizeable to a polyethnic Europe. Looking to European studies, Cully et al.'s (1999) national survey measured *perceived* workplace performance but did not quantify the impact of HR strategy on organizational outcomes. Addison et al. (2000) demonstrated that EI could be effective in increasing labour productivity and a firm's profits. Using data from Britain and Germany, Addison et al. examined the effects of different EI vehicles on organizational performance, as well as investigating the mediating influence of trade unions. The findings suggest that, in unionized workplaces, the link between EI and financial performance is likely to be less clear-cut because EI arrangements reflect union power rather than a competitive response to external factors. Addison's et al. study predicts that EI in non-union regimes in Britain will yield positive economic results for the firm, but the union–EI nexus is associated with negative outcomes. Finally, the German evidence indicated that mandatory EI is associated with higher productivity in larger organizations (employing more than 100 workers) and lower productivity gains in smaller workplaces.

Despite these interesting findings, Addison et al.'s (2000) study has limited value in demonstrating the link between HR strategy and performance because it examined only one HR practice and did not quantify the effect of coherent clusters of HR practices on overall organizational performance. The results therefore need to be read with some caution. As with all studies, the footnotes should be read. No hard financial data were collected – profit being measured subjectively – to allow a comparison of HR practices and economic performance. Also, there were no standardized measures of labour productivity and value added, which makes international comparison at best problematic. Furthermore, perceptual measures of firms' performance often result in respondents overstating the performance of their workplace (Cully et al., 1999). Finally, the study was unable to control for response bias; in simple terms, the researchers were unable to deal with the possibility that more successful establishments were systematically more likely to adopt EI strategies.

Buyens and De Vos (2001) conducted a qualitative study to measure the added value of the HR function as perceived by managers in Belgian organizations. The objective of the study was to investigate how the value of the HR function was perceived by three groups of managers – top managers, HR managers and line managers – within the sample of 256 organizations. Qualitative data were gathered through interviews, focus groups and a questionnaire. The researchers asked the different groups of managers to describe how they saw the value added of HR practices. Buyens and De Vos (2001) found that, for top managers, the HR function added value through its change programmes following restructuring and downsizing. HR managers, on the other hand, most frequently mentioned 'management of the employee' as the area in which the HR function delivered value to the organization. The findings suggested that line managers had 'a rather traditional view of the HR function' (Buyens and De Vos, 2001, p. 81) because a majority most frequently mentioned functional HR activities such as selection and training as the domain in which the HR function added value. Buyens and De Vos (2001, p. 81) acknowledged that the data were 'highly subjective in nature' and that the findings might be contingent on other factors such as size or industry. Moreover, the study was unable to quantify the magnitude of the value added of the HR function.

Den Hartog and Verburg's (2004) study of high-performance HR practices in the Netherlands demonstrated that national social institutions may decrease the effect of bundles of HR practices on an organization's performance. The study emphasized that the context in which companies operate may limit or enhance the distinctiveness and performance improvement synergies of HR practices. In the Netherlands, the employment relationship is highly regulated, trade union density and involvement is more extensive, unlike, for example, the USA, and Dutch labour laws ensure employee participation in workplace decision-making. Thus, the idea of a Dutch firm adopting a universal cluster of best HR practices to gain a competitive advantage is more problematic because they have less leeway to distinguish themselves from their competitive rivals.

Although Dutch laws set the boundaries, Den Hartog and Verburg's findings demonstrate that managers can, within these boundaries, design HR practices to suit the specific needs of their organization. Moreover, a combination of HR practices with an emphasis on employee development, the strict selection of employees and an overarching philosophy in terms of HR strategy had significant positive effects on organizational performance. Following studies by Huselid (1995) and others, Den Hartog and Verburg (2004) assessed the HR practice–performance link using a questionnaire completed by senior HR managers and chief executives. The data from 175 Dutch enterprises disclosed that employee skill and direction correlated positively and significantly with employee work motivation, or what the authors call 'going beyond contract', and economic outcome. Furthermore, autonomy showed a positive relationship with willingness to go beyond contract, and profit-sharing correlated positively with perceived economic performance, as did pay-for-performance (see Table 14.2 above).

Den Hartog and Verburg (2004) argued that their data evinced a commitment that resulted in Dutch workers doing more than was typically required in their contract or job description – going beyond contract – which accounted for enhanced economic outcomes. Importantly, work motivation was related to a specific set of HR practices fashioned to each specific context: 'The set of practices labelled 'Employee skill direction' … were positively related to workers' willingness to go beyond contract and perceived economic performance of the firm and negatively to absenteeism' (Den Hartog and Verburg, 2004, pp. 74–5). Finally, Den Hartog and Verburg acknowledged that future research should focus more on hard economic data rather than managers' 'perceptions' of economic performance, and should include data on workers' outcomes and voices.

STUDY TIP

Evaluating the value added of different HR strategies means having a good appreciation of research designs, HR measurements and the approaches to evaluating HR practices. Obtain a copy of Den Hartog and Verburg's (2004) article. What research design do the authors use? How do they seek to measure the value added of HR? Drawing on the material in this chapter, what are the strengths and weaknesses of the study?

An examination of the more recent empirical research reveals that the measurement of the value added of HR strategy and individual HR practices across studies is not consistent. This is a serious problem. The development of reliable and valid measures of HR strategic practices is needed to advance research. The notion of what constitutes 'superior performance' needs to be disaggregated, and, in order to gain a meaningful insight into what 'performance' means, the researcher and practitioner need to be able to 'compare and contrast performance measures at a variety of individual and organizational levels' (Truss, 2001, p. 1146). With these limitations in mind, recent studies have consistently pointed to the positive effects of complementary better HR practices. The upshot is that organizations implementing a package of internally consistent and mutually reinforcing HR practices experience significant improvements in performance. This suggests, however, an apparent paradox. If the pursuit of identifiable soft, better HRM practices leads to improved organizational performance, one would, from the perspective of economic rationality, expect such practices to be more widely used. This apparent paradox may result from the long-term investment costs associated with the resource-based approach to strategic HRM and the pressure on individual managers to achieve short-term financial results.

REFLECTIVE QUESTION

What do you think of this line of argument? If, indeed, high-commitment HR strategies significantly improve overall company performance, why does a relatively small proportion of workplaces adopt such an HR strategy?

Theorizing the human resource management–performance link

Although most HRM models provide no clear focus for any test of the HRM–performance link, it is commonly assumed that an alignment of organizational strategy and HRM strategy will improve organizational performance and competitiveness. How, therefore, can the positive association between HR strategy and organizational performance be explained? The resource-based strategic HRM model assumes a simple causal chain of soft HRM policies of empowerment and learning–employee commitment–synergy–improved organizational performance (Guest, 1997, 2000). This 'involvement–commitment cycle' is the reverse of the vicious circle of control that organizational theorists discussed in the early 1980s.

A core assumption of this approach is that organizational commitment and a cornucopia of motivational HR practices are significantly related to organizational performance (Beer et al., 1984; Wright et al., 2003). Thus, according to Beer et al.

(1984, p. 19), 'Increased commitment can result not only in more loyalty and better performance for the organization, but also in self-worth, dignity, psychological involvement, and identity for the individual.' Arthur (1994, p. 673) justified his results on the HRM–performance link by drawing upon behavioural control theory, and argued that by:

> Setting up a formal participation mechanism, and providing the proper training and rewards, a commitment system can lead to a highly motivated and empowered work-force whose goals are closely aligned with those of management. Thus the resources required to monitor employee compliance … can be reduced. In addition, employees under these conditions are thought to be more likely to engage in organizational citizenship behaviors, non-role, unrewarded behaviors that are believed to be, nonetheless, critical to organizational success.

Strategic HRM theorists have argued that the HRM contribution to organizational outcomes is a function of three interrelated processes. HR strategy, through a diverse range of key best practices, shapes employees' intellectual and physical assets and skills, enhances work motivation and provides the opportunity and the means for employees to contribute, for example through quality circles and joint consultation arrangements, to operational decision-making (Bamberger and Meshoulam, 2000; Boxall and Purcell, 2003; Eisenhardt, 1989; Freeman and Lazear, 1995; Snell, 1992; Wright and McMahan, 1992). Thus, prescriptions and measurements of HRM–employee performance are based on a number of well-grounded organizational behaviour theories including AMO theory, which states that performance is a function of employee ability, motivation and opportunity for employee voice (Boxall and Purcell, 2003, p. 20). These three interrelated processes are shown in Figure 14.8. Central to the model is the notion that HRM research is required to monitor and evaluate the effectiveness of HR strategy in order to ensure its contribution and value added to the organization.

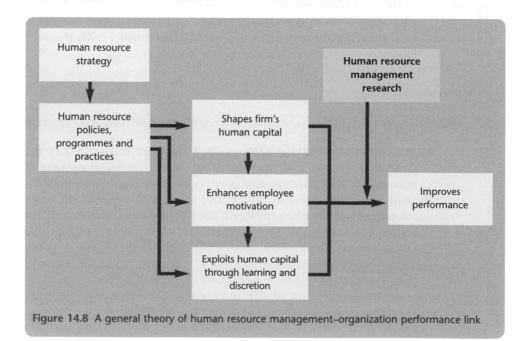

Figure 14.8 A general theory of human resource management–organization performance link

Despite advances in empirical research, our understanding of the nature of the HRM–organizational performance link is still somewhat limited because of a number of theoretical and methodological challenges facing researchers. First, the best practices perspective advocates a diverse mix of core HR practices to achieve superior performance, but there is no clear consensus on the meaning of specific best practices that should be included in the HRM–performance equation, and their consistency with each other within a bundle, and the claims that this model of HRM is universally applicable (Marchington and Grugulis, 2000). Second, it is unclear when a single HR practice is in fact a set or a bundle or a system that is being evaluated against performance variables (Den Hartog and Verburg, 2004). Efforts to identify a universal cluster of HR practices that differentiate successful organizations from less successful ones are analogous to the early leadership studies that attempted to identify a universal cluster of personality traits distinguishing leaders from followers. Both theoretical approaches tend to study social phenomena as if the organization were disembedded from the wider society. The best fit and best practice schools are typically silent on the inherent conflicts and paradoxical elements encountered in managing people. The societal effects on the analysis of best HR practices adds an additional theoretical perspective and new challenges for future research on HRM strategy–performance processes (Lane, 2000; Paauwe and Boselie, 2003).

In assessing the research on best HR practice, the more extreme universalist model is stymied by the societal effects approach. In effect, a diverse cluster of better HR practices will be used to manage employment relations based on national variations in social institutions and culture. But the societal effects approach does not invalidate best fit or best practice thinking. Detractors cannot seriously argue against the importance of the concept of best fit or specific contextual factors when managers choose their HR practices, or against the merits of best or better practices within specific contexts (Boxall and Purcell, 2003, p. 70). No responsible manager would advocate unlawful or dysfunctional HR practices. For example, in reward management, managers would be advised to design a job evaluation process that did not implicitly or explicitly discriminate against female employees. Thus, the concept of 'better' HR practice, when examined within a multivariate and social embeddedness framework, still plays an important role for understanding the principles of HRM.

Chapter summary

- We began this chapter by offering some quotes from HRM practitioners and by reviewing some of the literature arguing that the HRM function is going through a transition in which the evaluation of HRM is being recognized as both fundamental and necessary.

- We have suggested that, in an increasingly competitive environment and with HR specialists playing a role in the strategic planning process, those in charge of organizations are demanding accountability on the part of all functional areas, including the HR department. Identifying the extent of the alignment of organizational and HR strategies and developing HR practices to improve fit requires the measurement and evaluation of HR practices.

- The issue is whether HR professionals are capable of demonstrating their contribution and value added to other members of the management team in a quantifiable way, and of providing useful data and information that clearly indicate the outcomes of HR strategy in a meaningful manner comparable with those of other organizational departments. This of course requires that sound, ongoing evaluation be carried out, the results being reported and communicated throughout the organization.

● We have examined different ways of demonstrating the value added of HRM in terms of level of measurement, different research designs and evaluation techniques. Although these topics have been discussed separately, they are of course closely connected. We have also discussed the limitations of the research. For Legge (2001, p. 31), for example, much of the research on the HR high-commitment firm–performance link 'is at best confused and, at worst, conceptually and methodologically deeply flawed'. Our intent is to help the reader make sense of the research, and to critique and evaluate published research in the strategic HRM genre.

● The chapter examined the possibility of measuring individual-, team- and organization-level variables. Major research designs for investigating HR strategy–performance links include surveys, case studies, experimental studies and meta-analysis. Turning to evaluation, we examined statistical evaluation, financial evaluation and the use of HR audits and benchmarking when evaluating HR systems.

● Despite the methodological challenges associated with demonstrating the HR strategy and the organization–performance link, the different research designs, both quantitative and qualitative, and the limitations of the research, there is now a substantive body of literature demonstrating that HR strategy and practices can and do make a positive impact on a variety of organizational outcomes.

● A major challenge for HRM researchers is to continue not only to examine the value added of different HR strategies, but also to predict the magnitude of the value added of the HRM function for organizational outcomes more accurately and to make their research results meaningful to managers and HR practitioners.

Key concepts

● Epistemology

● HR measurement

● Experimental research

● Qualitative research

● HRM auditing

● Research design

● HRM benchmarking

● Return on investment

● HRM–performance link

Chapter review questions

1. What forces are driving the added-value movement in the field of HRM?

2. To what extent do you agree or disagree with the statement that 'The least important HR practices are measurable, whereas the most important HR practices are not.' Discuss.

3. Explain the statement that 'all evaluation methods require the measurement of some set of variables.'

4. What are the strengths and weaknesses of (a) the survey approach and (b) the case study approach to HRM research?

5. How effective is the HR audit for measuring an HR strategy's contribution to the finan-
    cial bottom line of a company?

6. How can the effect of HR strategy on organizational performance be explained?

Further reading

Ashton, D. and J. Sung (2002) *Supporting Workplace Learning for High Performance Working*. Geneva:
    International Labour Organization.

Buyens, D. and De Vos, A. (2001) Perceptions of the value of the HR function. *Human Resource
    Management Journal*, **11**(2): 70–89.

Fitz-enz, J. and Davison, B. (2002) *How to Measure Human Resources Management* (3rd edn). New York:
    McGraw-Hill.

Marchington, M. and Grugulis, I. (2000) 'Best practice' human resource management: perfect oppor-
    tunity or dangerous illusion? *International Journal of Human Resource Management*, **11**(6): 1104–24.

Nutley, S. (2000) Beyond systems: HRM audits in the public sector. *Human Resource Management
    Journal*, **10**(2): 21–38.

Shipton, H., West, M., Dawson, J., Birdi, K. and Patterson, M. (2006) HRM as a predictor of innova-
    tion. *Human Resource Management Journal,* **16**(1): 3–26.

Truss, C. (2001) Complexities and controversies in linking HRM with organizational outcomes. *Journal
    of Management Studies*, **38**(8): 1121–49.

Wood, S. (2006) Human resource management and performance in UK call centres. *British Journal of
    Industrial Relations*, **44**(1): 99–124.

Practising human resource management

Searching the web

On an individual basis, or working in a small group, pick two or three online HR-
related websites (e.g. www.jiscmail.ac.uk/lists/industrial-relations-research.html, www.
shrm.org/hrlinks, www.fdmmag.com/articles/03aco.htm, www.hrreporter.com or
www.peoplemanagement.co.uk). Search for articles on evaluating HRM and the
HRM–performance link. Based on your search:

1. List the research methods used, for example survey or case study, and the use of
   financial evaluation measures (e.g. ROI).
2. List the HR practices investigated.
3. Identify and discuss the factors that are encouraging the movement towards a
   value-added approach to HRM.

Bring this information to class and present your findings in an oral report.

HRM group project

Form a group of three or four students. The purpose of this group assignment is to
gain a better understanding of the HR audit and/or the benchmarking process.
Specifically:

1. Contact the HR department of one organization that conducts HR audits or HR benchmarking and is willing to discuss its auditing or benchmarking process with members of the group.
2. Design a series of questions to learn about the auditing or benchmarking process. In particular, be sure to gather information concerning each of the steps in the two processes outlined in the chapter. For example, describe the scope of the audit and identify what to benchmark (see Figure 14.6 above).
3. Analyse the results of your interviews. What conclusions can you make about the auditing or benchmarking process, and what conclusions can you make about the organization's HR department?

Each group member should take responsibility for researching the various aspects of the assignment. Present your findings to your class. For further information on benchmarking and best practices, go to www.human-resources.org.

Chapter case study

ALPHA HOTEL

Alpha Hotel is an exclusive all-season resort located in the Canadian Rockies, 90 minutes' drive west of Calgary. The hotel employs over 1100 employees during the winter skiing season and during the peak summer months. The HR department carries out its own recruitment and selection, administration of pay and benefits, customer service training, supervisory leadership training programmes and relations with the trade union covering the non-managers.

Andrew Bellamy, the newly appointed hotel manager, has received a mandate to ensure that Alpha Hotel remains a destination of choice for Japanese and European tourists, and to reduce operating costs without jeopardizing the hotel's strategic goal. After attending an executive management workshop on 'Accountability in human resource management', Andrew Bellamy added this item to the agenda for the next management meeting. The following table showing indices of HRM effectiveness in North American major hotels was attached to the agenda.

Table 1 Indices of human resource management effectiveness in North American hotels

Index	Hotels (n=2400)
Customer satisfaction	4.39
Overall productivity	3.99
Employee commitment	2.35
Employee satisfaction	4.01
Grievance rate	2.01
Absenteeism	4.20
Turnover	5.09

Note: All items are measured on a scale of 1 = very low; 6 = very high

At the monthly senior management meeting, individual reaction to Andrew's contribution included the following. Amy Finley, the assistant general manager, made a strong case for outsourcing the work of the HR department. Her final comment to the management team was: 'It's HR's job to demonstrate that it can do the work better and more cheaply than any other source. If it can't, then we should outsource the HR function.'

Rowena Phillips, the front-desk manager, did not argue strongly for outsourcing the HR function but asked a number of questions: 'Does HR follow best practices?' 'How do their programmes help to reduce our operating expenses?' 'How does our HR function compare with that of our main competitors?'

Ron Levine, the food services manager, was neutral but commented that the 'Wine appreciation course' for restaurant servers delivered in November by HR staff had been 'a great success', adding 'the wine sales increased substantially in the following three months over the Christmas period because the servers were able to 'upsell' the wine.' Ron went on to give some details on the design and delivery of the three one-day wine appreciation workshops. The total direct cost for the three workshops was $6,000. The indirect cost included the wages paid to the 60 servers (servers being paid $9 per hour) to attend the training. Wine sales increased by $23,000 per month in the high season between December and February.

Jean Marlow, the HR manager, agreed that it would be helpful to know the value added of her department but went on to say that 'Evaluating the contribution of HR programmes to the hotel's financial bottom line is too difficult and too time-consuming.'

Assignment

As corporate vice-president of HR for Alpha Hotels Inc., you must persuade Jean Marlow of the merits of measuring the HR contribution and demonstrate the value of the HR function to the Alpha Hotel management team. In your report:

1. Describe some of the things you would do to demonstrate the value added of the HRM department and its work to the organization, making sure that its accomplishments are presented in language that is convincing to the other managers. (Hint: look at Schuler's four-task HRM model, first discussed in Chapter 2, as a guide.)

2. State whether you would suggest conducting an HR audit or benchmarking to demonstrate the value added of the HRM department to the hotel.

Be sure to justify your recommendations.

HR-related skill development

A work-based learning intervention programme presents an overview of the learning activity that the manager or HR specialist is proposing to undertake. It should tell the reader why the work-based learning intervention is necessary, what costs are involved and how it will benefit the organization. In essence, the work-based learning intervention proposal underscores the whole notion of accountability in HRM.

Many managers, however, lack the basic knowledge and skills to craft such a proposal. To help you to develop this important management skill and to give you the experience of writing a work-based learning intervention proposal, we have devised a realistic case study that requires you to demonstrate your understanding of ROI. You can participate, at either individual or group level, in the exercise and develop an important HR skill by going to www.palgrave.com/business/brattonand-gold4 and clicking on 'Learning intervention proposal'.

Notes

1. Paul Juniper, President, HRP Associate of Ontario, Canada. 'President's Message'. *HR Professional*, February/March 2003, p. 9.
2. Michael Ford, President of the HR Institute of Alberta; quoted by Terrence Belford, HR focusing on how it can add value, *Globe and Mail*, 2002, March 25, p. B11.
3. Tim Epps, vice president, people systems for Saturn Corp., quoted by Phillips, J. (1996). *Accountability in Human Resource Management*. Houston: Gulf Publishing.
4. Peter Drucker. How to measure white-collar productivity. *Wall Street Journal*, 1985, November 26, p. 28; quoted by Phillips (1996, p. 5).

Chapter fifteen

Conclusion: Rebuilding trust and voice

John Bratton and Jeff Gold

'Instead of accepting the "superior wisdom" of experts, patients/customers/clients increasingly look upon those experts with a critical eye.'[1]

'The separate espionage episodes involving WestJet Airlines Ltd. and U.S. computer giant Hewlett-Packard Co. illustrate once again the need for strong, independent boards capable of ensuring that corporate officers adhere to the highest ethical standards and of taking tough action when they don't.'[2]

'At present findings are often polarized, with some commentators arguing that workers have little to gain from high commitment HRM, while others are more positive about the opportunities for workers.'[3]

'The idea of the "knowledge economy" appears to place the fundamentals of human resource management onto an entirely new footing.'[4]

'The practice of HRM must inevitably confront ethical dilemmas.'[5]

Chapter outline

- Reconstructing the moral profession of human resource management   p. 560
- Ethics in human resource management   p. 562
- Does HRM work? Embeddedness and divergence   p. 564
- Towards a practice perspective in HRM   p. 568
- Final comment   p. 572

Chapter objectives

After studying this chapter, you should be able to:

1. Describe the different ways in which the preceding chapters relate to one another
2. Explain the professional standing of those practising human resource management (HRM)
3. Explain how ethical principles can inform HRM policies and practices
4. Assess how HRM practice and theory is regarded by others
5. Explain the need for a practice perspective on HRM

For over 20 years, the term 'human resource management' (HRM) has been used to conceptualize a particular approach to managing the employment relationship and, frequently, as a contrast to 'personnel management'. We started this journey into HRM by examining its evolution and some of the theoretical models used in its study. It was acknowledged that all activity involving the management of the employment relationship, whether termed HRM or personnel management, involved ambiguity, tension, uncertainty and possible contradiction and paradox.

In Part One of the book, we emphasized that HRM views the workforce as the most important asset for generating value, increasingly through the creation of knowledge, which gives organizations a potential, sustainable competitive advantage. We pointed out that, starting from this premise, HRM decisions and practices impact on strategic goals and need to be integrated into the organization's strategy. We emphasized in Part Two that there is a range of external and internal contextual factors that affect and shape HR strategy and practices, organizational form and work experience. In Part Three, we endeavoured to describe and evaluate a range of HR practices used to attract, motivate, develop and maximize the inherent potential of the workforce. Finally, we examined the pressure to evaluate the contribution of HRM and the growing body of research that seeks to measure the HRM–organizational performance link. The purpose of this final chapter is to reflect on the major landmarks visited along the journey, attempt to draw general conclusions about HRM, and its current and future status, explore the ethical dimension of employment management and consider why a practice perspective on HRM is needed.

Reconstructing the moral profession of human resource management

Professional recognition is highly valued in Western economies, and throughout the 20th century, the number of people engaged in professional work steadily increased. In the UK, for example, the National Skills Task Force (2000) suggested a 50 per cent increase in the number of professional workers from 1981 to 1998, with a forecast of a further 20 per cent up to 2009. But not all professionals are the same, some clearly being more powerful than others or making claims in support of a powerful influence. For practitioners in a field of professional work, institutions – the professional associations – usually advance such claims, the strength of which symbolizes the status and power of the particular profession. In HRM (and personnel), 2000 saw the creation of the Chartered Institute of Personnel and Development (CIPD), following an earlier merger between the Institute of Training and Development and the Institute of Personnel Management. Although the new title suggested something of a compromise, the merger did reflect an attempt to enhance the status of practitioners and espouse an approach to practise what we would call HRM.[6] In addition, since autumn 2003, individual members have been able to consider themselves as 'chartered'.[7]

In Chapter 1, we discussed the change from 'personnel' to 'HRM'. To some, this change represented the use of a new label and emphasized the limited and piecemeal diffusion of the HRM style, with only islands of innovation in HRM. The sustainability of the HRM paradigm was also questioned. One set of perspectives therefore emphasizes the superficial nature and continuities of managing the employment relationship. For others, the changes represented a transformation of how people could and should be managed at work. This set of perspectives emphasized the differences between the stereotyped personnel and human resources (HR) models. Whereas personnel management evoked images of 'welfare' professionals interfering with and hindering the line manager, of reactive 'fire-fighting' management and of submitting to militant shop stewards, HRM emphasized strategic integration, the HR professional as a member of the senior management team, strategic planning and proactive management. It is the latter image that the CIPD seeks to promote, but what are the key elements of professional work and status, and how do HR professionals match such requirements?

According to Dietrich and Roberts (1997, p. 16), the starting point for professional work is the existence of clients facing complex issues and problems related to decision-making complexity in which such clients are 'incapable of pre-thinking all the issues involved with a decision because of the complexities involved'. This provides for the 'economic basis' of professionalism. Through their possession of specialist knowledge and skills, which is based on a particular kind of education and training, professionals make claims that they will help their clients to tackle and solve the problems they face. Continuing and successful practice allows a profession to acquire certain privileges that enhance its status and power. So how does HRM stack up? If we consider Friedson's (2001) idea of an ideal type of professionalism, a brief assessment can be made (Table 15.1).

Table 15.1 An ideal type of professionalism

Friedson's ideal type of professionalism criteria	Human resource management (HRM) in the UK
Specialized work that is grounded in a body of theoretically based, discretionary knowledge and skill that is given special status	Cross-disciplinary theoretical underpinning for all HR activities and ongoing attempts to improve practice. Dissemination of developments in knowledge via journals, conferences, electronic media and so on. No unified HRM theory, debates existing over whether such a theory can ever be formed. Generally low status at strategic levels of decision-making. Emerging evidence of high commitment/performance from HR activities, and the trend towards knowledge production and management could enhance status
Exclusive jurisdiction created and controlled by occupational negotiation	Continuing debates regarding who practises HRM – HR function or line manager responsibility? Specialized practice of some techniques. Considerable growth of the CIPD, with chartered status since 2000 for the professional body and chartered status for members since 2003. Exclusivity has, however, not yet been achieved; there is no regulation of a licence to practise
A sheltered position with labour markets based on the qualifying credentials of the occupation	CIPD does not regulate the point of entry for HR practitioners. Movement into HR may frequently occur through internal promotion. Growing requirement for CIPD qualifications, and the professional journal, *People Management*, is a key location for HR recruitment. The variegated character of HRM prevents total sheltering
A formal training programme to provide qualifying credentials	CIPD professional development scheme delivered throughout the UK. National standards regulate overall content at three levels – support, practitioner and advanced practitioner. Growing number of Masters degree programmes in HRM and related areas, usually delivered by academic HRM departments
An ideology that asserts a commitment to doing good-quality work	CIPD code of professional conduct for members, with internal disciplinary procedures for malpractice. Expulsion from the CIPD is possible, but this cannot prevent a continuation of practice (see Appendix B)

In terms of representing a profession, HRM and its professional association, the CIPD, have clearly made significant advances in both the extent of influence of some of the main ideas and the size of the CIPD's membership.[8] There remain, however, some interesting issues to consider with respect to HRM's professional status. For example, although the HRM profession may have made advances against other groups who lack professional status, there are still significant variations in status and authority within the professions, with HRM practitioners frequently finding their voices downgraded against those of other professionals such as accountants and lawyers. Abbott (1988, p. 9) has argued that the control of a profession 'lies in control of the abstractions that generate the practical techniques' and that 'only a knowledge system governed by abstractions can redefine its problems and tasks, defend them from interlopers, and seize new problems'. So what is the nature of the abstractions in HRM?

Here, it is useful to draw on the distinction made by Halliday (1987) between professionals who have technical authority relating to expertise in performing challenging tasks and providing specialized knowledge, and professionals with moral authority relating to the specification of norms that guide behaviour. It is argued that the 'exercise of moral authority in the name of expertise' is based on professional knowledge that is 'normative', with the consequence that 'its potential breadth of influence' is greater (Halliday, 1987, p. 40). Thus, in many organizations, it is frequently those professions which provide moral authority, for example corporate finance and law, that gain most influence and whose voices will be heard and proceed to dominate, even though this is often disguised as technical advice. However – and crucially – others feel they should acknowledge and accept such advice.

In contrast, HRM professionals in many organizations are less likely to command authority because they do not have sole control over the sources of professional knowledge and may rely on technical authority. By seeking to establish its status on semi-scientific grounds, often by resorting to a never-ending search for the latest techniques,[9] but without control over the sources of a unifying body of scientific knowledge and certifiable skills that defines the differential distribution of power, HR expertise can be challenged by others inside the organization, thereby undermining both the professionalization and the power of HR practitioners. In such a situation, HR practitioners face ongoing precariousness (Caldwell, 2001; Jacoby, 2004). In order to advance, HRM needs to develop the normative basis of its professional knowledge to provide a source of moral authority. The crucial issue here is whether HRM is moving in this direction.

Ethics in human resource management

Whether the HR practitioner can be a source of moral authority speaks to the growing interest in the debate around 'ethical stewardship' in decision-making and the role of the HR professional as 'a guardian of ethics' (Ashman and Winstanley, 2006; Winstanley and Woodall, 2000). Given the centrality of the employment relationship, one aspect of HRM that cries out for serious consideration is that of ethics. However, as Winstanley and Woodall (2000) point out, with the focus of research on strategy and efficacy, ethics has been largely left out of the HRM discourse (HRM in Practice 15.1).

HRM IN PRACTICE 15.1

DEFENCE PAINTS FASTOW AS GREEDY LIAR

BARRIE MCKENNA, *GLOBE AND MAIL*, 9 MARCH 2006, P. B15

In Andrew Fastow's mind, he was a loyal servant working with his bosses at Enron Corp. on an elaborate scheme to dupe investors. But lawyers for Enron founder Kenneth Lay and former chief executive office Jeffrey Skilling portrayed an even more sinister Mr. Fastow, the company's former finance chief, as they began cross-examining the prosecution's star witness yesterday in a Houston court.

During a sometimes testy exchange, Daniel Petrocelli, Mr. Skilling's lawyer, suggested Mr. Fastow, 44, was a greedy and manipulative liar. Mr. Fastow, who could spend up to a decade in jail after pleading guilty to consipiracy, didn't duck the accusation. 'I believe I was extremely greedy, and that I lost my moral compass, and

I've done terrible things that I very much regret,' Mr. Fastow said. Mr. Lay, 63, and Mr. Skilling, 52, are facing up to 25 years in jail for their role in the 2001 collapse of Enron.

> The steady growth and bright prospects 'was the outside view of Enron. The inside view of Enron was very different.'

Mr. Fastow has testified that he deceived his own wife, Lea, and even indirectly involved his children in the kickback schemes that earned him millions of dollars. Lea Fastow has already served a year in prison for failing to disclose income from Enron deals crafted by her husband on her taxes. During the six-week trial, prosecutors

have cast Mr. Lay and Mr. Skilling as key players in the manipulation of Enron's books by repeatedly telling outsiders that all was well at the energy trading giant, even as it spiralled toward calamity.

Under cross-examination, Mr Fastow admitted making similarly optimistic remarks to investors and being considered a hero for it. But he said it was an illusion. 'Within the culture of corruption Enron had, a culture that rewarded financial reporting rather than rewarding economic value, I believed I was being a hero. I was not. It was not a good thing. That's why I'm here today,' he said.

The steady growth and bright prospects 'was the outside view of Enron. The inside view of Enron was very different,' Mr Fastow said.

Morality is always of relevance in management. Managers and HR professionals may agonize over what is 'the right thing to do' in difficult cases, whether the issue is disciplinary action, the duty to accommodate, or knowingly exposing employees to a carcinogen when this could be prevented. Nevertheless, occasions arise on which HR professionals face difficult decisions that 'favour one stakeholder over another' (Beatty et al., 2003, p. 258). Ethicists suggest that morality and ethics are not the same. Whereas morality concerns societal beliefs and mores about right and wrong, whether on the part of an individual or a whole society, ethics is the critical study of the underlying moral principles and concepts utilized in determining whether individual or collective conduct is 'right' or 'wrong' and outcome is 'good' or 'bad'. Managers and HR professionals will ultimately rely on their own ethical values to determine the right thing to do. Unfortunately, American-based Enron Energy and WorldCom Inc., Canadian-based Bre-X and Italian-based Parmalat have become icons of unethical corporate conduct and emphasize the importance of ethics in management.

To begin to understand the role of ethics in HRM, we need to compare several important ethical principles that people have relied on in the past to make ethical decisions. Moral philosophers have identified five ethical principles that can be of use to managers and HR professionals in navigating through the tangled moral issues that often arise in the practice of employment management. These are the principles of:

- individual rights
- distributive justice
- utilitarianism
- the stakeholder
- care.

The *individual rights principle* reflects the belief that people have the right to free speech, to privacy, to freedom of conscience and to the due process of the law. The first imperative of this ethical position is that decision-makers should follow the principle of 'universality' – 'what is right for one individual is right for all.' Respect for individual rights requires that people never be treated as means, but always as ends. For this imperative to be satisfied, the employee 'must not be treated as a commodity but instead as a human being with an inalienable right to dignified treatment' (Adams, 2006, p. 15).

The *distributive justice principle* declares that decisions should be based on fairness, equity and impartiality, and asserts the maxim: 'Do unto others as you would have them do unto you.' The justice-based ethical principle emphasizes legally binding agreements to guarantee that justice and rights are upheld.

The *utilitarian principle* emphasizes outcomes and advises individuals to make decisions that result in the 'greatest good for the greatest number of people' as being the most moral. The *stakeholder principle* reflects the belief that the most moral decision takes into account the interests of the people who have a stake in the organization's affairs including, for example, employees and shareholders. The *care principle* determines the most morally correct action to be the one that is sensitive to the relationships between co-workers and the needs of the situation. The idea of the ethics of care is based on the assumption that estrangement from self or others causes moral indifference.

Most textbooks on business ethics make the traditional concepts of rights, justice and utilitarianism the centre of their analysis. For Winstanley and Woodall (2000), however, the stakeholder and care principles have much relevance to HRM. For example, recognizing that the employment relationship is characterized by asymmetrical power relations and structured antagonism (Clayton, 2000), employee voice and subordinates' involvement in decision-making, issues we examined in Chapters 11 and 12, are good starting points for debating ethics in HRM. Furthermore, we suggest that the stakeholder and care principles contribute to developing the normative framework of the profession's esoteric knowledge and moral authority.

HRM WEB LINKS

Check the website http://www.businessethics.com, from which you will be able to download information on ethics in business.

● Does HRM work? Embeddedness and divergence

The question 'Does HRM work?' is more than a debating point. Evidence that *better* HR practices can indeed contribute to the organization's performance or the bottom line has fundamental implications for whether or not an organization should invest in HR interventions, as well as for the HR profession. Let us assess the evidence here:

1. At the level of practice, do those with 'human resources' in their job title do anything different from personnel managers that might be considered an enhancement or a progression?
2. Is anything emerging, contextually or theoretically, that might help HR managers to improve their status in strategic discussions?
3. What is the response of those on the receiving end of HRM, that is, the employees and managers who are selected, rewarded, appraised, trained and so on?

To start to answer these questions, let us first consider the use of different job titles. The number of specialist practitioners who are more qualified has increased in line with the growth in the number of organizations using 'human resources' within a job title; specialist practitioners also have a greater involvement in designing plans and are found in greater numbers where employee development is more likely to feature in strategic plans. HRM is associated with more sophisticated practices such as personality testing, the use of attitude surveys and off-the-job training. Thus, the difference between 'HR' and 'personnel' does seem to matter, and HR specialists appear to have more credibility as professionals (Hoque and Noon, 2001).

Moving to the second question, many advocates of an HRM approach will be heartened by the fact that part of the credibility for HR professionalism might be concerned with an involvement in strategic planning. Indeed, since its first appearance in the USA in the 1980s, the importance of a strategic connection and the integration of key HR activities with strategy has been the distinguishing feature of HRM compared with personnel management (Purcell, 2001). Since that time, the ongoing research we examined in Chapter 14 appears to demonstrate that such a connection pays off. This work is important in two ways with respect to the stature of HRM professionalism:

1. The research demonstrating a positive association between strategic HRM and organizational performance adds to a body of theoretical knowledge that provides the foundation for professional status.
2. Such knowledge forms a repertoire of ideas and activities that serve to persuade others of the legitimacy of HRM.

Thus, HRM professionals are able to make claims about the efficacy of their involvement in strategic work on the basis of their expertise related to a particular body of knowledge, and from such expertise flows authority and status (Middlehurst and Kennie, 1997). The voice of HRM, therefore, *should* be heard. In recent years, such claims have been strongly associated with a link between HRM and organizational performance, especially the achievement of what is commonly referred to as 'high-performance' working realized through the contribution of high-commitment HRM practices. The 'breakthrough' studies reviewed by Ichniowski et al. (1996) in the USA, and the work of Guest (2000) and others in the UK and Paauwe (2004) in Holland, have been very important in this respect. Some doubts, however, remain. Let us take each of these in turn.

First, if there has been a breakthrough in terms of providing the evidence, any knowledge of the HRM–commitment/performance link seems to have fallen on deaf ears, as indicated by the surveys of Taylor (2002) and even Guest (2000). Particularly galling was the finding by Taylor (2002, p. 7) of little evidence of a 'coherent human resource management agenda', and the recent WERS 2004 results indicate a mixed take-up of high-commitment HRM practices, especially among smaller organizations (Kersley et al., 2006). Even the promise of the need for a high-skilled workforce with ample resources devoted to human resource development is proving to be difficult to fulfil (Lloyd and Payne, 2004). As Godard (2004) argues, high-performance organizations can work with practices that negatively affect employees and unions. It would thus seem that, in the UK, there is still some way to go before HRM professionals are able to voice claims that have a persuasive appeal equal to that of marketing and finance.

Second, as we emphasized in Chapters 6 and 14, there are problems with measuring performance at work when worker outcomes need to be included, and many argue for the need for multiple measures of performance to match the variety of goals and interests (Paauwe and Boselie, 2003). It would also seem that, depending on which measures are used, the results of a link between HRM and performance could, even in larger samples, be positive, neutral or even negative (Guest et al., 2003). Thus, a number of writers (e.g. Legge, 2001, 2005; Thompson and McHugh, 2002) continue to express doubts about the claims for a link, and even when a positive link is made between HRM activities and outcomes, there can be no certainty of the direction of causality. A cluster of HRM practices, for example, may be introduced as the result of favourable profits or overall organizational performance.

Legge (2001) highlights the complexity of any attempt to link HRM processes with organizational performance – however this is measured. Each organization has, for example, its own history, culture and experience, all of which influence in a unique way the choices and decisions that will be made. The accounting scandals in some prominent US corporations in 2002 further illustrate the difficulty of using valid and reliable organizational performance measurements. In arguing for the link between HRM and performance, there is a need to understand how the link actually works, what Bowen and Ostroff (2004) refer to as the 'strength' of the HRM system. Crucial here is the role of national business systems, local culture and organizational culture and the meanings made in everyday interactions.

Third, the ability of managers and HR professionals to secure and maintain a high commitment-based HRM system that will enhance organizational performance might be undermined or inhibited by the form of corporate governance under which managers operate. As Konzelmann et al. (2006) point out, a strategic approach to managing people requires employee cooperation to secure their commitment to the objectives of the organization and to leverage the full potential of employees' knowledge and capabilities. The researchers' core argument is that satisfying external shareholders' demands might prevent managers from making 'credible' commitments to the workforce, which in turn inhibits managers' ability to secure full cooperation from their employees, a prerequisite for effective HRM. There are parallels here with the early work of Armstrong (1989) and his analysis of how the long-term strategic aspirations of HRM can be subjugated to accounting controls and the conflicting priority of boosting shareholder value.

Appealing though such quantitative studies of HRM–performance links may be, there are significant problems associated with the idea of better or best practice HRM, in relation to both their competitive advantage when organizations are embedded in national business and employment networks, and the claims that the best practice HRM model is universally applicable. As we explained in Chapter 3, the employment relationship is shaped by national systems of employment legislation and the cultural contexts in which this operates. The widespread demonstrations in France in spring

2006 against precarious employment – *'Non à la précarité!'* – affirm the centrality of societal effects on HR practices. If we are to understand the nature of employment management, we need to understand the social relations and the dynamics of the society in which it is embedded. Owing to the intensified pace and extended scope of globalization processes, the notion of embeddedness has become a hot topic in HRM research. Longitudinal, more culturally informed and societal effects studies of better practice HRM are increasingly acknowledging that the issue of universally applying 'better practice' needs more careful nuance than has been the case hitherto and that national conceptions of better HRM practices remain dominant (see, for example, Brewster, 2001; Jacoby, 2005; Sparrow et al., 2004).

Contrary to the convergence hypothesis underpinning globalization, the idea that best HR practices have universal application is untenable when the HRM phenomenon is embedded in national institutional profiles and shared social values different from those in the USA or UK. Different national institutional networks, which comprise laws, frames of reference, core values, communication styles and norms, can explain the divergence between parent and host local companies, as can the disjuncture between best HR practices and the shared mindset of stakeholders.

Quantifying the HRM–performance link is, it seems, problematic when best practice and employment management are transferred and embedded in a different social milieux. Moreover, given that potential conflict and active cooperation elements are both inherent in the employment relationship, together with the differences in relative power that the latter generates, the capability of managers to create processes by which legitimate differences in stakeholder interests can be reconciled will determine the efficacy of best HR practices in the multifaceted reality of corporate capitalism (see, for example, Dobbin, 2005; Konzelmann, 2005; Sako, 2005). Therefore, if researchers and HR practitioners wish to demonstrate the contribution of HRM to organizational performance, there is a need for more case study research that takes account of the societal effects on HR practices as they are transplanted around the globe and translated locally into workable social relations.

HRM WEB LINKS

Check the workplace reorganization, HRM and corporate performance website at www.bbk.ac.uk/manop/research/mgesrc.shtml, from which you will be able to download various papers. David Guest's homepage is www.kcl.ac.uk/depsta/pse/mancen/staff/david_guest.htm. Papers by Casey Ichniowski and his colleagues can be found at www.nber.org/cgi-bin/author_papers.pl?author=casey_ichniowski, and Jaap Paauwe's homepage can be found at http://people.few.eur.nl/paauwe/.

In answer to the third question above, there are also a variety of views from those on the receiving end of HRM practices. Mabey et al. (1998b), in a collection of case studies, argued that the voice of such recipients has been underrepresented. They reported workplace accounts of HRM interventions, providing compelling insights into employment relations, and helped us move away from the somewhat moribund academic debate on soft versus hard HRM models. The case studies affirmed that significant changes had taken place at work under the guise of HRM. However, on the question of the delivery of HRM goals such as greater commitment and a unified culture, Mabey et al. (1998b, p. 237) concluded that, 'many of [HRM's] prized goals … remain unproven at best, and unfulfilled at worst'. But not all is doom and gloom:

the data also provided evidence that, for the 'majority of participants', the benefits arising from HRM interventions seem to 'outweigh the costs to the minority' (Mabey et al., 1998b, p. 240).

Guest (1999) also sought to evaluate employees' experiences of HRM, partly in response to criticisms from writers such as Legge.[10] In addition, he wanted to examine the particular influence of high-commitment/performance practices, which he felt was lacking in Mabey et al.'s (1998b) study. Using data from an annual survey of a stratified random sample of 1000 workers in the UK, conducted by the CIPD to examine the state of the employment relationship, Guest (1999) found that progressive HR practices were consistent with positive outcomes such as feelings of fair treatment, security and satisfaction with the job and motivation. Guest's conclusion was that a 'large proportion of the UK workforce' seemed to 'like' HR practices (Guest, 1999, p. 22), although he did acknowledge some of the limitations of the survey and the lack of evidence on strategic integration of the practices.

As Nichols et al. (2002) observed, however, employee satisfaction surveys, claiming to reveal either positive or negative views of the work situation, were rating not simply management practices, but also how workers perceived their own work situation relative to their local economic position, constraints and opportunities: everything cannot be reduced to management techniques. This was reinforced in a study by Edgar and Geare (2005) into employee attitudes, measured by organizational commitment, job satisfaction and organizational fairness, in turn affected by HR practices of good and safe working conditions, training and development, equal employment opportunities and recruitment and selection. Edgar and Geare found that attitudes were affected less by the quantity of HR practices and more by the way in which they were implemented, particularly by line managers.

It is doubtful that these studies will satisfy the methodological criticisms of Legge and others. Nevertheless, there remains a strong interest in finding out *whether* the link between HRM and performance works, and *how* it works, although there is also a fair degree of mystification. Boselie et al. (2005) examined over 100 studies from 1994 to 2003 and found an inconsistent picture of the meaning of HRM and what it was supposed to do. There is still a need for more longitudinal research (Marchington and Zegelmeyer, 2005), especially studies that consider more closely the direction of causality. There is also, we would suggest, a need to study more closely how and why, even in organizations that espouse HRM, there seem to be consistent barriers to progress that reinforce a lower status for HRM. Here, we advocate a move towards a practice perspective in HRM.

Towards a practice perspective in HRM

What do we mean when we advocate a practice perspective, and why do we do this? In recent years, in a number of management fields, partly in response to difficulty and contradiction in research findings, there has been a growing interest in what happens in practice, that is, the everyday processes and actions that occur. For example, there appears to be a thriving interest in how strategy is made and enacted in organizations, with a focus on activities that occur on a daily basis and relate to strategic outcomes.[11] In leadership, there is growing interest in how influence is exerted in practice and distributed throughout an organization instead of being seen as the prerogative of a single individual.[12] As we saw in Chapter 9, attention has also been given to how learning occurs and how knowledge is constructed in practice.

One of the appeals of a practice perspective in HRM is how the concern shifts from what is advocated by HRM specialists, through polices and procedures, to what is actually done or not done, as the case may be. A practice perspective considers 'the conditions of intelligibility' (Schatzki, 2001, p.1) of organizational life and the taking of action. This inevitably requires access to the various organizational agents who are deemed to have responsibility for or are required to respond to HR activities. Thus, a practice perspective implies a multivoiced approach to researching organizational life. The methods employed in such studies have to take account of this feature. It is thus no use simply asking HR managers for their opinions because it is the practice that needs to be accessed.

Why is this needed? As has been indicated above, the HRM project has had only partial success. Certainly, in some organizations, there has been a signifcant impact of HR practices that seek to engender high-performance working and high commitment. In most, however, this is not the case, and repeated efforts to persuade such organizations of the need to follow in this direction seem to have fallen on deaf ears or have failed to meet expectations. The reasons for this are often found in embedded cultural and historical factors that are manifest in daily interactions but often not fully appreciated by those present. For example, high-skill work is a key feature of the high-commitment ideal, yet there is a persistence of low-skill working that is accepted as the way to do work, and little awareness that this may be holding back progress or how and why this may be the case. There are many other facets of HR practice that may face the same fate. A practice perspective is therefore vital in order to reveal the apparent contradictions and tensions between what is stated and what is done under the heading of HRM.

At this point, we need to review what we have said about the nature of the employment relationship and address a number of issues that will help us to speculate on the future of HRM, while providing the reader with some analytical tools for studying the HRM literature. Although change is a defining feature of the 'new economy', the core characteristic of the capitalist employment relationship has not changed. As we first explained in Chapter 1, a set of tensions revolves around the buying and selling of human resources and the indeterminate nature of workers' physical or intellectual efforts in the labour process. In other words, the pay–effort bargain is inherently prone to conflict because workers still predominantly seek to maximize and employers to minimize pay. The leverage of human knowledge and skill to generate value is in turn mediated by antagonistic employment relations and technological and organizational change, whereas the accumulation of profit is mediated by product markets and global competition. These sets of complex relationships create patterns of conflict, accommodation and cooperation, and engender persistence in employment relations; they also cause both minor and fundamental change.

Another feature of the employment relationship emphasized throughout this text relates to the notion of paradox. We do not wish to rehearse all the arguments in the previous chapters but will instead cite a few examples:

- selection instruments designed to identify individuals possessing team traits, while espousing the need for independent and critical thinkers
- work regimes that call for critical reflection, creativity and experimentation, while insisting that workers maintain a 'zero defects' record
- employee participation schemes to enhance productivity but which exclude from any influential position the very people whom the formal participatory structure is supposed to empower

● learning organizations claiming to emancipate workers but maintaining electronic surveillance of operating procedures – computer-controlled autonomy (Bratton, 1992)

● reward systems that link pay and promotion to individual performance yet expect people to collaborate and share their knowledge and information with co-workers (ask your lecturer how this paradox may occur in a university setting).

Managers often appear to be caught between two contradictory imperatives – regulating human endeavours too tightly undermines workers' leverage potential, whereas empowering workers undermines management control. We have assumed that paradox is inherent in HRM practices and organizational structures. By illustrating and explaining how various paradoxes in HRM are produced and reproduced, we hope to encourage a greater understanding of and sensitivity towards managing the employment relationship in the future.

In addition, we wish to draw attention to the need for an understanding of historical trajectories in our study of HRM.[13] The foregoing chapters have emphasized the historical development of HRM and its current practices, which reaffirm Storey's (2001, p. 6) argument that HRM emerged in the 1980s as 'a historically situated phenomenon'. Whatever the claims of academics and practitioners to apparently 'new' HRM practices, most have deep historical roots: whether it is the 'discovery' of the importance of informal learning in the discourse on competitive advantage (recognized in the apprenticeship system of the Middle Ages); the 'discovery' that contract workers are less committed to the organization than permanent workers (well understood and documented by Niccolò Machiavelli in his book *The Prince*, written in 1513); the 'discovery' of the 'virtual' organization without face-to-face human activity, with people working at home and connected through electronic networks (resembling key structural elements of the preindustrial 'putting-out' system); or the 'discovery' that 'social partnerships' are advantageous to management faced with uncertainty in product markets and global competition (as researched by the Committee of Inquiry on Industrial Democracy, chaired by Lord Bullock, in 1977).

Thus, most of the important practices that make up the new HRM phenomenon are not all that new, and HRM is therefore a product of a set of complex forces at a particular point in the history of Western capitalism. In a field of management so variable and divergent, HRM cannot be understood in the context of simplistic linear models that expunge old practices and substitute new ones. Developments in HRM over the past 20 years may thus be seen as innovative and as evidence of change, but at the same time, when viewed through a historical lens, there is a realization of déjà vu.

We also need to emphasize one of the main features of our treatment of HRM throughout the book, first discussed in Chapter 1: the need to understand the importance of differing standpoints in management theory. The two standpoints we have presented in this book are mainstream, on the one hand, and critical on the other. An understanding that all aspects of managing the employment relationship can be investigated and interpreted from these different standpoints is an important analytical tool for evaluating the diverse range of HRM literature and how differing standpoints produce contradictory claims and conclusions related to HRM. In this context, it is legitimate to examine the recent growth of call centres from either the new economy or 'electronic sweatshop' perspective. A sensitivity to differing theoretical approaches to researching HRM therefore contributes to our ability to identify and understand the roots of apparent tensions, contradictions and paradoxes that pervade much of the literature on and experiences relating to HRM practices.

In our analysis of strategic HRM, we have emphasized that whether managers adopt a high-commitment HR strategy or a cost control HR strategy will depend upon the relative advantages of each vis-à-vis the 'master' strategy, and on whether inherently political regulations and pressure from organized workers encourage a high road approach to competitiveness. It follows logically from this premise that, when it comes to HR strategy, there is no universal or one best way, and the prediction that one HR strategy, generally assumed to be the high-commitment HR strategy, would be widely adopted by organizations across the economy seems theoretically unsound, given the complex dynamics operating in the global market. Put another way, if long-term profitability depends on the mobilization of human capital, and workers are seen as part of the solution rather than the problem, employers and managers are more likely to adopt a high-commitment HR strategy. On the other hand, the so-called new economy still contains scores of industries in which the business plan relies heavily on a low-paid, low-skilled and tightly controlled workforce: 'McWork'. In such enterprises, employers and managers tend to view workers as part of the problem rather than the solution.

In reviewing the evidence, we consider that the prospect is for the continued diversity of HR strategies. Some organizations will adopt the 'high road' to economic competitiveness using human capital and a high-commitment HR strategy, whereas others will continue to use a 'low road' and a traditional HR strategy; still more will use a combination of the various strategies for different occupational groups depending on the problems and opportunities confronting management. Diversity of HRM has thus been the defining feature of UK organizations in the past, and will probably continue to be so in the future. The gains made by HR professionals during the 1990s cannot be guaranteed; professional power is not a naturally occurring feature of our world and should be regarded as contingent and ephemeral. Professional power and the influence of HR specialists will rise and fall depending on how well they predict and respond to changing external and internal forces that influence and shape organizational strategies, as well as on how competent they are at demonstrating the value added by HRM to their colleagues.

Our final point concerns the problem of shareholder value-driven capitalism and corporate leadership and rewards. Although some have suggested that the greatest challenge facing HRM professionals is an internal issue – identifying and using credible evaluation methods, and convincing senior and middle management that HR activities do contribute significantly to organizational goals – we would also agree with those observers who suggest that internal issues revolving around the use of stock options for chief executives, and rewards contingent upon meeting 'hard' short-term financial targets, serve to undermine HRM (Armstrong, 1989; Legge, 1995; Sisson and Storey, 2000; Storey, 1995a, 2001). In the aftermath of accounting-related scandals in some US and Italian companies, stock option abuses, self-obsessed chief executive officers and other nefarious activities, this issue is even more pressing. A resource-based approach to sustainable competitive advantage, one requiring a high-skill, learning-oriented, high-performance workplace, is a long-term investment strategy (see Jacoby, 2005). As long as chief executives are either unable – due to shareholder pressures – or unwilling to invest in people because they have to meet short-term financial targets or wish to maximize their own inflated rewards from share options, the development and diffusion of high-performance practices designed to elicit employee cooperation and long-term commitment, and with it the ability to leverage human knowledge, creativity and skills, will continue to remain limited.

Final comment

Your journey through some theories and practices of HRM is now drawing to a close. Throughout this book, we have emphasized diversity in both the theory and the practices, endeavoured to make the field more transparent and relevant through vignettes, web-based sources and case studies, and, through the use of discussion questions, study tips and reflective questions, encouraged independent thinking and critical inquiry. The time has now come to reflect on what you have learned from this journey.

Adult education scholars emphasize the need for *reflection* as a critical component of the learning process. Reflection is like using a mirror to help us to look back on our actions and thought processes; reflective learning occurs where we have experiences and then step back from them to evaluate the learning we have experienced. There are several ways of carrying out reflection. One approach is to go systematically back through all you have learned so far. Another approach, however, is to look at the additional reading listed at the end of each chapter. Other sources of information, particularly material that tends to differ from the approach taken in this textbook, provide mirrors for us and allow us to look at topics from another perspective. Furthermore, other people – friends, relatives and co-workers – also provide mirrors for us, allowing us to understand HRM from another perspective, so talk to other people about the topics covered in this book.

Finally, your own experience of work is excellent material for reflection and can provide insightful information on and an understanding of HRM theory and practice. To help you start the reflection process, go back to the beginning of each chapter and consider whether you have personally achieved the major learning objectives.

Notes

1. Matzdorf et al. (1999, p. 94).
2. Editorial, *Globe and Mail*, October 6, 2006, p. A14.
3. Marchington and Zegelmeyer (2005, p. 7).
4. Storey and Quintas (2001, p. 345).
5. Winstanley and Woodall (2000, p. 278).
6. It is, however, noticeable that the new association did not incorporate 'human resource management' into its title, unlike the US-based Society for HRM.
7. The significance of this may be lost on non-UK readers, but to be called a chartered professional is highly symbolic in UK society.
8. In 2005, the membership of the CIPD had reached over 125,000, an increase of 60 per cent since 1996.
9. A visit to the CIPD's annual conference held in Harrogate, UK, will reveal a vast array of 'new' techniques on offer.
10. Guest highlights Karen Legge, Tom Keenoy and Hugh Willmott as being critical analysts of HRM.
11. See the *Journal of Management Studies*, 2003, **40**(1), for some of the key papers. Also check the website at www.strategy-as-practice.org/.
12. See Spillane, J. (2006) *Distributed Leadership*. San Francisco: Jossey-Bass.
13. We are indebted to Peter Sawchuk, University of Toronto, for his insight into historical trajectories and some of the historical links between HRM and informal learning. See Bratton et al. (2003).

Appendices

Appendix A

The European Union Social Charter

The Social Charter was adopted by all member states, except the UK, in December 1989. The Social Charter is not a legal text. It is a statement of principles by which governments agree to abide. They will be required each year to present a report on how they are implementing the Charter. Its aim is to highlight the importance of the social dimension of the single market in achieving social as well as economic cohesion in the EC.

The preamble of the Social Charter gives added weight to other international obligations such as ILO conventions. The preamble also includes a commitment to combat every form of discrimination, including discrimination on grounds of sex, colour, race, opinions and belief.

Summary of the rights set out in the Social Charter:

1. Freedom of movement throughout the Community with equal treatment in access to employment, working conditions and social protection.

2. Freedom to choose and engage in an occupation, which shall be fairly remunerated.

3. Improvement of living and working conditions, especially for part-time and temporary workers, and rights to weekly rest periods and annual paid leave.

4. Right to adequate social protection.

5. Right to freedom of association and collective bargaining.

6. Right to access to lifelong vocational training, without discrimination on grounds of nationality.

7. Right of equal treatment of men and women, especially in access to employment, pay, working conditions, education and training and career development.

8. Right to information, consultation and participation for employees, particularly in conditions of technological change, restructuring, redundancies, and for transfrontier workers.

9. Right to health protection and safety at the workplace including training, information, consultation and participation for employees.

10. Rights of children and adolescents, including a minimum working age.

11. Right for the elderly to have a decent standard of living on retirement.

12. Right of people with disabilities to programmes to help them in social and professional life.

Appendix B

CHARTERED INSTITUTE OF PERSONNEL AND DEVELOPMENT
Code of professional conduct and disciplinary procedures

The Chartered Institute of Personnel and Development (CIPD) is the professional association specialising in the management and development of people for the United Kingdom and the Republic of Ireland.

1 Mission

The mission of the Chartered Institute of Personnel and Development is:

1.1 to lead in the development and promotion of good practice in the field of the management and development of people, for application both by professional members and by their organisational colleagues

1.2 to serve the professional interests of members

1.3 to uphold the highest ideals in the management and development of people.

2 Objects

The objects for which the Institute is established are:

2.1 The promotion of the art and science of the management and development of people for the public benefit.

3 Purpose of this code

All the CIPD members of whatever grade of membership should be concerned with the maintenance of good practice within the profession and must commit themselves to this code of professional conduct which sets out the standards of professional conduct to which members must adhere. Attached to this code is a description of the procedure which will be applied to deal with any complaints arising.

4 Standards of professional conduct

CIPD members are expected to exercise relevant competence in accordance with the Institute's professional standards and qualifications.

4.1 CIPD members provide specialist professional knowledge, advice, support and management competence in the management and development of people. In all circumstances they:

4.1.1 must endeavour to enhance the standing and good name of the profession; adherence to this code of professional conduct is an essential aspect of this

4.1.2 must seek continually to improve their performance and update and refresh their skills and knowledge

4.1.3 must within their own or any client organisation and in whatever capacity they are working, seek to achieve the fullest possible development of people for present and future organisational needs and encourage self-development by individuals

4.1.4 must within their own or any client organisation and in whatever capacity they are working, seek to adopt in the most appropriate way, the most appropriate people management processes and structures to enable the organisation to best achieve its present and future objectives

4.1.5 must promote and themselves maintain fair and reasonable standards in the treatment of people who are operating within scope of their influence

4.1.6 must promote and themselves seek to exercise employment practices that remove unfair discrimination including but not limited to gender, age, race, religion, disability and background

4.1.7 must respect legitimate needs and requirements for confidentiality

4.1.8 must use due diligence and exercise high standards of timeliness, appropriateness and accuracy in the information and advice they provide to employers and employees

4.1.9 must seek to recognise the limitations of their own knowledge and ability and must not undertake activity for which they are not yet appropriately prepared or, where applicable, qualified.

4.2 In the public interest and in the pursuit of its objects, the Chartered Institute of Personnel and Development is committed to the highest possible standards of professional conduct and competency. To this end members:

4.2.1 are required to exercise integrity, honesty, diligence and appropriate behaviour in all their business, professional and related personal activities

4.2.2 must act within the law and must not encourage, assist or act in collusion with employers, employees or others who may be engaged in unlawful conduct.

5 Complaints

Any person, whether or not a member, may complain to the Institute that a member has been guilty of conduct which is not in accordance with the provisions of this code and/or where that conduct appears likely to bring discredit to the Institute or the profession. Such conduct will be considered under the terms of the disciplinary procedure.

CIPD professional conduct disciplinary procedure

1   Procedures for complaints

1.1 Complaints may be made against a member by:

- the Institute
- another member
- a third party

1.2 Any complaint made against a member must be made in writing under confidential cover and addressed to the Secretary of the Institute at its registered office. Complainants shall set out the circumstances forming the basis of the complaint, including the relationship, if any, between the complainant and the member concerned.

1.3 The Secretary shall at his/her discretion consult with the complainant and other parties, in particular, officers and members of the Institute, including the member concerned to determine whether a prima facie case has been made. If the Secretary concludes that there is a prima facie case, he/she shall then formally notify in writing the member concerned.

1.4 If the Secretary concludes that a prima facie case has not been made, he/she shall so advise the complainant, and at the Secretary's discretion the member concerned, in writing. The complainant may challenge the decision of the Secretary in writing to the member of the Nominations and Professional Conduct Committee designated to consider such appeals (designated member). This 'preliminary appeal' process will consist solely of the consideration of the information already submitted to the Secretary, the Secretary's own advice and written representations from the complainant and the member concerned. The designated member's decision shall be final and binding and there shall be no obligation to give written reasons for the decision.

1.5 If the Secretary decides in the first instance, or the designated member of the Nominations and Professional Conduct Committee on preliminary appeal considers a prima facie case has been made, the Secretary shall then notify in writing the member concerned of the nature of the complaint and the Secretary shall request the member concerned's written response within 28 days of the date of sending out the notification. Upon receipt of the response or at the end of the period, whichever is earlier, the Secretary shall refer the complaint and the member concerned's response, if any, to the Chair of the Nominations and Professional Conduct Committee. The Chair shall then instruct the Secretary to convene, as soon as reasonably practicable, a disciplinary panel.

2   Disciplinary panel

2.1 The power of making disciplinary decisions is vested in a disciplinary panel.

2.2 Disciplinary panels shall be drawn from members of the Nominations and Professional Conduct Committee. The Chair of the Nominations and Professional Conduct Committee shall not be a member of a disciplinary panel. The nominated panel members will appoint one of their number to act as their Chair.

2.3 A disciplinary panel will consist of not more than four and not less than three members including the Chair of the panel, each of whom shall have a primary vote. A panel may co-opt additional specialist advisers should it so decide, who will not have a vote. There will also be a Secretary for each panel who will normally be the Secretary of the Institute. In the event of a tied vote, the Chair does not have a casting vote.

3   Disciplinary panel hearings

3.1 Within 14 days of receiving a response, or after the lapse of 28 days from sending notification to the member concerned whichever is the lesser, the Secretary shall fix a date and place for the complaint to be heard by the disciplinary panel, giving at least 28 days notice to the member and complainant concerned or such other period as may be determined (unless otherwise agreed between all the parties). The place where the complaint will be heard will ordinarily be the headquarters of the CIPD.

3.2 At least 14 days before the disciplinary hearing, the panel must present in writing to the member concerned and all other parties involved the document supporting the complaint. The member concerned shall also have proper opportunity to bring witnesses and introduce at the hearing any relevant evidence he/she may consider fit. The person making the complaint will normally be required to appear before the hearing and given the opportunity of an explanation. Either or both parties may be accompanied by a full member (i.e. companion, fellow, or member) of the CIPD if he/she so wishes. Such a member shall attend as a supporter or adviser but not as a representative.

3.3 The hearing can, with the agreement of the parties, take place in the absence of one of the parties if, in the opinion of the disciplinary panel, there is no alternative to proceeding in this way. With the agreement of the parties, the hearing could be conducted by correspondence.

3.4 The disciplinary panel may make such further enquiries by correspondence or call witnesses or otherwise as it may think fit. This may involve an adjournment of the panel hearing for a reasonable period.

3.5 The disciplinary panel, after considering all available submissions, will determine their decision. If the panel decides that the case has not been substantiated, the complaint will be dismissed. The Secretary will in writing inform the person making the complaint and the member concerned.

3.6 Decisions of the disciplinary panel shall be by simple majority and can be made in the absence of the member concerned, provided they have been previously informed of the date of the hearing and nature of the complaint. In the event of a tied vote, the Chair shall not have a casting vote; in these circumstances the complaint shall be regarded as dismissed.

4 Powers of the disciplinary panel

The disciplinary panel shall have the following powers:

4.1 dismiss the complaint

4.2 exercise one or more of the following disciplinary decisions, in combination or as alternative:

4.2.1 warn, admonish or reprimand any member

4.2.2 call for a written undertaking from the member as to future conduct and performance, to provide for guidance from a senior colleague and specific training, and/or arrange for regular reporting

4.2.3 direct that a statement recording the complaint should be entered on the CIPD's personal record of the respondent for a defined time

4.2.4 review the member's eligibility for Institute office

4.2.5 re-designate a member in the Institute's membership grades

4.2.6 withdraw the benefits of membership of the Institute and the use of designatory letters for a defined time

4.2.7 call for the resignation of a member

4.2.8 expel a member from the Institute

4.2.9 make recommendations to the President of the Institute regarding publication of the decision.

5 Appeal system

5.1 It is open for a member against whom a complaint has been upheld in full or in part by a disciplinary panel and against whom a disciplinary decision has been made, to lodge an appeal to an appeals panel. Such appeal must be made in writing to the Secretary of the Institute at the registered office of the CIPD within 28 days of the date of notification of the disciplinary decision. The notice must set out the full grounds on which issue is taken with the disciplinary decision. The action decided upon will, at the discretion of the disciplinary panel, normally be suspended until after the appeal is heard.

5.2 The Secretary will notify the Chair of the Nominations and Professional Conduct Committee, as Chair of the appeals panel, of the appeal, and he/she will instruct the Secretary to convene an appeals panel.

5.3 The Secretary shall fix a date and place for the case to be heard, giving at least 28 days notice to the member concerned or such other period as may be agreed between all the parties.

5.4 The appeals panel will follow the same procedure as the disciplinary panel save that the member concerned may be represented by a third party who need not be a member of the Institute. Relevant documents will be circulated to all parties before the appeal hearing. The decision of the appeals panel will be final and by a simple majority; where no such majority is obtained, the appeal fails and the original decision stands.

5.5 The appeals panel may overturn the disciplinary decision, vary or uphold it.

5.6 The member concerned will be informed in writing within 14 days of the decision of the appeals panel.

6 Appeals panel

The appeals panel will consist of the Chair of the Nominations and Professional Conduct Committee, as Chair, and four other members of that committee. In the unavoidable absence or indisposition of the Chair, that person or the panel itself may nominate another member of the panel to act as Chair. No member may serve on the appeals panel who was previously involved in the disciplinary panel, in relation to the same matter.

7 Publication of decisions

7.1 Decisions by the Secretary and upon preliminary appeal by the Chair of the Nominations and Professional Conduct Committee shall be reported to that committee.

7.2 Decisions of the disciplinary panel (subject to paragraph 5.1) and of the appeals panel will be notified to the member against whom the complaint has been made and as soon as practicable to the council, and will be effective immediately. The extent of publication will be at the discretion of the President of the Institute, based on a recommendation from the disciplinary or appeals panel. Individuals in cases which have been dismissed will not be identified, but details of such cases may nevertheless be published. Members who have been the subject of disciplinary proceedings may request the President, at his/her discretion, to publish decisions on their behalf.

8 Readmittance

Before a member is readmitted following expulsion, the matter will be referred to the Nominations and Professional Conduct Committee.

Glossary

360° appraisal or feedback Feedback regarding performance from all aspects of the job.

Appraisal A process that provides analysis of a person's overall capabilities and potential, allowing informed decisions to be made for particular purposes.

Assessment An important part of the appraisal process whereby data on an individual's past and current work behaviour and performance are collected and reviewed.

Assessment centre The combination of assessment techniques at a single event to make judgements about people for selection and promotion and/or to provide feedback to employees on areas for development.

Attraction Favourable interaction between potential applicants and the images, values and information about an organization.

Autonomy The extent to which a job allows employees freedom and discretion to schedule their work and decide the procedures used to complete it.

Bargaining scope The range of issues covered by the subject matter of collective agreements.

Behaviour-anchored rating scale (BARS) A performance appraisal technique with performance levels anchored by job-related behaviours.

Best Value Provides a framework or benchmark for performance management in local government service provision in the UK.

Briefing groups Groups called together on a regular and consistent basis so that organization decisions and the reasons for them may be communicated. Group members may in turn meet with another briefing group so that information is systematically communicated down the management line.

Bureaucracy An organizational structure marked by rules and procedures, hierarchy of authority and division of labour.

Bureaucratic control An approach to performance management that formally seeks to measure an employee's behaviour at work, the outputs achieved from work or both.

Business process re-engineering A radical change of business processes by applying IT to integrate tasks.

Career management Activities and processes to match individual needs and aspirations with organization needs, set within an integrative framework.

'Careless worker' model Assumption that most accidents at work are due to an employee's failure to take safety seriously (or to protect him/herself).

Coaching A management activity to enhance the development of employees, with a particular emphasis on the transfer of learning from formal training courses into workplace activity.

Collective agreement The outcome of collective bargaining, it is an agreement between employers and trade unions respecting terms and conditions of employment. Unlike Canada and the USA, in the UK the agreement is not legally enforceable.

Collective bargaining An institutional system of negotiation in which the making, interpretation and administration of rules, and the application of the statutory controls affecting the employment relationship, are decided within union–management negotiating committees.

Communication The process by which information is exchanged between a sender and a receiver.

Comparative human resource management A field of study that focuses on providing insights and understanding into the nature of, and reasons for, differences in HR practice across national boundaries.

Competences The outcomes of work performance in an occupational area with specified performance criteria.

Competencies Underlying characteristics of a person which result in competent or effective performance taking into consideration the nature of the tasks and the organization context.

Computerized personnel information system The use of software to record manpower data and calculate measures such as turnover, absenteeism and staff profiles.

Control-based model A model of HR strategy that assumes the prime focus of managers is to monitor and control employee role performance. Accordingly, organizational structures and HR strategies are instruments and techniques to control all aspects of the labour process.

Cooperatives The joint ownership and management of an organization between its customers and/or employees.

Core workforce Workers with organization-specific skills and high discretionary elements in their work.

Corporate manslaughter A legal term referring to the unlawful killing of an employee without malice aforethought but involving the transgression of health and safety standards, which directly or indirectly causes death to a human being.

Corporate strategic international human resource management The HRM policies and practices developed at corporate office level for managing people within the company's subsidiaries at home and in other countries.

Culture The set of values, understandings and ways of thinking that is shared by the majority of members of a work organization, and is taught to new employees as correct.

Deindustrialization The contraction of the manufacturing sector of the economy.

Delayering Restructuring an organization by reducing the number of grades and levels of work.

Deskilling An initiative taken by management to redesign jobs that leads to a reduction in needed job skills due to job simplification and new technology.

Development The process of improvement or enhancement – of an organization or individuals – through learning and maturation.

Developmental approach (to appraisal) An attempt to harness the potential of employees through the discussion of the development needs of employees.

Developmental humanistic approach A view of people that focuses on their potential for learning.

Development centres The use of assessment techniques to provide feedback for development.

Diagnostic approach (to manpower planning) The use of manpower data to understand manpower problems so that appropriate action can be taken.

Distributive bargaining A system of activities instrumental to the attainment of one party's goals when they are in basic conflict with those of the other party, for example pay bargaining.

Diversity management An approach to managing people that recognizes differences between people and the value of difference as a source of productive potential within an organization.

Downsizing The laying-off of employees to restructure the business.

e-Assessment Online testing used for selection and other HR purposes.

e-HR The use of information and communication technology (ICT) to complete a range of human resource activities.

e-Learning Learning through the medium of technology such as email, the Internet and computer software packages.

Emergent learning Learning derived by interaction with evolving situations such as dealing with customers, and used in the formation and formulation of strategy.

Emotional labour Work that has a requirement for the display of particular emotions and the suppression of others.

Employability Ensuring that, through workplace learning, employees' skills are transferable from one organization to another, making them more employable and thus less dependent.

Employee assistance programme (EAP) A set of actions or activities established by an employer that seeks to help employees overcome their personal problems (e.g. marital difficulties, alcohol or drug abuse) that may be adversely affecting their work performance.

Employee communication The transmission of information, and the exchange of meaning, between management and employees.

Employee discipline A process initiated by management to encourage compliance with the organization's employment rules or standards.

Employee involvement Processes providing employees with the opportunity to influence decision-making on matters that affect them.

Employee participation Involves workers exerting a countervailing and upward pressure on management control. This does not, however, imply unity between managers and non-managers.

Employment relationship This describes the dynamic, interlocking economic, legal, social and psychological relations that exist between individuals and their work organizations.

Empowering Limited power sharing: the delegation of power or authority to subordinates.

Epistemology The study of knowledge and the justification of belief. Questions such as 'Which beliefs are justified and which are not?', 'What, if anything, can we know?' and 'Do researchers reflect reality or create it?' are at the centre of epistemology.

Equality A view that people should be treated equally regardless of race, ethnic origin, gender, sexual orientation and other social categorizations.

e-Recruitment A fast-changing facet of e-HRM that encompasses both online general recruitment agents (for example Monster, StepStone), and recruitment sites established by companies for advertising their own vacancies.

Ethics The code of moral principles and values that governs the behaviour of an individual or group with respect to what is right or wrong.

Evaluation An attempt to assess the value derived from training and development activities.

Expectancy theory A process theory of motivation, stating that employees will direct their work effort towards behaviours that they believe will lead to desired outcomes.

Experience-based interview The use of questions in selection interviews that examine past performance in real situations.

Experimental research This is used to provide evidence regarding cause-and-effect relationships within the workplace with as much control as possible.

Face validity How selection and assessment techniques appear to those subjected to them.

Flexibility An approach to work arrangements that allows variation in practice by time, location, skill and payment.

Flexible working A wide range of initiatives that allow variations in the employment relationship, work practices and working time.

Fordism The application of Taylorist principles of job design to work performed on specialized machines, usually based on flow-line production assembly work. First applied by Henry Ford.

Foucauldian analysis Refers to the application of Michel Foucault's concepts of taxinomia, mathesis, examination and confession to human resource management (HRM). The hypothesis is that HRM practices play a key role in constituting the self, in defining the nature of work, and in organizing and controlling employees.

Four-task model of HRM A term used to describe the four primary responsibilities of the HR function that guide the choice of specific HRM policies and practices.

Globalization A worldwide process of integration of national economies, political and social convergence in which national governments and time and space become less significant.

Global strategy The current set of plans, decisions and objectives that have been adopted to achieve the organization's goals in the international marketplace.

Goal-setting The process of setting targets and objectives to improve performance (individual, team, department, organization).

Grapevine The process of informal communication network within an organization.

Group technology The grouping of machines and workers to form a logical 'whole task' that can be performed with minimum interference.

Groupthink The tendency of members of a highly cohesive group to adhere to shared views so strongly that they totally ignore external information inconsistent with these views.

Health and Safety at Work etc. Act 1974 A broad-ranging UK Act that imposes general duties on employers, employees, self-employed, manufacturers and suppliers of articles and substances used in the workplace, in order to prevent accidents and improve health and welfare in the workplace.

Hierarchy of strategy Refers to different levels of planning, decision-making and objectives formulated at functional, business and corporate level in multinational firms.

HR measurement The careful and deliberate observations of HR and work practices for the purpose of identifying outcomes. In HRM quantitative research, measurement provides a consistent 'yardstick' for gauging differences in outcomes and more precise estimates of the degree of relationship between variables.

HRM auditing A process of evaluating the effectiveness of the HR function.

HRM benchmarking A form of auditing that enables organizations to gauge their own practices against those in 'excellent' organizations, to learn from other organizations about effective HR

strategies, and to identify what actions need to be taken in order to improve, relative to those organizations.

HRM–performance link A hypothesis concerned with establishing causal connections between relevant HR-related variables and individual, group and/or organizational performance.

Human capital theory The view that people are worth investing in as a form of capital: that people's performance and the results achieved can be considered as a return on investment and assessed in terms of cost and benefits.

Human relations movement A movement that grew out of the Hawthorne experiments conducted by Elton Mayo in the 1920s, which emphasizes the psychological and social aspects of job design.

Human resource accounting The measurement and expression of HRM activities in financial terms.

Human resource development A term used to indicate training and development as an organization's investment in the learning of its people as part of an HRM approach.

Human resource management That part of the management process that specializes in the management of people in work organizations.

Human resource planning An HRM approach to planning, set in the context of organizations' views of people as the source of competitive advantage.

Human resource strategy The patterns of decisions regarding human resource policies and practices used by management to design work and select, train and develop, appraise, motivate and control workers.

Ideal type A model or social construct that serves as a measuring rod against which specific cases can be evaluated.

Image projection A loose model of the values, personality and attitudes of potential employees directed at appropriate labour markets.

Industrial relations The processes of regulation and control over the collective aspects of the employment relationship.

Integration-responsiveness grid A model that assumes global competitive strategies face two critical pressures: standardization of product or service and the integration of production pressures for cost reductions *and* differentiation and flexible production pressures for local responsiveness.

Internal equity Refers to the pay relationships between jobs within a single organization. It is translated into practice using reward techniques, and focuses on comparing jobs and individuals in terms of their relative contributions to the organization's objectives.

Internal labour markets Hierarchies of jobs and conditions of employment that are determined by rules internal to the organization rather than by external competitive forces in the wider labour market.

International human resource management Refers to all HRM policies and practices used to manage people in companies operating in more than one country.

International strategy *see* global strategy.

Interventionist approach The government or its agents seek to influence decision-making in organizations and make decisions on training and development in the interests of the economy as a whole.

Japanization A term used to encapsulate the adoption of Japanese-style management techniques such as team or cellular production, just-in-time and total quality control systems in Western organizations.

Job analysis The systematic process of collecting and evaluating information about the tasks, responsibilities and context of a specific job.

Job characteristic model A job design model developed by Hackman and Oldham (1980) suggesting that five core job characteristics – skill variety, task identity, task significance, autonomy and feedback – result in positive work experience.

Job description Descriptions of tasks and responsibilities that make up a job, usually derived from job analysis.

Job design The process of combining tasks and responsibilities to form complete jobs, and the relationships of jobs in the organization.

Job enlargement The horizontal expansion of tasks in a job.

Job enrichment Processes that assign greater responsibility for scheduling, coordinating and planning work to the employees who actually produce the product.

Job evaluation A systematic process designed to determine the relative worth of jobs within a single work organization.

Job rotation The periodic shifting of a worker from one task to another to reduce monotony and/or increase skill variety.

Joint consultation The involvement of employee representatives in discussion and consideration of matters that affect employees.

Knowledge-based organization An organization that values the collection, dissemination and utilization of new knowledge, with a view to innovation and the development of what is known.

Knowledge management Management of information and knowledge to enhance organization activities.

Knowledge work Paid work that is of an intellectual nature, non-repetitive, result-oriented, and engaging scientific and/or artistic knowledge demanding continuous learning and creativity.

Labour markets The markets that provide labour for organizations and vary in terms of size, education and skills.

Labour market segmentation A method of classifying the ways in which organizations seek to employ different kinds of workers.

Labour process The process by which a product is created from raw materials through the application of human labour.

Leadership A process whereby an individual exerts influence upon others in an organizational context.

Learning The process of attaining new knowledge, expertise or skills resulting from the processing and ongoing reinforcement of information and experience.

Learning climate or environment Physical and psychosocial variables in an organization that affect the efficiency of employees in realizing learning potential.

Learning cycle A view of adult learning that emphasizes learning as a continuous process. It is usually associated with the work of Kolb (1984).

Learning movement Encompasses the recommendations, ideas and exhortations relating to human resource development and learning at work, plus the structures to support these.

Learning organization A concept representing an ideal of whole organization learning by all employees, and the use of learning to transform the organization.

Learning style The way in which individuals prefer different aspects and ways of learning to others.

Learning transfer Learning from human resource development activities transferred to workplace behaviour and performance.

Line manager responsibility The acceptance by line managers of responsibility for the development of subordinates.

Low-cost leadership A business strategy that attempts to increase market share by emphasizing low cost compared to competitors.

Low-quality product–low-skill equilibrium Finegold and Soskice's (1988) explanation of the UK's failure to educate and train its workforce to the same levels as its competitors.

McDonaldization (also known as 'McWork' or 'McJobs') Symbolizes the new realities of corporate-driven globalization that engulf young people in the 21st century, including simple work patterns, electronic controls, low pay, part-time and temporary employment.

Management A set of roles in a work organization and the activities and skills associated with them, which are primarily concerned with planning, directing and communicating to achieve specified goals.

Management strategy The long-term planning and decision-making activities related to meeting organizational goals.

Managerialist perspective An ideology concerned primarily with the maximization of employee commitment and motivation through the adoption of appropriate HRM practices.

Managerial prerogative A belief that management should have unilateral control within an organization.

Manpower planning Processes, techniques and activities to ensure the necessary supply of people is forthcoming to allow organization targets to be met.

Manpower planning techniques and modelling Application of statistical techniques to models of manpower stocks and flow, allowing calculation of manpower decisions.

Measurement In human resources research, the term 'measurement' means systematic observation of workplace practices for the purpose of describing events and outcomes in terms of the attributes composing the variable.

Mentoring Help given by a more senior or experienced member of staff, providing one-to-one, career-related guidance and encouragement to a less experienced colleague, with a focus on longer term learning and development.

Multidomestic strategy The current set of plans, decisions and objectives that have been adopted to achieve the organization's goals in the domestic marketplace.

Multisource feedback (MSF) Feedback from a variety of sources for appraisal and development.

Networking The process of establishing professional relations with individuals and groups both within and outside the workplace.

New unionism Is internally focused and places a renewed emphasis on the recruitment and organization of new union members. It also refers to a trade union organizing strategy.

Non-verbal communication The process of coding meaning through individual behaviour such as hand gestures or facial expressions.

Normative model A theoretical model that describes how managers should make choices and decisions and provides guidelines for reaching an ideal outcome for the organization.

Offshoring Moving production and service provision to countries with low wages but similar or even higher skills.

Online testing Virtual testing via the Internet.

Organizational communication The systematic provision of information to employees concerning all aspects of their employment and the wider issues relating to the organization in which they work.

Organizational politics Those activities that are not required as part of a manager's formal role, but that influence the distribution of resources for the purpose of promoting personal objectives.

Organization learning An explanation of learning at an organizational level. Emphasis is placed on the 'potential' that individuals and work groups have to learn, and the means – through job redesign, empowerment and changing leadership style – they have to achieve these goals.

Outsourcing Sourcing aspects of production or service process by setting up a contractual relationship with an external provider.

Panopticon The panopticon is a 12-sided polygon with a central observatory tower through which prison guards can observe the behaviour of inmates. For Michel Foucault, the panopticon provides the architectural image of society's disciplinary power. Over time, constant observation induces in the inmate a state of consciousness and reduces the need for discipline so that the surveillance is permanent in its effects, even when it is discontinued.

Paradigm A framework of thinking based on fundamental assumptions providing explicit and implicit views about the nature of reality.

Paradox of consequence Organizational behaviour that has unintended consequences quite different from or even in direct opposition to what was originally intended.

Pay equity Pay relationships among jobs both within an organization (internal equity) and between comparative or competing organizations (external competitiveness).

Pay model A heuristic (learning device) designed to facilitate our understanding of the complex links between an organization's business strategy, reward objectives, the different reward options and techniques and the effect of markets on reward management.

Pendulum arbitration Form of arbitration that prohibits the arbitrator from recommending a compromise solution. The arbitrator must find in favour of either the employer or the income.

Performance and development plan The linking of a business aim with an individual's key areas of responsibility, the competencies that are expected to be demonstrated in performing a role and measurable objectives.

Performance appraisal Analysis of an employee's capabilities and potential drawn from assessment data of past and current work, behaviour and

performance, allowing decisions to be made in relation to purpose, for example human resource development needs.

Performance contracts Details of what a jobholder agrees to accomplish over time.

Performance control approach (to appraisal) Means by which employee performance can be measured, monitored and controlled.

Performance management system A systematic attempt to link organizational strategy to employees through the integration of activities that assess, appraise, develop and reward employees.

Performance rating Judgements of performance in terms of personality attributes, results and work outcomes, and behaviour within performance.

Peripheral workforce Workers outside the core workforce, for example temporary or casual workers.

Personnel management A function of management that coordinates the human resource needs of an organization, including the designation of work, employee selection, training and development, rewards, performance assessment and union–management relations.

Personnel specification Profile of the requirements of a person to fill a job used as a framework to assess applicants. Requirements may be expressed as 'essential' or 'desirable'.

Pluralist perspective A view of workplace relations which assumes that management and employees have different goals but seek a reconciliation of such differences.

Point method A method to establish pay structures in the workplace that has three common characteristics: (1) compensable factors, with (2) factor degrees numerically scaled and (3) weights reflecting the relative importance of each factor.

Post-Fordism Describes the development from mass production assembly lines to more flexible manufacturing processes.

Postindustrial society/organization The thesis that posits that the modern Western industrial society is moving into a 'postindustrial' era, where traditional manual work will disappear and large bureaucratic work organizations will be replaced by smaller organizations, 'adhocracies', characterized by high levels of flexibility and participation in decision-making.

Postmodernism This refers to the flexible, anti-hierarchical organizational structures that have come to replace the 'modern' rigid, hierarchical organizational structures of the past.

Power A term denoting the ability to influence others' behaviour.

Precarious employment Employment contracts that are part-time, short-term or temporary agency work, and also known as 'non-standard' employment.

Profit-sharing A scheme through which employees are given a share of company profits.

Psychological contract A metaphor that captures a variety of largely unwritten expectations and understandings of the two parties – employees and their organization – about their mutual obligations.

Psychometric tests Techniques to measure certain aspects of a person's behaviour in order to try to assess their suitability for a particular job.

Qualitative research Refers to the gathering and sorting of information through a variety of techniques, including interviews, focus groups, observations and the use of archival data in organizational files, records or reports.

Quality circle A small group of employees who hold regular meetings to ensure that quality within the workplace is maintained and improved.

Realistic job previews An opportunity for applicants to obtain a realistic picture of a job through job sampling, video, shadowing and case studies.

Recruitment Processes to attract applicants within appropriate labour markets for vacant positions within an organization.

Re-engineering A cross-functional initiative by senior management involving fundamental redesign of business processes to bring about changes in organizational structure, culture, information technology, job design and the management of people.

Reliability A statistical measure of the extent to which a selection or assessment technique achieves consistency in what it is measuring over repeated use.

Research design A plan created by the HR researcher or professional in order to make choices about how to handle the most important HR variables and how to study them. HRM research designs usually take the form of survey research, case studies, experimental research or meta-analysis.

Resource-based model An HR strategy that leverages people's knowledge and distinctive competences as a source of competitive advantage.

Return on investment The calculation of the cost of a HR intervention, such as training or an employee participation arrangement, and its determined benefit in monetary terms.

Reward All forms of financial returns and tangible services and benefits that employees receive as part of the employment relationship.

Safety committee A body of employees elected and appointed for the specific function of effectively promoting, developing and monitoring health, safety and wellness in the workplace according to statutory duties, regulations and guidelines.

Safety policy A set of guidelines and procedures that maintain health and safety in the workplace.

Scientific management A process of determining the division of work into its smallest possible skill elements, and how the process of completing each task can be standardized to achieve maximum efficiency. Also referred to as Taylorism.

Selection Processes to establish the most suitable applicants for vacant positions within an organization from a number of applicants.

Selection interviews The oldest and most widely used method of employee selection.

Self-appraisal A review of one's own performance.

Self-managed team A group of employees with different skills who rotate jobs and assume managerial responsibilities as they produce an entire product or service.

Sexual harassment Repeated, unwelcome behaviour with a sexual content when such behaviour creates an intimidating or offensive working environment.

Shared responsibility model A view that the best way to reduce levels of occupational accidents and disease and improve health and safety at work lies in cooperation between employers and employees.

Social capital The value of relationships between people, embedded in network links that facilitate trust and communication vital to overall organizational performance.

Social Charter European legislation created in 1989 to protect and improve workers' health and safety, communications, employee involvement and employment equity across Europe.

Social partnership A labour–management partnership typically at enterprise level that encourages the parties to develop a 'mutual gain' or 'productive coalition'. Such partnerships are associated with 'high-performance, high-commitment work systems'.

'So far as is reasonably practicable' A legal term that refers to standards by which health and safety statutory duties are to be carried out. It means that the employer must weigh the time and cost, and so on of complying with a general duty against the health and safety risks involved.

Sophisticated modernism A style of industrial relations management that encourages union membership, membership participation in trade unions, workplace union organization, and joint union–management involvement in areas of common interest in order to gain acceptance for change, to maximize cooperation, and to minimize conflict.

Sophisticated paternalism A style of industrial relations management that does not take for granted that employees accept the organization's goal (unitary perspective) and therefore management devote considerable resources to ensuring that their employees have the 'right' attitude and approach.

Standard modernism A style of industrial relations management that is pragmatic or opportunist. Trade unions and workplace union organizations are recognized but union–management relations tend to be viewed primarily as a 'reactive' activity; it is assumed to be non-problematic until events prove otherwise.

Strategic human resource development The process of responding to and influencing organization strategy through learning and development.

Strategic human resource management The process of linking the human resource function with the strategic objectives of the organization in order to improve performance.

Strategic management Denotes a specific pattern of decisions and actions undertaken by the upper echelon of an organization in order to accomplish specific outcomes and/or performance goals.

Synergy The concept that the whole is greater than the sum of its parts. The condition that exists when a group interacts and learns and produces a group outcome that is greater than the sum of the individuals acting alone.

Systematic training model An approach to training encouraged by industrial training boards in the 1960s, based on a four-stage process of identifying training needs and specifying objectives, designing a programme, implementing training and evaluation.

Tacit knowledge Knowledge that is gained through doing rather than learned through being taught.

Taylorism A management control strategy named after F. G. W. Taylor. A systematic theory of management, its defining characteristic has been the identification and measurement of work tasks so that the completion of tasks can be standardized to achieve maximum efficiency (*see also* scientific management).

Teleworking Working at a distance from an employer's premises but maintaining contact via telecommunications.

Theoretical perspective A set of assumptions used to view society, the workplace and people's behaviour. A theoretical perspective serves as a model as to which questions researchers should ask and how they should interpret the answers.

Third-party intervention A person (e.g. mediator) or party (e.g. ACAS), besides the two primarily concerned (e.g. employer and employee or trade union), involved in settling a claim or dispute.

Time and motion study The systematic observation, measurement and timing of movements in the completion of tasks to identify more efficient work behaviour.

Trade union density The proportion of the workforce belonging to a union.

Training champions Senior managers who contribute to an organization's philosophy of support for training and development.

Transferable skills Skills that can be transferred from one position to another.

Transfer of learning The process of applying learning from training and development events to workplace behaviour.

Transformational leadership The ability of leaders to motivate followers to believe in the vision of organizational transformation or re-engineering.

Transformation process Behaviour by which an employee converts attributes, skills, knowledge and attitudes into work outcomes and results.

Transnational strategy *see* global strategy.

Union recognition strategy A management strategy to accept the legitimacy of a trade union role and of collective bargaining as a process for regulating the employment relationship. This contrasts with union exclusion, a strategy to curtail the role of trade unions, and union opposition, a strategy to maintain a non-union company.

Union structure The relationship between the parts of the union.

Unitarist perspective A view of workplace relations which assumes that management and employees share common goals.

Upward appraisal A form of appraisal based on feedback from staff to their managers.

Validity A statistical measure of the extent to which a selection or assessment technique actually measures what it sets out to measure. Criterion validity measures the results of a technique against criteria such as present success of existing employees (concurrent validity) and future performance of recruits (predictive validity).

Voluntarist approach Encouragement, rather than compulsion, to organizations to take responsibility for their own training and development and its finance.

Welfare management The acceptance by employers of responsibility for the general welfare of their employees.

Wellness All HR and health and safety programmes and inverventions that can assist an employee to live at her or his highest possible level as a whole person, including physical, social, emotional and spiritual, and expands an employee's potential to live and work more effectively.

Whistle-blowing Employee disclosure of illegal, immoral, or illegitimate practices on the part of the organization.

Work Physical and mental activity that is carried out at a particular place and time, according to instructions, in return for money.

Working arrangements Activities associated with the work–effort exchange: allocation of work, work teams, functional flexibility.

Work–life balance The need to balance work and leisure/family activities.

Workplace learning A metaphor for capturing formal, self-directed, collective and informal learning activities in the organization.

Workplace wellness Any voluntary health-improving programme and activity instigated by the employer to effect changes in non-occupational health behaviour.

Works council A council set up within the workplace in order to maintain peaceful and cooperative employment relations. It will normally consist of management, employees and union representatives, and establishes two-way communication between employees and management, and unions and management.

Bibliography

Aart Scholte, J. (2005) *Globalization: A Critical Introduction*. Basingstoke: Palgrave Macmillan.

Abbott, A. (1988) *The System of Professions*. Chicago: University of Chicago Press.

Abraham, S. E., Karns, L. A., Shaw, K. and Mena, M. A. (2001) Managerial competencies and the managerial appraisal process. *Journal of Management Development*, **20**(10): 842–52.

Accounting for People Task Force (2003) *Report of the Accounting for People Task Force*. London: Department for Trade and Industry.

Ackroyd, S. and Thompson, P. (1999) *Organizational Misbehaviour*. Thousand Oaks, CA: Sage.

Adams, R. J. (1995) Canadian industrial relations in comparative perspective. In M. Gunderson and A. Ponak (eds) *Union–Management Relations in Canada* (3rd edn) (pp. 495–526). Don Mills, Ontario: Addison-Wesley.

Adams, R. J. (2006) *Labour Left Out*. Ottawa: Canadian Centre for Policy Alternatives.

Adams, T. and McQuillan, K. (2000) New jobs, new workers? Organizational restructuring and management hiring decisions. *Relations Industrielles/Industrial Relations*, **55**(3): 391–413.

Adamson, S. J., Doherty, N. and Viney, C. (1998) The meanings of career revisited: implications for theory and practice. *British Journal of Management*, **9**(4): 251–9.

Addison, J., Siebert, W., Wagner, J. and Wei, X. (2000) Worker participation and firm performance. *British Journal of Industrial Relations*, **38**(1): 7–48.

Adler, L. (2002a) *Hire With Your Head*. Chichester: John Wiley & Sons.

Adler, N. J. (1984) Women do not want international careers: and other myths about international management. *Organizational Dynamics,* **13**: 66–79.

Adler, N. J. (1987) Pacific basin managers: a gaijin, not a woman. *Human Resource Management*, **26**(2): 169–92.

Adler, N. J. (1994) Competitive frontiers: women managing across borders. In N. J. Adler and D. N. Izraeli (eds) *Competitive Frontiers: Women Managers in a Global Economy* (pp. 22–40). Oxford: Blackwell.

Adler, N. J. (2002b) Global managers: no longer men alone. *International Journal of Human Resource Management*, **13**(5): 743–60.

Adler, N. J. (2005) Shaping history: global leadership in the twenty-first century. In H. Scullion and M. Linehan (eds) *International Human Resource Management* (pp. 281–97). Basingstoke: Palgrave Macmillan.

Advisory, Conciliation and Arbitration Service (1987) *Working Together: The Way Forward*. Leeds: ACAS.

Advisory, Conciliation and Arbitration Service (1988) *Labour Flexibility in Britain: The 1987 ACAS Survey*. London: ACAS.

Agashae, Z. and Bratton, J. (2001) Leader–follower dynamics: developing a learning organization. *Journal of Workplace Learning*, **13**(3): 89–102.

Aktouf, O. (1996) *Traditional Management and Beyond*. Montreal: Morin.

Alberga, T. (1997) Time for a check-up. *People Management*, 6 February: 30–2.

Albizu, E. and Olazaran, M. (2006) BPR implementation in Europe: the adaptation of a management concept. *New Technology, Work and Employment*, **21**(1): 43–58.

Alliger, G., Tannenbaum, S., Bennett, W., Traver, H. and Shotland, A. (1997) A meta-analysis of the relations among training criteria. *Personnel Psychology*, **50**: 341–58.

Almond, P. and Rubery, J. (2000) Deregulation and societal systems. In M. Maurice and A. Sorge (eds) *Embedding Organizations* (pp. 176–94). Amsterdam: Benjamin.

Amit, R. and Shoemaker, P. J. H. (1993) Strategic assets and organizational rent. *Strategic Management Journal*, **14**, 33–46.

Anakwe, U. P. (2002) Human resource management practices in Nigeria: challenges and insights. *International Journal of Human Resource Management*, **13**(7): 1042–59.

Anderson, B. A. (2005) Expatriate selection: good management or good luck? *International Journal of Human Resource Management*, **16**(4): 567–83.

Anderson, J. (ed.) (1981) *Cognitive Skills and their Acquisition*. Hillsdale, NJ: Laurence Erlbaum.

Anderson, J., Gunderson, M. and Ponak, A. (1989) *Union–Management Relations in Canada*. Don Mills, Ontario: Addison-Wesley.

Andolšek, D. M. and Štebe, J. (2005) Devolution or (de)centralization of HRM function in European organizations. *International Journal of Human Resource Management*, **16**(3): 311–29.

Antonacopoulou, E. (2001) The paradoxical nature of the relationship between training and learning. *Journal of Management Studies*, **38**(3): 327–50.

Antonacopoulou, E., Ferdinand, J., Graca, M. and Easterby-Smith, M. (2005) *Dynamic Capabilities and Organizational Learning: Socio-Political Tensions in Organizational Renewal*. AIM Working Paper Series. London: Advanced Institute of Management.

Appelbaum, E. and Batt, R. (1994) *The New America Workplace: Transforming Systems in the United States*. Ithaca, NY: ICR/Cornell University Press.

Appelbaum, S. H and Donna, M. (2000) The realistic downsizing preview: a management intervention in the prevention of survivor syndrome. Part I. *Career Development International*, **5**(7): 333–50.

Apprenticeships Task Force (2005) *Apprenticeships Task Force – Final Report*. London: Apprenticeships Task Force.

Argyris, C. and Schön D. A. (1978) *Organizational Learning: A Theory of Action Perspective*. London: Addison Wesley.

Aries, E. (1996) *Men and Women in Interaction: Reconsidering the Differences*. New York: Oxford University Press.

Armstrong, J. (1987) Human resource management: a case of the emperor's new clothes? *Personnel Management*, **19**(8): 30–5.

Armstrong, M. (1998) *Employee Reward*. London: Institute for Personnel and Development.

Armstrong, M. and Baron, A. (2004) *Managing Performance* (2nd edn). London: Chartered Institute of Personnel and Development.

Armstrong, P. (1989) Limits and possibilities for HRM in an age of management accountancy. In J. Storey (ed.) *New Perspectives on Human Resource Management* (pp. 154–66). London: Routledge.

Arnold, J. (1997) *Managing Careers into the 21st Century*. London: Paul Chapman.

Aronowitz, S. (2005) On the future of American labour. *Working USA: The Journal of Labor and Society*, **8**: 271–91.

Arthur, J. (1994) Effects of human resources systems on manufacturing performance and turnover. *Academy of Management Journal*, **37**, 670–87.

Arthur, M. B. and Rousseau, D. M. (eds) (2000) *The Boundaryless Career*. Oxford: Oxford University Press.

Arthur, W., Woehr, D. J. and Graziano, W. G. (2001) Personality testing in employment settings. *Personnel Review*, **30**(6): 657–76.

Arvey, R. D. and Campion, J. E. (1982) The employment interview: a summary and review of recent research. *Personnel Psychology*, **35**, 281–322.

ASH (2005) Smoking statistics: illness and death. www.ash.org.uk.

Ashman, I. and Winstanley, D. (2006) The ethics of organizational commitment. *Business Ethics: A European Review*, **15**(2): 142–53.

Ashton, D. and Felstead, A. (1995) Training and development. In J. Storey. (ed.) *Human Resource Management* (pp. 234–53). London: Routledge.

Ashton, D. and Sung, J. (2002) *Supporting Work-place Learning for High Performance Working*. Geneva: International Labour Organization.

Atkinson, J. S. (1984) Manpower strategies for flexible organizations. *Personnel Management*, August: 28–31.

Atkinson, J. S. (1985) The changing corporation. In D. Clutterbuck (ed.) *New Patterns of Work* (pp. 13–34). Aldershot: Gower.

Atkinson, J. S. and Meager, N. (1985) Introduction and summary of main findings. In Atkinson, J. S. and Meager, N., *Changing Work Patterns* (pp. 2–11). London: National Economic Development Office.

Atwater, L. E., Waldman, D. A., Atwater, D. and Cartier, P. (2000) An upward feedback field experiment: supervisors' cynicism, reactions and commitment to subordinates. *Personnel Psychology*, **53**(2): 275–97.

Bach, S. D. (2002) Public-sector employment relations reforms under Labour: muddling through on modernization? *British Journal of Industrial Relations*, **40**(2): 319–39.

Bacon, N. and Storey, J. (1993) Individualization of the employment relationship and the implications for trade unions. *Employee Relations*, **15**(1): 5–17.

Bacon, N. and Storey, J. (2000) New employee relations strategies in Britain: towards individualism or partnership? *British Journal of Industrial Relations*, **38**(3): 407–27.

Bae, J., Chen, S., Wan, T., Lawler, J. and Walumbwa, F. (2003) Human resource strategy and firm performance in Pacific Rim countries. *International Journal of Human Resource Management*, **14**(8): 1308–32.

Baglioni, G. and Crouch, C. (1991) *European Industrial Relations: The Challenge of Flexibility*. London: Sage.

Bain, G. S. and Price, R. (1983) Union growth: determinants, and density. In G. S. Bain (ed.) *Industrial Relations in Britain* (pp. 3–33). Oxford: Blackwell.

Bain, P. (1997) Human resource malpractice: the deregulation of health and safety at work in the USA and Britain. *Industrial Relations Journal*, **28**(3): 176–91.

Bain, P. and Baldry, C. (1995) Sickness and control in the office – the sick building syndrome. *New Technology, Work and Employment*, **10**(1): 19–31.

Baker, T. (1999) *Doing Well by Doing Good*. Washington: Economic Policy Institute.

Baldamus, W. (1961) *Efficiency and Effort: An Analysis of Industrial Administration*. London: Tavistock.

Baldwin, T. T. and Ford, J. K. (1988) Transfer of training: a review and directions for future research. *Personnel Psychology*, **41**, 63–105.

Ball, B. (1997) Career management competences – the individual perspective. *Career Development International*, **2**(2): 74–9.

Ball, K. (2001) The use of human resource information systems: a survey. *Personnel Review*, **30**(6): 677–93.

Bamber, G. and Lansbury, R. R. (1998) *International and Comparative Employment Relations: A Study of Industrialised Market Economies* (3rd edn). London: Sage.

Bamber, G., Ryan, S. and Wailes, N. (2004) Globalization, employment relations and human indicators in ten developed market economies: international data sets. *International Journal of Human Resource Management*, **15**(8): 1481–516.

Bamberger, P. and Meshoulam, I. (2000) *Human Resource Management Strategy*. Thousand Oaks, CA: Sage.

Bamberger, P. and Phillips, B. (1991) Organizational environment and business strategy: parallel versus conflicting influences on human resource strategy in the pharmaceutical industry. *Human Resource Management*, **30**, 153–82.

Banker, R. D., Field, J. M., Schroeder, R. G. and Sinha, K. (1996) Impact of work teams on manufacturing performance: a longitudinal field study. *Academy of Management Journal*, **39**(4): 867–90.

Barber, A. E. (1998) *Recruiting Employees: Individual and Organizational Perspectives*. Thousand Oaks, CA: Sage.

Barber, A. E. and Bretz, R. (2000) Compensation, attraction and retention. In S. Rynes and B. Gerhart (eds) *Compensation in Organizations: Current Research and Practice* (pp. 32–60). San Francisco, CA: Jossey-Bass.

Barber, A. E., Wesson, M. J., Roberson, Q. M. and Taylor, M. S. (1999) A tale of two job markets: organizational size and its effects on hiring practices and job search behaviour. *Personnel Psychology*, **52**(4): 841–67.

Barclay, J. (1999) Employee selection: a question of structure. *Personnel Review*, **28**(1/2): 134–51.

Barclay, J. (2001) Improving selection interviews with structure: organisations' use of 'behavioural' interviews. *Personnel Review*, **30**(1): 81–101.

Barlow, G. (1989) Deficiencies and the perpetuation of power: latent functions in management appraisal. *Journal of Management Studies*, **26**(5): 499–517.

Barnes, C. (1996) What next? Disability, the 1995 Disability Discrimination Act and the Campaign for Peoples' Rights. Text of the Walter Lessing Lecture, presented at the National Skill Bureau for Disabled Students, Annual Conference, 2 March, Leeds.

Barney, J. B. (1991) Firm resources and sustained competitive advantage. *Journal of Management*, **17**(1): 99–120.

Barney, J., Wright, M. and Ketchen, D. J. (2001) The resource-based view of the firm: ten years after 1991. *Journal of Management*, **27**: 625–41.

Barrett, J. T. (1996) Trade unions in South Africa: dramatic change after apartheid ends. *Monthly Labor Review*, **119**(5): 37–46.

Bartholomew, D. J. (1971) The statistical approach to manpower planning. *Statistician*, **20**, 3–26.

Bartlett, C. A. and Ghoshal, S. (1989) *Managing across Borders: The Transnational Solution*. Boston, MA: Harvard Business School Press.

Bartol, K. and Locke, E. (2000) Compensation. In S. Rynes and B. Gerhart (eds) *Compensation in Organizations: Current Research and Practice* (pp. 104–47). San Francisco, CA: Jossey-Bass.

Bass, B. M. (1985) *Leadership and Performance Beyond Expectations*. New York: Free Press.

Bassett, P. (1987) *Strike Free: New Industrial Relations in Britain*. London: Papermac.

Bassett, P. (1988) Non-unionism's growing ranks. *Personnel Management*, March: 16–19.

Batstone, E. (1984) *Working Order*. Oxford: Blackwell.

Batstone, E. and Gourlay, S. (1986) *Unions, Unemployment and Innovation*. Oxford: Blackwell.

Batstone, E., Levie, H. and Moore, R. (1987) *New Technology and the Process of Labour Regulation*. Oxford: Oxford University Press.

Bauer, T. N., Truxillo, D. M., Sanchez, R. J., Craig, J. M., Ferrera, P. and Campion, M. A. (2001) Applicant reactions to selection: development of the selection procedural justice scale (SPJS) *Personnel Psychology*, **54**(2): 387–421.

Beatty, R. W. and Schneier, C. E. (1996) New human resource roles to impact organizational performance: from partner to players. *Human Resource Management*, **36**(1): 29–37.

Beatty, R. W., Huselid, M. A. and Schneier, C. E. (2003) The new HR metrics: scoring on the business scorecard. *Organizational Dynamics*, **32**(2): 107–21.

Beaumont, P. (1991) Trade unions and HRM. *Industrial Relations Journal*, **22**(4): 300–8.

Beaumont, P. (1992) *Public Sector Industrial Relations*. London: Routledge.

Becker, B. and Gerhart, B. (1996) The impact of HRM on organizational performance: progress and prospects. *Academy of Management Journal*, **39**, 779–801.

Beckett, D. (2000) Making workplace learning explicit: an epistemology of practice for the whole person. *Westminster Studies in Education*, **23**: 41–53.

Beckett, D. and Hager, P. (2002) *Life, Work and Learning: Practice in Postmodernity*. London: Routledge.

Beer, M. and Cannon, M. (2004) Promise and peril in implementing pay-for-performance. *Human Resource Management*, **43**(1): 3–48.

Beer, M., Spector, B., Lawrence, P. R., Quin Mills, D. and Walton, R. E. (1984) *Managing Human Assets*. New York: Free Press.

Belanger, J., Edwards, P. and Wright, M. (1999) Best HR practice and the multinational company. *Human Resource Management Journal*, **9**(3): 53–70.

Belcourt, M., Wright, P. C. and Saks, A. M. (2000) *Managing Performance Through Training and Development* (2nd edn). Scarborough, Ontario: Nelson.

Bell, D. (1989) Why manpower planning is back in vogue. *Personnel Management*, July: 40–3.

Bell, E., Taylor, R. and Thorpe, R. (2002) Organisational differentiation through badging: Investors in People and the value of the sign. *Journal of Management Studies*, **39**(8): 1071–85.

Bell, E., Taylor, R. and Hoque, K. (2004) *Workplace Training and the High Skills Vision: Where Does Investors in People Fit?* SKOPE Research Paper No.45. Warwick: Warwick University, Centre for Skills, Knowledge and Organisational Performance (SKOPE).

Bendal, S. E., Bottomley, C. R. and Cleverly, P. M. (1998) Building a new proposition for staff at NatWest UK. In P. Sparrow and M. Marchington (eds) *Human Resource Management: The New Agenda* (pp. 90–105). London: Financial Times/Pitman.

Bengtsson, L. (1992) Work organization and occupational qualification in CIM: the case of Swedish NC machine shops. *New Technology, Work and Employment*, **7**(1): 29–43.

Bennison, M. (1980) *The IMS Approach to Manpower Planning*. Brighton: IMS.

Benschop, Y and Doorewaard, H. (1998) Covered by equality. The gender subtext of organizations. *Organization Studies*, **19**(5): 787–805.

Benson, J. (1996) Management strategy and labour flexibility in Japanese manufacturing enterprises. *Human Resource Management Journal*, **6**(2): 44–57.

Benson, J. (2006) Japanese management, enterprise unions and company performance. *Industrial Relations Journal*, **37**(3): 242–58.

Benson, J. and Zhu, Y. (1999) Markets, firms and workers in Chinese state-owned enterprises. *Human Resource Management Journal*, **9**(4): 58–74.

Benson, J., Debroux, P., Yuasa, M. and Zhu, Y. (2000) Flexibility and labour management: Chinese manufacturing enterprises in the 1990s. *International Journal of Human Resource Management*, **11**(2): 183–96.

Bentham, K. (2002) Employer resistance to union certification: a case study of eight Canadian jurisdictions. *Relations Industrielles/Industrial Relations*, **57**(1): 159–87.

Bentley, K. (2005) A healthy workplace: more than 'lunch and learns'. *Network*, July: 13–16.

Berg, B. (2007) *Qualitative Research Methods for the Social Sciences* (6th edn). Boston: Allyn & Bacon.

Berggren, C. and Nomura, M. (1997) *The Resilience of Corporate Japan: New Competitive Strategies and Personnel Practices*. London: Paul Chapman.

Bertua, C., Anderson, N. and Salgado, J. (2005) The predictive validity of cognitive ability tests: A UK meta-analysis. *Journal of Occupational and Organizational Psychology*, **78**, 387–409.

Betcherman, G., McMullen, K., Leckie, N. and Caron, C. (1994) *The Canadian Workplace in Transition*. Queen's University, Kingston, Ontario: IRC Press.

Bevan, S. (1991) *Staff Retention – a Manager's Guide*. Report 203. Brighton: IMS.

Beynon, H. (1984) *Working for Ford*. Harmondsworth: Penguin.

Billett, S. (2001) Learning through work: workplace learning affordances and individual engagement. *Journal of Workplace Learning*, **13**(5): 209–15.

Bin Idris, A. R. and Eldridge, D. (1998) Reconceptualising human resource planning in response to institutional change. *International Journal of Manpower*, **19**(5): 343–57.

Birdthistle, N. and Fleming, P. (2005) Creating a learning organization within the family business: an Irish perspective. *Journal of European Industrial Training*, **29**(9): 730–50.

Blanchard, O., Dornbusch, R., Krugman, P., Layard, R. and Summers, L. (1991) *Reform in Eastern Europe*. Cambridge, MA: MIT Press.

Blinder, A. (ed.) (1990) *Paying for Productivity*. Washington, DC: Brooking Institute.

Bloom, N., Conway, N., Mole, K., Möslein, K., Neely, A. and Frost, C. (2004) *Solving the Skills Gap*. London: Advanced Institute of Management Research.

Blum, S. (1997) Preventing culture shock. *Smythe Dorward Lambert Review*, Winter/Spring: 4–5.

Blundell, R., Dearden, L., Meghir, C. and Sianesi, B. (1999) Human capital investment: the returns from education and training to the individual, the firm and the economy. *Fiscal Studies*, **20**(1): 1–23.

Blyton, P. and Turnbull, P. (1992) HRM: debates, dilemmas and contradictions. In P. Blyton and P. Turnbull (eds) *Reassessing Human Resource Management* (pp. 1–15). London: Sage.

Blyton, P. and Turnbull, P. (1998) *The Dynamic of Employee Relations* (2nd edn). Basingstoke: Macmillan – now Palgrave Macmillan.

Boam, S. and Sparrow, P. (1992) *Designing and Achieving Competency*. Maidenhead: McGraw-Hill.

Bonache, J. and Fernandez, Z. V. (2005) International compensation: costs and benefits of international assignments. In H. Scullion and M. Linehan (eds) *International Human Resource Management* (pp. 114–30). Basingstoke: Palgrave Macmillan.

Bonney, N. (2005) Overworked Britons? Part-time work and work–life balance. *Work, Employment and Society*, **19**(2): 391–401.

Booth, R. (1985) What's new in health and safety management? *Personnel Management*, April: 17–23.

Boselie, P., Paauwe, J. and Jansen, P. G. W. (2001) Human resource management and performance: lessons from the Netherlands. *International Journal of Human Resource Management*, **12**(7): 1107–25.

Boselie, P., Dietz, G. and Boon, C. (2005) Commonalities and contradictions in HRM and performance research. *Human Resource Management Journal*, **15**(3): 67–94.

Bosquet, M. (1980) The meaning of job enrichment. In T. Nichols (ed.) *Capital and Labour* (pp. 370–80). Glasgow: Fontana.

Bottomore, T. B. and Rubel, M. (1956) *Karl Marx: Selected Writings in Sociology and Social Philosophy*. London: Penguin.

Boud, D. and Garrick, J. (eds) (1999) *Understanding Learning at Work*. London: Routledge.

Bowen, D. (1992) Bigger is better in Britain's battered industry. *Independent on Sunday*, 26 July.

Bowen, D. E. and Ostroff, C. (2004) Understanding HRM–firm performance linkages: the role of the 'strength' of the HRM system.

Academy of Management Review, **29**(2): 203–21.

Boxall, P. F. (1992) Strategic human resource management: beginnings of a new theoretical sophistication? *Human Resource Management Journal*, **2**(3): 60–79.

Boxall, P. F. (1995) Building the theory of comparative HRM. *Human Resource Management Journal*, **5**(5): 5–17.

Boxall, P. F. (1996) The strategic HRM debate and the resource-based view of the firm. *Human Resource Management Journal*, **6**(3): 59–75.

Boxall, P. F. (2003) HR strategy and competitive advantage in the service sector. *Human Resource Management Journal*, **13**(3): 5–20.

Boxall, P. F. and Purcell, J. (2003) *Strategy and Human Resource Management*. Basingstoke: Palgrave Macmillan.

Boydell, T. H. (1976) *Guide to the Identification of Training Needs* (2nd edn). London: BACIE.

Brady, T. and Davies, A. (2004) Building project capabilities: from exploratory to exploitive learning. *Organization Studies*, **25**(9): 1601–21.

Bramley, P. (1989) Effective training. *Journal of European Industrial Training*, 13.

Brannen, P., Batstone, E., Fatchett, D. and White, P. (1976) *The Worker Directors*. London: Hutchinson.

Bratton, J. (1991) Japanization at work: the case of engineering plants in Leeds. *Work, Employment and Society*, **5**(3): 377–95.

Bratton, J. (1992) *Japanization at Work: Managerial Studies for the 1990s*. Basingstoke: Macmillan – now Palgrave Macmillan.

Bratton, J. (1999) Gaps in the workplace learning paradigm: labour flexibility and job design. 1st International Conference on Researching Work and Learning, University of Leeds, UK.

Bratton, J. (2001) Why workers are reluctant learners: the case of the Canadian pulp and paper industry. *Journal of Workplace Learning*, **13**(7/8): 333–43.

Bratton, J. (2005) Work redesign and learning at work: a win–win game? In E. Poikela (ed.) *Osaaminen ja Kokemus – työ, oppiminen ja kasvatus*. Tampere, Finland: Tampere University Press.

Bratton, J., Grint, K. and Nelson, D. (2004) *Organizational Leadership*. Mason, OH: South-Western Thompson.

Bratton, J., Helm-Mills, J., Pyrch, T. and Sawchuk, P. (2003) *Workplace Learning: A Critical Introduction*. Toronto: Garamond Press.

Braverman, H. (1974) *Labour and Monopoly Capital*. New York: Monthly Review Press.

Brewster, C. (1992) Starting again: industrial relations in Czechoslovakia. *Human Resource Management Journal*, **3**(3): 555–74.

Brewster, C. (1994) European HRM: Reflection of, or challenges to, the American concept. In P. S. Kirkbride (ed.) *Human Resource Management in Europe* (pp. 56–89). London: Routledge.

Brewster, C. (1995) Towards a 'European model' of human resource management. *Journal of International Business Studies*, First Quarter: 1–21.

Brewster, C. (2001) HRM: 'the comparative dimension'. In J. Storey (ed.) *Human Resource Management: A Critical Text* (pp. 255–71). London: Thompson Learning.

Brewster, C. and Scullion H. (1997) A review and an agenda for expatriate HRM. *Human Resource Management Journal*, **7**(3): 32–41.

Brewster, C., Hegewisch, A. and Mayne, L. (1994) Trends in European HRM: signs of convergence? In P. Kirkbride (ed.) *Human Resource Management in Europe* (pp. 114–32). London: Routledge.

Brewster, C., Larsen, H. and Mayrhofer, W. (1999) Human resource management: a strategic approach. In C. Brewster and H. Larsen (eds) *Human Resource Management in Northern Europe* (pp. 225–71). Oxford: Blackwell.

Brewster, C., Mayrhofer, W. and Morley, M. (eds) (2000) *New Challenges for European Human Resource Management*. New York: St Martins Press.

Brewster, C., Tregaskis, O., Hegewisch, A. and Mayne, L. (1996) Comparative research in human resource management: a review and an example. *International Journal of Human Resource Management*, **7**(3): 585–604.

Brewster, C., Wood, G., Brookes, M. and Van Ommeren, J. (2006) What determines the size of the HR function? A cross-nation analysis. *Human Resource Management*, **45**(1): 3–21.

Broderick, R. and Boudreau, J. W. (1992) HRM, IT and the competitive edge. *Academy of Management Executive*, **6**(2): 7–17.

Broughton, A. and Gilman, M. (2001) European industrial relations in 2000: a chronicle of events. *British Journal of Industrial Relations*, **32**(5): 494–516.

Brown, A. (2005) Implementing performance management in England's primary schools. *International Journal of Productivity and Performance Management*, **54**(5/6): 468–81.

Brown, J. S. and Duguid, P. (1991) Organizational learning and communities-of-practice: toward a unified view of working, learning and innovation. *Organization Science*, **2**(1): 40–7.

Brown, M. (2001) Unequal pay, unequal responses? Pay referents and their implications for pay level satisfaction. *Journal of Management Studies*, **38**(6): 879–96.

Brown, M. and Heywood, J. (2005) Performance appraisal systems: determinants and change. *British Journal of Industrial Relations*, **43**(4): 659–79.

Brown, W. (1988) The employment relationship in sociological theory. In D. Gallie (ed.) *Employment in Britain* (pp. 33–66). Oxford: Blackwell.

Brown, W. (1989) Managing remuneration. In K. Sisson (ed.) *Personnel Management in Britain* (pp. 249–70). Oxford: Blackwell.

Brown, W. (2000) Putting partnership into practice in Britain. *British Journal of Industrial Relations*, **38**(2): 299–316.

Brown, W., Deakin, S. and Ryan, P. (1997) The effects of British industrial relations legislation. *National Institute Economic Review*, **161**: 69–83.

Brown, W., Deakin, S., Nash, D. and Oxenbridge, S. (2000) The employment contract: from collective procedures to individual rights. *British Journal of Industrial Relations*, **38**(4): 611–29.

Bryson, A. (2004) Management responsiveness to union and nonunion worker voice in Britain. *Industrial Relations*, **43**(1): 213–41.

Buchanan, D. A. (1997) The limitations and opportunities of business process re-engineering in a politicized organizational climate. *Human Relations*, **50**(1): 51–72.

Buckingham, G. (2000) Same indifference. *People Management*, **6**(4): 44–6.

Budhwar, P. S. and Boyne, G. (2004) Human resource management in the Indian public and private sectors: an empirical comparison. *International Journal of Human Resource Management*, **15**(2): 346–70.

Budhwar, P. S. and Debrah, Y. (2005) International HRM in developing countries. In H. Scullion and M. Linehan (eds) *International Human Resource Management* (pp. 259–78). Basingstoke: Palgrave Macmillan.

Bullock, Lord (1977) *Report of the Committee of Inquiry on Industrial Democracy*. Cmnd 6706. London: HMSO.

Burawoy, M. (1979) *Manufacturing Consent: Changes in the Labour Process Under Monopoly Capitalism*. Chicago: Chicago University Press.

Burchell, B., Day, D., Hudson, M., et al. (1999) *Job Insecurity and Work Intensification: Flexibility and the Changing Boundaries of Work*. York: Joseph Rowntree Foundation.

Burke, J. (1985) *The Day the Universe Changed*. Boston, MA: Little, Brown.

Burkett, H. (2005) ROI on a shoestring: evaluation strategies for resource-constrained environments or ROI on a shoestring. *Industrial and Commercial Training*, **37**(2): 97–105.

Butler, A. B. and Skattebo, A. L. (2004) What is acceptable for women may not be for men: The effect of family conflicts with work on job performance ratings. *Journal of Occupational and Organizational Psychology*, **77**: 553–64.

Buyens, D. and De Vos, A. (2001) Perceptions of the value of HR function. *Human Resource Management Journal*, **11**(3): 70–89.

Byers, P. Y. (ed.) (1997) *Organizational Communication: Theory and Behavior*. Boston: Allyn & Bacon.

Byrne, D. (1998) *Complexity Theory and the Social Sciences*. London: Routledge.

Cable, D. M. and Parsons, C. K. (2001) Socialization tactics and person–organization fit. *Personnel Psychology*, **54**(1): 1–23.

Caldwell, R. (2001) Champions, adaptors, consultants and synergists: the new change agents in HRM. *Human Resource Management Journal*, **11**(3): 39–52.

Caligiuri, P. M. and Tung, R. (1999) Comparing the success of male and female expatriates IToma V.S.-based company. *International Journal of Human Resource Management*, **10**(5): 763–82.

Caligiuri, P. M., Lazarova, M. and Tarique, L. (2005) Training, learning and development in multinational organizations. In H. Scullion and M. Linehan (eds) *International Human Resource Management* (pp. 71–90). Basingstoke: Palgrave Macmillan.

Callaghan, G. and Thompson, P. (2001) Edwards revisited: technical control and worker agency in call centres. *Economic and Industrial Democracy*, **22**: 13–37.

Campbell, D. J. and Lee, C. (1988) Self-appraisal in performance evaluation. *Academy of Management Review*, **13**(2): 3–8.

Campbell, M. (1999) *Learning Pays and Learning Works*. London: National Advisory Council for Education and Training Targets.

Campion, M. A., Palmer, D. K. and Campion, J. E. (1997) A review of structure in the selection interview. *Personnel Psychology*, **50**: 655–702.

Cannell, M. (2002) Class struggle. *People Management*, **8**(5): 46–7.

Cannon, M. and Witherspoon, R. (2005) Actionable feedback: unlocking the power of learning and performance improvement. *Academy of Management Executive*, **19**(2): 120–34.

Cappelli, P. (1984) Competitive pressures and labor relations in the airline industry. *Industrial Relations*, **24**: 316–18.

Cappelli, P. and Chalykoff, J. (1985) The effects of management industrial relations strategy: results of a survey. In J. Anderson, M. Gunderson and A. Ponak (1989) *Union–Management Relations in Canada*. Don Mills, Ontario: Addison-Wesley.

Cappelli, P. and Singh, H. (1992) Integrating strategic human resources and strategic management. In D. Lewin, O. S. Mitchell and P. Sherer (eds) *Research Frontiers in Industrial Relations and Human Resources* (pp. 165–92). Madison, WI: Industrial Relations Research Association.

Carless, S. A. (2005) Person–job fit versus person–organization fit as predictors of organizational attraction and job acceptance intentions: a longitudinal study. *Journal of Occupational and Organizational Psychology*, **78**: 411–29.

Carrick, P. and Williams, R. (1999) Development centres – a review of assumptions. *Human Resource Management Journal*, **9**(2): 77–92.

Carrington, L. (2005) The ex-factor. *People Management*, 10 February: 36–8.

Carter, A. (2001) *Executive Coaching: Inspiring Performance at Work*. Report no. 379. Sussex: Institute for Employment Studies.

Caruth, D. and Handlogten, G. (2001) *Managing Compensation: A Handbook for the Perplexed*. Westport, CT: Quorum.

Castells, M. (1996) *The Rise of the Network Society*. Oxford: Blackwell.

Castells, M. (2000) Information technology and global capitalism. In W. Hutton and A. Giddens (eds) *On the Edge: Living with Global Capitalism* (pp. 52–74). London: Cape.

Caulkin, S. (2001) The time is now. *People Management*, **7**(17): 32–4.

Ceci, S. and Williams, W. (2000) Smart bomb. *People Management*, **6**(17): 32–6.

Centre for Labour–Management Development (2001) Progressive Discipline. Toronto, CLMD.

Chalmers, N. (1989) *Industrial Relations in Japan: The Peripheral Workforce*. London: Routledge.

Chamberlain, N. and Kuhn, J. (1965) *Collective Bargaining* (2nd edn). New York: McGraw-Hill.

Champy, J. (1996) *Reengineering Management: The Mandate for New Leadership*. New York: Harper-Collins.

Chandler, A. (1962) *Strategy and Structure*. Cambridge, MA: MIT Press.

Chapman, D. and Zweig, D. (2005) Developing a nomological network for interview structure: antecedents and consequences of the structured selection interview. *Personnel Psychology*, **58**: 673–702.

Charles, N. and James, E. (2003) The gender dimensions of job insecurity in a local labour market. *Work, Employment and Society*, **17**(3): 531–52.

Charlwood, A. (2002) Why do non-union employees want to unionize? Evidence from Britain. *British Journal of Industrial Relations*, **40**(3): 463–91.

Charmaz, K. (2000) Grounded theory: objectivist and constructivist methods. In N. Denzin and Y. Lincoln (eds) *Handbook of Qualitative Research* (2nd edn) (pp. 509–35). Thousand Oaks, CA: Sage.

Chartered Institute of Personnel and Development (2003) *Managing Careers Survey*. London: CIPD.

Chartered Institute of Personnel and Development (2005a) *Human Capital Reporting: An Internal Perspective*. London: CIPD.

Chartered Institute of Personnel and Development (2005b) *Recruitment, Retention and Turnover*. London: CIPD.

Chartered Institute of Personnel and Development (2005c) *Performance Management*. London: CIPD.

Chartered Institute of Personnel and Development (2005d) *Training and Development*. London: CIPD.

Chartered Institute of Personnel and Development (2006a) *Offshoring and the Role of HR*. London: CIPD.

Chartered Institute of Personnel and Development (2006b) *Reward Management: Survey Report*. London: CIPD.

Chiaburu, D. and Tekleab, A. (2005) Individual and contextual influences on multiple dimensions of training effectiveness. *Journal of European Industrial Training*, **29**(8): 604–26.

Child, J. (1972) Organizational structure, environment and performance: the role of strategic choice. *Sociology*, **6**(1): 331–50.

Child, J. (1994) *Management in China in the Age of Reform*. Cambridge: Cambridge University Press.

Chisholm, P. (2001) Redesigning work. *MacLean's*, 5 March: 16–19.

Chiu, W., Thomson, D., Mak, W. and Lo, K. L. (1999) Re-thinking training needs analysis. *Personnel Review*, **28**(1/2): 77–90.

Chomsky, N. (1999) *Profit over People*. New York: Seven Stories Press.

Chossudovsky, M. (2003) *The Globalization of Poverty and the New World Order*. Pincourt: CRG.

Chou, B. K. (2005) Implementing the reform of performance appraisal in China's civil service. *China Information*, **19**(1): 39–65.

Cin, B.-C., Han, T.-S. and Smith, S. (2003) A tale of two tigers: employee financial participation in Korea and Taiwan. *International Journal of Human Resource Management*, **14**(6): 920–41.

Clark, I. and Almond, P. (2004) Dynamism and embeddedness: towards a lower road? British subsidaries of American multinationals. *Industrial Relations Journal*, **35**(6): 536–56.

Clark, J. (ed.) (1993) *Human Resource Management and Technical Change*. London: Sage.

Clark, T. and Pugh, D. (2000) Similarities and differences in European conceptions of human resource management. *International Studies of Management and Organizations*, **29**(4): 84–100.

Clark, T., Grant, D. and Heijltjes, M. (2000) Researching comparative and international human resource management. *International Studies of Management and Organization*, **29**(4): 6–23.

Clarke, L. (1997) Changing work systems, changing social relations. *Relations Industrielles/Industrial Relations*, **52**(4): 839–61.

Clarke, N. (2003) The politics of training needs analysis. *Journal of Workplace Learning*, **15**(4): 141–53.

Clarke, N. (2004) HRD and the challenges of assessing learning in the workplace. *International Journal of Training and Development*, **8**(2): 140–56.

Clarke, N. (2006) Why HR policies fail to support workplace learning: the complexities of policy implementation in healthcare. *International Journal of Human Resource Management*, **17**(1): 190–206.

Clarke, T. (1977) Industrial democracy: the institutional suppression of industrial conflict. In T. Clarke and L. Clements (eds) *Trade Unions under Capitalism* (pp. 351–82). London: Fontana.

Clarke, T. and Dopp, S. (2001) *Challenging McWorld*. Ottawa: Canadian Centre for Policy Alternatives.

Clarke, T. and Hermens, A. (2001) Corporate developments and strategic alliances in e-learning. *Education + Training*, **43**(4): 256–67.

Clausen, C. and Lorentzen, B. (1993) Workplace implications of FMS and CIM in Denmark and Sweden. *New Technology, Work and Employment*, **8**(1): 21–30.

Claydon, T. (1989) Union de-recognition in Britain in the 1980s. *British Journal of Industrial Relations*, **27**(2): 214–24.

Clayton, T. (1998) Problematizing partnerships: the prospects for a cooperative bargaining agenda. In P. Sparrow and M. Marchington (eds) *Human Resource Management: The New Agenda* (pp. 180–92). London: Financial Times Management.

Clayton, T. (2000) Employee participation and involvement. In D. Winstanley and J. Woodall (eds) *Ethical Issues in Contemporary Human Resource Management* (pp. 208–23) Basingstoke: Palgrave – now Palgrave Macmillan.

Clegg, H. (1976) *Trade Unionism Under Collective Bargaining*. Oxford: Blackwell.

Clegg, H. (1979) *The Changing System of Industrial Relations in Great Britain*. Oxford: Blackwell.

Clegg, S. R. (1990) *Modern Organizations: Organization Studies in the Postmodern World*. London: Sage.

Clegg, S. R. and Dunkerley, D. (1980) *Organization, Class and Control*. London: Routledge & Kegan Paul.

Clegg, S. R. and Hardy, C. (eds) (1999) *Studying Organizations: Theory and Method*. London: Sage.

Cloke, K. and Goldsmith, J. (2002) *The End of Management and the Rise of Organizational Democracy*. San Francisco, CA: Jossey-Bass.

Clutterbuck, D. and Megginson, D. (2005) How to create a coaching culture. *People Management*, 21 April: 44–5.

Coates, D. (1975) *The Labour Party and the Struggle for Socialism*. Cambridge: Polity Press.

Coffield, F., Moseley, D., Hall, E. and Ecclestone, K. (2004) *Learning Styles and Pedagogy in Post-16 Learning: A Systematic and Critical Review*. Wiltshire: Learning and Skills Research Centre.

Coleman, S. and Keep, E. (2001) Background literature review for PIU project on workforce development.www.cabinet-office.gov.uk/innovation/2001/workforce/literaturereview.pdf.

Colling, T. (1995) Experiencing turbulence: competition, strategic choice and the management of human resources in British Airways. *Human Resource Management*, **5**(5): 18–32.

Colling, T. (2005) Managing human resources in the networked organization. In S. Bach (ed.) *Managing Human Resources* (pp. 90–112). Oxford: Blackwell.

Collins, C. and Han, J. (2004) Exploring applicant pool quantity and quality: the effects of early recruitment strategies, corporate advertising and firm reputation. *Personnel Psychology*, **57**: 685–717.

Collins, J. M. and Muchinsky, P. M. (1993) An assessment of the construct validity of three job evaluation methods: a field experiment. *Academy of Management Journal*, **36**, 895–904.

Conger, J. and Kanungo, R. (eds) (1988) *Charismatic Leadership*. San Francisco: Jossey-Bass.

Conley, H. (2002) A state of insecurity: temporary work in the public services. *Work, Employment and Society*, **16**(4): 725–37.

Connerley, M. L., Carlson, K. D. and Mecham, R. L. (2003) Evidence of differences in applicant pool quality. *Personnel Review*, **32**(1): 22–39.

Contu, A., Grey, C. and Örtenblad, A. (2003) Against learning. *Human Relations*, **56**(8): 931–52.

Conway, H. E. (1987) *Equal Pay for Work of Equal Value Legislation in Canada: An Analysis*. Ottawa: Studies in Social Policy.

Cook, J. and Crossman, A. (2004) Satisfaction with performance appraisal systems. *Journal of Managerial Psychology*, **19**(5): 526–41.

Cook, M. (1994) *Personnel Selection and Productivity*. Chichester: Wiley.

Cooke, F. L. (2000) *Human Resource Strategy to Improve Organisational Performance: A Route for British Firms?* Working Paper 9. Economic and Social Research Council Future of Work Programme. Swindon: ESRC.

Cooke, F. L. (2004) Foreign firms in China: modelling HRM in a toy manufacturing corporation. *International Journal of Human Resource Management*, **14**(3): 31–52.

Cooke, W. N. (2005) Exercising power in a prisoner's dilemma: transnational collective bargaining in an era of corporate globalization? *Industrial Relations Journal*, **36**(4): 283–302.

Coopey, J. (1996) Crucial gaps in the 'learning organization'. In K. Starkey (ed.) *How Organizations Learn* (pp. 348–67). London: International Thomson Business.

Coriat, B. (1980) The restructuring of the assembly line: a new economy of time and control. *Capital and Class*, (11): 34–43.

Coulson, A. (1999) Local business representation: can we afford TECs and chambers? *Regional Studies*, **33**(3): 269–73.

Council for Excellence in Management and Leadership (2002) *Managers and Leaders: Raising Our Game*. London: CEML.

Coupar, W. and Stevens, B. (1998) Towards a new model of industrial partnership. In P. Sparrow and M. Marchington (eds) *Human Resource Management: A New Agenda* (pp. 145–59). London: Financial Times Management.

Cowling, A. and Walters, M. (1990) Manpower planning – where are we today? *Personnel Review*, **19**(3): 3–8.

Coyle-Shapiro, J. and Kessler, I. (2000) Consequences of the psychological contract for the employment relationship: a large-scale survey. *Journal of Management Studies*, **37**(7): 903–30.

Coyle-Shapiro, J. A.-M., Shore, L., Taylor, M. S. and Tetrick, L. (2005) *The Employment Relationship*. Oxford: Oxford University Press.

Craig, M. (1981) *Office Worker's Survival Handbook*. London: BSSR.

Crane, D. (ed.) (1994) *The Sociology of Culture*. Cambridge, MA: Blackwell.

Crawford, M. (1995) *Talking Differences: On Gender and Language*. Thousand Oaks, CA: Sage.

Cressey, P. (1998) European works councils in practice. *Human Resource Management Journal*, **8**(1): 67–81.

Cross, B. and Travaglione, A. (2004) The times they are a-changing: who will stay and who will go in a downsizing organization? *Personnel Review*, **33**(3): 275–90.

Crossan, M. M. (1999) An organizational learning framework: from intuition to institution. *Academy of Management Review*, **24**(3): 522–38.

Crouch, C. (1982) *The Politics of Industrial Relations* (2nd edn). London: Fontana.

Crow, G. (2005) *The Art of Sociological Argument*. Basingstoke: Palgrave Macmillan.

Cullen, L. (2002) *A Job To Die for: Why so Many Americans Are Killed, Injured or Made Ill at Work and What To Do About It*. Monroe, ME: Common Courage Press.

Cully, M., O'Reilly, A., Woodland, S. and Dix, G. (1998) The 1998 Workplace Employee Relations Survey, first findings. www.dti.gov.uk/emar.

Cully, M., Woodland, S., O'Reilly, A. and Dix, G. (1999) *Britain at Work*. London: Routledge.

Cunningham, S., Ryan, Y., Stedman, L., Bagdon, K., Flew, T. and Coaldrake, P. (2000) *The Business of Borderless Education*. Canberra: Department of Education, Training and Youth Affairs.

Curnow, B. (1986) The creative approach to pay. *Personnel Management*, October: 32–6.

Czerny, A. (2004) Not so quick and easy. *People Management*, 26 February: 14–15.

Daft, R. (2001) *Organization Theory and Design* (7th edn). Cincinnati, OH: South-Western.

Dalen, L. H., Stanton, N. A. and Roberts, A. D. (2001) Faking personality questionnaires in personnel selection. *Journal of Management Development*, **20**(8): 729–41.

Dancy, J. (1985) *Introduction to Contemporary Epistemology*. Oxford: Blackwell.

Danford, A., Richardson, M. and Upchurch, M. (2005) *New Unions, New Workplaces: Strategies for Union Revival*. London: Taylor & Francis.

Daniel, W. W. and Millward, N. (1983) *Workplace Industrial Relations in Britain*. London: Heinemann.

Daniel, W. W. and Millward, N. (1993) Findings from the Workplace Industrial Relations Surveys. In J. Clark (ed.) *Human Resource Management and Technical Change* (pp. 943–77). London: Sage.

Daniels, K. and Macdonald, L. (2005) *Equality, Diversity and Discrimination*. London: Chartered Institute of Personnel and Development.

Davidow, W. H. and Malone, M. S. (1992) *The Virtual Corporation: Structuring and Revitalizing the Corporation for the 21st Century*. New York: Harper Business.

Davidson, M. J. and Cooper, C. L. (1992) *Shattering the Glass Ceiling*. London: Paul Chapman.

Dawson, M. (2005) Costa's 'filter' gets the right employees. *Human Resource Management International Digest*, **13**(4): 21–2.

Debono, J. (2001) Sexual harassment in employment: an examination of decisions looking for evidence of a sexist jurisprudence. *New Zealand Journal of Industrial Relations*, **26**(3): 329–40.

De Cieri, H. and Dowling, P. (1999) Strategic human resource management in multinational enterprises: theoretical and empirical developments. In P. Wright, L. Dyer, J. Boudreau and G. Milkovich (eds) *Research in Personnel and Human Resource Management* (pp. 305–27). Stanford, CT: JA Press.

De Cieri, H., Holmes, B., Abbott, J. and Pettit, T. (2005) Achievements and challenges for work/life balance strategies in Australian organizations. *International Journal of Human Resource Management*, **16**(1): 90–103.

Deery, S. (1995) The demise of the trade union as a representative body? *British Journal of Industrial Relations*, **33**(4): 537–43.

Deery, S. and Kinnie, N. (2004) *Call Centres and Human Resource Management: A Cross-national Perspective*. Basingstoke: Palgrave Macmillan.

Delaney, J. T. and Huselid, M. A. (1996) The impact of HRM practices on perceptions of organizational performance. *Academy of Management Journal*, **39**(4): 949–69.

Delbridge, R. and Whitfield, K. (2001) Employee perceptions of job influence and organizational participation. *Industrial Relations*, **40**(3): 472–89.

Delery, J. and Doty, H. (1996) Modes of theorizing in strategic human resource management: tests of universalistic, contingency and configurational performance predictions. *Academy of Management Journal*, **39**: 802–35.

Delsen, L., Benders, J. and Smits, J. (2006) Choices within collective labour agreements *à la Carte* in the Netherlands. *British Journal of Industrial Relations*, **44**(1): 51–72.

De Menezes, L. and Wood, S. (2006) The reality of flexible work systems in Britain. *International Journal of Human Resource Management*, **17**(1): 106–38.

Denham, D. (1990) Unfair dismissal law and the legitimation of managerial control. *Capital and Class*, (41): 32–41.

DeNisi, A. and Kluger, A. (2000) Feedback effectiveness: can 360-degree appraisal be improved? *Academy of Management Executive*, **14**(1): 129–39.

Den Hartog, D. N. and Verburg, R. M. (2004) High performance work systems, organizational culture and firm effectiveness. *Human Resource Management Journal*, **14**(1): 55–78.

Denzin, N. and Lincoln, Y. (2005) *Handbook of Qualitative Research* (3rd edn). Thousand Oaks, CA: Sage.

Department for Education and Employment (1991) *Education and Training for the 21st Century*. White Paper. Sheffield: DfEE.

Department for Education and Employment (1998) *The Learning Age: A Renaissance for a New Britain*. Green Paper. Sheffield: DfEE.

Department for Education and Employment (2000) *Labour Market and Skill Trends*. Sheffield: DfEE.

Department for Education and Skills (2003) *21st Century Skills – Realising our Potential: Individuals, Employers, Nation*. London: DfES.

Department for Education and Skills (2005) *Skills: Getting on in Business, Getting on at Work*. London: DfES.

Department of Employment (1974) *Company Manpower Planning*. Manpower Papers 1. London: HMSO.

Department of Trade and Industry (2003) *Flexible Working*. London: DTI.

Department of Trade and Industry (2004) *The UK Contact Centre Industry: A Study*. London: DTI.

Department of Trade and Industry (2005a) *People, Strategy and Performance: Results from the Second Work and Enterprise Business Survey*. London: DTI.

Department of Trade and Industry (2005b) *Inside the Workplace: First Findings from the 2004 Work-*

place *Employment Relations Survey (WERS 2004)*. London: DTI.

Department of Work and Pensions (2005) *Opportunity Age*. London: DWP.

Des, G. G. and Shaw, J. D. (2001) Voluntary turnover, social capital and organizational performance. *Academy of Management Review*, **26**: 446–56.

Despres, C. and Hiltrop, J. (1995) Human resource management in the knowledge age: current practice and perspectives on the future. *Employee Relations*, **17**(1): 9–23.

Devanna, M. A., Fombrun, C. J. and Tichy, N. M. (1984) A framework for strategic human resource management. In C. J. Fombrun, N. M. Tichy and M. A. Devanna (eds) *Strategic Human Resource Management* (pp. 3–18). New York: John Wiley & Sons.

Dex, S. (1988) Gender and the labour market. In D. Gallie (ed.) *Employment in Britain* (pp. 281–309). Oxford: Blackwell.

Dickens, C. (1859 [1952]) *A Tale of Two Cities*. London: HarperCollins.

Dickens, L. (1994) Wasted resources? Equal opportunities in employment. In K. Sisson (ed.) *Personnel Management: A Comprehensive Guide to Theory and Practice in Britain*. Oxford: Blackwell.

Dickens, L. (1998) What HRM means for gender equality. *Human Resource Management Journal*, **8**(1): 23–45.

Diekma, A. B. and Eagly, A. H. (2000) Stereotypes as dynamic constructs: women and men of the past, present, and future. *Personality and Social Psychology Bulletin*, **26**: 1171–88.

Dietrich, M. and Roberts, J. (1997) Beyond the economics of professionalism. In J. Broadbent, M. Dietrich and J. Roberts (eds) *The End of the Professions?* (pp. 14–33). London: Routledge.

Ding, D. and Warner, M. (1999) Re-inventing China's industrial relations at enterprise level: an empirical field study in four major cities. *Industrial Relations Journal*, **30**(3): 243–60.

Ding, D., Goodall, K. and Warner, M. (2000) The end of the 'iron rice-bowl': whither Chinese human resource management. *International Journal of Human Resource Management*, **11**(2): 217–36.

Disney, R. (1990) Explanations of the decline in trade union density in Britain: an appraisal. *British Journal of Industrial Relations*, **28**(2): 165–77.

Dixon, N. (1992) Organizational learning: a review of the literature with implications for HRD professionals. *Human Resource Development Quarterly*, **3**(1): 29–49.

Dixon, N. (1994) *The Organizational Learning Cycle: How We Can Learn Collectively*. Maidenhead: McGraw-Hill.

Dobbin, F. (2005) Is globalization making us all the same? *British Journal of Industrial Relations*, **43**(4): 569–76.

Doeringer, P. B. and Piore, M. J. (1971) *Internal Labour Markets and Manpower Analysis*. Lexington, MA: D. C. Heath.

Dohery, N. and Tyson, S. (2000) HRM and employee well-being: raising the ethical stakes. In D. Winstanley and J. Woodall (eds) *Ethical Issues in Contemporary Human Resource Management* (pp. 102–15). Basingstoke: Palgrave Macmillan.

Donnelly, E. (1987) The training model: time for a change. *Industrial and Commercial Training*, May/June: 3–6.

Donnelly, E. and Dunn, S. (2006) Ten years after: South African employment relations since the negotiated revolution. *British Journal of Industrial Relations*, **44**(1): 1–29.

Donovan, Lord (1968) *Royal Commission on Trade Unions Employers' Association*. Cmnd 3623. London: HMSO.

Dore, R. (1973) *British Factory, Japanese Factory*. London: Allen & Unwin.

Dowlen, A. (1996) NLP – help or hype? Investigating the uses of neuroliguistic programming in management learning. *Career Development International*, **1**(1): 27–34.

Dowling, P. J., Welch, D. and Schuler, R. (1999) *International Journal of Human Resource Management: Managing People in the International Context* (3rd edn). Cincinatti, OH: South-Western.

Down, S. and Smith, D. (1998) It pays to be nice to people. *Personnel Review*, **27**(2): 143–55.

Drache, D. (1995) The decline of collective bargaining: is it irreversible? *Proceedings of the XXXIst ACRI/CIRA*, pp. 101–22.

Drohan, M. (2000) Technology comes with a price: stress and depression. *Globe and Mail*, 11 October: B15.

Drucker, P. F. (1993) *Post-capitalist Society*. London: Butterworth Heinemann.

Dulewicz, V. and Higgs, M. (2000) Emotional intelligence: a review and evaluation. *Journal of Managerial Psychology*, **15**(4): 341–72.

Dundon, T., Wilkinson, A., Marchington, M. and Ackers, P. (2004) The meaning and purpose of employee voice. *International Journal of Human Resource Management*, **15**(6): 1149–70.

Dwelly, T. and Bennion, Y. (2003) *Time To Go*

Home: Embracing the Home-working Revolution. London: Work Foundation.

Dyck, D. E. (2002) *Disability Management: Theory, Strategy and Industrial Practice* (2nd edn). Markham, Ontario: Butterworths.

Easterby-Smith, M., Burgoyne, J. and Araujo, L. (eds) (1999) *Organizational Learning and the Learning Organization.* London: Sage.

Easterby-Smith, M., Snell, R. and Gherardi, S. (1998) Organizational learning: diverging communities of practice. *Management Learning,* **29**(3): 259–72.

Ebbinghaus, B. and Waddington, J. (2000) United Kingdom/Great Britain. In B. Ebbinghaus and J. Visser (eds) The *Societies of Europe: Trade Unions in Western Europe Since 1945* (pp. 705–56). Basingstoke: Macmillan – now Palgrave Macmillan.

Edgar, F. and Geare, A. (2005) HRM practice and employee attitudes: different measures – different results. *Personnel Review,* **34**(5): 534–49.

Edvinsson, L. and Malone, M. S. (1997) *Intellectual Capital.* London: Piatkus.

Edwards, J. (2000) Technological discontinuity and workforce size: an argument for selective downsizing. *International Journal of Organizational Analysis,* **8**(3): 290–308.

Edwards, P. K. (1985) *Managing Labour Relations Through the Recession.* Warwick: University of Warwick, Industrial Relations Research Unit.

Edwards, P. K., Geary, J. and Sisson, K. (2001) Employee invovement in the workplace: transformative, exploitative or limited and controlled? In J. Bélanger, G. Murray and P.-A. Lapointe (eds) *Work and Employment Relations in the High Performance Workplace.* London: Cassell/Mansell.

Edwards, R. (1979) *Contested Terrain: The Transformation of the Workplace in the Twentieth Century.* London: Heinemann.

Edwards, T. and Kuruvilla, S. (2005) International HRM: national business systems, organizational politics and the international division of labour in MNCs. *International Journal of Human Resource Management,* **16**(1): 1–21.

Egri, C. P. and Pinfield, L. T. (1999) Organizations and the biosphere ecologies and environments. In S. Clegg, C. Hardt and W. Nord (eds) *Managing Organizations: Current Issues* (pp. 209–33). London: Sage.

Eisenhardt, K. M. (1989) Agency theory: an assessment and review. *Academy of Management Review,* **14**, 57–74.

El Akkad, O. (2005) *Globe and Mail,* 22, July, p. B7.

Elenkov, D. (1998) Can American management concepts work in Russia?: a cross-cultural comparative study. *California Management Review,* **40**(4): 133–56.

Elger, T. and Smith, C. (1994) *Global Japanization?* London: Routledge.

Elias, P. and Purcell, K. (2003) *Measuring Change in the Graduate Labour Market.* Research Paper no. 1. Bristol: Employment Studies Research Institute.

Emmott, M. and Hutchinson, S. (1998) Employment flexibility: threat or promise? In P. Sparrow and M. Marchington (eds) *Human Resource Management: A New Agenda* (pp. 229–44). London: Financial Times Management.

Eraut, M. (2000) Non-formal learning and tacit knowledge in professional work. *British Journal of Educational Psychology,* **70**: 113–36.

Etzioni, A. (1988) *The Moral Dimension.* New York: Free Press.

European Trade Union Confederation Factsheet: Working Time Directive. www.etuc.org/a/504.

Eva, D. and Oswald, R. (1981) *Health and Safety at Work.* London: Pan Original.

Evans, A. L. and Lorange, P. (1989) The two logics behind human resource management. In P. Evans, Y. Doz and A. Laurent (eds) *Human Resource Management in International Firms.* Basingstoke: Macmillan – now Palgrave Macmillan.

Evans, J. A., Kunda, G. and Barley, S. A. (2004) Beach time, bridge time, and billable hours: the temporal structure of technical contracting. *Administrative Science Quarterly,* **49**: 1–38.

Evered, R. D. and Selman, J. C. (1989) Coaching and the art of management. *Organizational Dynamics,* Autumn: 16–32.

Exworthy, M. and Halford, S. (1999a) Professionals and managers in a changing public sector: conflict, compromise and collaboration. In M. Exworthy and S. Halford (eds) *Professionals and the New Managerialism in the Public Sector* (pp. 1–17). Buckingham: Open University Press.

Exworthy, M. and Halford S. (eds) (1999b) *Professionals and the New Managerialism in the Public Sector.* Buckingham: Open University Press.

Farnham, D. (1990) *Personnel in Context.* London: Institute of Personnel Management.

Farrell, D. (2005) Offshoring: value creation through economic change. *Journal of Management Studies,* **42**(3): 675–83.

Faux, J. and Mishel, L. (2000) Inequality and the global economy. In W. Hutton and A. Giddens (eds) *On the Edge: Living with Global Capitalism* (pp. 93–111). London: Jonathan Cape.

Fayol, H. (1949) *Administration Industrielle et Générale/General and Industrial Management.* London: Pitman.

Feldman, D. C. and Klass, B. S. (2002) Internet job hunting: a field study of applicant experiences with online recruiting. *Human Resource Management,* **41**(2): 175–92.

Felstead, A. and Ashton, D. (2000) Tracing the links: organizational structures and skill demands. *Human Resources Management Journal,* **10**(3): 5–20.

Felstead, A. and Gallie, D. (2004) For better or worse? Non-standeard jobs and high involvement work systems. *International Journal of Human Resources Management,* **15**(7): 1293–316.

Felstead, A. and Jewson, N. (1999) Flexible labour and non-standard employment: an agenda of issues. In A. Felstead and N. Jewson (eds) *Global Trends in Flexible Labour* (pp. 1–20). Basingstoke: Macmillan – now Palgrave Macmillan.

Felstead, A., Jewson, N., Phizacklea, A. and Walters, S. (2002) Opportunities to work at home in the context of work–life balance. *Human Resource Management Journal,* **12**(1): 54–76.

Feltham, R. (1992) Using competencies in selection and recruitment. In S. Boam and P. Sparrow (eds) *Designing and Achieving Competency.* (pp. 89–103). Maidenhead: McGraw-Hill.

Fenwick, T. (2003) Flexibility and individualisation in adult education work: the case of portfolio educators. *Journal of Education and Work,* **16**(2): 165–84

Fenwick, T. (2004) Toward a critical HRD in theory and practice. *Adult Education Quarterly,* **54**(3), 193–209.

Fenwick, T. (2006) Contradictions in portfolio careers: work design and client relations. *Career Development International,* **11**(1): 65–79.

Ferner, A., Almond, P., Colling, T. and Edwards, T. (2005) Policies on union representation in US multinationals in the UK: between micro-politics and macro-institutions. *British Journal of Industrial Relations,* **43**(4): 703–28.

Fernie, S., Metcalfe, D. and Woodland, S. (1994) *Does Human Resource Management Boost Employee Management Relations?* London School of Economics CEP Working Paper 546. London: LSE.

Findlay, P., McKinlay, A., Marks, A. and Thompson, P. (2000) Flexible when it suits them: the use and abuse of teamwork skills. In S. Procter and F. Mueller (eds) *Teamworking* (pp. 222–43). Basingstoke: Macmillan – now Palgrave Macmillan.

Finegold, D. and Soskice, D. (1988) The failure of training in Britain: analysis and prescription. *Oxford Review of Economic Policy,* **4**(3): 21–53.

Fitz-enz, J. (1995) *How to Measure Human Resource Management.* New York: McGraw-Hill.

Fitz-enz, J. (2000) *The ROI of Human Capital.* New York: AMACOM.

Fitz-enz, J. and Davison, B. (2002) *How to Measure Human Resources Management* (3rd edn). New York: McGraw-Hill.

Flamholz, E. (1985) *Human Resource Accounting.* Los Angeles: Jossey-Bass.

Flynn, R. (1999) Managerialism, professionalism and quasi-markets. In M. Exworthy and S. Halford (eds) *Professionals and the New Managerialism in the Public Sector* (pp. 18–36). Buckingham: Open University Press.

Fombrun, C. J., Tichy, N. M. and Devanna, M. A. (eds) (1984) *Strategic Human Resource Management.* New York: John Wiley & Sons.

Foot, D. and Stoffman, D. (1996) *Boom, Bust and Echo: How To Profit from the Demographic Shift.* Toronto: Macfarlane Walker & Ross.

Ford, J. (2006) Discourses of leadership: gender, identy and contradiction in the UK public sector organization. *Leadership,* **2**(1): 77–99.

Forrester, K. (2005) Learning for revival; British trade unions and workplace learning. *Studies in Continuing Education,* **27**(3): 259–72.

Fox, A. (1985) *Man Mismanagement* (2nd edn). London: Hutchinson.

Freeman, R. B. and Lazear, E. P. (1995) An economic analysis of works councils. In J. Rogers and W. Streeck (eds) *Works Councils: Consultation, Representation and Cooperation in Industrial Relations.* Chicago: University of Chicago Press.

Freeman, R. B. and Pelletier, J. (1990) The impact of industrial relations legislation on British union density. *British Journal of Industrial Relations,* **28**(2): 141–64.

Frege, C. M. (2002) A critical assessment of the theoretical and empirical research on works councils. *British Journal of Industrial Relations,* **40**(2): 221–48.

Friedman, A. (1977) *Industry and Labour: Class Struggle at Work and Monopoly Capitalism.* London: Macmillan.

Friedson, E. (2001) *Professionalism.* Cambridge: Polity Press.

Frits, K. and MacDuffie, P. (1996) The adoption of high-involvement work practices. *Industrial Relations,* **35**(3): 423–55.

Fröbel, P. and Marchington, M. (2005) Team-working structures and worker perceptions: a cross-national study in pharmaceuticals. *International Journal of Human Resource Management*, **16**(2): 256–76.

Fuller, A. and Unwin, L. (2003) Fostering workplace learning: looking through the lens of apprenticeship. *European Educational Research Journal*, **2**(1), 41–55.

Fuller, A., Ashton, D., Felstead, A., Unwin, L., Walters, S. and Quinn, M. (2003) *The Impact of Informal Learning at Work on Business Productivity*, London: DTI.

Furnham, A. (2004) Performance management systems. *European Business Journal*, **16**(2): 83–94.

Fyfe, J. (1986) Putting people back into the manpower planning equation. *Personnel Management*, October: 64–9.

Gabriel, Y. (2000) *Storytelling in Organizations*. Oxford: Oxford University Press.

Gagnon, S. and Cornelius, N. (2000) Re-examining workplace equality: the capabilities approach. *Human Resource Management Journal*, **10**(4): 68–87.

Gallie, D. (2005) Work pressure in Europe 1996–2001: trends and determinants. *British Journal of Industrial Relations*, **43**(3): 351–75.

Gamble, J. (2003) Transferring human resource practices from the United Kingdom to China: the limits and potential for convergence. *International Journal of Human Resource Management*, **14**(3): 369–87.

Gamble, J., Morris, J. and Wilkinson, B. (2004) Mass production is alive and well: the future of work and organization in east Asia. *International Journal of Human Resource Management*, **15**(2): 397–409.

Garavan, T. N. (1997) The learning organization: a review and an evaluation. *Learning Organization*, **4**(1): 18–29.

Garavan, T. N. and McGuire, D. (2001) Competencies and workplace learning: some reflections on the rhetoric and the reality. *Journal of Workplace Learning*, **13**(4): 144–63.

Garavan, T. N., Heraty, N. and Barnicle, B. (1999) Human resource development: current issues, priorities and dilemmas. *Journal of European Industrial Training*, **23**(4/5): 169–79.

Garavan, T. N., Morley, M., Gunnigle, P. and Collins, E. (2001) Human capital accumulation: the role of human resource development. *Journal of European Industrial Training*, **25**(2–4): 48–68.

Garrick, J. (1998) *Informal Learning in the Workplace*. London: Routledge.

Garrick, J. (1999) The dominant discourses of learning at work. In D. Boud and J. Garrick (eds) *Understanding Learning at Work* (pp. 216–29). London: Routledge.

Garvey, B. and Williamson, B. (2002) *Beyond Knowledge Management*. Harlow: Pearson Education.

Gascó, J. L., Llopis, J. and González, M. (2004) The use of information technology in training human resources. *Journal of European Industrial Training*, **28**(5): 370–82.

Gattiker, U. E. and Cohen, A. (1997) Gender-based wage differences. *Relations Industrielles/Industrial Relations*, **52**(3): 507–29.

Geary, J. F. and Dobbins, A. (2001) Teamworking: a new dynamic in pursuit of management control. *Human Resource Management Journal*, **11**(1): 3–23.

Gennard, J., Steele, M. and Miller, K. (1989) Trends and developments in industrial relations law: trade union discipline and non-strikers. *Industrial Relations Journal*, **20**(1): 5–15.

Geppert, M. and Williams, K. (2006) Global, national and local practices in multinational corporations: towards a sociopolitical framework. *International Journal of Human Resource Management*, **17**(1): 49–69.

Gerhart, B. (2000) Compensation strategy and organizational performance. In S. Rynes and B. Gerhart (eds) *Compensation in Organizations: Current Research and Practice* (pp. 151–94). San Francisco: Jossey-Bass.

Gewirth, A. (1991) Human rights and the prevention of cancer. In D. Poff and W. Waluchow (eds) *Business Ethics in Canada* (2nd edn) (pp. 205–15). Scarborough, Ontario: Prentice Hall.

Gibb, S. (1998) Exploring career chaos: patterns of belief. *Career Development International*, **3**(4): 149–53.

Gibb, S. (2003) Line manager involvement in learning and development: small beer or big deal? *Employee Relations*, **25**(3): 281–93.

Giddens, A. (1984) *The Constitution of Society*. Berkeley, CA: University of California Press.

Giddens, A. (1990) *The Consequencies of Modernity*. Cambridge: Polity Press.

Giddens, A. and Hutton, W. (2000) In conversation. In W. Hutton and A. Giddens (eds) *On the Edge. Living with Global Capitalism* (pp. 1–51). London: Jonathan Cape.

Giles, A. and Iain, H. (1989) The collective agreement. In J. Anderson, M. Gunderson and A. Ponak (eds) *Union–Management Relations in Canada* (2nd edn). Don Mills, Ontario: Addison-Wesley.

Giles, A. and Starkman, A. (2001) The collective agreement. In M. Gunderson, A. Ponack and D. Taras (eds) *Union–Management Relations in Canada* (4th edn) (pp. 272–313). Toronto: Addison-Wesley Longman.

Gillani, B. B. (2003) *Learning Theories and the Design of E-Learning Environments.* Lanham, MD: University Press of America.

Gilman, M. and Marginson, P. (2002) Negotiating European Works Councils: contours of constrained choice. *Industrial Relations Journal,* **33**(1): 36–51.

Glasbeek, H. (1991) The worker as a victim. In D. Poff and W. Waluchow (eds) *Business Ethics in Canada* (2nd edn) (pp. 199–204). Scarborough, Ontario: Prentice Hall.

Godard, J. (1991) The progressive HRM paradigm: a theoretical and empirical re-examination. *Relations Industrielles/Industrial Relations,* **46**(2): 378–99.

Godard, J. (2004) A critical assessment of the high-performance paradigm. *British Journal of Industrial Relations,* **42**(2): 349–78.

Godard, J. (2005) *Industrial Relations: The Economy and Society* (3rd edn). Concord, Ontario: Captus Press.

Godard, J. and Delaney, J. T. (2000) Reflections on the 'high performance' paradigm's implications for industrial relations as field. *Industrial and Labor Relations Review,* **53**(3): 482–502.

Gold, J. and Hamblett, J. (1999) Emotions, values and rhetorical performance: a detailed description of a conflict within a human resource management team. In T. Abma (ed.) *Telling Tales: On Evaluation and Narrative* (pp. 131–50). Stamford, CT: JAI Press.

Gold, J. and Smith, V. (2003) Advances toward a learning movement: translations at work. *Human Resource Development International,* **6**(2): 139–52.

Gold, J., Rodgers, H. and Smith, V. (2003a) What is the future for the human resource development professional? A UK perspective. *Human Resource Development International,* **6**(4): 437–455.

Gold, J., Devins, D. and Johnson, S. (2003b) What is the value of mentoring in a small business? Using narrative evaluation to find out. *British Journal of Guidance and Counselling,* **31**(1): 51–62.

Gold, J., Thorpe, R., Woodall, J. and Sadler-Smith, E. (2006) Continuing professional development in the legal profession: a practice-based-learning perspective. *Management Learning* (in press).

Goleman, D. (1997) *Emotional Intelligence.* New York: Bantam Books.

Gollan, P. J. (2000) Non-union forms of employee representation in the United Kingdom and Australia. In B. E. Kaufman and D. G. Taras (eds) *Non-Union Employee Representation; History, Contemporary Practice and Policy* (pp. 410–49). New York: M. E. Sharpe.

Gollan, P. J. (2002) So what's the news? Management strategies towards non-union employee representation at News International. *Industrial Relations Journal,* **33**(4): 316–31.

Gollan, P. J. (2006) Editorial: Consultation and non-union employee representation. *Industrial Relations Journal,* **37**(5): 428–37.

Gomez-Mejia, L. and Balkin, D. (1992) *Compensation, Organizational Strategy, and Firm Performance.* Cincinnati, OH: South-Western.

Gospel, H. F. (1994) *Markets, Firms and the Management of Labour in Modern Britain.* Cambridge: Cambridge University Press.

Gospel, H. F. and Littler, C. R. (eds) (1983) *Managerial Strategies and Industrial Relations.* London: Heinemann.

Gospel, H. F. and Palmer, G. (1993) *British Industrial Relations* (2nd edn). London: Routledge.

Grant, D. and Oswick, C. (1998) Of believers, atheists and agnostics: practitioner views on HRM. *Industrial Relations Journal,* **29**(3): 178–93.

Gratton, L. (1997) Tomorrow people. *People Management,* 24 July: 22–7.

Gratton, L. (2000) A real step change. *People Management,* **6**(6): 26–30.

Gratton, L. (2005) Managing integration through cooperation. *Human Resource Management,* **44**(2): 151–58.

Gray, G. and Guppy, N. (1999) *Success Surveys: Research Methods and Practice.* Toronto: Harcourt.

Green, F. (1997) *Review of Information on the Benefits of Training for Employees.* Research Report no. 7. Sheffield: Department for Education and Employment.

Green, F. (1999) Training the workers. In P. Gregg and J. Wadsworth (eds) *The State of Working Britain* (pp. 127–46). Manchester: Manchester University Press.

Green, F. and Ashton, D. (1992) Skill shortage and skill deficiency. *Work, Employment and Society,* **6**(2): 287–301.

Green, F., Machin, S. and Wilkinson, D. (1998) Trade unions and training practices in British workplaces. *Industrial and Labour Relations Review,* **52**(2): 179–95.

Green, F., Mayhew, K. and Molloy, E. (2003) *Employer Perspectives Survey.* Warwick University:

Centre for Skills, Knowledge and Organisational Performance (SKOPE).

Green, J. (1998) Employers learn to live with AIDS. *HR Magazine*, **43**(2): 62–7.

Gregg, P. (1973) *A Social and Economic History of Britain, 1760–1972* (7th edn). London: Harrap.

Greider, W. (2002) China is winning the new 'race to the bottom' in wages. *Canadian Centre for Policy Alternatives Monitor*, **9**(1): 30–1.

Grey, C. (2005) *Studying Organizations*. London: Sage.

Grey, C. and Mitev, N. (1995) Reengineering organizations: a critical appraisal. *Personnel Review*, **24**(1): 6–18.

Grint, K. (1995) *Management*. Cambridge: Polity Press.

Grint, K. (2005) *Leadership: Limits and Possibilities*. Basingstoke: Palgrave Macmillan.

Grint, K. and Willcocks, L. (1995) Business process re-engineering in theory and practice: business paradise regained? *New Technology, Work and Employment*, **10**(2): 99–108.

Gröjer, J.-E. and Johanson, U. (1998) Current development in human resource accounting and costing. *Accounting, Auditing and Accountability*, **11**(4): 495–505.

Grote, R. (1996) *The Complete Guide to Performance Appraisal*. New York: American Management Association, pp. 204–79.

Groves, K. (2005) Linking leader skills, follower attitudes, and contextual variables via an integrated model of charismatic leadership. *Journal of Management*, **31**(2): 255–77.

Grugulis, I. (2002) *Skill and Qualification: The Contribution of NVQs to Raising Skill Levels*. SKOPE Research Paper no.36. Winter, Warwick University: Centre for Skills, Knowledge and Organisational Performance (SKOPE).

Grugulis, I., Vincent, S. and Hebson, G. (2003) The rise of the 'network organization' and the decline of discretion. *Human Resource Management Journal*, **13**(2): 45–59.

Grundy, T. (1994) *Strategic Learning in Action*. Maidenhead: McGraw-Hill.

Grzeda, M. M. (1999) Re-conceptualizing career change: a career development perspective. *Career Development International*, **4**(6): 305–11.

Guba, E. G. and Lincoln, Y. S. (1989) *Fourth Generation Evaluation*. London: Sage.

Guest, D. E. (1986) Worker participation and personnel policy in the UK: some case studies. *International Labour Review*, **125**(6): 406–27.

Guest, D. E. (1987) Human resource management and industrial relations. *Journal of Management Studies*, **24**(5): 503–21.

Guest, D. E. (1989) HRM: implications for industrial relations. In J. Storey (ed.) *New Perspectives on Human Resource Management* (pp. 41–55). London: Routledge.

Guest, D. E. (1990) Human resource management and the American dream. *Journal of Management Studies*, **27**(4): 377–97.

Guest, D. E. (1991) Personnel management: the end of orthodoxy? *British Journal of Industrial Relations*, **29**(2): 149–75.

Guest, D. E. (1995) Human resource management, trade unions and industrial relations. In J. Storey (ed.) *Human Resource Management: A Critical Text* (pp. 110–41). London: Routledge.

Guest, D. E. (1997) Human resource management and performance: a review and research agenda. *International Journal of Human Resource Management*, **8**(3): 263–76.

Guest, D. E. (1998) Beyond HRM: commitment and the contract culture. In P. Sparrow and M. Marchington (eds) *Human Resource Management: The New Agenda* (pp. 37–51). London: Financial Times/Pitman.

Guest, D. E. (1999) Human resource management – the workers' verdict. *Human Resource Management Journal*, **9**(3): 5–25.

Guest, D. E. (2000) Piece by piece. *People Management*, **6**(15): 26–30.

Guest, D. E. (2001) Industrial relations and human resource management. In J. Storey (ed.) *Human Resource Management: A Critical Text* (2nd edn) (pp. 96–113). London: Thomson Learning.

Guest, D. E. and Conway, N. (2002) Communicating the psychological contract: an employer perspective. *Human Resource Management Journal*, **12**(2): 22–38.

Guest, D. E., Davey, K. and Patch, A. (1998) *The Impact of New Forms of Employment Contract on Motivation and Innovation*. London: Economic and Social Research Council.

Guest, D. E., Michie, J., Conway, N. and Meehan, M. (2003) Human resource management and corporate performance in the UK. *British Journal of Industrial Relations*, **41**(2), 291–314.

Guirdham, M. (2005) *Communicating Across Cultures at Work*. Basingstoke: Palgrave Macmillan.

Gunderson, M., Ponak, A. and Taras, D. (eds) (2001) *Union–Management Relations in Canada* (4th edn). Toronto: Addison Wesley Longman.

Gunnigle, P., Turner, T. and D'Art, D. (1998) Counterpoising collectivism: performance-related pay and industrial relations in greenfield sites. *British Journal of Industrial Relations*, **36**(4): 565–79.

Gunnigle, P., Murphy, K. R., Cleveland, J. Heraty, N. and Morely, M. (2002) Localization in human resource management: comparing American and European multinational corporations. *Advances in International Management*, **14**: 259–84.

Guthrie, J. P. and Hollensbe, E.C. (2004) Group incentives and performance: a study of spontaneous goal setting, goal choice and commitment. *Journal of Management*, **30**(2): 263–84.

Hackman, J. R. and Oldham, G. R. (1980) *Work Redesign*. New York: Addison-Wesley.

Hager, P. (2003) Lifelong learning in the workplace? Challenges and issues, work and lifelong learning in different contexts. Paper delivered at the 3rd International Conference of Researching Work and Learning, Tampere, Finland. Tampere: University of Tampere, Department of Education.

Halachmi, A. (2002) Performance measurement and government productivity. *Work Study*, **51**(2): 63–73.

Hale, R. (2000) To match or mis-match? The dynamics of mentoring as a route to personal and organisational learning. *Career Development International*, **5**(4): 223–34.

Hales, C. P. (1986) What do managers do? A critical review of the evidence. *Journal of Management Studies*, **23**(1): 88–115.

Hall, D. T., Zhu, G. and Yan, A. (2002) Career creativity as protean identity transformation. In M. Peiperl, M. Arthur and N. Anand (eds) *Career Creativity: Explorations in the Remaking of Work* (pp. 159–79). Oxford: Oxford University Press.

Hall, M. and Marginson, P. (2005) Trojan horse and paper tigers. Assessing the significance of European Works Councils. In B. Harley, J. Hyman & P. Thompson (eds) *Participation and Democracy at Work* (pp. 204–21). Basingstoke: Palgrave Macmillan.

Hall, P. and Soskice, D. (2001) *Varieties of Capitalism*. Oxford: Oxford University Press.

Hall, S. (1998) The great moving nowhere show. *Marxism Today*, November/December: 9–14.

Hall, S. and Jacques, M. (1989) *New Times*. London: Lawrence & Wishart.

Halliday, T. C. (1987) *Beyond Monopoly: Lawyers, State Crises and Professional Empowerment*. Chicago: University of Chicago Press.

Halman, F. and Fletcher, C. (2000) The impact of development centre participation and the role of individual differences in changing self-assessments. *Journal of Occupational and Organizational Psychology*, **73**, 423–42.

Hamel, G. and Prahalad, C. K. (1994) *Competing for the Future*. Boston: Harvard Business School.

Hammer, M. (1997) *Beyond Reengineering*. New York: HarperCollins.

Hammer, M. and Champy, J. (1993) *Reengineering the Corporation*. London: Nicholas Brealey.

Hammer, M. and Stanton, S. (1995) *The Reengineering Revolution: A Handbook*. New York: Harper Business Press.

Handy, C. (1994) *The Age of Paradox*. Boston: Harvard Business School Press.

Handy, L., Devine, M. and Heath, L. (1996) *360° Feedback: Unguided Missile or Powerful Weapon?* Berkhamsted: Ashridge Management Research Group.

Hansen, M. T., Mors, M. L. and Løvas, B. (2005) Knowledge sharing in organizations: multiple networks, multiple phases. *Academy of Management Journal*, **48**(5): 776–93.

Harland, C., Knight, L., Lamming, R. and Walker, H. (2005) Outsourcing: assessing the risks and benefits for organisations, sectors and nations. *International Journal of Operations and Production Management*, **25**(9): 831–50.

Harley, B., Hyman, J. and Thompson, P. (2005) *Participation and Democracy at Work*. Basingstoke: Palgrave Macmillan.

Harper, S. C. (1983) A developmental approach to performance appraisal. *Business Horizons*, September/October: 68–74.

Harri-Augstein, S. and Webb, I. M. (1995) *Learning To Change*. Maidenhead: McGraw-Hill.

Harrington, B., McLoughlin, K. and Riddell, D. (1998) Business process re-engineering in the public sector: a case study of the Contributions Agency. *New Technology, Work and Employment*, **13**(1): 43–50.

Harris, M. M. (1989) Reconsidering the employment interview: a review of recent literature and suggestions for future research. *Personnel Psychology*, **42**: 691–726.

Harris, P. and Moran, R. (1991) *Managing Cultural Differences*. London: Gulf Publications.

Harzing, A. W. (2000) An empirical analysis and extension of the Bartlett and Ghoshal typology of multinational companies. *Journal of International Business Studies*, **31**(1): 101–20.

Hassard, J. and Parker, M. (1993) *Postmodernism and Organizations*. London: Sage.

Hassard, J., Morris, J. and Sheehan, J. (2004) The 'third way': the future of work and organization in a 'corporatized' Chinese economy. *International Journal of Human Resource Management*, **15**(2): 314–30.

Haunschild, A. (2003) Humanization through discipline? Foucault and the goodness of employee health programmes. *Journal of Critical Postmodern Organization Science*, **2**(3): 46–59.

Hausknecht, J., Day, D. and Thomas, S. (2004) Applicant reactions to selection procedures: an updated model and meta-analysis. *Personnel Psychology*, **57**: 639–83.

Hawkins, K. W. (1995) Effects of gender and communications content on leadership in small task-oriented groups. *Small Group Research*, **26**: 234–50.

Health and Safety Commission/Department of the Environment, Transport and the Regions (2000) *Revitalizing Health and Safety. Strategy Statement.* London: DETR.

Health and Safety Executive (2005) Health and Safety Statistics, 2003/04. Available at www.hse.gov.uk/statistics/2005.

Heckscher, C. (1994) Defining the post-bureaucratic type. In C. Heckscher and A. Donnelon (eds) *The Post-bureaucratic Organisation*. Thousand Oaks, CA: Sage.

Heckscher, C. and Donnelon, A. (eds) (1994) *The Post-bureacratic Organization*. Thousand Oaks, CA: Sage.

Heery, E. (2000) The new pay: risk and representation at work. In D. Winstanley and J. Woodall (eds) *Ethical Issues in Contemporary Human Resource Management* (pp. 172–88). Basingstoke: Macmillan – now Palgrave Macmillan.

Heery, E. (2002) Partnership versus organizing: alternative futures for British trade unionism. *Industrial Relations Journal*, **33**(1): 20–35.

Heery, E. (2004) The trade union response to agency labour in Britain. *Industrial Relations Journal*, **35**(5): 434–50.

Heery, E. (2005) Sources of change in trade unions. *Work, Employment and Society*, **19**(1): 91–106.

Heery, E. and Salmon, J. (2000) *The Insecure Workforce*. London: Routledge.

Heery, E., Conley, H., Delridge, R., Simms, M. and Stewart, P. (2004) Trade union responses to non-standard work. In G. Healy, E. Heery, P. Taylor and W. Brown (eds) *The Future of Worker Representation* (pp. 127–50). Basingstoke: Palgrave Macmillan.

Helgesen, S. (1995) *The Female Advantage: Women's Ways of Leadership*. New York: Doubleday.

Heller, F., Puslc, E., Strauss, G. and Wilpert, B. (1998) *Organizational Participation: Myth and Reality*. Oxford: Oxford University Press.

Hendry, C. (1994) The single European market and the HRM response. In P. Kirkbride (ed.) *Human Resource Management in Europe* (pp. 93–113). London: Routledge.

Hendry, C. (2000) Strategic decision making, discourse, and strategy as a social practice. *Journal of Management Studies*, **37**(7): 955–77.

Hendry, C. and Pettigrew, A. (1990) Human resource management: an agenda for the 1990s. *International Journal of Human Resource Management*, **1**(1): 17–44.

Henkens, K., Remery, C. and Schippers, J. (2005) Recruiting personnel in a tight labour market: an analysis of employers' behaviour. *International Journal of Manpower*, **26**(5): 421–33.

Herbert, S. (1991) Organisation markets. *Journal of Economic Perspectives*, **5**(33).

Herriot, P. (1998) The role of human resource management in building a new proposition. In P. Sparrow and M. Marchington (eds) *Human Resource Management: A New Agenda* (pp. 106–16). London: Financial Times Management.

Herriot, P. and Fletcher, C. (1990) Candidate-friendly, selection for the 1990s. *Personnel Management*, February: 32–5.

Herriot, P., Manning, W. E. G. and Kidd, J. M. (1997) The content of the psychological contract. *British Journal of Management*, **8**(2): 151–62.

Hertz, N. (2002) *The Silent Takeover: Global Capitalism and the Death of Democracy*. London: Arrow.

Herzberg, F. (1966) *Work and the Nature of Man*. Chicago, IL: World Publishing.

Heyes, J. (2000) Workplace industrial relations and training. In H. Rainbird (ed.) *Training in the Workplace* (pp. 148–68). Basingstoke: Macmillan – now Palgrave Macmillan.

Hill, C. W. and Jones, G. R. (2004) *Strategic Management Theory: An Integrated Approach* (6th edn). Boston, MA: Houghton Mifflin.

Hillage, J. and Moralee, J. (1996) *The Return on Investors*. Report no. 314. Brighton: Institute for Employment Studies.

Hillier, Y. (1997) Competence based qualifications in training, development and management. *Journal of Further and Higher Education*, **21**(1): 33–41.

Hirsh, W. (1990) *Succession Planning: Current Practice and Future Issues*. Report no.184. Brighton: Institute of Management Studies.

Hirsh, W. and Jackson, C. (1997) *Strategies for Career Development: Promise, Practice and Pretence*. Report no. 305. Brighton: Institute for Employment Studies.

Hirsh, W. and Tamkin, P. (2005) *Planning Training for your Business*. Report no. 422. Brighton: Institute of Employment Studies.

Hobsbawm, E. (1968) *Industry and Empire*. London: Weidenfeld & Nicolson.

Hobsbawm, E. (1995) *Age of Extremes*. London: Abacus.

Hochschild, A. R. (1983) *The Managed Heart: Commercialization of Human Feeling*. Berkeley, CA: University of California Press.

Hochschild, A. R. (2000) Global care chains and emotional surplus value. In W. Hutton and A. Giddens (eds) *On the Edge: Living with Global Capitalism* (pp. 130–46). London: Jonathan Cape.

Hochschild, A. R. (2003) *The Second Shift*. New York: Penguin.

Hochschild, A. R. and Machung, A. (1989) *The Second Shift: Working Parents and the Revolution at Home*. New York: Viking.

Hofstede, G. (1980) *Culture's Consquences: International Differences in Work-related Values*. London: Sage.

Hogarth, T. (1993) Worker support for organizational change and technical change. *Work, Employment and Society*, **7**(2): 45–63.

Hogarth, T., Hasluck, C., Pierre, G., Winterbotham, M. and Vivien, D. (2001) *Work–Life Balance 2000: Results from the Baseline Study*. Department for Education and Employment Research Report no. 249. London: DfEE.

Holbeche, L. (1998) *Motivating People in Lean Organizations*. Oxford: Butterworth Heinemann.

Holbeche, L. (1999) *Aligning Human Resources and Business Strategy*. Oxford: Butterworth Heinemann.

Hollenbeck, J. (2000) A structural approach to external and internal person–team fit. *Applied Psychology: An International Review*, **49**(3): 534–49.

Holman, D. (2000) A dialogical approach to skill and skilled activity. *Human Relations*, **53**(7): 957–80.

Holman, D., Pavlica, K. and Thorpe, R. (1997) Rethinking Kolb's theory of experiential learning in management education: the contribution of social constructionism and activity theory. *Management Learning*, **28**(2): 135–48.

Holmberg, I. and Strannegård, L. (2005) Leadership voices: the ideology of 'The New Economy'. *Leadership*, **1**(3): 353–74.

Hom, P. W., Griffeth, R. W., Palich, L. E. and Bracker, J. S. (1999) Revisiting met expectations as a reason why realistic job previews work. *Personnel Psychology*, **52**(1): 1–16.

Hoogvelt, A. (2001) *Globalization and the Post-colonial World* (2nd edn). Basingstoke: Palgrave Macmillan.

Hoque, K. (1999) Human resource management and performance in the UK hotel industry. *British Journal of Industrial Relations*, **37**(3): 419–43.

Hoque, K. (2003) All in all, it's just another plaque on the wall: the incidence and impact of the Investors In People standard. *Journal of Management Studies*, **40**(2): 543–71.

Hoque, K. and Noon, M. (2001) Counting angels: a comparison of personnel and HR specialists. *Human Resource Management Journal*, **11**(3): 5–22.

Hoque K., Taylor, S. and Bell, E. (2005) Investors in People: market-led voluntarism in vocational education and training. *British Journal of Industrial Relations*, **43**(1): 135–53.

Huczynski, A. and Buchanan, D. (2001) *Organizational Behaviour* (4th edn). Harlow: Pearson Education.

Huczynski, A. and Buchanan, D. (2004) *Organizational Behaviour* (5th edn). Harlow: Pearson Education.

Huffcutt, A. I., Weekly, J. A., Wiesner, W. H., DeGrout, T. G. and Jones, C. (2001) Comparison of situational and behavior description interview questions for higher-level positions. *Personnel Psychology*, **54**(3): 619–44.

Hughes, N. C. (2002) *China's Economic Challenge: Smashing the Rice Bowl*. New York: M. E. Sharpe.

Huselid, M. A. (1995) The impact of HRM practices on turnover, productivity, and corporate financial performance. *Academy of Management Journal*, **38**(3): 635–72.

Huseman, R. C. and Goodman, J. P. (1999) *Leading with Knowledge: The Nature of Competition in the 21st Century*. Thousand Oaks, CA: Sage.

Hutchinson, S., Purcell, J. and Kinnie, N. (2000) Evolving high commitment management and the experience of the RAC call centre. *Human Resource Management Journal*, **10**(1): 63–78.

Hutton, W. (1996) *The State We're in*. London: Vintage.

Hutton, W. (1997) *The State to Come*. London: Vintage.

Hutton, W. and Giddens, A. (eds) (2000) *On the Edge: Living with Global Capitalism*. London: Jonathan Cape.

Huws, U. (1997) *Teleworking: Guidelines for Good Practice*. Report no. 329. Brighton: Institute for Employment Studies.

Hyman, R. (1975) *Industrial Relations: A Marxist Introduction*. Basingstoke: Macmillan – now Palgrave Macmillan.

Hyman, R. (1987) Trade unions and the law: papering over the cracks? *Capital and Class*, (31): 43–63.

Hyman, R. (1988) Flexible specialization: miracle or myth? In R. Hyman and W. Streeck (eds) *New Technology and Industrial Relations* (pp. 48–60). Oxford: Blackwell.

Hyman, R. (1989)*The Political Ecomony of Industrial Relations*. Basingstoke: Macmillan – now Palgrave Macmillan.

Hyman, R. (1994) Industrial relations in Western Europe: an era of ambiguity? *Industrial Relations Journal*, **33**(1): 1–24.

Hyman, R. (1997a) Editorial. *European Journal of Industrial Relations*, **3**(1): 5–6.

Hyman, R. (1997b) The future of employee representation. *British Journal of Industrial Relations*, **35**(3): 309–36.

Hyman, R. (1999) National industrial relations systems and transnational challenges: an essay review. *European Journal of Industrial Relations*, **5**(1): 89–110.

Hyman, R. and Mason, B. (1995) *Managing Employee Involvement and Participation*. London: Sage.

Hyman, J., Baldry, C., Scholarios, D. and Bunzel, D. (2003) Work–life balance in call centres and software development. *British Journal of Industrial Relations*, **41**(2): 215–39.

Ichniowski, C., Kochan, T., Levine, D., Olson, C. and Strauss, G. (1996) What works at work: overview and assessment. *Industrial Relations*, **35**(3): 299–333.

Iles, P. and Salaman, G. (1995) Recruitment, selection and assessment. In Storey, J. (ed.) *Human Resource Management* (pp. 203–33). London: Routledge.

Ilgen, D. R., Fisher, C. D. and Taylor, M. S. (1979) Consequences of individual feedback on behavior in organizations. *Journal of Applied Psychology*, **64**(4), 349–71.

Income Data Services (2003) *Pay and Conditions in UK Call Centres*. London: Income Data Services.

Industrial Relations Services (1998) *Partnership in Practice at Legal and General*. IRS Employment Trends no. 650. London: IRS.

Industrial Relations Services (2001) *Competency Frameworks in UK Organisations*. London: IRS.

Industrial Relations Services (2003a) Sharpening up recruitment and selection with competencies. *IRS Employment Review*, **782**: 42–9.

Industrial Relations Services (2003b) Performance management; policy and practice. *Employment Trends*, **781**: 12–19.

Institute of Personnel and Development (1996) *The Lean Organisation: Managing the People Dimension*. London: IPD.

Institute of Personnel and Development (1997) *Overqualified and Underemployed?* London: IPD.

Institute of Personnel Management (1981) *Representative Structures*. London: IPM.

International Labour Organization (2000) High performance working: research project overview. http://www.ilo.org/public/english/employement/skills/training/casest/overivew.htm (accessed 2 May 2002).

Jackson, C. (1996) *Understanding Psychological Testing*. Leicester: BPS Books.

Jackson, T. (2002) Reframing human resource management in Africa: a cross-cultural perspective. *International Journal of Human Resource Management*, **13**(7): 998–1018.

Jacoby, S. M. (2005) *The Embedded Corporation: Corporate Governance and Employment Relations in Japan and the United States*. Princeton, NJ: Princeton University Press.

Jaffee, D. (2001) *Organization Theory: Tension and Change*. Boston: McGraw-Hill.

James, P. and Walters, D. (2002) Worker representation in health and safety: options for regulatory reform. *Industrial Relations Journal*, **33**(2): 141–56.

Jansen, B. and Jansen, K. (2005) Using the web to look for work. *Internet Research*, **15**(1): 49–66.

Jenkins, C. and Sherman, B. (1979) *The Collapse of Work*. London: Eyre Methuen.

Jewson, N. and Mason, D. (1986) The theory and practice of equal opportunities policies: liberal and radical approaches. *Sociological Review*, **34**(2): 307–34.

Johanson, U. (1999) Why the concept of human resource costing and accounting does not work. *Personnel Review*, **28**(1/2): 91–107.

Johanson, U. and Nilson, M. (1996) *Human Resource Costing and Accounting and Organisational Learning*. Report no. 1995:1. Stockholm: Personnel Economics Institute.

Johnson, G. (1987) *Strategic Change and the Management Process.* Oxford: Blackwell.

Johnson, S., Campbell, M., Devins, D., Gold, J. and Hamblett, J. (2000) *Learning Pays.* Sheffield: National Advisory Council for Education and Training Targets.

Jones, E. (2005) The politics of Europe 2004: solidarity and integration. *Industrial Relations Journal,* **36**(6): 436–55.

Jones, O. (1997) Changing the balance? Taylorism, TQM and the work organization. *New Technology, Work and Employment,* **12**(1): 13–23.

Judge, T. A. and Cable, D. M. (1997) Applicant personality, organizational culture and organization attraction. *Personnel Psychology,* **50**: 359–94.

Judt, T. (2005) *Postwar: A History of Europe since 1945.* New York: Penguin.

Jurgens, U. (1989) The transfer of Japanese management concepts in the international automobile industry. In S. Wood (ed.) *The Transformation of Work?* (pp. 204–18). London: Unwin Hyman.

Kamenou, N. and Fearfull, A. (2006) Ethnic minority women: a lost voice in HRM. *Human Resource Management Journal,* **16**(2): 154–72.

Kamoche, K. (1996) Strategic human resource management within a resource-capability view of the firm. *Journal of Management Studies,* **22**(2): 213–33.

Kaplan, R. and Norton, D. (2000) *The Strategy-focused Organization: How Balanced Scorecard Companies Thrive in the New Business Environment.* Boston, MA: Harvard Business School Press.

Kasl, E., Marsick, V. and Dechant, K. (1997) Teams as learners. *Journal of Applied Behaviour Science,* **33**(2): 227–46.

Kato, T. and Morishima, M. (2003) The nature, scope and effects of profit sharing in Japan: evidence from a new survey data. *International Journal of Human Resource Management,* **14**(6): 942–55.

Kaufman, D. (2006) The role of executive coaching in performance management. *Handbook of Business Strategy* **7**(1): 287–91.

Keenoy, T. (1990) Human resource management: rhetoric, reality and contradiction. *International Journal of Human Resource Management,* **1**(3): 363–84.

Keenoy, T. and Anthony, P. (1992) HRM: metaphor, meaning and morality. In P. Blyton and P. Turnbull (eds) *Reassessing Human Resource Management* (pp. 233–55). London: Sage.

Keep, E. (1989) Corporate training policies: the vital component. In J. Storey (ed.) *New Perspectives in Human Resource Management* (pp. 109–25). London: Routledge.

Keep, E. (1999) *Employer Attitudes Towards Adult Learning.* Skills Task Force Research Paper no. 15. London: Department for Education and Employment.

Keep, E. (2004) Trapped on the low road? *Adults Learning,* February: 16–17.

Keep, E. (2005) Skills and training. In S. Bach (ed.) *Managing Human Resources* (pp. 211–36). Oxford: Blackwell.

Keith, M. (2000) Sexual harassment case law under the Employment Contracts Act 1991. *New Zealand Journal of Industrial Relations,* **25**(3): 277–89.

Kelly, J. E. (1985) Management's redesign of work: labour process, labour markets and product markets. In D. Knights, H. Willmott and D. Collinson (eds) *Job Design: Critical Perspectives on the Labour Process* (pp. 30–51). Aldershot: Gower.

Kelly, J. E. (1988) *Trade Unions and Socialist Politics.* London: Verso.

Kelly, J. E. (1996) Union militancy and social partnership. In P. Ackers, C. Smith and P. Smith (eds) *The New Workplace and Trade Unionism* (pp. 77–91). London: Routledge.

Kelly, J. E. (1998) *Rethinking Industrial Relations: Mobilisation, Collectivism and Long Waves.* London: Routledge.

Kelly, J. E. (2005) Industrial relations approaches to the employment relationship. In J. A.-M. Coyle-Shapiro, L. Shore, S. Taylor and L. Tetrick (eds) *The Employment Relationship: Examining Psychological and Contextual Perspectives* (pp. 48–64). Oxford: Oxford University Press.

Kelly, J. E. and Bailey, R. (1989) Research note: British trade union membership, density and decline in the 1980s. *Industrial Relations Journal,* **20**(1): 54–61.

Kennerley, M. and Neely, A. (2002) A framework of the factors affecting the evolution of performance measurement systems. *International Journal of Operations and Production Management,* **22**: 1222–45.

Kersley, B., Alpin, C., Forth, J., Bryson, A., Bewley, H., Dix, G. and Oxenbridge, S. (2005) *Inside the Workplace: First Findings from the 2004 Workplace Employment Relations Survey (WERS 2004).* London: DTI/ESRC/ACAS/PSI.

Kersley, B., Alpin, C., Forth, J., Bryson, A., Bewley, H., Dix, G. and Oxenbridge, S. (2006) *Inside the*

Workplace: Findings from the 2004 Workplace Employment Relations Survey. London: Routledge.

Kessels, J. W. M. (1996) *Corporate Education: The Ambivalent Perspective of Knowledge Productivity*. Leiden University: Centre for Education and Instruction.

Kessels, J. W. M. (2001) Learning in organisations: a corporate curriculum for the knowledge economy. *Futures*, **33**(6): 497–506.

Kessler, I. (1994) Performance pay. In K. Sisson (ed.) *Personnel Management* (2nd edn). Oxford: Blackwell.

Kessler, I. (1995) Reward systems. In J. Storey (ed.) *Human Resource Management: A Critical Text* (pp. 254–79). London: Routledge.

Kessler, I. (2001) Reward system choices. In J. Storey (ed.) *Human Resource Management: A Critical Text* (2nd edn) (pp. 206–31). London: Thomson Learning.

Kessler, S. and Bayliss, F. (1995) *Contemporary British Industrial Relations* (2nd edn). Basingstoke: Macmillan – now Palgrave Macmillan.

Kettley, P. (1997) *Personal Feedback: Cases in Point*. Report no. 326. Brighton: Institute for Employment Studies.

Kettley, P. and Reilly, P. (2003) *e-HR: An Introduction*. Report no. 398. Brighton: Institute of Employment Studies.

Kidd, J., Xue, L. and Richter, F.-J. (2001) *Maximizing Human Intelligence Deployment in Asian Business*. Basingstoke: Palgrave Macmillan.

Kim, S. and Briscoe, D. (1997) Globalization and a new human resource policy in Korea: Transformation to a performance based HRM. *Employee Relations*, **19**(4): 298–308.

Kinnie, N. J. and Arthurs, A. J. (1996) Personnel specialists' advanced use of information technology. *Personnel Review*, **25**(3): 3–19.

Kirkbride, P. S. (ed.) (1994) *Human Resource Management in Europe*. London: Routledge.

Kirkpatrick, D. L. (1983) Four steps to measuring training effectiveness. *Personnel Administrator*, November: 19–25.

Kirton, G. and Green, A. (2000) *The Dynamics of Managing Diversity*. Oxford: Butterworth Heinemann.

Klass, B., Gainey, T., McClendon, J. and Yang, H. (2005) Professional employer organizations and their impact on client satisfaction with human resource outcomes: a field study of human resource outsourcing in small and medium enterprises. *Journal of Management*, **31**(2): 234–54.

Klein, N. (2000) *No Logo*. London: Flamingo.

Kline, T. (1999) *Remaking Teams*. San Francisco, CA: Jossey-Bass.

Knight, K. and Latreille, P. (2000) Discipline, dismissals and complaints to employment tribunals. *British Journal of Industrial Relations*, **38**(4): 533–55.

Knights, D. and Willmott, H. (eds) (1986) *Gender and the Labour Process*. Aldershot: Gower.

Kochan, T. E. and Dyer, L. (1995) HRM: an American view. In J. Storey (ed.) *Human Resource Management: A Critical Text* (pp. 332–51). London: Routledge.

Kochan, T. E., Batt, R. and Dyer, L. (1992) International human resource studies: a framework for future research. In D. Lewlin, O. Mitchell and P. Sterer (eds) *Research Frontiers – Industrial Relations and Human Resources* (pp. 309–37). Madison: University of Wisconsin, Industrial Relations Association.

Kochan, T. E., Katz, H. and McKersie, R. (1986) *The Transformation of American Industrial Relations*. New York: Basic Books.

Kolb, D. A. (1984) *Experiential Learning*. Englewood Cliffs, NJ: Prentice Hall.

Kolk, N., Born, M. and van den Flier, H. (2003) The transparent assessment centre: the effects of revealing dimensions to candidates. *Applied Psychology: An International Review*, **52**(4): 648–68.

Kono, T. (1984) *Strategy and Structure of Japanese Enterprise*. London: Macmillan.

Konzelmann, S. (2005) Varieties of capitalism: production and market relations in the USA and Japan. *British Journal of Industrial Relations*, **43**(4): 593–603.

Konzelmann, S., Conway, N., Trenberth, L. and Wilkinson, F. (2006) Corporate governance and human resource management. *British Journal of Industrial Relations*, **44**(3): 541–67.

Korczynski, M. (2002) *Human Resource Management in Service Work*. Basingstoke: Palgrave Macmillan.

Kotter, J. (1990) *A Force for Change*. New York: Free Press.

Kotter, J. (1996) *Leading Change*. Boston, MA: Harvard Business.

Koubek, J. and Brewster, C. (1995) Human resource management in turbulent times: HRM in the Czech Republic. *International Journal of Human Resource Management*, **6**(2): 223–47.

KPMG (1996) *Learning Organisation Benchmarking Survey*. London: KPMG.

Kramer, R. M. and Tyler, T. R. (1996) *Trust in Organizations: Frontiers of Theory and Research.* Newbury Park, CA: Sage.

Kraut, A. (1996) An overview of organizational surveys. In A. Kraut (ed.) *Organizational Surveys* (pp. 1–17). San Francisco, CA: Jossey-Bass.

Kristof, A. L. (1996) Person–organization fit: an integrative review of its conceptualizations, measurement, and implications. *Personnel Psychology*, **49**: 1–49.

Kumar, P. and Schenk, C. (2006) *Paths to Union Renewal.* Peterborough, Ontario: Broadview Press.

Kuttner, R. (2000) The role of governments in the global economy. In W. Hutton and A. Giddens (eds) *On the Edge: Living with Global Capitalism* (pp. 147–63). London: Jonathan Cape.

Kuwahara, Y. (1998) *Employment Relations in Japan.* In G. Bamber and R. Lansbury (eds) *International and Comparative Employment Relations* (pp. 249–79). London: Sage.

Kydd, B. and Oppenheim, L. (1990) Using human resource management to enhance competitiveness: lessons from four excellent companies. *Human Resource Management Journal*, **29**(2): 145–66.

Lado, A. and Wilson, M. (1994) Human resource systems and sustained competitive advantage: a competency-based perspective. *Academy of Management Review*, **19**: 699–727.

Lane, C. (2000) Understanding the globalization strategies of German and British multinational companies. In M. Maurice and A. Sorge (eds) *Embedding Organizations* (pp. 189–208). Amsterdam: John Benjamin.

Lank, E. (2002) Head to head. *People Management*, **8**(4): 46–9.

Lansbury, R. and Baird, M. (2004) Editorial: Researching HRM and employment relations in a global context: choosing appropriate methodologies. *International Journal of Human Resource Management,* **15**(3): 429–32.

Lash, S. and Urry, J. (1987) *The End of Organized Capitalism.* Cambridge: Polity Press.

Latham, G. P., Saari, L. M., Pursell, E. D. and Campion, M. A. (1980) The situational interview. *Journal of Applied Psychology*, **65**: 422–27.

Lave, J. and Wenger, E. (1991*) Situated Learning.* Cambridge: Cambridge University Press.

Lawler, E. E. (1990) *Strategic Pay: Aligning Organizational Strategies and Pay Systems.* San Francisco: Jossey-Bass.

Lawler, E. E. (1995) The new pay: a strategic approach. *Compensation and Benefits Review*, July–August: 64–54.

Learning and Skills Council (2005) *National Employers Skills Survey 2004.* Coventry: LSC.

Lee, B. and Cassell, C. (2004) A study of accountability in work-based learning: the learning representative initiative in the UK. *Management*, **8**: 171–81.

Legge, K. (1989) Human resource management: a critical analysis. In J. Storey (ed.) *New Perspectives on Human Resource Management* (pp. 21–36). London: Routledge.

Legge, K. (1995) *Human Resource Management: Rhetorics and Realities.* Basingstoke: Macmillan – now Palgrave Macmillan.

Legge, K. (1998) The morality of HRM. In C. Mabey, D. Skinner and T. Clark (eds) *Experiencing Human Resource Management* (pp. 14–30). London: Sage.

Legge, K. (2001) Silver bullet or spent round? Assessing the meaning of the 'high commitment'/performance relationship. In J. Storey (ed.) *Human Resource Management* (pp. 21–36). London: Thomson Learning.

Legge, K. (2005) *Human Resource Management: Rhetorics and Realities* (anniversary edn). Basingstoke: Palgrave Macmillan.

Lepak, D. P. and Snell, S. A. (1999) The strategic management of human capital: determinants and implications of different relationships. *Academy of Management Review*, **24**(1): 1–18.

Levinson, H. (1970) Management by whose objectives? *Harvard Business Review*, July/August: 125–34.

Levy, D. L. (2005) Offshoring in the new global political economy. *Journal of Management Studies*, **42**(3): 685–93.

Li, J. (2003) Strategic human resource management and MNEs' performance in China. *International Journal of Human Resource Management*, **14**(2): 157–73.

Liff, S. (1997a) Constructing HR information systems. *Human Resource Management Journal*, **7**(2): 18–31.

Liff, S. (1997b) Two routes to managing diversity: individual differences or social group characteristics. *Employee Relations*, **19**(1): 11–26.

Liff, S. (2000) Manpower or human resource planning – what's in a name? In S. Bach and K. Sisson (eds) *Personnel Management* (3rd edn) (pp. 93–110). Blackwell: Oxford.

Liff, S. and Dickens, L. (2000) Ethics and equality: reconciling false dilemmas. In D. Winstanley and J. Woodall (eds) *Ethical Issues in Contemporary Human Resource Management* (pp. 85–101).

Basingstoke: Macmillan – now Palgrave Macmillan.

Lincoln, J. and Kalleberg, A. (1992) *Culture Control and Commitment*. Cambridge: Cambridge University Press.

Lindkvist, L. (2004) Governing project-based firms: promoting market-like processes within hierarchies. *Journal of Management and Governance*, **8**: 3–25.

Linehan, M. (2000) *Senior Female International Managers: Why so Few?* Aldershot: Ashgate.

Linehan, M. (2005) Women in international management. In H. Scullion and M. Linehan (eds) *International Human Resource Management* (pp. 181–201). Basingstoke: Palgrave Macmillan.

Linehan, M. and Mayrhofer, W. (2005) International careers and repatriation. In H. Scullion and M. Linehan (eds) *International Human Resource Management* (pp. 131–55). Basingstoke: Palgrave Macmillan.

Littler, C. R. (1982) *The Development of the Labour Process in Capitalist Societies*. London: Heinemann.

Littler, C. R. and Salaman, G. (1984) *Class at Work: The Design, Allocation and Control of Jobs*. London: Batsford.

Littler, C. R., Wiesner, R. and Dunford, R. (2003) The dynamics of de-layering: changing management structures in three countries. *Journal of Management Studies*, **40**(2): 225–56.

Lloyd, C. (1997) Microelectronics in the clothing industry: firm strategy and the skills debate. *New Technology, Work and Employment*, **12**(1): 36–47.

Lloyd, C. and Payne, J. (2004) *Just Another Bandwagon? A Critical Look at the Role of the High Performance Workplace as Vehicle for the UK High Skills Project*. SKOPE Research Paper no. 49. Warwick: ESRC Research Centre on Skills, Knowledge and Organisational Performance (SKOPE).

Locke, E. A., Feren, D. B., McCaleb, V., Shaw, K. and Denny, A. (1980) The relative effectiveness of four methods of motivating employee performance. In K. D. Duncan, M. Gruneberg and D. Wallis (eds) *Changes in Working Life*. London: Wiley.

Locke, R. and Thelen, K. (1995) Apples and organges compared: contextualised comparisions and the study of comparative politics. *Politics and Society*, **23**(3): 337–67.

Long, R. J. (2002) *Strategic Compensation in Canada* (2nd edn). Scarborough, Ontario: Thomson Learning.

Loveridge, R. (1983) Labour market segmentation and the firm. In J. Edwards, C. Leek, R. Loveridge, R. Lumley, J. Mangan and M. Silver (eds) *Manpower Planning: Strategy and Techniques in an Organisational Context* (pp. 155–75). Chichester: John Wiley & Sons.

Lowe, G. (2000) *The Quality of Work*. Don Mills, Ontario: Oxford University Press.

Lowstedt, J. (1988) Prejudices and wishful thinking about computer aided design. *New Technology, Work and Employment*, **3**(1): 30–7.

Lucas, R., Marinova, M., Kucerova, J. and Vetrokova, M. (2004) HRM practice in emerging economies: a long way to go in the Slovak hotel industry? *International Journal of Human Resource Management*, **15**(7): 1262–79.

Luthar, V. and Luthar, H. (2002) Using Hofstede's cultural dimensions to explain sexually harassing behaviours in an international context. *International Journal of Human Resource Management*, **13**(2): 268–84.

Lyon, P. and Glover, I. (1998) Divestment or investment? The contradictions of HRM in relation to older employees. *Human Resource Management Journal*, **8**(1): 56–68.

Mabey, C. and Iles, P. (1991) HRM from the other side of the fence. *Personnel Management*, February: 50–3.

Mabey, C., Salaman, G. and Storey, J. (eds) (1998a) *Human Resource Management: A Strategic Introduction*. Oxford: Blackwell.

Mabey, C., Skinner, D. and Clark, D. (eds) (1998b) *Experiencing Human Resource Management*. London: Sage.

McCarthy, A. M. and Garavan, T. N. (2001) 360° feedback processes: performance improvement and employee career development. *Journal of European Industrial Training*, **25**(1): 5–32.

McCarthy, J. and Goffin, R. (2004) Measuring job interview anxiety: beyond weak knees and sweaty palms. *Personnel Psychology*, **57**: 607–37.

McClurg, L. N. (2001) Team rewards: how far have we come? *Human Resource Management*, **40**(1): 73–86.

McCormack, B. (2000) Workplace learning: a unifying concept. *Human Resource Development International*, **3**(3): 397–404.

McCracken, M. and Wallace, M. (2000) Towards a redefinition of strategic HRD. *Journal of European Industrial Training*, **24**(5): 281–90.

MacDuffie, J. P. (1995) Human resource bundles and manufacturing performance: organizational logic and flexible production systems in the world of auto industry. *Industrial and Labor Relations Review*, **48**: 197–221.

McGoldrick, J. and Stewart, J. (1996) The HRM–HRD nexus. In J. McGoldrick and J. Stewart (eds) *Human Resource Development* (pp. 9–27). London: Pitman Publishing.

McGoldrick, J., Stewart, J. and Watson, S. (2001) Theorizing human resource development. *Human Resource Development International*, **4**(3): 343–56.

McGregor, D. (1957) An uneasy look at performance apprasisal. *Harvard Business Review*, **35**(3): 89–94.

McGregor, D. (1960) *The Human Side of Enterprise*. New York: McGraw-Hill.

McHenry, R. (1997a) Tried and tested. *People Management*, 23 January: 32–7.

McHenry, R. (1997b) Spurring stuff. *People Management*, 24 July: 28–31.

Machin, S. (2000) Union decline in Britain. *British Journal of Industrial Relations*, **38**(4): 631–45.

Machin, S. and Vignoles, A. (2001) *The Economic Benefits of Training to the Individual, the Firm and the Economy: The Key Issues*. London: Centre for the Economics of Education.

McIlroy, J. (1991) *The Permanent Revolution? Conservative Law and the Trade Unions*. Nottingham: Spokesman.

MacInnes, J. (1985) Conjuring up consultation. *British Journal of Industrial Relations*, **23**(1): 93–113.

MacInnes, J. (1987) *Thatcherism at Work*. Milton Keynes: Open University Press.

McIvor, R. (2005) *The Outsourcing Process: Strategies for Evaluation and Management*. Cambridge: Cambridge University Press.

McKendrick, E. (1988) The rights of trade union members: part I of the Employment Act 1980. *Industrial Law Journal*, **17**(3): 141–61.

Mackie, K. S., Holahan, C. and Gottlieb, N. (2001) Employee involvement management practices, work stress, and depression in employees of a human services residential care facility. *Human Relations*, **54**(8): 1065–92.

McKiernan, P. and Carter, C. (2004) The millennium nexus, strategic management at the crossroads. *European Management Review*, **1**: 3–13.

McKinlay, A. and Taylor, P. (1998) Through the looking glass: Foucault and the politics of production. In A. McKinlay and K. Starkey (eds) *Foucault, Management and Organizational Theory* (pp. 173–90). London: Sage.

McLoughlin, I. and Clark, J. (1988) *Technological Change at Work*. Milton Keynes: Open University Press.

McMillan-Capehart, A. (2005) A configurational framework for diversity: socialization and culture. *Personnel Review*, **34**(4): 488–503.

McNabb, R. and Whitfield, K. (2001) Job evaluation and high performance work practices: compatible or conflictual? *Journal of Management Studies*, **38**(2): 293–312.

Macpherson, W. (1999) *The Stephen Lawrence Inquiry*. London: Stationery Office.

McShane, S. L. (1990) Two tests of direct gender bias in job evaluation ratings. *Journal of Occupational Psychology*, **63**: 129–40.

McShane, S. L. (2006) *Canadian Organizational Behaviour* (6th edn). Boston: Irwin.

Madsen, S. R. (2003) Wellness in the workplace: preparing employees for change. *Organization Development Journal*, **21**(1): 46–55.

Maitra, S. and Sangha, J. (2005) Intersecting realities: young women and call centre work in India and Canada. *Women and Environments*, Spring/Summer: 40–2.

Malloch, H. (1997) Strategic and HRM aspects of kaizen: a case study. *New Technology, Work and Employment*, **12**(2): 108–22.

Mallon, M. and Walton, S. (2005) Career and learning: the ins and the outs of it. *Personnel Review*, **34**(4): 468–87.

Mankin, D. P. (2001) A model for human resource development. *Human Resource Development International*, **4**(1): 65–85.

Mann, S. and Holdsworth, L. (2003) The psychological impact of teleworking: stress, emotion and health. *New Technology, Work and Employment*, **1**(3): 196–211.

Mannion, E. and Whittaker, P. (1996) European Passenger Services Ltd – assessment centres for recruitment and development. *Career Development International*, **1**(6): 12–16.

Marchington, M. (1980) *Responses to Participation at Work*. Aldershot: Gower.

Marchington, M. (1982) *Managing Industrial Relations*. Maidenhead: McGraw-Hill.

Marchington, M. (1987) A review and critique of research on developments in joint consultation. *British Journal of Industrial Relations*, **25**(3): 339–52.

Marchington, M. (1995) Involvement and participation. In J. Storey (ed.) *Human Resource Management: A Critical Text* (pp. 280–305). London: Routledge.

Marchington, M. (2001) Employee involvement. In J. Storey (ed.) *Human Resource Management: A Critical Text* (pp. 232–52). London: Thomson Learning.

Marchington, M. and Grugulis, I. (2000) 'Best practice' human resource management: perfect opportunity or dangerous illusion? *International Journal of Human Resource Management*, **11**(6): 1104–24.

Marchington, M. and Wilding, P. (1983) Employee involvement inaction? *Personnel Management*, December: 73–82.

Marchington, M. and Wilkinson, A. (2000) Direct participation. In S. Bach and K. Sisson (eds) *Personnel Management: A Comprehensive Guide to Theory and Practice*. Oxford: Blackwell.

Marchington, M. and Zegelmeyer, S. (2005) Foreword: linking HRM and performance – a never-ending search? *Human Resource Management Journal*, **15**(4): 3–8.

Marchington, M., Goodman, J., Wilkinson, A. and Ackers, P. (1992) *Recent Developments in Employee Involvement*. Employment Department Research Series no. 1. London: HMSO.

Marginson, P. and Wood, S. (2000) WERS98 special issue: Editor's introduction. *British Journal of Industrial Relations*, **38**(4): 489–99.

Marsick, V. and Watkins, K. E. (1999) Envisioning new organisations for learning. In D. Boud and J. Garrick (eds) *Understanding Learning at Work* (pp. 199–215). London: Routledge.

Martin, R. and Cristescu-Martin, A. (1999) Industrial relations in transformation: Central and Eastern Europe in 1998. *Industrial Relations Journal*, **30**(4): 387–402.

Martin, R. and Cristescu-Martin, A. (2002) Employment relations in Central and Eastern Europe in 2001. *Industrial Relations Journal*, **33**(5): 523–35.

Martin, J. N. and Nakayama, T. K. (2000) *Intercultural Communications in Context* (2nd edn). Mountain View, CA: Mayfield.

Martinez Lucio, M. and Weston, S. (1992) Human resource management and trade union responses: bringing the politics of the workplace back into the debate. In P. Blyton and P. Turnbull (eds) *Reassessing Human Resource Management* (pp. 215–32). London: Sage.

Maslow, A. (1954) *Motivation and Personality*. New York: Harper & Row.

Matlay, H. (2004) Contemporary training initiatives in Britain: a small business perspective. *Journal of Small Business and Enterprise Development*, **11**(4): 504–13.

Matzdorf, F., Price, I. and Green, M. (1999) Barriers to organizational learning in the chartered surveying profession. *Property Management*, **18**(2): 92–113.

Maurice, M. and Sorge, A. (eds) (2000) *Embedding Organizations*. Amsterdam: John Benjamins.

Mayerhofer, H., Hartmann, L., Michelitsch-Riedl, G. and Kollinger, I. (2004) Flexpatriate assignments: a neglected issue in global staffing. *International Journal of Human Resource Management*, **15**(8): 1371–89.

Mayfield, M., Mayfield, J. and Lunce, S. (2003) Human resource information systems: a review and model development. *Advances in Competitiveness Research*, **11**(1): 139–51.

Mayhew, C. and Quinlan, M. (1997) Subcontracting and occupational health and safety in the residential building industry. *Industrial Relations Journal*, **28**(3): 192–205.

Mayo, A. (1991) *Managing Careers*. London: Institute of Personnel Management.

Mayo, A. (1998) Memory bankers. *People Management*, 22 January: 34–8.

Mayo, A. (2002) A thorough evaluation. *People Management*, **8**(7): 36–9.

Mayo, A. (2004) *Creating a Learning and Development Strategy*. London: Chartered Institute of Personnel and Development.

Mayrhofer, W., Brewster, C., Morley, M. and Gunnigle, P. (2000) Communication, consultation and the HRM debate. In C. Brewster, W. Mayrhofer and M. Morley (eds) *New Challenges for European Human Resource Management* (pp. 222–44). Basingstoke: Macmillan – now Palgrave Macmillan.

Mearns, K. and Hope, L. (2005) *Health and Well-being in Offshore Environment: The Management of Personal Health*. Research Report no. 305, London: Health and Safety Executive.

Megginson, D. (2000) Current issues in mentoring. *Career Development International*, **5**(4): 256–60.

Megginson, D. and Clutterbuck, D. (1995) *Mentoring in Action*. London: Kogan Page.

Megginson, D. and Pedler, M. (1992) *Self Development*. Maidenhead: McGraw-Hill.

Merriam, S. and Simpson, E. (1995) *A Guide to Research for Educators and Trainers of Adults*. Malabar, FL: Krieger.

Merrick, N. (2001) Wel.com aboard. *People Management*, **7**(10): 26–32.

Meyer, H. H., Kay, E. and French, J. R. P. (1965) Split roles in performance appraisal. *Harvard Business Review*, **43**: 123–29.

Mezirow, J. (1991) *Transformative Dimensions of Adult Learning*. San Francisco: Jossey-Bass.

Michaels, E., Handfiled-Jones, H. and Axelrod, B. (2001) *The War for Talent*. Boston: Harvard Business School Press.

Michie, J. (1992) Unlucky 13 for the economy. *Observer*, 5 April: 35.

Michie, J. and Sheehan, M. (2005) Business strategy, human resources, labour market flexibility and competitive advantage. *International Journal of Human Resource Management*, **16**(3): 445–64.

Michie, J. and Sheehan-Quinn, M. (2001) Labour market flexibility: human resource management and corporate performance. *British Journal of Management*, **12**(4): 287–305.

Middlehurst, R. and Kennie, T. (1997) Leading professionals: towards new concepts of professionalism. In J. Broadbent, M. Dietrich and J. Roberts (eds) *The End of the Professions?* (pp. 50–68). London: Routledge.

Miles, R. and Snow, C. (1984) Designing strategic human resources systems. *Organizational Dynamics*, Summer: 36–52.

Miliband, R. (1969) *The State in Capitalist Society*. London: Weidenfeld & Nicolson.

Milkovitch, G. and Newman, J. (2004) *Compensation* (8th edn). New York: McGraw-Hill.

Miller, L., Rankin, N. and Neathey, F. (2001) *Competency Frameworks in UK Organizations*. London: Chartered Institute of Personnel and Development.

Miller, P. (1987) Strategic industrial relations and human resource management – distinction, definition and recognition. *Journal of Management Studies*, **24**(4): 347–61.

Mills, A. and Simmons, T. (1995) *Reading Organizational Theory*. Toronto: Garamond.

Mills, A. and Tancred, P. (eds) (1992) *Gendering Organizational Analysis*. Newbury Park, CA: Sage.

Millward, N. and Stevens, M. (1986) *British Workplace Industrial Relations 1980–1984*. Aldershot: Gower.

Millward, N., Bryson, A. and Forth, J. (2000) *All Change at Work: British Employee Relations 1980–1998*. London: Routledge.

Millward, N., Stevens, M., Smart, D. and Hawes, W. (1992) *Workplace Industrial Relations in Transition*. Aldershot: Dartmouth Press.

Miner-Rubino, K. and Cortina, L. M. (2004) Working in a context of hostility towards women: implications for employees' well-being. *Journal of Occupational Health Psychology*, **9**(2): 107–22.

Mintzberg, H. (1973) *The Nature of Managerial Work*. London: Harper & Row.

Mintzberg, H. (1978) Patterns in strategy formation. *Management Science*, **24**(9): 934–48.

Mintzberg, H. (1987) Crafting strategy. *Harvard Business Review*, July/August: 66–75.

Mintzberg, H. (1989) *Mintzberg on Management*. New York: Collier/Hamilton.

Mintzberg, H. (1990) The design school: reconsidering the basic premises of strategic management. *Strategic Management Journal*, **11**: 171–95.

Mintzberg, H. (2005) *Managers not MBAs*. New York: Berrett-Koehler.

Mintzberg, H., Ahlstrand, B. and Lampel, J. (1998) *Strategic Safari: A Guided Tour Through the Wilds of Strategic Management*. New York: Free Press.

Mok, K., Wong, L. and Lee, G. (2002) The challenges of global capitalism: unemployment and state workers' reactions and responses in post-reform China. *International Journal of Human Resource Management*, **13**(3): 399–415.

Mole, K. F. (2004) *International Review of Business Support and Brokerage: A Report to the Small Business Service*. Warwick: Centre for Small and Medium Sized Enterprises.

Monks, J. (1998) Foreword. In C. Mabey, C., Skinner and D. Clark (eds) *Experiencing Human Resource Management*. London: Sage.

Monks, K. and McMackin, J. (2001) Designing and aligning an HR system. *Human Resource Management Journal*, **11**(2): 57–72.

Montgomery, J. and Kelloway, K. (2002) *Management of Occupational Health and Safety* (2nd edn). Scarborough, Ontario: Nelson Thomson Learning.

Moore, H. L. (1995) The future of work. *British Journal of Industrial Relations*, **33**(4): 657–78.

Morden, T. and Bowles, D. (1998) Management in South Korea: a review. *Management Decisions*, **36**(5): 316–30.

Morgan, G. (1997) *Images of Organization*. London: Sage.

Morley, M., Brewster, C., Gunnigle, P. and Mayrhofer, W. (2000) Evaluating change in European industrial relations: research evidence on trends at organizational level. In C. Brewster, W. Mayrhofer and M. Morley (eds) *New Challenges for European Human Resource Management*. New York: St Martin's Press.

Morrell, K. M., Loan-Clarke, J. and Wilkinson, A. J. (2001) Unweaving leaving: the use of models in the management of employee turnover. *International Journal of Management Reviews*, **3**(1): 219–44.

Morrell, K. M., Loan-Clarke, J. and Wilkinson, A. J. (2004) Organisational change and employee turnover. *Personnel Review*, **33**(2): 161–73.

Morrison, E. W. and Robinson, S. L. (1997) When employees feel betrayed: a model of how psychological contract violation develops. *Academy of Management Review*, **22**(1): 226–56.

Mueller, C., De Coster, S. and Estes, S. (2001) Sexual harassment in the workplace. *Work and Occupations*, **28**(4): 411–46.

Mumford, A. and Gold, J. (2004) *Management Development*. London: Chartered Institute of Personnel and Development.

Munro, A. and Rainbird, H. (2000) The new unionsism and the new bargaining agenda: UNISON–employer partnerships on workplace learning in Britain. *British Journal of Industrial Relations*, **38**(2): 223–40.

Munro, A. and Rainbird, H. (2004) Opening doors as well as banging tables: an assessment of UNISON/employer partnerships on learning in the UK public sector. *Industrial Relations Journal*, **35**(5): 419–33.

Munro-Fraser, J. (1971) *Psychology: General, Industrial, Social*. London: Pitman.

Murakami, T. (1995) Introducing team working: a motor industry case study from Germany. *Industrial Relations Journal*, **26**(4): 293–304.

Murphy, C. and Olthuis, D. (1995) The impact of work reorganization on employee attitudes towards work, the company and the union. In C. Schenk and J. Anderson (eds) *Re-shaping Work: Union Responses to Technological Change* (pp. 76–102). Toronto: Ontario Federation of Labour.

Murray, G. (2001) Unions: membership, structures, actions, and challenges. In M. Gunderson, A. Ponak and D. Taras (eds) *Union–Management Relations in Canada* (4th edn) (pp. 79–116). Toronto: Addison Wesley Longman.

Murray, G. (2005) Like a phoenix? Sources of renewal in the organized study of work and employment. Selected papers from the XLIth Annual CIRA Conference (pp. 11–21). Concord, Ontario: Captus Press.

Mwita, J. I. (2000) Performance management model. *International Journal of Public Sector Management*, **13**(1): 19–37.

National Skills Task Force (1998) *Towards a National Skills Agenda*. London: Department for Education and Employment.

National Skills Task Force (2000) *Skills for All: Research Report from the National Skills Task Force*. London: Department for Education and Employment.

Needle, D. (2004) *Business in Conext* (4th edn). London: Thomson.

New Earnings Survey (2005) National statistics online. www.statistcs.gov/uk/cci.

Newell, S. (2005) Recruitment and selection. In S. Bach (ed.) *Managing Human Resources* (pp. 115–47). Oxford: Blackwell.

Newell, S. and Shackleton, V. (2000) Recruitment and selection. In S. Bach and K. Sisson (eds) *Personnel Management* (3rd edn) (pp. 111–36). Oxford: Blackwell.

Newell, S., Robertson, M., Scarbrough, H. and Swan, J. (2002) *Managing Knowledge Work*. Basingstoke: Palgrave Macmillan.

Newton, T. and Findlay, P. (1996) Playing God? The performance of appraisal. *Human Resource Management Journal*, **6**(3): 42–58.

Ng, Y. C. and Siu, N. (2004) Training and enterprise performance in transition: evidence from China. *International Journal of Human Resource Management*, **15**(4): 878–94.

Nichols, T. (ed.) (1980) *Capital and Labour*. London: Fontana.

Nichols, T. (1986) *The British Worker Question: A New Look at Workers and Productivity in Manufacturing*. London: Routledge & Kegan Paul.

Nichols, T. (1990) Industrial safety in Britain and the 1974 Health and Safety at Work Act: the case of manufacturing. *International Journal of the Sociology of Law*, **18**: 371–42.

Nichols, T. and Beynon, H. (1977) *Living with Capitalism: Class Relations and the Modern Factory*. London: Routledge & Kegan Paul.

Nichols, T., Sugur, N. and Demir, E. (2002) Globalized management and local labour: the case of the white-goods industry in Turkey. *Industrial Relations Journal*, **33**(1): 68–85.

Nkomo, S. M. (1988) Strategic planning for human resources – let's get started. *Long Range Planning*, **21**(1): 66–72.

Noble, C. (1997) International comparisons of training policies. *Human Resource Management Journal*, **7**(1): 5–18.

Nonaka, I. and Takeuchi, H. (1995) *The Knowledge-creating Company*. Oxford: Oxford University Press.

Nonaka, I., Toyama, R. and Nagata, A. (2000) A firm as a knowledge creating entity: a new perspective on the theory of the firm. *Industrial and Corporate Change*, **9**(1): 1–20.

Noon, M. (1992) HRM: a map, model or theory? In P. Blyton and P. Turnbull (eds) *Reassessing Human Resource Management* (pp. 16–32). London: Sage.

Nutley, S. (2000) Beyond systems: HRM audits in the public sector. *Human Resource Management Journal*, **10**(2): 21–38.

O'Donoghue, J. and Maguire, T. (2005) The individual learner, employability and the workplace. *Journal of European Industrial Training*, **29**(6): 436–46.

Office for National Statistics (2005) Labour Force Survey available from www.statistics.gov.uk/StatBase/Source.asp?vlnk=358&more=y, accessed 5 March 2006.

O'Hagan, E., Gunnigle, P. and Morley, M. (2005) Issues in the management of industrial relations in international firms. In H. Scullion and M. Linehan (eds) *International Human Resource Management: A Critical Text* (pp. 156–78). Basingstoke: Palgrave Macmillan.

O'Hagan, E. (2002) *Employee Relations in the Periphery of Europe*. Basingstoke: Palgrave Macmillan.

Oliver, N. and Wilkinson, B. (1988) *The Japanization of British Industry*. Oxford: Blackwell.

Olsen, K. and Kalleberg, A. (2004) Non-standard work in two different employment regimes: Norway and the United States. *Work, Employment and Society*, **18**(2): 321–48.

Organization for Economic Co-operation and Development (1996) *The Knowledge-based Economy*. Paris: OECD.

Organization for Economic Co-operation and Development (1997) *The Internationalisation of Higher Education*. Paris: OECD.

Organization for Economic Co-operation and Development (2004) *Employment Outlook*. Paris: OECD.

Örtenblad, A. (2004) The learning organization: towards an integrated model. *Learning Organization*, **11**(2): 129–44.

Osterman, P. (1995) How common is workplace transformation and who adopts it? *Industrial and Labor Relations Review*, **47**: 173–87.

Ouchi, W. (1979) A conceptual framework for the design of organizational control mechanisms. *Management Science*, **25**(9): 833–48.

Ouchi, W. (1981) *Theory Z: How American Companies Can Meet the Japanese Challenge*. Reading, MA: Addison-Wesley.

Paauwe, J. (2004) *HRM and Performance: Achieving Long-Term Viability*. New York: Oxford University Press.

Paauwe, J. and Boselie, P. (2003) Challenging 'strategic HRM' and the relevance of the institutional setting. *Human Resource Management Journal*, **13**(3): 56–70.

Paauwe, J. and Boselie, P. (2005) HRM and performance: what next? *Human Resource Management Journal*, **15**(4): 68–83.

Pahl, R. E. (ed.) (1988) *On Work: Historical, Comparative and Theoretical Approaches*. Oxford: Blackwell.

Paik, Y., Vance, C. and Stage, H. (1996) The extent of divergence in human resource practice across three Chinese national cultures: Hong Kong, Taiwan and Singapore. *Human Resource Management Journal*, **6**(2): 20–31.

Palys, T. (1997) *Research Decisions: Quantitative and Qualitative Perspectives*. Toronto: Harcourt Brace.

Panteli, N. and Dawson, P. (2001) Video conferencing meetings: changing patterns of business. *New Technology, Work and Employment*, **16**(2): 88–99.

Parker, B. and Caine, D. (1996) Holonic modelling: human resource planning and the two faces of Janus. *International Journal of Manpower*, **17**(8): 30–45.

Parker, J., Mars, L., Ransome, P. and Stanworth, H. (2003) *Social Theory: A Basic Tool Kit*. Basingstoke: Palgrave Macmillan

Pascale, R. T. and Athos, A.G. (1986) *The Art of Japanese Management*. Harmondsworth: Penguin.

Payne, S. and Huffman, A. (2005) A longitudinal examination of the influence of mentoring on organizational commitment and turnover. *Academy of Management Journal*, **48**(1): 158–68.

Pearson, R. (1991) *The Human Resource*. Maidenhead: McGraw-Hill.

Pedler, M. and Aspinall, K. (1996) *Perfect PLC?* Maidenhead: McGraw-Hill.

Pedler, M., Boydell, T. and Burgoyne, J. (1988) *The Learning Company Project Report*. Sheffield: Employment Department.

Pedler, M., Burgoyne, J. and Boydell, T. (1991) *The Learning Company: A Strategy for Sustainable Development*. Maidenhead: McGraw-Hill.

Pendleton, A. (1997a) The evolution of industrial relations in UK nationalized industries. *British Journal of Industrial Relations*, **35**(2): 145–72.

Pendleton, A. (1997b) What impact has privatization had on pay and employment? *Relations Industrielles/Industrial Relations*, **52**(3): 554–82.

Penn, R., Lilja, K. and Scattergood, H. (1992) Flexibility and employment patterns in the paper industry: an analysis of mills in Britain and Finland. *Industrial Relations Journal*, **23**(3): 214–23.

Penrose, E. T. (1959) *The Theory of the Growth of the Firm*. Oxford: Blackwell.

Performance and Innovation Unit (2001) *In Demand: Adult Skills for the 21st Century*. London: Performance and Innovation Unit, Cabinet Office. www.piu.gov.uk/2001/workforce/report/ index.html.

Perrow, C. (1986) *Complex Organizations: A Critical Essay*. New York: Random House.

Peters, T. and Waterman, R. (1982) *In Search of Excellence*. New York: Harper & Row.

Pettigrew, A., Sparrow, P. and Hendry, C. (1988) The forces that trigger training. *Personnel Management*, December: 28–32.

Pettijohn, L. S., Parker, S., Pettijohn, C. E. and Kent, J. L. (2001) Performance appraisals: usage, criteria and observations. *Journal of Management Development*, **20**(9): 754–71.

Pfeffer, J. (1994) *Competitive Advantage Through People: Understanding the Power of the Workforce*. Boston, MA: Houghton Mifflin.

Pfeffer, J. (1998) *The Human Equation*. Boston, MA: Harvard Business School Press.

Pfeffer, J. (2005) Changing mental models: HR's most important task. *Human Resource Management*, **44**(2): 123–8.

Pfeffer, J. and Salancik, G. (1977) Organizational context and the characteristics and tenure of hospital administrators. *Academy of Management Journal*, **20**: 74–88.

Pfeffer, J. and Salancik, G. (1978) *The External Control of Organizations: A Resource Dependency Perspective*. New York: Harper & Row.

Phillips, J. (1996a) Measuring the ROI: the fifth level of evaluation. *Technical and Skills Training*, April: 10–13.

Phillips, J. J. (1996b) *Accountability in Human Resource Management*. Houston, TX: Gulf Publishing.

Phillips, J. (2005) Measuring up. *People Management*, 7 April: 42–3.

Phillips, J. M. (1998) Effects of realistic job previews on multiple organizational outcomes: a meta-analysis. *Academy of Management Journal*, **41**(6): 673–90.

Phillips, P. and Phillips, E. (1993) *Women and Work: Inequality in the Canadian Labour Market*. Toronto: Lorimer.

Phillips, R. (1995) Coaching for higher performance. *Executive Development*, **8**(7): 5–7.

Pickard, J. (1997) Vacational qualifications. *People Management*, 10 July: 26–31.

Pickard, J. (2001) When push comes to shove. *People Management*, **7**(23): 30–5.

Piore, M. and Sabel, C. (1984) *The Second Industrial Divide*. New York: Basic Books.

Plachy, R. J. (1987) Writing job descriptions that get results. *Personnel*, October: 56–63.

Platt, L. (1997) Employee work–life balance: the competitive advantage. In F. Hesselbein, M. Goldsmith and R. Beckhard (eds) *The Drucker Foundation, the Organization of the Future*. San Francisco: Jossey-Bass.

Pollard, E. and Hillage, J. (2001) *Exploring e-Learning*. Report no. 376. Brighton: Institute for Employment Studies.

Pollert, A. (1988) Dismantling flexibility. *Capital and Class*, (34): 42–75.

Pollert, A. (1991) *Farewell to Flexibility?* Oxford: Blackwell.

Pollitt, C. (2000) Is the emperor in his new underwear?: an analysis of the impacts of public management reform. *Public Management*, **2**(2): 181–99.

Pollitt, D. (2005a) E-recruitment gets the Nike tick of approval. *Human Resource Management International Digest*, **13**(2): 33–5.

Pollitt, D. (2005b) Testing graduates at Lloyds TSB. *Human Resource Management International Digest*, **13**(1): 12–14.

Poon, J. (2004) Effects of performance appraisal politics on job satisfaction and turnover intention. *Personnel Review*, **33**(3): 322–34.

Porter, M. (1980) *Competitive Strategy*. New York: Free Press.

Porter, M. (1985) *Competitive Advantage: Creating and Sustaining Superior Performance*. New York: Free Press.

Posthuma, R., Morgeson, F. and Campion, M. (2002) Beyond employment interview validity: a comprehensive narrative review of recent research and trends over time. *Personnel Psychology*, **55**: 1–82.

Potosky, D. and Bobko, P. (2004) Selection testing via the internet: practical considerations and exploratory empirical findings. *Personnel Psychology*, **57**: 1003–34.

Powell, W. and DiMaggio, P. (eds) (1991) *The New Institutionalism in Organizational Analysis*. Chicago: University of Chicago Press.

Prahalad, C. K. and Doz, Y. L. (1987) *The Multinational Mission: Balancing Local Demands and Global Vision*. New York: Free Press.

Prahalad, C. K. and Hamel, G. (1990) The core competencies of the corporation. *Harvard Business Review*, **68**(May–June): 79–91.

Pratt, D. D. (1998) Alternative frames of understanding. In D. D. Pratt (ed.) *Five Perspectives on Teaching in Adult and Higher Education* (pp. 33–53). Malabar, FL: Krieger.

Premack, S. L. and Wanous, J. P. (1985) A meta-analysis of realistic job preview experiments. *Journal of Applied Psychology*, **70**(4): 706–19.

Priestland, A. and Hanig, R. (2005) Developing first level leaders. *Harvard Business Review*, **83**(6): 112–20.

PRI Project (2004) *The Working Poor and the Role of Precarious Employment*. Ottawa: IDRC.

Proctor, S. and Mueller, F. (eds) (2000) *Teamworking*. Basingstoke: Macmillan – now Palgrave Macmillan.

Prokopenko, J. (1994) The transition to a market economy and its implications for HRM in Eastern Europe. In P. S. Kirkbride (ed.) *Human Resource Management in Europe* (pp. 147–63). London: Routledge.

Pryce, V. and Nicholson, C. (1988) The problems and performance of employee ownership firms. *Employment Gazette*, **96**(6): 53–8.

Psoinos, A. and Smithson, S. (2002) Employee empowerment in manufacturing: a study of organizations in the UK. *New Technology, Work and Employment*, **17**(2): 132–48.

Pudelko, M. (2006) A comparison of HRM systems in the USA, Japan and Germany in their socio-economic context. *Human Resource Management Journal*, **16**(2): 123–53.

Pulakos, E. D. and Schmitt, N. (1995) Experienced-based and situational questions: studies of validity. *Personnel Psychology*, **48**: 289–309.

Pulignano, V. and Stewart, P. (2006) Bureaucracy transcended? New patterns of employment regulation and labour contol in the international automotive industry. *New Technology, Work and Employment*, **21**(2): 90–106.

Pun, K. F. and White, A. S. (2005) A performance measurement paradigm for integrating strategy formulation: a review of systems and frameworks. *International Journal of Management Reviews*, **7**(1): 49–71.

Punnett, B., Crocker, O. and Stevens, M. (1992) The challenge for women expatriates and spouses: some empirical evidence. *International Journal of Human Resource Management*, **3**(3): 585–92.

Purcell, J. (1989) The impact of corporate strategy on human resource management. In J. Storey (ed.) *New Perspectives on Human Resource Management* (pp. 67–91). London: Routledge.

Purcell, J. (1995) Corporate strategy and its link with human resource management strategy. In J. Storey (ed.) *Human Resource Management: A Critical Text* (pp. 63–86). London: Routledge.

Purcell, J. (1999) Best practice and best fit: chimera or cul-de-sac? *Human Resource Management Journal*, **9**(3): 26–41.

Purcell, J. (2001) The meaning of strategy in human resource management: a critical text. In J. Storey (ed.) *Human Resource Management* (pp. 59–77). London: Thomson Learning.

Purcell, J. (2003) Foreward. *Human Resource Management Journal*, **13**(3): 3–4.

Purcell, J. (2004) Foreward. *Human Resource Management Journal*, **14**(2): 2–3.

Purcell, J. and Ahlstrand, B. (1994) *Human Resource Management in the Multi-divisional Company*. Oxford: Oxford University Press.

Purcell, J. and Sisson, K. (1983) Strategies and practices in the management of industrial relations. In G. Bain (ed.) *Industrial Relations in Britain* (pp. 95–120). Oxford: Blackwell.

Pye, M., Cullinane, J. and Harcourt, M. (2001) The right to refuse unsafe work in New Zealand. *New Zealand Journal of Industrial Relations*, **26**(2): 199–216.

Quah, D. (1997) Weightless economy packs a heavy punch. *Independent on Sunday*, May 18: 4.

Quintanilla, J. and Ferner, A. (2003) Multinationals and human resource management: between global convergence and national identity. *International Journal of Human Resource Management*, **14**(3): 363–8.

Rainbird, H. (2000) Training in the workplace and workplace learning: introduction. In H. Rainbird (ed.) *Training in the Workplace* (pp. 1–17). Basingstoke: Macmillan – now Palgrave Macmillan.

Randell, G. (1994) Employee appraisal. In K. Sisson (ed.) *Personnel Management* (pp. 221–52). Oxford: Blackwell.

Rarick, C. A. and Baxter, G. (1986) Behaviourally anchored rating scales (bars): an effective performance appraisal approach. *SAM Advanced Management Journal*, Winter: 36–9.

Redman, T., Snape, E., Thompson, D. and Ka-Ching Yan, F. (2000) Performance appraisal in an NHS hospital. *Human Resource Management Journal*, **10**(1): 48–62.

Reed, M. I. (1989) *The Sociology of Management*. Hemel Hempstead: Harvester Wheatsheaf.

Reed, M. I. (1993) Organizations and modernity: continuity and discontinuity in organization theory. In J. Hassard and M. Parker (eds) *Post-modernism and Organizations* (pp. 163–82). London: Sage.

Rees, I. (1998) *Mainstreaming Equality in the European Union: Education, Training and Labour Market Policies*. London: Routledge.

Rees, W. D. (1998) Communication. In M. Poole and M. Warner (eds) *Handbook of Human Resource Management* (pp. 488–91). London: Thomson Business.

Reilly, B., Paci, P. and Holl P. (1995) Unions, safety committees and workplace injuries. *British Journal of Industrial Relations*, **33**(2): 275–87.

Reilly, P. (2005) Get the best from knowledge workers. *People Management*, **29**(September): 52–3.

Reilly, R. R., Smither, J. W. and Vasilopoulos, N. L. (1996) A longitudinal study of upward appraisal. *Personnel Psychology*, **46**: 599–612.

Reinharz, S. (1988) Feminist distrust: problems of context and content in sociological work. In D. N. Berg and K. K. Smith (eds) *The Self in Social Inquiry*. Newbury Park, CA: Sage.

Rendall, P. (1986) Stuck in the middle. *Chief Executive*, September.

Richbell, S. (2001) Trends and emerging values in human resource management. *International Journal of Manpower*, **22**(3): 261–8.

Riesman, C. K. (1993) *Narrative Analysis*. Thousand Oaks, CA: Sage.

Rifkin, J. (1996) *The End of Work*. New York: Tarcher/Putnam Press.

Rinehart, J. W. (2006) *The Tyranny of Work*. Toronto: Thomson Nelson.

Risher, H. (1978) Job evaluation: mystical or statistical. *Personnel*, **55**: 23–36.

Rix, M. and Gold, J. (2000) 'With a little help from my academic friend': mentoring change agents. *Mentoring and Tutoring*, **8**(1): 47–62.

Robbins, S. P. (1989) *Organizational Behavior* (4th edn). London: Prentice Hall.

Robbins, S. P. (1990) *Organization Theory* (3rd edn). Englewood Cliffs, NJ: Prentice Hall.

Robens, Lord (1972) *Safety and Health at Work*. Cmnd 5034. London: HMSO.

Roberts, G. (1997) *Recuitment and Selection*. London: Institute of Personnel and Development.

Robertson, I. T., Baron, H., Gibbons, P., MacIver, R. and Nyfield, G. (2000) Conscientiousness and managerial performance. *Journal of Occupational and Organizational Psychology*, **73**(2): 171–81.

Roche, W. and Geary, J. (2002) Advocates, critics and union involvement in workplace partnerships: Irish airports. *British Journal of Industrial Relations*, **40**(4): 659–88.

Rodger, A. (1970) *The Seven Point Plan* (3rd edn). London: NFER.

Rolfe, H. (1986) Skill, deskilling and new technology in the non-manual labour process. *New Technology, Work and Employment*, **1**(1): 37–49.

Rose, M. (1988) *Industrial Behaviour*. London: Penguin.

Rose, M. (2000) Target practice. *People Management*, **6**(23): 44–5.

Rousseau, D. M. (1995) *Psychological Contracts in Organizations: Understanding Written and Unwritten Agreements*. Thousand Oaks, CA: Sage.

Rousseau, D. M. and Ho, V. T. (2000) Psychological contract issues in compensation. In S. L. Rynes and B. Gerhart (eds) *Compensation in Organizations: Current Research and Practice* (pp. 273–310). San Francisco, CA: Jossey-Bass.

Rowley, C. and Bae, J. (2002) Globalization and transformation of human resource management in South Korea. *International Journal of Human Resource Management*, **13**(3): 522–49.

Rowley, C., Benson, J. and Warner, M. (2004) Towards an Asian model of human resource management? A comparative analysis of China, Japan and South Korea. *International Journal of Human Resource Management*, **14**(4): 917–33.

Royle, T. (2005) The union recognition dispute at McDonald's Moscow food-processing factory. *Industrial Relations Journal*, **36**(4): 318–32.

Rubery, J. (1988) Employers and the labour market. In D. Gallie (ed.) *Employment in Britain* (pp. 251–80). Oxford: Blackwell.

Rubery, J., Smith, M. and Fagen, C. (1999) *Women's Employment in Europe: Trends and Prospects*. London: Routledge.

Rynes, S. and Gerhart, B. (eds) (2000) *Compensation in Organizations: Current Research and Practice*. San Francisco: Jossey-Bass.

Sako, M. (2005) Does embeddedness imply limits to within-country diversity? *British Journal of Industrial Relations*, **43**(4): 585–92.

Sako, K. and Tierney, A. (2005) *Sustainability of Business Service Outsourcing: The Case of Human Resource Outsourcing (HRO)* AIM Working Paper. London: Advanced Institute of Management.

Saks, A. M. (2000) *Research, Measurement, and Evaluation of Human Sources*. Scarborough, Ontario: Nelson/Thompson Learning.

Salaman, G. (1979) *Work Organizations: Resistance and Control*. London: Longman.

Salaman, G. (1981) *Class and the Corporation*. London: Fontana.

Salamon, M. (1987) *Industrial Relations: Theory and Practice*. London: Prentice Hall.

Salgado, J. F. (1997) The five factor model of personality and job performance in the European Community. *Journal of Applied Psychology*, **82**(1): 30–43.

Sano, Y. (1993) Changes and continued stability in Japanese HRM systems: choice in the share economy. *International Journal of Human Resource Management*, **4**(1): 11–27.

Sass, R. (1982) Safety and self-respect. *Policy Options*, July–August: 17–21.

Saul, J. R. (2005) *The Collapse of Globalism*. Toronto: Viking.

Saunders, D. (2006) The year the right turned pink. *Globe and Mail*, January 7: F3.

Sayer, A. (1986) New developments in manufacturing: the just-in-time system. *Capital and Class*, (30): 43–72.

Scarbrough, M. and Elias, J. (2002) *Evaluating Human Capital. CIPD Research Report*. London: Chartered Institute of Personnel and Development.

Scarbrough, H. and Swan, J. (2001) Explaining the diffusion of knowledge management: the role of fashion. *British Journal of Management*, **12**(1): 3–12.

Schafer, D. (1996) *Stress Management for Wellness* (3rd edn). Chico, CA: Harcourt Brace.

Schatzki, T. R (2001) Introduction. In T. R. Schatzki, K. Knorr Cetina and E. Von Savigny (eds) *The Practice Turn in Contemporary Theory*, (pp. 1–14.) London: Routledge.

Schmidt, F. L. (2002) The role of general cognitive ability and job performance: why there cannot be a debate. *Human Performance*, **15**: 187–210.

Schneider, B. (1987) The people make the place. *Personnel Psychology*, **40**: 437–53.

Schneider, B. (1999) Research in the workplace: whose knowledge is it anyway? In Conference Proceedings, *How to Keep Your Intellectual Capital* (pp. 56–71). Calgary: University of Calgary.

Schneider, R. (2001) Variety performance. *People Management*, **7**(9): 26–31.

Scholarios, D. and Marks, A. (2004) Work–life balance and the software worker. *Human Resource Management Journal*, **14**(2): 54–74.

Schön, D. A. (1983) *The Reflective Practitioner: How Professionals Think in Action*. London: Maurice Temple Smith.

Schonberger, R. (1982) *Japanese Manufacturing Techniques: Nine Hidden Lessons in Simplicity*. London: Collier Macmillan.

Schramm, J. (2002) A hard lesson to learn. *People Management*, **8**(8): 32–4.

Schuler, R. S. (1989) Strategic human resource management and industrial relations. *Human Relations*, **42**(2): 157–84.

Schuler, R. S. (1990) Repositioning the human resource function: transformation or demise? *Academy of Management Executive*, **4**(3): 49–60.

Schuler, R. S. (1992) Strategic human resource management: linking people with the strategic needs of the business. *Organizational Dynamics*, **21**: 18–31.

Schuler, R. S. and Jackson, S. (1987) Linking competitive strategies and human resource management practices. *Academy of Management Executive*, **1**(3): 209–13.

Schuler, R., Dowling, P. and De Cieri, H. (1993) An integrative framework of strategic international human resource management. *Journal of Management*, **19**(2): 419–59.

Schuler, R. S., Jackson, S. and Storey, J. (2001) HRM and its links with strategic management. In J. Storey (ed.) *Human Resource Management: A Critical Text* (2nd edn) (pp. 114–30). London: Thompson Learning.

Schultz, T. W. (1981) *Investing in People: The Economics of Population Quality*. Berkeley, CA: University of California Press.

Scott, M. (1998) *Value Drivers*. Chichester: Wiley.

Scott, S. G. and Einstein, W. O. (2001) Strategic performance appraisal in team-based organizations: one size does not fit all. *Academy of Management Executive*, **15**(2): 107–16.

Scott, W. R. (2003) *Organizations: Rational, Natural, and Open Systems* (5th edn). Upper Saddle River, NJ: Prentice Hall.

Scullion, H. (1995) International human resource management. In J. Storey (ed.) *Human Resource Management: A Critical Text* (pp. 352–82). London: Routledge.

Scullion, H. (2001) International human resource management. In J. Storey (ed.) *Human Resource Management: A Critical Text* (2nd edn) (pp. 288–313). London: Thompson Learning.

Scullion, H. and Linehan, M. (eds) (2005) *International Human Resource Management: A Critical Text* (2nd edn). Basingstoke: Palgrave Macmillan.

Scullion, H. and Paauwe, J. (2005) Strategic HRM in multinational companies. In Scullion, H. and Linehan, M. (eds) *International Human Resource*

Management: A Critical Text (2nd edn) (pp. 22–46). Basingstoke: Palgrave Macmillan.

Scullion, H. and Starkey, K. (2000) The changing role of the corporate human resource function in the international firm. International Journal of Human Resource Management, 11(6): 1061–81.

Sebbens, T. D. (2000) Rising tides, leaky boats: the influence of downsizing on wage levels. New Zealand Journal of Industrial Relations, 25(2): 119–50.

Selwyn, N. M. (2004) Selwyn's Law of Employment (13th edn). London: Butterworths.

Selznick, P. (1957) Leadership and Administration. New York: Harper & Row.

Senge, P. (1990) The Fifth Discipline. New York: Doubleday.

Sennett, R. (1998) The Corrosion of Character. New York: Norton.

Sewell, G. (1998) The discipline of teams: the control of team-based industrial work through electronic and peer surveillance. Administrative Science Quarterly, 43: 406–69.

Sewell, G. (2005) Doing what comes naturally? Why we need a practical ethics of teamwork. International Journal of Human Resource Management, 16(2): 202–18.

Shalley, C. E., Zhou, J. and Oldham, G. (2004) The effects of personal and contextual characteristics on creativity: Where should we go from here? Journal of Management, 30(6): 933–58.

Shaw, J. D., Duffy, M. K., Johnson, J. L. and Lockhart, D. E. (2005) Turnover, social capital losses and performance. Academy of Management Journal, 48(4): 594–606.

Sheffield, J. and Coleshill, P. (2001) Developing best value in a Scottish local authority. Measuring Business Excellence, 5(2): 31–8.

Shen, J. (2006) Factors affecting international staffing in Chinese multinationals (MNEs). International Journal of Human Resource Management, 17(2): 295–315.

Shen, J. and Edwards, V. (2004) Recruitment and selection in Chinese MNEs. International Journal of Human Resource Management, 15(4): 814–35.

Shenkar, O. (1995) Global Perspectives on Human Resource Management. Englewood Cliffs, NJ: Prentice Hall.

Sherwood, R. (2001) Workers turn off autopilot and take charge on assembly lines of the 21st century. Globe and Mail, September 3: B7.

Shibata, H. (2000) The transformation of the wage and performance appraisal system in a Japanese firm. International Journal of Human Resource Management, 11(2): 294–313.

Shibata, H. (2002) Wage and performance appraisal systems in flux: a Japan–United States comparison. Industrial Relations, 41(4): 629–52.

Shipton, H., West, M., Dawson, J., Birdi, K. and Patterson, M. (2006) HRM as a predictor of innovation. Human Resource Management Journal, 16(1): 3–26.

Shiva, V. (2000) The world on the edge. In W. Hutton and A. Giddens (eds) On the Edge: Living with Global Capitalism (pp. 112–29). London: Jonathan Cape.

Shotter, J. (1993) Cultural Politics of Everyday Life. Toronto: University of Toronto Press.

Sianesi, B. and Van Reenan, J. (2000) The Returns to Education: A Review of the Macro-economic Literature. London: Centre for the Economics of Education.

Simpson, B. (1986) Trade union immunities. In R. Lewis (ed.) Labour Law in Britain (pp. 161–94). Oxford: Blackwell.

Singh, K. (2003) Strategic HR orientation and firm performance in India. International Journal of Human Resource Management, 14(4): 530–43.

Singh, R. (1997) Equal opportunities for men and women in the EU: a commentary. Industrial Relations, 28(1): 68–71.

Singh, V. (2002) Managing Diversity for Strategic Advantage. London: Council for Excellence in Management and Leadership.

Sisson, K. (ed.) (1989) Personnel Management. Oxford: Blackwell.

Sisson, K. (1993) In search of HRM. British Journal of Industrial Relations, 31(2): 201–9.

Sisson, K. (ed.) (1994) Personnel Management (2nd edn). Oxford: Blackwell.

Sisson, K. (1995) Human resource management and the personnel function. In J. Storey (ed.) Human Resource Management: A Critical Text (pp. 87–109). London: Routledge.

Sisson, K. and Storey, J. (2000) The Realities of Human Resource Management: Managing the Employment Relationship. Buckingham, Oxford University Press.

Sklair, L. (2002) Globalization: Capitalism and its Alternatives (3rd edn). New York: Oxford University Press.

Sloman, M. (2002) The e-Learning Revolution: From Propositions to Action. London: Chartered Institute of Personnel and Development.

Sloman, M. (2005) Training to Learning. London: Chartered Institute of Personnel and Development.

Sloman, M. and Reynolds, J. (2002) Developing the e-learning community. Paper presented to the Third Conference on Human Resource Development: Research and Practice Across Europe, Edinburgh, January.

Smeaton, D. (2003) Self-employed workers: calling the shots or hesitant independents? A consideration of the trends. *Work, Employment & Society*, **17**(6): 379–91.

Smethurst, S. (2004) The allure of online. *People Management*, 29 July: 38–40.

Smith, A. (1776 [1982]) *The Wealth of Nations*. Harmondsworth: Penguin.

Smith, A. (2001) Perceptions of stress at work. *Human Resource Management Journal*, **11**(4): 74–86.

Smith, A. R. (1980) *Corporate Manpower Planning*. London: Gower Press.

Smith, I. (1992) Reward management and HRM. In P. Blyton and P. Turnbull (eds) *Reassessing Human Resource Management* (pp. 169–84). London: Sage.

Smith, P. and Morton, G. (1993) Union exclusion and the decollectivization of industrial relations in contemporary Britain. *British Journal of Industrial Relations*, **31**(1): 97–114.

Smith, P. and Morton, G. (2001) New Labour's reform of Britain's employment law: the devil is not only in detail but in the values and policy too. *British Journal of Industrial Relations*, **39**(1): 119–38.

Smith, P. and Morton, G. (2006) Nine years of New Labour: neoliberalism and workers' rights. *British Journal of Industrial Relations*, **44**(3): 401–20.

Smither, J., London, M. and Reilly, R. (2005) Does performance improve following multisource feedback? A theoretical model, meta-analysis, and review of empirical findings. *Personnel Psychology*, **58**: 33–66.

Smither, J., London, M., Flautt, R., Vargas, Y. and Kucine, I. (2003) Can working with an executive coach improve multi-source feedback ratings over time? A quasi-experimental field study. *Personnel Psychology*, **56**(1): 23–44.

Smither, J., Reilly, R., Millsap, R., Pearlman, K. and Stoffey, R. (1993) Applicant reactions to selection procedures. *Personnel Psychology*, **46**: 49–76.

Sneade, A. (2001) Trade union membership 1999–2000: an analysis of data from the certification officer, and The Labour Force Survey, *Labour Market Trends*, September: 433–41.

Snell, S. A. (1992) Control theory in strategic human resource management: the mediating effect of administrative information. *Academy of Management Journal*, **35**: 292–327.

Snell, S. A., Youndt, M. A. and Wright, P. M. (1996) Establishing a framework for research in strategic human resource management: merging source theory and organizational learning. *Research in Personnel and Human Resources Management*, **14**: 61–90.

Soltani, E., ven der Meer, R. and Williams, T. (2005) A contrast of HRM and TQM approaches to performance management: some evidence. *British Journal of Management*, **16**(3): 211–30.

Sparrow, P. (1996) Too good to be true. *People Management*, 5 December: 22–7.

Sparrow, P. (2000) New employee behaviours, work designs and forms of work organization: what is in store for future work? *Journal of Management Psychology*, **15**(3): 202–18.

Sparrow, P. and Budhwar, P. (1997) Competition and change: mapping the Indian HRM recipe against worldwide patterns. *Journal of World Business*, **32**: 224–42.

Sparrow, P. and Marchington, M. (1998) *Human Resource Management: The New Agenda*. London: Financial Times/Pitman.

Sparrow, P., Brewster, C. and Harris, H. (2004) *Globalizing Human Resource Management*. London: Routledge.

Spychalski, A. C., Quiñones, M. A., Gaugler, B. B. and Pohley, K. (1997) A survey of assessment center practices in the United States. *Personnel Psychology*, **50**, 71–90.

Squires, G. (2001) Mangement as a professional discipline. *Journal of Management Studies*, **38**(4): 473–87.

Standing, G. (1997) Globalization, labour flexibility and insecurity: the era of market regulation. *European Journal of Industrial Relations*, **3**(1): 7–37.

Stanfield, C., Campbell, M. and Giles, L. (2004) *The UK Workforce: Realising our Potential*. London: Sector Skills Development Agency.

Stern, E. and Sommerlad, E. (1999) *Workplace Learning, Culture and Performance*. London: Institute of Personnel and Development.

Sternberg, R. J. and Horvath, J. A. (eds) (1999) *Tacit Knowledge in Professional Practice: Researcher and Practitioner Perspectives*. Mahwah, NJ: Lawrence Erlbaum Associates.

Stewart, R. (1998) Managerial behaviour. In M. Poole and M. Warner (eds) *Handbook of Human Resource Management* (pp. 147–63). London: Thomson Business.

Stewart, J. and Knowles, V. (1999) The changing nature of graduate careers. *Career Development International*, **4**(7): 370–83.

Stewart, J. and Knowles, V. (2000) Graduate recruitment: implications for business and management courses in HE. *Journal of European Industrial Training*, **25**(2): 98–108.

Stiglitz, J. E. (2002) *Globalization and its Discontents*. New York: Norton.

Stohl, C. and Cheney, G. (2001) Participatory processes/paradoxical practices. *Management Communications Quarterly*, **14**(3): 349–407.

Stokes, A. (2001) Using tele-mentoring to deliver training to SMEs: a pilot study. *Education and Training*, **43**(6): 317–24.

Storey, J. (ed.) (1989) *New Perspectives on Human Resource Management*. London: Routledge.

Storey, J. (1992) *Developments in the Management of Human Resources*. Oxford: Blackwell.

Storey, J. (ed.) (1995a) *Human Resource Management: A Critical Text*. London: Routledge.

Storey, J. (1995b) Human resource management: still marching on or marching out? In J. Storey (ed.) *Human Resource Management: A Critical Text* (pp. 3–32). London: Routledge.

Storey, J. (2001) Human resource management today: an assessment. In J. Storey (ed.) *Human Resource Management: A Critical Text* (2nd edn) (pp. 3–20). London: Thompson Learning.

Storey, J. and Quintas, P. (2001) Knowledge management and HRM. In J. Storey (ed.) *Human Resource Management: A Critical Text* (2nd edn) (pp. 339–63). London: Thomson Learning.

Storey, J., Cressey, P., Morris, T. and Wilkinson, A. (1997) Changing employment practices in UK banking: case studies. *Personnel Review*, **26**(1): 24–42.

Storey, J., Quintas, P., Taylor, P. and Fowle, W. (2002) Flexible employment contracts and their implications for product and process innovation. *International Journal of Human Resource Management*, **13**(1): 1–18.

Strauss, G. (1998) An overview. In F. Heller, E. Pusic, G. Strauss and B. Wilpert (eds) *Organizational Participation: Myth and Reality* (pp. 8–39). Oxford: Oxford University Press.

Strebler, M., Robinson, D. and Heron, P. (1997) Getting the best out of your competencies. Report no. 334. Brighton: Institute for Employment Studies.

Stredwick, J. and Ellis, S. (2005) *Flexible Working* (2nd edn). London: Chartered Institute of Personnel and Development.

Stredwick, J. and Ellis, S. (1998) *Flexible Working Practices*. London: Institute of Personnel Development.

Streeck, W. (1987) The uncertainties of management in the management of uncertainty. *Work, Employment and Society*, **1**: 281–308.

Streeck, W. (1996) Comment on Ronald Dore. *Industrielle Beziehungen*, **3**: 187–96.

Streeck, W. and Visser, J. (1997) The rise of the conglomerate union. *European Journal of Industrial Relations*, **3**(3): 305–32.

Sturges J. and Guest, D. (2004) Working to live or living to work? Work/life balance early in the career. *Human Resource Management Journal*, **14**(4): 5–20.

Sukert, A. (2000) Marionettes of globalization: a comparative analysis of legal protections for contingent workers in the international community. *Syracuse Journal of International Law and Commerce*, **27**(2): 403–77.

Sung, J. and Ashton, D. (2005) *High Performance Work Practices: Linking Strategy and Skills to Performance Outcomes*. London: Department of Trade and Industry/Chartered Institute of Personnel and Development.

Suutari, V. and Brewster, C. (2003) Repatriation: empirical evidence from a longitudinal study of careers and expectations among Finnish expatriates. *International Journal of Human Resource Management*, **14**(7): 1132–51.

Sveiby, K. E. (1997) *The New Organizational Wealth: Managing and Measuring Organizational Wealth*. San Francisco, CA: Berrett-Koehler.

Swanson, R. A. (2001) HRD and its underlying theory. *Human Resource Development International*, **4**(3): 299–312.

Swinburne, P. (2001) How to use feedback to improve performance. *People Management*, **7**(11): 46–7.

Sydow, J., Lindkvist, L. and DeFillippi, R. (2004) Project-base organizations, embeddedness and repositories of knowledge: editorial. *Organization Studies*, **25**(9): 1475–89.

Tahvanainen, M. and Suutari, V. (2005) Expatriate performance management in MNCs. In H. Scullion and M. Linehan (eds) *International Human Resource Management* (pp. 91–113). Basingstoke: Palgrave Macmillan.

Tamkin, P., Barber, L. and Hirsh, W. (1995) Personal development plans: case studies of practice. Report no. 280. Brighton: Institute for Employment Studies.

Tamkin, P., Barber, L. and Dench, S. (1997) From admin to strategy: the changing face of the HR function. Report no. 32. Brighton: Institute for Employment Studies.

Tamkin, P., Giles, L., Campbell, M. and Hillage, J. (2004) *Skills Pay: The Contribution of Skills to Business Success*. Brighton: Institute for Employment Studies.

Tan, J.-S. (1998) Communication, cross-cultural. In M. Poole and M. Warner (eds) *Handbook of Human Resource Management* (pp. 492–97). London: Thomson Business.

Tannen, D. (1993) *You Just Don't Understand: Women and Men in Conversation*. London: Virago.

Taras, D. and Kaufman, B. (2006) Non-union employee representation in North America: diversity, controversy and uncertain future. *Industrial Relations Journal*, **37**(5): 513–42.

Taras, D., Ponak, A. and Gunderson, M. (2001) Introduction to Canadian industrial relations. In M. Gunderson, A. Ponak and D. Taras (eds) *Union–Management Relations in Canada* (4th edn) (pp. 1–24). Toronto: Addison Wesley Longman.

Taylor, C. (2001) Windows of opportunity. *People Management*, **7**(5): 32–6.

Taylor, H. (1991) The systematic training model: corn circles in search of a spaceship? *Management Education and Development*, **22**(4): 258–78.

Taylor, P., Baldry, C., Bain, P. and Ellis, V. (2003) A unique working environment: health, sickness and absence management in UK call centres. *Work, Employment and Society*, **17**(3): 435–58.

Taylor, R. (2002) *Britain's World of Work – Myths and Realities*. Swindon: Economic and Social Research Council.

Taylor, S. (1998) *Employee Resourcing*. London: Institute of Personnel Development.

Taylor, S. and Napier, N. (1996) Working in Japan: lessons from women expatriates. *Sloan Management Review*, **37**: 125–44.

Taylor, S., Beechler, S. and Napier, N. (1996) Toward an integrative model of strategic international human resource management. *Academy of Management Review*, **21**(4): 959–85.

Teague, P. and Grahl, J. (1992) *Industrial Relations and European Integration*. London: Lawrence & Wishart.

Templer, A. J. and Cawsey, T. F. (1999) Rethinking career development in an era portfolio careers. *Career Development International*, **4**(2): 70–6.

Temporal, P. (1978) The nature of non-contrived learning and its implications for management development. *Management Education and Development*, **9**: 20–3.

Terry, M. (1995) Trade unions: shop stewards and the workplace. In P. Edwards (ed.) *Industrial Relations*. Oxford: Blackwell.

Thomas, C. and Wallis, B. (1998) Dŵr Cymru/ Welsh water: a case study in partnership. In P. Sparrow and M. Marchington (eds) *Human Resource Management: A New Agenda* (pp. 160–70). London: Financial Times.

Thompson, M. (2001) The management of industrial relations. In M. Gunderson, A. Ponak and D. Taras (eds) *Union–Management Relations in Canada* (4th edn) (pp. 117–41). Toronto, Addison Wesley Longman.

Thompson, P. (1989) *The Nature of Work* (2nd edn). Basingstoke: Macmillan – now Palgrave Macmillan.

Thompson, P. (1993) Postmodernism: fatal distraction. In J. Hassard and M. Parker (eds) *Postmodernism and Organizations* (pp. 183–203). London: Sage.

Thompson, P. and McHugh, D. (2002) *Work Organisations: A Critical Introduction* (3rd edn). Basingstoke: Palgrave Macmillan.

Thompson, P. and Wallace, T. (1996) Redesigning production through teamworking. *International Journal of Operations and Production Management*, **16**(2): 103–18.

Thompson, P. and Warhurst, C. (eds) (1998) *Workplaces of the Future*. Basingstoke: Macmillan – now Palgrave Macmillan.

Thomson, N. and Millar, C. (2001) The role of slack in transforming organizations. *International Studies of Management and Organization*, **31**(2): 65–83.

Thornhill, A., Saunders, M. N. K. and Stead, J. (1997) Downsizing, delayering – but where's the commitment. *Personnel Review*, **26**(1): 81–98.

Thurley, K. and Wood, S. (1983) Business strategy and industrial relations strategy. In K. Thurley and S. Wood (eds) *Industrial Relations and Management Strategy*. Cambridge: Cambridge University Press.

Thursfield, D. (2000) *Post-Fordism and Skill*. Aldershot: Ashgate.

Tichy, N. and Devanna, M. (1986) *The Transformational Leader*. New York: John Wiley & Sons.

Tipper, J. (2004) How to increase diversity through your recruitment practices. *Industrial and Commercial Training*, **36**(4): 158–61.

Tomaney, J. (1990) The reality of workplace flexibility. *Capital and Class*, (40): 97–124.

Toplis, J., Dulvicz, V. and Fletcher, C. (2005) *Psychological Testing* (4th edn). London: Chartered Institute of Personnel and Development.

Torbiörn, I. (2005) Staffing policies and practices in European MNCs: strategic sophistication, culture-bound policies or ad hoc reactivity? In

H. Scullion and M. Linehan (eds) *International Human Resource Management* (pp. 47–68). Basingstoke: Palgrave Macmillan.

Torrington, D. (1998) Discipline and dismissals. In M. Poole and M. Warner (eds) *The Handbook of Human Resource Management* (pp. 498–506). London: International Thomson Business Press.

Toulson, P. K. and Dewe, P. (2004) HR accounting as a measurement tool. *Human Resource Management Journal*, **14**(2): 75–90.

Towers, B. (1989) Running the gauntlet: British trade unions under Thatcher, 1979–1988. *Industrial and Labor Relations Review*, **42**(2): 296–313.

Towers, B. (1992) Two speed ahead: social Europe and the UK after Maastricht. *Industrial Relations Journal*, **23**(2): 83–9.

Townley, B. (1989) Employee communication programmes. In K. Sisson (ed.) *Personnel Management* (pp. 329–55). Oxford: Blackwell.

Townley, B. (1994) *Reframing Human Resource Managment*. London: Sage

Trades Union Congress (1986) *Health and Safety at Work: TUC Course Book for Union Reps* (4th edn). London: TUC.

Trades Union Congress (1999) *Partners for Progress: New Unionism in the Workplace*. London: TUC.

Trades Union Congress (2000) *Focus on Recognition*. London: TUC.

Trades Union Congress (2002) New record high for employers recognizing unions. TUC press release, 21 January. www.tuc.org.uk/organization/tuc.

Trapp, R. (2004) Older and wiser. *People Management*, 23 December: 40–1.

Trapp, R. (2005) The mirror has two faces. *People Management*, 19 May: 40–2.

Trethewey, A. (1997) Organizational culture. In P. Y. Byers (ed.) *Organizational Communication: Theory and Behavior*. Boston: Allyn & Bacon.

Truss, C. (2001) Complexities and controversies in linking HRM with organizational outcomes. *Journal of Management Studies*, **38**(8): 1121–49.

Truss, C., Gratton, L., Hope-Hailey, V., Stiles, P. and Zaleska, J. (2002) Paying the piper: choice and constraint in changing HR functional roles. *Human Resource Management Journal*, **12**(2): 39–63.

Tsang, E. W. (1994) Human resource management problems in Sino-foreign joint ventures. *Employee Relations*, **15**(9): 1–14.

Tsui, A. A. and Wu, J. B. (2005) The new employment relationship versus the mutual investment approach: implications for human resource management. *Human Resource Management*, **44**(2): 115–21.

Tulip, S. (2004) Hired education. *People Management*, 30 September: 46–9.

Tung, R. (1988) *The New Expatriates*. Boston, MA: Ballinger.

Tung, R. (1998) A contingency framework for selection and training of expatriates revisited. *Human Resource Management Review*, **98**(8): 23–38.

Turnbull, P. (1986) The Japanisation of British industrial relations at Lucas. *Industrial Relations Journal*, **17**(3): 193–206.

Turnbull, R. S. and Elliott, C. (2005) *Critical Thinking in Human Resource Development*. London: Routledge.

Turner, G. (1996) Human resource accounting – whim or wisdom? *Journal of Human Resource Costing and Accounting*, **1**(1): 63–73.

Tyson, D. E. (1996) *Profit Sharing in Canada: The Complete Guide to Designing and Implementing Plans that Really Work*. Toronto: John Wiley.

Tyson, S. (1995) *Human Resource Strategy*. London: Pitman.

Tziner, A., Joanis, C. and Murphy, K. R. (2000) A comparison of three methods of performance appraisal with regard to goal properties, goal perception and ratee satisfaction. *Group and Organization Management*, **25**(2): 175–90.

Ulrich, D. (1997) *Human Resource Champions*. Boston, MA: Harvard Business School Press.

Ulrich, D. and Beatty, R. W. (2001) From partner to players. *Human Resource Management*, **40**(4): 293–307.

Ulrich, L. and Trumbo, D. (1965) The selection interview since 1949. *Psychological Bulletin*, **63**: 100–16.

Undy, R., Ellis, V., McCarthy, W. E. J. and Halmos, A. M. (1981) *Change in Trade Unions*. London: Hutchinson.

Vallas, S. (1999) Re-thinking post-Fordism: the meaning of workplace flexibility. *Sociological Theory*, **17**(1): 68–85.

van Vijfeijken, H., Kleingeld, A., van Tuijl, H., Algera, J. and Thierry, H. (2002) Task complexity and task, goal, and reward interdependence in group performance management: a prescriptive model. *European Journal of Work and Organizational Psychology*, **11**(3): 363–83.

Veng Seng, C., Zannes, E. and Pace, R. W. (2002) The contributions of knowledge management to workplace learning. *Journal of Workplace Learning*, **14**(4): 138–47.

Verhaar, C. H. A. and Smulders, H. R. M. (1999) Employability in practice. *Journal of European Industrial Training*, **23**(6): 268–74.

Verlander, E. G. (1985) The system's the thing. *Training and Development*, April 20–3.

Verma, A. (1995) Employee involvement in the workplace. In M. Gunderson and A. Ponak (eds) *Union–Management Relations in Canada* (3rd edn) (pp. 281–308). Don Mills, Ontario: Addison-Wesley.

Verma, A. and Taras, D. (2001) Employee involvement in the workplace. In M. Gunderson, A. Ponak and D. Taras (eds) *Union–Management Relations in Canada* (4th edn) (pp. 447–85). Don Mills, Ontario: Addison-Wesley.

Verma, A., Kochan, T. and Wood, S. (eds) (2002) Editor's introduction. *British Journal of Industrial Relations*, **40**(3): 373–84.

Visser, J. and Waddington, J. (1996) Industrialization and politics: a century of union structural developments in three European countries. *European Journal of Industrial Relations*, **2**(1): 21–53.

Von Krogh, G. (2003) Knowledge sharing and the communal resources. In Easterby-Smith, M. and Lyles, M. A. (eds) *The Blackwell Handbook of Organizational Learning and Knowledge Management* (pp. 372–92). Oxford: Blackwell.

Vosko, L. (2000) *Temporary Work: The Gendered Rise of a Precarious Employment Relationship*. Toronto: University of Toronto Press.

Vroom, V. H. (1964) *Work and Motivation*. New York: Wiley.

Vygotsky, L. S. (1978) *Mind in Society: The Development of Higher Psychological Processes*. Cambridge, MA: Harvard University Press.

Waddington, J. (1988) Business unionism and fragmentation within the TUC. *Capital and Class*, (36): 7–15.

Waddington, J. (1992) Trade union membership in Britain, 1980–1987: unemployment and restructuring. *British Journal of Industrial Relations*, **30**(2): 7–15.

Waddington, J. and Whitston, C. (1994) The politics of restructuring: trade unions on the defensive in Britain since 1979. *Relations Industrielles/ Industrial Relations*, **49**(4): 794–817.

Wagner, R. F. (1949) The employment interview: a critical summary. *Personnel Psychology*, **2**: 17–46.

Wajcman, J. (1998) *Managing Like a Man*. University Park, PA: Pennsylvania State University Press.

Wajcman, J. (2000) Feminism facing industrial relations in Britain. *British Journal of Industrial Relations*, **38**(2): 183–201.

Wall, T. D. and Wood, S. J. (2005) The romance of human resource management and business performance, and the case for the big science. *Human Relations*, **58**(4): 429–61.

Wallace, M. (1989) Brave new workplace: technology and work in the new economy. *Work and Occupations*, **16**(4): 363–92.

Wallis, E., Stuart, M. and Greenwood, I. (2005) Learners of the workplace unite!: an empircal examination of the UK trade union learning representative initiative. *Work, Employment and Society*, **19**(2): 234–83.

Walters, D. (1987) Health and safety and trade union workplace organization: a case study in the printing industry. *Industrial Relations Journal*, **18**(1): 40–7.

Walters, D. (2004) Worker representation and health and safety in small enterprises in Europe. *Industrial Relations Journal*, **35**(2): 169–86.

Walters, M. (ed.) (1995) *The Performance Management Handbook*. London: Institute of Personnel Development.

Walton, R. (1985) From control to commitment in the workplace. *Harvard Business Review*, March/April: 77–84.

Warde, A. (1990) The future of work. In J. Anderson and M. Ricci (eds) *Society and Social Science: A Reader* (pp. 86–94). Milton Keynes: Open University Press.

Warner, M. (1996) Human resources in the People's Republic of China: the 'three systems' reforms. *Human Resource Management Journal*, **6**(2): 32–43.

Warner, M. (1997) Management–labour relations in the Chinese economy. *Human Resource Management Journal*, **7**(4): 2–22.

Warner, M. (2002) Globalization, labour markets and human resources in Asia-Pacific economies: an overview. *International Journal of Human Resource Management*, **13**(3): 384–98.

Warner, M. (2004) Human resource management in China revisited: introduction. *International Journal of Human Resource Management*, **15**(4): 617–34.

Watson, T. (1986) *Management, Organization and Employment Strategy*. London: Routledge & Kegan Paul.

Watson, T. (1994) Recruitment and selection. In Sisson, K. (ed.) *Personnel Management* (pp. 185–252). Oxford: Blackwell.

Watson, T. (1999) Human resourcing strategies. In J. Leopold, L. Harris and T. Watson (eds) *Strategic Human Resourcing* (pp. 17–38). London: Pitman.

Watson, T. (2004) HRM and critical social sciences. *Journal of Management Studies*, **41**(3): 447–67.

Webb, D. and Collis, C. (2000) Regional development agencies and the 'new regionalism' in England. *Regional Studies*, **34**(9): 857–64.

Weber, M. (1968 [1922]) *Economy and Society*. New York: Bedminster.

Wedderburn, Lord (1986) *The Worker and the Law* (3rd edn). Harmondsworth: Penguin.

Weichman, D. and Ryan, A. (2003) Reactions to computerized testing in selection contexts. *International Journal of Selection and Assessment*, **11**: 215–29.

Weick, K. and Westley, F. (1996) Organizational learning: affirming an oxymoron. In S. Clegg, C. Hardy and W. Nord (eds) *Handbook of Organization Studies* (pp. 190–208). London: Sage.

Weinstein, M. and Obloj, K. (2002) Strategic and environmental determinants of HRM innovations in post-socialist Poland. *International Journal of Human Resource Management*, **13**(4): 642–59.

Welbourne, T. and Trevor, C. (2000) The roles of departmental and position power in job evaluation. *Academy of Management Journal*, **43**(4): 761–71.

Wells, D. (1993) Are strong unions compatible with the new model of human resource management? *Relations Industrielles/Industrial Relations*, **48**(1): 56–84.

Wells, G. (1999) *Dialogic Inquiry: Towards a Sociocultural Practice and Theory of Education*. New York: Cambridge University Press.

Wenger, E. C. and Snyder, W. M. (2000) Communities of practice: the organizational frontier. *Harvard Business Review*, January–February: 139–45.

Wheatley, M. (1994) *Leadership and the New Science*. San Francisco: Berrett-Koehler.

Wheelen, T. and Hunger, J. (1995) *Strategic Management and Business Policy* (5th edn). New York: Addison-Wesley.

Whiddett, S. and Hollyforde, K. (2003) *A Practical Guide to Competencies*. London: Chartered Institute of Personnel and Development.

Whipp, R. (1999) Creative destruction: strategy and organizations. In S. Clegg, C. Hardy and W. Nord (eds) *Managing Organizations: Current Issues* (pp. 11–25). London: Sage.

Whitley, R. (1999) *Divergent Capitalism: The Social Structuring and Change of Business Systems*. Oxford: Oxford University Press.

Whittaker, D. H. (1990) *Managing Innovation: A Study of British and Japanese Factories*. Cambridge: Cambridge University Press.

Whittington, R. (1993) *What is Strategy and Does it Matter?* London: Routledge.

Wickens, P. (1987) *The Road to Nissan*. London: Macmillan – now Palgrave Macmillan.

Wiggins, J. S. (ed.) (1996) *The Five-factor Model of Personality*. New York: Guildford Publications.

Wilk, S. and Cappelli, P. (2003) Understanding the determinants of employer use of selection methods. *Personnel Psychology*, **57**: 103–24.

Wilkinson, A. and Ackers, P. (1995) When two cultures meet: new industrial relations at Japanco. *International Journal of Human Resource Management*, **6**(4): 1039–60.

Williams, A. (1993) *Human Resource Management and Labour Market Flexibility*. Aldershot: Avebury.

Williams, S. (1999) Policy failure in education and training: the introduction of National Vocational Qualifications (1986–1990) *Education and Training*, **41**(5): 216–26.

Willman, P. (1996) Merger propensity and merger outcomes among British unions, 1986–95. *Industrial Relations Journal*, **27**(4): 331–7.

Willmott, H. (1984) Images and ideals of managerial work. *Journal of Management Studies*, **21**(3): 349–68.

Willmott, H. (1995) The odd couple?: re-engineering business processes; managing human relations. *New Technology, Work and Employment*, **10**(2): 89–97.

Wilson, F. (1994) Introducing new computer-based systems into Zenbank. *New Technology, Work and Employment*, **9**(2): 115–26.

Wilson, J. P. and Western, S. (2000) Performance appraisal: an obstacle to training and development. *Journal of European Industrial Training*, **24**(7): 384–90.

Wilson, R. and Hogarth, T. (2003) *Tackling the Low Skills Equilibrium: A Review of Issues and Some New Evidence*. London: Department of Trade and Industry.

Winstanley, D. and Woodall, J. (eds) (2000) *Ethical Issues in Contemporary Human Resource Management*. Basingstoke: Macmillan – now Palgrave Macmillan.

Winter, J., Neal, J. and Waner, K. (2001) How male, female and mixed gender groups regard interaction and leadership differences in the business communication course. *Business Communication Quarterly*, **64**(3): 43–58.

Witherspoon, P. D. (1997) *Communicating Leadership*. Boston: Allyn & Bacon.

Witz, A. (1986) Patriarchy and the labour market: occupational control strategies and the medical division of labour. In D. Knights and H. Willmott (eds) *Gender and the Labour Process* (pp. 14–35). Aldershot: Gower.

Womack, J., Jones, D. and Roos, D. (1990) *The Machine that Changed the World*. New York: Rawson Associates.

Wong, M. L. (2001) The strategic use of contingent workers in Hong Kong's economic upheaval. *Human Resource Management Journal*, **11**(4): 22–37.

Wood, I., Rodgers, H. and Gold, J. (2004) Picturing prejudice: learning to see diversity. Paper presented at the Fifth HRD Conference, Limerick University, May.

Wood, S. (1995) The four pillars of HRM: are they connected? *Human Resource Management Journal*, **5**(5): 49–59.

Wood, S. (2000) The BJIR and industrial relations in the new millennium. *British Journal of Industrial Relations*, **38**(1): 1–5.

Wood, S. (2006), Human resource management and performance in UK call centres. *British Journal of Industrial Relations*, **44**(1): 99–124.

Wood, S. and Godard, J. (1999) The statutory union recognition procedure in the Employment Relations Bill: a comparative analysis. *British Journal of Industrial Relations*, **37**(2): 203–44.

Wood, S., Moore, S. and Willman, P. (2002) Third time lucky for statutory recognition in the UK. *Industrial Relations Journal*, **33**(3): 215–33.

Woodall, J. (2001) Editorial. *Human Resource Development International*, **4**(3): 287–90.

Woodhams, C. and Lipton, B. (2006) Gender-based equal opportunities policy and practice in small firms: the impact of HR professionals. *Human Resource Management Journal*, **16**(1): 74–97.

Woodruffe, C. (1992) What is meant by a competency? In S. Boam and P. Sparrow (eds) *Designing and Achieving Competency* (pp. 16–30). Maidenhead: McGraw-Hill.

Woodruffe, C. (2000) *Development and Assessment Centres* (3rd edn). London: Chartered Institute of Personnel and Development.

Wright, M. (1996) The collapse of compulsory unionism? Collective organization in highly unionized British companies, 1979–1991. *British Journal of Industrial Relations*, **34**(4): 497–513.

Wright, P. M. and McMahan, C. G. (1992) Theoretical perspectives for strategic human resource management. *Journal of Management*, **18**: 295–319.

Wright, P. M., Gardner, T. M. and Moynihan, L. M. (2003) The impact of HR practices on the performance of business units. *Human Resource Management Journal*, **13**(3): 21–36.

Yammarino, F. J. and Atwater, L. E. (1997) Implications of self–other rating agreement for human resources management. *Organizational Dynamics*, **25**(4): 35–44.

Yanow, D. (2000) Seeing organizational learning: a 'cultural' view. *Organization*, **7**(2): 247–68.

Yanow, D. (2004) Translating local knowledge at organizational peripheries. *British Journal of Management*, **15**(1): 9–25.

Youndt, M. A., Snell, S. A., Dean, J. W. and Lepak, D. P. (1996) Human resource management, manufacturing strategy and firm performance. *Academy of Management Journal*, **39**: 836–66.

Yukl, G. (2002) *Leadership in Organizations* (5th edn) Englewood Cliffs, NJ: Prentice Hall.

Zhou, J. and Martocchio, J. (2001) Chinese and American managers' compensation award decisions: a comparative study. *Personnel Psychology*, **54**(1): 115–45.

Zhu, C. and Dowling, P. (2002) Staffing practices in transition: some empirical evidence from China. *International Journal of Human Resource Management*, **13**(4): 569–97.

Zorn, T. E., Christensen, L. and Cheney, G. (1999) *Do We Really Want Constant Change?* San Francisco: Berrett-Koehler.

Index

Name index

Subject index